Global Report on Human Settlements

The United Nations Centre for Human Settlements (Habitat) was established in 1979 as a result of the consolidation of several United Nations offices and programmes, some of which had been in operation since the very inception of United Nations assistance to social and economic development in developing countries. Operating from Nairobi with a global mandate, the Centre is the focal point for human settlement activities within the United Nations system. Under the guidance of the United Nations Commission on Human Settlements, and within the framework of biennial work programmes, the Centre co-ordinates human settlements activities, publishes research studies, provides training support, disseminates human settlements information, and executes human settlements projects in co-operation with member governments—currently (1986), 161 projects in 77 countries. The Centre is also the secretariat for the 1987 International Year of Shelter for the Homeless.

Global Report on Human Settlements

United Nations Centre for
Human Settlements
(Habitat)

Published by
OXFORD UNIVERSITY PRESS
for the
UNITED NATIONS CENTRE FOR HUMAN SETTLEMENTS (HABITAT)
1987

Oxford University Press, Walton Street, Oxford OX2 6DP
Oxford New York Toronto
Delhi Bombay Calcutta Madras Karachi
Petaling Jaya Singapore Hong Kong Tokyo
Nairobi Dar es Salaam Cape Town
Melbourne Auckland
and associated companies in
Beirut Berlin Ibadan Nicosia

Oxford is a trade mark of Oxford University Press

Published in the United States
by Oxford University Press, New York

British Library Cataloguing in Publication Data
United Nations. Centre for Human
Settlements (Habitat)
Global report on human settlements.
1. Anthropo-geography
I. Title
307   GF101
ISBN 0–19–828622–8
ISBN 0–19–828602–3 Pbk

Library of Congress Cataloging in Publication Data
Data available

Set by Wyvern Typesetting Ltd, Bristol

Printed in Great Britain by
Butler and Tanner Ltd,
Frome and London

Foreword

The present report has been prepared to document global human settlements conditions and trends and to assist member governments in improving their settlement policies, plans, and programmes. It is also dedicated to those who—in spite of limited means, and facing financial and physical odds—are at this moment building or improving their own habitat; to those whose wisdom and inspiration prompted the world community to embrace the concept of human settlements; and to the planners and builders who believe that the world can become a better place to live in.

Little more than ten years ago, the member states of the United Nations held a Conference named Habitat: United Nations Conference on Human Settlements. The Conference resulted in the adoption of a set of recommendations for national and international action and in the establishment of the United Nations Centre for Human Settlements (Habitat).

Many events have occurred since the Conference. Some observers will argue, no doubt very convincingly, that the world has not become a better place. Others will maintain, no doubt with much reason, that our global community, well into the Third United Nations Development Decade, is confronted with problems of a magnitude and a complexity never faced before. A good number among the students and practitioners of human settlements development warn us about the formidable and growing obstacles which lie between us and our disturbingly evasive 'moving target': a satisfying living and working environment for the present and future members of the world's community. This report attempts to document these realities responsibly and objectively. Yet the economic crises experienced and somehow survived during the past decade have also taught us to give more credit to the inner strengths of our fellow human beings, and to the ability of men, women, and children to build a better world for themselves.

So, in the midst of a yet unsolved world recession, of a growing indebtedness of the developing world, of a persistent retrenchment of the more affluent from the duty and commitment to aid weaker nations and communities, this report wishes to convey a sense of hope in the future, and an exhortation to join in a truly worthwhile and engaging challenge: that of building—as we move into the twenty-first century—a world where everyone, man, woman, and child, can live in a home they are not ashamed of; where everyone can enjoy a minimum of space, privacy, security, and protection; where all have access to water and sanitation good enough not to impair one's health, or that of one's children; where the entire community can exercise a right to enjoy health, cultural, and educational facilities; where everyone can share a sense of pride in living in settlements, be they small villages or large cities, planned and developed through common efforts and for the common good.

I believe that this challenge can be met. I am also confident that the present report will make a major contribution to show how engaging this challenge is, and to show appropriate and affordable strategies to meet it.

DR ARCOT RAMACHANDRAN
Under-Secretary-General
Executive Director

Contents

PART IV   Conclusion

List of Boxes

List of Figures

List of Tables

Introduction

At its thirty-fourth session, in December 1979, the General Assembly of the United Nations decided (resolution 34/114) that the quinquennial housing survey called for by a previous resolution (2598, xxiv) should become the *Global Report on Human Settlements* and should provide a complete review of human settlements conditions, including an analysis of the forces and trends accounting for both their present development and their continuing creation, maintenance, and improvement. In order to meet this goal, the *Report* was to analyse worldwide and regional developments, trends, and prospects in the field of human settlements. The *Report* would also:

• Provide a basic source of information on the global and regional conditions of settlements, which would be of value to individual countries and international agencies in shaping their policies and programmes.

• Encourage and maintain a general interest in and contribute to the understanding of the evolving nature of settlements, the interrelatedness of their parts, and the significance of settlement systems in providing settings for social, economic, and physical development.

• Provide a periodic updating and synthesis of all information generated by the United Nations Centre for Human Settlements (Habitat) and of other information available to it from sources inside and outside the United Nations system.

The *Report* presents its findings in four parts. Part I (Human Settlements: A Strategy for Development) introduces the concept of human settlements as it is understood today. Emphasis is placed on the notion that human settlements development, maintenance, and improvement constitute both one of the fundamental aims of and one of the basic prerequisites for equitable and sustainable development. An attempt has been made to outline the evolution of the past decade's theoretical and practical approaches to human settlements policy and planning, with particular reference to strategies for the improvement of the living conditions of the poor and disadvantaged.

Part II (Global Conditions, Trends, and Prospects) responds to the prime purpose set down in the project's mandate—to analyse world-wide and regional developments, trends, and prospects in the field of human settlements. It is composed of three chapters: the first describes global trends, i.e. the conditions and trends which are similar in all regions of the world, the second is devoted to the developed countries, and the third covers the developing countries. Here, some of the most acute differences become clear and set the tone for the next part of the report.

Part III (Key Policy Areas in Settlements Development) is based on the conclusion emerging from the analysis of human settlements conditions, trends, and prospects that the greatest problems of the world's human settlements system are in developing countries. While human settlements conditions have largely stabilized in developed countries, the developing countries are going to be subjected to demographic and physical changes never witnessed before. Moreover, it is in the developing regions that the greatest challenges to economic and social stability will have to be met.

The eight chapters of this part are devoted to key policy areas requiring the attention of national and subnational governments. These policy issues are principally oriented to the situation in developing countries but they are not of concern to developing countries alone. The key policy areas are: national development and its relationship to human settlements; resource mobilization, mainly focusing on the financing of human settlements; institutional needs for rational human settlements management; settlements management, including planning, development, operation, maintenance, and improvement of the physical structure of settlements; building materials and construction technologies and their relationship to development;

options for the provision of affordable infrastructure; the management of land resources; and the delivery of shelter, particularly to the poor majorities of the developing countries. These issues are seen as policy areas where vigorous action is needed to raise the level of efficiency of human settlements and to address the core issue highlighted by this *Report*—the living conditions of the poor and disadvantaged.

Part IV (Conclusion) describes the measures that are to be used to build and operate the cities of the developing countries beyond the year 2000 and summarizes some of the main arguments in favour of an innovative concept of human settlements development as a strategy for strengthening the economic, social, and physical structures of developing countries. A focus on human settlements can be a means of shifting priorities from outmoded development models to a new model based on community participation and technological self-sufficiency, leading eventually to economic growth and equitable access to benefits. This process is seen as the only one likely to meet the needs of developing countries over the next decades.

Part I

Human Settlements: A Strategy for Development

1 People, Habitat, and Development

The definition of human settlements is elusive, particularly because most people, although perfectly capable of grasping the concept, are normally unable to describe it. One of the main problems is that this term—as with 'culture' or 'civilization' or 'development'—offers the temptation of defining it in the widest encompassing terms. However, in the simplest terms, human settlements are where organized human activity takes place. At first glance, defining human activity as 'organized' could appear to be a tautology, but the reference to 'organization' is needed as a reminder that human settlements are often conceived and invariably developed and used as systems.

Human settlements, in today's world, are all pervasive, and settlement systems have progressively extended from very limited enclaves to the whole surface of the earth. This report —the *Global Report on Human Settlements*—is defined as global not only because it has to do with all countries of the world but also because it is based on the concept of one global human settlements system. This concept is not new, but growing interdependence among countries evidences its special current importance. Human settlements function as a system at the global, regional, subregional, national, and subnational scale—down to the lowest unit of human habitation. This view of human settlements also introduces another central concept: human settlements are not simply housing or, for that matter, merely the physical structure of a city, town, or village but an integrated combination of all human activity processes—residence, work, education, health, culture, leisure, etc.—and the physical structure that supports them.

Human settlements and the systems they form are the expression of a nation's society, of its values, and of its achievements. The great civilizations of the past are largely, if not exclusively, renowned for the great human settlements they were able to produce. However, the values and symbols expressed by the great nations and civilizations of the past were the product of selected and privileged élites. Today, different parameters are employed to assess societal and global achievements. It is taken for granted that cities can be built and individual buildings erected on a scale and of a nature never seen before: technology has advanced to a point where very few obstacles exist, at least in theory, to the improvement of human settlements and human settlements systems beyond recognition. Because of this, judgement criteria have shifted from the appreciation of isolated achievements of élite societal groups to the measurement of the overall conditions enjoyed by an entire human settlements system and of a whole society.

Emphasis is placed here on 'settlement conditions', as opposed to living conditions. Whereas the expression 'living conditions' generally applies to the personal environment, settlement conditions extend to all those components of the physical environment with which an individual or a community comes into contact and which are used on a regular basis for the whole range of human activities—the individual dwelling and its related services, the dwelling's immediate surroundings, community facilities, transportation and communication networks, and so on. It is essential to keep in mind that the quality of dwellings and related services, although of great importance, is only one of the factors to be considered. Furthermore, the argument of this report is that one of the main criteria by which a society's values and achievements can be measured is the settlement conditions of its weakest social groups.

Economists and development analysts will be the first to acknowledge that economic development demands physical infrastructure (ports, airports, roads, railways, power lines, communications) and efficient social services (including centres capable of handling administration and disseminating knowledge). Therefore, the need for settlement nodes to function at an optimally efficient level is universally accepted. Yet, no individual settlement, and therefore no national or subnational settlements system, can function efficiently if policy-makers allow settlement conditions to deteriorate beyond control and without a semblance of rationality.

Human settlements are not simply indicators of societal achievement: they are also a country's fixed capital asset. Public investments in human settlements development—unlike investments in 'productive' sectors, which more often than not suffer rapid obsolescence—are rarely wasted. Although much could be said about the criteria used by governments to determine the nature and distribution of human settlements investment (particularly in terms of social equity, environmental considerations, and efficiency), it can be safely argued that investment in human settlements invariably contributes to the improvement of a society's ability to respond to basic development needs, such as shelter, education, health, mobility, and, generally, productive output. No national economy, anywhere, can afford an inefficient human settlements system, since human settlements are the backbone of development. People, habitat, and development are parts of an indivisible whole.

2 Changing Thinking on Human Settlements: Turning Challenge into Opportunity

The purpose of this chapter is to highlight the changing context of human settlements and to document changing thinking on human settlements policies and planning, thus setting the scene for subsequent chapters. Since development and change in human settlements cannot be separated, either conceptually or analytically, from processes of economic and social development, a review of changing thinking on human settlements must, by definition, incorporate an assessment of recent development trends.

Since the late 1970s, the world has witnessed a recession of a magnitude unknown in half a century. Given the high degree of integration in the world economy, no nation, whether market economy or centrally planned, has been able to isolate itself from the recession's impacts nor from its profound effects on political and social institutions. The combination of falls in output, sluggish rates of economic growth, persistent inflation, and high unemployment is a phenomenon new to the 1980s. While economists are divided on both causes and remedies, most share the view that the 'development crisis' is rooted in structural problems that constitute a challenge to economic theory, social processes, and political decision-making.

The impacts of the development crisis have been severe in the industrialized countries, but they have been most dramatic in the developing countries, as a consequence of the dependent nature of their development patterns. The limitations of the models that have moulded the development efforts of most developing countries and shaped the growth of human settlements within them have become apparent in the past decade. It has become increasingly clear, for example, that, in a highly integrated world economy, a nation's development prospects are as much conditioned by the terms of participation in the international economic system as by internal processes of accumulation and distribution. The terms of participation, however, are far from being equal: the international economic system has evolved with in-built and self-propelling mechanisms that work to the disadvantage of the developing countries. These mechanisms, with their origins in a different historical period, constitute obstacles to processes of economic and social development which developing countries, without the co-operation of the developed countries, can do very little to overcome.

It has also become apparent that the inequalities that characterize the relations between rich and poor countries are still often internalized in national power structures and condition the relationships between rich and poor people within developing countries. The very processes that lock national economies into the world economic system are able, if left to their own devices, to block full national economic participation by the poorest groups. Experience has shown that without purposefully designed redistributive mechanisms there can be no guarantees that the benefits of development will reach the poor through 'trickle-down' processes.

It has also become clear that high growth in output from manufacturing no longer translates into high rates of labour absorption, one of the central tenets of the labour-surplus growth model. While some developing countries have achieved impressive rates of industrial growth, such growth has not been matched by growth of employment. There are many reasons for low rates of labour absorption, but most of them are found in the dependent nature of much of the industrialization that has taken place in developing countries. The stage has been reached where, with current rates of labour absorption, industrial output in the developing countries would need to increase by around 40 per cent per annum for the next 10 years, if new entrants to the labour market and those currently unemployed are to be absorbed by the industrial sector. In the past five years, there has been virtually no increase at all.

The modernization model has been responsible for important biases in national development strategies, some of which have left indelible

Box 2.1 The impact of the global recession on developing countries

The world has experienced two recessions in the past two decades. These recessions have caused considerable hardships in the industrialized countries, but their impact on the developing countries has been critical. The consequences of the 1979–83 recession, less sharp but more prolonged than that of 1973–5, have effectively brought development efforts to a standstill in many developing countries. The severity of the economic problems that currently confront the developing countries is clearly evident by reference to the indicators traditionally employed to measure economic development.

Growth of GDP and trade

After two years of very low growth (0.5 per cent per annum), real output in the developing countries increased by 2.0 per cent in 1984 and by 2.4 per cent in 1985, with a growth rate of 3 per cent expected in 1986. Growth forecasts for 1986 for non-oil-producing developing countries were 4.5 per cent, from 3.3 per cent in 1985.

The growth of exports declined from 11.7 per cent in 1984 to 3.4 per cent in 1985 for non-oil-producing developing countries. World market prices, particularly of primary commodities, decreased, resulting in a decline of the terms of trade for developing countries of 1.1 per cent in 1985. Only late in 1986 and early in 1985 was some relief felt by different groups of developing countries—first, by a number of the heavily indebted countries, which benefited from the decline in interest rates and a fall in the value of the dollar, and secondly by the oil-importing countries, which benefited from the break in the price of oil in the first quarter of 1986. Despite a rise in coffee prices, the prices of non-oil primary commodities as a group fell by 11 per cent in 1985.

For the group as a whole, the weighted average rate of inflation, which rose from 25 to 27 per cent in 1980–2 to about 37 per cent in 1984, accelerated to almost 40 per cent in 1985. Little progress has been made in reducing inflation over the past two to three years, a period during which the

corresponding rate of price increases in industrial countries was cut by more than a third.

The decline in dollar price of non-oil commodity exports from the developing countries in 1985 was caused partly by slow demand growth since early 1985 in industrial countries. Exports of manufactures from developing countries rose by only 3.3 per cent, compared with 6.6 per cent in 1984. Countries that rely heavily on the US market, particularly in Latin America and East Asia, were most affected. Continued weakness in the oil market, with increased production by high-income countries, reduced the export revenues of oil-exporting developing nations by almost 5 per cent.

The current-account deficit of developing countries amounted to $34 billion in 1985, down slightly over the year before, and more than $50 billion less than the peak deficit of $91 billion in 1982. Declines in lending, small increases in export revenues, and declines in terms of trade resulted in an increase in non-oil-producing developing-country imports of only 3.3 per cent in volume, down from 5.2 per cent in 1984.

External debt

Developing countries have been compelled to borrow heavily, in order to cushion themselves from some of the worst effects of the global recession and to secure the funds required to maintain development efforts. The growth of their indebtedness has been particularly marked since the mid-1970s. In the period 1974–84, it increased from $140 billion to nearly $700 billion. In 1982, the combined debt of the developing countries surpassed, for the first time, the total value of their exports. The 1980s have also witnessed a significant worsening of debt-service ratios, which are today twice as onerous as a decade ago. The deterioration of debt-servicing has its origins in declining terms of trade and stagnating export performance. As the figures presented here indicated, debt has become an extremely severe problem since 1975.

imprints on human settlements development. An emphasis on the 'modern' sector has led to a preoccupation with large towns and cities, the places where the industrial development that has taken place has been very largely concentrated. Because the modern sector was conceived of in terms of large towns and cities, economic development strategies were strongly biased in their favour, and the attention that rural settlements and rural areas received was often limited to the expansion of cash-crop pro-

duction. Food production for local consumption has received little attention, with the consequence that it has stagnated in many countries.

Prospects for human settlements in the context of the present development crisis

These general economic trends, which are certainly not encouraging, have inspired many development analysts to reach pessimistic con-

Box 2.1 continued

Table 1. Debt indicators for developing countries

	1970	1975	1980	1981	1982	1983	1984	1985
Total debt outstanding and disbursed (billions of dollars)	68.4	168.6	431.6	492.5	552.4	629.9	674.1	711.2
Ratio of total debt to export earnings	99.4	76.4	90.1	97.5	116.4	134.3	130.4	135.7
Debt service ratio (ratio of interest payments and amortization to exports)	13.5	11.1	16.1	17.7	20.7	19.4	19.8	21.9

Source: World Bank, *World Development Report 1986.*

Table 2. Economic indicators for developing countries, 1980–1986

	1980	1981	1982	1983	1984	1985[a]	1986[b]
Growth of output[c]							
All developing countries	3.5	1.3	0.3	0.8	2.0	2.4	3.0
Non-oil-producing developing countries	5.0	1.7	0.6	1.9	3.8	3.3	4.5
Growth of per capita GDP[c]							
All	3.0	0.2	−0.8	−1.3	1.4	0.9	0.4
Non-oil-producing	2.4	0.8	0.3	0.6	3.1	2.7	2.3
Growth of exports[c]							
All	−4.0	−5.7	−8.1	2.9	7.1	0.4	3.8
Non-oil-producing	9.1	6.5	0.7	8.3	11.7	3.4	4.3
Growth of imports[c]							
All	8.5	7.1	−4.2	−3.2	2.2	−0.3	−0.6
Non-oil-producing	6.5	1.5	−5.5	1.6	5.2	3.3	5.1
Terms of trade[c]							
All	16.7	3.0	−1.2	−3.9	1.2	−2.2	−11.7
Non-oil-producing	−5.9	−5.3	−2.6	0.2	1.5	−1.2	3.6
Balance of payments[d]							
All	27.9	−49.2	−90.9	−58.9	−35.1	−34.1	−69.3
Non-oil-producing	−67.1	−80.2	−65.3	−44.1	−26.5	−27.6	−20.3
Consumer prices[c]							
All	27.1	26.0	24.5	32.7	37.4	39.3	25.9
Non-oil-producing	32.2	30.6	28.0	37.1	47.6	53.0	30.6

[a] Preliminary estimates.
[b] Forecasts.
[c] Percentage change from preceding year.
[d] Billions of US dollars.

Sources: IMF, *World Economic Survey* (Washington DC, 1986). United Nations, *World Economic Survey 1986* (New York, 1986).

clusions on the prospects for human settlements development. In many countries, the past decade has witnessed a narrowing of planning horizons and an erosion of the capacity for purposeful planning. Some countries have deliberately chosen to dismantle planning mechanisms and to de-emphasize, in practice if not necessarily in theory, the need for co-ordinated and integrated decision-making. Such trends have not always been conducive to effective settlement policy-making and planning.

In both developed and developing countries, there has been disenchantment with settlements policies and plans which have promised more than they could deliver. Settlements have grown with only scant respect for the master plans laboriously prepared to guide their development. Deconcentration and decentralization policies have failed to curtail the growth of primate cities. New national capitals that promised much have delivered little at exaggerated cost. Rural development programmes have

Box 2.2   Africa's economic and social crisis

Nowhere are the prospects of the poor and disadvantaged more uncertain than in the low-income countries of Africa. In many of them, development efforts have ground to a halt, and the stage has been reached where survival of tens of millions of people can no longer be taken for granted. The continent's predicament is one of formidable dimensions in which political, economic, and social problems are inextricably linked. Difficulties have been compounded by the severe effects of global recession, adverse climatic conditions (including the most serious droughts in living memory in some countries), and the decline in productivity of biological systems. It is also the region with the highest rates of population growth and rural–urban migration.

The region is becoming poorer. Per capita real GDP declined by 4.7 per cent in 1983, and by a further 1.6 per cent and 1.3 per cent in 1984 and 1985, respectively. Although the region's terms of trade improved slightly during the 1983–4 period, the decline in the prices of non-oil primary commodities led to a 5.6 per cent deterioration in 1985 in the terms of trade of the low-income African countries. The volume of exports registered a fall of 16.1 per cent in 1981—the largest since 1974—but recovered in the period 1983–5. The export volume increased by 6.1 per cent in 1985, but the purchasing power of exports in 1985 was much lower than in 1977 because non-oil commodity prices were much weaker in 1985 than had been expected. These prices declined by some 11 per cent, in US dollar terms, compared with the projection of 2.25 per cent decline.

The region's debt is increasing, and its capacity to pay its creditors is declining. Total debt at the end of 1985 amounted to $168.6 billion, $120 billion of which had been disbursed. Over the period 1973–83, total disbursed debt increased at an annual average rate of 18 per cent, far exceeding the growth of output and exports. As a result of the hardening of the overall terms of debt and stagnation in exports, the region's debt–service ratio increased from 13.6 per cent in 1980 to 27 per cent in 1985. While the region's indebtedness has increased, aid has decreased from $13.1 billion to $8.9 billion between 1983 and 1984, a fall that is even bigger in real terms.

Trends in agriculture have become a particular source of concern. While most countries in Africa are potentially able to support their populations, expansion of food production has failed to match population growth. In the 1970s, agricultural production increased at less than 2 per cent per annum (1.2 per cent in the case of cereals), while the demand for food increased by more than 3 per cent per annum. In only four countries did domestic food production increase faster than the demand for food. For the region as a whole, real earnings from crops and livestock declined by 2 per cent per annum throughout the decade, while imports of agricultural products increased by 9 per cent, with the share of food in total imports reaching 20 per cent for the first time in 1980. Total imports in 1984 are estimated at 5.3 million tons, with a food-aid component of nearly 3 million tons. Immediate crop prospects in about one-third of the region's countries are poor.

The economies of all countries and the survival prospects of many poor people have suffered from the degradation and loss of agricultural soils, the destruction of vegetal cover, the desertification of pasture lands, and the depletion of groundwater. In efforts to survive, populations have resorted to the cultivation of marginal lands with fragile soils, reduced fallow periods, and overgrazed rangelands. More than 2.5 million hectares of savannah are estimated to have been destroyed in 1983 alone, while deserts in some parts of the region are advancing by 10 kilometres a year. Topsoil losses, in countries with some of the worst food problems, have been estimated to be in excess of 1 billion tons per year.

The growth of poverty and hunger and the erosion of the productivity of biological systems have greatly exacerbated the continent's chronic health and nutritional problems. In the Sahelian subregion, protein–energy malnutrition is believed to affect 20–30 per cent of all pre-school children, and some 40 per cent of all pre-school children and 60 per cent of pregnant women are estimated to suffer from nutrition anaemia. Diet deficiencies combined with poor environmental hygiene and the lack of potable water contribute to a high incidence of infectious diseases and high child-mortality rates, both of which have been increasing in recent years. Generally, a higher proportion of the population of African countries is undernourished than in other developing regions, and, while Africa has only one-sixth of the population of the developing countries, the majority of the cases of infant deaths occur in the region.

Africa's current social and economic crisis cannot be resolved by short-term and remedial measures alone. It demands a long-term commitment of resources aimed at developing the infrastructure that can support sustainable economic and social development. It will be impossible to develop the required infrastructure without the existence, at the country level, of a spatial framework that can guide investments in the economic and social sectors and which is able to reconcile the often-competing needs that stem from agricultural and industrial development and from environmental protection. Human settlements policies provide such a framework. Human settlements policies alone cannot solve Africa's crisis, but there can be no lasting solution to the region's problems without them.

Source: 'Critical Economic Situation in Africa: Report of the Secretary General on the Critical Social and Economic Situation in Africa', document prepared for the special session of the General Assembly, 27–31 May 1986. IMF, *World Economic Survey* (Washington, 1986).

failed to reduce income inequalities. Urban housing policies have been unable to provide shelter at costs that intended beneficiaries can reasonably afford. Such failures have exposed the weaknesses in traditional approaches to planning and encouraged the search for policies that are based on an understanding of what is feasible as well as desirable.

The past decade has been favourable neither to sustained social and economic development nor to the emergence of the integrated and comprehensive approaches advocated for human settlements development. It has exposed the limitations of the model that many developing nations have chosen to guide their development, and called into question the conventional wisdom that has shaped settlements policies and plans. It has also witnessed a search for pragmatic approaches to settlements development, less ambitious in aspiration, more attuned to resource scarcities, and more realistic in appraisal of what is possible than those of a decade ago. Generalized models and deterministic blueprints for human settlements development are giving way to strategies that reflect specific historical experience and the constellation of problems and opportunities that exist in every country.

Changing thinking on the urban poor

While the past decade has indicated the limitations of conventional planning, it has dispelled

---

Box 2.3   The 'trickle-down' model of development

The limitations of the models that have moulded the development efforts of most developing countries and shaped the growth of human settlements within them have become increasingly apparent in the past decade.

The most favoured model, the 'trickle-down' model of development, was developed in the 1950s and 1960s, a period of rapid decolonization and of unprecedented economic expansion on a world scale. Most of the newly independent nations were able to share in this growth; throughout the 1950s, the developing countries attained annual average growth rates of nearly 5 per cent, rising to 6 per cent during the 1960s. These rates of growth were consistently higher than the 4 per cent achieved by the developed countries over the same 20-year period.

The high expectations were predicated on a model that assumed the universality of prevalent economic development thinking. The model implicitly regarded developing countries as developed countries at an early stage of development and as equal competitors in a development race. In this linear view of the development process, all countries were assumed to start at more or less the same point and to be confronted with more or less the same obstacles. Some countries, the model's logic dictated, would simply move more quickly than others in the race to become developed. The direction to be followed was mapped out by the North American and European academic community, and the speed at which the obstacles could be negotiated would be determined by the carrots and sticks to be found in the hands of strengthened national institutions and entrepreneurial classes, expanding transnational corporations, and bilateral and multilateral aid agencies.

The economic theory that underpinned the modernization model and the development strategies derived from it was labelled the 'labour-surplus growth process'. The theory contended that concentration on the development of the 'modern' sector would gradually eliminate the 'traditional' or 'backward' sector as surplus labour was drawn off to work in the modern sector. The latter was conceived of as the engine of growth capable of powering economic and social development, and the traditional sector as the cheap fuel that was required to propel the engine. The development of the modern sector required the exploitation of new resources, the production of cash crops for export and local processing, and, especially, the creation of a manufacturing base able to produce goods for the local market within the framework of import substitution. The 'traditional' sector tended to be regarded as a sea of poverty and backwardness with isolated islands that contributed to the modernization drive through the production of exportable cash crops. The distribution of the benefits of development, in the form of equitable income distribution and improved access to social services, would be guaranteed by 'trickle-down' processes. Such processes would ensure that the urban and rural poor would not only reap some of the benefits of development but would also, over time, be moulded into a growing legion of factory workers, secretaries, professionals, and governmental administrators.

The successes of the model, however, have been more than offset by its failures. Its most serious failure has been its very limited capacity to provide the poor with productive employment. After three decades of development efforts, the number of people living in poverty, without a reliable source of income and without any real prospect of securing the work that could provide it, is greater than ever before.

most of the reservations about the issue which possibly constitutes the greatest challenge to human settlements development for decades to come—the potential contribution that the people are able to make to the development of human settlements in an environment of scarcity. Thinking on migration, urbanization, and the provision of shelter for the urban poor has, for example, undergone significant change. In the 1950s and early 1960s, migration and urbanization tended to be viewed negatively. Reactions to both were conditioned by the dominant economic model that distinguished between a modern sector, defined mainly in terms of manufacturing industry, and a traditional sector, conceived as a sea of rural poverty and backwardness. The model interpreted migration in terms of poor and backward peasants who flocked to the city in search of jobs in the modern sector. The 'engine of growth', however, was soon flooded by its own fuel, since there were more labourers than there were jobs for them.

Widely held perceptions about migrants, the work they resorted to, and the settlements they built included the following:

• The new urban poor possessed insufficient education, training, or skills to secure employment, and their backgrounds made them unemployable in the city. By flooding to the city, they constituted an economic drain on the nation, whereas they could be effectively used in 'gainful employment' in agricultural production. They belonged on the farm, not in the city.

• The unemployed and unemployable in the city resorted to meaningless work. In order to survive, they were reduced to being shoeshine boys, hawkers, beggars, prostitutes, and the like. Such occupations contributed nothing to the growth of the modern sector, and those who existed in the informal sector constituted a parasitic enclave in the city that fed off the modern sector and impeded its growth.

• Because their illiteracy rates were high, their educational levels low, their skills virtually non-existent and their culture rural-based, the poor were unable to participate in urban life and had little to offer the city.

• Migrants flocked to the city in indiscriminate and uncontrolled ways, and their reasons for migrating were often poorly defined. While they knew what they were leaving behind, they had little idea of what to expect in the city, and they severed their links with the rural areas without establishing a basis for assimilation in the city. The move was irrevocable, and, once it had taken place, the peasant was stuck in the city: there was no going back and nowhere else to go.

• They were the hungriest and most poorly housed. The settlements they built were chaotic, unorganized, and unorganizable, and they were not only a public health risk and a blot on the landscape but also fertile breeding grounds for organized and petty crime, juvenile delinquency, prostitution, family breakdown, and illegitimacy. They were also seen as hotbeds of political unrest and the breeding grounds for social disruption.

The early studies of migrants, slums, and squatter settlements were largely descriptive. Few were based on empirical analysis, and even fewer gave more than passing reference to the structural processes through which patterns and systems evolve. They strongly reflected the norms, values, and expectations of Western researchers who borrowed concepts derived from the study of poverty in the slums of North American and European cities.

These essentially negative views of rural–urban migration, squatters, and the settlements of the poor gave rise to such expressions as 'ring of misery', 'creeping cancers', and 'slums of despair'. They also gave rise to such concepts as:

• *The culture of poverty*. Derived from studies of poverty in North American ghettos, this view stressed that unemployment, low levels of education, and non-participation in urban institutions and city life prevented the urban poor from seizing the opportunities that exist in the city. Because it was transmitted to later generations, it was difficult to break out of the culture of poverty.

• *Rural–urban dichotomy*. This was a concept which asserted that the rural backgrounds and traditions of migrants isolated them in the city and made it impossible for them to participate in urban social and economic life. The impediments of a rural background meant that urban opportunity was almost bound to pass the migrant by.

• *Marginality*. Squatters and slum dwellers were defined in terms of their marginal position in the city. They were considered economically marginal because they contributed little to production and even less to economic growth. They were socially marginal because they were unable to participate in or were excluded from formal organizations and urban institutions. They were culturally marginal because their origins, customs, values, and behaviour prevented them from entering the mainstream of urban life. They were politically marginal because they were unable to influence processes of resource allocations and decision-making. They were geographically marginal because they lived in settlements on the fringes of cities, often in places which were of little interest to others.

A succession of recent studies has shown that these early views, while not necessarily without foundation, were at best half-truths. The findings of a wide range of empirical studies have not only challenged or discredited early beliefs but also contributed to a sophisticated and positive image of migrants and slums and squatter settlements. These studies have analysed in detail the patterns and processes of city growth and the framework within which the urban poor, especially squatters, live and work. While it is both difficult and hazardous to attempt to generalize the findings of such a large body of research, the following descriptions can be considered to hold true with respect to patterns of migration, squatter settlements, and the informal sector.

Patterns of migration

Decisions to migrate are seldom arbitrary. While always involving individuals, decisions may be collective, involving kinship groups and even rural communities as a whole. When migration is voluntary, migrants tend to be 'positively selected' from their home populations; while this degree of selectivity may change over time, rural migrants generally comprise the 'vital' and enterprising elements of the rural population. In the case of migration for employment, young adults almost always predominate, since they tend to be not only physically strong but also adaptable to the demands placed upon them by the urban environment.

The overwhelming majority of people migrate for economic reasons, and in most cases the move is justified. On the whole, migrants do succeed in increasing their income and improving their standard of living. Work can be found within a period of two months, and those who start out with undesirable and low-paid jobs are often able to find other jobs over time. There is no evidence that migrants are confined to marginal employment, or that they contribute disproportionately to urban unemployment. There is evidence to suggest that, over time, the employment-related differences between migrants and non-migrants with the same age, sex, and educational level tend to disappear.

Migrants are not necessarily lost in the city, nor are they alone. There are numerous mechanisms for promoting assimilation and adjustment upon arrival, including kinship groups and voluntary associations. As with the urban born, migrants may be securely anchored in networks of kinship and friendship, and, far from being uprooted and disconnected from their rural home, migrants are likely to maintain contact with their own community through a network of reciprocal relationships and obligations. They have a high capacity for adaptation and are usually able to adopt urban patterns of behaviour without forgetting how things were done at home and the reasons for doing them. Rural values do not necessarily disappear or disintegrate: while distance may develop between migrants and their rural ways, migrants neither abandon nor lose the ability to enter into social relationships governed by rural norms. They are able to behave in urban and rural ways as the situation dictates.

Migrants tend to move in step-wise progression through the urban hierarchy, especially in Latin America: it is mainly in Africa that migration involves a sharp 'leap' from a small village to a distant city. Not all moves to the city are permanent: there is reverse migration, circular migration, and floating migration. Migration is not necessarily a once-and-for-all move: several moves may be made over a lifetime. Although a country's urban system may share in migratory movement, individual cities will not do so equally: migration will be concentrated on the area where the structure of opportunity is perceived to be greatest—traditionally, the nation's capital or a very large city. This perception has so far been largely justified but may change in the future: in some countries, there is recent evidence of increased migration to intermediate cities.

Migration may have beneficial effects that are larger than those for the individual migrant. The remittances that the successful migrant is able to send home, for example, may help improve the distribution of income between urban and rural areas. Similarly, the increased demand for food from growing urban populations can serve to stimulate agricultural production.

The squatter settlement

Squatter settlements are not marginal: they make significant contributions to the city as a whole. Squatters add to the city's labour force, consume some of its production, and house themselves at little direct cost to the city. There is a considerable degree of integration between squatter communities and the 'mainstream' of urban life, and many levels of interaction between the formal and informal sectors. There is political, economic, social, and cultural integration, but in all cases it is characterized by structural inequality. It is not the lack of integration that is a problem but rather the conditions and terms that govern the participation of the poor.

Box 2.4   Types of low-income settlements

The popular image of the city in the developing countries is one of a central business district and a collection of middle-income and upper-income neighbourhoods set in a sea of squatter settlements peopled by desperately poor migrants drawn from rural areas. However, there is hardly a city in the developing countries that fits this stereotype. The popular conception does not begin to capture the diversity that exists in the types of accommodation occupied by low-income groups and the settlements they build. A partial listing of urban residential settlement types would need to include at least the following:

● *'Back-to-back' housing* (the *callejon* in Mexico, *vecindad* in Mexico, and *conventillo* in Chile). These consist of a series of horizontal one-room and two-room rental units with shared water and sanitation facilities, often built around courtyards or accessible only through entryways. They are usually occupied by families who pay rent.

● *Government 'temporary' or emergency housing* (the *barracas populares* in Brazil, *villas de emergencia* in Chile, and *jhuggi-jhompri* colonies in northern India). This type of accommodation is provided by government agencies to rehouse people displaced as a result of natural disaster, political action (refugees), or eviction. In Latin America, emergency housing usually takes the form of barracks, although it may comprise large single buildings. In Africa and parts of Asia it may comprise tented camps. While officially designated 'temporary', such accommodations may exist for decades and become part of a city's housing stock.

● *'Occupational' settlement* (the *conjunto* in Brazil). This is an accommodation, often of poor physical standard, built by enterprises for low-income workers. This type may also include dwellings built by an agency, labour union, association, or other collectivist group for its members. These residential enclaves inevitably tend to have a high degree of occupational specialization.

● *Tilted plots without services* (the *barrios piratas* in Colombia, *suburbios* in Brazil, and *colonias populares* in Mexico). These are expanses of simple, separate, privately owned houses with very little in the way of supporting infrastructure and services. The houses are laid out more or less according to a predetermined plan but may range from little more than hovels to consolidated housing.

● *'Urban villages'*. These are small rural settlements engulfed by cities in the course of their growth. The villages are usually devoid of services, even though the new development that surrounds them may be reasonably well served. Such villages are much in evidence in Indian cities: about 110 villages, with 250,000 people, have been engulfed by Delhi alone. Jakarta is made up of an interlinked series of *kampungs* and has been called the largest village in the world.

● *'Floating settlements'*. The best known examples are the boat communities in Hong Kong and Bangkok.

● *Camps on garbage* (the *ciudades perdidas* of Mexico City). These are peopled by those who live and work on municipal garbage dumps, living virtually on and off the garbage. Tolerated by the dump administration, people build their shelter in and from the city's refuse.

● *Roof dwellers* (*turgurios de azoteas* in Mexico City). In a number of Latin American countries, people rent space on flat roofs of single-family houses or apartment blocks, and build themselves shacks. They are usually located in dense areas, close to places of work.

● *Pavement dwellers*. These are the absolutely homeless who live and sleep on the streets, often in spaces they have 'claimed' to be their own. Calcutta and Bombay each have

Squatter settlements are neither unorganized nor unorganizable: on the contrary, they tend to be highly organized places. Capacities for self-organization have part of their explanation in the illegal nature of the community, since the threat of eviction creates common interests that must be defended. The organization of the community is likely to be strongly influenced by its recognized leaders.

While the physical appearance of the settlement may be homogeneous, it may be very heterogeneous from a social point of view. Squatter settlements are seldom limited to a single social rank or even class, and often display a broad spectrum of occupations and social strata. While squatter settlements are a manifes-

tation of poverty, they are not necessarily synonymous with it.

Squatters *per se* are neither radicals nor conservatives: they can be normal responsible citizens, if given the opportunity to participate in the decisions that affect them. Communities are seldom unidimensional: they are usually complex, varied, and, in part, situationally oriented, and play different political games opportunistically.

The squatter settlement is a solution to shelter problems in a highly restricted housing market. The root cause of squatting cannot be found in the nature of the squatters themselves but rather in their limited resources and their lack of access to conventional housing. In this situation,

---

Box 2.4 continued

an estimated 200,000 or more pavement dwellers, and they exist in many other cities. A variation of this group is formed by abandoned or runaway children who live off the streets and have no fixed home. The most publicized group, though not necessarily the largest, are the *gamines* of Bogota.

• *Mosque dwellers*. In some cities, in Western Asia in particular, people without a permanent home sleep in city mosques. Some mosques in Cairo are visited every night by up to 2,000 people.

• *Converted structures*. All manner of structures once used for other purposes have been claimed for low-income housing. Such structures include palaces abandoned by the rich in parts of Western Asia: where one family and its retainers once lived, there may now be 30 or 40 families, each occupying a small part of an interior courtyard, a bedroom, or a kitchen outbuilding.

• *Inner-city slums* (the *tugurios* of Latin American cities, *chawls* of Indian cities, *medinas* of the Arab world, and shophouse tenements of South-east Asia). This is not a type of accommodation but rather a generic term representing a wide range of accommodation, including entrepreneurial rooming houses built as single constructions with the specific intent of creating very small units for the maximization of rents, temporary rental space in the form of cheap rooming houses, hotels and pensions ostensibly for transient populations, and a very wide range of apartment buildings and converted structures, often with shared facilities.

• *Squatter settlements* (the *bidonvilles* in former French colonies, *barong-barongs* in the Philippines, *gecekondus* in Turkey, *barriadas* or *pueblos jovenes* in Lima, *favelas* in Brazil, *jhuggi-jhompri* in the north of India, and *katchi abadis* in

Pakistan). Squatter settlements are also referred to as spontaneous settlements, in reference to the absence of governmental aid and control; uncontrolled settlements, in reference to their lack of regulation; shantytowns, in reference to the poor quality of construction; popular settlements, in recognition of the fact that they are inhabited by low-income people; marginal settlements, in reference to the role their inhabitants are assumed to play in urban society and to their location within the city; and transitional settlements, as an expression of a positive view suggesting that they can, over time, become consolidated and permanent settlements. Squatter settlements share one distinguishing feature: they are built on land that does not belong to those who build the houses. The land is invaded by them, sometimes by individuals or small groups, and sometimes as a result of collective action. Such possession with respect to land held without title is the origin of the term 'squatter'.

While far from comprehensive, the above list serves to show that there are many types of low-income settlement and that, within broad types, there may be so much variation as to defy generalization.

Each type of or subtype has its own delivery system, each has its own unique set of organizational, social, economic, and environmental characteristics and patterns, and each fulfils different types of settlement needs. Treating all types as a single category serves to compound confusion and makes it impossible to understand the dynamics of large settlements in the developing countries and their housing markets.

Source: United Nations Centre for Human Settlements (Habitat), *The Residential Circumstances of the Urban Poor in Developing Countries* (New York: Praeger, 1981).

squatting constitutes a rational solution. There are valid reasons for the sites selected by squatters, and location usually determines housing choice. The squatter settlement, as with the inner-city slum, is often a staging area for the urban poor. It offers more than shelter: it can form the 'base camp' for strategies that enable the poor not only to survive but to climb out of poverty.

Squatters have demonstrated that they have the skills, motivation, and, sometimes, the resources to provide basic shelter for themselves. In favourable circumstances, they are able to produce solid houses as well as to consolidate their communities, and even in cases where they are exposed to the perpetual risk of eviction they have shown a readiness to invest in houses and communities. The growth and improvement of squatter communities are most marked in Latin American cities, less so in African cities. The difference not only is a function of the age of the settlements—squatting was taking place in Latin American cities in the 1940s, whereas it did not become widespread in Africa until the 1960s—but also appears linked to social and economic aspects of a city's and nation's development.

Squatters are able to develop their own market mechanisms and are able to provide themselves with building materials largely appropriate to their needs. They are able to organize themselves and use mutual aid and self-help in building not only houses but also community facilities. Squatter settlements are pervasively family places, and much of the social interaction and mutual aid revolves around exchanges and transactions of an economic and social sort among households and along kinship and friendship lines emanating from such households.

The informal sector

The informal sector is not a separate, parasitic enclave, but an integral part of the urban economy and a positive contributor to economic growth. There can be a high degree of integration between the formal and informal sectors, and a point can be reached where the dividing lines between them become blurred. The formal

Box 2.5   The main characteristics of the informal sector

While the concept of the informal sector defies rigorous definition, it is where very large numbers of people, especially the urban poor, earn or seek to earn their living. Estimates made for different cities in Africa, Asia, and Latin America suggest that between 40 and 70 per cent of the urban labour force works in the informal sector, with women being predominant in some cities.

The informal sector was brought to the attention of policy-makers by an ILO mission to Kenya in 1972,[1] although the ideas behind it and the expression itself were in currency earlier.[2] The mission report argued that the informal sector was able to provide a wide range of low-cost and labour-intensive goods and services, and that it was not confined to peripheral employment or even to specific kinds of economic activity. Rather, the informal sector was defined as a 'way of doing things' exactly the opposite of the formal sector that was characterized by:

- Ease of entry.
- Reliance on indigenous resources.
- Family ownership of enterprises.
- Small scale of operation.
- Labour-intensive and adapted technology.
- Skills acquired outside the formal school system.
- Unregulated and competitive markets.

Since the publication of the Kenya mission report, the informal sector has been the subject of considerable research and debate. Some research has been critical of the concept, especially its dualistic connotations. It is now widely accepted that the dividing lines between formal and informal economic activity may be so blurred as to have become meaningless, although the relationships tend to be characterized by inequality.

However defined, the informal sector is recognized as a positive contributor to economic growth and essential to the survival strategies of the urban poor. Despite its importance, the sector is largely ignored and rarely supported by urban development strategies, and sometimes actively discouraged by developing-country governments. Given conceptual and definitional problems, programmes and projects designed to support the informal sector are difficult to formulate and implement, although economic activity within the informal sector is sufficiently diverse to justify a range of supportive measures.[3]

1. ILO, *Employment, Incomes and Inequality: A Strategy for Increasing Productive Employment in Kenya* (Geneva, 1972).
2. Credit for the introduction of the term 'informal sector' into the development studies literature is usually given to Keith Hart. See his 'Informal Income Opportunities and the Structure of Urban Employment in Ghana', *Journal of Modern African Studies*, 2/1 (1973).
3. See R. Bromley, 'The Urban Informal Sector: Why Is It Worth Discussing?' *World Development*, 6/9–10 (1978).

sector is dependent upon the informal market for some of its goods and services and for cheap labour, while the informal sector is dependent upon the formal sector for parts for its products. However, the informal sector is usually in an inferior and subservient position, because it tends to produce low-cost inputs for the formal sector. The informal sector effectively subsidizes the formal sector, because earning differentials between the sectors are substantial, even at comparable levels of age and education.

The degree of integration between the formal and informal sectors appears to differ according to levels of development. It seems to be greatest in Latin America and some Asian cities, and lowest in African cities. In the former, there is, for example, a tradition of subcontracting to informal-sector workers; in the latter, this process is still poorly developed.

Much economic activity in the informal sector is economically efficient and profitable. The sector is able to provide the full range of skills needed to provide goods and services for a large section of the urban poor, and, because of its labour-absorptive capacities, it is able to sustain large numbers of people, but often at very low levels of consumption. It is an essential source of goods and services for people who are unable to fulfil their needs through the formal sector. The assumption that the informal sector is the exclusive province of the poor is not wholly correct.

Despite these facts, governmental policies continue to be strongly biased towards the formal sector and its development. The formal sector typically enjoys tariff and quota protection, market protection, privileged access to foreign exchange and low-cost credit. The informal sector enjoys no such benefits and is often deprived of such basic services as water, electricity, and credit. It is not only is denied formal privileges but also may be the object of governmental harassment and restriction, most evident in periodic attempts to round up hawkers and to deposit them in places where they offer no competition to formal enterprises. The main advantages of the informal sector reside in such areas as capacities to escape taxation and social security charges, and to bypass laws regulating wages, working conditions, and job security. Entrepreneurs in the informal sector have

reasons to evade the law, and some governments, in tacit recognition of the importance of the sector, have reasons to allow them to do so.

Unresolved issues

The findings of a large body of research have thrown a favourable light on migration, squatter settlements, and the informal sector. They convey a more positive picture than the one that preceded it, going so far as to suggest that cities have become as dependent on the poor as the poor have been on cities. It is a picture that suggests that it is time to regard squatter settlements, slums, and the informal sector not as the biggest problem of but as the basic answers to urbanization, unfulfilled shelter needs, and growing unemployment. There is no denying, however, that this positive picture is one that contains a number of unresolved questions, and, given the projected growth of population, urbanization, poverty, and inequality, it cannot be assumed that what applies today will necessarily apply 20 years hence.

Migrants move because they perceive opportunity. This opportunity has existed in cities and large towns but it may not do so in future, since migrants will have to compete with the city's own growing population. The most vital and enterprising rural people may always wish to move, but 10 years hence they may have nowhere to go. Patterns of migration reveal as much about rural areas as they do about towns and cities, and the story they tell is a disturbing one. It is all too frequently one of growing landlessness, poverty, and homelessness. While the streets of the city were never paved with gold, they were always preferable to the tracks that led nowhere in rural areas, and a struggle that offered at least the hope of improvement was preferable to one that did not. Despite commitments to rural development, the countries in which the standards of living of the rural poor are improving are still in a minority.

The informal sector 'works' for the urban poor for no other reason than it has to: there is no alternative to it. For many, however, it 'works' on the basis of highly competitive survival strategies that involve all the members of the family, sometimes depriving children of all but the most basic education. The strategies are highly parti-cularistic, involving marriage alliances, patron–client relations, and even migration. When the strategies work, the poor make a living; when they do not, the poor have to adjust. Adjustment normally means going without. How many people the informal sector can absorb without completely eroding the survival strategies of the poor is a debatable question. Certainly, there are cities where the need for the informal sector to absorb increasing numbers of workers has already led to a marked deterioration in incomes and living standards. A point can be reached where consumption is reduced to virtually nothing, insufficient to guarantee the barest survival. As the sector swells, as poverty becomes widespread, and as survival strategies become aggressively competitive, the informal sector could become self-destructive.

There are also problems at both 'ends' of the informal sector. The 'top end' of the sector has been able to grow and develop in part because it has subsidized the formal sector. Should the two become directly competitive, it may not be allowed to develop further. It is probable that governments will find it difficult to resist press-ures for measures that seek to regulate and contain the activities of informal sector entrepreneurs and the networks they draw on. The top end of the informal sector has been able to grow in the past, but its capacity for future growth may be restricted. Problems at the other end of the informal sector seem destined to become severe. It is here that the informal sector fades into serious underemployment and seasonal, casual, and coolie labour, including the pettiest of trading and prostitution. In this part of the informal sector, life is not moulded by co-operation and mutual aid: its laws are those of survival of the fittest.

Squatters can improve their settlements when conditions are favourable, but, without signifi-cant changes in governmental attitudes and poli-cies, poverty may increase and give way to destitution—trends that will curtail opportuni-ties for consolidation. Pavement-dwellers are among those who cannot be expected to respond to appeals to improve their dwellings. The pros-pect is that, in many cities, there will be a sizeable and growing group that is too busy surviving to worry about 'consolidation'.

The squatter and the slum dweller are not necessarily 'radicals', but this does not mean to say that they are incapable of becoming a radical force. A violent reaction to persistent poverty cannot be discounted simply because it has not yet occurred. The behaviour of the urban poor is not preordained, but has to be understood in terms of their perceptions of problems and opportunities. If, in this perception, there is little or no space for reasoned hope, the poor may no longer be prepared to accept the subordination and exploitation that form an inescapable part of their poverty. They will challenge the structures that perpetuate power and inequality, and because they are concentrated and most visible in the city, it is in the city that authority will be challenged.

In order to be discontented with the city, one has to live within its confines. The city in devel-oping countries is strikingly full of the young, and it is among the young that dissatisfaction may be highest. Like their parents, they will share a profound desire to be treated as people rather than problems but, unlike their parents, they may not be ready to accept a future that promises little more than miserable rewards and, at best, prolonged survival.

Governments would appear to have two main options. They can seek to co-opt and contain social protest, turning emerging movements into a new constituency; or they can seek to mobilize the creative energies contained in the move-ments and harness them to broad purposes of economic and social development. The first option will be easy, but the results uncertain. The second option will be difficult, involving as it does a reorientation of development priorities and strategies, but its results are likely to prove long-lasting and compatible with the sustainable development that is urgently required.

Part II

Global Conditions, Trends, and Prospects

3 Population and Urbanization Trends

While the challenge posed by human settlements and by the forces and processes that underlie their growth differ greatly in the developed and developing countries, there are certain demographic and urbanization trends that they share, albeit unequally. The trends analysed below are based upon projections and estimates prepared by the United Nations Population Division.[1] While United Nations population and urbanization projections and estimates are acknowledged as the most authoritative available, they must nevertheless be interpreted with considerable caution. They are extrapolations of observed data on fertility and mortality rates, sex ratios, life expectancies, and rural–urban migration, and the statistical base of some of the estimates is undeniably weak. The urbanization projections are, for example, dependent upon country definitions of urban areas, which range from 100 to 20,000 or more inhabitants. In some cases, part of the statistical basis for estimates is not simply empirically weak but purely hypothesized. Finally, their very nature excludes assumptions concerning the desirability of the trends defined or criteria for evaluating their realism.

Trends do not necessarily depict the future. They can, however, suggest the shape of things to come—the scale of the challenge ahead. In the case of the trends outlined below, the scale of the challenge posed to human settlements by population and urbanization trends is daunting. Viewed globally, it must be defined as one of unprecedented dimensions.

Population trends

Some 2,000 years ago, the world's population probably numbered around 300 million, and it took around 1,500 years to double. Only in the eighteenth century did it begin to grow significantly: from about 1750, at the outset of Europe's industrial revolution, until the twentieth century it grew at the unprecedented average rate of 0.5 per cent per annum. By 1900, the world's population had reached about 1.7 billion—a six-fold increase in 150 years. From then on, the rate of growth doubled, remaining at about 1.5 per cent per annum until 1950. In the 35 years since then it has grown at around 1.9 per cent per annum: in these 35 years the world's population almost doubled, to reach 4.8 billion in 1985. Another relevant phenomenon is the constant change in the distribution of the world's population between developed and developing regions. Between 1750 and the early 1900s, population growth was concentrated in today's developed countries. Since 1950 it has been increasingly concentrated in the developing countries.

The momentum built into population growth will ensure its continuation for decades to come. It is almost certain that an additional 80–90 million children will be born every year until well into the next century. The end of the twentieth century could witness the high point of several centuries of accelerated growth, and while demographic expectations are for a gradual decline in growth rates until world population stabilizes at some time in the twenty-second century, the immediate prospect is for some 6.1 billion people by the year 2000, increasing to 8.2 billion by the year 2025, or a 71 per cent increase in a period of 40 years. By the year 2000, 8 out of 10 people will be living in today's developing countries—nearly one-half of them in China and India.

When population growth will end is a matter of speculation. The main single determinant is declining fertility. Fertility levels have declined rapidly, and are now close to, or even below, the levels necessary for the maintenance of the population at its present size in Europe, Northern America, Japan, and the Soviet Union. Among the developing countries, fertility decline has occurred in Eastern Asia and in much of Latin America.

Demographic projections published by the World Bank in 1984 suggest a hypothetical

Box 3.1   The world's most populous nations

The 25 most populous countries in 1960 and 1985 are given below, together with projections for the year 2000. The listings of countries show considerable stability: all but three of the countries listed in 2000 appear in the list for 1960. Between 1960 and 1985, Argentina lost its place to the Islamic Republic of Iran, while between 1985 and 2000, Poland and Spain are expected to be replaced by Ethiopia and Zaire.

The 25 largest countries accounted for around 80 per cent of the world's total population in 1960, but their share is projected to fall to around 77 per cent by the turn of the century. China and India together already accounted for nearly 36 per cent of the world's population and 53 per cent of the population of the developing countries in 1960. In the year 2000, the share of these two countries in the world's total population will still stand at 36 per cent, while their share of the developing countries' total population could still be as high as 46 per cent.

The nine largest developed countries accounted for 80 per cent of the total population of the developed countries in 1960, and this figure is projected to apply at the turn of the century.

Table 1. Ranking of countries by population, 1960, 1985, and 2000

1960		1985		2000	
Country	Population (millions)	Country	Population (millions)	Country	Population (millions)
1 China	657.3	China	1,059.5	China	1,255.9
2 India	442.3	India	758.9	India	961.5
3 USSR	214.3	USSR	278.4	USSR	314.8
4 USA	180.7	USA	238.0	USA	268.2
5 Indonesia	96.2	Indonesia	166.4	Indonesia	211.4
6 Japan	94.1	Brazil	135.6	Brazil	179.5
7 Brazil	72.6	Japan	120.7	Nigeria	161.9
8 Germany, Fed. Rep.	55.4	Pakistan	100.4	Bangladesh	145.8
9 United Kingdom	52.6	Bangladesh	101.1	Pakistan	141.0
10 Bangladesh	51.6	Nigeria	95.2	Japan	129.7
11 Italy	50.2	Mexico	79.0	Mexico	109.2
12 Pakistan	50.1	Germany, Fed. Rep.	60.9	Viet Nam	79.9
13 France	45.7	Viet Nam	59.7	Philippines	74.1
14 Nigeria	42.3	Italy	57.3	Ethiopia	66.5
15 Mexico	37.1	United Kingdom	56.1	Thailand	65.5
16 Viet Nam	34.7	France	54.6	Turkey	65.4
17 Spain	30.3	Philippines	54.5	Iran	65.2
18 Poland	29.6	Thailand	51.4	Egypt	63.9
19 Philippines	27.9	Turkey	49.3	Germany, Fed. Rep.	59.5
20 Turkey	27.5	Egypt	46.9	Italy	58.6
21 Thailand	26.9	Iran	44.6	France	57.2
22 Egypt	25.9	Korea, Rep. of	41.3	United Kingdom	56.4
23 Korea, Rep. of	25.0	Spain	38.5	Korea, Rep. of	51.0
24 Burma	21.7	Poland	37.2	Burma	48.5
25 Argentina	20.6	Burma	37.2	Zaire	47.6

Source: United Nations, *Urban and Rural Population Projections 1950–2025: The 1984 Assessment* (New York, 1986).

stabilized population of around 11 billion by 2150, with a doubling of today's population to 9.8 billion by the middle of the next century. While the population of today's developed countries is expected to increase by 200 million by that time, the population of today's developing countries is projected to grow by 4.8 billion—from 3.6 billion in the mid-1980s to 8.4 billion in 2050.[2]

The most alarming feature of all population projections concerns anticipated rates of growth in the world's poorest countries and regions —those in which the pace of development has either slowed dramatically or stopped. According to the Bank's projections, India's population will not stabilize until it reaches 1.7 billion, a figure comparable to the total population of all developing countries in 1950. Bangladesh, one of the world's poorest countries, will have a stable population of 450 million, while Nigeria's population will not stabilize until it reaches 650 million. Ethiopia, the scene of the worst famine in a decade, is projected to grow from its present population of around 35–40 million to 230 million, Zaire from 32 million to 170 million, and Kenya from 20 million to 150 million.[3] Together, sub-Saharan Africa and Southern Asia, the world's poorest regions, would, when and if world population stabilizes, account for 50 per cent of the world's population, compared with 30 per cent today.

Urbanization trends

Population growth is more than matched by the pace of urbanization. In the mid-eighteenth century, the first period in human history to witness sustained and accelerated population growth, no more than 3 out of every 100 persons lived in towns. It was only in 1900 that the first country—the United Kingdom—became predominantly urban. Even by 1920, only an estimated 14 per cent of the world's population lived in urban areas,[4] but by 1950 the proportion had reached one-quarter, and by 1980 it stood at around 40 per cent. If present trends continue, nearly half the world's population will live in towns and cities at the turn of the century, and the figure could reach 60 per cent by 2025. By that time, as many people could be living in towns and cities as are alive in the world today (see Table 3.1). Given the growth of population, these percentages translate into very large numbers of people. Between 1980 and 2000, the num-

ber of urban dwellers is projected to increase by 1.1 billion; by 2025 there could be 4.9 billion people living in urban areas, 3.2 billion more than in 1980.

Patterns of population growth inevitably mean that it will be in the developing countries that urban population will increase most rapidly. Urban settlements in the developing countries are at present growing three times faster than those in the developed countries, and 85 per cent of the growth in the world's urban population between 1980 and 2000 is projected to take place in the developing countries. The figure for the period 1980–2025 is very close to 90 per cent.

Of course, these averages conceal very significant regional variations, not just between developed and developing countries but also between the regions of the world (see Fig. 3.1). Nevertheless, they herald a change of truly dramatic dimensions. In 1960, the developing countries as a group were still overwhelmingly rural, with only one in five of all people living in urban areas, and there were 30 countries in which less than 10 per cent of the total population lived in urban settlements. By 1985, there were only 10 such countries, and by the year 2000 there may be no more than two (Bhutan and Cape Verde). Between 1960 and 1980, the number of countries in which urban residents became the majority almost doubled, from 45 to 82, and in the 20 years to 2000, it will rise to about 125. By the turn of the century, more than 39 per cent of the population of the developing countries is projected to be living in urban areas.

Table 3.1 The growth of world and urban population, 1950–2025

	World population (millions)	Urban population (millions)	Urban population as % of total
1950	2,516	734	29.2
1960	3,019	1,032	34.2
1970	3,693	1,371	37.1
1980	4,450	1,764	39.6
1990	5,246	2,234	42.6
2000	6,122	2,854	46.6
2010	6,989	3,623	51.8
2020	7,822	4,488	57.4
2025	8,206	4,932	60.1

Source: United Nations, *Urban and Rural Population Projections 1950–2025: The 1984 Assessment* (New York, 1986).

Table 3.2 Urban population in developed and developing countries, 1950–2025

	Developed countries		Developing countries	
	Urban population (millions)	% of total	Urban population (millions)	% of total
1950	447	53.8	287	17.0
1960	571	60.5	460	22.2
1970	698	66.6	673	25.4
1980	798	70.2	966	29.2
1990	877	72.5	1,357	33.6
2000	950	74.4	1,904	39.3
2010	1,011	76.0	2,612	46.2
2020	1,063	77.2	3,425	53.1
2025	1,087	77.8	3,845	56.5

Source: United Nations, *Urban and Rural Population Projections 1950–2025: The 1984 Assessment* (New York, 1986).

Box 3.2   The urbanization of the earth

All regions of the world, with the exception of Africa and Asia, are already predominantly urban. In 1980, North America, Europe including USSR, Oceania, and Latin America had 73.9, 67.7, 71.5, and 65.4 per cent urban population, respectively, compared to Africa's 27.0 per cent and Asia's 26.6 per cent urban.

The different regions, however, exhibited markedly contrasting patterns in their levels of urbanization. In terms of the developing and developed regions, the gap between their respective levels of urbanization has been narrowing. While the developed regions were predominantly urban (60.5 per cent) in 1960 and continued steadily to increase their level of urbanization to 70.2 per cent in 1980, the developing countries has a much lower level in 1960 (22.2 per cent urban), increasing to 29.2 per cent in 1980. If the present trends in urbanization persist, it is expected that the two levels will be much closer by year 2020.

Table 1. Percentage of urban population, by regions, 1960–2020

	1960	1980	2000	2020
World total	34.2	39.6	46.6	57.4
Developed regions	60.5	70.2	74.4	77.2
North America	69.9	73.9	74.9	76.7
Europe incl. USSR	56.9	67.7	73.4	76.7
Oceania	66.3	71.5	71.4	75.1
Developing regions	22.2	29.2	39.3	53.1
Africa	18.8	27.0	39.0	52.2
Asia	21.5	26.6	35.0	49.3
Latin America	49.3	65.4	76.8	83.0

Source: United Nations, *Urban and Rural Population Projections 1950–2025: The 1985 Assessment* (New York, 1986).

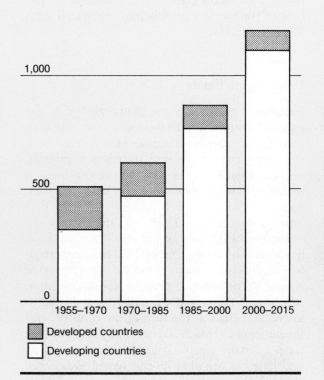

Fig. 1 Urban population increment, 1955–2015 (in millions)

Developed countries
Developing countries

From a level of less than 20 per cent in 1960, the African region—the least urbanized region—was 27.0 per cent urbanized in 1980, and is projected to have 39.0 per cent of the total population living in urban areas by the turn of the century. The proportion urban in the year 2020 in Africa will be 52.2 per cent.

Latin America had a level of urbanization of 49.3 per cent in 1960, the highest among the developing regions, and this level increased to 65.4 per cent in 1980 and is projected to increase to 76.8 per cent by the year 2000—a level comparable to that of the developed countries.

In absolute terms, the world's urban population increased by 612 million between 1970 and 1985. Some 77 per cent of this increase was contributed by developing countries. Between 1985 and the year 2000, the world's urban population is projected to increase by a further 871

Again, these percentages mean millions of additional people living in cities. In the next 25 years, the urban population of the developing countries could increase by 1.5 billion, double the present level. By 2025, the number is projected to grow to more than 3.8 billion, 2.7 billion more than in 1985, by which time the urban population of the developing countries would almost equal the world's total population around 1975 (see Table 3.2).

As in the case of population growth, it is in today's poorest countries that urbanization will be particularly rapid. Whereas in the past 15 years the urban population of the developing countries as a whole has been growing at around 3.5 per cent per annum, the rate of growth in the

Box 3.2 continued

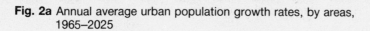

Fig. 2a Annual average urban population growth rates, by areas, 1965–2025

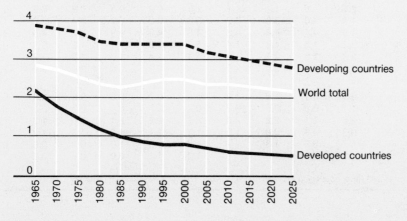

Fig. 2b Annual average rural population growth rates, by areas, 1960–2025

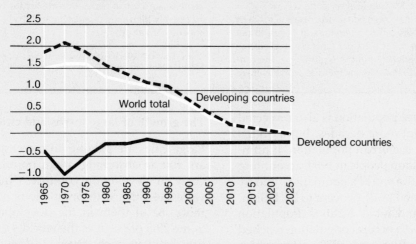

world's poorest countries, China and India excepted, has been close to 5 per cent—a figure that is projected to continue for several decades. In 1950, there were only 150 million people living in the towns and cities of the poorest countries, and all but 25 million of them were to be found in China and India. Today, the urban population of the poorest countries stands at more than 500 million, accounting for nearly one-half the urban population of the developing countries. By the year 2000, the urban population of today's poorest countries is projected almost to double, and by 2020 it could be in the order of 1.8 billion people—a fourfold increase in less than four decades. Of these 1.8 billion people, 1.2 billion would be living in the towns of China and India.

Table 2. Urban and rural population, annual average growth rate, by world regions 1960–2025 (percentages)

	1960–1965	1965–1970	1970–1975	1975–1980	1980–1985	1985–1990	1990–1995	1995–2000	2000–2005	2005–2010	2010–2025
Urban											
North America	2.1	1.6	1.1	1.1	1.0	0.9	0.9	0.8	0.8	0.8	0.8
Latin America	4.4	4.0	3.9	3.6	3.3	3.0	2.7	2.4	2.2	1.9	1.8
Africa	4.3	4.4	4.4	4.9	4.8	4.9	4.9	4.7	4.5	4.3	3.9
Europe (including USSR)	2.2	1.8	1.6	1.4	1.3	1.2	1.1	1.0	0.8	0.7	0.6
Oceania	2.8	2.6	2.1	1.5	1.4	1.4	1.3	1.3	1.2	1.2	1.2
Asia	3.4	3.3	3.4	2.9	2.8	2.9	3.0	3.1	3.0	2.9	2.7
Rural											
North America	0.1	−0.2	1.0	1.0	0.8	0.7	0.6	0.5	0.3	0.3	0.2
Latin America	1.1	0.8	0.5	0.2	0.1	0.1	0.1	0.1	0.1	0.0	−0.1
Africa	2.0	2.1	2.2	2.3	2.2	2.2	2.1	2.0	1.8	1.6	1.3
Europe (including USSR)	−0.3	−0.9	−0.8	−1.0	−1.1	−1.1	−1.2	−1.2	−1.2	−1.3	−1.4
Oceania	0.7	0.5	1.3	1.7	1.4	1.3	1.0	0.7	0.5	0.3	0.0
Asia	1.9	2.2	1.9	1.5	1.3	1.1	0.9	0.6	0.2	−0.2	−0.4

Source: United Nations, *Urban and Rural Population Projections 1950–2025: The 1984 Assessment* (New York, 1986).

million, of which 760 million will come from developing countries. The trends of urban population increments for the world and developing countries are upward, while that for developed countries is downward.

During the period 2000–15, cities in the developing countries will be expanding at the rate of almost 74 million people a year, or 202,000 people every day.

The world's annual average rate of urbanization reached 3.7 per cent in the late 1950s; afterwards, it began to fall slowly, stabilizing at today's 2.4 per cent. It is expected to continue around this level until the beginning of the century after which it will begin to decline. The world average of 2.4 per cent masks significant regional variations. Growth rates range from under 1 per cent per annum in North America to nearly 5 per cent for Africa.

Historically, such rates are not high: rates in excess of 3 per cent per annum were attained in Western Europe at the height of the Industrial Revolution. The dramatic increases in the world's urban population are not the consequence of excessively high growth rates but of the absolute numbers of people involved.

Source: United Nations, *Urban and Rural Population Projections 1950–2025: The 1984 Assessment* (New York, 1986).

The world's rural population is also projected to grow for several more decades, but at much slower rates than the urban population. It numbered around 2 billion people in 1960, accounting for 66 per cent of the world's population, and by 1980 it had increased by 35 per cent to 2.7 billion. According to the United Nations Population Division, the growth of rural population reached a peak between 1965 and 1970, after which growth rates began to decline. The world's rural population is expected to reach a peak in absolute numbers around the year 2010, when it should stand at around 3.4 billion people—all but 320 million of them in the developing countries. After 2010, the absolute number of people living in rural areas is projected to decline very slowly. At present, the least developed countries account for 75 per cent of the developing countries' rural population, and this figure is projected to apply in the year 2000.

The growth of large towns and cities

Large cities are playing an increasingly important role in absorbing urban populations, especially in developing countries. In 1960, there were 114 cities with populations of 1 million or more, 62 of them in the developed countries. Some 29.5 per cent of the world's urban population lived in such cities—27.3 per cent in the developed countries and 28.4 per cent in the developing countries. Between 1960 and 1980, the number of 'million' cities doubled to 222, their numbers increasing from 62 to 103 in the developed countries and from 52 to 119 in the developing countries (see Table 3.3 and Fig. 3.2). In 1980, 34 per cent of the world's urban population lived in cities with more than 1 million people. The number of 'million' cities is projected to increase still further, to 408 in the year 2000, and to 639, nearly three times their present

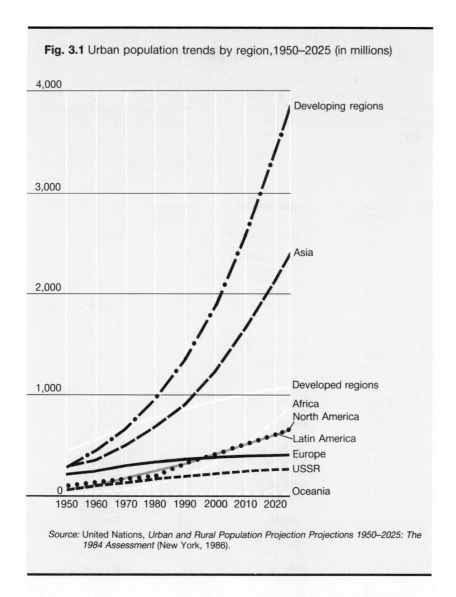

Fig. 3.1 Urban population trends by region,1950–2025 (in millions)

Developing regions

Asia

Developed regions
Africa
North America
Latin America
Europe
USSR
Oceania

Source: United Nations, *Urban and Rural Population Projection Projections 1950–2025: The 1984 Assessment* (New York, 1986).

number, by 2025. Nearly all of the growth, some 87 per cent, is projected to take place in the developing countries. By 2025, almost half of the urban population in the developing countries, some 2.2 billion people, is projected to be living in cities with more than 1 million people.

Most spectacular is the anticipated growth of cities with more than 4 million people. Such cities were unknown in history until only a century ago, when London reached that figure. By 1960, the number of cities with more than 4 million people had reached 19, with 10 of them in the industrialized countries; some 13.4 per cent of the world's urban population lived in them. By 1980, they almost doubled in number to 35,

most of the growth taking place in the developing countries, and the share of the urban population living in such cities increased to 15.8 per cent. The number of '4 million' cities is projected to nearly double by the year 2000, and to increase nearly four times by 2025. While the number of people living in these very large cities is expected to decline in relative terms in the developed countries, it is expected to increase significantly in the developing countries. By 2025, more than 1.2 billion people—28.2 per cent of the urban population of the developing countries—could be living in '4 million plus' cities (see Table 3.4 and Fig. 3.3).

The growth of large cities does not, however,

Box 3.3   The world's 25 largest agglomerations, 1960–2000

The size of cities was once regarded as an index of development. Today, many of the world's most rapidly growing cities can be found in the least-developed and poorest countries. As indicated in Table 1, fewer than half of the world's 25 largest agglomerations were to be found in developing countries in 1960, and only 4 were to be found in low-income developing countries. By the year 2000, 20 of the world's largest agglomerations will be in developing countries, and 8 of them will be in countries that are at present classified as low-income (see Table 2).

Table 1. Ranking of city agglomerations by population, 1960, 1980, and 2000

1960		1980		2000	
Agglomeration	**Population (millions)**	**Agglomeration**	**Population (millions)**	**Agglomeration**	**Population (millions)**
1 New York/NE New Jersey	14.2	Tokyo/Yokohama	17.7	Mexico City	25.8
2 London	10.7	New York/NE New Jersey	15.6	São Paulo	24.0
3 Tokyo/Yokohama	10.7	Mexico City	14.5	Tokyo/Yokohama	20.2
4 Shanghai	10.7	São Paulo	12.8	Calcutta	16.5
5 Rhein–Ruhr	8.7	Shanghai	11.8	Greater Bombay	16.0
6 Beijing	7.3	London	10.3	New York/NE New Jersey	15.8
7 Paris	7.2	Buenos Aires	10.1	Seoul	13.8
8 Buenos Aires	6.9	Calcutta	9.5	Tehran	13.6
9 Los Angeles/ Long Beach	6.6	Los Angeles/ Long Beach	9.5	Shanghai	13.3
10 Moscow	6.3	Rhein–Ruhr	9.5	Rio de Janeiro	13.3
11 Chicago/NE Indiana	6.0	Rio de Janeiro	9.2	Delhi	13.2
12 Tianjin	6.0	Beijing	9.1	Jakarta	13.3
13 Osaka/Kobe	5.7	Paris	8.7	Buenos Aires	13.2
14 Calcutta	5.6	Osaka/Kobe	8.7	Karachi	12.0
15 Mexico City	5.2	Greater Bombay	8.5	Dhaka	11.2
16 Rio de Janeiro	5.1	Seoul	8.5	Cairo/Giza	11.1
17 São Paulo	4.8	Moscow	8.2	Manila	11.1
18 Milan	4.5	Tianjin	7.7	Los Angeles/ Long Beach	11.0
19 Cairo/Giza	4.5	Cairo-Giza	6.9	Bangkok	10.7
20 Greater Bombay	4.2	Chicago/NE Indiana	6.8	Osaka/Kobe	10.5
21 Philadelphia	3.7	Jakarta	6.7	Beijing	10.4
22 Detroit	3.6	Milan	6.7	Moscow	10.4
23 Leningrad	3.5	Manila	6.0	Tianjin	9.1
24 Naples	3.2	Delhi	5.9	Paris	8.7
25 Jakarta	2.8	Baghdad	3.9	Baghdad	7.4

Source: United Nations, *Urban and Rural Population Projections 1950–2025: The 1984 Assessment* (New York, 1986).

Table 2. Distribution of city agglomerations by country type, 1960, 1980, and 2000

	1960	1980	2000
Developed countries	14	10	5
Developing countries	11	15	20
Low-income developing countries	4	5	8

Source: United Nations, *Urban and Rural Population Projections 1950–2025: The 1984 Assessment* (New York, 1986).

Table 3.3   The growth of cities with more than 1 million inhabitants, 1960–2025

	Number of 'million' cities			'Million' cities as % urban population		
	In world	In developed countries	In developing countries	In world	In developed countries	In developing countries
1960	114	62	52	29.5	27.3	28.4
1980	222	103	119	34.0	33.4	34.6
2000	408	129	279	40.8	34.0	44.2
2025	639	153	486	43.2	32.6	46.4

Source: United Nations, *Estimates and Projections of Urban, Rural, and City Populations 1950–2025: The 1982 Assessment* (New York, 1984).

Table 3.4   The growth of cities with more than 4 million inhabitants, 1960–2025

	Number of '4 million' cities			'4 million' cities as % urban population		
	In world	In developed countries	In developing countries	In world	In developed countries	In developing countries
1960	19	10	9	13.4	14.2	12.5
1980	35	13	22	15.8	14.1	17.2
2000	66	16	50	19.9	13.4	23.2
2025	135	21	114	24.6	12.8	28.2

Source: United Nations, *Estimates and Projections of Urban, Rural, and City Populations 1950–2025: The 1982 Assessment* (New York, 1984).

stop here. Beyond the '4 million' cities are 'supercities' or 'megacities' that are taking urban policy-making and planning into completely uncharted territory. In 1980, there were seven agglomerations with populations in excess of 10 million, three of them in the developed countries. If present trends continue, there will be 22 by the turn of the century, and all but 4 of them will be in developing countries. The largest, Mexico City and São Paulo, could have

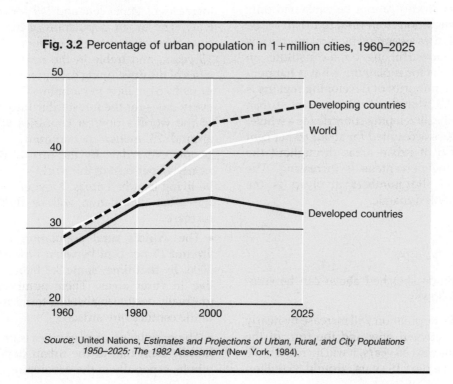

Fig. 3.2 Percentage of urban population in 1+million cities, 1960–2025

Source: United Nations, *Estimates and Projections of Urban, Rural, and City Populations 1950–2025: The 1982 Assessment* (New York, 1984).

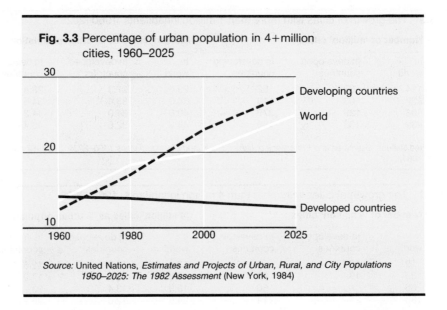

Fig. 3.3 Percentage of urban population in 4+million cities, 1960–2025

Source: United Nations, *Estimates and Projects of Urban, Rural, and City Populations 1950–2025: The 1982 Assessment* (New York, 1984)

populations around 25 million. As would be expected, given population growth and urbanization trends, the poorest cities in the world are prominent among those that are projected to grow most rapidly and to very large sizes.

Contrary to much popular belief, the growth of urbanization and city populations in the developing countries cannot be explained only in terms of migration from rural to urban areas. The image of cities swamped by rural migrants is undeniably a powerful one, but it constitutes an inadequate basis for explaining what is happening. Only in a minority of developing regions is migration the dominant element of urban growth. For the developing countries as a whole, natural increase accounted for about 60 per cent of the growth of urban areas throughout the 1960s, and the percentage is increasing. The sheer size of the numbers involved is the principal growth dynamic.

Conclusions

The main trends sketched above can be summarized as follows:

• The world's population will increase by nearly 27 per cent between now and the turn of the century. In the next 40 years, it will increase by 70 per cent. In the next 15 years, around 85 million

people per annum—230,000 every day—will be added to the world's population, and 8 out of every 10 of them will be citizens of developing countries.

• The world's urban population will increase by nearly 870 million between 1985 and the end of the century and by 2.9 billion by the year 2025, increases of 44 per cent and 149 per cent respectively. The urban population of the developing countries will increase by 66 per cent in the next 15 years, and treble in the next 40 years. The cities of the developing countries are projected to grow by 51 million per annum—140,000 persons every day—for the foreseeable future. The cities of the world's poorest countries will grow by around 25 million per annum, or by 68,000 people every day. By the turn of the century, nearly 47 per cent of the world's population will be living in urban areas. Most of the growth in the urban population will be due to natural increase.

• The world's rural population will grow by around 15 per cent between now and the year 2000. By that time, some 3.3 billion people will live in rural areas. Their numbers will very gradually decline in absolute terms from the turn of the century onwards.

• The population of large cities is growing more rapidly than that of the urban population as a whole, especially in the developing countries. If

Box 3.4   How large can cities become?

The United Nations periodically makes projections for the growth of the world's cities. These projections are based on demographic trends relating to the growth of national and city populations. Projections based on demographic factors can give startling results, as indicated in the graph opposite. Many of the largest cities in the developing countries are projected to double in size in the next 15 years. By the turn of the century, Mexico City, and São Paulo could have around 25 million inhabitants, Bombay and Calcutta might have passed the 15 million mark, while Bangkok, Beijing, Buenos Aires, Cairo, Delhi, Dhaka, Jakarta, Karachi, Manila, Rio de Janeiro, Shanghai, Seoul, and Tehran could each be home to more than 10 million people.

How realistic are such projections? They say nothing about the desirability or the technical feasibility of the numbers involved. They do, however, imply a very great deal, and rest on various assumptions that must be called into question. They assume that rapidly growing cities can be supplied with water and energy: some of the cities listed above are already experiencing severe difficulties in this area. They imply that very large cities can be supplied with food at prices their populations can afford: in some of the above cities, the urban poor already spend up to 80 per cent of all they earn on the purchase of food, and food scarcities would mean rising prices, placing food beyond the reach of millions of people. Perhaps most important of all, the projections assume that rapidly expanding populations can be provided with productive employment: yet some 40 per cent of the urban poor are without it today, and in some of the world's poorest cities—usually among the most rapidly growing—up to 70 per cent of the population is dependent upon reliable jobs in the informal sector.

Table 1. Population growth of large cities, 1950–2000 (in millions)

	1950	1960	1970	1980	1990	2000
Africa						
Cairo/Giza	3.5	4.5	5.7	6.9	8.6	11.1
Kinshasa	0.2	0.5	1.2	2.2	3.3	5.0
Lagos	0.4	0.7	1.4	2.8	4.8	8.3
Asia						
Beijing (Peking)	6.7	7.3	8.3	9.1	9.3	10.4
Shanghai	10.4	10.7	11.4	11.8	12.0	13.3
Bombay (Greater)	3.0	4.2	6.0	8.5	11.8	16.0
Calcutta	4.5	5.6	7.1	9.5	12.5	16.5
Delhi	1.4	2.3	3.6	5.9	9.1	13.2
Madras	1.4	1.7	3.1	4.4	6.0	8.2
Karachi	1.0	1.8	3.1	5.2	8.2	12.0
Jakarta	1.8	2.8	4.5	6.7	9.5	13.3
Seoul	1.1	2.4	5.4	8.5	11.7	13.8
Manila	1.6	2.3	3.6	6.0	8.3	11.1
Bangkok/Thonburi	1.4	2.2	3.3	5.0	7.4	10.7
Tehran	1.0	1.8	3.3	5.8	9.4	13.6
Dhaka	0.4	0.7	1.5	3.4	6.5	11.2
Europe						
Moscow	4.8	6.3	7.1	8.2	9.5	10.4
Latin America						
Mexico City	3.1	5.2	9.1	14.5	20.3	25.8
Rio de Janeiro	3.5	5.1	7.2	9.2	11.4	13.3
São Paulo	2.8	4.8	8.2	12.8	18.8	24.0
Greater Buenos Aires	5.3	6.9	8.5	10.1	11.7	13.2

Source: United Nations. *Urban and Rural Population Projections, 1950–2025: The 1984 Assessment* (New York, 1986).

present trends continue, close to half the urban population of the developing countries will be living in cities with more than 1 million people by 2025. One in four of them will be living in cities with more than 4 million inhabitants.

• The next few decades will witness the emergence of 'supercities' in the developing countries of a size never experienced in human history. Many of the largest agglomerations—perhaps one-third of the largest 25—will be in countries which are today among the world's least developed.

These trends indicate the magnitude of the global problem posed by human settlements —the sheer size of the challenge that confronts policy-makers. At a time of financial stringency, an additional 30,000 urban dwellers must be accommodated every day in the developed countries, but developing countries have the task of providing shelter, services, and work in cities for an additional 140,000 people every day. They must seek to do this when more than 300 million are already without productive employment, 700 million people live in absolute or relative poverty, and development prospects for

many of them appear more constrained than ever before. This is the scale of the challenge ahead.

Notes

1. The United Nations Population Division assesses urban and rural populations on a country-by-country basis every two years, usually for the period 1950–2025. This chapter is based on the 1982 assessment (published in 1984), and the 1984 assessment (published in 1986).
2. World Bank, *World Development Report 1984* (New York: Oxford University Press, 1984), 2–5.
3. Ibid., 254–5 (Table 19).
4. B. Renaud, *National Urbanization Policy in Developing Countries* (New York: Oxford University Press, 1981), 13.

4 The Developed Countries

High levels of urbanization have been one of the most distinctive characteristics of human settlements systems in the developed countries since the Second World War. This is true of both market-economy and centrally planned countries. More than 70 per cent of the population of developed countries today live in urban areas, although, as indicated in Table 4.1, this average disguises significant variations. The urban population of the developed countries is expected to reach nearly 75 per cent of the total population by 2000; by that date, 950 million people will be living in cities, approximately 110 million more than at present. Nearly 45 per cent of this growth is projected to take place in the developed centrally planned countries, some of which, e.g. the USSR, have been urbanizing very rapidly. Only in Latin America have urbanization rates in the post-war period been higher than in the developed centrally planned countries.

Urbanization trends in the developed countries are projected to continue into the next century. The urban population is expected to grow by 113 million in the first two decades of the next century, by which time 77 per cent of the population of the developed countries will live in urban areas. The coming decades will witness a change in the distribution, however, with Europe's share progressively decreasing and the share of the USSR increasing. As indicated in Table 4.2, one-quarter of the urban population of the developed countries is projected to be living in the USSR in 2020, compared with 18 per cent in 1960.

The trend towards increasing urbanization in the developed countries is being accompanied by some significant demographic trends, the most important of which are:

- *Declining rates of population growth.*

- *Increasing average age*—nearly one person in six was 60 years or older in 1980, and this is expected to reach one in five by the year 2000.

- *Decreasing family sizes*—households of one and two persons accounted for some 50 per cent of the total number of households in the early 1980s.

Table 4.1 Urbanization trends in the developed countries by region, subregion, and selected countries, 1960–2020

	1960		1980		2000		2020	
	Urban population (millions)	% total	Urban population (millions)	% total	Urban population (millions)	% total	Urban population (millions)	% total
North America	139	69.9	186	73.8	223	74.9	258	76.7
United States	126	70.0	168	73.7	200	74.6	233	76.4
Canada	12	68.9	18	75.7	22	76.9	26	78.9
Europe	259	60.9	340	70.2	385	75.1	412	78.8
Northern Europe	58	76.7	70	85.0	74	88.3	76	90.2
Western Europe	96	71.4	121	78.9	127	81.2	126	82.9
Southern Europe	58	49.5	84	60.5	104	68.1	119	75.0
Eastern Europe	46	47.9	65	59.4	80	66.7	92	71.1
USSR	105	48.8	167	63.1	222	70.7	264	73.8
Japan	59	62.5	89	76.2	101	77.8	106	80.0
Australia/New Zealand	10	79.8	15	85.3	19	85.8	23	88.4
Australia	8	80.6	13	85.8	16	85.9	19	88.6
New Zealand	2	76.0	3	83.3	3	85.1	4	87.2
Total	571	60.5	798	70.2	950	74.4	1,063	77.2

Source: United Nations, *Urban and Rural Population Projections 1950–2025: The 1984 Assessment* (New York, 1986).

Note: Combined country totals may not equal subregional totals due to rounding of figures.

Table 4.2 Share of urban population by region and country, 1960–2020 (per cent)

	1960	1980	2000	2020
Europe	45.3	42.6	40.6	38.7
North America	24.3	23.3	23.4	24.3
USSR	18.4	21.0	23.4	24.8
Japan	10.3	11.2	10.6	10.0
Australia/New Zealand	1.7	1.9	2.0	2.2
Total developed areas	100.0	100.0	100.0	100.0

Source: United Nations, *Urban and Rural Population Projections 1950–2025: The 1984 Assessment* (New York, 1986).

These trends are in evidence in both the market-economy and centrally planned countries. As indicated in Table 4.3, the trends towards population stabilization are particularly marked in Northern Europe and Western Europe where the population of most countries is expected to decline in absolute terms from the turn of the century. The population of five countries—Denmark, the Federal Republic of Germany, Hungary, Luxembourg, and Sweden—is already shrinking, and a similar trend will soon be evident in Austria and Switzerland.

In the market-economy countries, changes in patterns of urbanization are no less important than demographic trends. In many market-economy countries, urbanization is being directed away from metropolitan areas and large cities. In Western Europe, with the exception of some Mediterranean countries, 70 per cent or

Table 4.3 Average annual growth rates of total population by region, subregion, and selected country, 1960–2025 (per cent)

	1960–1970	1970–1980	1980–1990	1990–2000	2000–2010	2010–2025
United States of America	1.27	1.05	0.87	0.77	0.66	0.64
Canada	1.79	1.18	1.05	0.79	0.61	0.59
Europe	0.78	0.53	0.22	0.28	0.14	0.07
Northern Europe	0.58	0.22	0.12	0.08	0.00	0.01
Denmark	0.74	0.39	0.00	−0.08	−0.23	−0.32
Finland	0.39	0.37	0.38	0.18	0.03	−0.03
Ireland	0.41	1.41	1.22	1.17	0.97	0.84
Norway	0.80	0.53	0.23	0.09	0.04	0.07
Sweden	0.73	0.33	−0.01	−0.17	−0.21	−0.21
United Kingdom	0.54	0.09	0.04	0.03	−0.04	−0.01
Western Europe	0.97	0.36	0.09	0.08	−0.12	−0.17
Austria	0.55	0.08	0.00	0.01	−0.10	−0.10
Belgium	0.52	0.22	0.10	0.06	0.03	0.03
France	1.04	0.59	0.32	0.30	0.14	0.08
Germany, Fed. Rep. of	0.91	0.14	−0.21	−0.15	−0.39	−0.45
Netherlands	1.27	0.83	0.42	0.22	−0.02	−0.11
Switzerland	1.56	0.10	0.10	−0.08	−0.29	−0.37
Southern Europe	0.78	0.89	0.44	0.45	0.26	0.13
Greece	0.55	0.93	0.45	0.35	0.20	0.10
Italy	0.64	0.64	0.09	0.19	−0.04	−0.16
Portugal	−0.23	1.36	0.65	0.62	0.46	0.38
Spain	1.09	1.03	0.61	0.61	0.44	0.29
Yugoslavia	1.02	0.91	0.69	0.54	0.33	0.20
Eastern Europe	0.66	0.58	0.50	0.46	0.40	0.32
Bulgaria	0.79	0.40	0.43	0.31	0.24	0.22
Czechoslovakia	0.51	0.64	0.34	0.47	0.43	0.34
German Dem. Rep.	−0.10	−0.19	0.09	0.16	0.16	0.12
Hungary	0.37	0.34	−0.05	0.06	−0.01	−0.08
Poland	1.00	0.86	0.80	0.58	0.51	0.40
Romania	1.01	0.87	0.70	0.71	0.57	0.51
USSR	1.20	0.94	0.95	0.76	0.69	0.64
Japan	1.03	1.13	0.59	0.47	0.25	0.00
Australia	1.97	1.58	1.29	1.09	0.87	0.78
New Zealand	1.73	1.17	0.89	0.79	0.57	0.46
Developed regions	1.03	0.82	0.62	0.54	0.42	0.36

Source: United Nations, *Urban and Rural Population Projections 1950–2025: The 1984 Assessment* (New York, 1986).

more of population growth in the 1960s and 1970s took place in towns with 50,000 or fewer inhabitants,[1] and a large number of metropolitan areas are reporting population losses and the decentralization of economic activities. In the period 1960–80, 30 out of 78 metropolitan areas in the United Kingdom experienced population losses, 27 out of 53 in the Federal Republic of Germany, and 23 out of 84 in Italy.[2] However, there is much variation both between and within the market-economy developed countries, and the exact causes of the changes that are taking place have yet to be established. Urbanization with diffusion and dispersal of population and economic activity is recognized as a complex process that involves changes in patterns of economic structure (particularly in manufacturing), labour mobility, and urban–urban migration, as well as in technological and sociocultural factors.

The traditional source of employment of many inner-city residents—manufacturing industry—has been increasingly lost. In the majority of big cities in the developed market-economy countries, the number of manufacturing jobs has decreased, sometimes dramatically. Some jobs have been lured away to greenfield sites, often making use of incentives provided under urban containment policies. Many of them, however, have just disappeared as a consequence of structural changes in manufacturing. As a result, up to one-third of the population in some cities may be unemployed.

The consequence, in some circumstances, has been the growth of inner-city poverty. In the United Kingdom, for example, more than half of all the inhabitants of the country's inner cities live in areas of concentrated poverty, and in London one-quarter of all families are estimated to live below the nation's poverty line. The concentration of poverty in the city has also been marked in the United States. Between 1950 and the mid-1970s, for example, about 1.8 million middle-class whites—nearly one-quarter of the population—left New York City for the suburbs and small communities, to be replaced by almost the same number of poor members of racial minorities.

In many large cities in the developed market-economy countries, employment generation and the improvement of housing and living condi-

---

Box 4.1   Non-spatial policies affecting urban growth

There is growing recognition among policy-makers that many national policies that are urban in neither character nor intent can have significant impacts on the form and rate of urban growth. Such policies include:

● *Fiscal policies.* Policies with respect to such issues as tax relief on mortage-interest payments and taxation levels relating to automobile ownership and use have had an impact on the way in which cities have developed.

● *Industrial policies.* Decisions on whether to support certain industries, such as ship-building, steel, and textiles, or certain categories of the labour market, carry important spatial consequences, since the industries concerned tend to be very unevenly distributed.

● *Defence policies.* Decisions to expand or reduce defence expenditures have similar spatial consequences, since important defence contractors also tend to be concentrated in certain cities and regions.

● *Equalization policies.* Policies resulting in intragovernmental transfers will favour some urban areas signficantly.

● *Agricultural policies.* Policies designed to promote the capitalization of agriculture directly affect the size of the agricultural labour force and, therefore, rural–urban migration.

● *Immigration policies.* Such policies tend to affect some cities more than others, especially in respect of labour markets, housing programmes, and social structures.

Experience has shown that the effects on patterns of urban growth of some of the above policies may be more significant than those of urban policies themselves. This requires that governments afford great importance to the evaluation of urban impacts by the agencies responsible for such policies and, where necessary, formulate urban development policies to include realistic assessments of the urban effects of non-spatial national policies.

---

tions are central issues in urban development and human settlements policies. Formulating appropriate responses to inner-city decline has become a policy concern of many governments, a concern made acute by the growing realization that past urban development and containment policies have contributed to the growth of the problems that must today be confronted. Policy responses to inner-city decline include incentives to attract population, especially young families and single people, and small enterprises to central areas, in order to re-establish demographic balance, to create employment, and to enlarge tax revenues. 'Gentrification' of run-down inner-city residential areas has been welcomed by governments and city authorities, although there is evidence that this process has curtailed the supply of housing available to underprivileged groups.[3]

The trends described above are not much in evidence in the developed market-economy countries of Southern Europe. While central-area decline has become apparent in some Italian cities, most countries in the region are confronted with human settlements policy issues distinct from those of the most developed and urbanized market-economy countries.[4] This is especially so in the case of Greece and Portugal and is to some degree so in Italy and Spain.

First among the challenges confronting these four countries is the lack of adequate urban housing, a challenge accentuated by the fact that conventional housing is beyond the reach of substantial numbers of people. In the case of Italy, the lack of housing is illustrated by the dramatic increase in co-habitation over the past decade—from 1.1 million families in 1971 to 2.1 million families in 1981. This was accompanied by a 35 per cent fall in private-sector housing construction over the same period—the result of a rapid rise in inflation, financing costs, and land prices, and of the introduction of new building and rental regulations. The lack of housing and urban services has been aggravated by such factors as internal migration, inadequacy of institutional and organizational structures, insufficiency of financial resources, and the relative lack of land for urban development. In Portugal, the housing shortage was exacerbated by the repatriation of close to 1 million citizens from former overseas territories after 1975, which put a great strain on inadequate public resources.

Urbanization and human settlements development have followed a different process in the developed centrally planned economies. The period since the Second World War has been one of rapid urbanization and industrialization, although the pace of both slowed in the second half of the 1970s, as it did in the market-economy countries. In 1980, around 60 per cent of the population of the centrally planned economies lived in urban areas, but differences between individual countries were significant—ranging from 77 per cent in the case of the German Democratic Republic to 51 per cent in Romania. The patterns of urbanization and industrialization have been largely planned.

At the end of the Second World War, most centrally planned countries, including the USSR, were predominantly rural, and industrial and urban infrastructure was poorly developed. The process thus proceeded in four main phases:

1. The concentration of investment for rapid industrialization in centres where the required supporting infrastructure was already available or could be created quickly, mainly in the country's large cities.
2. The planned growth and expansion of established centres.
3. The containment of the growth of expanding centres, the stimulation of the growth of small centres, and the creation of new centres, particularly in underdeveloped regions.
4. The development of rural centres based mainly on the establishment of agro-processing industries.

Human settlements policies in the centrally planned countries have thus been guided by the objective of building a system of settlements to foster industrialization and the growth of production. However, while the processes and policy concerns differ from those of the developed market-economy countries, the main human settlements issues and problems approximate those of the market-economy countries.

Urban upgrading

In the market-economy countries, especially in Europe, urban revitalization policies aim at urban upgrading and renewal, improvement of the housing stock (including the rehabilitation of old housing), replacement or rehabilitation of ageing urban infrastructure, including roads, water-supply and sewerage mains, and transport facilities, and provision of educational and recreational facilities. They also include inducements to reverse out-migration and programmes to re-establish residential zones in the city core. Policies targeted specifically at environmental upgrading are aimed at reducing air and noise pollution and at creating green zones. These policies have in many countries been combined with urban traffic controls to reduce traffic flows, open pedestrian zones, and allow for recreational use of residential zones, particularly by children.

Most upgrading programmes in the developed market-economy countries stress the need for co-operation between the public and private sectors. National governments, and in some cases local authorities, provide financing, in the form of loans, grants, and subsidies, to private developers as well as individuals. The public sector is expected to play a supportive and facilitating role.

Many of the developed market-economy countries which have experienced inner-city decline have incorporated economic revitalization measures in their urban upgrading policies, and responsibility for the implementation of such measures has been mainly vested in city authorities. The exercise of such responsibilities has required additional measures to increase the powers of local authorities to assist industry. In the EEC region, the Community's Social Fund has been used to finance revitalization measures, while in the United States of America local communities have relied on state funds, federal block grants and Urban Development Action Grants

---

Box 4.2   Italy: changing approach to urban renewal

Urban renewal in Italy became an issue of national concern in the 1950s, and was initially seen in terms of renovating ancient urban settlements and the *centri storici* (historic cores) of cities. The approach was initially formulated in 'cultural terms' by an élite of intellectuals and progressive town-planners interested in the preservation of historical and architectural values. Limited as it was, this approach spared most inner-city cores from the bulldozer. In addition, appreciation of the value of the old urban fabric has grown to such an extent that urban renewal projects based on comprehensive demolition and reconstruction, as envisaged only 20 years ago, would be unthinkable today. At the same time, however, a process has been taking place of expulsion of low-income residents of 'historic cores' and their replacement with commercial and professional activities and high-income residents.

In recent years, the issues have radically changed. First, protests from local inhabitants resisting the speculative expulsion process have taken the form of organized movements (neighbourhood committees, politically involved groups advocating their 'housing rights', etc.). Such groups have, in many instances, successfully resisted the threat of expulsion. Secondly, the concept of 'historic cores' has evolved from that of precious heritage to be preserved in its original form, regardless of social implications, to an important and active feature of the city, a vital and crucial element of the urban fabric.

Source: United Nations Economic Commission for Europe, *Urban Renewal and the Quality of Life*, ECE/HBP/31 (Geneva/New York, 1980), 31.

Box 4.3   New York City: 'self-help' urban improvement programmes

Inner-city problems have led to a wide range of citizen initiatives modelled on the principle of self-help. Such initiatives have been particularly numerous in the United States. Of the many examples, one of the most interesting is the Davidson Community Center in the West Bronx section of New York City.

The area has a population of about 143,000 people. Half of the population is made up of migrants from Puerto Rico and of blacks who moved there during the 1960s and early 1970s from the south of the country and from northern cities. Over a third of the population receives public assistance.

The Davidson Community Center, which began operation in a burned-out store on Davidson Avenue, is recognized by both the neighbourhood and the city as an important community resource. With a paid staff and volunteers, supplemented by teachers assigned by the Board of Education and recreational leaders from various city youth programmes, the Center organizes and implements a wide range of community-development programmes covering information, training, and referral and counselling for problems related to housing, welfare, education, and employment. Its housing programme organizes tenants' groups, secures legal aid, and helps relocate families from derelict and fire-scarred buildings. The Center has been able to identify target areas for neighbourhood rehabilitation under the city's housing and community-development programme. A neighbourhood patrol programme it initiated to lower street crime is now used by New York Police Department as a showcase in neighbourhood crime prevention and has been duplicated in 50 neighbourhoods throughout the city. The Center is also active in organizing citizens to identify needs and programmes to aid the West Bronx.

The vital signs of the West Bronx are improving both physically and socially because of the Davidson Community Center. A neighbourhood which was 'crawling towards destruction', in the words of the founder of its self-help citizens' group, appears to be heading in a new direction.

Source: United Nations Economic Commission for Europe, *Urban Renewal and the Quality of Life*, ECE/HBP/31 (Geneva/New York, 1980), 41–2.

(UDAG), and funds such as the Ford Foundation to underwrite the costs of local economic development.

The success of revitalization policies is, to a large extent, dependent on co-operation among public agencies as well as on the creation of a working partnership between the public and private sectors, often in conjunction with support from community and voluntary organizations. The United Kingdom has attempted to enlist the private sector in this effort through programmes and institutions such as the Financial Institutions Group, the Urban Development Programme (modelled on UDAG),

Inner Enterprises, and the Enterprise Trusts. Urban development corporations have also been established in large centres, such as London and Liverpool, to reverse the process of decay and to stimulate employment creation, especially in the industrial sector. Industrial development policies have tended to stress small-scale firms rather than large enterprises, and special attention has been given to attracting high-technology industries which are able to retain their competitive edge.

The economic difficulties experienced in most developed market-economy countries in the past decade have given an impetus to rehabilitation

Box 4.4   The United Kingdom: revitalizing inner cities

In April 1977, the Government of the United Kingdom announced new policy measures designed to combat inner-city decline, reversing the orientation of previous policies that had stressed decongestion and urban containment. The measures announced were guided by the following goals:

● To improve the physical fabric of inner cities and to make their environment attractive for housing existing residents and for attracting new investment.

● To alleviate social problems through concerted action by public authorities and community care.

● To secure a new balance between inner-city areas and city regions, in terms of population and jobs.

● To match the skills of inner-city residents with employment opportunities.

● To provide the types of houses that people want.

The instruments to achieve these goals were defined in the Inner Urban Area Act adopted in 1978, and implemented under the overall responsibility of the Secretary of State for the Environment.

The Act designated seven so-called 'Partnership Areas' in the inner cities most urgently in need of co-ordinated central and local government action for socio-economic and physical revitalization. 'Programme Authorities' were also established in 15 other cities, where local authorities were to be given additional support to develop and implement improvement programmes. Partnership Committees and Programme Authorities were given new powers and additional finance to:

● Assist private industry and commerce with loans or grants for the acquisition of land and the development of infrastructure.

● Make loans and grants for site clearance and prepara-

tion, environmental improvements, and the conversion or improvement of buildings for housing and other purposes.

● Subsidize the rent of buildings and the interest on loans incurred by firms with less than 50 workers for land acquisition or the building of new premises and infrastructure.

The Inner Urban Areas Act also gave wide powers to local authorities for the economic revitalization of inner-city areas when these could meet the criteria established under the Act for designation as development areas. In these cases, however, no additional public resources were provided.

An addition to revitalization legislation was made in 1981, when a law was passed creating 'Enterprise Zones'. The most unorthodox of policy instruments, enterprise zones are areas in which existing and new firms are provided with special investment incentives and concessions. They are exempted from land tax, property tax, and tax on new plant and equipment. Permit systems and planning procedures are drastically liberalized, although health, safety, and pollution standards are maintained. Enterprise zones are created for a period of 10 years and may not exceed 200 hectares. As of 1984, enterprise zones had been created in 11 inner-city areas: eight in England and one each in Scotland, Wales, and Northern Ireland. Measures to reverse economic decline are supplemented by social and educational programmes organized in close co-operation with community groups and non-governmental organizations.

While the new legislation has achieved promising results in some inner cities, it is as yet too early to determine whether it will be able to help reverse long-established processes of decline.

Source: United Kingdom monograph on the human settlements situation and related trends, economics, and policies, prepared for United Nations Commission for Europe, Committee on Housing, Building, and Planning, 1982.

and revitalization programmes. Many countries have found it difficult to finance comprehensive urban development schemes during periods of recession and cutbacks in public expenditures, and have opted for rehabilitation programmes instead. Also, some have experienced disillusionment with the results of city planning in the post-war period, which has in part been held responsible for inner-city decay and a gradual reduction in the habitability of urban areas. This has been particularly evident in the failure of many high-rise public housing schemes which have been found to be socially and economically undesirable.

Urban upgrading policies in some European countries, particularly the Federal Republic of Germany, France, Netherlands, and the United Kingdom, have had to consider the existence of low-income ethnic minorities. Migrants from the Mediterranean area, as in the case of the Federal Republic of Germany, France, and the Netherlands, or immigrants from the Commonwealth, as in the United Kingdom, tend to inhabit old, substandard housing in the inner cities. In some urban areas in the Federal Republic of Germany, up to 25 per cent of all children belong to 'guest worker' families, and similar concentrations of minority groups can be found in parts of such cities as Birmingham, London, Paris, and Rotterdam. While the number of guest workers in some cities has declined following repatriation measures adopted by some countries in the face of recession (more than 1 million 'guest workers' left Western Europe between 1973 and 1977), such minorities can be expected to place demands in the future on social services, particularly education, as well as to require urban development policies that are sensitive to their needs, especially in respect of affordable and decent housing. Current policies have generally failed to display such sensitivity.

Few European countries with large migrant-worker populations have adopted long-term urban development policies that meet the needs of large minorities in the inner city. This failure can perhaps be explained by the apparent belief that problems will eventually disappear through such measures as repatriation, integration, and immigration controls. This belief appears unfounded: migrant populations seem destined to remain large—4.6 million in the Federal

---

Box 4.5 Austria: improving the urban environment

During the past decade, the Austrian Government has devoted high priority to the improvement of the country's housing stock and the quality of the built environment. A human settlements policy statement of 1975 identified a number of priorities in these areas. They included conservation of the housing stock worthy of being preserved, prevention of city-centre housing conversion to offices and retail stores (a process which has accelerated the depopulation of urban centres), broad rights to the occupiers of dwellings, and equitable housing prices and rental costs.

Specific measures have included provisions in the Rent Act of 1982 which allows landlords to levy a fee against their tenants as a contribution to the maintenance of the residential building. This law is specifically aimed at protecting the stock of urban rental units, particularly old multistorey apartment buildings. Another measure aimed at the rehabilitation of housing stock permits regional and local authorities to guarantee loans for the improvement of residential buildings.

A special housing scheme launched in 1982 provides for construction and financing subsidies to a limited number of dwellings for low-income groups. This measure is a recognition of the fact that rising building costs are placing the purchasing price of new housing beyond the reach of those with modest incomes. The costs of the subsidy are shared by national and regional governments, and the recipient's contribution is deliberately kept low.

Another subsidy programme is the Young Families Housing Act, which provides young couples with temporary low-cost accommodation. This programme is designed to provide shelter at minimal cost to young couples while they accumulate the necessary capital to find a permanent solution to their housing needs. If necessary, the government, through local authorities, provides a direct subsidy to the beneficiaries to enable them to pay minimal rent.

These and other programmes aimed at the improvement of residential buildings and at urban renewal in general are designed with the aim of conserving and renewing old town centres and preserving them as residential neighbourhoods. Subsidy or loan programmes, including those for the modernization and upgrading of inhabited old dwellings, also serve as subsidies for the building industry, particularly hard hit by the world recession. Such subsidies contribute to the creation of employment and serve to stimulate economic growth.

Republic of Germany, 3.5 million in France—and failure to deal with their problems could result in urban social tensions.

The qualitative improvement of the housing stock and the urban environment are concerns of urban development policies in the centrally planned countries. Economic growth and social development, along with high wages and expectations, have resulted in a demand for high-quality housing and variations in dwelling types. This has been especially the case in those centrally planned countries in which emphasis has been on multi-dwelling units constructed either by the state or by co-operatives. While this demand for quality and choice has emerged after great strides have been made towards meeting basic housing needs, the quantitative demand for housing is still not fully met (with the possible exception of the German Democratic Republic). Demand for both quantity and quality in housing has produced pressure on the resources of the centrally planned countries, particularly since the high costs that qualitative housing policies entail cannot be recovered through the low rents charged for housing. Improvement in the quantity and quality of the housing stock is beginning to be seen as a complex policy issue which calls for new investments, replacement and modernization of existing housing stock, mobilization of savings, and close co-ordination between housing and economic policies.

Most centrally planned countries began to adopt long-term strategies aimed at improving the existing housing stock in the early 1970s. The principal components of these strategies have been the raising of housing standards and the renovation and modernization of old housing stock. In Czechoslovakia, Hungary, and the USSR, for example, construction standards have been raised in the socialized sector (state and co-operatives) with regard to floor area, equipment, finish of dwellings, and environmental impact. Poland has also approved high standards for housing developments in urban areas. In the past few years, a topic of constant debate and discussion at governmental level has been the diversification of building types and the upgrading of their equipment (fixtures, appliances, etc.).

The other aspect of this new policy trend has been the emphasis on reducing the difference in quality between new and old housing, either through renovation and upgrading or demolition of that part of the old housing stock that would prove too costly to upgrade. Much debate has taken place over the right balance between upgrading and demolition, but renovation is beginning to attract attention, in part owing to

---

Box 4.6   The evolution of housing policies in the developed countries

In the developed market-economy and centrally planned countries, quantitative housing needs have been largely met. In the region covered by the member states of the Economic Commission for Europe (ECE), excluding the USSR,* the housing stock grew from 265 to 345 dwellings per thousand population in the period 1950–80, although considerable variations exist within the region. Table 1 indicates that there are also considerable differences in the quality of national housing stocks, for example:

● *There are differences in the average size of dwellings.* Sizes are smaller in Eastern Europe and Southern Europe than in North America and Western Europe. Between 1950 and 1980, the average size of dwellings increased most rapidly in the market-economy countries (from 3.5 to 4.5 rooms). Total usable residential floorspace increased from 1.5 billion to 2.2 billion square metres in the ECE region in the period 1970–80.

● *There are differences in the age of the housing stock.* In the industrialized countries as a group, more than 50 per cent of all dwellings were constructed after 1945; in some countries, it is more than two-thirds. Some of the oldest stocks of housing can be found in the centrally planned economies: in the German Democratic Republic and Yugoslavia, more than half of all dwellings were built before 1914.

● *There are differences in the composition of dwellings types* (multistorey flats, low-rise housing, etc.) and in patterns of ownership.

Housing policies in both market-economy and centrally planned countries have been characterized by shifts from quantitative objectives to qualitative ones. Housing-policy trends in both groups of countries include the following:

● Shifts in policy to cover the total housing stock (i.e. away from preoccupation with the construction of new dwellings only), accompanied by emphasis on qualitative objectives in existing urban areas. Policies increasingly cover neighbourhood levels of amenities and environmental considerations. Both market-economy and centrally planned countries justify shifts with economic as well as social arguments.

● Changes in subsidy systems to make them flexible, moving away from subsidies for dwellings to subsidies for individuals.

● Efforts to promote owner occupation, so as to mobilize domestic savings, limit public subsidies, and reduce maintenance costs.

Housing policy has become very complex in all industrialized countries and is seeking to widen its

Box 4.6 continued

Table 1. Comparative housing situation in selected developed countries

	Dwellings per 1,000 inhabitants in 1981	New dwellings constructed per 1,000 inhabitants		Average rooms per dwelling 1981	Useful floor space per dwelling (m²)		% in 1- or 2- dwelling houses 1981
		1960	1980		1960	1981	
Western Europe	407	7.6	6.4	4.3	68	92	65
Austria	410	6.0	6.8	4.2	68	89	41
Belgium	387[a]	5.3	...[b]	5.3[a]	77	171[a]	70[a]
Denmark	424	6.1	5.9	4.9	88	103	71
Finland	385	7.1	10.4	4.0	59	89	37
France	436	6.9[c]	7.3[c]	3.9	64	...[d]	64
Germany, Fed. Rep.	418	10.4	6.3	4.7	71	99	65
Ireland	268	2.1	8.1	5.6	88	101	96
Luxembourg	382	6.0	5.5	5.0	...	120	70
Netherlands	348	7.3	7.9	4.2	81	97	75
Norway	376	7.5	9.1	4.7	76	98	69
Sweden	440	9.1	6.5	4.9	69	111	66
Switzerland	424	9.4	6.7	3.9	67	98[e]	36
United Kingdom	388	5.9	4.5	4.5	...	66[f]	73
Southern Europe	332	4.9	4.6	3.5	...	88	27
Greece	350[g]	5.8	4.5	3.4	64	108[g]	56
Italy	338[g]	5.8	4.5	4.1[g]	...	...	24[h]
Portugal	...	3.2	4.1	5.0[a]	...	134	56
Spain	350[g]	4.2	7.0	3.5[g]	65	91[g]	4[h]
Yugoslavia	278[g]	4.1	6.2	2.4[g]	48	69[g]	59[a]
Eastern Europe	329	5.7	7.6	3.3	53	64	26
Bulgaria	327	6.3	8.4	2.3	56	62	15
Czechoslovakia	361	6.1	8.8	3.7	59	71	31
German Dem. Rep.	412[a]	4.7	7.2	2.9	55	63	17
Hungary	331[g]	5.8	8.3	3.3	57	70	43
Poland	277	4.8	6.1	3.8	57	64	25
Romania	...	7.3	8.9	...	46	57[g]	...
USSR	266[a]	12.9	7.7	2.3[a]	42	52	27[a]
North America							
Canada	351	6.9	7.5	4.9	99	112	64
United States	390	7.2	6.6	5.3	105	120[i]	69

[a] In 1980.
[b] Dwellings begun in 1980, 4.9 per cent; 1981, 3.4 per cent.
[c] Includes boarding houses.
[d] Living space: 73.
[e] In 1976.
[f] Does not include private sector.
[g] In 1979.
[h] In 1977.
[i] In 1978.

Source: Intergovernmental Documentation Centre on Housing and Environment for the Countries of the United Nations Economic Commission for Europe (IDCHEC), Paris.

horizons. At the same time, policies are being shaped by the need to find cost-effective solutions, a need resulting from economic difficulties.

*The ECE includes, in addition to the countries of Europe, the USA and Canada as well as the USSR, but the figures presented here do not include those for the USSR.

the recognition that such renovation can be cost effective, and that improved old neighbourhoods often provide a more attractive habitat than new housing developments.

Such improvement programmes have included new standards not only for upgraded buildings but also for neighbourhoods: in the German Democratic Republic, for example, the improvement of old housing is closely tied to neighbourhood improvement. Funding such modernization is taking a great share of housing investment in the centrally planned countries. Bulgaria, for example, devotes 30 per cent of total housing investment to the modernization of existing housing and urban infrastructure. In the USSR, the government funds the improvement not only of state-built housing but also of co-operative and private housing.

Given the low level of rents in the centrally planned countries, high investments in the upgrading of old housing stock and qualitative improvements in new housing mean that an increased share of net investment will go to the construction sector, thus diverting state funds away from other economic sectors. The issue of state subsidies for rental housing and the determination of fair levels of rent is likely to remain a central policy issue. Governments, especially in Czechoslovakia, Hungary, Poland, and Romania, have adopted policies to increase total funds available for housing by tapping the accumulated savings of the population, in part by charging high fees for such services as electricity, water, and gas.

Increases in personal income in most of the centrally planned countries have made it possible for individuals to invest their own resources in a dwelling, either through housing co-operatives or as individual house-owners. This has resulted in a boom in individual construction, particularly in Bulgaria, Hungary, and Romania. In the case of Bulgaria, this trend is backed by official policy which encourages individual house-ownership, as long as such ownership is not used for personal profit or gain. This trend has confronted public authorities and policy-makers with the need to decide whether to support individual and co-operative construction through national financing institutions: such a policy would be economically beneficial, since over the long term such subsidies would be less costly than subsidizing state-owned housing, especially since the owners (co-operatives or individuals) would be responsible for maintenance. In addition to encouraging the use of personal resources for construction, with grants and subsidies, governments have also increasingly resorted to the sale of state-built housing on credit, in order to recover the cost of construction and to encourage savings for the purchase of housing.

Regional development and decentralization

One of the most persistent policy trends in both the market-economy and centrally planned countries has been the redistribution of regional activities. This trend has been generally characterized by two main emphases—the containment of large city growth, and the development of depressed or underdeveloped regions. Policy measures to achieve these ends have been varied, ranging from industrial dispersion policies to the creation of growth centres and new towns.

In the market-economy countries, policies aimed at limiting the growth of very large cities and controlling urban sprawl have been mainly intended to direct growth of designated locations and to decentralize economic activity. Countries have adopted a variety of measures, including legal prohibitions and financial disincentives to capital investment in large centres, as in the case of Denmark, the Federal Republic of Germany, and the United Kingdom, and financial and other incentives aimed at promoting the development of designated growth areas and centres. Some countries, notably France and the Netherlands, have gone so far as to specify the optimum future populations of important settlements and have planned accordingly.

While some countries have a tradition of policies designed to redistribute urban growth which extends over nearly half a century, in others it is a relatively recent concern. This is the case in such countries as Belgium, Hungary, Ireland, Italy, and Luxembourg. Italy's plans to create 30 growth centres as part of its Project 80 policy, were, however, abandoned.

Concern for controlling the growth of large cities has been accompanied in most developed

countries by attempts to redress regional disparities and income inequalities. Regional differences exist in almost all developed countries;
some are so large that when combined with
ethnic, cultural, and linguistic differences they
may pose a threat to long-term political stability.
In the EEC region as a whole, the income differential between the wealthiest and poorest
regions, adjusted for differences in the costs of
living, is in the order of 3:1, although greater
differences can be found within individual
countries.

Box 4.7   Bulgaria: promoting house-ownership in a centrally planned economy

Centrally planned economies are often associated with
state-built or co-operative-built rental accommodation.
While this remains the dominant form of housing in most
centrally planned economies, the majority of such
countries are seeking to mobilize personal savings for
house construction, and some are actively encouraging
private house-ownership, providing this is not used for
personal profit or gain. Bulgaria is such a country.

House construction in Bulgaria takes four main forms:

• *State-controlled building construction*, financed out of the
state budget or subsidized from the special funds of the
People's Councils (subnational administrative organs),
state institutions, and economic organizations. These
residential units remain state property and are intended
mainly for rental housing.

• *Housing construction under the auspices of the People's
Councils*. This housing is intended mainly for sale, and
construction is executed through the use of state financing
in the form of credit. These dwellings are sold to citizens
who do not already own a private dwelling.

• *Co-operative residential housing construction* financed
through the personal savings and loans of members of
construction co-operatives. These houses remain privately
owned.

• *Individual house construction* by individuals or groups of
individuals who do not already own a private dwelling.

This differentiated approach makes it possible for the state
to reduce its own investment in housing thereby freeing
resources for investment in other sectors. It is also seen as
being responsive to different housing needs, as well as
compatible with efforts to improve the quality of the
nation's housing stock.

Source: National monograph on the human settlements situation
and related trends and policies, prepared for the 43rd Session of
the Committee on Housing, Building and Planning on the United
Nations, Economic Commission for Europe by the Peoples'
Republic of Bulgaria, Ministry of Construction and Architecture,
Sofia, 1982.

Most market-economy countries are applying
policy instruments to stimulate growth in their
depressed or underdeveloped regions. In the
United Kingdom, for example, these include
capital subsidies, tax allowances, and the use of a
system of industrial location controls. Italy has
used a comprehensive approach to the development of the *Mezzogiorno*, with emphasis on
incentives to stimulate industrialization-led
economic growth, the creation of social and
physical infrastructure, and a diversified economic base. Finland has emphasized similar policies in the pursuit of the development of its
northern regions, which suffered from a rural
exodus during the rapid expansion of the urban
areas in the southern part of the country during
the 1960s. By subsidizing the location of
industrial investment in the north, Finland is
attempting to develop the region economically
and to create the basis for balanced national
demographic development. Canada has made
efforts to develop medium-sized cities within the
framework of regional development strategies,
particularly in the eastern areas of the country.
Given the relatively undeveloped state of great
parts of that country and its low population
density, the trend in human settlements
development has to a large degree been
determined by policies that have directed investment to extractive industries which have opened
up resource frontiers and brought about rapid
expansion of settlement activities.

Some market-economy countries have sought
to advance regional development through
administrative decentralization, usually through
local government reforms and the creation of
regional authorities. Local government reforms
have often sought to amalgamate small municipalities as a strategy to deal with urban fiscal
problems by making use of the economies of
scale. The extent of such reforms is evidenced by
the figures for selected countries in Table 4.4.
Only in Denmark, Italy, and the Netherlands
have local-government reforms been accompanied by a substantial increase in the power
of local governments, especially in their powers
to generate revenues which usually remain
under direct and indirect government control.
The same applies to the regional authorities that
have been established in some market-economy
countries to co-ordinate human settlements poli-

Table 4.4 Reduction in the number of local governments, selected countries, 1960–1980

	1960	1980
Austria	5,000	2,300
Belgium	2,500	596
Denmark	1,200	277
Germany, Fed. Rep. of	24,000	8,500
Norway	750	450
Sweden	2,500	279
United Kingdom	1,500	548

Source: OECD, Urban Policies for the 1980s (Paris, 1980), 40.

cies. Although all indications are that the trend towards decentralization will continue, as witnessed by the policies of Belgium, Denmark, Ireland, and the Netherlands, the emphasis is likely to be on efficient programme delivery rather than on the devolution of real powers to local and regional authorities.

The experience of the market-economy developed countries in their efforts to contain urban growth and promote regional development has thus been mixed. Efforts have been frustrated by the difficulties experienced by governments and public authorities in guiding market forces. Experience has shown that decentralization and decongestion policies involving the movement of employment sources over short distances from the central city have been more successful than interregional decentralization policies. The former often work with market forces, the latter against them.

In the USSR spatial planning is linked to the achievement of socio-economic development and to the attainment of nationally determined production targets. The USSR has developed a Master Plan for Residential Distribution which is closely linked to production targets, and is designed to establish a unified system of population distribution based on regional and cluster systems of human settlements. It restricts the growth of large cities, provides for the development of small and medium-sized towns and cities (between 10,000 and 100,000 inhabitants), and attempts to establish a regional balance in the levels of economic development and services. Other considerations in developing this strategy have been the specific needs of under-populated and underdeveloped regions, such as

the Northern sub-Arctic region, the Far East, and Siberia, as well as a desire to rationalize inter-regional and intraregional manpower migration. In so far as this plan is designed to achieve the most effective spatial distribution of the country's labour resources for national economic development over the next two decades, it represents a continuation of the existing trend of subordinating human settlements planning to economic planning. Over the past decades, this has resulted in the development of new urban regions and human settlements systems in areas of the USSR targeted for intensive economic development.

This type of long-term planning is also found in other centrally planned countries. Poland has developed a national physical plan as an integral part of its macro socio-economic planning effort. Elaborated between 1972 and 1974, it outlines town and country planning goals up to 1990. It projects the development of a polycentric settlements network designed to maximize national economic development and to reduce regional imbalances. This plan is to be facilitated by the territorial restructuring of the country for administrative purposes which divides Poland into functional urban regions. Similar administrative reforms have recently been undertaken in Czechoslovakia with the same goals in mind.

All the centrally planned countries have attempted to establish a human settlements hierarchy linked to a system of production. This structure is designed to allow for the controlled growth of urban centres through deliberate policies of locating investment in centres designated for growth, and limiting investment in others. Lately, this strategy has been used to limit the expansion of large towns and to encourage the development of small and medium-sized towns. In the case of Hungary, this has been expanded to include rural centres, principally through the development of agro-industries which will stimulate employment opportunities in the rural areas and slow rural–urban migration to the principal cities. Such migration has altered the age structure of many small towns and villages in Hungary, as the young have left to find work in the urban industrial centres. As in the USSR, the development of a settlements hierarchy as part of the economic planning process is attempting to distribute manpower according to regional production needs.

The new emphasis on the development of small and medium-sized towns in the centrally planned countries (and even rural centres in the cases of the German Democratic Republic and Hungary) is in part an attempt to reverse the imbalances created by the rapid growth of urban centres during the 1950s and 1960s, a pattern of urbanization which was encouraged by the national economic policies of the time which stressed rapid industrial development around centres with existing infrastructure and services. This was particularly true of Bulgaria, Hungary, Poland, and Romania, all of which were predominantly rural societies prior to the Second World War. While all countries appear optimistic about the prospect for the success of the new strategy over the next two decades, it remains to be seen whether deconcentration and decentralization will yield the anticipated results in practice.

Transport policies

The important role of transport in regional and urban development is widely recognized. The construction of railways in the last century and the rising tide of motorization in this century have had profound impacts on human settlements patterns. The impacts were first visible in the United States of America, not only in the spread of suburbanization but also in the effects of national road-building programmes. The development of the Interstate Highway System, initiated in the mid-1950s, served to promote national economic integration by speeding up the movement of goods between states. It also provided improved connections between urban peripheries and the central city, thus fuelling the process of suburbanization.

The initial response of most market-economy countries to the growth of car ownership is well known. To accommodate the growing numbers of motor vehicles, cities invested in urban highways, including costly motorway systems, and in parking facilities—trends that changed the shape of many cities, especially their central areas. Few cities, however, were able to keep pace with the demands made by vehicular traffic. Traffic congestion and a growing appreciation of social and environmental costs as well as economic costs led to questioning in many countries, notably in Europe, of the wisdom of the policies that were being pursued. Support for public transport has become widespread among policy-makers, and many cities have chosen to invest in public-transport systems.

The 1973 oil crisis gave impetus to the development of public transport and encouraged some governments to postpone or even abandon expensive road-building programmes. The severe economic difficulties experienced in many countries since then, however, have compelled some governments to reduce their support for public-transport systems with high investment requirements. The need for energy conservation and reduced public spending has led an increasing number of market-economy countries to place emphasis on management-oriented urban transportation policies. These policies usually attempt to improve the quality of the urban environment by seeking to achieve balance between the use of private automobiles, public transport, and other modes. The experience of several cities in Austria, Belgium, Denmark, France, Italy, the Netherlands, Sweden, and the United Kingdom, among others, has demonstrated the potential of this approach.

While most market-economy countries in Europe have a long tradition of support for public transport, in North America the situation is mixed. In some of the old, densely settled, and populous cities, public transport gained an early foothold and has never completely lost it, whereas in many parts of the country's southern and western regions it is still in an early stage of development. There also seems little doubt that the automobile lobby in the United States has been more effective than lobbies in Europe and Japan in resisting pressures to limit the use of automobiles and to promote public transport. The jobs of 13 million Americans are linked directly or indirectly to the production and use of automobiles, and 7 of the nation's 10 largest enterprises either manufacture automobiles or are in business to supply them with fuel.

Although the interrelationships between transport and land use are clearly recognized, there have not been many instances in the market-economy countries of successful management of transport demand through human settlements planning, or of the use of transport investments to guide settlements development (with Sweden and, partly, the United Kingdom being two of the notable exceptions). The reverse is usually the case. Transport policies have often served to reinforce existing trends (such as suburbanization) rather than to challenge them.

In the centrally planned countries, transport policies have been actively used to achieve settlements and economic planning objectives. The development of national human settlements systems has been accompanied by the creation of transport infrastructure linking the points within the systems. In towns and cities as well as in rural areas, public transport is by far the most important mode of travel to work and for other purposes. The dependence on public mass transport is reflected in the low rates of car ownership, partly as a result of deliberate governmental policies. Only in the 1970s was there a significant reversal of this trend in some centrally planned countries: however, relatively high prices for motor vehicles and ceilings on their production and sale continue to ensure that their use will be primarily for leisure activities.

The almost exclusive dependence by commuters on mass public transport has resulted in elaborate planning forms and standards. In the USSR, transport-planning standards specify a distance of no more than 500 metres between the commuter's house and the pick-up point. Transport planning also has as an objective the limitation of time spent in commuting to and from workplaces, and some countries, such as the USSR, have established normative requirements that urban commuters spend no more than a specific amount of time in work trips, with transport networks having to be laid out accordingly.

While public transport will continue to receive high priority in the centrally planned economies, planners will need to give increasing attention to the problems caused by the growing number of automobiles. With car ownership still at a relatively low level, automobile use is concentrated in cities, with corresponding problems of congestion and air pollution. In some cities, urban traffic flow and parking demands are emerging as important issues which will need to be addressed within the framework of human settlements policies.

Environmental policies

The list of environmental issues linked, directly or indirectly, to human settlements development is long and growing. For example, urban decay and inner-city decline have contributed to a lowering of environmental standards in central areas. Industrial development brings problems of pollution and of toxic wastes, some of which have been indiscriminately disposed of and now constitute health hazards. Mass motorization creates its own environmental problems, the full seriousness of which—health hazards of lead emissions in exhaust gases and the contribution of exhaust fumes to acid rain—is only beginning to be understood. There are environmental problems associated with national energy problems, most apparent in the siting of nuclear power stations and the disposal of radioactive wastes. No country, whether market-economy or centrally planned, has been able to come to grips with all these and similar problems, although all governments now accept the need for environmental legislation and for incorporating environmental considerations in human settlements policies.

In the market-economy countries, two main types of environmental policy have been pursued. The first has embodied policy measures designed to reduce levels of pollution and to conserve areas of historical importance as well as to set aside areas for recreation and leisure activities. Some countries, such as the Federal Republic of Germany and the Netherlands, have enacted environmental legislation based on the 'polluter pays' principle. Similar legislation was passed in the United States in the 1970s, but its implementation has been far from uniform. Countries such as Greece, Italy, Portugal, and Spain have weak or practically non-existent pollution legislation. Both Italy and Spain, however, have been successful in preserving the historic areas of their cities from often destructive urban development, whereas such developments have gone ahead with considerable insensitivity in Belgium and France, and in some towns and cities in the Federal Republic of Germany and the United Kingdom. The second policy trend has been the weighing of environmental factors in the formulation of urban policies, particularly in relation to land-use planning, housing, and transport. During the late 1960s, most countries moved away from the wholesale clearance of rundown areas and ambitious urban road schemes, not least because of their enormous cost and often disappointing results, although the timing and extent of this change have varied from country to country. The Netherlands, for example, first legislated to stimulate the improvement of property as early as 1962.

While considerable progress has been made in some market-economy countries in the environmental field, there is concern that further progress might be halted in a period of slow-down of economic activities. Industry, in particular, has recently put pressure on governments to relax the enforcement of environmental protection legislation in order to reduce production costs—a trend that has been most in evidence in the United States but is in no way restricted to it. It has, however, been demonstrated—and this was the conclusion of the International Conference on Environment and Economics organized by the OECD in June 1984—that the environment and the economy, if properly managed, are mutually reinforcing, and are supportive of and supported by technological innovation.

While concern for environmental issues may be diminishing in many market-economy countries in view of the economic situation, it is figuring prominently in the centrally planned countries. This concern may to some extent be a reflection of the neglect of environmental issues in the past. There seems little doubt that the centrally planned economies—the USSR in particular—have experienced some very serious environmental problems, the consequence of making environmental considerations subservient to the strategic objective of increasing output in both the industrial and agricultural sectors.

Conclusions

In the developed market-economy countries, it is clear that policy-makers have often failed to anti-cipate events with significant impacts on human settlements as well as some of the consequences of their policies. Urban policies have often had the effect of decreasing rather than enhancing the quality of life in human settlements, especially in the case of socially and economically disadvantaged groups. While almost all market-economy countries have satisfied quantitative housing needs, some qualitative needs, particularly of minority groups, non-nuclear families, and persons living alone, have yet to be met.

Despite some efforts at regionalization and local-government reform, many countries continue to lack effective administrative structures and institutional arrangements to execute human settlements policies. Lack of co-ordination among agencies at the national level has had a negative impact on policy implementation in a number of countries, and regionalization has generally failed to produce institutions with effective powers. The extent to which governments should seek to direct or regulate private investment in urban areas remains an issue in most countries.

Policy-makers and governments in general have demonstrated some adaptability and responsiveness to new issues and demands on the part of activist groups and the general public. Evidence of this is to be found in environmental regulations, measures to preserve historic areas, housing subsidies to individuals rather than to dwellings, and the shift to 'qualitative' policies in general. In many market-economy countries, however, the parliamentary process has at times resulted in a discontinuity in specific policies and a slow-down in the application of existing legislation. Economic recession has also eroded support for legislation in some areas, notably environmental protection.

It appears safe to assume that, given current economic difficulties and ideological preferences as well as the often disappointing results of large-scale urban renewal projects, governments and city authorities will in future undertake projects of a smaller scale than those of a decade or two ago. This applies not only to urban renewal projects but also to public-transport systems. The problems of concentrated poverty in the inner cities of the advanced market-economy countries seems destined to remain an important issue which cannot be resolved by urban development policies alone.

With respect to the centrally planned economies, the nature of their planning systems, in principle, provides the political authority and the policy instruments required to address the issue of human settlements development. Human settlements policies are linked to economic planning, although the latter dominate the former. The shortcomings of human settlement development in centrally planned countries are most apparent at the micro level. Some of the housing that has been provided has qualitative shortcomings, a fact that is recognized by most governments, and the centrally planned countries still have to meet quantitative housing needs while upgrading the existing housing stock. Some also have to repair the damage done, particularly to the natural environment, during the period of very rapid industrialization when human settlement and environmental considerations tended to be subservient to the strategic objective of expanding output.

Notes

1. See R. Drewett and A. Rossi, 'General Urbanization Trends in Western Europe', in L. H. Klassen, W. T. Molle, and J. H. P. Paelinck, *Dynamics of Urban Development* (Farnborough: Gower, 1981).
2. See Peter Hall, 'Changing Urban Hierarchies in the Development Process: An International Comparison', *Habitat International*, 7 (1983), 129–35.
3. See P. Clay, *Neighbourhood Renewal* (Lexington, Mass.: Heath, 1979); and P. Levy, 'Neighbourhoods in a Race with Time', in S. Laska and D. Spain, *Back to the City: the making of a movement* (New York: Pergamon, 1980).
4. See 'Human Settlements Problems—Southern Europe', in *Human Settlements: Key Factor in Economic and Social Development*, Economic Bulletin for Europe, 35/1 (1983), ch. 13.

5 The Developing Countries

The diversity that exists among developed countries is more than matched by the diversity among developing countries. They range in size from China and India, that together account for nearly two-fifths of the world's population, to small states, some 50 of which have populations of under 1 million. They differ in terms of their economic structures and political and social systems as well as their historical experience. There are developing countries that seem destined to join the ranks of the developed countries, and those where development appears to have ground to a halt or where it can no longer keep pace with population growth. There is no generalization about the developing countries that holds true, no 'rule' that does not have its exceptions.

This is to point to the difficulties in describing human settlements conditions, trends, and policy issues in developing countries. The diversity can only be captured by a review of individual countries—a review of the type that clearly falls beyond the scope of this work. We therefore necessarily make use of broad statements and point to global trends, even though there will be countries to which they do not immediately apply.

Population

The world's population is expected to increase by nearly 1.3 billion between 1985 and the year 2000.[1] More than 90 per cent of this growth—an increment of 1.2 billion people—is projected to take place in the developing countries. The average annual rate of population growth in the developing countries is some three times higher than in the developed countries. In the period 1980–5, the population of the developing countries increased at an annual rate of 2.01 per cent, compared with 0.64 per cent in the developed countries.

The average for the developing countries as a whole from 1980 to 1985 disguises significant regional variations, ranging from 2.92 per cent per annum in the case of Africa to 1.21 per cent per annum in East Asia, a figure that reflects China's modest growth rate of 1.23 per cent. Growth rates are in fact declining in all the world's developing regions with the exception of Africa. For the developing countries as a whole, annual population growth rates at the turn of the century are projected to be in the order of 1.70 per cent, falling to 1.37 per cent by 2020, a figure reached in the developed countries before 1950. From the period 1980–5 to 2000–5, Latin America's population growth rate is expected to decline from 2.27 per cent per annum to 1.55 per cent, East Asia's from 1.21 per cent to 0.84 per cent, and South Asia's from 2.16 per cent to 1.51 per cent. Africa's annual rate of population growth is expected to increase throughout the 1980s, and thereafter fall to reach 2.99 per cent by the turn of the century. Growth rates in excess of 2.20 per cent per annum, equivalent to more than a doubling of population every 35 years, are expected to persist until after 2020: in 2020, 38 of the 56 countries and territories that make up the African region are expected still to have annual population growth rates in excess of 2.20 per cent. As indicated in Table 5.1, the rapid rates of population growth in Africa will increase the region's share of the world's total population from around 9 per cent in 1960 to 19 per cent in 2020.

In 1960, the developing countries together accounted for 69 per cent of the world's total population. By 1980, the share had increased to 74 per cent, and should reach close to 80 per cent by the turn of the century. As indicated in Table 5.2, in 1960 more than 4 out of 10 of the world's urban population lived in the developing countries, and by the year 2000 the figure will be close to 7 out of 10.

Population growth rates will also ensure that the population of the developing countries remains overwhelmingly young. Around 40 per cent of the population falls within the 0–14 years age-group, and another 20 per cent is aged

Table 5.1   The growth of world population by region, 1960–2020

	1960		1980		2000		2020	
	Population (millions)	% of total	Population (millions)	% of total	Population (millions)	% of total	Population (millions)	% of total
Africa	280	9.3	479	10.8	872	14.2	1,468	18.8
Latin America	217	7.2	361	8.1	546	8.9	735	9.4
East Asia	791	26.2	1,176	26.4	1,475	24.1	1,679	21.5
South Asia	877	29.0	1,408	31.6	2,074	33.9	2,686	34.3
Oceania	16	0.5	23	0.5	30	0.5	36	0.5
Europe (incl. USSR)	639	21.2	750	16.9	827	13.5	881	11.3
Northern America	199	6.6	252	5.7	297	4.9	337	4.3
Developing countries	2,074	68.7	3,313	74.4	4,845	79.1	6,446	82.4
Developed countries	945	31.3	1,137	25.6	1,277	20.9	1,377	17.6
World	3,019	100.0	4,450	100.0	6,122	100.0	7,822	100.0

Source: United Nations, *Urban and Rural Population Projections 1950–2025: The 1984 Assessment* (New York, 1986).

Note: The figures for developed and developing countries are not sums of the above subregions since the classifications used in the compilation of the two sets of data are different.

Table 5.2   Share of developing countries in world urban and rural population, 1960–2020 (percentages)

	1960	1980	2000	2020
Total population	68.7	74.5	79.1	82.4
Urban population	44.6	54.8	66.7	76.3
Rural population	81.2	87.4	90.0	90.6

between 15 and 24 years. Between 1980 and 2000, the number of persons in the 0–14 age-group in the developing countries is expected to increase from 1.3 billion to 1.6 billion, or by nearly 25 per cent. Some 80 per cent of this growth is projected to take place in urban areas, where the population of this age-group is expected to increase by nearly 15 million per year, compared with only 1 million per year in rural areas.[2]

Urbanization

In 1950, less than 300 million people lived in towns and cities in the developing countries. The figure of 500 million was reached in the early 1960s, and by 1985 the number had more than doubled to 1.1 billion. In the next 15 years, the urban population is expected to increase by 760 million, or by more than 50 million every year. The urban population is expected to continue to grow, reaching close to 4 billion around the year 2025, a figure comparable to the world's total population in 1975.

For the developing countries as a whole, the annual average rate of urbanization is declining. From approximately 5.2 per cent per annum in the late 1950s, it fell to approximately 3.4 per cent in the early 1980s. It is projected to decline very slowly, averaging 3.4 per cent in the 1990s and falling to about 2.8 per cent by around 2025. By this time, all the developing regions will be predominantly urban.

Such rates are not high by historical standards. What makes them unique is the sheer size of the population of the developing countries. Today, a mere 1 per cent increase in migration rates from rural to urban areas can result in an additional 25 million urban inhabitants every year.

These global figures conceal significant regional variations, the most important of which are discussed below.

Regional variations

Africa

Africa is the world's least urbanized region, with only 30 per cent of its population at present living in towns and cities. It has, however, the world's highest urbanization rates, averaging around 4.6 per cent per annum throughout the 1970s. The annual average rate of urbanization is not expected to decrease to 3 per cent until after 2025.

The rates of growth of urbanization combined with high population growth rates will ensure a dramatic increase in the region's urban population. As shown in Table 5.3, this is expected to increase from 129 million in 1980 to more than 765 million by the year 2020, by which time over 52 per cent of the region's population will be living in towns and cities.

Differences in urbanization growth rates within the region are shown in table 5.3 and in Figs. 5.1a and 5.1b and 5.2. Southern Africa is already predominantly urban, while in Eastern and Western Africa, only approximately 20–25 per cent of the population live in urban areas. By the year 2020, approximately 60–70 per cent of the population of Northern and Southern Africa is expected to be living in towns and cities, while the figures for Eastern and Western Africa are projected to be 40–50 per cent. The annual average rates of growth of urban populations in Eastern and Western Africa are, however, the highest in the region, although the rates for both are in decline. Growth rates in Eastern Africa were around 7 per cent per annum during most

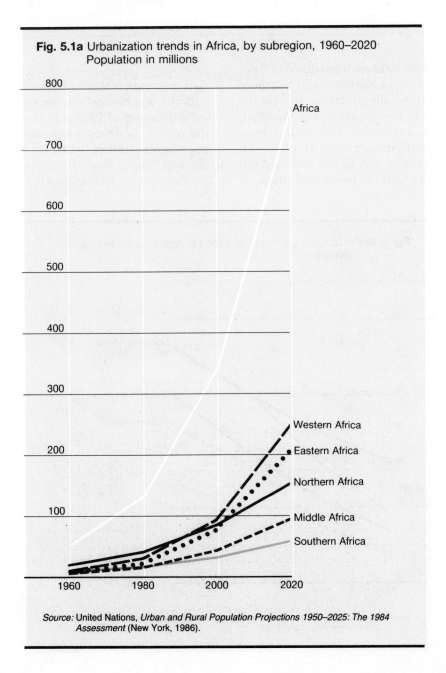

Fig. 5.1a Urbanization trends in Africa, by subregion, 1960–2020
Population in millions

Africa
Western Africa
Eastern Africa
Northern Africa
Middle Africa
Southern Africa

Source: United Nations, *Urban and Rural Population Projections 1950–2025: The 1984 Assessment* (New York, 1986).

Table 5.3   Urbanization trends in Africa, by subregion

	1960		1980		2000		2020	
	Urban population (millions)	% of total	Urban population (millions)	% of total	Urban population (millions)	% of total	Urban population (millions)	% of total
Eastern Africa	5.8	7.3	21.5	15.1	77.5	32.0	206.0	42.6
Middle Africa	5.9	18.0	16.4	31.6	43.9	51.4	95.3	61.7
Northern Africa	20.9	32.1	43.0	39.9	88.8	50.6	154.1	63.0
Southern Africa	8.8	42.3	16.3	49.6	33.2	60.9	59.5	71.0
Western Africa	11.2	13.8	32.0	22.2	96.7	34.9	250.8	50.0
Total	52.6	18.8	129.3	27.0	340.1	42.3	765.6	52.2

Note: The regional and subregional grouping of countries is in accordance with United Nations practice.

of the 1970s and are unlikely to go down to 5 per cent until after 2010. In Northern and Southern Africa, natural population increase will be the dominant factor in the growth of urbanization, while in Western and Eastern Africa, which have some of the fastest-growing cities in the world, rural–urban migration will be the most significant factor in the growth of towns and cities.

Asia

Asia is a region with very great differences in patterns of urbanization. Because of the statistical dominance of China, India, and Indonesia, the region combines a very low level of urban population growth with the world's largest absolute population. In most of the region, natural increase has become the dominant factor

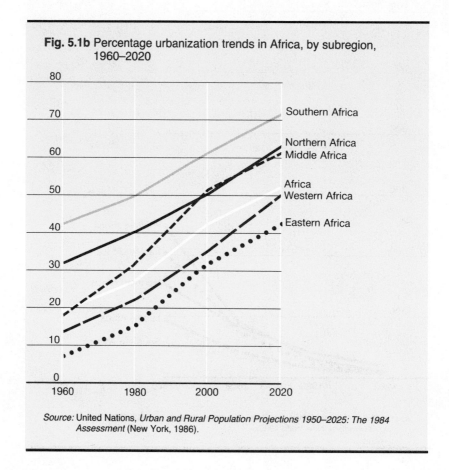

Fig. 5.1b Percentage urbanization trends in Africa, by subregion, 1960–2020

Source: United Nations, *Urban and Rural Population Projections 1950–2025: The 1984 Assessment* (New York, 1986).

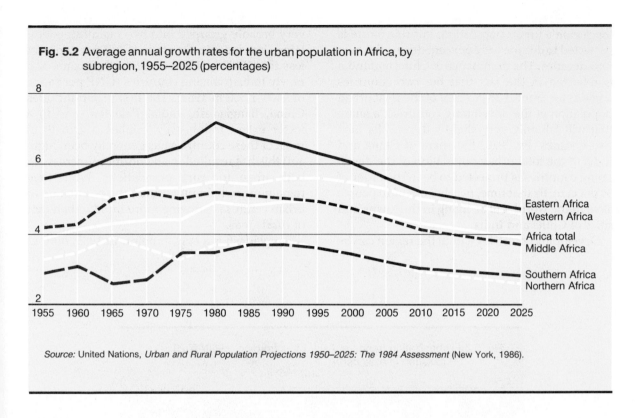

Fig. 5.2 Average annual growth rates for the urban population in Africa, by subregion, 1955–2025 (percentages)

Eastern Africa
Western Africa
Africa total
Middle Africa
Southern Africa
Northern Africa

Source: United Nations, *Urban and Rural Population Projections 1950–2025: The 1984 Assessment* (New York, 1986).

in the growth of urban populations, particularly in South-eastern and Southern Asia. An indication of subregional differences is given in Tables 5.4, and Figs. 5.3a and 5.3b and 5.4.

Asia's urban population is growing at an average rate of around 3 per cent per annum. It doubled in the period 1960–80 from 359 million to 688 million. The average rate of growth of the urban population is not expected to change significantly between 1980 and the year 2000, which implies a further doubling of the urban population to 1.2 billion in the next 20 years.

The dominant position of China and India is reflected in their share of the region's total population. In 1960, the two countries together accounted for 1.1 billion of the region's 1.7 billion people, or approximately two-thirds of the total. This share is likely to remain above 60 per cent until well into the next century. In 1960, China and India together accounted for 57 per cent of

Table 5.4 Urbanization trends in Asia, by subregion and selected country, 1960–2020

	1960		1980		2000		2020	
	Urban population (millions)	% of total	Urban population (millions)	% of total	Urban population (millions)	% of total	Urban population (millions)	% of total
East Asia	198	25.0	331	28.1	485	32.9	770	45.8
China	125	19.0	203	20.4	315	25.1	570	39.7
South Asia	161	18.4	358	25.4	757	36.5	1,381	51.4
South-eastern Asia	40	17.6	87	24.0	184	35.5	334	50.7
Southern Asia	103	17.3	220	23.2	466	33.6	863	48.6
India	79	18.0	161	23.4	330	34.2	591	49.8
Western Asia	18	32.9	51	51.6	107	64.0	185	73.9
Total	359	21.5	688	26.6	1,242	35.0	2,151	49.3

Source: United Nations, *Urban and Rural Population Projections 1950–2025: The 1984 Assessment* (New York, 1986).

the region's urban population, but this figure is projected to decline to 52 per cent during the next four decades. The dominance of China and India is reflected in the fact that the two countries account for around 38 per cent of the total urban population of the developing countries, a share that will fall only very slightly during the next two decades. By 2020, the share of China and India of the total urban population of the developing countries is projected to be in the order of 34 per cent: by that time, nearly 3 out of 10 people alive in the world will be living in the towns and cities of China and India.

Developing countries within the region can be

very broadly grouped into two main categories: large, low-income countries (GNP per capita of less than $400 in 1983) and middle-income and newly industrializing countries (GNP per capita of $400–1,500 in 1983). The first group includes China, Bangladesh, India, Pakistan, and to a lesser extent Indonesia. Population growth in most of these countries has generally been high, and this has resulted in an enormous increase in both urban and rural populations. While they remain overwhelmingly rural, the population of urban centres is growing more rapidly than that of rural areas.

Bangladesh is a case in point. In 1985, only 12

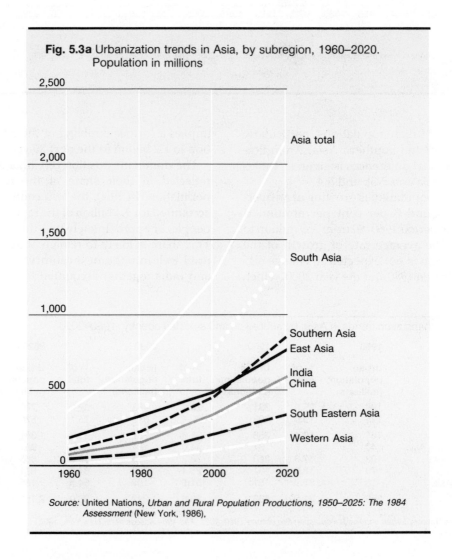

Fig. 5.3a Urbanization trends in Asia, by subregion, 1960–2020. Population in millions

Source: United Nations, *Urban and Rural Population Productions, 1950–2025: The 1984 Assessment* (New York, 1986),

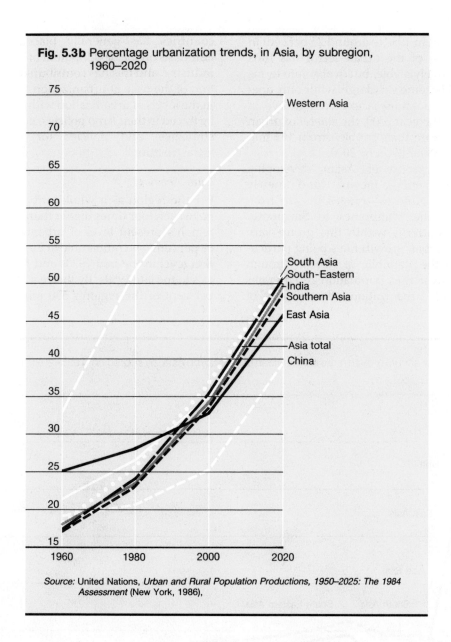

Fig. 5.3b Percentage urbanization trends, in Asia, by subregion, 1960–2020

Source: United Nations, *Urban and Rural Population Productions, 1950–2025: The 1984 Assessment* (New York, 1986),

per cent of the country's 100 million people lived in urban areas, but by the year 2000 a little less than 2 people in 10 are projected to be living in towns and cities—still making it one of the world's least urbanized countries. However, while the country's total population has been growing at between 2.3 and 2.8 per cent per annum since the late 1950s, the urban population grew at more than 6 per cent per annum during the 1960s and early 1970s. These growth rates translate into very large future urban and rural populations. The urban population is projected to increase from 9 million in 1980 to 27 million in 2000, or by nearly 1 million people per annum. Over the same period, the country's rural population is projected to grow from 79 million to 119 million, or by 2 million people every year.

In India, the rural population increased by 60 per cent between 1960 and 1985, while the country's urban population increased by 140 per cent. The level of urbanization increased from about 17 per cent in 1950 to around 25 per cent in 1985. The share of the urban sector has thus remained relatively stable, but in absolute terms the sector has become very large: while only one-third of the population is expected to live in urban areas in the year 2000, the *number* of urban dwellers will more than double—from 161 million in 1980 to 330 million by 2000.

The second group of Asian developing countries—the middle-income and newly industrializing countries—ranges in size from Thailand and the Philippines to Singapore. Urbanization patterns within this group vary considerably, urban growth rates being particularly high in the Republic of Korea. Though differing greatly in their population growth rates and levels of urbanization, this group of

countries has generally placed considerable emphasis on the development of export-oriented industry, and this has contributed to an acceleration of the pace of urbanization. The differences in the levels of urbanization within the group can be traced to their rural policies, economic growth strategies, and policies for investment in infrastructure.[3]

Latin America

For the region as a whole, urban growth rates have been four times higher than rural rates. The region's present level of urbanization—around 69 per cent—is comparable to Europe's urbanization level in the mid-1970s and to North America's in the late 1950s. By the year 2000, around 77 per cent of the region's 550 million people are

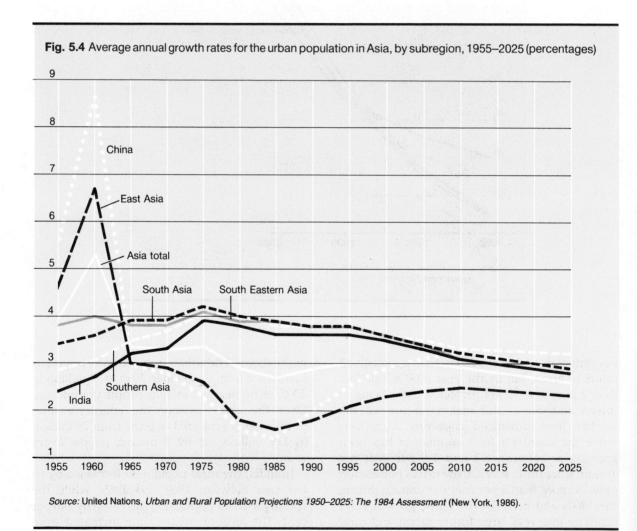

Fig. 5.4 Average annual growth rates for the urban population in Asia, by subregion, 1955–2025 (percentages)

Source: United Nations, *Urban and Rural Population Projections 1950–2025: The 1984 Assessment* (New York, 1986).

projected to be living in urban areas. Urbanization trends and growth rates for subregions within Latin America are shown in Table 5.5 and Figs. 5.5a and 5.5b and 5.6.

Urbanization levels within the region varied in 1985 from 55.5 per cent in the case of the Caribbean to 84.3 per cent in Temperate South America (Argentina, Chile, and Uruguay). Only Australia, New Zealand, North America, and the countries of Northern Europe had levels of urbanization in 1985 that were higher than the level of Argentina, Chile, and Uruguay com-

bined. It is noticeable, however, that all subregions were predominantly urban in 1985, and that all but the Caribbean had reached or were approaching this condition a quarter of a century ago.

Noteworthy also are the dominant positions of Mexico and Brazil within their respective subregions. In 1960, Mexico's urban population accounted for approximately 83 per cent of Central America's urban population, and the figure is projected to be only slightly lower in the year 2000. Similarly, Brazil accounted for 60 per

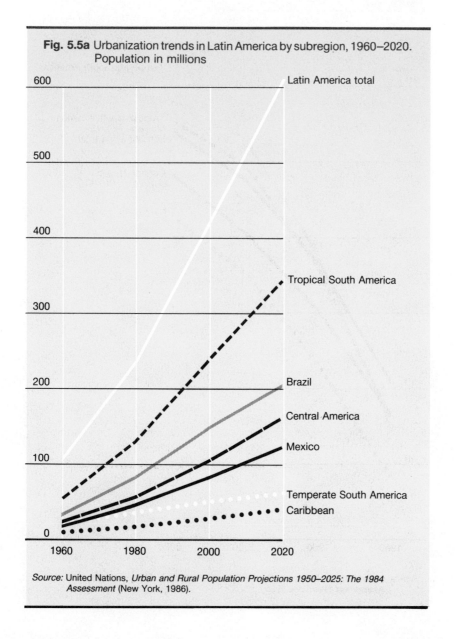

Fig. 5.5a Urbanization trends in Latin America by subregion, 1960–2020. Population in millions

Source: United Nations, *Urban and Rural Population Projections 1950–2025: The 1984 Assessment* (New York, 1986).

cent of the total urban population of the 10 countries that make up Tropical South America, and this share is projected to apply at the turn of the century.

Urban growth rates in all subregions are declining, and with the exception of the Caribbean have been doing so since the late 1940s. All subregions, excluding Temperate South America, have annual rates of urban growth of between 2.8 and 3.7 per cent, rates that are projected to decline to 2.0–2.5 per cent by the turn of the century. Temperate South America's growth rate has averaged 2 per cent since the late 1960s and is projected to fall to 1 per cent in the early years of the next century. In the countries that make up this group, the city-to-city mobility

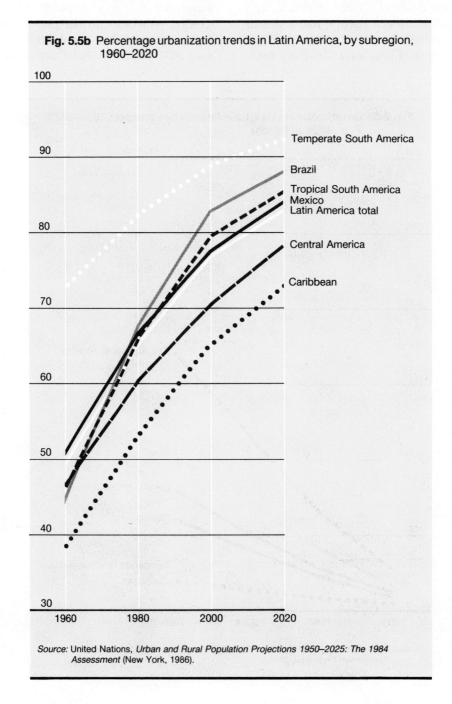

Fig. 5.5b Percentage urbanization trends in Latin America, by subregion, 1960–2020

Source: United Nations, *Urban and Rural Population Projections 1950–2025: The 1984 Assessment* (New York, 1986).

of an already urbanized population is becoming an increasingly significant factor in urbanization patterns.

Trends by types of developing countries

Other variations can be identified within broad groupings of developing countries. Figure 5.7

Table 5.5 Urbanization trends in Latin America, by subregion and selected country, 1960–2020

	1960		1980		2000		2020	
	Urban population (millions)	% of total	Urban population (millions)	% of total	Urban population (millions)	% of total	Urban population (millions)	% of total
Caribbean	8	38.5	16	53.2	27	64.8	40	72.6
Central America	23	46.7	56	60.4	105	70.6	163	78.3
Mexico	19	50.8	46	66.4	84	77.4	123	84.0
Temperate South America	22	72.7	35	82.3	49	88.6	62	92.0
Tropical South America	54	46.1	130	66.0	239	79.4	345	85.3
Brazil	33	44.9	82	67.5	148	82.7	206	88.0
Total	107	49.3	236	65.4	420	76.8	610	83.0

Source: United Nations, *Urban and Rural Population Projections 1950–2025: The 1984 Assessment* (New York, 1986).

Fig. 5.6 Average annual growth rates for the urban population in Latin America, by subregion, 1955–2025 (percentages)

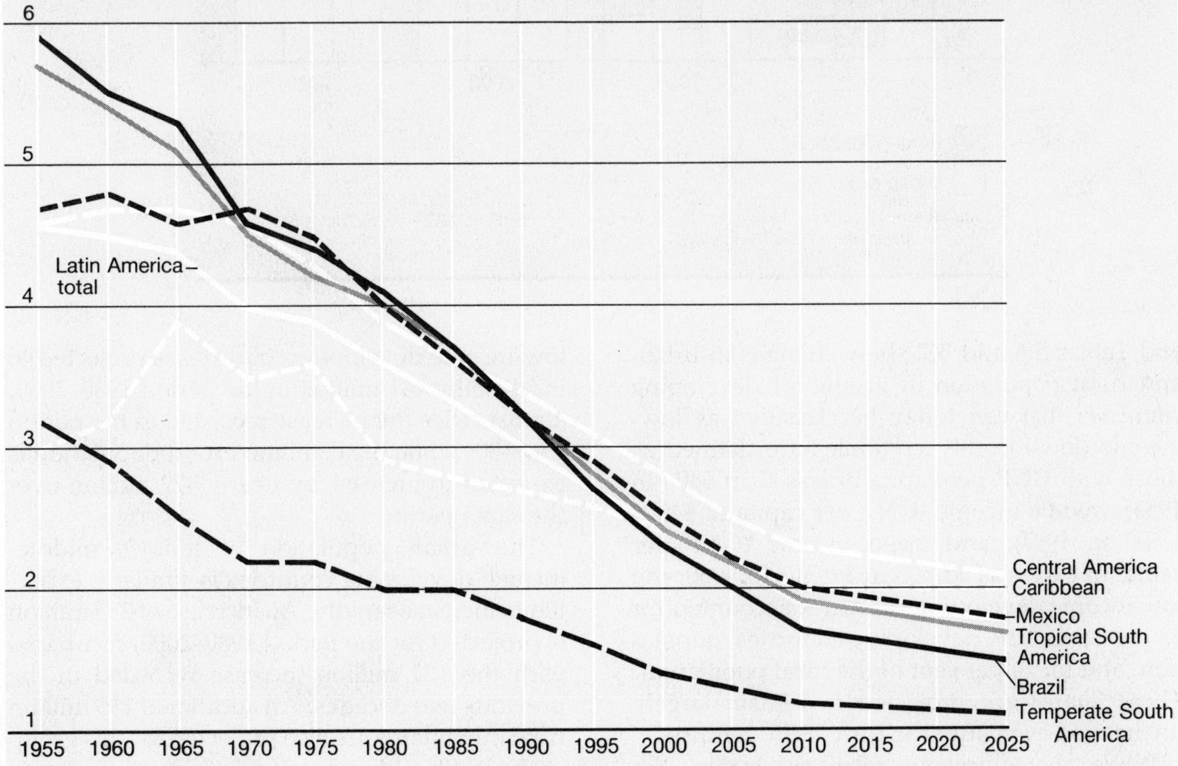

Source: United Nations, *Urban and Rural Population Projections 1950–2025: The 1984 Assessment* (New York, 1986).

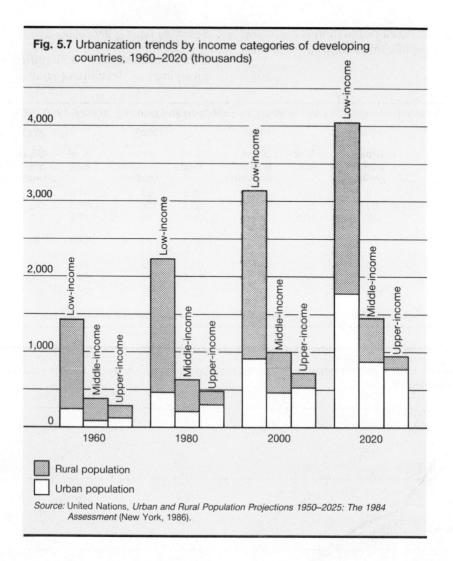

Fig. 5.7 Urbanization trends by income categories of developing countries, 1960–2020 (thousands)

Rural population

Urban population

Source: United Nations, *Urban and Rural Population Projections 1950–2025: The 1984 Assessment* (New York, 1986).

and Tables 5.6 and 5.7 show changes in urban and rural population in groups of developing countries that can today be classified as low-income (low-income economies are defined as those with GNP per capita of less than $400 in 1983), middle-income (GNP per capita of $400–1,500 in 1983), and upper-income (GNP per capita in excess of $1,500 in 1983).[4] In 1960, the low-income developing countries accounted for 53 per cent of the developing countries' population, and for 74 per cent of the rural population. These shares are projected to remain largely unchanged even after the turn of the century.

While shares remain relatively stable, the absolute numbers of people involved in the changes that are projected to take place are very considerable. The urban population of today's

low-income developing countries is projected to increase by 441 million in the period 1980–2000, almost twice the increase recorded in the period 1960–80, while the combined rural population is expected to increase by nearly 472 million over the same period.

The urban population of today's middle-income developing countries is similarly expected to increase rapidly. An increase of 253 million is projected for the period 1980–2000, compared with the 122 million increase recorded in the previous two decades. An additional 115 million rural inhabitants are also projected for this group in the last two decades of this century.

Upper-income developing countries are projected to increase their urban population by nearly 235 million in the period 1980–2000, com-

Table 5.6 Urban and rural population in developing countries, by income level and region, 1960–2020 (thousands)

	1960			1980			2000			2020		
	U	R	% U	U	R	% U	U	R	% U	U	R	% U
Low-income developing countries	245	1,189	17.1	466	1,769	20.9	908	2,242	28.8	1,774	2,274	43.8
Africa	13	121	10.0	40	185	17.8	125	293	29.9	321	404	44.3
Asia	231	1,066	17.8	424	1,580	21.2	779	1,943	28.6	1,444	1,863	43.7
Latin America	1	3	25.0	1	4	20.0	4	6	40.0	9	8	52.9
Middle-income developing countries	92	282	24.6	214	413	34.1	466	528	46.9	868	577	60.1
Africa	27	88	23.5	64	138	31.7	162	203	44.4	352	260	57.5
Asia	40	158	20.2	95	227	29.5	200	267	42.8	346	257	57.4
Latin America	25	34	42.4	55	44	55.6	104	53	66.2	167	55	75.2
Oceania	—	2	—	1	3	25.0	1	5	16.7	3	5	37.5
Upper-income developing countries	132	163	44.7	294	183	61.6	529	185	74.1	770	176	81.4
Africa	12	18	40.0	24	25	49.0	48	34	58.5	85	37	69.7
Asia	28	47	37.3	71	57	55.5	141	61	69.8	217	60	78.3
Latin America	81	73	52.6	180	76	70.3	312	68	82.1	433	62	87.5
Europe	11	25	30.6	18	24	42.9	26	21	55.3	34	16	68.0
North America	—	—	—	—	—	—	—	—	—	—	—	—
Oceania	—	—	—	—	1	—	1	1	50.0	1	—	—
Total[a]	460	1,614	22.2	966	2,347	29.2	1,904	2,941	39.3	3,425	3,021	53.1

Source: United Nations, *Urban and Rural Population Projections 1950–2025: The 1984 Assessment* (New York, 1986).

Note: U = urban, R = rural.

[a]The sum of low-income, middle-income, and upper-income developing countries does not tally with the total for all developing countries as the classification used in compilation are different.

Table 5.7 Annual average rate of change in urban and rural populations in developing countries, by income level, 1950–2020 (percentages)

Low-income developing countries	1950–1960		1960–1970		1970–1980		1980–1990		1990–2000		2000–2010		2010–2020	
	U	R	U	R	U	R	U	R	U	R	U	R	U	R
Africa	5.4	1.9	5.5	2.0	5.5	2.3	5.7	2.3	5.6	2.3	5.1	1.9	4.5	1.5
Asia	4.9	1.3	3.2	2.1	2.9	1.8	2.8	1.3	3.3	0.8	3.3	0.0	3.0	−0.4
Latin America	4.3	1.4	4.5	1.6	4.5	1.7	4.7	1.8	4.8	1.7	4.6	1.3	4.2	1.0
Middle-income developing countries														
Africa	3.6	2.0	4.1	2.3	4.5	2.3	4.7	2.0	4.6	1.8	4.2	1.5	3.8	1.2
Asia	4.4	1.8	4.3	2.0	4.3	1.6	3.9	1.1	3.6	0.6	3.0	0.0	2.6	−0.3
Latin America	4.4	1.5	4.2	1.5	3.6	1.2	3.4	1.0	3.0	0.7	2.6	0.4	2.3	0.2
Oceania	8.1	1.6	10.0	1.7	4.6	2.0	4.1	2.1	4.3	1.6	4.4	1.0	4.0	0.6
Upper-income developing countries														
Africa	3.5	1.0	3.3	1.5	3.4	1.8	3.6	1.8	3.5	1.3	3.1	0.5	2.7	0.2
Asia	5.0	1.8	5.0	1.4	4.5	0.5	3.8	0.5	3.0	0.3	2.4	0.1	2.0	−0.2
Latin America	4.6	1.1	4.2	0.6	3.8	−0.2	3.1	−0.6	2.4	−0.6	1.8	−0.4	1.6	−0.4
Europe	2.9	0.2	2.6	−0.4	2.5	0.0	2.0	−0.5	1.7	−0.8	1.4	−1.2	1.2	−1.4
North America	1.9	4.2	2.5	4.1	2.0	0.1	1.7	−0.3	1.4	−0.4	1.2	−0.5	1.1	−0.7
Oceania	4.7	2.0	4.7	1.8	3.9	0.8	3.1	0.4	2.4	−0.3	1.9	−0.8	1.5	−1.1

Source: United Nations, *Urban and Rural Population Projections 1950–2025: The 1984 Assessment* (New York, 1986).

Note: U = urban, R = rural.

pared with an increase of around 165 million in the preceding 20 years. Their combined rural population is, however, in decline.

Tables 5.8 and 5.9 disaggregate the broad groupings of developing countries found in Tables 5.6 and 5.7 into subgroups of developing countries, classified according to type of economy. Both these tables illustrate the high levels of urbanization of the industrializing and oil-exporting developing countries in comparison with other categories of developing countries. It is especially noteworthy that the highest rate of urban population growth between 1960 and 1980 was experienced by the oil-exporting developing countries. During those two decades, their annual average rate of change of urban population was twice that of the rate for developing countries as a whole.

As for the market-economy and centrally plan-ned developing countries, both groupings are projected to have virtually the same percentage of urbanized population by 2020, although the percentage will continue to be slightly higher for the centrally planned economy countries. Urbanization patterns in the centrally planned group are dominated by China, while patterns in the market-economy group strongly reflect the position occupied by India. When these two countries are excluded from calculations, it can be seen that both groups of low-income countries urbanized at rates well in excess of 4 per cent per annum during the 1960s and 1970s. The urbanization rates of the low-income, centrally planned developing countries exceeded those of low-income market-economy countries for the first time in the late 1980s, and United Nations projections indicate that they are likely to be 4.9 per cent per annum during the

Table 5.8 Urban and rural population in developing countries, by type of economy, 1960–2020 (thousands)

	1960			1980			2000			2020		
	U	R	% U	U	R	% U	U	R	% U	U	R	% U
All developing countries[a]	460	1,614	22.2	966	2,347	29.2	1,904	2,941	39.3	3,425	3,021	53.1
Low-income developing countries	245	1,189	17.1	466	1,769	20.9	908	2,242	28.8	1,774	2,274	43.8
Middle-income developing countries	92	282	24.6	214	413	34.1	466	528	46.9	868	577	60.1
Upper-income developing countries	132	163	44.7	294	183	61.6	529	185	79.4	770	176	81.4
High-income, oil-exporting developing countries	2	5	28.6	11	6	64.2	27	7	78.3	46	9	83.6
Market-economy developing countries	302	932	24.5	681	1,339	33.7	1,399	1,698	45.2	2,472	1,798	57.9
Market-economy, low-income developing countries												
Including India	105	540	16.3	227	803	22.0	498	1,053	32.1	983	1,112	46.9
Excluding India	26	177	12.8	65	276	19.1	168	419	28.6	392	516	43.2
India	79	363	17.9	161	527	23.4	330	634	34.2	591	595	49.8
Centrally planned developing countries												
Including Albania and Yugoslavia	164	696	19.1	295	1,023	22.4	520	1,256	29.3	974	1,233	44.1
Centrally planned, low-income developing countries												
Including China	140	650	17.7	240	966	19.9	409	1,188	25.6	791	1,162	40.5
Excluding China	15	117	11.4	36	173	17.3	95	247	27.7	220	296	42.6
China	125	533	19.0	203	793	20.4	315	941	25.1	570	866	39.7

Source: United Nations, *Urban and Rural Population Projections 1950–2025: The 1984 Assessment* (New York, 1986).

Note: U = urban, R = rural.

[a]The sum of low-income, middle-income, oil-exporting, and upper-income developing countries does not tally with the total for all developing countries as classifications used in compilation are different.

Table 5.9 Annual average rate of change in urban and rural populations in developing countries, by type of economy, 1960–2025 (percentages)

	1950–1960		1960–1970		1970–1980		1980–1990		1990–2000		2000–2010		2010–2025	
	U	R	U	R	U	R	U	R	U	R	U	R	U	R
All developing countries[a]	4.7	1.4	3.8	2.0	3.6	1.7	3.4	1.3	3.4	0.9	3.2	0.4	2.8	0.1
Low-income developing countries	4.9	1.4	3.3	2.1	3.1	1.9	3.1	1.4	3.6	1.0	3.6	0.3	3.3	0.0
Middle-income developing countries	4.2	1.8	4.2	2.0	4.2	1.8	4.0	1.4	3.8	1.0	3.4	0.7	3.0	0.4
Upper-income developing countries	4.4	1.1	4.2	0.8	3.8	0.3	3.3	0.1	2.6	0.0	2.1	−0.1	1.8	−0.3
High-income, oil-exporting countries	7.6	1.1	8.4	1.3	8.6	1.1	5.4	1.2	3.9	1.3	3.1	1.2	2.5	0.9
Market-economy developing countries	3.9	1.9	4.1	1.9	4.1	1.7	3.8	1.4	3.4	1.0	3.1	0.5	2.8	0.2
Centrally planned developing countries	6.4	0.9	3.3	2.1	2.5	1.8	2.5	1.2	3.2	0.9	3.4	0.1	3.1	0.2
Market economy, low-income														
Including India	3.0	2.0	3.6	2.1	4.1	1.9	3.9	1.6	4.0	1.1	3.7	0.5	3.3	0.2
Excluding India	4.8	1.8	4.8	2.1	4.5	2.3	4.7	2.3	4.8	1.9	4.6	1.4	4.1	0.9
India	2.5	2.0	3.2	2.0	3.9	1.7	3.6	1.2	3.5	0.6	3.2	−0.1	2.8	−0.4
Centrally planned, low-income														
Including China	6.8	0.9	3.1	2.2	2.3	1.8	2.2	1.2	3.2	0.8	3.5	0.1	3.2	−0.2
Excluding China	4.2	1.6	4.5	1.9	4.2	2.0	4.7	1.9	4.9	1.6	4.6	1.1	4.1	0.8
China	7.2	0.8	2.9	2.2	2.0	1.8	1.7	1.1	2.7	0.6	3.1	−0.2	2.9	−0.6

Source: United Nations, *Urban and Rural Population Projections 1950–2025: The 1984 Assessment* (New York, 1986).

Note: U = urban, R = rural.
[a] The sum of low-income, middle-income, oil-exporting and upper-income developing countries does not tally with the total for all developing countries as classifications used in compilation is different.

1990–2000 period, remaining above those of low-income, market-economy developing countries.

The inclusion of China and India significantly changes the picture. India's rate of urbanization reached 3.9 per cent per annum in the 1970s, while China's declined throughout the 1960s and 1970s to reach 1.7 per cent in the early 1980s (Table 5.10). However, while India's rate of urbanization is projected to decline until year 2000, China's is projected to increase in the 1990s as a result of the new economic policies being pursued. As a consequence, the differences in the rates of urbanization between low-income, centrally planned and market-economy developing countries, defined to include the world's two most populous nations, can be expected to narrow until they disappear by the turn of the century.

Table 5.10 Urban average annual growth rates in low-income centrally planned and market-economy developing countries (percentages)

	1950–1960	1960–1970	1970–1980	1980–1990	1990–2000
Market-economy	3.9	4.1	4.1	3.8	3.4
Market-economy minus India	4.8	4.8	4.5	4.7	4.8
India	2.5	3.2	3.9	3.6	3.5
Centrally planned	6.4	3.3	2.5	2.5	3.2
Centrally planned minus China	4.2	4.5	4.2	4.7	4.9
China	7.2	2.9	2.0	1.7	2.7

Source: United Nations, *Urban and Rural Population Projections 1950–2025: The 1984 Assessment* (New York, 1986).

The components of urban population growth

The two causes of urban population growth are the natural increase of urban populations and migration. Migration is overwhelmingly internal and voluntary, but in some regions transnational and impelled migration may be a significant factor. For example, since 1967, Amman has received an estimated 250,000 refugees; and in Africa at the beginning of the 1980s there were an estimated 2.7 million refugees, displaced from 14 countries to 22 other countries. This figure does not include another 1.4 million people who were displaced by wars and unrest but had not left their own country.[5]

Most people who choose to leave their country do so in search of work. One estimate made in the late 1970s placed the world-wide total of people working outside their own country at around 20 million: 12 million of them were from the developing countries.[6]

Differences in the levels of development and distribution of economic opportunities within regions also result in voluntary migration. In Latin America, people from the poorest three countries—Bolivia, Colombia, and Paraguay—migrate to the richest two—Argentina and Venezuela. One-fourth of Venezuela's labour force is made up of immigrants, many of whom entered illegally. In West Africa, workers from Burkina Faso, Guinea, and Mali emigrate to Côte d'Ivoire, Ghana, and Senegal, while workers from Ghana are employed in Nigeria. Migrants make up about 20 per cent of the labour force in Côte d'Ivoire and form the majority of agricultural wage-labourers and unskilled urban workers.[7] In the mid-1960s, the average per capita income in Abidjan was almost 19 times that of Burkina Faso. Since then the differential appears to have grown, and even the poorest parts of Côte d'Ivoire have income levels higher than those prevailing in Burkina Faso.[8]

International migration has also been accompanied by replacement migration. In some Middle East countries a large part of the national labour force is working abroad, while at the same time the country is importing labour from neighbouring countries for specific tasks. Likewise, large numbers of Mexicans have emigrated to the United States, while Mexico itself is the target of people from small Central American countries.

While international migration is a significant factor in the growth of cities in some developing countries, it is internal voluntary migration that remains the crucial variable. The relationships between rural–urban migration and natural increase in urban populations have been studied by demographers in various settings and over several decades. Although comprehensive data are not available, and the existing studies employ different methodologies, it appears that natural increase has become the most important source of urban population growth, especially in the urbanized developing countries. In several countries of Latin America, for example, it has been found that, in the 1950s, net migration was the prime source of urban population growth, but analyses of recent periods point to a reversal between natural increase and net migration in their contributions to urban population growth.

A study by the United Nations Population Division largely supported those findings for a number of developing countries in Africa, Asia, and Latin America for the 1960–70 period. According to the study, the contribution of natural increase to urban population growth, on average, exceeded that of net migration in 29 developing countries during the 1960s. The study also showed substantial variations among countries as well as within countries for which more than one observation period was available. Recent findings have been widely interpreted as an indication that natural increase rather than net migration is the crucial variable for urban population growth in the developing countries. While there seems little doubt that this is becoming the case, there are countries in which, as indicated in Table 5.11 rural–urban migration remains the dominant factor.

The growing emphasis on natural increase may lead to neglect of the complexity of the relationships between natural increase, migration, and urban population growth. First, attention must be called to the fact that the reported relative importance of the two components of growth are country averages. There is a wide variation among developing countries, as well as within countries over time, in terms of the proportions of urban growth attributable to those two components: the migration increase ranges

Table 5.11 Share of net migration in urban growth in selected developing countries, 1970–1975 (percentages)

	Annual average urban growth	Share of migration	Annual average population growth
Papua New Guinea	10.1	74.3	2.6
Yemen	8.0	76.3	1.9
Kuwait	8.2	24.4	6.2
United Republic of Tanzania	7.5	64.4	2.7
Nigeria	7.0	64.3	2.5
Colombia	4.9	43.1	2.8
Mexico	4.6	23.4	3.5
Brazil	4.5	35.5	2.9
Venezuela	3.9	20.5	3.1
Argentina	2.0	35.0	1.3
Thailand	5.3	45.3	2.9
Philippines	4.8	41.7	2.8
Indonesia	4.7	48.9	2.4
Sri Lanka	4.3	60.5	2.1
India	3.8	44.7	1.7

Source: United Nations Population Division.

from 7.3 per cent in Uruguay to 62 per cent in Turkey. Secondly, in most countries where policy-makers are concerned with the growth of urban population, that concern is especially pronounced with respect to the largest cities. As shown by the study of metropolitan areas, the contribution of net migration to the growth of 25 large metropolitan areas in selected developing countries during the 1960s exceeded its contribution to urban areas in general by 42 per cent, with a range of 13 per cent in Peru and 199 per cent in Chile. Finally, net rural–urban migration flows are the result of two-way movements: gross migration is usually considerably larger than net migration. It has also been shown that rural–urban migration is characterized by a different age structure from urban–rural migration. Even small migration flows can thus have an important impact on urban areas. For example, migrants to urban areas are concentrated in the young adult ages (15–29 years of age), and migration thus disproportionately increases the urban labour supply.

For these reasons, migration indeed remains a crucial factor for urban population growth. Furthermore, should continued progress be made in the reduction of natural increase, net migration may well emerge again as the prime source of urban population growth. In any event, the low level of urbanization in many developing countries virtually assures a substantial flow of rural–urban migrants in the coming decades.

The growth of large cities and the concentration of urban population

Rapid urbanization in the developing countries has generally been accompanied by the even more rapid growth of large cities. The trend towards increased concentration is in evidence in all developing regions with the single exception of China (see Table 5.12). The trend is especially pronounced in Africa: whereas, in 1985 only about 7 per cent of the urban population lived in cities above 4 million, the proportion is expected to increase to 20 per cent by the end of this century, and to 34 per cent by 2025. During the same period, the number of cities in this category will grow from 2 in 1985 to 11 in 2000 and to 36 in 2025.

The proportion of the urban population in middle-sized cities is not projected to change significantly in most developing regions (except for Melanesia, Micronesia, and Polynesia, where the proportion is likely almost to double, from 10.2 to 19.4 per cent, during the 1970–2025 period). The smallest towns are expected to account for a steadily decreasing share of the urban population in all developing regions, with an especially sharp decrease in Africa and South Asia. It should be noted, however, that despite the increasing concentration of the urban population in all developing regions except China, at least 50 per cent of the urban popula-

Table 5.12   Percentage distribution of urban population by city-size class, area, and region, 1970–2025

	Under 1 million				1 million–3,999,999				4 million and above			
	1970	1985	2000	2025	1970	1985	2000	2025	1970	1985	2000	2025
World total	68.2	64.5	59.2	56.8	18.0	18.6	20.9	18.7	13.7	17.0	19.9	24.6
Developed regions	67.5	66.3	66.1	67.4	18.3	19.6	20.6	19.8	14.2	14.1	13.4	12.8
Developing regions	69.0	63.2	55.8	53.6	17.8	17.8	21.0	18.3	13.2	19.1	23.2	28.1
Africa	81.1	68.7	55.5	50.5	12.3	24.1	24.6	15.6	6.6	7.3	19.8	33.9
Latin America	64.7	57.4	51.7	52.7	15.0	16.1	20.2	17.6	20.3	26.4	28.1	29.7
China	64.3	65.6	65.6	61.9	19.1	21.5	20.8	20.6	16.6	12.9	13.5	17.5
Other East Asia	51.1	47.2	38.6	41.3	26.6	10.8	23.3	27.6	22.3	42.1	38.1	31.1
South Asia	72.8	64.9	55.1	53.0	19.8	15.1	19.8	18.6	7.4	20.0	25.1	28.4
Melanesia, Micronesia, and Polynesia	84.7	76.4	73.6	74.8	10.2	16.2	19.5	19.4	5.2	7.4	6.9	5.9

Source: United Nations, *Estimates and Projections of Urban, Rural, and City Population 1950–2025: The 1982 Assessment* (New York, 1984).

tion is expected to live in urban areas with fewer than 1 million persons in 2025.

Urban centres with fewer than 100,000 persons accounted for the greatest share of the urban population in the 'below 1 million' category among the developing countries in 1980 (see Table 5.13). Almost two-fifths of all urban residents lived in towns smaller than 100,000 population, the proportion ranging from 76.8 per cent in Melanesia–Micronesia–Polynesia to 18.7 per cent in Other East Asia (which is the only region where cities with 100,000–499,999 persons account for a larger share of the urban population than the smallest urban category). Except for East Asia, over 50 per cent of all urban residents lived in urban centres with 500,000 or fewer inhabitants in 1980.

The location of the world's largest cities is shifting from the developed to the developing countries. In 1970 nearly half the world's largest 25 cities were located in the developed countries,

but the number dropped to 9 in 1985 and is expected to decrease to 6 by the end of this century. By then, Mexico City and São Paulo will be the world's two largest cities, with projected populations of 26 and 24 million, respectively.

Some very large cities are growing at very high rates. During the 1970s, the 12 largest agglomerations in the developing countries grew at an average rate of almost 3 per cent per annum, although some, such as Jakarta, Mexico City, São Paulo, and Seoul, grew at an annual rate of 4 per cent or above. The growth of Mexico City and São Paulo is especially remarkable; in both countries it exceeded the total rate of urban growth registered during the 1970s, thus continuing the increasing domination of the two agglomerations in their respective countries. This growth can only be explained in terms of rural–urban migration. In Mexico, for example, migration accounted for approximately one-quarter of the country's growth in urban popula-

Table 5.13   Proportion of urban population in city-size classes below 1 million inhabitants, by region, 1980 (percentages)

	Under 100,000	100,000–499,000	500,000–999,000	Total under 1 million
World	38.1	18.0	9.9	66.0
Developed regions	36.8	20.5	9.4	66.7
Developing regions	39.1	15.9	10.4	65.4
Africa	42.3	18.7	11.6	72.6
Latin America	37.5	15.1	8.4	61.0
China	46.0	7.1	12.2	65.3
Other East Asia	18.7	22.5	5.7	46.9
South Asia	37.2	19.6	10.8	67.6
Melanesia, Micronesia, and Polynesia	76.8	23.2	0.0	100.0

Source: United Nations Population Division.

Box 5.1 Urbanization trends in China

Few countries have demonstrated the same determination as China to ensure that national processes of social and economic development do not result in rapid urbanization. A comparison of 1964 and 1982 census data allows an assessment to be made of how far this objective has been achieved.

Between 1964 and 1982, the country's urban population——defined as inhabitants of settlements as small as 2,500—increased from 18.4 per cent to only 20.6 per cent. This very modest growth is thrown into sharp relief by China's industrial performance over the same period. While per capita domestic product during the 1960s and 1970s increased by around 5 per cent per annum, the share of industry in gross domestic product increased from approximately 40 per cent in 1964 to more than 35 per cent in 1982. The contribution of agriculture over the same period fell 32 per cent to less than 20 per cent. Such figures indicate that the country's objective has been very largely attained, and the country's achievements, when measured against trends in other developing countries, can be considered remarkable. Such a judgement is not entirely shared by the government. Its own comment on the efforts it has made to control urbanization has been that 'greater efforts are needed' to overcome the disproportionate growth of towns and cities.

Before the foundation of the People's Republic of China in 1949, China's industrial infrastructure was mainly concentrated in the country's largest cities. While this is still the case, concentration has been reduced in relative terms through policies aimed at the decentralization of industrial development. This policy has been instrumental in containing the growth of large cities. Between 1964 and 1982, the three largest cities—Beijing, Tianjin, and Shanghai—grew very slowly (see Table 1).

The census data also show that the highest rates of population growth were recorded in the country's sparsely populated inland provinces. These grew at 2.6 per cent per annum in 1964 and 3.5 per cent in 1982. Interestingly, they also indicate that the densely populated south-eastern provinces, where a high proportion of the urban population lives in medium-sized cities (for example, Anhui, Jiangxi, and Fujian), recorded high rates of growth, while north-eastern provinces, with several coastal cities of more than 1 million inhabitants (for example, Shandong and Liaoning), recorded below-average growth rates up to 1982. This suggests a considerable degree of success in controlling the growth of large cities and in promoting the growth of medium-sized cities.

With almost 80 per cent of China's population living in villages and small towns of up to 2,500 inhabitants, the slow pace of urbanization could only have been made possible by enabling many millions of rural dwellers to shift to non-agricultural occupations for their main source of income. The experience gained in this area may represent the most important lesson that can be gained from China's 25 years of development without rapid urbanization.

Table 1. Growth of main cities in China, 1964–1982

	Population in 1982 (millions)			Annual average growth rate, 1964–82 (%)	Natural population increase 1981 (%)
	City	Municipal county	Total		
Beijing	5.6	3.6	9.2	1.1	1.2
Tianjin	5.2	2.6	7.8	1.2	1.3
Shanghai	6.3	5.6	11.9	0.5	1.0
China	—	—	1,003.9	2.1	1.5

tion. In Mexico City, however, it accounted for more than one-half. Every year, 360,000 babies are born in the city, while 400,000 people migrate to it.

It has been argued that the growth of cities into megacities will result in uncontrollable and unmanageable conurbations. However, size is not the most important parameter for manageability. Large cities are not unmanageable because they are large, nor are small cities necessarily easy to manage because they are small. What happens is that growth magnifies the negative impacts of mistakes, delays, and omissions, so that it is in large cities that failures are particularly visible. Failures in small settlements, although equally important, tend to be less in focus and can more easily be ignored.

For this reason, urbanization has often come to be equated with the growth of the largest cities, which is a misconception of the process.

Urbanization is the process by which a national population shifts from rural occupations to urban occupations, and hence from rural settlements to urban settlements—of all sizes. It is important to emphasize the point that the settlement pattern of a country encompasses urban settlements of all sizes, from small service centres to primate cities. Urbanization is not brought about mainly by farmers moving to the large cities: it is brought about by natural growth of urban populations, by transformation of rural settlements into urban settlements, and by complex migration shifts of rural residents to a variety of urban centres. It is not a demographic issue, and it cannot be approached through demographic analysis: it is an issue of location economics, and it can only be understood as an expression of human settlements development patterns.

Rural development

In most developing countries, differences in levels of economic activity and of human settlements development have contributed to the growth of very large cities and their metropolitan areas. While rural development may figure

---

Box 5.2   Mega-cities: profile of Calcutta

Mega-cities are cities that are expected to have populations of at least 8 million inhabitants by the year 2000. India's largest city, Calcutta (according to United Nations estimates, the eighth largest city in the world in 1980), had a population of more than 9 million in 1980. The Calcutta Metropolitan District (the CMD) had a population of about 10 million. For the long term, the Calcutta Metropolitan Development Authority (CMDA) has projected a population of 14.7 million for the CMD by the year 2001. According to United Nations estimates, the city of Calcutta could reach 16.5 million by 2000.

Calcutta has been frequently cited by journalists throughout the world as an example of urban pathology, or of what the future may hold for other cities in developing countries with rapid urban growth. Numerous articles have discussed the scores of thousands of pavement dwellers on the Calcutta streets, the visible evidence of widespread unemployment and absolute poverty, and the severe congestion and infrastructure deficits.

Although Calcutta remains, in economic terms, one of the poorest cities in India (indeed, one of the poorest in the world), it has mounted a very large infrastructure and public-investment programme, and has made considerable progress during the past decade in addressing some of the city's most serious infrastructure deficits. This capacity is explained by the combination of a strong development authority (the CMDA) and massive financial support from the International Development Association (IDA). Under the aegis of the CMDA, since 1970, the city's water-distribution network has been improved to the point where one-half of the population has access to piped water (previously it was one-third); the sewerage network has been extended; drainage, which was one of the city's most intractable problems, has been much improved; several hundred schools, particularly primary schools, have been constructed or rebuilt; and there has been the beginning of a shift from a curative, hospital-based health-care system to a preventive, primary health-care approach. Although Cal-

cutta's slums are among the worst in India, slum-improvement efforts, involving the construction of paved internal roads, electrification, and the provision of water standpipes and sanitary latrines, have improved living conditions for nearly 1.7 million persons.

Although the CMDA's successes in the public works area, and especially in the provision of primary infrastructure, have generated indirect benefits for the metropolitan population, they have not contributed directly to increasing incomes and purchasing power. This is clearly the challenge facing Calcutta's planners. Any improvement in levels of living will require a high rate of economic development. Unfortunately, the current economic climate in Calcutta does not seem to favour the achievement of this objective. The industrial base is rather narrow, with a substantial weight of industries insufficiently diversified and with too few new product lines. The central government's ban on new large and medium-scale industries in large cities may obstruct efforts to attract new firms unless the state is able to obtain exemptions.

Decisions on optimal planning strategies for the CMD and the rest of urban West Bengal cannot be well-informed unless policy-makers have a clear view of the future population of the CMD, of medium-term and long-term economic trends in the metropolitan economy, and of the future pattern of urbanization in the state. At present this information is largely missing. Estimates of future population have been derived from simple projections, and there has been little study of urbanization in West Bengal. Attempts to integrate economic and physical planning within the CMD and to formulate an urbanization strategy for the state have yet to be made by state and CMDA planners. Without these analyses, planning for the CMD is likely to be, at best, only partly effective.

Source: United Nations, *Population Growth and Policies in Mega-cities: Calcutta*, ST/ESA/SER.R/61.

prominently in a nation's official development strategy, the resources and efforts devoted to it are often insufficient. As indicated in Table 5.14, disparities in developing countries are consistently greater than those in developed countries. While, in developed countries, the disparity between the richest and poorest areas is usually under 1:3, in such countries as Argentina, the Islamic Republic of Iran, and Venezuela, the disparity is in the range of 1:9 to 1:10.

However measured, disparities tend to be extreme. In terms of medical provision, education, health, industrial activity, or financial transactions, certain areas demonstrate a marked superiority over others. In Senegal, for example, nearly 80 per cent of industrial enterprises, 66 per cent of salaried employees, and 80 per cent of all doctors are concentrated in the Dakar area, where 16 per cent of the country's population live. In Pakistan, Karachi generates 42 per cent of the industrial value-added and holds 50 per cent of all bank deposits, while accounting for 6 per cent of the national population. Mexico City accounts for 24 per cent of the country's population but in 1975 was responsible for 46 per cent of all commercial sales, 55 per cent of service activities, and 52 per cent of industrial production.

Disparities tend to be small in the centrally planned developing countries, although they are still in evidence. In China, for example, personal consumption was estimated in 1979 at $244 per capita in urban areas as against $111 per capita in rural areas, a ratio that has been achieved in some market-economy developing countries in Asia. Despite a commitment to reducing the urban–rural gap, urban per capita incomes were estimated to have increased at the rate of 2.9 per cent per annum between 1957 and 1979, while rural incomes increased by 1.6 per cent. The quality of educational and health facilities also appears much higher in urban areas than rural areas, notwithstanding the innovations made by China in bringing health services to rural areas.[9]

Many governments in the developing countries have committed themselves to redressing urban–rural inequalities, and plans have usually afforded high priority to the containment of the growth of large cities and the promotion of rural development. Examples include the development of depressed or undeveloped areas (the Brazilian Amazon and north-eastern areas, and the western area of the Republic of Korea); the improvement of rural settlements to support rural development (Colombia, Indonesia, Kenya, Malaysia); the development or creation of settlements to explore newly discovered mineral resources (east coast of Mexico, the Amazon area in Brazil); the restructuring of

Table 5.14 Disparities in per capita gross regional product within selected developed and developing countries, 1976

	Richest area ($)	Poorest area ($)	Ratio
United Kingdom	3,667	2,566	1.43
Netherlands	4,032	2,578	1.56
Belgium	4,380	2,616	1.67
Korea, Republic of	582	270	2.16
Italy	3,384	1,538	2.20
India	217	97	2.24
Germany, Federal Republic of	7,022	2,683	2.62
Japan	5,555	1,900	2.92
Malaysia	730	202	3.62
Mexico	1,067	198	5.39
Thailand	1,358	215	6.34
Colombia	1,342	199	6.75
Argentina	3,706	397	9.33
Iran, Islamic Republic of	3,132	313	10.07
Brazil	1,102	109	10.14

Source: B. Renaud, *National Urbanization Policies in Developing Countries* (New York: Oxford University Press, 1979), 118.

Note: To facilitate comparison, all figures have been converted into US dollars.

metropolises (São Paulo in Brazil and Seoul in the Republic of Korea); intensification policies for river basins (India, Mexico); and the development of border areas for strategic reasons.

Rural development figures prominently among the national priorities of most developing countries, including Bangladesh, Botswana, Central African Republic, Ecuador, Pakistan, Thailand, Tonga, and Zambia. The focus of policies range from land-redistribution schemes (Nicaragua) to rationalization of the location of rural facilities (Bhutan) and development of agro-industries (Costa Rica). Some countries, such as Mali and Somalia, are implementing 'villagization' schemes, based on the regrouping

of rural population in organized settlements, with the objective of expanding agricultural production and improving the access of the rural population to basic infrastructure and facilities. Rural housing and rural centre upgrading programmes are also being undertaken in Burkina Faso, Côte d'Ivoire, Kenya, Malawi, and Senegal.

The integration of rural areas and urban centres is being pursued in Papua New Guinea through the creation of a system of small towns to support rural development. Ghana and Kenya are seeking to promote rural development and expand agricultural productivity through the development of a hierarchy of villages and

---

Box 5.3   Kenya: a District focus for rural development

One of the development strategies adopted by the Government of Kenya under its 1983/4–1987/8 National Development Plan is rural development with a District focus. This is a process whereby project planning and implementation responsibilities are exercised at the local level, with efforts co-ordinated by District Development Committees (DDCs) under the chairmanship of the District Commissioner. The process transfers decision-making authority to the local level, thus helping to ensure an improved approach to the selection of priorities and opportunities for people to participate in development efforts in their own communities.

Under the new strategy, all ministries and other public agencies are required to indicate the resources allocated annually to each District. This requirement helps guarantee an equitable allocation of limited national development funds, with the aim of enabling all Districts to develop their own social and economic potentials, according to their natural assets and comparative advantage. Local authorities are required to identify projects, but because some have traditionally experienced chronic management shortcomings they are able under the new strategy to draw directly upon expertise that exists at the District level. To ensure sound financial management, local authorities are also required to produce budgets and five-year development plans in line with those of the central government.

The Ministry of Local Government (MLG) is entrusted with the responsibility for guiding, assisting, and controlling local authorities in carrying out their new developmental and administrative functions, and for co-ordinating the development plans prepared at the local level. In exercising this responsibility, MLG works in close consultation with other governmental agencies, notably the Ministry of Works, Housing, and Physical Planning, the Ministry for Water Development, and the National Housing Corporation. MLG has initiated a number of studies designed to improve co-ordination between DDCs and

local authorities. These studies cover such issues as local-government financing, improvements in revenue-collection procedures, methods for measuring the productivity of and demand for local-authority services, employment creation, urban transport planning, investment strategies, and forward budgeting. It has also established a training programme designed to improve the skills of local-authority officers. The training programme also involves local political leaders, with an emphasis on identifying local needs and the programmes and projects required to meet them.

The first action taken by MLG was to require all local authorities to prepare a Local Authority Development Programme (LADP) during the current five-year plan period. LADPs cover such issues as population trends and the employment situation, and contain appraisals of the management capabilities and financial status of the local authority. The LADPs are designed to assist local political leaders and officials to assess needs, identify target groups, set priorities, and select projects. Once the LADP is approved, MLG uses it as a basis for allocating resources. To assist local authorities in this exercise, MLG has prepared manuals on the preparation and management of the LADP. A Workbook for Councillors has also been prepared in Swahili.

Kenya's new District focus for rural development should not only improve co-ordination between different levels of government in the resource-allocation process but also make it possible to identify both the institutional weaknesses within local authorities and the measures required to overcome them. Because the District provides spatial linkage between urban and rural areas, the District focus policy provides an important framework also for human settlements development.

towns. This is expected to result in the improvement of housing, infrastructure, and services, and better access to urban markets.

Ethiopia's large resettlement programme is based upon the creation of new rural settlements. It provides for the development of villages in the area to be settled, supported by a land-distribution scheme and the creation of rural co-operatives. Under the programme, rural settlements are provided with basic facilities, including schools, clinics, workshops, offices, stores, water supply, and flour mills, and are expected to become productive fairly quickly. The self-contained communities have an area of 1,520 hectares and house 500 families on plots of 1,000 square metres. Some 30 hectares are reserved for village facilities, 1,000 hectares are designated for communal crops, 135 hectares for forestry, 200 hectares for grazing, 70 hectares for soil and water conservation, and 35 hectares for seed and seedling production.

Rural housing and self-help systems are being stimulated in Algeria and Benin, where efforts are being made to upgrade rural settlements through the provision of improved social infrastructure using simple construction techniques and local materials. In southern Chad, a project is being implemented to build a training-centre network in rural communities to disseminate modern agricultural techniques. The project also aims at improving rural housing and infrastructure, through the improvement of building techniques and the use of local materials.

Despite the wide range of policies being pursued, results have usually proved disappointing. Governments have often lacked the will to implement such policies, especially where these are perceived as conflicting with the imperatives of national economic growth and with the interests of powerful urban-based groups and rural élites. Furthermore, there is evidence that attempts to limit the growth of very large cities and to deconcentrate economic activity may damage prospects for economic growth, especially at low levels of development, as well as contribute to the growth of poverty. For such reasons, policy issues in a number of areas may need to be redefined.

Employment

Problems of access to decent shelter, basic services, and food are rooted in poverty, which is itself conditioned by the availability of productive employment. The creation of employment has greatly lagged behind population growth in the vast majority of the developing countries, although estimation of the number of the numbers involved is frustrated by lack of reliable and consistent data. Studies conducted during the 1970s and early 1980s suggest considerable variations in unemployment levels, and official estimates of unemployment rates in seven Asian cities range from 16.9 per cent for Sri Lanka to 1.3 per cent for Thailand. The official unemployment rate for most developing countries around mid-1980 shows that 15 to 20 per cent of the labour force are unemployed. For women, the rate often goes as high as 30 per cent.[10]

Unemployment levels are only a crude measure of poverty, since even many of those employed exist on very meagre incomes. In Mexico City, for example, the official unemployment rate was 8 per cent in 1984, but nearly one-half of the city's population existed on less than $4 per day. Similarly, Indian cities have low official unemployment rates (often under 2 per cent), but a World Bank study found that 98 per cent of the population of Madras had an annual average income of less than $125. In none of the cities studied—Ahmedabad, Bogota, Madras, Nairobi, and Seoul—did more than 40 per cent of the population earn above this level.[11] Employment may often mean underemployment, and figures for underemployment are even more difficult to ascertain than for those for unemployment. Estimates made by the ILO (International Labour Office) in the mid-1970s, however, suggest that between one-fifth and one-quarter of urban working populations in the developing countries are without regular employment.[12]

If the employment situation in many developing countries is already problematic, it seems destined to become very much worse. ILO projections show that the labour force of the developing countries can be expected to increase from 1.2 billion in 1980 to 1.9 billion by the year 2000. Around 700 million new jobs will therefore need to be created just to maintain existing employment levels. Given demographic trends, the projected rate of increase for the next two decades is almost twice that of the previous two decades.

The scale of the unemployment problem facing developing countries can be indicated by estimates for Central America. To accommodate rising populations, some 1.2 million new jobs need to be created each year. During the 1970s, the United States succeeded in creating 2 million jobs annually with an economy 15 times greater than the combined economies of the region. Most formidable of all are the employment problems in Africa: the region must create 10 million new jobs a year with an economy one-tenth the size of that of the United States.

The construction sector

Economic growth is directly related to the level and efficiency of fixed capital formation. In developing countries, the share of fixed capital formation pertaining to construction can be as high as 80 per cent. Therefore, the construction sector should be regarded as one of the backbones of the development process. An indication of this situation is that in most developing countries, the annual growth in construction is higher, and often considerably so, than growth of population and gross domestic product (GDP) (see Table 5.15).

Building materials constitute the single largest

Table 5.15 Annual growth rates in real GDP, construction, and building materials production, selected developing countries, 1975–1980 (percentages)

	Argentina	Egypt[a]	India	Kenya[a]	Republic of Korea	Malaysia	Mexico	Saudi Arabia	Thailand
Population	1.3	2.7	2.0	4.2	1.6	2.4	3.6	2.8	2.4
GDP	2.0	8.6	3.4	5.2	7.6	8.6	6.6	9.3	7.6
Construction	6.8	28.0	1.8	4.4	12.2	12.6	7.2	11.4	14.3
Building materials production[b]									
Plywood	−2.8	−6.9	7.2	3.4	3.4	3.9	18.2	...	11.8
Glass	...	...	10.2	...	13.3	...	5.6	...	...
Building bricks of clay	...	−9.2	...	−4.4	−6.3	...	...	...	...
Quicklime	...	1.8	17.3	...	16.0	...	...	22.8	...
Cement	6.3	0.4	1.8	7.4	9.1	10.2	7.9	23.8	6.2
Asbestos and cement Articles	...	...	5.8	...	...	...	6.9	...	...
Concrete blocks			...	46.8	43.7	...		...	...
Crude steel, ingots	4.9	23.1	3.5	...	23.2	...	6.2	...	14.0
Angles, shapes, etc.	...	...	...	...	19.3	7.6	4.2	...	...
Aluminium	43.3	167.2	2.0	...	3.7	...	1.3	...	...
Nails, screws, etc.	...	6.2	0.8	...	24.5	...	...	...	...
GDP/capita	0.7	5.8	1.4	0.9	5.9	6.0	2.9	6.2	5.0
Construction/capita	5.4	24.4	−0.2	0.2	10.5	10.0	3.4	8.3	11.6
Building materials production (per capita)[b]									
Plywood	−4.0	—	5.2	−0.7	1.8	1.5	14.0	...	9.2
Glass	...	...	8.0	...	11.3	...	1.9	...	...
Building bricks	...	...	...	−8.3	−7.6	...	...	...	...
Quicklime	...	−11.6	14.9	...	14.5	...	...	19.3	...
Cement	5.0	−11.6	−0.2	3.0	7.4	7.6	4.1	20.3	3.7
Asbestos and cement Articles	...	−2.2	3.7	...	...	...	3.1	...	...
		—							
Concrete blocks	...		1.5	40.9	41.3	...	...	...	...
Crude steel, ingots	3.5	...	...	...	21.3	...	2.4	...	11.3
Angles, shapes, etc.	...	19.9	—	...	17.5	5.3	0.5	...	...
Aluminium	41.4	...	—	...	3.7	...	−2.2	...	...
Nails, screws, etc.	...	123.6	—	...	22.9	...	...	...	...

Note: Growth in GDP and construction calculated at constant currency values.

[a] Annual growth rate, 1975–9.
[b] Measured in physical output.

input to construction, accounting for about 50 to 80 per cent of the total value of construction, but in developing countries, a large proportion of items are imported. For instance, it is estimated that building materials alone account for 5 to 8 per cent of the total value of imports in Africa —representing an expenditure of about $2.5 billion. In most instances, imported materials constitute the primary or basic materials used in construction: Portland cement, galvanized iron or aluminium roofing sheets, and steel are examples of these basic materials. In cases where these materials are not imported as finished products, the main inputs and the production technology are imported.

Energy is a critical factor in the production of building materials. Energy consumption in the production of materials such as steel, Portland cement, lime, and fire-clay bricks is high, sometimes representing over 50 per cent of production costs. The impact of rising energy prices on the cost of building materials, even in industrialized countries such as Finland, France, Greece, Portugal, and Yugoslavia, has led to the price of Portland cement increasing by 300 to 400 per cent between 1970 and 1980. Because of their low value/weight ratio, the cost of transporting materials over long distances from production points to consumption points can be as critical as the initial production cost. Developing countries are particularly vulnerable to this negative factor in the distribution of building materials because of the high cost or scarcity of fuel and the under-developed nature of road infrastructure and transportation systems. Thus, it is estimated that in Botswana, Honduras, and the Sudan, after 100 miles of transport the cost of transporting Portland cement exceeds its production cost.

Another reason for the high cost and limited supply of materials in developing countries is that there is often a high degree of wastage or wrong application. Reinforced concrete technology, for instance, is very popular in construction, but in many countries it is wastefully applied in low-strength construction and in simple basic structures. Portland cement has become the main building agent for mortars and plasters, but the mixtures produced are often stronger than needed for the function they serve.

Despite the high incidence of importation, there is considerable output of building materials at the local level in developing countries. For almost every significant building material, developing countries collectively improved their share of global production from 1970 to 1980 (see Tables 5.16 and 5.17a and 5.17b). For example, the African region increased cement production by about 64 per cent, while Asia's increase was about 136 per cent. Notable examples were Indonesia, with a tenfold increase of production during the decade, and Nigeria and the Republic of Korea, with increases of nearly 300 per cent.

For domestic production of building materials, there is a distinction to be made between a truly indigenous production based on locally available inputs, and a system of production which can best be called import reproduction, i.e. every input is imported and assembled locally. Both systems of production are to be found in developing countries. In some countries, such as Brazil, China, India, Mexico, and the Republic of Korea, basic materials, including Portland cement and fired-clay products, are produced with almost every input based on locally available resources. On the other hand, there are also numerous examples of domestic production units where installed plants, raw materials, labour, management, and even repair and maintenance capabilities are all imported, while the use of locally produced, low-cost building materials is largely ignored or often discouraged.

In most developing countries, there is a component of the construction sector which can best be described as the informal or traditional sector, predominantly providing for the construction needs of the rural population and the urban poor. This sector, which includes building materials producers, artisans, small-scale contractors, and a vast array of operators in various aspects of construction, plays a vital role in development. For instance, in Indonesia, the use of lime-pozzolana mortars is the norm, and in some parts of the country locally found limestone is used for the semi-industrialized production of lime in vertical kilns made from local materials and using firewood for fuel. Natural pozzolana is extracted by hand, sieved, and mixed with lime to make blocks of lime-pozzolana. In Sri Lanka, small-scale traditional units produce bricks, country tiles, sand, and lime totalling more than 35 per cent by value of building materials used in the country. In China,

Table 5.16 Building materials: production in developing countries, 1972 and 1981

ISIC	Material	Units	Africa^a 1981	1972	Latin America^b 1981	1972	Asia^c 1981	1972	Developing countries as % of world total^d 1981	1972
369204	Cement	MMT	26	15	26	14	197	94	28.5	18.1
369901	Asbestos–cement articles	TMT	353	222	1,529	1,364	830	449	39.8	32.0
369910	Concrete blocks and	TMT	666	248	...	...	310	310	1.7	1.3
369913	bricks	TMT	12	186	129	...	...	310	...	...
369916	Concrete pipes	TMT	1,465	807	3,403	3,055	1,570	1,570	9.1	9.2
369101	Concrete other products	MU	499	2,410	4,593	4,418	18,879	7,875	23.9	13.9
369104	Building bricks of clay	MU	4	5	892	863	455	469	40.0	39.0
369107	Tiles, roofing, clay	TSM	9,928	2,650	152,859	38,135	41,297	9,418	34.8	13.5
290119	Tiles, floor and wall	TMT	1,663	1,207	6,319	4,142	2,782	2,247	...	...
321901	Clay	TSM	...	...	...	...	514	1,952	...	...
290116	Floor covering	MMT	4	4	12	7	7	6	...	...
290113	Gravel and crushed stone	TMT	7,203	3,612	42,774	20,358	25,559	9,455	...	...
290110	Sand, silica, and quartz	TMT	9,363	8,752	98,863	40,934	119,569	45,850	...	...
	Limestone flux and									
331101	calcareous stone	TCM	464	949	355	500	704	592	20.9	22.4
331104	Wooden railway sleepers	TCM	533	402	13,257	7,725	17,878	14,065	10.1	6.5
331107	Sawnwood, coniferous	TCM	5,428	2,604	14,014	8,111	31,935	22,908	45.9	32.3
331110	Sawnwood, broadleaved	TCM	300	294	364	191	544	501	28.1	26.0
331113	Veneer sheets	TCM	2	2	20,793	24,243	...	...	...	...
331116	Blockboard	TCM	1,252	333	1,467	1,058	7,098	3,649	24.8	17.9
331122	Plywood	TCM	185	122	1,613	611	673	285	6.1	3.8
352101	Particle board	TMT	6	26	...	17	137	25	...	...
352104	Paints, cellulose	TMT	5	7	125	171	87	15	...	...
352107	Paints, water	TMT	87	59	244	281	133	134	...	...
362001	Paints, other	TMT	...	...	171	87	1,797	204	32.6	4.1
	Glass, drawn or blown in									
362004	rectangles, unworked	TMT	...	21	12	891	...	...	...	...
	Glass, cast, rolled, drawn,									
362007	or blown	TMT	...	1	1,069	540	...	...	...	...
	Glass, safety or									
371019	toughened or laminated	TMT	1,984	636	21,500	15,003	57,901	35,032	12.1	8.3
	Crude steel, ingots									

Source: UN Yearbook of Industrial Statistics, ii (1981).

Note: Many production figures are based on UN estimates and some countries are not included in the totals at all. Also, as there is wide variation in the definitions of the product groups, some outputs are inevitably allocated to the wrong categories.

^a Excluding South Africa.

^b Latin America includes all countries of North America and South America, with the exceptions of Canada, the United States, and Puerto Rico.

^c Excluding Japan and Israel.

^d The developing countries of Europe have not been included.

Abbreviations: TMT = thousand metric tons
TCM = thousand cubic metres
TSM = thousand square metres
MU = million units

80 per cent of building materials, including bricks, tiles, fly-ash, sand, and stone, are produced by the traditional sector.

In principle, most of the imported materials currently in wide use can be replaced by locally produced, cheap materials. For example, lime and various pozzolanas can replace Portland cement in a number of applications, while fired-clay roofing tiles and fibre-cement roofing sheets can substitute for aluminium and galvanized iron roofing sheets. This is already occurring in some countries, such as China, India, Indonesia, and Malaysia. The problem is that knowledge about the production and use of innovative building materials which can be locally produced is limited to a few laboratories and research institutions. The gap in technology transfer, within a country and between countries, for wide-scale adoption of innovative materials is a result of several related factors. For instance,

Table 5.17a Production of and trade in all building materials, 1975, 1980, and estimated 1985 (constant 1975 billion US dollars)

	Production			Imports			Exports		
	1975	1980	1985	1975	1980	1985	1975	1980	1985
Total	277,069	326,267	394,063	26,311	37,051	45,824	24,494	34,496	42,786
Developed market economies	190,837	211,529	251,721	16,103	23,865	29,013	21,954	30,412	37,175
North America	49,383	57,157	70,664	2,959	4,106	6,977	3,123	4,381	5,664
Europe North	84,191	91,588	107,040	10,956	17,004	18,594	14,762	20,353	23,986
Europe South	13,337	15,126	17,647	1,057	1,182	1,419	924	1,698	2,234
Japan	36,291	40,789	48,688	448	816	899	2,691	3,577	4,638
Other developed	7,635	6,869	7,682	683	757	1,124	184	403	653
Developing countries	34,589	52,270	66,122	7,518	10,744	13,887	1,609	2,821	4,464
Latin America	11,807	17,446	21,215	1,424	1,831	2,391	389	731	974
Tropical Africa	3,342	3,860	4,347	1,019	1,077	1,382	120	143	166
North Africa	2,995	4,462	5,355	1,086	1,311	1,615	14	13	23
West Asia	5,367	8,964	10,650	2,346	3,839	4,876	193	305	450
South Asia	6,102	7,435	9,580	180	396	602	110	127	234
East Asia (Mfg)	2,991	6,631	10,237	770	1,377	1,927	572	1,164	2,167
South-east Asia	1,985	3,472	4,738	693	913	1,094	211	338	450
Centrally planned economies	51,643	62,468	76,220	2,690	2,442	2,924	931	1,263	1,147
European	46,795	53,459	65,286	2,367	2,012	2,461	827	1,036	909
Asian	4,848	9,009	10,934	323	430	436	104	227	238

Table 5.17b Shares and annual growth rates (percentages)

	Production					Imports					Exports				
	Share			Growth		Share			Growth		Share			Growth	
	1975	1980	1985	1975–1980	1980–1985	1975	1980	1985	1975–1980	1980–1985	1975	1980	1985	1975–1980	1980–1985
Total	100.0	100.0	100.0	3.3	3.8	100.0	100.0	100.0	7.0	4.3	100.0	100.0	100.0	7.0	4.4
Developed market economies	68.8	64.8	63.8	2.0	3.5	61.2	64.4	63.3	8.1	3.9	89.6	88.1	86.8	6.7	4.0
North America	17.8	17.5	17.9	2.9	4.3	11.2	11.0	15.2	6.7	11.1	12.7	12.7	13.2	7.0	5.2
Europe North	30.3	28.0	27.1	1.6	3.1	41.6	45.8	40.5	9.1	1.8	60.2	59.0	56.0	6.6	3.3
Europe South	4.8	4.6	4.4	2.5	3.1	4.0	3.1	3.0	2.2	3.7	3.7	4.9	5.2	12.9	5.6
Japan	13.0	12.5	12.3	2.3	3.6	1.7	2.2	1.9	12.7	1.9	12.0	10.3	10.8	3.8	5.3
Other developed	2.7	2.1	1.9	−2.0	2.2	2.5	2.0	2.4	2.0	8.2	0.7	1.1	1.5	16.9	10.1
Developing countries	12.4	16.0	16.7	8.6	4.8	28.5	28.9	30.3	7.4	5.2	5.4	8.1	10.4	11.8	9.6
Latin America	4.2	5.3	5.3	8.1	3.9	5.4	4.9	5.2	5.1	5.4	1.5	2.1	2.2	13.4	5.9
Tropical Africa	1.2	1.1	1.1	2.9	2.4	3.8	2.9	3.0	1.1	5.1	0.4	0.4	0.3	3.5	3.0
North Africa	1.0	1.3	1.3	8.2	3.7	4.1	3.5	3.5	3.8	4.2	—	—	—	−1.4	12.0
West Asia	1.9	2.7	2.7	10.8	3.5	8.9	10.3	10.6	10.3	4.8	0.7	0.8	1.0	9.5	8.0
South Asia	2.2	2.2	2.4	4.0	5.2	0.6	1.0	1.3	17.0	8.7	0.4	0.3	0.5	2.9	13.0
East Asia (Mfg)	1.0	2.0	2.5	17.2	9.0	2.9	3.7	4.2	12.3	6.9	2.3	3.3	5.0	15.2	13.2
South-east Asia	0.7	1.0	1.2	11.8	6.4	2.6	2.4	2.3	5.6	3.6	0.8	0.9	1.0	9.8	5.8
Centrally planned economies	18.6	19.1	19.3	3.8	4.0	10.2	6.5	6.3	−1.9	3.6	3.8	3.6	2.6	6.2	−1.9
European	16.8	16.3	16.5	2.6	4.0	8.9	5.4	5.3	−3.1	4.1	3.3	3.0	2.1	4.6	−2.5
Asian	1.7	2.7	2.7	13.1	3.9	1.2	1.1	1.0	5.8	1.4	0.4	0.6	0.5	16.8	0.9

Source: UNIDO secretariat computations.

Box 5.4   Making building codes work

Building codes are often an obstacle to construction activities in low-income settlements. Such codes typically prohibit the use of the building materials used by the poor. As a result, there is usually an absence of standards and specifications designed to guide quality control in production and use of traditional materials, with the further result that tender and contracting procedures are not used to promote the inclusion of traditional materials in low-cost construction projects carried out by governmental agencies.

Building codes that forbid the use of earth as a construction material have particularly limited the opportunities to build cheap shelter in urban low-income settlements. Resistance to the use of earth as a building material is widespread. The United Kingdom Building Research Station's *Model Regulations for Small Buildings*, for example, emphasizes that unburnt earth blocks or bricks, wattle and daub walls, and *pise de terre* should be excluded for use in small buildings. In developing countries, notably in rural areas, these materials are not merely the only materials that are available, they are also perfectly adequate for most construction needs, provided they are used in the right way.

Defects in building codes have negative effects on the housing situation of the urban and rural poor, illustrated by the low quality of building materials and construction techniques utilized in low-income settlements. Sometimes, resource inputs utilized in the production of building materials for low-income settlements have been wasted because no appropriate specifications were drawn up to guide the production process. Most existing codes favour import-based construction materials which, despite their high cost or scarcity, often become imposed as the only choice available to the low-income builder. Thus, attempts to introduce improved traditional building materials have been hampered.

It is necessary to correct these defects so as to improve the housing situation of the urban and rural poor. Efforts in this direction should bear in mind the need to promote standards rather than rigidly enforce regulatory measures in low-income settlements. In promoting reformulated regulations, consideration should be given to the socio-cultural values of low-income target groups.

Box 5.5   Construction activities in the informal sector

In most developing countries, the informal sector is largely responsible for the provision of shelter in low-income settlements. Because informal-sector construction activity is inadequately enumerated and seldom accounted for in government statistics, it is difficult to estimate its contribution to the construction sector and to economic development. Estimates made for some countries, however, leave little doubt that the contribution can be very substantial.

In Kenya, for example, the construction of traditional dwellings in 1976 contributed almost 60 per cent of gross fixed capital formation, while the informal construction sector contributed around 30 per cent to the gross domestic product generated by construction between 1969 and 1978. In Côte d'Ivoire, it has been estimated that informal construction activity accounted for 30 per cent of the value added by the construction sector, for 39 per cent of the intermediate consumption of materials and services, and for 35 per cent of the total value of the output of the construction sector.

As with other economic activities in the informal sector, construction is labour-intensive and generates both employment and opportunities for the acquisition of skills. In brickmaking, for example, the labour requirement for the production of 10 million bricks per annum ranges from 160 men in small-scale traditional units to only 8 in a modern, highly automated factory. Hence, small units use 20 times as much labour as large units for the production of the same volume of output. Similarly, an investment of KSh1 million in the manufacturing sector of the informal economy in Nairobi is estimated to yield 5,500 jobs and KSh2,250,000 worth of output, compared to 500 jobs and only KSh744,000 worth of output from an equivalent investment in the formal manufacturing sector.

Despite its contribution to general development and the specific provision of affordable shelter for low-income groups, the informal construction sector enjoys few of the benefits of the formal sector. The disbenefits to the sector find expression in the low quality of products and services, high costs of production, and, in some cases, patterns of economic activity which have few positive effects on other sectors of the economy.

most building research institutions in developing countries lack the comprehensive structure required to translate their findings into commercial production. The link between investors, manufacturers, and research institutions is at times non-existent.

Shelter

The great shelter problem in the developing countries is the shortage of affordable housing for the low-income majority of households in urban areas. This has resulted in proliferation of slums and squatter settlements. Accurate statistics on their extent are difficult to obtain, partly because of definitional problems and inadequate methods of data collection. Moreover, many city authorities undoubtedly underestimate the extent of inadequate housing, either because they ignore communities outside the city's administrative boundaries or because they do not enumerate them correctly. Even so, estimates indicate that in many cities in developing countries, 40 to 50 per cent of the inhabitants are living in slums and informal settlements (see Table 5.18).

It has been estimated that 17 per cent of the world's stock of housing is made up of one-room shelters, of which some three-quarters are to be found in the developing countries. Some 42 per cent of rural and 35 per cent of urban dwellings in Africa are single rooms, and their average density of occupation is estimated at 2.23 persons. In Asia, the average number of persons per room is 2.17, although nearly one-third of all dwellings in the region have three or more persons per room. In Latin America and the Caribbean, the average is 1.76 persons.[13]

Such averages conceal more than they reveal, since, as averages, they underestimate the housing conditions of the poor in urban and rural settlements. The poor make up for low household incomes by intensively occupying space and by making do with little. The most extreme form of multiple occupation is the 'shift system' of bed hiring, but the most common form is households sharing the same room. In India, for example, it has been estimated that two-fifths of the urban population live in one-room shelters with an average occupancy of nearly five persons. A survey of housing conditions in Kanpur revealed that three-quarters of all dwellings had no windows, and two-thirds became waterlogged when it rained heavily.[14] One-half of Calcutta's families live in one-room shelters devoid of almost all amenities, while in Greater Bombay an estimated 77 per cent of households, with an average size of 5.3 persons, live in one room. In Mexico City, nearly one-third of all families sleep in a single room, and 40 per cent have no or very inadequate sanitation.[15]

Even countries that have made great efforts to provide decent accommodation for their people are finding it increasingly difficult to keep pace with the demand for housing and have been compelled to lower standards. In Shanghai, a city that has grown relatively slowly, public authorities built 20 million square metres of residential floorspace for 2 million people in 156 housing estates. However, 70,000 dwellings are still required for families living in substandard accommodation, mostly in the central part of the

Table 5.18 Estimates of the percentage of city populations in informal settlements in 1980

	Total population (000s)	In informal settlements	
		Number (000s)	%
Addis Ababa, Ethiopia	1,668	1,418	85
Luanda, Angola	959	671	70
Dar es Salaam, United Republic of Tanzania	1,075	645	60
Bogota, Colombia	5,493	3,241	59
Ankara, Turkey	2,164	1,104	51
Lusaka, Zambia	791	396	50
Tunis, Tunisia	1,046	471	45
Manila, Philippines	5,664	2,666	40
Mexico City, Mexico	15,032	6,013	40
Karachi, Pakistan	5,005	1,852	37
Caracas, Venezuela	3,093	1,052	34
Nairobi, Kenya	1,275	421	33
Lima, Peru	4,682	1,545	33
São Paolo, Brazil	13,541	4,333	32

Source: United Nations, *Patterns of Urban and Rural Population Growth*, Population Studies 68 (New York, 1980), 125–54, Table 48; and numerous country publications and published studies.

city, where space per capita is under 2 square metres.

While large cities in some developing countries have been growing at rates of up to 10 per cent per annum, slums and squatter settle-ments in some of them have been growing twice as quickly. Around one-half of the urban popula-tion of the developing countries—some 600 mil-lion people—live in very poor quality housing. Given present rates of growth, this number can be expected at least to double by the year 2000. That the problems associated with slums and squatter settlements are already beginning to assume unmanageable proportions is evident.

Box 5.6   Yemen Arab Republic: catching up with present demands

Until 1982, Yemen had virtually no schools, hospitals, or clinics. There was no centralized water-supply or sewerage system, and the country's only diesel generators were confined to the royal palace in Sana'a. The first paved road was not built until 1960; until then, there were only dirt tracks for off-road vehicles. The country's primitive har-bours could only accommodate lighters, and all goods were hand-carried ashore. There was not, however, a serious housing problem, since Yemenis have a long tradition of building sophisticated houses from indigenous materials.

The main problem was overwhelmingly one of lack of services and infrastructure. Progress in providing infrastructure in a country very largely dependent on remit-tances received from Yemenis working in Western Asia has been slow. According to World Health Organization stat-istics published in 1985, only 2.2 million of the country's 6.4 million people, or 34.4 per cent of the total population, had access to water supply. The consumption of electricity has gone up from 38 kilowatt hours per capita in 1981 to 46 kilowatt hours per capita in 1984, but this is still very low compared to other countries in the region.

Although Yemen is still very largely a rural country, urban population is increasing rapidly. The population living in Sana'a, the capital, and in the other main towns increased from 910,000 in 1980 to 1,370,000 in 1985. If present trends continue, more than 3.6 million Yemenis could be living in towns by the end of the century. While the urban population has been growing at around 8.2 per cent per annum, the growth of squatter settlements around the main towns has been faster still.

The government has a struggle on two fronts—to catch up with centuries of neglect, and to cope with the demands of a growing and urbanizing population. Although a poor country, Yemen has made considerable efforts to improve living conditions and levels of service in Sana'a. It is now turning its attention to Hoeidah, Yemen's second largest city. Under a project supported by the International Development Association (IDA) it is engaged in upgrading Ghuleil, the largest squatter settlement in Hodeidah, and in developing 1,650 new serviced plots.

Services have so far been provided free of charge. The country's serious financial and economic difficulties, however, today compel the government to charge for the services that are being provided. The money raised will be used to maintain the existing services as well as to provide new ones.

Water supply and sanitation

The importance of providing safe and adequate drinking water and sanitation has gained in-creasing international attention. The principal reason is the appreciation that people cannot achieve a quality of life consistent with human dignity unless they have access to safe drinking water and sanitation, and, to a lesser extent, solid-waste disposal facilities. Perhaps the most notable international effort in seeking to increase coverage of the provision of water supply and waste disposal was initiated with the launching of the United Nations International Drinking Water Supply and Sanitation Decade in 1980. The Decade called for safe water and adequate sanitary facilities to be made available to all rural and urban areas by 1990. Despite the world economic recession experienced during the initial years of the Decade and the concomitant slowing-down of economic activity, both in industrialized and in developing countries, some progress has been made throughout the world in extending drinking water and sani-tation to urban and rural populations. Table 5.19 summarizes the situation regarding coverage on a regional and global basis in 1980 and 1983.

On a global scale, approximately 71 per cent of the urban population (excluding China) have access to drinking water supplies. The avail-ability of most services is higher in urban areas than in rural areas, and drinking-water supply is no exception. At present, only 41 per cent of the rural population have convenient access to safe drinking-water supplies.

With regard to sanitation, approximately 59 per cent of the world's urban population (exclud-ing China) were served in 1983. Thus, in spite of rapid urban population increases, the percent-age of urban population receiving sanitation services was increased substantially from an estimated 1980 level of 49 per cent. This increase constitutes a reversal of a declining trend observed in the previous 10 years. Unfortunately, with regard to rural sanitation facilities, coverage declined during the first three years of the 1980s from 14 per cent to 12 per cent. This trend emphasizes the need for promoting of sanitation in rural settlements.

As the statistics above show, urban areas have traditionally been better provided than rural areas with water-supply and sanitation services. This general observation hides the deficiencies occurring in low-income urban settlements, however. No reliable statistics are available on the extent of water-supply and sanitation coverage in these settlements, but the limited information available would indicate gross shortfalls in both services. Urban slums are generally better endowed with basic infrastructure than urban squatter areas, but some squatter settlements are now being provided with basic services under comprehensive squatter-settlement upgrading schemes.

Old urban slums are usually located near the centres of large cities, but recent slum areas exist on the urban peripheries. Slum properties are usually served by municipal utility networks, but, because of the age of many slums and the problems of overcrowding, services are deteriorating and cannot cope with the demand made on them. Water supply sometimes takes the form of a single tap in each house, but what it often amounts to is a public standpipe shared by hundreds of people. Sanitation frequently consists of a primitive household system, such as the bucket conservancy system, and is usually available on a communal basis only. Municipal servi-

Table 5.19 Water supply and sanitation coverage, by region, 1980 and 1983 (population in millions)

	Population		Water-supply				Sanitation			
	1980	1983	1980		1983		1980		1983	
			Pop'n served	%	Pop'n served	%	Pop'n served	%	Pop'n served	%
Africa[a]										
Urban	135	160	89	66	91	57	73	54	88	55
Rural	334	356	76	22	103	29	67	20	64	18
Total	469	516	162	34	194	38	140	29	152	29
Asia and the Pacific[b]										
Urban	428	493	278	65	330	67	175	41	237	48
Rural	1,064	1,109	277	26	488	44	117	11	100	9
Total	1,492	1,602	555	37	818	51	292	29	337	21
Latin America and the Caribbean[c]										
Urban	234	254	183	78	215	85	131	56	203	80
Rural	124	126	52	42	62	49	25	20	25	20
Total	358	380	235	66	277	73	156	44	228	60
Western Asia[d]										
Urban	27	30	25	94	29	95	22	80	28	93
Rural	21	24	9	41	12	50	4	18	6	21
Total	48	54	34	69	41	76	26	51	34	63
Totals										
Urban	824	937	575	70	665	71	401	49	556	59
Rural	1,543	1,615	441	27	665	41	213	14	195	12
Total	2,367	2,552	986	42	1,330	52	614	26	751	29

Source: United Nations, 'Report of the Secretary General on the UN International Drinking Water Supply and Sanitation Decade, A/40/108, E/1985/49 (New York, 1986), 20.

[a]Members of the Economic Commission for Africa.
[b]Members of the Economic and Social Commission for Asia and the Pacific, excluding China.
[c]Members of the Economic Commission for Latin America and the Caribbean.
[d]Members of the Economic and Social Commission for Western Asia.
Note: No comparative data are available for the region of the United Nations Economic Commission for Europe and North America.

Box 5.7   Slums and squatter settlements

Africa

Bangui (Central African Republic). Estimated population 500,000 in 1985. Around three-quarters of Bangui's population lives in self-built housing referred to as *habitat spontane*. The city's sewerage system was constructed in 1946, when the population was 26,000, and has never been expanded. Almost all squatter settlements are dependent on pit latrines and lack electricity and dependable supplies of water. None of the settlements is the result of conscious planning, and their inhabitants have no title to the land they occupy.

Cairo, Egypt. Estimated population 7.7 million in 1985. Severe overcrowding, lack of basic services, and deteriorating housing conditions characterize many parts of this rapidly expanding city. More than 1 million people are estimated to live in the cemeteries of the city, while many others sleep in mosques. Only 10 per cent of the city's population are able to afford low-cost housing provided through public programmes.

Freetown, Sierra Leone. Estimated population 480,000 in 1985. Most of the city's rapid increase in population has been accommodated in unplanned residential areas. The absence of affordable housing and rapidly increasing land prices have forced low-income groups into very high density housing areas in and near the city's centre and onto sites ill-suited for housing, such as river banks, steep hills, the tidal zone, and even the sides of garbage dumps. A 1978/9 household survey revealed that only 20 per cent of households in the metropolitan area had a water tap inside their houses and only 5 per cent had access to flush toilets. Most of the city is not served by sewers, and the sewage that is collected is discharged untreated into the sea.

Lusaka, Zambia. Estimated population 740,000 in 1985. Some 350,000, around one-half of the city's population, live in squatter settlements or illegal residential developments. The squatter settlements have grown rapidly in the past two decades, and many have populations of 20,000 to 50,000. Despite the efforts that are being made to upgrade the settlements, the social and physical infrastructure in many of them remains rudimentary.

Nairobi, Kenya. Estimated population 1.2 million in 1985. An estimated 110,000 unauthorized dwellings house around 40 per cent of the city's population. The city's largest squatter settlement, Mathare Valley, grew from 4,000 inhabitants in 1964 to more than 50,000 in 1971 and is today occupied by at least 100,000 people. Many small areas with unauthorized constructions have grown at comparable rates. Typically, squatter settlements have very high densities, their structures are rudimentary, and water supply and sewage-disposal facilities are either elementary or non-existent. Few settlements have access roads or street lighting.

Nouakchott, Mauritania. A small town with 5,000 inhabitants in 1965, it grew to 135,000 in 1977, and since then the population has doubled. Most of the very large increase in population has been housed in illegal shanty or tent settlements. Since 1972, the government has distributed 7,000 unserviced plots, and an estimated 64 per cent of the city's population today live in self-built settlements on these plots and in unauthorized settlements. More than two-thirds of the city's inhabitants have no direct access to water; the bulk of the city's population is compelled to purchase water of questionable quality from water vendors at a price up to 100 times that paid by those with piped water connections.

Ouaguadougou, Burkina Faso. Estimated population 310,000 in 1985. Around 60 per cent of the city's population live in a wide belt of 'spontaneous settlements' built around the centre. The settlements typically lack access to piped water, sanitation, and electricity, and their inhabitants have no tenure to the land they occupy.

Tunis, Tunisia. Estimated population 1.3 million in 1985. A 1978 study revealed that 135,000 people were living in the city's old town centre (*medina*) and its two *faubourgs* at a density of 500 persons per hectare, with some 40 per cent of all households living in a single room. Another 300,000 people lived in squatter settlements at an average density of 925 persons per hectare. The *medina* and the squatter settlements, which together housed 45 per cent of the city's population, accounted for a little more than 10 per cent of the city's total residential area. Just under one-third of the population, predominantly upper-income and middle-income groups, lived in garden suburbs that accounted for nearly two-thirds of the city's total residential area.

Asia

Ankara, Turkey. Estimated population 2.9 million in 1985. Around two-thirds of Ankara's population live in spontaneous settlements called *gecekondus*. While some *gecekondu* areas have developed into consolidated settlements, surveys conducted in the mid-1970s revealed the poor quality accommodation in many of them. Around 40 per cent of the housing in *gecekondus* in the inner areas of the city are less than 30 square metres in area and consist of one or two rooms. Around one-third of the dwellings are shared by two or more households. Some 60 per cent are without their own water supply, and only 15 per cent have an internal toilet.

Bombay, India. Estimated population 10.1 million in 1985. Some 3.5 million slum dwellers live on about 8,000 acres of Bombay's land—over 400 persons an acre. By current trends, 75 per cent of Bombay's population will be living in slums by the turn of the century. Some 100,000 people already live on the pavements, which is still less than in Calcutta, where an estimated 600,000 people sleep every night in the streets. Bombay also contains the world's biggest slum, a sprawling conglomeration of shanties called Dharavi.

From a survey of about 4,000 households in nine slums in Bombay, we know that nearly 40 per cent of households live 2 to 4 persons in one room, another 35 per cent have 5 to 9 persons in one room, and 1 per cent have 10 or more persons living in one room. No house has a private toilet, and a quarter of the households do not even have access to community toilets and use the open spaces around the slum. Over a third have no drainage facilities, and another 40 per cent have uncovered drains. This lack of amenities makes the slum environment extremely prone to disease.

Colombo, Sir Lanka. Estimated population 610,000 in 1985. Estimates indicate that around 25,000 households live in squatter settlements in Colombo City, and another 25,000 in shanties in the urban area. In addition, nearly 29,000 households are estimated to live in substandard tenements built by the private sector at very high densities in inner-city slums. In total, between 50 and 60 per cent of Colombo's population live in substandard accommodation, usually without adequate supporting services.

Hong Kong. Estimated population 5.1 million in 1985. An ambitious public housing programme reduced the squatter population from 411,000 in 1964 to 274,000 in 1976. However, there has been a large increase in squatting in the past decade as a result of the arrival of an estimated 200,000 legal and illegal immigrants. A clearance programme initiated in 1980 resulted in the removal of 46,000 people from squatter settlements and yielded 210 hectares of land for development. Of the people removed, 31,300 were allocated permanent housing, and the reminder temporary housing. Despite these and related efforts, there were more than 300,000 squatters living in the urban areas of Hong Kong Island and Kowloon and in three new towns in the New Territories in 1982. The number of squatters was higher than in 1976.

Karachi, Pakistan. Estimated population 6.7 million in 1985. Karachi has two distinct types of unauthorized housing, both of which house several hundred thousand people. The first are settlements built on invaded land, of which there are around 120, many built on the banks of water courses. The second type is formed by the unauthorized subdivision of government land by private persons. Some such subdivisions, such as Baldia, Orangi, and Mahmoodabad, have become very large and are occupied by tens of thousands of people.

Latin America

Bogota, Colombia. Estimated population 4.5 million in 1985. Close to 70 per cent of the housing stock is substandard, and around one-half of the population lives in squatter settlements and *urbanizaciones piratas*—illegal subdivisions which have accounted for around 60 per cent of all residential construction over the past two decades. A 1977 survey of 135 'pirate subdivisions' found that more than one-half lacked sewers, and more than one-third lacked water and electricity. The city's total housing shortage was estimated in the same year at nearly 250,000 units.

El Salvador. A 1975 study revealed that 63 per cent of the housing stock of the country's five largest cities was produced illegally or through informal arrangements. Nearly two-thirds of all housing comprises rented rooms in tenements, illegal subdivisions, and squatter settlements. Unserviced illegal subdivisions accommodate close to half of the country's urban population, while a further 9 per cent live in *tuqurios*, typically a collection of squatter huts built on invaded land, including public rights-of-way, steep gullies, and dry river beds.

Guayaquil, Ecuador. Estimated population 1.3 million in 1985. In 1975, some 60 per cent of the city's population lived in squatter communities built over tidal swamplands. These communities, known as *suburbios*, are mostly made up of bamboo and timber houses built on poles above the mud and polluted waters of the tidal zone. The houses are connected by a complex system of timber catwalks which also link them to the shore: in some cases, dry land is a 40-minute walk away. About one-third of the city's population is unable to afford the down-payment on a government-provided low-cost house.

Lima, Peru. Estimated population 5.7 million in 1985. Approximately one-half of the city's population lives in inner-city slums (*tuqurios*), and another quarter in squatter settlements (*pueblos jovenes*). *Pueblos jovenes* have increased rapidly and today number over 300, ranging in size from a few families to Villa El Salvador, with well over 100,000 inhabitants. Some settlements have been built over public garbage dumps.

Mexico City, Mexico. Estimated population 17.3 million in 1985. At least 7 million people live in some form of uncontrolled or unauthorized settlement. One-third of the city's families live in one-room shelters devoid of almost all amenities, and 80 per cent of all the dwellings in the city display some form of physical irregularity.

São Paulo, Brazil. Estimated population 15.9 million in 1985. Up to 2 million people are estimated to live in very substandard accommodation in inner-city slums and squatter settlements, and two-thirds of the families entering the labour market are unable to afford formal housing. Around 3 million people obtain their water from wells sunk into a watertable heavily polluted with sewage. Partly because of this the infant mortality rate has almost doubled in 15 years. Nearly half the children living in the city's slums and squatter settlements are undernourished.

ces in slum areas are poor, and landlords are unwilling and tenants unable to improve existing water-supply and sanitation systems. The high densities of urban slums, besides presenting gross hazards to health, often represent potential fire hazards, especially because the distribution of water is intermittent and of insufficient pressure.

Squatter settlements have grown on sites unsuitable for conventional development and are often located in inaccessible areas such as flood plains, swamps, and steep hillsides. Services in these areas are often non-existent, and opportunities for connecting to municipal utility networks are poor. Population densities in squatter settlements vary greatly but are generally lower than those in urban slums. While this has a positive effect in terms of reduced exposure to diseases spread by overcrowding, the per capita cost of providing water supply, and to a lesser extent sanitation (except for sewerage) is, none the less, high.

Squatters in different parts of the world use a wide variety of water-supply sources. Natural springs have often encouraged squatter settlements, but in densely populated urban areas if such springs remain unprotected they become a hazard to health. Shallow wells, although convenient, are easily contaminated where sanitation is poor and facilitate the transmission of water-borne diseases. Standpipes connected to the municipal supply are sometimes used for squatters who have reasonable access to them, but very large settlements cannot be served by such inadequate, improvised facilities. Sale of water from mobile tankers is another frequent source of supply, but communities served in this way usually pay more for their supply than those connected to the municipal supply network.

Sanitation in squatter settlements, where it exists at all, is very primitive. Some residents simply use near-by wasteland or water bodies, while others carry the waste to dumping grounds. Bucket latrines are widely used in many Asian and certain African squatter settlements, and collected excreta are often transported in unhygienic conditions and dumped on the periphery of the settlement or in the nearest watercourse or refuse site. Dry-pit and wet-pit latrines are sometimes used where space is available, but such latrines are often installed by householders with little technical orientation, and the usual consequence is pollution of surface water or groundwater.

The problem of supplying water and sanitation to rural populations in developing countries is exacerbated by the large number of communities lacking these services. Although most rural settlements have developed where water is available, many rural residents still have to travel large distances to a water source. Not all areas have groundwater resources—generally the most satisfactory form of supply for small communities in terms of both quality and cost—and surface supplies pose serious health problems, particularly in densely populated countries. Until recently, rural water-supply schemes were not always designed to provide for basic needs at minimum cost, and the systems installed are often either too sophisticated for rural people to manage or too costly for them to operate. Consequently, many such systems lie idle.

Solid-waste disposal

The need for the collection and disposal of solid waste in urban settlements is far from adequately recognized. Uncollected refuse accumulates in drains, roads, and open spaces, disrupting community life and creating additional problems in the operation of other public services. Solid wastes normally have a low concentration of disease-causing organisms, but in low-income areas where faeces are dumped together with refuse the wastes are a danger to health.

There are no reliable statistics on the extent of solid-waste management coverage in developing countries. Usually, between 25 and 55 per cent of all waste generated in large cities is collected by municipal authorities entrusted with its disposal. As is the case with water supply and sanitation, even this minimal level of waste-disposal service is not provided to the slums and squatter settlements that accommodate the majority of the urban poor. Very often no form of refuse-disposal service is provided, and refuse is either dumped on the limited common space available for circulation within these communities or in unofficial dumping grounds, such as verges of watercourses.

Where surface drains are provided, these serve as convenient disposal points.

A low-income community's perception of the need for an appropriate solid-waste collection and disposal system is even lower than is the case for sanitation. Inhabitants of scattered rural settlements normally dispose of solid wastes by dumping. Because the production of waste is low, the need for an institutionalized system of collection and disposal is minimal. The small quantities of predominantly organic refuse are often separated at source for animal feed, and in a few cases for production of organic compost. Public awareness of proper methods for disposal to arrest pest proliferation and avoid disease transmission is, however, greatly needed in these settlements.

Governments in developing countries have problems in financing systems of solid-waste collection and disposal because the possibility of cost recovery is normally very low. This is especially true for low-income urban communities. However, the potential for recovery and re-use of waste materials is yet to be realized in most developing countries, and opportunities for reducing operating costs through such reclamation are good.

Transport

The number of cities in developing countries affected by serious transport difficulties is steadily growing. Urban growth, combined with motorization, has placed great demands on city budgets. Heavy investments are needed in roads, parking facilities, and public-transport infrastructure. It has not been possible to meet this rapidly growing demand, even in cities where a significant part of total public investment has been directed to the transport sector. Also, the distribution of investment has not always benefited the greatest number: in all cities in developing countries, the number of people affected by inadequate facilities for pedestrians and by inadequate public transport greatly exceeds the number affected only by traffic congestion and parking problems. In Bogota, a low-income adult travels for 127 minutes per day in comparison to 83 minutes for a high-income traveller.

However, the urban poor make fewer trips than other urban residents, and their mobility is generally limited to essential purposes, such as work and education. A very high share of trips are on foot and by other means of unmotorized transport, and the proportion of walk trips is especially high for low-income groups. In Bombay, the proportion of walk trips for low-income groups exceeds 80 per cent, in comparison to about 25 per cent for the highest income group.

In contrast to the situation in developed countries, the proportion of income that a poor family in a developing country spends on transport is higher than that of any other income group. In some countries, a low-income family spends about one-tenth of its total income on transport, while in the case of the lowest income group this proportion may be as high as 30 per cent.[16] The interdependence between accessibility and employability is of particular importance. The lack of affordable access to different sources of employment results in lack of effective job search or in acceptance of substandard wages in places located close to low-income housing. Similarly, limited access to educational institutions and other social services places low-income groups at a disadvantage compared with better-off groups. The combination of these deficiencies causes feelings of isolation and frustration.

The causes of the present inadequacies of transport systems can be found both within and outside the transport sector. First, there is often a lack of harmonization between the human settlements pattern (the distribution of population and activities) and the transport system: in urban areas, separation of activities, often imposed by zoning practices, creates the need for excessively long trips. Secondly, resources available to the transport sector as a whole are inadequate, and they are usually allocated in such a manner that long-distance transport is favoured over local transport. Lastly, the scarce resources available are not used in the most effective manner because of the inefficient division of tasks between modes of transport, the use of inappropriate and inefficient transport modes and technologies, the inadequate maintenance of facilities and transport equipment, and the inefficient management of traffic and public-transport operations. Most of these causes relate to prevailing human settlements and transport policies.

The growth of motorization and resulting urban traffic flows have so far directed the attention of authorities towards increasing road capacity. There are at least five good reasons why current policies relating to the accommodation of motor traffic should be questioned. First, the construction of main roads has diverted funds and technical resources away from other forms of investment in the sector which might have benefited society as a whole. Secondly, the cost to the community of motor traffic in the centres and main arteries of cities is very high. The price system has failed to maintain an efficient balance between the cost of supplying transport facilities and the cost of using them, and where the vehicle owner does not bear the full cost of the use of a congested road, he is not discouraged from undertaking trips by private vehicle even when they are clearly not indispensable. Thirdly, to make room for new highways, houses are demolished, pavements narrowed, and travel on foot made dangerous and inconvenient. Fourthly, where traffic-management measures have been used instead of or in addition to capital improvements to reduce traffic congestion, constraints have often been placed on unmotorized modes of travel (such as cycle-rickshaws) and on pedestrian movement. Fifthly, of great significance in the long term, accommodating motorized traffic on high-speed links has a profound impact on city form, to the disadvantage of the poor.

These disadvantages to urban low-income groups are not necessarily created intentionally by city authorities. In the face of growing congestion, it might seem at first glance that road investments and motor-vehicle-oriented traffic management represent the only options. However, even in the wealthiest cities of the developed countries, it is not possible to purchase congestion-free motoring, and the emphasis of transport strategy has therefore swung away from capital investment towards constraint and control based on administrative and pricing measures.

In rural areas, many farms are not served directly by public roads, so that off-farm transport is required to carry supplies and crops between the farm and the roadside, as well as along roads to or from markets and supply points. The problems faced by small farmers in moving produce and materials are exacerbated by a shortage of appropriate vehicles. Very few have access to motorized transport.

The extent of the use of handcarts, pack animals, animal carts, bicycle derivatives, etc. varies from country to country and from region to region. Animals are widely used in Latin America, North Africa, and, particularly, in Asian countries. However, even in areas with a long tradition of animal use, headloading and backloading are still the predominant way of moving goods for most of the rural poor, and in many countries this is done mostly by women. When heavy loads must be moved long distances, most small farmers are limited to three options: selling to and purchasing from itinerant traders at the roadside; participating in a co-operative or marketing organization which arranges collection and delivery of goods; or hiring space on a bus, truck, or pick-up (with the farmer usually accompanying his goods).

Although rural roads are particularly needed for the conveyance of goods, personal movement often predominates. Despite a large demand for personal travel, access to public passenger-transport facilities is usually limited. Yet, where public-transport services are available, they are often unaffordable to many potential passengers.

Since 1945, investment in rural highways has brought considerable changes in rural road systems. Even so, most developing countries lag behind the rest of the world in terms of the density and quality of their road networks. By the end of the 1960s, basic trunk road networks had been completed in many developing countries, and during the 1970s attention turned to the provision of extensive secondary and feeder-road networks. Labour-based methods of low-cost road construction were introduced in some countries. However, the effects of public investment in access roads have not been as positive as expected, because of insufficient co-ordination with other rural development activities, too much emphasis on high-quality design, the use of capital-intensive construction technology, and neglect of maintenance.

The most important point, however, is that the problem of providing rural areas with appropriate vehicles and transport aids was almost totally neglected. As a result, the majority of the rural population is prevented from owning personal means of transport, and the development of rural access roads has mostly benefited large and medium-sized farms. One of the main causes for the existing situation is that vehicles and other transport equipment are generally considered beyond the scope of governmental interests. Issues such as the appropriateness or adequacy of the current vehicle stock, means of overcoming constraints on the supply of vehicles, and the need for investment in different types of vehicles are generally ignored.

Current transport policies have generally not resulted in the anticipated improvements in the quality of life and productivity. In particular, investments in transport have not facilitated the solution of emerging transport problems, as the conventional policy focus on roads and motor vehicles usually takes little account of the needs of the underprivileged majority and often works against their interests. Foreign exchange is required to import vehicles, and the consumption of fuel, mainly in the transport sector, has become a heavy burden to oil-importing countries. The revision of these policies is particularly crucial in view of the continued and dramatic increases in the urban population of developing countries.

Energy

In many developing countries, the bulk of the population depends mainly on non-commercial fuels. The financial problems of people below the poverty line result in their use of fuelwood and/or animal dung which are the most easily available and cheapest fuels they can get. However, the exploitation of forests and natural fertilizers leads to environmental degradation, which reduces the productivity of the soil in the long run. Hence, energy-use patterns increase poverty, and there is a vicious circle which links poverty to energy. In oil-importing countries, oil-based commercial fuels are beyond the reach of not only low-income but even some middle-income families.

Most of the developing countries are not endowed with commercial fuels such as oil, natural gas, and coal. Non-commercial fuels, namely, firewood, charcoal, animal dung, and vegetable residues, are the primary energy sources for rural households, agriculture, transportation, industries, services, and construction. The proportion of consumption for domestic use in rural settlements varies from 30 to 70 per cent of the total primary energy consumption. This is because of the low level of primary energy consumption in the agricultural, transportation and industrial sectors.

The following observations can be made on domestic energy-consumption patterns in rural settlements of the developing countries:

• In Asia, where 69 per cent of the world's population live, the rural population consumes less than 1 million kilocals (3.4 gigajoules) per capita per annum in the domestic sector.

• In Africa, fuelwood is used for over 90 per cent of primary energy needs, and annual per capita consumption in the rural domestic sector stands at 2.2 million kilocals (9.5 gigajoules).

• In Latin America, primary energy consumption in the domestic sector is substantially higher than in Asia and Africa, at 4 million kilocals (18.2 gigajoules) per capita per annum.

• In all developing regions, fuelwood is by far the most important source of primary energy for domestic use in rural areas.

In Africa, as in Asia, non-commercial fuels account for the greatest share of energy consumption. There are hardly any data on rural energy-consumption patterns among Latin America's 126 million (1980) rural inhabitants, but from the rudimentary figures available it appears that wood and other vegetable matter are the main fuels used by most Latin American rural populations. Studies of rural energy-consumption patterns in Brazil, Colombia, Mexico, and Peru indicate that fuelwood is the main source of primary energy, and that the per capita consumption of energy in the domestic sector in rural settlements is almost twice the per capita consumption in Asia or Africa.

As many developing countries have given electrification priority during the past few decades, some countries have spent as much as 20 per cent of their capital budgets on electrification, with a considerable proportion of the funds

---

Box 5.8   Domestic energy consumption in the developing countries: the case of India

A commonly held misconception is that firewood, dung, agricultural wastes, and other non-commercial sources are used almost entirely in villages and rural areas. In fact, as much as 45 per cent of the energy consumed in towns and cities in India comes from non-commercial sources, with more than 70 per cent used for cooking. In villages, the number of households that are partly or completely dependent on non-commercial sources of energy for cooking is as high as 99 per cent.

Of the non-commercial sources, firewood is the most important. It provides 50 per cent of the energy used for cooking in towns and cities, and 70 per cent in villages. The rapidly increasing prices of such fuels as coal and kerosene, combined with the destruction of woodlands and forests, imply that the rural and urban poor will find it increasingly difficult to secure sufficient supplies of the energy needed for cooking at prices they can afford. Shortages of non-commercial sources of energy not only will add to the costs of existence but could also result in a deterioration in health and nutritional standards.

Source: India's Environment: A Citizen's Report (New Delhi: Centre for Science and Environment, 1982).

---

going to rural electrification programmes. However, most rural communities are still without electricity, and in those that do have it, the low-income groups cannot afford it. It is therefore crucial to determine the proper role of rural electrification in satisfying rural requirements by establishing the uses for which electricity is economical and socially justified and investigating the comparative costs of other decentralized energy systems.

So far, surveys to examine the basic energy-consumption patterns of the urban poor have not produced adequate results. Since many slum and squatter-settlement dwellers are rural migrants with limited resources, they resort, as in rural settlements, to traditional ways of satisfying their energy needs. Firewood and charcoal obtained from the surrounding rural areas are commonly used in the semi-rural squatter settlements located on the outskirts of large urban communities in Africa. Families in the squatter communities of large urban centres in Asia have to rely on oil products for their cooking needs, owing to the extremely limited availability of firewood and charcoal. Squatter settlements in South Asia use dried animal wastes, sometimes mixed with coal dust, as a fuel for cooking. Bottled gas and oil products, such as kerosene, are becoming increasingly important among the squatter communities of Asia and Latin America, and are primarily used for cooking and lighting. Generally, the use of electricity, where available, is limited to lighting and the powering of small appliances.

The annual per capita energy consumption of the urban poor in developing countries does not differ significantly from that of the rural poor. However, with rising incomes, the energy-consumption patterns of urban households in developing countries are starting to change, and fuelwood is being replaced by kerosene and kerosene by gas and electricity for cooking and lighting.

Environment

The relationships between human settlements and natural environments are complex at both the village and the metropolitan levels. Inefficient use of natural resources by burgeoning populations is putting resource systems under stress in a broad range of settlements, but most visibly in large urban areas. These areas draw heavily on natural resources such as water, forests, and soils, and if improperly managed they discharge wastes in a fashion that distorts natural biogeochemical cycles. Where long-term development consequences of environmental degradation are understood and the rate of urbanization is matched by the rate of economic development, measures to avoid acute degradation can be easily taken. Where urban growth assumes massive proportions while rates of overall development are low, environmental conditions are often severely affected.

Most environmental attention is focused on pollution control and hazard management. There is an obvious reason for this, since pollution has an immediate and visible impact on living conditions, and it can be tackled by short-term remedial measures which are politically attractive and administratively uncomplicated. There is even a justification for this, in the sense that conditions have deteriorated so badly in some places that emergency action is called for.

In Mexico City, for example, 130,000 factories

Box 5.9   Urban growth of massive proportions: Mexico City

Even a decade ago, the health risk of breathing the air in Mexico's capital was equated to smoking two packs of cigarettes a day. Owing to the thin air of the mountain plateau on which Mexico City is located, car engines emit about twice as much carbon monoxide and hydrocarbon pollutants as they would at sea level. Moreover, the high mountains surrounding the plateau trap industrial and combustion-engine pollutants above the city, only to be periodically dispersed on windy days. Only in December 1983 did the Mexican Senate, for the first time, establish factory pollution limits.

These problems, which are particularly acute in Mexico City, occur in other megacities. One of the main reasons for late reaction to the problems is the necessity to deal with other priority issues, such as employment, housing, water supply, and sewerage. For instance, at least 2 million inhabitants of Mexico City lack piped water in their houses, and city authorities are facing large expenditures to maintain sufficient water supply for the growing millions of citizens. Most of the 1 billion gallons of water currently supplied every day have to be pumped from reservoirs located at a large distance from and situated at much lower altitudes than the city. Overexploitation of subsoil water supplies in the metropolitan area has caused parts of the most densely built-up city centre to sink by 3–10 metres over the past few decades. This subsidence is playing havoc with water mains and sewerage systems. Some 20 per cent of houses lack any form of sewerage. The appropriate treatment of liquid and solid urban wastes must also be included in the list of elementary environmental needs which the city authorities, in spite of immense infrastructural outlays, have not been able to keep up with.

For all these reasons, ecological planning and environmental protection have now become a political issue, and their inclusion in action programmes of the new government has been given extensive publicity. However, it is questionable—particularly in view of Mexico's present international debt problem—whether Mexico City will be able to bear the astronomical costs of the programmes.

and 3 million motor vehicles produce an estimated 4 kilogrammes of noxious chemicals every week for each of the city's 18 million people. Such pollution has hazardous effects far beyond the area of its occurrence: hinterland environmental impacts of air pollution include damage to vegetation and falling crop yields. In China, for example, air pollution from Lanzhou (an industrial city) has destroyed fruit trees in surrounding villages. Datepalms flowered but did not bear fruit, pumpkins failed to mature, and livestock contracted oral cavities which ulcerated, perforated, and kept them from eating, causing high death rates.[17] Considerable damage has been reported to the Samsoon Plains in the Republic of Korea, once an important rice-producing area, from power, petrochemical, and fertilizer plants. There are grounds for believing that such problems have been exacerbated by the transfer of polluting industries from developed to developing countries.[18] Firms involved in the manufacture of asbestos have shifted their operations to Latin America (notably Brazil and Mexico), and the Republic of Korea has been displacing Japan as a source of asbestos textiles for North American markets as new regulations on this industry have been introduced in Japan.[19]

In China, the industrial sector is the dominant consumer of fossil fuels and it is concentrated in around 20 cities, all of which have serious air-pollution problems. Lung-cancer mortality in China is 4–7 times higher in cities than in the nation as a whole, and the difference appears largely attributable to heavy air pollution.[20] The city of Cubatao, in Brazil, has been known for many years as the Valley of Death. The city contains a high concentration of heavy industry and has very high levels of stillborn births, tuberculosis, pneumonia, bronchitis, emphysema, and asthma, and a high infant mortality rate, all of which have been linked to air pollution.[21] Malaysia's highly urbanized Klang Valley, which includes Kuala Lumpur, has 2–3 times the air-pollution level recorded in cities in North America.

The disposal of city wastes can have environmental impacts that reach beyond the immediate hinterland. Fisheries damaged or destroyed by liquid effluents from city-based industries are becoming increasingly common. Worsening water pollution is threatening the livelihoods of millions of river fishermen in India. In a 158-kilometre stretch of the Hooghly River, for example, the average fish yield in polluted zones is about one-sixth of that in unpolluted zones. In Malaysia, the livelihood of many fishermen who depended on rivers and lakes has been severely undermined by water pollution, while fishermen in inshore waters have reported large reductions in catches in coastal areas affected by industrial effluents and oil. In Lake Maryut, close to the city of Alexandria in Egypt, fish production has declined by about 80 per cent owing to discharges of industrial and domestic effluents.[22] Other cases where industrial effluents have severaly damaged local fisheries include the Han River in the Republic of Korea; the Li Jiang River in Guilin, Hangzhou Bay, and the Wunjin County section of the Grand Canal in China;[23] and Rio de Janeiro's Guanabara Bay.[24]

River pollution from city-based industries and untreated sewage can lead to serious health problems in settlements located downstream. One example is the River Bogota which flows through Colombia's capital. At the town of Tocaima, 120 kilometres downstream, the river has been found to have an average faecal bacteria coliform count of 7.3 million, making it totally unfit for drinking or cooking. In a village close to Tocaima, the river was reported in 1980 to be black and, despite its distance from Bogota, to smell of sewage and chemicals. Nearly all the children have skin sores or growths from swimming in it.[25] The La Paz River, which flows through Bolivia's capital, has become so polluted that horticultural production downstream of the city has had to be curtailed.[26] Regional impacts of water pollution can even extend to international water bodies. In the Persian Gulf—a small, shallow, salty, and almost landlocked sea—rapid urban and industrial growth on its shores is helping to endanger one of the world's most fragile ecosystems. While the great danger of marine pollution comes from oil, especially from tanker deballasting and tank washing, raw sewage from the rapidly expanding coastal cities and industrial liquid wastes dumped untreated into the Gulf are also having a considerable impact, as is the concentration of desalination plants along the coast.

More than a hundred developing countries have established national environmental agencies of one kind or another. Many, however, are weak and small institutions, mandated to play co-ordinating roles and without independent authority. Sound and effective environmental policies have yet to emerge in most countries. Enforcement of environmental law and regulations tends to be a haphazard process heavily dependent on the

Box 5.10   Ethiopia's environment: can it recover?

In 1984, in Ethiopia, 3 million people were faced with starvation. In large parts of the country, it had not rained for three or, even, four years, and in these areas there was no food or water. Nothing was growing, and animals were dying by the thousands.

Drought was the most visible and prominent ingredient of Ethiopia's predicament, yet it was not the only one. Underlying the country's predicament and conditioning, the survival prospects of the rural poor is the erosion of the productive capacity of the biological systems that support life. In the case of Ethiopia, these appear to have deteriorated to such an extent that it is legitimate to raise the question of whether they can ever recover.

The destruction that has taken place is most evident in deforestation and soil erosion. Ethiopia's steep highlands and parts of its plains were once covered by dense forests: less than a century ago, about half the country had forest cover. This figure fell to about 15 per cent 20 years ago, and today no more than 3 per cent of Ethiopia's land area is covered by forests. If this trend continues, the country will be without forest cover in a few years' time. The loss of forest cover has resulted in massive soil erosion, especially in the country's erosion-prone highlands. As early as the 1960s, FAO estimated national soil loss at nearly 1 billion tons per year, equivalent to 32 tons every second. Today the figure is probably lower, not because there is less erosion but because Ethiopia has probably lost much of its topsoil. It is to be found in the rivers of Egypt, Somalia, and Sudan, and at the bottom of the Mediterranean and the Red Sea.

The fertility of the remaining soil is being affected by the country's firewood problems. In much of the countryside, firewood supplies have been exhausted, and animal dung and the straw from harvests are used instead. As a result, very little organic matter is being returned to the soil which is becoming poor and infertile, unable to support human and animal populations.

Ethiopia was once a fertile country, but much of it no longer is. The average daily per capita intake of food energy fell by 13 per cent during the 1970s, and in 1980 the supplies of food energy met only 74 per cent of requirements. Where is the extra food to come from? No matter how much fertilizer is applied, it is impossible to grow food on the barren bedrock of the Ethiopian highlands. The semi-arid low rangelands, less affected by erosion, have little water. They are also the home of pastoralists who have expanded their herds, both to support a growing population and as an insurance against drought and hunger. The expanding herds are placing new pressure on the productivity of the vulnerable rangelands.

Ethiopia's predicament should serve as a warning to other countries because it exemplifies the interactions between people, poverty, and the natural environment. The equations that link them may appear abstract on paper, but that they exist in reality is evidenced by the plight of Ethiopia.

political power of those who violate the regulations and on the extent to which the government is under pressure to stop pollution.

This will certainly continue to be the case as long as environmental emphasis is given to negative approaches, such as controlling and clearing up pollution. What will be needed is a new view of the environment as a development resource to be managed for optimal benefits along with all other resource inputs to the development process. It is popular to refer to the 'impact of human settlements on the environment', as though the environment were some independent entity separate from human beings and their way of life. The fact is, however, that human beings live in human settlements, and the real question to be faced is how the environment can support human settlements to the greatest long-term benefit of the people who live in them.

To speak of 'protecting' the environment against the human race is to reflect a distorted sense of priorities. The task is to find sustainable ways of using the environment to benefit the world's population. The issue of 'affordability' of environmental programmes will then simply cease to apply.

Conclusions

The global picture that emerges is that basic human settlements needs are largely being met in the developed countries but that the situation in developing countries gives cause for considerable concern, with needs being met neither in urban nor in rural settlements. While the scale of unfulfilled needs has already reached disturbing dimensions in the towns and cities of developing countries, the situation in rural areas is often even worse, a factor that in part explains the growth of urban areas. It is the towns and cities of the developing countries, however, that will grow most rapidly, some of them becoming so large as to take them into policy territory which is completely uncharted. Given urbanization trends, poverty seems almost certain to grow rapidly in urban areas, and the economic advantages traditionally enjoyed by the poor in towns and cities can no longer be taken for granted.

There is little evidence in the majority of developing countries to suggest that negative trends are being reversed and that human settlements situations, in either urban or rural areas, are being improved. The picture that emerges is one of a challenge not being met and of governments losing ground in their efforts to meet it. When demographic and urbanization trends are imposed upon the present human settlements situation and the conditions that prevail in cities, towns, and villages, the problems take on forms that threaten to become unmanageable.

Some of the problems cannot be solved by human settlements policies, however defined. They have their roots in poverty and the structures and processes that create and maintain it. Such problems demand deliberate decisions that favour the poor and the disadvantaged, and they must be addressed at the level of a nation's development strategy. However, human settlements, as creators and distributors of wealth, have a vital role to play, as do the policies that underpin their development.

Notes

1. The population and urbanization trends analysed in this chapter are based on United Nations, *Estimates and Projections of Urban, Rural and City Populations 1950–2025: The 1982 Assessment* (New York, 1985).
2. United Nations, *Age and Sex Structure of Urban and Rural Populations 1970–2000: The 1980 Assessment* (New York, 1982).
3. For a discussion of the differences, see B. Renaud, *National Urbanization Policy in Developing Countries* (New York: Oxford University Press, 1979); and ESCAP, *Study and Review of the Human Settlements Situation in Asia and the Pacific.* Vol. 1, *Regional Overview of the Human Settlements Situation* (Bangkok, 1983).
4. Classification according to World Bank, *World Development Report 1985* (Washington DC, 1985).
5. United States Commission on Refugees, *1980 World Refugee Survey* (New York, 1980).
6. A. Tonelson, 'Migration: People on the Move', *The Inter Dependent* (July/Aug., 1979).
7. Kathleen Newland, *International Migration: The Search for Work*, Worldwatch Paper 33 (Washington DC: Worldwatch Institute, 1979).
8. Heather Joshi, H. Lubell, and J. Mouly, *Abidjan: Urban Development and Employment in the Ivory Coast* (Geneva: ILO, 1976).
9. See R. Murphey, *The Fading of the Maoist Vision: City and Country in China's Development* (London: Methuen, 1980).
10. International Labour Organization, *Yearbook of Labour Statistics* (Geneva, 1986).

11. World Bank, *A Task for Life: Housing for Low-income Families* (Washington DC, 1974).

12. See P. Bairoch, *Urban Unemployment in Developing Countries* (Geneva: ILO, 1973).

13. United Nations, *World Housing Survey 1974* (New York, 1975).

14. R. P. Misra (ed.), *Million Cities of India* (Delhi: Vikas Publishing House, 1978).

15. B. Stokes, *The Global Housing Prospect*, Worldwatch Paper 46 (Washington DC: Worldwatch Institute, 1982).

16. D. A. C. Maunder *et al.*, *Household and Travel Characteristics in Two Residential Areas of Delhi, India, 1979*, Transport and Road Research Laboratory, Supplementary Report 673 (1981), 7.

17. V. Smil, *The Bad Earth: Environmental Degradation in China* (New York: M. E. Sharpe; London: Zed Press, 1984).

18. See Jane H. Ives (ed.), *The Export of Hazard* (Boston: Routledge and Kegan Paul, 1985).

19. See B. I. Castleman, 'The Export of Hazardous Factories to Developing Nations', *International Journal of Health Services*, 9/4 (1979), 569–97.

20. Smil, *The Bad Earth*.

21. H. J. Leonard, 'Politics and Pollution from Urban and Industrial Development', in H. J. Leonard (ed.), *Diversifying Nature's Capital: The Political Economy of Environmental Abuse in the Third World* (New York, 1981).

22. A. Hamza, 'Management of Industrial Hazardous Wastes in Egypt', *Industry and Environment*, 4 (1983), 28–32.

23. Smil, *The Bad Earth*.

24. Leonard, 'Politics and Pollution'.

25. Gloria Moreno, *Drinking Water: Black with Foam on Top* (London: Earthscan Feature, 1980).

26. USAID, *Report on Peruvian 'Pueblos Jovenes' Problems and Possibilities for USAID IIPUP Technical Assistance* (Washington DC: Office of Housing and Urban Programs, Agency for International Development, 1979).

Part III

Key Policy Areas in Settlements Development

6 National Development

Human settlements are affected by virtually the entire range of economic and social policies formulated at the national level. Such policies have a direct effect on income and employment, and both of these have indirect effects on settlements. Policies on imports, on the value of the currency, on the growth of industrial and agricultural output, and on the distribution of investments between sectors all affect, sometimes in unintended ways, the development of human settlements.

The relationships between economic policy and human settlements development are increasingly recognized, and many countries are seeking to establish policy frameworks which integrate the two. Centrally planned developing countries have attempted to link human settlements planning with economic development goals in order to achieve an improved spatial distribution of population and economic activity and to reduce subnational inequalities. Market-economy developing countries, several with UNCHS (Habitat) technical co-operation, are also increasingly engaging in national spatial and physical planning. In Bangladesh, for example, the Ministry of Planning and the Ministry of Urban Development are co-operating in the preparation of a National Housing and Human Settlements Policy aimed at mobilizing the scarce resources available to respond to high rates of population growth and urbanization and the resulting critical housing and human settlements problems. The National Physical Plan under preparation is designed to provide a framework for the integration of population growth and economic development and for the identification of sectoral priorities and the allocation of development funds. Indonesia, one of the world's most rapidly urbanizing countries, is involved in an economic and spatial planning exercise which sets out to concentrate investment in a hierarchy of key cities linked by a transport network. The resultant national spatial plan will guide the allocation of funds in all urban areas and the composition of spatially disaggregated investment programmes. Malaysia has also embarked on the preparation of a national spatial plan designed to establish a hierarchy of settlements and a framework for investment decisions. The formulation of national spatial development policies is also under way in, among other countries, Madagascar, Malawi, Mexico, and Uganda.

The integration of national economic and human settlements policies has also been attempted in countries which have undertaken agrarian transformation or rural resettlement schemes. In Iraq, for example, the implementation of land reform, particularly in the country's central and southern regions, has involved not only land distribution but also an attempt to transform traditional villages into planned service and production centres within the organizational framework of co-operative and collective farms. This effort to raise agricultural production is being accompanied by investments in infrastructure, particularly irrigation systems. In the Syrian Arab Republic, the agricultural development of the Upper Euphrates region in the north of the country is based upon a combination of infrastructure development (the Euphrates Dam, irrigation works, electrical power generation and distribution) and the establishment of a network of rural settlements in which agricultural production is organized on a co-operative basis. The overall economic objective is to raise agricultural productivity, especially in foodgrains, both for domestic consumption and export. The Côte d'Ivoire has also embarked on an ambitious rural development programme that involves the creation of a planned hierarchy of settlements.

Developing countries implementing resettlement programmes with a strong emphasis on the development of human settlements include Brazil, Colombia, Egypt, Ethiopia, Indonesia, Malaysia, Peru, the Philippines, and Venezuela. In Indonesia and the Philippines, the economic development of the outer islands is to be achieved, in part, through planned settlements built for people transferred from densely populated regions. Brazil is basing the economic development of the Amazon basin, which accounts for one-half of the country's land area, on a planned system of human settlements to be populated by migrants from disadvantaged areas, notably north-eastern Brazil. An extensive network of roads will link the settlements, pro-

---

Box 6.1   Brazil: the search for an integrated approach

The two key federal institutions with an interest in human settlements are the Ministry of the Interior, which is responsible for regional development, housing, water supply, and environment, and the Ministry of Planning, which has strong control over resource-allocation procedures. The respective roles and powers of these two ministries have changed over time according to the political situation. The National Housing Bank (BNH) has an important role in allocating funds for housing the poor and providing employment for low-income groups.

Attempts were made to produce a National Urban Policy under the Ministry of the Interior, while the Ministry of Planning has devised procedures, through the establishment of the Financiadora de estudos e Projetos (FINEP), to allocate funds to development projects which link macro-economic and sectoral plans with their social and spatial components. However, the municipalities were not successfully incorporated in these approaches, and the desired sectoral co-ordination was not achieved. Under the National Development Plan 1974–9, another attempt was made to devise a national urban policy in which regional economic differences, intraurban problems, and the foci of national socio-economic policy could be reconciled. Rural planning problems and those of health, welfare, and community development were deliberately excluded.

On the administrative side, this second National Urban Policy proposed that there should be a minister in the President's Office responsible for co-ordination, a Ministry for Urban Development, and a National Council for Urban Development (CNDU), representing all federal public agencies and presided over by the Minister of Planning. The fact that CNDU had control of some 30 per cent of investment funds ensured some degree of success in co-ordinating the intragovernmental effort. However, integration with established agencies was not so straightforward. BNH, for example, remains essentially a sectoral housing agency, and very rarely is it involved in comprehensive urban development.

In September 1979, CNDU approved a National Spatial Policy which defined strategies for each region in the country and is the basis for national policies on urban development from the period 1980 to 1985. CNDU now has the legal powers to direct the federal funds that go into a specific area.

Box 6.2   Promoting the development of secondary and intermediate cities

There can be no universally valid definition of what constitutes an intermediate or secondary city. If measured in terms of their populations, thresholds must necessarily be determined by the national settlement system and each settlement's place within it. In some countries, especially small ones, the category could include small towns of 5,000 people, while in such countries as China and India, it would need to be extended to include cities with a population of around 500,000.

The importance of the role played by small settlements in national settlement systems is indicated by the fact that, in 1980, around 80 per cent of the urban population of developing countries lived in settlements with a population of less than 100,000. Other reasons for the growing attention being paid to them are:

● Intermediate-sized settlements are the centres with which most rural people and rural enterprises interact. It is through them that the rural population is linked to national markets.

● Subnational and subregional levels of governmental administration are usually located in small and intermediate centres. Strengthening such centres can contribute to developing institutional capabilities for the planning and management of human settlements and to ensuring that locally defined needs are met.

● Many national priorities, such as increasing agricultural production or productivity and reducing food imports, demand increased investments in infrastructure and services within small and intermediate centres or their rural hinterlands.

● Through an improved understanding of conditions and trends in small and intermediate settlements, governments are able to appraise development opportunities and constraints, particularly important when 'growth centres' are to be designated.

Developing countries that are actively seeking to promote the development of small and intermediate cities include the following:

● *Ecuador.* The National Development Plan 1980–4 emphasizes the need to support the growth of 16 'intermediate cities' (with between 40,000 and 200,000 inhabitants in 1981) so as to strengthen their role as centres of urban subsystems and alternatives for international migration. There are also plans for 'minor' cities (with between 10,000 and 40,000 inhabitants in 1981), to promote rural services and agro-industries, and for rural centres (3,000–10,000 inhabitants). Governmental plans include improved co-ordination between central planning and municipal action; industrial-location policy; programming of urban infrastructure; a cadastral and planning programme aimed at rationalizing municipal affairs; and improving the tax base of small and intermediate centres.

Box 6.2 continued

• *India*. Various government initiatives have sought to encourage the development of relatively small centres. The Sixth Five-Year Plan (1980–5) introduced a government-sponsored scheme for the 'Integrated Development of Small and Medium Towns', which arose out of recommendations from a task force set up in 1975. The scheme provides for central loan assistance on a matching basis with state and local government (40:40:20) to support land acquisition and development, traffic and transport improvement, industrial-estate development, and services for rural hinterlands. The state government has to fund slum improvements, water-supply and sanitation improvements, and preventive health-care facilities. As of 1 April 1983, projects for 230 towns had been approved.

• *Indonesia*. During the 1979–83 Plan, 10 large cities, 40 small cities (50,000–100,000 inhabitants), and 150 towns were chosen for *kampung* improvement programmes, with improved water supply, sewerage, drainage, and solid-waste removal/treatment. The public housing and serviced-site programmes were to be decentralized. The National Housing Agency (PERUMNAS) is currently implementing projects in some 30 centres.

• *Kenya*. Seven small or intermediate centres were selected as growth centres in the 1970–4 Plan, two were added in the 1974–8 Plan, and a further nine in the 1979–83 Plan. The 18 growth centres are to receive priority in social and economic infrastructure investment. Differing roles have been assigned to them. For instance, Machakos and Thika, both close to Nairobi, are to receive industrial investment, while Garissa, Isiolo, Kapenguria, and Narok are to be developed as 'gateway towns' linking arid and semi-arid areas to more developed regions and their markets. The 1974–8 and 1979–83 Plans also outlined a national service centre hierarchy through which the government aims to reach 90 per cent of the population with 86 urban centres (not including the 11 large urban centres), 420 market centres, 1,015 local centres, and 150 rural centres. Each category aims at a different mix of services and infrastructure for the surrounding area.

• *Nicaragua*. The Housing and Human Settlements Ministry (MINVAH), set up in 1979, has defined a national urban system with a national centre, 9 regional centres (20,000–100,000 inhabitants), 19 secondary centres (10,000–20,000 inhabitants), and, below these, service centres and base villages. The distribution of investments in urban infrastructure and services will be made through this system. Measures will also seek to direct investment away from the Pacific coast and Managua, and to decentralize industry, especially towards centres with limited agricultural potential. The government also aims to strengthen regional and local government and to promote people's participation in, for instance, municipal affairs.

• *Panama*. A programme for the development of integrated urban systems was prepared in 1976, its aim being to strengthen urban centres in inner areas of the country, so that migration to the capital would be decreased. It has 14 subprogrammes which include promoting small industries, agro-industries, and industrial parks in small and intermediate centres, and preparing master plans.

• *Philippines*. As part of a long-term national settlements policy, 346 settlements have been identified as potential growth centres: these should serve as focal points for intraregional and interregional transport and communications networks and help encourage urban development away from Manila. For the first 5–10 years of this plan (first outlined in the early 1970s), 30 centres were to be given top priority, including 2 metropolitan centres (Cebu and Davao), 8 regional centres, 15 subregional centres (including 4 in the Manila Bay Metropolitan Region), and 5 growth centres also within this metropolitan region. New industrial developments within a 50-kilometre radius of the centre of Manila City centre are to be restricted.

• *Thailand*. The Fifth Plan (1982–6) designated five regional cities in the three poorest regions which will receive investments in infrastructure (roads, drainage, flood protection, solid-waste disposal sites), revenue-earning facilities (including markets, fishing ports, and industrial estates), slum improvement, and institutional development. Efforts are also being made to develop 'subregional' cities and their peripheral rural communities.

• *United Republic of Tanzania*. The villagization programme envisaged complementary development of nine regional 'growth centres'—substantial urban centres and regional headquarters. The nine growth centres were first identified in the 1969–74 Plan, and include Dodoma which is being developed as the national capital. Various measures have sought to stimulate their development, including improved infrastructure and fiscal incentives to attract public and private enterprises. The Small Industries Development Organization is developing industrial estates in the nine growth centres and other regional capitals. The 1976–81 Plan sought to support the development of basic consumer-goods industries and to promote and develop small and medium industries in regional and subregional (district) headquarters. Two-fifths of the budget and the civil service has been decentralized to the regional level.

viding access to the Amazon basin for settlers and facilitating the movement of capital equipment and agricultural and forestry products.

The linking of national economic development goals and human settlements policies is, if not explicit, at least implicit in those countries in which the development of intermediate and secondary cities is afforded priority. Such countries include Chile, China, Ecuador, India, Indonesia, Kenya, Nepal, Nicaragua, Panama, Peru, the Philippines, Thailand, Tunisia, and the United Republic of Tanzania. One of the main aims of strategies that seek to promote the development of intermediate cities is to establish attraction points for rural–urban migration which can serve as countermagnets to large urban centres and promote integrated rural development.

The difficulties being encountered in promoting the development of small and intermediate cities are some of the problems that have become apparent in the efforts being made to integrate spatial and economic planning. In the past decade, little progress has been made, for example, in evaluating the implications of core economic policies for human settlements development. Despite the growing concern for spatial planning, there is little evidence of settlement policies that are shaped to any real extent by national economic imperatives.

Part of the problem continues to reside in the different professional concerns and preoccupations of economic and spatial planning. When effective, economic planning is able to influence the growth and composition of output, but it is still largely unaware of and sometimes indifferent to the effects of economic decisions on the distribution of population or ensuing settlement and service needs. Spatial planning, on the other hand, is largely concerned with the distribution of population but has little access to and knowledge of the mechanisms which produce and sustain the distribution.

Problems are aggravated by the lack of data. Developing market-economy countries seldom collect the data required for planners to make informed recommendations about the location of economic activity, except on the crudest grounds (the availability of raw materials, transport, water, energy, etc.). Consequently, settlement costs are seldom elaborated in detail, and national spatial plans rarely give expression to national economic imperatives. National urban development plans may make provision for a planned hierarchy of settlements, but in reality may be based on very few concrete social and economic data. As a result, the proposed distribution of the urban population appears arbitrary when compared to the needs of production.

Problems of information are compounded by the underlying problem of theory, especially in the developing countries. There is no framework of adequate generalizations about the location of economic activity, partly because the locational pattern is in virtually continuous change. Yet, without such a theory, there are few clear criteria with which to appraise the forces of concentration and dispersal and to determine what would be an efficient and beneficial distribution of population. This conceptual gap has, in most countries, been filled by theories derived from the experience of European countries. A number of intellectual prejudices associated with this heritage continue to colour human settlements policies and planning, even though there is little demonstration of their relevance. It is still widely accepted, for example, that it is both possible and desirable to plan for a 'balanced' urban hierarchy in market-economy countries and that 'hinterlands' sustain the modern metropolis through the exchange of raw materials for urban industrial production. The heritage also finds expression in the continuing preoccupation with 'optimum' city size (where size is measured by nothing more than the population residing within arbitrary administrative boundaries), and in the propagation of such generic misconceptions as 'parasitic cities' or 'over-urbanized countries'.

To stress these points is to stress the importance of the relationships between economic plans and human settlements policies. It is also to point to the difficulties in ensuring their effective integration. Efforts to improve integration will need to recognize that national economic planning agencies in developing and developed countries usually enjoy considerably more authority and are hierarchically superior to institutions vested with responsibilities for human settlements policies and programmes. For this reason, the greatest promise for narrowing the gap between economic planning and spatial planning would appear to reside not in broadening human settlements policies to include economic planning but in seeking to ensure that the spatial dimensions of development are incorporated in socio-economic planning, especially at the macro level. Ways in which this can be actively promoted include the following:

• *Broadening the interdisciplinary nature of technical teams entrusted with national economic planning* to include human settlements disciplines such as urban and regional planning, physical and economic geography, and land management.

• *Paying particular attention to the spatial components and implications of the national economic development plan.* This may require the preparation of a national physical plan the main purpose of which should be to provide a spatial framework for determining public-sector investment and guiding private-sector investment.

• *Devising mechanisms for designing and implementing human settlements components* in specific development programmes and projects.

• *Devising monitoring and evaluation mechanisms* that make it possible to assess the impact of human settlements on processes of social and economic development and vice versa.

Conclusions

Economic development strategies and human settlements policies are both concerned with the creation of conditions conducive to sustainable economic and social development. Strengthening the linkages between economic development and human settlements policies can be expected to result in the improvement of both, enhancing their individual and combined contributions to the process of raising standards of living and the quality of life. Improved integration would also help overcome some of the problems traditionally associated with resource allocation and budgetary procedures. The need for agencies to compete for scarce resources for their own programmes and projects would be reduced. Instead, there would be emphasis on participation in the overall process of national economic and social development.

7 Settlements Management

In the human settlements context, management means the whole complex of actions involved in planning, programming, budgeting, developing, operating, and maintaining a settlement. Since the provision of basic services not only improves living conditions but also enhances the capabilities of settlements to contribute to economic growth, attempts have been made at establishing linkages between settlement management and economic planning at national and local levels. For instance, employment generation is one of the objectives that many local governments recently have been including in their development plans: it is assumed that part of any additional family income will be spent to finance the upgrading and maintenance of settlement conditions at the individual and community level, thus adding to the settlement's facilities while relieving local government of some of its financial burdens. There is no universal model for settlement management: development strategies and institutional arrangements for and in human settlements will respond to specific political structures and to changing needs and opportunities. Management methods for settlements in developing countries should therefore be continuously adjusted to match capacities and constraints.

Planning as an element of management

Initially, planning focused only on the physical aspects of settlement development, indicating mainly desired land-use distributions and transport networks. This type of planning is known as indicative planning because although it could indicate the desired direction it lacked control over the factors contributing to change. Frequently, plans were drafted by teams based in the academic world or in planning agencies with no decision-making powers and with little or no influence over the forces that were building the settlement. Despite their technical sophistication, plans had few links to socio-economic reality, carried no provisions for public consultation, and provided no implementation tools.

Notwithstanding the fact that they did not live up to expectations, indicative plans have contributed to the understanding of the functioning of individual settlements, of the magnitude of their problems, and of their opportunities for development. In some cases, where land-use control has been effective, indicative planning has ensured some order in the physical growth of the settlement, and has sometimes been capable of containing undesirable change. However, the failure of plans to do what they could not do and were not designed to achieve—to provide a good quality of life for all in rapidly growing settlements—is one of the causes of a pronounced decline in the popularity of conventional settlement planning among policy-makers and practitioners.

While criticism of indicative planning continues, examples exist in many parts of the world of other planning devices which show promise of meeting real development needs. Where there is a will to manage settlement development, planning can organize not only the spatial configuration of a settlement but also its social, economic, and financial aspects. Innovative planning can achieve development objectives, improve living conditions, and efficiently deliver basic services.

Planning can thus also be seen as a management tool. It follows that whenever managing mechanisms are lacking or inadequate, they must be created or improved as part of the planning process. Despite the many generalized criticisms made regarding the failure of planning, it is an indispensable and powerful tool in the hands of those institutions that have clearly defined their development strategies and have a will to take the lead in the development process.

A settlement plan is no more and no less than a political decision backed by technical and legal solutions. Different approaches can be developed in accordance with the political system a society has adopted and in accordance with the

Box 7.1   Local planning as an instrument for government action: Cali, Colombia

Cali is one of the few cities which seems to have coped remarkably well with rapid population growth. Since the late 1970s, although the concentration of poverty appears to have increased and not even the informal housing market has enabled the lower third of the population to become houseowners, incomes have risen, absolute poverty has declined, nutrition has improved, the supply of housing has increased faster than population, and people have obtained access to public services, including water, sewage, power, and transport. While part of this was fortuitous, sound management policies also played a significant role. For instance, the expansion of employment opportunities achieved in Cali suggests that rapid growth does not necessarily imply high unemployment rates, given appropriate job-creation policies. Generally, public-sector action in Cali has proved that rapid urban growth can be managed.

The main lesson to be learned from the Cali experience is the value of local planning in a strategic perspective. There are historic reasons that account for Cali's relative success in urban management. In the early 1930s, local governments in Colombia were granted more powers than before. Subsequently, administrative institutions were reformed, public enterprises for specific services were created, and the notion of planning for development was strengthened. Administrative reform and legislative development became a semi-permanent process during this period, consolidating an already well-developed institutional structure. The first planning office was established in the early 1950s, and several important municipal service and utility companies were set up in the 1960s. However, up to the late 1960s, urban planning in Cali centred only on the physical aspects of development.

In 1979, a review of the general development plan and the restructuring of the municipal planning office within the framework of comprehensive administrative reform based on the National Law for Urban Reform, which established criteria for development planning in cities with over 200,000 inhabitants, initiated a new stage. The main reforms included:

● The establishment of the Municipal Development Policies Council (CONPAL) composed of the managers of all state corporations and decentralized organizations.

● The creation of a fiscal code through which budget becomes associated with programmes and projects.

● Reform of the system of taxation of industrial and commercial activities.

● Updating of the urbanization statute.

● Upgrading of the municipal planning office to a Department of Municipal Planning.

● Establishment of a social security corporation (SICALI) financed through a 5 per cent quota of industrial and commercial taxation.

● Creation of a public recreation corporation, with 70 per cent financial support from the private sector.

● Establishment of new urban-development and service-delivery institutions, including a mass transit organization (PROTRANS), a freight and motor-trucks terminal (CENCAO), a regional slaughterhouse, and a solid waste disposal/recycling agency.

During that same period, Colombia underwent a change in its centralized national planning system. As a result, the Valle del Cauca Department started developing an integrated regional development plan. A subregional planning system was developed through an agreement signed by the municipality of Cali, Valle Department, Emcali, and the Cauca Valle Commission (CVC). At the urban level, the Cali Urban and Metropolitan Comprehensive Development Plan (PIDECA) launched a development strategy based on the co-ordination of the public and private sectors and aimed at objectives of social equity and economic efficiency, taking advantage of the climate for 'national change' and of political support for the development process. This participative context ensured its legitimization and its acceptance within a mixed-economy and representative-democracy framework, and avoided conflicts in the implementation phase.

The public-participation mechanisms adopted by Cali are designed to support the technical organization of the planning system. Approximately 70 per cent of Cali neighbourhoods and 80 per cent of its subneighbourhood units have been in contact with the various levels of the local administration, which on the basis of such contacts has adopted technical solutions to fulfil the community's expressed needs and goals. The population at large, labour unions, and professional organizations participate in the assessment of problems and needs. Within the public sector, all levels of the administration have been integrated in the process of assessment, programming, and selection of urban development options.

Sources: Rakesh Mohan, 'The City Study: Understanding the Developing Metropolis', *Research News* (World Bank, Fall/Winter 1984); Jaime Ahumada, *El gobierno y la administracion local en la planification del desarrllo* (ILPES, October 1984).

---

planning objectives, policies, and strategies chosen—for example, the relative degree of participation of public and private sectors in the settlement development process. Approaches can range from the extreme alternatives of leaving settlement development to the free action of market forces, with the public sector only providing minimal support, to relying on the public sector as the sole development agent. Most countries follow intermediate approaches that may include different mixtures of the following options:

- Direct implementation of programmes.
- Regulation and control of private activities.
- Promotion and facilitation of private activities.
- Negotiation with the private sector.
- Partnership between the public and the private sector.

Radical extremes seldom occur and in most cases there are several agents of development acting with degrees of involvement in different fields of action. These agents of settlement development are mainly the public administration at the national, subnational, and local levels, the land-owners, the developers, the financial agents, the building sector, the productive forces, and the residents.

Planning should not only decide public-sector action but also guide private-sector participation, indicating the fields open to private initiative and encouraging actions that will contribute to the general welfare. At the same time, planning should restrict private-sector actions which may be detrimental to the community as a whole. Settlement management should ensure that developers get their fair share of profit for participating in the building process, but not at the expense of the future nor of the disadvantaged.

Programming and budgeting

For planning to achieve its full potential, it must be associated with programming and budgeting. The programming process involves all those

---

Box 7.2   Incremental approach to urban development in Indonesia

The *Kampung* Improvement Programme (KIP) was initiated in Jakarta at the municipal level in 1969. Subsequently, with assistance from the World Bank and other international agencies, it has spread to other Indonesian cities and towns. KIP has emerged as an effective strategy because of the government's awareness that it could not meet human settlements needs through the centralized construction of modern flats and houses, and that urban renewal would have incurred impossibly high costs. In addition, the loss of huge amounts of housing stock was perceived as counter to the aim of improving human settlements.

Community participation, from the preparatory and planning stages through to implementation and maintenance, has been the fundamental strategy to ensure the optimum flow of benefits from the scarce funding available. At the community level, programming and implementation are carried out through existing governmental structures and community organizations. Community organizations are used as channels for community programme activities, and particularly for the selection and implementation of projects funded by direct grants.

Kampung residents are also trained and encouraged to participate in the operation and maintenance of the infrastructure and facilities constructed during the improvement programme. For certain maintenance works the participation can be individual, but for others the whole community has to be involved. Individual tasks include the clearing of drains and cutting of grass adjacent to building lots. Community projects—such activities as cleaning open spaces, playgrounds, and public baths and toilets—can be done by the residents themselves or by labour that they pay for.

Thus, through a state–community partnership, KIP has progressively upgraded the living conditions of a large urban population. From the standpoint of scale, number of beneficiaries, and number of towns and cities affected, KIP is one of the world's outstanding slum-improvement programmes.

This experience has guided the adoption of an incremental approach to urban physical development in the recently approved UNCHS/UNDP National Urban Development Strategy Project undertaken by the government of Indonesia. The general principle is that initial service provision should be given at minimum standards which can be improved incrementally by or with the participation of the residents in accordance with increases in density. The role of the government is seen as one of providing encouragement and the minimum basis for community action. Different approaches have been recommended for the different areas: a guided land-development approach for new urban fringe areas; a low-standard guided development approach for low-density *kampung* areas; and the traditional KIP approach for high-density *kampungs*. The same principles have also been recommended for inner-city urban renewal projects which should be almost completely financed by the private sector.

Source: Indonesia Directorate of City and Regional Planning, Indonesia Directorate General of Human Settlements, United Nations Development Programme (UNDP), United Nations Centre for Human Settlements (Habitat), Indonesia National Urban Development Strategy (NUDS) Final Report (September 1985).

Box 7.3   Public- and private-sector partnership in settlements management

Individuals, organizations, and community groups with different resources and needs all have a role to play in the urban development process. In this connection, an interesting approach is one of partnership between public authorities and communities for the provision of services. Under such an arrangement, the public sector will ensure the functioning of the city as a whole, and the community will ensure the provision of services at the household level. This kind of enterprise cannot be undertaken in partnership with a sectoral administration at national level, so that it emphasizes the importance of decentralizing and strengthening local administration.

In many countries, the participation of the private sector is sought not only in physical development activities but also in the provision of basic services, such as transport, communications, solid-waste collection and recycling, and provision of various utilities. This approach may present advantages as long as satisfactory quality levels are ensured, and provided that services are made available at affordable prices. However, in order to derive benefits from private-sector participation in the delivery of basic services, the public sector must be able to maintain its role in establishing quality standards and enforcing them.

Detailed assessments should be made of the performance and capabilities of the public sector in providing the same services at comparable quality and costs, and careful assessment needs to be made as to where the margins of competitiveness of the private sector lie. Often, reductions in service costs are made at the expense of employee wage levels. Similarly, high efficiency of the private sectors in providing a specific service is often found in the most lucrative sectors, while the unattractive ones requiring subsidies are left to the public sector.

The participation of the private sector in the provision of basic services can take very different forms: among them are direct private initiatives, concessions, subcontracts, and mixed enterprises. In some cases, the private sector may be granted the exploitation of a public natural resource, as long as such resource is upgraded and reverts to public use in due time. There have also been successful cases where the private sector has been granted the right to process and recycle urban solid waste, as long as collection was undertaken.

The argument that is most frequently used to favour the private sector over the public sector in physical development or in the provision of basic services is that what impedes efficiency in the public sector is the high level of corruption. The private sector can indeed control illegal practices at the intermediate levels, but the search for profits at top managerial and ownership levels can be equally harming, and in fact is often the prime cause of malpractice on the part of public officials. Probably the best way of avoiding corrupt practices on the part of local government officials is to make managers accountable to the public in one form or other.

interventions, public or private, that need to be undertaken in order to implement settlement plans. These interventions include the acquisition and preparation of land, the provision of basic services, and the construction and maintenance of buildings and infrastructure. The programme not only identifies each action and quantifies its costs but also establishes priorities and sequences to ensure the optimization of the implementation process. Feasibility of implementation should be assessed according to the investment capabilities of all the agents involved in the process.

Programmes should provide the frame of reference for the budgeting of all branches of the administration involved directly or indirectly in settlement development. Similarly, programming should include all projects to be undertaken by the private sector as a result of negotiations with the public administration. The inclusion of private-sector development in the programming process is often not easy, mainly because it requires high levels of communication between public and private sectors, but it is essential if there is to be coherence in the settlement development process.

Operation and maintenance

In a period of economic constraints, the rational utilization of what already exists in the built environment of human settlements deserves much more attention than it has received in the past. The development of approaches to the operation, maintenance, and rehabilitation of housing and infrastructure is a difficult task which requires political commitment on the part of national and local governments. Too often, massive investments in infrastructures and structures have been largely nullified by failure to operate the installations properly and by lack of measures to keep them in good condition and maximize their working life. Both working maintenance, to ensure peak efficiency of operation, and rehabilitation of obsolescent installations, at the point where their useful life can be economically extended, are needed. It is regrettably common to see decisions deferred to the point where rehabilitation ceases to be a viable option, so that agencies are then forced into high expenditures for total replacement which could have been avoided.

Building deterioration has reached alarming proportions in the inner-city areas of many developed and developing countries. In the process, valuable assets are lost, making the housing shortage even more serious than it need be. The poor management of water-supply systems causes excessive losses of water and energy, thus depleting water resources and increasing costs to authorities. Neglect in the maintenance of sanitation and solid-waste collection systems creates health hazards and increases pollution. In many countries, the existing road networks are deteriorating faster than they are being expanded. The effective capacity of urban roads is reduced by inefficient traffic management, so that congestion occurs even in countries with relatively low car-ownership ratios. In some countries, owing to poor servicing and maintenance, more than half of the public-transport vehicles are often immobilized, and their inefficient operation further reduces the capacity offered to users. Recreational and other common areas go unattended and degenerate into unsightly places.

Many operational, maintenance, and user difficulties are caused by inappropriate design of buildings and services, which have largely followed Western models and do not take into account users' habits. Frequently, cheapest first-cost solutions are chosen even though they may require disproportionately greater future expenditures. The adoption of sophisticated technologies involving imported components may create operational and maintenance problems owing to shortage of maintenance equipment, spare parts, and skilled personnel, and to lack of understanding among users.

Community participation is probably one of the most promising lines of approach for hard-pressed administrations faced with growing maintenance demands. There should therefore be educational and training programmes to give people a basic understanding of how to use and maintain buildings and services. For instance, co-operation among all users is necessary for the effective operation of water-supply and sanitation systems. There is also a great potential for direct community participation through labour in rehabilitation and repair works, with resulting

employment, income generation, and enhancement of skills.

For developing countries, the importance of rehabilitation and maintenance cannot be overstressed. First of all, the cost of rehabilitating existing housing stock and infrastructure is considerably less than the cost of constructing new buildings and infrastructure, even though deci-

---

Box 7.4　Training for human settlements development in Sri Lanka

The primary emphasis of the DANIDA/UNCHS* Training Programme is on training the professional staff members of local governments and housing agencies in the formulation and implementation of community participation strategies. Once trained, the staff members are expected to become facilitators of community action at the grass-roots level.

As a rule, DANIDA/UNCHS training programmes are held 'on location' in settlement projects. This makes it possible to adapt the training to the actual needs of the professional staff members involved in the projects and to obtain feedback from the communities. In addition, the Training Programme for Community Participation aims to facilitate exchange of experiences of community participation in low-income housing projects both through training courses and through the dissemination of information.

In Sri Lanka, community participation already plays an important role in the improvement of slums and shanty settlements in Colombo. Community development councils (CDCs) have been established in many shanty towns, but there are no guidelines for professional staff of central agencies and local authorities on how to work with them. The National Housing Development Authority (NHDA)—the agency responsible for implementation of the Rural and Urban Housing Subprogrammes of the Million Houses Programme—therefore asked the Training Programme to develop models for community action to improve housing conditions in urban areas, to test these models by training community leaders, in particular in demonstration-project areas, to develop training material for community leader workshops, and to train NHDA staff to extend these models to community leaders in other areas on a large scale.

The Training Programme subsequently implented in Sri Lanka focused on two aspects of community participation:

- The construction of infrastructure by the community.
- The maintenance of infrastructure by the community.

Community construction of infrastructure

The National Housing Development Authority implements two types of low-income housing projects in urban areas:

sion-makers tend to give priority to new construction. Secondly, loss of valuable housing for low-income groups can be prevented, costly relocations reduced, and disruption of social fabric minimized. Large-scale demolition in inner-city areas should be avoided, this type of intervention being confined to individual buildings beyond repair. Existing building regulations, codes, and standards should be reviewed and modified to ensure their appropriateness for promoting rehabilitation, particularly rehabilitation to suit cost levels acceptable to different income groups. Thirdly, effective operation and maintenance of existing settlement plant is a prerequisite for the efficient use of public and private resources. Thus, although programmes

---

Box 7.4 continued

slum and squatter settlement upgrading projects, and sites-and-services schemes. In both, the provision of infrastructure (roads, drains, water supply, communal or individual toilets, communal bathrooms) is an important component. Experience shows that when commercial contractors are involved in this, the tender procedure tends to be rather time-consuming, the quality of the work is often poor, and the community does not feel any responsibility to supervise the work or to look after the maintenance of the infrastructure once it has been completed, as it has not been actively involved in the preparation of the project.

In collaboration with the Urban Housing Division of the NHDA, the Training Programme has developed a procedure for the construction of infrastructure by the community. The basic idea is to give the contract for the work to the area CDC instead of to a commercial contractor. NHDA staff members give the CDC all necessary technical assistance, and the CDC can keep the profit for the community development fund. The procedure was developed in three workshops for community leaders organized in the two IYSH demonstration project areas—Wanathamulla and Navagamgoda.

In the Wanathamulla project, NHDA worked closely with the Save the Children Federation, which also assisted in the construction of a bathing well as a first example of community construction of infrastructure. In Navagamgoda, residents were already involved in the construction of drains through an official agreement between the NHDA and the CDC of that area.

On the basis of these experiences, a manual was printed which describes the procedure and contains sample forms to be used by the community and the NHDA, and is to form part of the training material for community leader workshops. Posters explaining the procedure have been designed and tested in workshops, and can now be used by NHDA staff members in conduct training courses for community leaders. A training film on the construction of infrastructure by the community has also been prepared. The Training Programme will train the staff of the Urban Housing Division to conduct workshops for community leaders on this subject. Such workshops will become an integral part of the implementation of projects where the community constructs infrastructure.

Community maintenance of infrastructure

Until now, the maintenance and repair of infrastructure have always been considered the task of local authorities. However, this has often meant that maintenance has been carried out at long and irregular intervals. Moreover, the cost of such maintenance and repair operations is rather high. NHDA has therefore decided to give the responsibility to the community and to individual households.

In order to be able to look after the maintenance and repair of amenities, the community must know how to utilize the infrastructure provided, how to maintain it, how to carry out small repairs, and whom to contact if large repairs are necessary. These are the basic contents of the workshops for community leaders on infrastructure maintenance. Posters have been prepared, illustrating the technical requirements for the maintenance of infrastructure, and the parties involved in utilization and maintenance—the individual household, the user unit (all the households sharing one amenity), the community, and the local authorities. During the workshops, technical requirements are explained to the community leaders, who are then asked to formulate a proposal defining the maintenance responsibilities for each of the parties. Maintenance tasks are also illustrated in two posters for distribution in the project areas: one poster for the individual household, and one for the maintenance operator. The maintenance operator is designated by the CDC (which has to decide whether to pay him or not) to look after the common amenities in the area and to carry out small repairs. In the maintenance workshops, as well as in other community leader workshops, leaders from areas with successful community activities are being invited and trained as trainers. In this way, a pool of community leaders/trainers will be created for the community leader training programme, in addition to the pool of NHDA staff/trainers.

*Danish International Development Agency/United Nations Centre for Human Settlements (Habitat).

for intensified rehabilitation and improved operation are difficult to implement, they are cost-effective in the long run and should be given high priority.

A change in government's policy orientation is needed. Emphasis at the national and local level should be shifted from a capital-investment bias to a balanced approach in which a significant part of resources is allocated to optimizing use of existing assets through permanent maintenance and rehabilitation. Governments should stimulate the development of rehabilitation techniques in the construction industry and improve supplies of materials and components. Similarly, training for community participation in maintenance should be made available. New approaches to financing systems are needed for rehabilitation projects, which should as far as possible be based on the principles of cost recovery in order to eliminate misuse of scarce resources. Donors and international agencies should direct their assistance programmes towards an emphasis on the effective use of existing capital stock in human settlements. Furthermore, it is crucial that maintenance be carried out on a continuing basis—as preventive maintenance—rather than as a crisis response to repair breakdowns.

Community participation

Developing countries differ in the degree and quality of public participation in their settlement management process. The best way for any administration to prove that it represents the interests of those that it administers is to establish the necessary mechanisms to allow and encourage participation, and to adopt a well-designed system of communication and information so as to make the development process easily understandable. Public participation should be instituted as a permanent feature of the management process, supported by the necessary legal framework, and integrated in the management structure.

Only participatory management can guarantee the success of plans, in terms of ensuring that the goals and strategies adopted respond to the needs and aims of the population and receive adequate community support. Only through

---

Box 7.5 Public-sector management: democracy and pragmatism in Botswana

The vast, pastoral country of Botswana has experienced one of the fastest rates of urbanization in the world. Before independence in 1966, Botswana had only two small towns and a number of large villages. Since then, the old towns have grown rapidly, a capital city has been founded, and two other towns have been established near mining developments in the north of the country.

The stated objectives of Botswana's development policy are rapid economic growth, economic independence, sustained development, and social justice. Considerable achievements have been made in terms of economic growth as Botswana moved quickly from a traditional economy based on cattle rearing to a dualistic one led by a small but vigorous modern sector. However, the impressive quantitative and qualitative gains of economic growth have not fundamentally changed the life of most of the rural population.

Public-sector management in Botswana must be examined in the light of two fundamental qualities that characterize the political process in the country: democracy and pragmatism. The nature of governmental procedures and practice in Botswana not only allows a dialogue on policy-making but also ensures a remarkable degree of bureaucratic accountability to Parliament. Botswana's system of public management is rightly considered one of the most successful in Africa, if success is measured by the capacity of a system to formulate and implement strategies and programmes for economic and social development.

While still a developing country, Botswana stands out in many respects—it has a functioning democratic system, the lines of authority are defined, civil servants are accountable to Parliament, control over financial management is enforced, plans and planning are linked to budgetary control, technical assistance is utilized effectively, parastatals

---

such identification can the mobilization of all the necessary human resources and creative energy to undertake development tasks be ensured. Participatory management not only mobilizes the general public but also contributes to mobilizing the political, technical, and administrative actors directly involved.

There are several stages in which public participation constitutes a positive contribution to the settlement management process. Different stages of the development process will incorporate different degrees of public participation, but the most common stages are the following:

• *Participation in planning*—in the definition of objectives, strategies, and priorities.

are managed on commercial principles, and by and large there is order, logic, efficiency, and probity in the conduct of governmental business. Botswana's practice of open discussion and of interaction between professional analysts, senior civil servants, and politicians is an essential component in understanding the nature of development planning in Botswana. The consultation process is not limited to central government: it starts at the village level (the *kgotla* meeting and the village development committees) and is also present at the district level (district councils and district development committees), and substantial efforts are made to ensure that the consultation process is integrated from the village through district to central government and back again. There is a dialogue at all levels with regard to the plan and the budget until agreement is reached on realistic levels of expenditures. Policies contained in the plan are not immutable, although modification of the plan or substantial alteration in one of its projects has to be fully discussed and justified.

At the local level, there are three types of authorities: the tribal administration, the land boards, and the town and district councils. All of them play an important role in providing service, executing statutory functions, and—especially in the case of the councils—assisting in the formulation of public policy. They are considerably more healthy than the local authorities in most other African countries. Yet, despite this reasonable record compared with other African states, all three types of local authority are far from healthy. They are still poorly staffed, under-financed, and barely able to carry out their statutory functions without considerable assistance from central government agencies. Efficiency in public-sector delivery has yet to descend to the local level, even though the structures to allow it have been established.

• *Participation in programming and budgeting*—guaranteeing the effective employment of resources to fulfil objectives.

• *Participation in implementation*—creating responsibility for maintenance and management.

• *Participation in operational activities*—securing more cost-effective and efficient maintenance and management.

Human-resource inputs

Human resources are generally the most abundantly available resource in developing countries. However, there is a strong need for improving capabilities and adapting skills to the needs that settlement development strategies require. Moreover, the best trained and most efficient personnel are normally concentrated in central government positions, and often only minimally qualified officers are assigned to local governments, especially in peripheral areas. Government recognition of training as a strategy to increase the supply of efficient personnel is crucial.

The complex issues involved in human settlements development call for a wide spectrum of training programmes, ranging from the development of managerial and technical skills to the strengthening of community organization and participation. Such programmes, however, in order to be effective, have to be practically oriented and specially designed to meet the needs of specific urban policies. Moreover, the final objective of training programmes should not be just the creation of large numbers of trained individuals but the creation of institutions capable of formulating and executing human settlements policies and programmes. Unfortunately, the tendency has been to focus on the problems of human settlements development from the standpoint of professional planners, financial managers, and civil engineers. Simple operational and maintenance needs of basic services seem to have been neglected, in spite of the fact that the training of service personnel can have a direct impact on the quality of life of a great number of low-income urban and rural residents.

An important part of the improvement of human resources for management is the improvement of the public's knowledge of the functioning of the administration, of the rights and opportunities of participating in and benefiting from the development process, and of rights and obligations as voters, taxpayers, and consumers of services provided by the managing authority. This also requires special training and mobilization, as does the development of building skills for self-help schemes.

Not all developing countries have the necessary resources for training their public officials. There is a widespread lack both of experienced trainers and of suitable training materials. Overseas training is expensive, caters for relatively few, and is in the majority of cases irrelevant to local development needs. The best way to channel international assistance in this field is not through provision of direct training programmes but through improvement of indigenous training capabilities. Special care must be taken to adapt programmes to local needs, specific cultural characteristics, and the development strategies and management options chosen. Moreover, even though development aid may be of significance as a contribution, training responsibilities should lie mainly within the developing countries themselves.

Another important issue related to urban management personnel is that of the incentives needed to attract and keep managers in public service. Depending on the type of society and the category of the public officer, incentives can vary from political, social, or professional motivation, through remunerations and other compensations, to career development and promotion opportunities. Most often, it is the remuneration level that acts as the primary incentive, and local government salaries should be harmonized with those of central government and the private sector. Also, increased responsibilities and social status should go hand in hand with improved salaries. Theoretically, this should not imply additional costs to the public administration since costs should be recovered through increased efficiency in service delivery and revenue collection.

The distribution of management responsibilities: decentralization

Settlement management is undertaken at different administrative levels: national, subnational, municipal, and, sometimes, submunicipal. Depending on the existing administrative structures and on the development options that a country may have adopted, responsibilities will be distributed differently among these administrative levels. In most countries, there will be some strategic development sectors that require central planning and management, while other sectors may only require central guidance or technical support but can otherwise be approached at the local level. Most of the sectors related to the improvement of local living conditions and to the management of the environ-

ment, even though they may follow national guidelines, are best managed at the local level. In general terms, development management should be decentralized to the level of most efficient service delivery, project implementation, and community involvement, both in terms of participation in the decision-making process and in terms of control of the development process.

Nevertheless, local management of decentralized development should be seen in a broad framework of national development strategies for the benefit of the country as a whole. Therefore, local development objectives and policies ought to be co-ordinated with those of higher levels of government. For this to be effective, central governments should maintain some monitoring of local plans and local management performance, while at the same time taking care that controls do not slow or otherwise hinder local development.

Often, decentralization measures are simply the transfer to local government of some functions previously performed by central government. Almost invariably, the most difficult form of decentralization to achieve is the transfer of the financial and human resources needed to undertake such new responsibilities. The simultaneous decentralization of responsibilities, decision-making powers, and resources is essential to efficient development management, and local authorities must convince central governments of the need to act coherently in the decentralization process. On the other hand, local authorities in metropolitan areas or in large cities must understand that, because of the scale involved, decentralization processes should continue to flow downwards to district and/or neighbourhood levels.

Most often, neither the institutions nor the legal capabilities to put the distribution of responsibilities into effect are adequate. In such cases, an initial phase of administrative reform or the creation of new and complementary administrative and legal structures may be needed in order to acquire missing capabilities. Another essential factor to the success of decentralized development management is the decentralization of the political process: local authorities are most effective when they represent local aspirations and when the local

Box 7.6   Central support for effective decentralization in Venezuala

In Latin America, local authorities have been enormously strengthened in recent decades by quasi-autonomous municipal developing institutions (MDIs) set up with central government funds, often supplemented by financial or technical support from multilateral or bilateral aid agencies. MDIs provide stable and efficient mechanisms through which national and international institutions can confidently channel funds for the development of municipal infrastructure. By developing their own expertise and often their own training and technical advisory facilities, municipal development institutions have helped to transform previously moribund local authorities into dynamic vehicles of change.

One of the best examples of MDIs is the Foundation for Community Development and Municipal Improvement (Fundacion para el Dessarrollo de la Comunidad y Fomento Municipal, FUNDACOMUN) created as a development and co-ordinating agency to give technical and financial assistance to local governments and low-income urban settlements. Its current activities are developed within the context of the sixth National Plan and Joint Social Programmes. In the area of social development, the main objectives of FUNDACOMUN are the improvement of living conditions in low-income communities and promotion of community organization in order to enhance participation in the process of local development.

The administrative mechanism and implementation instrument through which projects are implemented —'comprehensive planning'—has three basic aspects:

- *Interinstitutional co-ordination* based on a consistent and concerted multisectoral effort to solve the problems of depressed low-income urban settlements.

- *Direct community participation* in assessment, planning, and implementation.

- *Practical projects* supported by financial and technical assistance from public and/or private organizations.

In the area of social development, the comprehensive plan is the administrative mechanism of the joint social programme which addresses all the factors related to marginal areas. These include infrastructure, adequate housing, training, education, culture, and participation in the benefits of the production process. Its programmes include:

- *The establishment of community facilities* which serve as centres for social integration and intergovernmental co-ordination, for the delivery of basic services, such as health, education, nutrition, security, and recreation.

- *Programmes for progressive habitat improvement* which include planned layout for the development of low-income areas, basic infrastructure provided by the public sector, and improvement of the area through community effort.

- *Low-income credit programmes* for upgrading dwellings. Financing is provided jointly by FUNDACOMUN and by the National Housing Institute (Instituto Nacional de la Vivienda—INAVI). Loans are available only for families in the poor urban *barrios* in settlements designated by the integral plans and in accordance with the priorities established by the community of each *barrio*.

In the area of municipal development, the purpose is to improve local government efficiency. Technical and financial assistance to local governments is given by FUNDACOMUN by means of agreements in a variety of areas, including administrative reforms, budgeting, public services, legal assistance, urban planning, land registration, community development, training, and employment generation. Special consideration is given to improving city management and public services in small and medium-size cities.

In the area of training and human-resource development, the need to implement programmes to complement actions in the municipal and community development areas encouraged FUNDACOMUN to create, within its own structure, the Centre for Studies in Local Development and Municipal Management (Centro de Estudios de Desarrollo Local y Administracion Municipal—CEDLAM). CEDLAM has already trained thousands of municipal employees at managerial, technical, administrative, and service levels, as well as community organizers. In the area of information, FUNDACOMUN has created the Centre for Documentation and Information on Marginality and Municipal Development (Centro de Documentacion e Informacion Sobre Areas Marginales y Municipalismo, CEDISAM), a permanent service of production, dissemination, and exchange of information, which understands information to be an instrument for development. In the area of international co-operation, FUNDACOMUN participates in technical assistance, training, research, and information exchange with the International Union of Local Authorities (IULA), the Brazilian Institute of Municipal Administration (IBAM), and the Spanish Institute for Studies on Local Administration (IEAL).

Sources: Allen, Hubert J. B., 'Enhancing decentralization for *development*', 27th Congress of the International Union of Local Authorities (Rio de Janeiro, Brazil, 1985).

Fundacomun, Que es y que hace FUNDACOMUN? (Caracas, Venezuela, n.d.).

Illarmendi, A. 'Integral Plan: An Experience with Public Participation and Housing in Venezuela', in Thomas L. Brair, ed. *Strengthening Urban Management* (Plenum Press, 1985).

Lordello de Mello, Diego, 'Modernizacion de los gobiernos locales en America Latina', *Revista interamericana de planificacion* (SIAP, June 1983).

Box 7.7   Improving the effectiveness of development assistance to human settlements: the World Bank experience

There is increasing awareness of the need for co-ordinated decentralization of all phases of development management, even when development is supported by external official aid. Recently, several agencies have issued statements to the effect that in order for aid to urban development to become effective, it is necessary to negotiate not only with the central government, which will be responsible financially, but also with the local governments that will be involved in the implementation of the projects. Additionally, there is a growing interest in urban management enhancement as a way to increase city authorities' capacity to implement multisectoral or city-wide programmes and improve cost recovery, tax collection, and maintenance of infrastructure. The World Bank, among others, has stressed the need to identify ways of improving the effectiveness of urban assistance in contributing to strengthening urban management and building up municipal institutions that will be self-sufficient and able to guide future uses of development assistance.

The first generation of World Bank-financed urban projects was targeted, almost without exception, to low-income people who were designated as the direct beneficiaries of project improvements in housing, transport, and urban services. However, it was clear that Bank-supported urban investment, based on a project-by-project, site-by-site approach, was only a small portion of the investment needed to meet urban deficits. As perceived by the Bank, the long-term impact of its work involved the ability to leave behind changed policies in governmental agencies that would enable them to multiply low-cost housing and infrastructure projects without outside help.

An early problem detected by the Bank was that the projects tended to ignore existing municipal structures while depending for implementation on investment agencies interested in low-income programmes rather than in wider problems of urban administration. As a consequence, the implementing agencies were rarely in a position to ensure that new policies would be continued by national and municipal governments. Once the project was completed, the municipal administration was left with the task, which it seldom fulfilled, of operating and maintaining the new services.

Urban population growth coupled with the physical expansion of cities reinforced thinking that external assistance to the urban sector should address the question of strengthening local institutional capacity. External resources would never be sufficient to meet local needs, but a necessary condition for efficient urban growth was improved local capacity to plan and finance urban development. In fact, the new approach necessarily broadens the benefits to a larger group than the very poor.

The focus of Bank-supported projects thus began to shift from delivering services at a project site to supporting an implementing agency's ability to deliver services city-wide. Several 'integrated projects', such as three projects in Calcutta, India, involved the delivery of a variety of urban-service components, and were intended explicitly to develop a city-wide institutional framework capable of co-ordinating complex urban tasks crossing administrative and jurisdictional lines. Recently, the Bank's new focus on urban management has been strengthened by increased attention to the fundamental role of cities in the economic performance of developing countries.

In December 1985, the World Bank held a Conference on 'Improving the Effectiveness of Urban Assistance: Lessons from the Past'. Together with the representatives of 15 bilateral and multilateral donors, delegates from more than 40 developing countries looked back on the past decade of urban development experience in the developing countries and evaluated urbanization trends, priorities for urban assistance programmes, and strategies to address future urban needs in developing countries. The Conference's main conclusions were as follows:

- As urban productivity is an integral part of economic growth, improved efficiency of cities is critical not only to national but global economic growth.

- Urbanization is not only inevitable but in fact desirable, provided that people are productively absorbed in cities.

- Resource needs for urban investment are critical, but mobilization will have to be principally a local responsibility; attention must therefore be focused on municipal institutions and management.

- Urban assistance must address not only the problems of neighbourhoods but the ability of the city to manage the process of its growth.

Sources: World Bank, *Urban Edge* (Washington DC, March 1985, Nov. 1985, Feb. 1986); World Bank, *Improving the Effectiveness of Urban Assistance* conference documents (Washington DC, Dec. 1985).

---

communities that have participated in the process of setting them in their position of power hold them accountable for their actions.

Conclusions

Efficient settlements do not only mean improved living conditions within the settlements themselves: they are also crucial to achieving national development goals. Efficiency can only be reached through the integration of physical planning and resource management in a continuous process. Crucial elements in this process include:

• Relating planning to the factors that contribute to settlement change.

• Political support and commitment.

• Rationalization of relationships between local government and other levels of public administration.

• Legal and institutional support consonant with development objectives and strategies.

• Finding new financial resources and improving financial control.

• Improving the level and performance of managers, and creating incentives to keep them in public service.

• Democratizing the management process.

• An effective land policy to determine the rights and obligations of landowners and developers and to provide the mechanisms to make land available to the public sector.

However, probably, the most important factor is the identification of the public sector with the aims and aspirations of the people. If local government could establish itself as a direct advocate for the people, its powers would be irresistible and it would be in a position to make enormous contributions to national development.

8 Settlements Institutions

Institutional structures

To be effective, human settlements policies and plans must be rooted in an appropriate institutional structure, embodying political, administrative, and technical instruments and arrangements. Without enabling legislation, rules, and regulations, and without adequate administrative procedures, settlements policies and programmes can be neither formulated nor implemented. The institutional arrangements adopted by nations to meet human settlement challenges inevitably display great diversity.[1] The variations result from the way in which challenges and problems are perceived and defined, and from the process through which institutions and decision-making arrangements have evolved.

The diversity in responses and experience makes it difficult to isolate and generalize characteristics, and suggests that there can be little scope for deterministic blueprints for institutional design. Some countries, such as Costa Rica, Mexico, and the Philippines, have chosen to emphasize a comprehensive approach, establishing Ministries for Human Settlements in the process. Other countries, such as Kenya and Sri Lanka, have chosen to define settlement problems mainly in terms of the need to provide affordable shelter and have tailored their institutional response to meet this narrow focus. Countries like The Gambia and Guinea have concentrated on strengthening their institutions for settlement development. In each case, the institutional framework adopted has necessarily reflected the specific set of settlement problems confronting the individual nation.

Brazil and Mexico, for example, are characterized by profound subnational inequalities, and attempts to reduce them have figured prominently in their human settlements policies. Such policies have been comprehensive in scope, but the past decade has revealed that the search for comprehensive approaches does not always result in effective settlements programmes and plans. While the complexity and trans-sectoral nature of human settlements problems have to be recognized, it must also be admitted that comprehensive approaches add to the difficulties of horizontal and vertical co-ordination.

The experience of Mexico and the Philippines, where stress has been placed on the development of a unitary approach, serves to show that the creation of 'super' settlement institutions may lead to the solution of perceived settlement problems, but may also create new ones. 'Bigger' does not necessarily mean 'better' in the important area of co-ordination: 'bigger' only becomes

---

Box 8.1 The Gambia and Guinea: strengthening settlements institutions

As many other developing countries, The Gambia and Guinea are confronted by the problems associated with rapid urban growth and the need to develop the skills and institutional capabilities to manage urban development. Both countries have recently embarked on IDA-supported projects to strengthen settlement planning institutions.

In The Gambia, the emphasis is on developing the basic skills required for formulating and implementing settlement policies and plans—skills that are in short supply in a country with a total population of around 600,000. The emphasis on skills development has meant that considerable attention will be given to training. This will cover land and property valuation, accounting and finance, land management, physical planning, architecture, and draughtsmanship. Whenever possible, training in these areas, if it cannot be given in The Gambia, will take place in other African countries.

In Guinea, the focus is on strengthening the institutions responsible for planning and administering urban development in Conakry, the nation's capital, the rapid growth of which—from 100,000 in 1958 to 700,000 in 1983—has been largely unplanned. The centrepiece is the creation of an Urban Planning Unit in the Ministry of Construction and Housing, with training and technical assistance geared to the development of capacities to identify, design, evaluate, and implement investment projects. A mechanism will also be established for funding urban services in Conakry from local revenues and for improving and maintaining the city's physical infrastructure.

'better' in an institutional structure where there are hierarchically superior organizations with powers and a mandate respected by other organizations. National settlement institutions may be superior in theory but not necessarily in practice.

Comprehensive approaches can also be frustrated by the policies and predilections of large enterprises that often enjoy special privileges and may have a history that has afforded them a powerful position in a national decision-making structure. In Mexico, for example, the national oil company, responsible for generating a substantial portion of the country's foreign-exchange earnings, is sufficiently powerful to decide its own investment priorities and to implement them, even when they conflict with the nation's human settlements policy. Similarly, in Brazil, the National Housing Bank, the oldest and most important housing-finance institution in the country, does not participate directly in efforts to improve co-ordination and develop integrated approaches to human settlements development.

Of course, problems of co-ordination are not limited to comprehensive settlement approaches. They can also exist when settlement problems are defined in narrow, sectoral terms. The proliferation of agencies with responsibilities for housing in Kenya, for example, has not been accompanied by clear delimitation of agency responsibilities and rationality in resource-allocation procedures. Agencies are expected to co-operate, but the mechanisms that are required to bring such co-operation about have yet to be devised.

It is also clear that institutional arrangements for settlement planning, whether comprehensive or sectoral, can only be effective when they provide access to financial resources. As pointed out in the previous chapter, resources are often controlled at the national level, where allocation priorities are decided, but are usually in greatest demand at the local level, where revenue-generation potential is often weak. Relationships between central government and local authorities in many countries are often far from harmonious, with central governments reluctant to relinquish control of allocation procedures and often critical of financial and administrative machinery at the local level, and local authorities

resentful of their dependent position and often taking the view that they are unable to improve financial and administrative management without support from the central government.

The dependent position of local authorities and project-implementing agencies makes them particularly vulnerable to shifts in the allocation priorities of central government. This vulnerability has been amply demonstrated by the decisions of many governments, in both developed and developing countries, to reduce public expenditure, in the interest of balanced budgets, and to redirect investment priorities to sectors in which they believe returns will be high and immediate. Governmental support for human settlements development has accordingly declined, and this has eroded the capacities of human settlements institutions. Given the procedures through which funds are generated and disbursed, the erosion of institutions has been particularly evident at the local level, and this situation will prevail until such time as governments become convinced of the economic value of investment in human settlements, and, no less important, local authorities are given autonomy in resource mobilization.

There is a trend in institutional arrangements to the decentralization of decision-making responsibilities in the field of human settlements, a trend in evidence in both developed and developing countries. Decentralization can take and has taken different forms and may be motivated by political factors as well as by considerations of efficiency. Some of the main types of decentralization have included 'constitutional' decentralization, in which powers are transferred to local political groups, 'regional' decentralization, with powers transferred to area-based institutions, and 'sectoral decentralization', with powers transferred to programme- and project-implementing agencies.

'Constitutional' decentralization suggests a formal involvement by local authorities in plan preparation and resource allocation, while 'regional' decentralization involves a top-down approach whereby regional branches of central government departments or *ad hoc* area-based agencies, such as urban development corporations, are set up to handle human settlements programmes at the subnational level. The area-

Box 8.2   Mexico: institutional decentralization

Key issues of human settlements planning in Mexico are the population growth rate, rural–urban migration, and concentration of migration in the three metropolitan areas of Mexico City, Guadalajara, and Monterrey. Outside these areas of concentration, much of the rest of the population is highly dispersed in very small communities. The oil price rise of 1973 transformed economic development and industrial location prospects in Mexico, and four industrial ports (Coatzacoalcos, Ciudad Madero, Salina Cruz, and Lazaro Cardenas) were designated as growth centres. Decentralization by concentration was the essence of the strategy formulated in the National Urban Development Plan (PNDU). Human settlements problems of low-income housing, urban land supply, environmental conditions, and so on, could, it was maintained, be ameliorated because new economic activities provided an opportunity to achieve large-scale shifts in the distribution of population.

The Ministry of Budgeting and Programming (SSP) is intended to exercise a key co-ordinating function, particularly in respect of the economic and financial aspects of government programmes. Up to 1982, the Ministry of Human Settlements (SAHOP) was the principal human settlements executing agency, composed of three divisions: human settlements, road construction, and urban services (and was thus a classic combination of old-established public works activities with a new-born interest in human settlements planning). With the change of government in Mexico in 1982, SAHOP was dissolved and replaced by the Ministry of Urban Development and Ecology, which will exercise many of the functions and responsibilities of SAHOP.

Many decentralized institutions are also involved in human settlements, as for example the Urban Development Corporation for Lazaro Cardenas, the Department of the Federal District, the Institute for National Workers' Housing Fund (INFONAVIT), and the National Institute for Community Development and Popular Housing (INDECO).

The starting point of a human settlements policy in Mexico was the PNDU, and this was co-ordinated by a National Commission for Urban Development in the Office of the Presidency. However, this overall framework for the spatial organization of the national development policy now rests in what is, in effect, only one of three divisions in one of the many ministries which administer governmental expenditures. Difficulties have arisen in implementing the national policy, partly because central vested interests have been against what is essentially a decentralizing strategy, but also because the institution charged with enforcing the plan needed either direct control over the assignment of public expenditure or the administrative authority to impose its criteria on other bodies. The human settlements division of SAHOP has neither.

Incorporating the spatial dimension in the sectoral assignment of governmental resources has not been effective because (*a*) the department of regional programming within the SPP had not developed a system for calculating regional priorities by the time the original distribution of resources within the federal administration took place; and (*b*) expenditure programmes tend to be planned incrementally, with inertia built in from year to year. Institutions with large budgets can thus apply their own priorities, once resources have been assigned, and the spatial dimension can be conveniently forgotten. The extreme example in Mexico was the state-owned oil company PEMEX, which decided to construct a fifth industrial port at Dos Bocas—a location which had appeared in none of the central government planning documents.

---

based approach taken by those agencies distinguished them from the third category, 'sectoral decentralization'. These are locally based but essentially sectoral activities, and include, for example, the local implementation of national housing policies through a national housing corporation or through local improvement projects.

Another policy trend in evidence in both developed and developing countries is the creation of new institutions and arrangements designed to bring about private-sector involvement in human settlements development, particularly in the area of housing finance. In the centrally planned economies of Eastern Europe, this has mainly taken the form of efforts to mobilize private savings. There is also an increasing tendency towards public- and private-sector co-operation in the development of urban land, for example. These trends are, in part, the consequence of strict controls on public spending and of the search for cost-effective solutions to settlement problems.

Strengthening co-ordination mechanisms

Constraints to the strengthening of co-ordination mechanisms are many and various. The role and activities of individual agencies may, for example, reflect political necessity rather than a concern with long-term development strategies.

Box 8.3   Sri Lanka: decentralizing decision-making on human settlements

The emphasis in human settlements policy in Sri Lanka is on housing. Policy changes in 1977 resulted in a new programme to construct 100,000 houses (half of them in rural areas), and a shift from an essentially regulatory approach to a development-oriented one. New legislation and important institutions have emerged from the programme. Examples include the National Housing Development Authority (NHDA), which is in charge of both urban and rural low-income shelter, the Urban Development Authority (UDA), the Building Materials Manufacturing Corporation, and the Housing Bank.

In 1983, the emphasis of the public housing programme shifted from supplying and delivering houses to an enabling process. The new Million Houses Programme aims to keep solutions at affordable levels through realistic costs and standards. Incremental construction, using locally available materials and traditional technology, is now encouraged, and the process of decision-making has been decentralized. Under the new programme, funds available from the national budget for investment in housing activities are allocated to the districts. The District Development Councils (DDCs) in turn allocate these resources, together with resources received from other sectoral ministries, to the *gramodaya mandala* (village councils), and the latter are responsible for the preparation of an investment plan bringing together all forms of public investment in the village. These Village Plans together form the District Development Plan.

This provides an interesting example of the way in which a human settlements approach can be integrated at the lowest level in the administrative hierarchy.

Institutional responsibilities may be jealously guarded, with institutions reluctant to relinquish traditional autonomy in the interests of improved co-ordination. Vested interests and bureaucratic inefficiencies frustrate efforts to strengthen co-ordination mechanisms, as does the paucity of trained manpower. Co-ordination is further impaired by frequent changes in governmental policy. However, three main approaches to the problem of co-ordination have been applied in the past decade.

• *Creation of new institutions.* The approach tried most often in the developing countries has been the creation of a new institution which consolidates human settlements functions and vested with responsibilities for co-ordination. In order for such an arrangement to produce results, the institution must have a clear mandate, have access to adequate funding, and be vested with authority respected by other institutions. When these prerequites are not met, the institution will prove ineffective.

• *Ad hoc arrangements at the programme and project level.* This approach, deliberate in its rejection of new institutions and seeking to establish formal and informal mechanisms that promote communication and co-operation between existing institutions, is used extensively in market-economy developed countries. Such mechan-

---

Box 8.4   Kenya: the local authority set-up

Modelled in the British tradition, local authorities in Kenya are semi-autonomous governmental units with prescribed rights and obligations under the Local Government Act. The Ministry of Local Government is responsible for overseeing their operations, financing, and management. At present, local authorities consist of municipal, town, county, and urban councils.

Municipal councils are established in the large centres, including Nairobi, and are supposed to be financially capable of offering a wide range of services to their residents, including water supply, sewerage, roads, and housing, and educational, health, and fire services. They are followed in status and range of services by town councils in medium-sized towns; county councils, whose areas of jurisdiction cover the districts (except for municipal and town councils' areas); and urban councils which are the smallest institutional entities and come under the jurisdiction of county councils. The urban councils are considered to be in transition to town councils.

Local authorities have a special relationship with the District Development Councils (DDCs), which identifies development projects before forwarding them to the Ministry for Local Government for funding. This process enables the DDCs to co-ordinate local authority projects with other development activities in the district and ensure that they are in accordance with district development priorities.

The local authorities fulfil an important function in that they are the institutions closest to the people. Thus, they enable the government to become responsive to the needs and wishes of the people. Secondly, they are of critical importance in implementing Kenya's economic development strategy as they oversee the urban centres which are the focus of industrial activity and provide the linkages for rural production and marketing. The management efficiency of urban centres has a direct bearing on the achievement of national economic development objectives in agriculture, industry, and services.

Source: Z. P. Omwando, *Housing and Urban Development Digest, East and Southern Africa* (Nairobi, US Agency for International Development, 1985).

isms include advisory groups, standing and joint committees, programme and project teams, and task forces with members drawn from different agencies. Experience shows that this approach is able to facilitate horizontal and vertical co-ordination, and it has the advantage of providing flexibility, drawing upon the skills, competence, and specializations of agencies as and when required. However, a prerequisite for this approach is the existence of well-developed and well-staffed agencies, and not all developing countries can meet this requirement.

• *Creation of intermediary bodies.* This approach involves the creation of a governmental agency or department which acts as an intermediary between central government, sectoral agencies, and local authorities. Typically, the agency is situated within or is responsible to the Ministry of Local Government. While the position of the agency in the institutional hierarchy may enable it to strengthen horizontal and, especially, vertical co-ordination, experience has shown that it may lack the authority to play a forceful role.

The creation of new institutions

Many countries have found it necessary to create new institutions to give special attention to some of the concerns in human settlements. These are mainly in the sectors of housing, water supply, sanitation, urban development, transport, and finance, but have also included organizations for building materials and pollution control. These organizations can be governmental undertakings (departmental), statutory bodies, public-owned companies, or, in rare cases, registered societies or co-operatives. In the area of housing finance, considerable efforts have been made to mobilize private-sector funds by involving commercial banks, insurance companies, and savings-and-loan societies in new types of institutional arrangements. In theory at least, such bodies command great flexibility, are reasonably autonomous, are not prone to procedural bottlenecks and delays, can raise resources outside the governmental budget, and can be made accountable for specific performance.

As indicated earlier, however, institutions created to deal specifically with human settlements development often prove to be stronger on paper than they are in practice. To be effective, settlement institutions, especially those with comprehensive mandates, require high-level political support, authority and autonomy which are respected by other institutions, access to resources and power to decide how they should be used, and staffs of professionals who are both competent and motivated. The absence of any one of these requirements can seriously weaken the institution. Experience has shown that, in the human settlements field especially, institutions can quickly lose credibility.

Human settlements institution-building may also be accompanied by institutional destruction. The creation of new institutions does not create trained manpower or the skills required to tackle complex settlements problems. What it can do is drain trained manpower from existing institutions, weakening them in the process and adding to the problem of too many jobs chasing too few people, which is still prevalent in developing countries. Therefore, before establishing new institutions, governments should be convinced that there is a clear need—a need that cannot be met by modifying the present institutional structure—as well as specific and obvious advantages.

Strengthening local authorities

The experience of the past decade indicates that the need to strengthen local authorities is an important issue. When local authorities are weak, human settlements development is bound to suffer. There are many causes of weakness, including inadequacy of funds made available by central government, inability or unwillingness to generate local revenues, poorly developed capacities for operational and fiscal management, paucity of trained manpower, and lack of career prospects for those who choose to work at the local level. It is at this level, however, that human settlements policies and plans are implemented, and it is here that the burdens placed on settlement institutions are growing most rapidly.

Governments should carefully consider the critical role of local bodies in the formulation and implementation of policies, strategies, and plans for human settlements. Measures to support local government imply an additional flow of resources from central government as well as the broadening of local revenue-raising powers. However, a number of measures, mostly of a legal nature, can be taken which do not necessarily imply the allocation of additional financial resources. Some of these measures deal with planning, administration, and training, as described below.

Settlements administration

While governments must pay primary attention to the most pressing and visible problems of the provision of basic services to their growing populations, they cannot lose sight of the equally important long-term need for efficient administration. Some of the basic principles of sound administration are:

• Organizational structure in tune with their defined functions.
• Power and authority commensurate with responsibility.
• Managers accountable for specific programmes.
• Service delivery constantly monitored, and systems of rewards and punishments institutionalized.
• Continuity and stability of personnel, and ongoing training.
• Availability of qualified staff, and appropriate arrangements to encourage secondment and exchange of staff.

The centralization of public-contact functions has tended to overload the administrative capacity of metropolitan and other large urban centres, producing inefficiency and unproductive use of essential manpower. The decentralization of these services, such as payment of taxes and fees, applications for licences and permits, requests for the connection of essential public services, and the handling of inquiries and complaints, can be accomplished by establishing administrative offices in residential neighbourhoods. Such offices could be staffed in part by volunteers from community organizations.

Establishing such neighbourhood municipal offices could provide the following:

• Improved delivery of administrative services.
• Direct contact between local government officials and residents.
• Reduction of public-contact functions at central offices, enabling employees to concentrate on vital planning and administrative functions.
• Information on neighbourhood issues and problems on the basis of which policies can be formulated.
• Openings for community participation through staffing basic administrative services, which can increase the efficiency of local government by freeing manpower for other purposes.

Training for settlements development

The complex issues involved in human settlements development, particularly at the local level where projects and programmes are implemented, call for considerable training. The spectrum of such training should be very wide, reflecting the scope of human settlements concerns, and should create the technical skills to meet all needs, from the operation of services to the formulation of policy and programmes at the highest levels of administration. What is important, however, is for training to be practically oriented and related to relevant policy areas.

Moreover, the objective of any training programme should be the creation not just of large numbers of trained *individuals* but of trained and effective *organizations* which can efficiently formulate and execute human settlements policies and programmes. This last point cannot be overstressed, since in many developing countries there is the paradox of public bodies, administrative agencies, and ministries that are ineffective even though they are staffed by administrators and professionals trained in prestigious universities and technical institutes, many of them foreign. With their professional preparation, these individuals should positively influence the performance of their organizations but they often have not been able to do so. This seems to indicate that low performance levels in a public agency cannot simply be reversed by injecting into that organization a handful of individuals trained outside the system. Rather, this must be accomplished by training and management processes internal to the organization which affect all staff from the point of recruitment on. An effective agency, therefore, is not simply the sum of its individual parts but is composed of individuals who are moulded by the organization to interact and perform their tasks along pre-established lines in order to reach collective goals.

Conclusions

It must be underscored that many professionals in technical fields are unprepared for practical administrative tasks, problem-solving, and project implementation, all of which are supposedly basic everyday functions of local authorities. This deficiency is accentuated by the fact that many professionals are often placed in key posts in agencies immediately after completing university-level training, without acquiring the practi-

cal administrative experience needed to be effective on the local level. This phenomenon is particularly common in small developing countries, where there are only a few experienced professionals to draw from, and in countries where the absence of an administrative apparatus to execute development policies necessitates the creation of new agencies and ministries to carry out ambitious sectoral development programmes. Training should also target low-level and middle-level technical and administrative staff, particularly in local agencies where human settlements policies are executed. The absence of an effective support staff to implement policies can easily outweigh the presence of a core of highly trained professionals within any organization.

Note

1. For a review of the institutional arrangements adopted, see UNCHS (Habitat), *Human Settlements Policies and Institutions: Issues, Options, Trends, and Guidelines* (Nairobi, 1984), ch. 5.

9 Settlements Financing

However well-conceived human settlements strategies, policies, and programmes may be, their implementation will depend upon both the amount and the nature of resources (human, material, and financial) to be applied to them. In developing countries, human and material resources are frequently of importance equal to if not greater than the purely financial, with skill, ingenuity, and sheer hard work often making up for shortages of funds, but the quality and quantity of the human resources available for settlements activity frequently depend on national or local commitment to the improvement of educational and training institutions. The increasing need to train professional and technical cadres according to criteria compatible with national development goals increases the burden placed on national development budgets. Therefore, the distinction between financial and non-financial resources can become an artificial one: in the final analysis, the main issue is not how to find financing for the execution of programmes, but how to improve resource mobilization to serve the goals of national settlement development. The mobilization of non-financial resources is mentioned elsewhere in this study: this chapter aims at illustrating some of the bottlenecks experienced by developing countries in attempting—and frequently failing—to mobilize the financial resources necessary to carry out high-priority settlement programmes. Three areas are singled out for special attention: the public financing of infrastructure and services, the mobilization of savings, and the financing of low-income shelter.

Investments, investors, and financing needs

The types of investment for human settlements development can be classified in four main categories:

- *Infrastructure*, including roads, water supply, sanitation, surface-water drainage, street lighting, and electrification.
- *Superstructures* required for services, such as schools, clinics, hospitals, churches, police and fire stations, etc.
- *Industrial and commercial structures*, such as office buildings, shops, stores, factory buildings, etc.
- *Residential structures*, i.e. multiple dwellings, individual houses, for rental or owner occupancy.

Responsibility for these different investment categories and for the decisions with regard to priorities, location, and size of investment and financing rests with different investors.

In socialist systems, all these investments are controlled by the central government, which allocates investment funds. There is a wide range of delegation of authority to local government, public-sector enterprises, ministries, etc., which all act as investors in implementing the socio-economic development plan. However, in the final analysis, investment funds are allocated through investment budgets which are co-ordinated through the central government according to investment priorities and the availability of funds.

In market-oriented economies, investment responsibilities are distributed between the private and public sector. The latter provides what is termed 'public goods and services', which have certain characteristics which make them unsuitable for delivery through market forces: (*a*) they require extensive investment in distribution networks and can therefore, practically, only be provided by a monopoly; (*b*) basic social policies require the distribution of certain services to all members of the society, and no person can be excluded from their consumption. Governments therefore provide the investments for infrastructure development as well as the superstructures required for administration, education, health services, etc., while investments in industry and commerce are normally the responsibility of private-sector enterprises.

In both developed and developing countries, housing has increasingly become a private-sector activity, regardless of the level of income of its end-users. The production of dwelling units as a market commodity for sale or rental to middle- and upper-income groups has always taken up the largest share of the formal housing sector, but in developing countries a distinctive feature of settlement development is the production of shelter by the informal sector—a sector which has similar objectives to the formal sector but which functions according to different modalities and has its own financing requirements. However, this very large share of settlement development in developing countries occurs without control and against the buildings codes and regulations of the authorities, and with unsatisfactory results.

Financing requirements in the housing sector are basically of two types:

• *Prospective final owners require long-term finance*, since the life-span (and thus the amortization period) of the asset are very long, usually 15 to 25 years and, sometimes, more.

• *Developers, who create an asset for resale, require short- to medium-term finance* for the period from land acquisition to sale of the final product.

While short-term finance is, in most countries, readily available to developers on capital markets, the provision of end-financing is problematic, the main issues being the long term of the loan and the slow amortization of the capital.

Sources of capital for human-settlement investments

The sources of finance are, for all investors, basically three: *current savings*, *accumulated assets* (in whatever form held), and *credit* provided by finance institutions. The origin and availability of these financial resources differ for different investors. As far as current savings are concerned, *government savings* are defined as current income from taxation, fees, charges, etc., less current consumptive expenditures, so that their availability for investment depends on revenue generation and control of expenditures; *private-sector savings* are retained profits: and *private-*

household savings are income less consumptive expenditures. Investors may also have accumulated assets which can be converted into investment capital. *Government assets* largely represent infrastructure investments and are therefore unsaleable, but one asset which can be sold in the course of development is land, an avenue frequently followed in low-income housing projects. *Private enterprises* may have financial assets at their disposal and finance new investments out of depreciation on existing assets, which in principle is a form of conversion of assets. *Private households'* accumulated assets are financial savings or intrafamily transfers, i.e. savings of other family members (particularly for low-income groups). The main source of investment finance, however, is the financial sector, which acts as the intermediary between investors in need of capital and organizations, institutions, and individuals with surplus financial resources.

Theoretically, developing countries can avail themselves of an alternative source to supplement their human settlements budget, i.e. external finance in the form of either international aid or foreign credit. However, the amount and reliability of aid resources, and even the advisability of drawing on this source, are questionable. A very recent UNCHS (Habitat) analysis indicates that only 5.5 per cent of international aid goes to shelter and shelter-related programmes and projects in the developing countries, and the implementation of human settlements projects through international funding is not necessarily consistent with the priorities of recipient countries if the funding received must be repaid in hard currencies.

The central question, therefore, is how to mobilize internally the financial resources needed to meet investment demands posed by human settlements development and to make the technical options described elsewhere in this study feasible.

Public-sector financing of infrastructure and services

Investments in the development of infrastructure and services are, with few exceptions, directly in the realm of the public sector, i.e. the government, its public works agencies, and its local authorities, through direct investments, loans, and subsidies. Direct investment is funded through allocations in the investment budget, of which a large share is financed through public borrowing on the financial market. Loans to private or public institutions are an indirect form of investment enabling mostly parastatal corporations to fulfil their role in implementing government policies. Such loans can be linked to the financing efforts of the institution itself, thus initiating and supporting larger investments than governments could complete by direct investment. Subsidies are granted by governments in various forms, most frequently in the form of tax exemption but often also as low-interest loans. These indirect subsidies reduce the revenue from taxation or interest (compared to market interest rates), but they are concealed, in that such losses do not appear in the budget.

Virtually all local governments in both developed and developing countries are responsible for providing a range of basic services, such as markets and abattoirs, street lighting, garbage collection, fire protection, public open spaces, libraries, and cemeteries. In most countries, they are also partly or fully responsible for providing basic physical infrastructure in the form of roads, potable water supply, sewerage systems, and drainage works, while telephone and electricity services are typically the responsibility of high-level (state or national) governmental agencies or parastatal corporations. However, there are wide variations between countries, and frequently between cities within countries.[1] With the rapid growth of urban centres and the increasing demand for the infrastructure and services which local authorities are expected to provide, a gap opens between perceived service needs and financial resources, frequently referred to as the urban fiscal gap.[2]

One of the central issues in the discussion of governmental financing of human settlements infrastructure is the problem of the apportionment of responsibilities and financial resources between central and local governments. In most developing countries, responsibility for investment in human settlements development is shared between local and higher-level authorities. Central governments influence the planning and investment phase of local service provision by controlling the ability of local authorities to borrow, providing capital grants or loans, or taking direct responsibility for investment programmes. Other means of central government control are special development agencies or autonomous corporations for the provision of services. One of the most striking administrative features of cities in the developing world is the extensive overlap of responsibilities, with all levels of government and a number of agencies typically involved in the provision of a particular service.[3]

While there is usually some local autonomy in the provision and financing of certain services, governmental systems in most developing countries are highly centralized, and control over available resources ultimately lies with central government. In rural areas, central governments deliver and finance most services directly, whereas in urban areas, local governments are generally financed through a system of grants or shared taxes. These finances are then supplemented by additional sources of revenue, such as property taxes and various licensing fees and charges. However, the fact remains that in most urban areas in developing countries, local authorities find themselves responsible for a host of services with insufficient financial resources at their disposal. Policies aimed at strengthening local authorities' capability to mobilize resources should look, first, into the possibility of increasing revenues from the taxes that are almost universally allocated to them, such as property or real-estate taxes, taxes on automobile use (road tax), taxes on business, and other taxes.

Revenue collection at the local level

Local government's ability to generate revenue through taxation is severely limited because central governments insist on the prerogative of imposing taxes and determining tax rates. The only substantial revenue source which is almost universally at the disposal of local authorities is property taxation. Although this is the most important single source of human settlements financing accessible to local authorities, it has shortcomings in its potential to increase revenues. Since the tax base—the amount of land—does not grow automatically with real income growth or inflation, there must be periodic reassessments to update property values. This is an administrative problem, because local governments fall behind in carrying out reassessments owing to lack of suitably trained staff. Thus, old property values remain on the tax rolls, and revenue losses are substantial.[4]

Another problem is the notoriously low rate of tax collection. Evidence on this is not readily available, since local government records on revenue-collection performance are not reliable, and the specific reasons for poor revenue-collection performance differ among local authorities. However, common elements can be found, the most important being the absence of effectively enforced penalty measures for non-payment or unduly delayed payment. Collection problems may stem from inadequacy of staff as well as from the structure of the tax: wide variations in the equity of property-tax assessments (i.e. in the ratio of the assessed value to the market value) are a typical obstacle in this respect. Another frequently cited problem is that many tax delinquents simply do not have the capacity to pay. Some governments in developing countries have begun to deal with these problems with a variety of reform measures. The most effective one, however, appears to be strict enforcement, including prompt identification of delinquent payers, rapid legal procedures, and automatic tax liens on delinquent property.[5]

Other forms of taxation, for instance on the use of automobiles, although well suited to urban areas, have been little used by developing countries. Car ownership has increased significantly in most developing countries and is largely concentrated among high-income groups, but taxes on automobiles do not cover costs of road networks, parking space, and traffic regulation, let alone generate surplus revenues for the development of urban services. Automobile taxation has the advantage that it can be made progressive and used to promote public transport, an investment of particular benefit to the poor.[6]

While data on betterment levies in developing countries are still inadequate, a few successful experiences have shown their potential for the financing of land development. Under the often-cited programmes of the Republic of Korea and of Colombia,[7] land is assembled and reparcellated, and infrastructure is provided in the form of roads and water-supply and sewerage installations. Landowners must surrender part of their holding for public use as payment for the improvements received on the retained land, and investment costs are recovered through resale of the surrendered land. While these programmes do not necessarily provide services specifically designed to benefit low-income households, they make financial resources available for other public-sector investments and can be used, for instance, to cross-subsidize low-income housing.

Central governments should encourage local authority efforts to generate revenues—especially since such actions can enhance equitable income distribution at the local level—and to strengthen local management capabilities. Appropriate methods would include incentives to improve local authorities' revenue generation through performance-linked grant systems, and assistance in organizing borrowing from financial institutions. Such support could help secure the capital required for investments in fixed infrastructure as well as reduce the demands for grant and loan funds from central government.

Programmes of this sort already operate in Brazil and India, illustrating how national financing of infrastructure investments can be linked to local revenue generation and administrative performance. This approach transforms the traditional system of transfers from central to local government from one of annual handouts covering deficits and centrally planned and funded investments into one of reliably sourced finance for locally planned and managed services and infrastructure.

Cost recovery

A factor in human settlements financing which has assumed increasing importance over the past few years is the question of cost recovery on capital investments or subsidies. In the past it was frequently ignored, but growing concern with the effectiveness of public investment has made it a concern in much current development work, the aim being to ensure that public invest-

Box 9.1   India: linking capital-works grants to fiscal performance

The State of West Bengal has recently begun to devolve increasing responsibilities for urban management to the 39 municipalities that make up the Calcutta metropolitan area. The main aim of a new programme, supported by the World Bank, is to create a system of checks and incentives to reduce local governments' financial dependence on the state. Under the Revised Grant Structure implemented by the state government in April 1983, fiscal performance targets are set for each municipality. Grants for new capital investment are linked to fiscal performance, particularly improved efficiency in property-tax collection, which is the most important source of municipal revenue. Expenditure targets are also set.

Each of the 39 municipalities received its full capital allotment in the first year of the programme, and the linkage system has begun to operate. Municipal bodies that were within their revenue-deficit targets for the first year will receive the capital investment as originally scheduled, those whose deficits exceed the targets will receive a reduced proportion of capital investment, and those with revenue surpluses will receive an additional matching capital grant. Any additional capital works contemplated by municipalities gaining the bonus allotment are subject to the same appraisal process as other investments.

While the state will still cover all municipal deficits, those exceeding projected deficits will be penalized by a reduction of capital investment grants. The logic behind the programme is that municipalities performing well will be able to recover additional investment costs and can therefore receive increased investment allocations, while municipalities performing poorly will need to improve revenue collection before new investments will be financed. Thus, the programme provides a very strong incentive for municipalities to improve their financial management.

Box 9.2   Paraná, Brazil: new mechanisms for financing capital investments

The State of Paraná in the south of Brazil has been experiencing rapid economic growth in the last decade, and planning authorities have attempted to promote the development of small towns as markets for farm produce and centres for the distribution of farm inputs and services for the surrounding population. One of the problems was how to devise a system of revenue generation and allocation capable of providing most of the resources needed by such small urban centres. Most municipal expenditures are financed from a 20 per cent share in a state-collected turnover tax, but this system tends to favour large cities.

In 1983/84, two new mechanisms were introduced to provide financial support for capital improvements in the state's 287 towns with a population of less than 50,000. First, fiscal resources are to be transferred from the state's annual budget to municipalities in proportion to their urban population and their growth trends. Expectations concerning future development are thus incorporated in decisions on the distribution of state resources. Secondly, funds are to be made available to these municipalities as loans from the state, which uses funds borrowed from the World Bank for this purpose. Lending is to be on the basis of assessment of the municipality's creditworthiness and its ability to operate and maintain the facilities in which the money is invested. Each year's credit will be linked to the municipality's revenue performance during the previous year. Under the provisions of the scheme, outstanding debt may not exceed 70 per cent of the past year's total revenue, new debt may not exceed 20 per cent of the year's revenue, and debt service may not exceed 15 per cent of the previous year's revenue. All figures are to be adjusted for inflation.

The new mechanisms provide a strong incentive to increase local revenues, especially from property tax, in order to increase investment. They also provide incentives for improved urban management and fiscal performance.

ment in development is recovered during its lifespan and from beneficiaries. In many countries, it has proved impossible to administer, but considerable attention will have to be devoted to it in the coming years.

One aspect which remains little explored and less understood relates to investments undertaken in connection with low-income settlement projects by the creation of infrastructure and services, which unless carefully monitored can become hidden subsidies to high-income settlements. Infrastructure provision for low-income settlements is often financed through mechan-

isms which involve initial loans, recoverable from the eventual residents over a period of years. The bringing of services—piped water, sewerage, electricity, telephones, storm drainage, roads, and street lighting—and the building of community facilities, such as schools and administrative centres, are costly undertakings, and if they benefit households outside the immediate settlement served, such households should bear an appropriate share of the expenses.

Cost recovery may operate through user charges, premium payments, local taxation, levies on rental property, head taxes, or other fiscal instruments. Conventional accounting wisdom demands—apparently quite reasonably— that such charges be levied on the people who occupy the site. As the quantity of land available for settlements within or near to urban centres declines and land costs escalate, new settlements are being located far from the centre, very often in areas traditionally seen as attractive for high-cost, commuter-type developments. The provision of infrastructure in such new, low-income settlements has an important effect in valorizing adjacent sites. First, the cost to those wishing to develop an adjoining site will be lowered, since in most cases they will only have to cover the cost of extending and connecting to an existing system. In addition, since low-income settlements are generally of medium to high density, their infrastructure provision is relatively 'heavy duty'; 'high-cost' developments tend to be built at low densities, particularly in suburban areas, and are thus relatively easy to link to existing heavy-duty systems without the need to increase capacities. So the cost per connection is considerably lower, reflecting only a charge for access to an existing system and not the total cost of provision of the facility. Thus, while the infrastructure costs are largely borne by public authorities and the intended beneficiaries in low-income settlements, the developers and occupants of nearby 'high-cost' schemes may reap real rewards both in initial cost savings and in being under no obligation to contribute to cost recovery.

Similar situations occur when derelict, unused, or underused inner-city sites are upgraded and provided with new infrastructure and services. Public investment in the provision or upgrading of services in urban revitalization or improvement programmes, the costs of which are to be recovered from the eventual residents, can be a factor in revalorizing adjacent inner-city areas, which can thus benefit from such actions without in any way contributing to cost recovery. Patterns of private land acquisition and hoarding are often the result of insider knowledge or inspired guesswork about future programmes of this type.

Improved services to and valorization of nearby sites thus become a charge on the people who can least afford them, while the advantages may accrue to people who contribute nothing to the capital expenditure involved. At a time when the burden of financing infrastructure may put adequate housing beyond the reach of those who need it most, considerable care must be taken to design the cost-recovery process so that it does not become yet another hidden subsidy of the rich by the poor.

Mobilization of savings

Neither the public nor the private sector is likely to provide long-term savings to the financial system—in fact, both are usually net borrowing sectors. The substantial deposits which they may hold with financial institutions are usually of short maturity to meet the financial demands of business transactions. It is the private-household sector which has to provide the pool of long-term savings to the financial system.

The development of the financial system depends on the ability of the system to attract savings from households in the form of deposits, savings accounts, and capital-market instruments. Three basic conditions are required for the functioning of the financial system: economic or monetary stability, a real return on financial investment, and confidence in the security and stability of financial institutions. It is probably less the lack of savings than the lack of these basic preconditions which has left capital markets underdeveloped even in countries which have enjoyed rapid economic progress during the last decades.

Battling inflation is therefore of high priority, and some countries have been more or less successful at it. Among the unsuccessful countries, a number (e.g. Colombia, Brazil, and Israel) have resorted to monetary adjustment of capital-market instruments, with transactions calculated in constant-value currency units and actual payments being made after multiplying the constant-value units by the reference index. Such a system, while not fighting the causes of inflation, allows capital markets to function.

Closely linked to the need to control inflation is the need to offer a real return on financial investments. This means that interest rates offered need to be higher than the rate of inflation—a condition which has led to high interest rates in most countries. For long-term investments, as required for human-settlements finance, finance institutions have introduced loans with variable interest rates so as to be able to adjust the return on investment to the cost of funds. Government regulation of interest rates on deposits and loans is not conducive to the mobilization of financial resources unless these set rates conform to market forces. Mostly rates are set too low, making financial assets unattractive and fostering the development of informal mechanisms which generally lack security and only deal in short-term funds. The result is a scarcity in the long-term funds needed to finance housing and infrastructure investment.

Confidence in the ability of financial institutions depends on the management of these institutions, the supervision of lending practices, and so on. Public confidence in the banking sector could be strengthened by governments through compulsory insurance of deposits and savings against default of finance institutions, but such regulation must be sensitively handled.

A number of instruments are available to mobilize savings, and some of them are particularly suitable for providing the type of resources required for long-term financing of human settlements investments.

Forced savings

In many developing countries, forced savings—mostly, contributions to provident funds—constitute the most important form of household savings. While such funds are usually managed as governmental or parastatal organizations, the contributing households are the real owners so the accumulated resources are considered to be household savings. Contributions, in the form of payroll deductions, are borne by employers and employees in varying proportions. Since contributions depend on formal employment, the coverage of the labour force by such funds depends largely on the degree of development of the formal sector—up to 100 per cent in developed countries, but varying enormously in developing countries to below 20 per cent in some countries with large rural populations and recently established systems.

The savings held with such funds have three characteristics which make them an ideal resource base for human settlements financing: (a) they are available as medium- to long-term capital; (b) they are held as financial assets and provide a steady inflow of capital over time; (c) the investment is closely controlled by governmental regulations to ensure security of the investment. There are two ways to channel funds from this source into the human settlements sector. First, public-sector institutions could issue debentures which could fulfil the security requirements, and, secondly, mortgage-backed securities could be developed. Such financial instruments can then be acquired by provident funds. Some developing countries have introduced special provident funds, such as the Fondo de Garantia de Tiempo de Servicio (FGTS) in Brazil and the Home Development Mutual Fund (HDMF) in the Philippines, where the receipts are specifically earmarked for human settlements investment. National housing-finance institutions manage these funds and are able to provide credit for infrastructure investments and housing loans.

Contractual savings

A special form of contractual savings is the saving-for-housing scheme. Schemes of this type have been successful in some European countries, for instance the *Bausparkassen* in the Federal Republic of Germany or building societies in the United Kingdom, but have rarely been emulated in developing countries. These contractual savings programmes have some interesting features. By accepting interest rates lower than the going market rates on savings, the saver acquires the right to take out a loan at a fixed low interest rate when the savings contract is fulfilled. The very important advantage of this is to isolate housing loans from market interest-rate fluctuations. Among the main obstacles to the introduction of such savings schemes in developing countries are the following:

• The savings period of three to five years required before loans are granted exceeds the planning horizon of most low-income people.

• Lack of a steady income flow from informal-

Box 9.3   Housing finance on a massive scale: the National Housing Bank of Brazil

One of the most sophisticated and well-known finance systems for housing, infrastructure, and urban development in developing countries is that of Brazil. Established in 1964 as a means to counterbalance the depression and unemployment caused by anti-inflationary policies and to relieve the large housing deficit, the National Housing Bank (BNH) draws its funds from the large unemployment fund (FGTS) made up of compulsory contributions from employers amounting to 8 per cent of gross salary for each employee. Since employees cannot have access to their accounts until dismissed, the BNH can count on extremely large financial resources. The Savings and Loans System (SBPE) controlled by the BNH allows the indexing of savings accounts and thus attracts additional funds in the form of private savings. The principle of relying on the private sector instead of building directly has been one of the reasons for the success of the programme. Not only can private enterprise offer consistently low prices for housing, but throughout this period special building techniques have been developed that allow rapid and cheap construction. Governmental activities are thus mainly limited to the management of the system.

Between 1964 and 1982, the Housing Finance System (SFH) provided funds for the construction of 4.1 million new units, about half of which were built after 1979. This represented a total investment of $15.8 billion. The funds allocated to local governments for the construction or expansion of water-supply and sewerage systems were $5.1 billion, of which $3.1 billion was after 1979. This provided funding to 2,521 of the 3,954 municipalities in Brazil.

The financial programmes supported by the SFH are extremely varied and cover income levels from the minimum salary upwards. Low-income financing has subsidized interest rates and long repayment periods. As the amount of the loan increases, payment periods get shorter and interest rates higher. Thus, an equilibrium is achieved, with high-income groups subsidizing the interest on low-income loans. Although all loans are indexed, monthly payments are also linked to the minimum salary, thereby maintaining the same proportion of the family income (25 to 30 per cent, according to the income level). This has allowed the system to finance housing for all categories of employees down to a minimum salary of about $100 per month.

Details of the main housing finance schemes are summarized below:

• *PROMORAR* upgrades inadequate housing, mainly in slums and squatter areas. It finances all aspects of redevelopment, including land acquisition, infrastructure installation, and promotion of community development with the objective of avoiding the removal of families from the site.

• *PROFILURB* allows for the acquisition of urban plots which are already linked to water-supply, sewerage, and electricity reticulation systems. It is available for income groups with up to five times the minimum salary.

• *COHABs* (Popular Housing Companies) carry out popular housing programmes for families with up to five times the minimum salary. The COHABs are managed by municipal and state governments and were the earliest programmes to be implemented (1965). The usual scheme is to promote the construction of housing projects on government-owned land. Although usually located on the urban periphery, the low cost of these mass-produced housing units determines a high demand, and in some cities the demand exceeds supply.

• *CO-OPERATIVES* is a programme that finances members of housing co-operatives, both those open to the public or those catering for a particular group (syndicates, clubs, professionals, etc.).

• *PROSINDI* finances low-income, unionized workers earning less than six times the minimum salary. The housing development is similar to the COHAB schemes, although higher salary levels allow better housing units to be provided.

• *PROHASP*, operated through housing co-operatives, is aimed at financing the housing needs of civil servants at all income levels.

• PROHEMP supports the investment of BNH funds through private firms to finance the production and/or marketing of housing for their employees, members, or contributors. It is designed to support housing schemes close to job locations for the employees of large companies.

• *PLACAR*, the main rural housing programme, is designed to provide loans with subsidized interest for the building or upgrading of dwellings and infrastructure for

---

sector employment can exclude precisely those people who most need loans from eligibility to borrow.

• Economic instability and fear that inflation will erode the real value of the contracted loan sum discourage participation.

• The supply of suitable dwelling units which

can be acquired with the contracted loan when it falls due is often insufficient.

• Unreasonable restrictions are imposed on the quality and standards of dwellings for which loans may be granted.

Promoting saving-for-housing schemes in developing countries would therefore require sup-

influence the flow of funds from such institutions. A large share of their financial resources are invested in government bonds since they are the only instruments which provide the necessary guarantees to fulfil the security regulations imposed by governments. A good example is found in India, where the Life Insurance Corporation (LIC) and General Insurance Corporation are tightly controlled in their investment policies. Here, part of the accumulated funds is directed into the housing sector and channelled through the National Housing and Urban Development Corporation (HUDCO) to human settlements investment.

Box 9.3 continued

small producers and rural workers, even without formal land tenure.

Other programmes include loans for private developers, individual housing loans (CICAP), urbanization programmes (PROAREAS), community equipment financing (PROEC), tenants' programmes, and condominium programmes. There are also programmes to finance the training of manpower for the building industry and to finance urban planning and urban development (expansion of infrastructure, urban services and facilities, urban renewal, etc.). The Sanitation Finance System is also managed by the BNH which raises funds and provides loans for local governments to build, expand, or upgrade their water-supply, sewerage, drainage, and waste-disposal systems. Furthermore, there are programmes to finance the acquisition of building materials by private consumers (much used in self-help schemes), and to provide finance to companies that produce, distribute, or transport building materials.

From 1964 to the present, the SFH has financed nearly all the 'financiable' housing projects. This has led to a diversification of objectives, with increasing resources being applied to urban development projects in support of the National Urban Development Council. However, a large part of the population in the informal sector is still unable to gain access to the finance system, although in some cases the BNH also administers other resources (foreign aid and loans, other social funds) to provide some subsidized housing.

The success of the Brazilian housing finance system has attracted the interest of other developing countries which find the approach more suited to their needs than the programmes used in developed countries. The BNH provides technical assistance and economic support to other Latin American and African countries. The largest schemes are with Algeria (support to build 100,000 housing units, including infrastructure), Jamaica (20,000 housing units), and Ecuador (to support the establishment of a housing-finance system).

Source: UNCHS (Habitat), *Human Settlements Policies and Institutions: Issues, Options, Trends, and Guidelines* (Nairobi, 1984).

Other savings

The mobilization of free savings requires an extensive network of branch institutions to reach out to savers. The Sri Lankan National Savings Bank, for instance, operates through 53 branches and close to 4,000 post offices and subpost offices, and carries about 8 million separate accounts on its books—an astonishing figure in a country with a total population of 15 million. Incentives for savers and depositors are high interest rates (12 to 16 per cent) and some tax exemption on the returns. Surprisingly, this savings effort is not linked to a lending programme: almost all investments (98 per cent) are in government securities. Given the high interest rates offered, channelling part of these funds into housing finance would require high repayment rates, and would thus preclude the financing of shelter for low-income groups unless an interest subsidy could be made available to borrowers.

A different approach to mobilizing household savings is the development of community-based finance institutions (CBFIs), such as credit unions, housing co-operatives, or local building societies. In many countries, these organizations have been successful in mobilizing resources from predominantly low-income members and in offering short-term loans. A recent study of the co-operative sector in Jamaica, Kenya, and Zambia showed that a substantial portion of these loans is already invested in the improvement of housing.[8] The study concluded that the demand for long-term finance from the members of such community-based finance institutions

portive measures, such as a direct link with the housing-delivery system, and, in inflationary environments, the protection of savings through an adequate monetary policy.

Insurance companies are also important accumulators of contractual savings, and through detailed regulation of the modes of investment of their required reserves, governments are able to

can only be met by linking up with national finance systems, and the potential of such linkages between national housing development banks and low-income communities should be recognized in formulating strategies intended to meet the housing-finance needs of the poor.

Housing-finance institutions

Implementation of housing-finance policies required efficient institutional arrangements. Many developing countries have established housing-finance institutions, frequently with the specific objective of assisting low-income groups in financing dwelling units; however, few have succeeded. Studies of housing-finance systems indicate that financing institutions make a very limited contribution to total housing investment —for instance, in Tunisia from 1975 to 1980, it was only one-sixth; in Thailand (1981), one-third; and in the Philippines (1977), one-quarter.[9]

Moreover, institutional finance is almost exclusively available to high-income groups. First, institutions normally operate as conventional mortgage lenders, requiring a legal title to land, proof of steady income, down-payments of 20 per cent and more, and other restrictive eligibility criteria. Secondly, these institutions do not have sufficient capability to mobilize resources and depend largely on governmental allocations. Thirdly, project-implementing agencies bypass these institutions (receiving project funds directly through budget allocation) and administer loan schemes for beneficiaries directly or through co-operating local authorities. Finally, they have no contact with the borrowing public because they cannot afford costly branch networks.

There are, of course, exceptions—one of the most successful being HUDCO in India. During the past 10 years, HUDCO has been able to expand its operations dramatically. Based on a government directive requiring all finance institutions and insurance corporations to invest a certain percentage of their portfolio in the housing sector, HUDCO offers debentures which these institutions buy to fulfil this obligation. These resources are then lent to state and municipal housing institutions and co-operative

organizations for urban and housing development. In recent years, HUDCO has been able to finance well over 250,000 dwelling units annually. India's Housing Finance Development Corporation (HFDC) has also made significant contributions in this field. It was founded in 1977 with the support of the International Finance Corporation of the World Bank group, the Aga Khan Foundation, and the Industrial Credit and Investment Corporation of India, Ltd, with the objective of mobilizing financial resources for financing acquisition or construction of dwelling units in India. Based on an authorized share capital of Rs250 million, of which Rs100 million have so far been subscribed and paid up, the HFDC has been able to mobilize substantial financial resources.

A different but equally promising approach was taken by the government of the Philippines when it introduced a secondary-mortgage system. The National Home Mortage Finance Corporation (NIIMFC) offers refinancing facilities to private mortgage-originating banks, financing itself through the sale of mortgage-participation certificates. The scheme is linked to the Home Development Mutual Fund which mobilizes resources through a payroll tax, and fund-members are the target group of the house-loan scheme. Both institutions have so far had a limited impact on the solution of the housing problem, but they appear to have taken steps in the right direction.

In a number of other countries—Egypt, Kenya, and Sri Lanka, for example—steps have been taken to integrate existing housing-finance institutions with the delivery system for housing for low-income groups. This is usually linked to specific housing projects in the following way: funds for housing loans are deposited with a branch office opened in the project area to manage the housing-loan scheme and create additional business in the area. This approach has the great advantage that a financial institution can branch out following a business operation created by a project rather than creating branches which may not be able to attract the necessary business to sustain themselves.

Box 9.4   Successful schemes for housing finance in India

Housing and Urban Development Corporation of India, Ltd.

Table 1. Resource allocation

	% of resources
Economically weaker section	30
Low-income group	25
Middle-income group	25
High-income group and other urban development	20

Table 2. Resource mobilization

	Rs million
Secured debentures	1,661
Unsecured debentures	100
Borrowing from Life Insurance Corporation	730
Borrowing from General Insurance Corporation	640
Equity	520
Reserves and surplus	415

Table 3. Lending policy

	Monthly income (Rs)	Loan ceiling (Rs)	Interest (%)	Amortization period (years)
Economically weaker section	<50	5,000–12,000	4.0–5.0	20
Low-income group	350–600	20,000	8.0	15
Middle-income group	600–1,500	50,000	10.5–11.5	12
High-income group and other	>1,500	60,000	12.5	10

Table 4. Dwelling units financed

	Units (000s)	Percentage
Economically weaker section	1,350	72.4
Low-income group	300	16.1
Middle-income group	170	8.9
High-income group and other	50	3.6
Total	1,870	100.0

Housing Finance Development Corporation, Ltd.

Table 5. Resource mobilization

	Rs millions
Own bond issues	200
Loans and bonds from/with insurance companies	280
Banks	282
Loans under the USAID Housing Guarantee Programme	300
International Finance Corporation	18
Certificates of deposit	1,764
Loan-linked deposit scheme	12
Home savings plan (new)	—
Total	2,856

Table 6. Resource allocation

	Rs millions
Individuals	1,945
Corporation and co-operative societies	387
Others	15
Total	2,347

Sources: H. U. Bijlani, *Case Study on Non-conventional Finance* (Nairobi: UNCHS/Habitat, 1983); S. K. Sharma, *Housing the Millions: The Hudco Approach* (1985); Housing Development Finance Corporation, Ltd, *Eighth Annual Report, 1984–5.*

Financing low-income housing

Problems such as the mobilization of financial resources, the economic viability of finance institutions and housing agencies, the security and recovery of loans, and the reduction of subsidies all emphasize the need for realistic interest rates, requirements of land titles as collateral, protection from the effects of inflation, and efficient financial management. Little consideration is given to considering the role of shelter as a basic need, or its potential for the redistribution of wealth and the socio-economic development of the poor. Reconciling the requirements of housing-finance institutions with the requirements of low-income groups for access to affordable loans raises the question of how financial services can be adapted to the requirements of the incremental construction process through which the majority of low-income households build their houses.

Only high-income groups are able to comply with the terms and conditions of conventional housing loans. The vast majority of households in developing countries create their own shelter, inadequate as it may be, over extended periods through progressive or phased investment. Studies of the financing mechanisms of informal investment in housing show that individual savings, particularly of the rental income from letting single rooms, form the main basis of such investment, frequently complemented by loans or gifts from friends and relatives. Detailed studies of the terms and conditions under which such informal, intrafamily transfers have yet to be made. The informal money market, money lenders, and pawnshops are only rarely used, probably because of the high costs of usury interest, repayment conditions, and lack of collateral.

The main obstacle for institutional financing in this sector is the lack of collateral. Tenure of occupied land ranges from squatting through various forms of renting to ownership in illegal subdivisions and, very rarely, full legal ownership. Under such tenure conditions, long-term conventional lending of large sums is excluded. What can be offered are multiple small short-term loans, based on purchased building materials as collateral. Through the granting of repeated loans, the progressive investment process could be substantially accelerated.

Box 9.5　Low-income housing pilot projects in Zimbabwe

The government of Zimbabwe, through the Ministry of Construction and National Housing (MCNH), and the United Nations Development Programme (UNDP), through the United Nations Centre for Human Settlements (Habitat), is implementing a Low-Income Housing Pilot Project in Kwekwe and Gutu, with funding for capital costs from the United States Agency for International Development (USAID). This joint multilateral technical co-operation project is characterized by a number of innovative features.

One such feature is provision for the expansion of the domestic thrift potential for low-income home finance through an appropriate arrangement with the Beverley Building Society. This is expected to give low-income families increased access to home-ownership finance and will also encourage them to use existing institutions to enhance their savings capacity and limited financial resources.

The capital cost of a fully serviced site in Kwekwe is about $Z1,254. This cost will be recovered in monthly instalments over a period of 25 years at an interest rate of 9.75 per cent per annum using progressive annuity. The building loan will depend upon the income of the beneficiary, and could range from $Z1,000 to $Z3,000. This loan will be recovered in monthly instalments over a period of 25 years at an interest rate of 12.50 per cent per annum using progressive annuity. The first-year monthly repayments for an average building loan of $Z2,000 and the capital infrastructure costs will be about $Z22.50. In the case of Gutu, the first-year monthly repayments for an average building loan of $Z2,000 and the capital infrastructure costs of $Z1,530 will be about $Z24.10. The monthly repayments do not include any recurrent costs and supplementary charges. These range from $Z3.00 in Gutu to $Z12.50 per month in Kwekwe—depending upon the total local authority investment in public works programmes for trunk infrastructure, recurrent costs, and individual household's consumption of water, sewerage, electricity, and so on. The monthly repayments and affordability are based upon the assumption that beneficiaries can afford to spend 20 to 25 per cent of their income for housing.

Community-based finance institutions (CBFIs), as discussed above, are another approach to the introduction of formal loan arrangements in the informal housing sector. With membership drawn from the community, close neighbourhood relationships, and solidarity around a goal of common concern, a CBFI can start to mobilize savings and foster community development in multiple respects. Thus, CBFIs can provide a point of entry for

expanding the financial system, and subsequently the housing-finance system, to the so
far unserviced group of self-employed and
casual workers who have no access to housing-
finance institutions.

Conclusions

The development of a housing-finance system
capable of financing shelter for the majority of
the world's population—the poor in developing
countries—requires a three-pronged approach:
the mobilization of resources at the national as
well as the beneficiary levels; the creation of
financial intermediaries with the ability to channel funds into the human settlements sector and
to the households most in need of financial
assistance; and the development of loan and
savings schemes adapted to the needs and
financial capacities of low-income groups.

Notes

1. United Nations, *Meeting of the* Ad Hoc *Group of Experts on Ways and Means of Establishing or Strengthening Financial Institutions for Human Settlements Financing and Investment.* Report of the Executive Director to the United Nations Commission on Human Settlements, Fourth Session (Nairobi, 1981), 6–7.
2. J. F. Linn, 'Urban Finance in Developing Countries'. Paper presented at the Meeting of the *Ad Hoc* Group of Experts on Ways and Means of Establishing or Strength-ening Financial Institutions for Human Settlements Financing and Investment (Nairobi, 1981).
3. Ibid., 9.
4. United Nations, *Human Settlements Finance and Manage-ment.* Report of the Executive Director to the United Nations Commission of Human Settlements, Third Ses-sion (Mexico City, 1980), 28–9.
5. Ibid., 28.
6. Ibid., 32.
7. Ibid., 31.
8. UNCHS (Habitat), *Community-based Finance Institutions* (Nairobi, 1984).
9. B. Renaud, 'Housing and Financial Institutions in Devel-oping Countries'. Discussion Paper, Urban Development Department, World Bank (Washington DC, 1982), 22.

10 Land

The rapid pace of urbanization projected for developing countries, especially for those of Central America, Africa, and South Asia, has already been amply described, and some of the implications have been discussed in earlier sections of this study. The projected increase of the built-up urban areas in developing countries between now and the end of the century is estimated to be around 118 per cent. This doubling of the physical size of the urban areas of the developing countries between 1980 and 2000 implies an increase in demand for residential plots from all income groups, locations for industry and commerce, and land for public buildings and projects at a scale and rapidity which has no precedent in the history of urban growth and development in the industrialized countries (see Table 10.1).

Given these trends and projections, it is clear that the question of land supply and the management of urbanized land will be one of the key issues, if not the central issue, of urban develop-

ment in the countries of Africa, Asia, and Latin America in the coming years. Land is the starting point for all settlement development and it provides the physical location for shelter, commerce, industry, roads, transport systems, social infrastructure, and other public services. Yet, most developing countries are ill-prepared for the coming dramatic expansion of their settlements and the subsequent demand for land, since most do not possess the legislation, policies, procedures, institutions, trained personnel, or financial resources to ensure that land will be supplied for settlement development at the pace and on the scale required.

The limited capacity to meet the complexity of the policy challenge posed by the land issue in developing countries is creating a bottleneck in settlement policy which will become increasingly severe in the coming years unless governments adopt immediate measures to clear it. These measures must emphasize efficient land management and ensure that future govern-

Table 10.1 Projected increases in the built-up area of selected cities and regions by the year 2000

	Initial period				Year 2000		Increase in built-up area	
	Year	Population (000s)	Built-up area (hectares)	Gross density	Population (000s)	Built-up area (hectares)	Annual (hectares)	% increase over base year
Hong Kong	1973	3,691	11,749	314	5,210	16,590	180	41
Ahmadabad, India	1980	2,451	10,073	243	5,196	21,380	565	112
Tunis, Tunisia	1975	960	4,560	211	1,994	9,450	196	107
Djakarta, Indonesia	1979	6,500	31,304	208	16,591	79,760	2,307	155
Lagos, Nigeria	1976	3,050	16,177	189	11,950	63,230	1,960	291
Moscow, USSR	1975	7,408	41,160	180	9,087	50,480	373	23
Bogota, Colombia	1981	4,550	28,260	161	11,663	72,440	2,325	156
Colombo, Sri Lanka	1980	586	3,803	154	1,125	7,310	366	92
Mexico City, Mexico	1970	8,889	58,000	153	31,025	202,780	4,826	250
Tehran, Iran	1966	2,720	18,000	151	11,329	75,030	1,677	316
Bangkok, Thailand	1981	5,331	44,428	120	11,936	99,470	2,897	124
Valencia, Venezuela	1981	730	12,167	60	1,387	23,120	576	90
Developing regions	1980	972,408	8,103,400	120	2,115,558	17,659,650	476,310	118
Developed regions	1980	834,401	6,953,340	120	1,092,470	9,103,920	107,530	31
World total	1980	1,806,809	15,056,740	120	3,208,028	26,733,570	583,840	78

Sources: United Nations, *Patterns of Urban and Rural Population Growth*, Population Studies 68 (New York, 1980), 125–54, Table 48; and numerous country publications.

Note: In calculating the estimated built-up area for the year 2000, densities are assumed to remain the same during the intervening period. Densities for regions were independently estimated, based on existing densities in towns of different sizes.

mental interventions are on the scale required for the land market to function efficiently and deliver land into the hands of large developers, small builders, building co-operatives, individual houseowners, and all the other agents producing shelter. Moreover, public authorities must strengthen their capacity to acquire land for the construction of public buildings and physical and social infrastructure on the scale that will be required over the next decades.

Considering the pace of urban growth since 1950, land markets have so far been extraordinarily adaptive. Given that the cities and urban regions of the developing countries have increased their populations as much as sixfold over the past three decades, what is surprising is not that they now face serious problems but that they function at all. But the fact that they have functioned so far does not mean they will continue to be able to do so as the future demand for land will occur under very different conditions from those of the past decades, especially with respect to the supply of land for shelter for the low-income majority.

From the physical point of view, one explanation for the initial capacity to absorb the influx may lie in what has been termed the 'porous'

quality of cities in many developing countries in the period following the Second World War, which marked the starting point of the urbanization process. The centres of these cities were, in many cases, occupied by large structures that could be converted into small units for residential and office uses. Moreover, dwellings in the centres of towns were often on large plots suitable for the construction of additional structures; and public authorities and other institutions owned large tracts of centrally located land which could be used for the construction of shelter and other physical structures and facilities. In other words, most cities in the developing countries had been built up in an unplanned, loosely structured fashion that left many empty spaces in the physical urban fabric which could be built up over time.

These conditions still persist in many African cities, but in most large cities of other developing regions the situation is changing rapidly. As a product of three decades of rapid urban growth, central-city locations have enormously increased in price. Sites have become too expensive for low-income residential occupancy, and great pressure has developed to expel existing residents and activities. Most city centres are

Table 10.2   Increases in urban land prices compared with increases in consumer price indices for selected cities and countries

	Period	Increase in land price		Increase in consumer price index		Real land price increase	
		As multiple of original	Annual (%)	As multiple of original	Annual (%)	As multiple of original	Annual (%)
Japan							
All cities	1976–81	4.93	37.6	1.36	6.3	3.63	29.4
Tokyo (residential areas)	1976–81	4.35	34.2	1.36	6.3	3.20	26.2
San Salvador, El Salvador (land for social housing)	1975–77	2.75	40.0	1.43	12.7	1.92	24.2
Seoul, Republic of Korea	1963–74	26.10	34.5	3.43	11.9	7.61	20.2
New Delhi, India (middle-income residential area)	1957–77	77.28	24.3	3.43	6.4	22.53	16.9
Caracas, Venezuela	1973–77	2.50	25.7	1.38	8.4	1.81	16.0
Large cities, France (residential suburbs)	1975–77	…	…	…	…	1.54	9.0
Manila, Philippines	1973–77	2.18	21.5	1.65	13.3	1.32	7.2
12 metropolitan areas, USA	1975–80	1.97	14.5	1.45	7.7	1.36	6.3
All cities, Federal Republic of Germany	1970–80	2.67	10.3	1.65	5.1	1.62	4.9
Urban areas, Norway (land for terrace housing)	1965–81	6.96	12.9	3.22	7.6	2.16	4.9
Lagos, Nigeria (public land)	1960–70	4.20	15.4	3.20	12.3	1.31	2.8

Sources: Country publications and other published studies. Where consumer price index was given, estimates were obtained from World Bank, *World Tables* (2nd edn., Washington DC, 1980).

undergoing a process of densification, primarily reflecting skyrocketing demand for commercial and office space which itself is the result of the economic growth and development experienced by most developing countries until at least the middle of the past decade (see Table 10.2).

If cities are to continue to be efficient platforms for economic growth and to accommodate the demands for land, shelter, and services of an ever-increasing number of residents, radical changes will be required to accomplish the transition of managed urban development. The land-delivery system in developing countries is hampered by a number of factors:

• *Land is often not perceived as a commercial good*, and hence there is little concept of land having a use-value for a particular purpose in a particular place at a particular time. Conventional market forces therefore do not function well in bringing land into settlement use.

• *Information about land is unreliable* because the market in land is weak, and commercial land trading is not geared to a large volume of transactions. Price structures are therefore haphazard and capricious, and those needing land have no institutional system for locating it where and when it is needed.

• *Land is often the only avenue for investment* in developing countries, and funds are channelled into land purchases simply as a saving mechanism. Hoarding and speculation therefore distort the land-supply process.

• *Land transactions are hampered by unclear laws* on ownership, use-rights, transfer formalities, and mortgage procedures. The acquisition of land for development can therefore be an enormously cumbersome, time-consuming, and, not infrequently, uncertain process.

• *Public authorities usually have no co-ordinated programme for extending the infrastructure* that will convert raw land into usable land. Land developers are therefore unable to plan ahead for an assured flow of buildable land at predictable prices.

Governments will have to tackle all of these issues in order to set up a reliable land-supply mechanism for their settlements.

Even when this has been done, some special attention will probably still be needed to the problem of land for low-income shelter. The transition to what some observers have labelled 'the second stage or urbanization' in developing countries will have particularly negative consequences for the methods by which the poor have obtained land for shelter in the past. In fact, a review of these methods shows that they are being exhausted. Since low-income groups will continue to constitute the majority of people in the settlements of the developing countries, it is essential to examine how the urban poor, in particular, have gained access to land in the past, and how these channels are being circumscribed, altered, or dramatically reduced in efficacy by economic and other factors.

The premiss of all human settlements strategies is, of course, that land will be available for the construction of all settlement elements, particularly for housing. The remainder of this chapter reviews a variety of options which governments may wish to consider in the formulation of their urban land policies, focusing on measures to increase the supply of urban land and on administrative reforms to reduce land-supply distortions. Their aim is to ensure that adequate supplies of land are made available for all builders, and that land markets function efficiently. The great problem will remain that of ensuring a supply of land for low-income housing. It is clear that public authorities cannot assume a passive attitude towards the issue of land supply in the decades ahead. With supply tight, demand high, and urban growth continuing, public authorities must establish new enabling mechanisms which will ensure land delivery as needed.

Actions by public agencies

There is rarely an absolute shortage of land: there is generally a supply bottleneck in the delivery of affordable serviced land in appropriate locations. One of the principal factors causing this artificial shortage is the lack of institutional, managerial, and financial capacity to increase the supply of serviced land. There is no doubt that accelerated expansion of basic urban infrastructure, combined with the expansion of transport networks to newly urbanized areas, is one of the principal means by which the problems of scarcity and high land prices can be met.

The ability of public authorities to extend basic services and transport systems is, to a very large degree, based on the financial capacity to do so, and this in turn will depend on the degree to which public agencies recover the costs of these infrastructure programmes from the increase in land values that they generate. Although such recovery mechanisms will vary from country to country and will be determined by local conditions, they will have to include some form of taxation that will ensure that the property owners who gain through the construction of infrastructure and the extension of transport systems pay a reasonable share of the cost of the construction and expansion of service networks. Particularly in cities with high demand and shortages of serviced land, the value added to the property will be far greater than the construction costs. In such cases, both the owners and the public agency gain.

Implementing such cost-recovery schemes will not be easy. They involve not only difficult political decisions but also the solution of a whole array of administrative and technical problems. Until some mechanisms for cost recovery and for property taxation in general are established, it will be difficult to increase the land supply and reduce the current high cost of urban land.

Public–private-sector co-operation

Despite the increasing commercialization of urban land markets, informal land-delivery systems still provide a very important proportion of the total land being supplied for shelter. Particularly in the case of unauthorized land subdivisions, there appears to be some scope for public intervention to improve performance and curb abuses. Evidence suggests that private subdividers operate more speedily and efficiently than government bureaucracies, and it should be possible to legitimize the basic activity of such subdividers while imposing on them the responsibility for preparing street alignments and plot layouts which are suitable for future expansion of basic services. The joining of private initiative with a supportive govern-

mental framework can, under certain conditions and assuming an effective administrative capacity at the city level, be cost-effective. The objective should be not to block informal systems of land delivery but to direct them in such a way that they operate in the public interest. This, of course, implies a firm managerial role for local government.

The same observation can be made regarding relationships between the formal private construction and land-development sector and the public sector. So far, governments have placed few demands on private developers regarding the provision of basic services and amenities. What will be necessary in the future is that both government and private developers establish a pattern of co-operation in land development that will provide a mix of incentives and disincentives and allow for the final outcome of land and urban development to be in harmony with the general interest.

Limiting land speculation

Releasing sufficient amounts of land for settlement development will also depend on reducing the degree to which land is used as a store of capital in the market-economy developing countries. Land is considered one of the safest forms of investment as a hedge against actual or anticipated inflation in virtually all these countries, and it is acquired by investors not with its physical use in mind but rather as a form of security against economic uncertainty. Some countries, mostly the developed market-economy countries but also some developing countries, have established a regulatory and taxation system which discourages this form of investment in land. In the majority of developing countries, however, investment in land as security has distorted urban development patterns. For example, in Greater Buenos Aires, more than half of all existing plots remain vacant, and in Brazil vacant lots represent one-third of the total area of cities.

It has been argued that land speculation is a normal and natural phenomenon which may actually have some beneficial effect by keeping in reserve a supply of land which can be put on the market at some future date. However, in developing countries, urban land markets do not function in ways which can ensure that land is brought into the market in an economically rational manner. Given this situation, it may be necessary for governments to consider measures to create investment opportunities with similar security and rate of return. This may be difficult to achieve, but if successful it would increase the supply of land for all income groups.

Such measures must be combined with other steps to ensure that land ceases to be such an attractive form of speculative investment. These disincentives could include:

• *Taxation*, to bring the profitability of land transactions in line with the returns from other investments with similar levels of risk.

• *Credit controls*, to prevent the lending of funds for the purchase of land which will not be immediately developed. (Such controls can never function perfectly but could prevent excessive speculations.)

• *Price freezing*, but this could be counterproductive in the long run since it might create more severe market distortions than those that it is intended to remedy.

Administrative reforms

There is no doubt that many of the current distortions in the urban land supply have been the result of inaction on the part of public authorities, owing to the absence of machinery to supervise the land market. In some areas, radical changes in thinking and procedures will be called for.

Efficient use of the existing land supply

One of the central questions of urban development is the degree of regulation that should be imposed on the process. There is no doubt that governments have a legitimate right and obligation to prevent the mushrooming of urban slums, but it is equally true that standards that are too high impose prohibitive costs on the low-income groups who will continue to constitute the majority of urban residents in most developing countries. When resolving this issue, public authorities must be guided by the fundamental objective of increasing the total amount of affordable land, since only adequate supply will, in the end, guarantee affordable prices. The adoption of appropriate standards is a fundamental step in achieving land-distribution and land-use efficiency.

Modernization of cadastral and land registration systems

It is evident that the operation of land markets has been negatively affected by the lack of good and up-to-date cadastral (land boundary) records as well as registration of titles. The systems existing in many, if not most, developing countries were established at a time of slow urban growth and have not kept up with the pace of the past two decades. Delays in land transfers, registration of titles, and so on have slowed down investment and construction, and because of intervening inflationary effects such delays have, in many instances, severely affected development costs. Since the security of registered title, with clear delineation of boundaries, is essential in all forms of land development, cadastral and land registration systems are important to economic development as physical infrastructure. Therefore, it is alarming that so many developing countries still have not taken the necessary steps to create modernized and efficient cadastral and land registration systems.

Inventories of publicly owned land

In many developing countries, the exact level of public land holdings is not known. This does not mean that when these holdings are identified they should be sold for development purposes, but rather that these inventories should set the basis for an interministerial and interagency policy concerning land and land supply. Moreover, such inventories could also facilitate transfers of land between governmental agencies, thus speeding up land development, especially for public infrastructure and buildings.

Box 10.1   Land cadastre: prerequisite for urban development

Cities in the developing world are finding that their land-registry agencies are unable to keep up with the volume of land transactions and rapidly changing patterns of land use associated with accelerated urban growth. As a result, a number of other problems have arisen, such as inability of cities to increase their revenue base, distortions of urban land markets, and delays in urban development projects.

Creating an up-to-date and efficient cadastre can do much to alleviate these problems. A cadastre is an official register of the location, boundaries, ownership, value, and other attributes of land. It must systematically cover all parcels within the defined area and be regularly updated. A cadastral survey is the demarcation of parcel boundaries; it may involve ground surveys, aerial photography, and data from existing maps. A cadastral map is based on the survey findings.

There are three basic types of cadastres: fiscal, legal, and multipurpose:

● *Fiscal cadastre.* A record of the information necessary for levying property taxes, including parcel location and value. Often, the information is not as precise as that required for a legal cadastre. Frequently, the occupant of the parcel is identified for tax purposes, and no effort is made to determine the legal owner.

● *Legal cadastre.* A register identifying the legal owner and precise boundaries of each land parcel. Establishing a legal cadastre requires both fixing parcel boundaries through surveying and mapping, and fixing legal rights, which may involve negotiations among involved parties and a judicial determination of ownership.

● *Multipurpose cadastre.* A relatively new development that incorporates, in one source, the legal and fiscal cadastre data plus information on land use, infrastructure, buildings, soil, and other factors. Each parcel must be assigned a unique identifier, so that all the information can be related to the same plot.

The quantity, breadth, and detail of the data to be included in a cadastre can thus vary, depending on its uses. Whatever the system adopted, public authorities will have to make a commitment to a continuous effort, involving *Source:* World Bank.

investment in staff and other resources. The benefits of such an undertaking can include:

● *Increased generation of revenue from city taxes.* A cadastre which lists the boundaries and market value of land parcels and identifies the individuals who own them and have an obligation to pay taxes on them is a prerequisite for the assessment and collection of property taxes. Especially now that cities are faced with increasing fiscal constraints, increased generation of revenue at the city level can help offset reduction of financial resources coming from central government. Of course, establishing a fiscal cadastre is not in itself sufficient: what is also needed is the political will to undertake the collection of property taxes and to provide sufficient manpower to update records and assessments.

● *Smoother functioning of urban land markets.* Systematic identification of the boundaries and legal ownership of land parcels is critical to the smooth functioning of urban land markets. The absence of such information produces long and unnecessary delays in the transfer of land parcels. This effectively removes a large percentage of urban land from the market, thus producing an upward surge in land prices.

● *More rapid assembly of land for development projects.* A cadastral system is also necessary in order for public authorities to carry out urban development projects. Inadequacies in the land registration system make it very difficult, time-consuming, and costly to assemble land for infrastructure, shelter, industry, and roads. Such delays raise project costs and can affect the choice of the project site.

● *Improved housing for the poor.* Experience in developing countries has repeatedly shown that secure title encourages the urban poor to mobilize resources that would otherwise not have been tapped for the improvement of their shelter. Since loans are usually extended on the basis of security provided by property, a cadastral system can widen and increase access to credit.

In light of the needs of the cities of developing countries, it may be appropriate that land registration systems be built around a legal cadastre which establishes actual landownership. Other data, particularly those related to taxation, could then easily be fed into such a system.

Legislation for compulsory acquisition

Since in many countries, the legal definition of acquisition in the public interest is very narrow, such procedures tend to be slow. Although land acquisition by public authorities should never be undertaken as a blanket measure, the increasingly tight urban land market and the prospects of urban growth may make it imperative that public authorities be given the instruments to

acquire land for the purposes of building essential social and physical infrastructure.

Land for housing the poor

The problem of delivering land for the supply of low-income shelter is a special issue in the promotion of a functioning land market. A survey of the mechanisms of land supply for low-income house-builders in the developing countries and of the gradual transformation of these mechanisms must take into account two considerations: (*a*) mechanisms of land supply for the urban poor are location-specific, making it difficult to generalize; and (*b*) land-supply mechanisms tend to change over time, principally as a reflection of the emergence of land as a commodity. As urban land changes from being just a place to settle to being a capital asset, its supply and value will be ruled by the laws of supply and demand rather than by considerations of social justice and equity.

The literature on the mechanisms for supply of urban land to low-income groups usually divides these into three categories: non-commercial, commercial, and administrative. *Non-commercial* refers to situations where those who build on the land do not pay for ownership or use-rights, or pay in the form of 'voluntary gifts' determined by social custom. In other words, there is no monetary transfer price attached to the land. Even if people are expected to pay, such payments are tied to the 'worth' of the person and not to the commercial value of the land. *Commercial mechanisms* for land supply are those of the land market, where the monetary transfer price of land is determined by supply–demand equilibrium, and access to building plots is conditioned by the ability to pay. One key aspect of commercial transfers of land is that it is the

---

Box 10.2   Public intervention in urban land markets: new approaches

In some developing countries, governments have experimented with measures designed to influence the behaviour of the urban land market:

● *Land readjustment* has become a vehicle for servicing and rationalizing land delivery at the city's periphery. Under land-readjustment programmes, unserviced land is surrendered to public authorities which subsequently provide it with basic infrastructure, parks, schools, etc. Part of the serviced land is returned to the previous owner who is able to develop it for profit. The remainder of the land is sold by the public agency to private developers at a price that provides for the full recovery of initial development costs and subsequent operating costs. The sale of serviced land to private developers is subject to conditions covering land use, density requirements, and other planning criteria.

If correctly undertaken, land readjustment is able to serve both public and private interests. Land readjustment is practised widely in the Republic of Korea and is also used to a limited degree in some cities in India. Several experiments in land readjustment have been carried out in Kenya, but their impact has been minimal, and the administrative and political problems involved have discouraged planners and administrators from pursuing it. The most serious deficiency is that, as practised in the developing countries, land readjustment makes land available for high-income and not for low-income housing.

● *Land banking* is another approach which some developing countries have introduced. Land banking refers to the acquisition and maintenance by public authorities of stocks or banks of land which are sufficiently large to meet future public-sector development needs. Malaysia and Singapore have implemented particularly ambitious land-banking schemes, designed to secure sites for new towns, while some other developing countries have used land banking to acquire sites with a high potential for housing on the periphery of cities. Ecuador, Chile, India, and Turkey have employed this option to build up land reserves.

The paucity of finance has proved an obstacle to the wide application of land-banking as well as to other efforts to generate finance through various types of joint-venture arrangements. In Colombia, for example, joint ventures have been established between a government mortgage bank, construction companies, and social security institutions. The mortgage bank, as the owner of large areas of urban land, uses 'expensive' money from social security funds to develop land for the construction of housing units, the sale of which produces profits for the bank. These profits are then used to buy new land for urban renewal projects to be undertaken by the bank itself or by private development companies. There is yet little evidence, however, to suggest that the bank's activities can be directed towards the satisfaction of the land needs of low-income groups.

● *Systems of land leasing* which aim at recovering increased urban land values and at creating land reserves for future development are also being increasingly employed. In Burma, all land is state land, and individual rights to land are established by grants, leases, and licences. Leaseholds run from 5 years to a maximum of 90 years and reflect the use to which the land is to be put and the extent and nature of developments on adjoining land. Landowners in Fiji are prohibited by law from selling communal land: such land can only be made available for use by leasing through the Native Land Trust Board. Leasehold tenure is often the most effective means of controlling publicly held land and encouraging its appropriate use. It calls, however, for efficient administrative arrangements and effective lease conditions, both of which have to be used in conjunction with fiscal and land-tenure measures if the objectives of public land policies are to be achieved.

owner who receives title to property, since it is not land which commands a price but land ownership. *Administrative* mechanisms are the means available to public authorities to acquire and dispose of land, change its form of tenure, and regulate its use and development. Public authorities rarely interfere with the market in the process of acquiring land or in allocating building plots. An example is the fringe locations of most sites-and-services projects, and the plot charges for the beneficiaries. Administrative power is the main expression of governmental action in urban land management.

Non-commercial sources

Customary land

In some developing countries, rapid urban growth occurred at a time when large tracts of land were not yet in the hands of individual owners or commercial entrepreneurs. In many parts of Africa and in the islands of the Pacific Ocean, tribes and ethnic communities retained their customary right to use and administer land and to allocate it according to prevailing social customs. The term 'customary land' can also be used to include the communal land holdings found in Islamic countries. In Latin America, by contrast, customary land holdings are rare. Communal land tenure was widespread in Central America before the turn of the century, but it disappeared with the arrival of commercialized export-oriented agriculture, primarily coffee production. As a rule, customary or communal land cannot be commercialized or alienated, and its use is restricted to members of the community, whether tribal, ethnic, or religious.

With the increase of migration to urban areas, customary land in and around the city became the focal point of settlement and shelter construction. This process would usually take place along the following lines. First, migrants belonging to the same community, tribe, or ethnic group would request temporary or permanent building plots on the basis of their filial ties with the urban community. Later, friends or acquaintances from within the city or tenants of the established occupants on the customary land would also apply, thus opening up the customary land to a broad stratum of urban low-income groups. Access, at least initially, was still controlled by the local traditional hierarchy, whether religious or otherwise, but today this important mechanism for the supply of cheap or no-cost building land is being eroded by three processes:

- *As settlements grow, the trading of occupied plots is no longer in the hands of chiefs or other traditional authorities,* but instead is undertaken by the occupants themselves. Land prices are established, and new arrivals are faced with an increasingly commercialized process of land development rather than the previous allocation system. As the pursuit of monetary gain becomes widespread, many residents develop rental housing themselves rather than offer the plots to new arrivals for shelter construction. One of the reasons for this change is that the monetary requirements of living in an urban economy are such that residents must turn to whatever resources are available to increase their income.

- *The growing sophistication and organization of tribal groups and other communities is increasing their tendency to reserve land for lucrative urban developments.* In Fiji, for example, the Native Lands Development Corporation is now the sole developer of native lands, disposing of serviced sites at market prices.

Box 10.3   Customary land

Port Moresby, Papua New Guinea. The Motu urban villagers in Port Moresby have long-standing traditional trading links with tribes from the Gulf Province. Because of these traditional links, many migrants from the Gulf Province have now been permitted to settle in and build houses at the edge of Port Moresby's urban villages.

Blantyre, Malawi. In order to get a building plot in Ndirande, a settler needs to be introduced to the local chief. Accompanied by a long-established resident who has proved to be a reliable and outstanding member of the community, the applicant will explain the reasons why he would like to settle there, the general area where he would like to live, the size of the plot he needs, and the type of house he would like to build. If the chief agrees, he will walk with the petitioner to the proposed site, talk it over with the people already settled there, and mark out the new plot with stones.

• *Governments increasingly view customary and communal land as an archaic form of land tenure out of step with the development of a modern economy and society.* In some African countries, governments have already taken legal steps to acquire African trust land and transfer it to the domain of 'public land'. Similar processes have taken place in other countries and regions in the past, as in Central America, and it is reasonable to expect that economic forces and administrative regulations will continue to erode the supply of customary land over the next decades.

Government land reserves

Many colonial governments alienated large tracts of native land which then reverted to the post-independence government in the form of public or state land. In Islamic countries, because of long-standing legal traditions, large tracts of land are, at least nominally, held by the government. Laws regulating the tenure and disposal of government land reserves tend to vary from country to country, but the very size of these land holdings, the absence of legal stipulations for their use, and the difficulty of policing them make land reserves an easy target for spontaneous settlement, particularly on the urban fringe.

In Lima, for example, the high proportion of unauthorized settlement development has resulted from the widespread ambiguity of land titles. This ambiguity results in part from a homesteading system that allows individuals to establish ownership of public land for agriculture and mining. Similarly, most land in rural Turkey had for generations been owned by the state, and villagers had use-rights to holdings they farmed or lived on. For migrants coming from these areas to the cities, such forms of settlement were an accepted and legitimate procedure, and the availability of unclaimed government land enabled them to act on this traditional basis.

Whether the result of organized invasions, gradual encroachments, or occupations undertaken with the tacit agreement of government, squatter settlements have grown rapidly on government land reserves, especially where such land was in large supply. Contrary to popular thinking, the role of public authorities in encouraging the growth of these settlements has been far from marginal. In fact, public authorities often played a crucial role in 'directing' these occupations on to undesirable sites and away from locations of commercial value. According to a very conservative estimate, 500,000 people, representing more than one-sixth of the total population of metropolitan Lima, live in settlements in the formation of which the government played a crucial role.

However, three factors, discernible in differing degrees in different countries and locations, are circumscribing the availability of government land reserves as a source of no-cost land for the construction of shelter. The first one is that squatter-settlement sites soon assume the characteristics of the urban commercial land market, as plots are sold or subdivided for sale to others. For example, a household survey conducted in Valencia, Venezuela, revealed that the people who had bought plots in the settlement, once the invasion was a *fait accompli*, far outnumbered the original 'invaders'. In Ankara, Turkey, when land in the private freehold and *gecekondu* markets was adequate to meet the demand, the two existed as distinct and separate entities; in the former, land was priced according to its location, while, in the latter, land was distributed largely through a network of personal contacts. With increasing pressure on land in both markets, developers quickly found ways of acquiring land originally settled by *gecekondus* and developing it for middle- and upper-income groups. What these two examples illustrate is a general tendency towards 'privatization' of squatter settlements developed on government land reserves, a tendency which quickly accelerates once these settlements are legalized and serviced as a consequence of settlement-upgrading programmes.

Another way by which the occupation of government land reserves is becoming commercialized is through illegal subdivision of the land by commercial entrepreneurs and political middle-men prior to occupation. Plots are sold to future occupiers, and, sometimes, some basic facilities are provided. Often these subdivisions and subsequent occupations are based on collusion and co-operation between commercial and political interests. In South Asia, in particular, such 'spontaneous' settlements on government land reserves have become targets for political patronage and vote-gathering, when legalization or service provision becomes a burning issue at election time. Finally, the supply of free land in government land reserves in or near urban areas is being curtailed, through its use by public authorities for sites-and-services projects or sale to private developers.

Abandoned properties

In some urban areas in developing countries, abandoned properties became a significant source of non-commercial land supply for the urban poor, particularly in the aftermath of armed conflict, domestic political upheaval, or the withdrawal of colonial authorities. Such events gave rise to opportunities whereby abandoned properties could become focal points for the development of squatter settlements. It is, however, clear that the appropriation of

abandoned properties by urban low-income settlers is a passing phenomenon, since governments quickly move to establish 'law and order' and end the arbitrary occupation of properties.

Marginal land

Over the past decades, squatter settlements have mushroomed on land not suitable for housing to the extent that squatter settlements scattered over flood plains, marshland, hill-slopes, and other sites unsuitable for habitation have come to typify the shelter conditions of urban low-income groups. Settlements appear on such marginal lands for two principal reasons, both of which are intimately connected with the increasing commercialization of the urban land supply. First, when no land is available for the construction of shelter through administrative measures or non-commercial means, those who cannot afford to pay even minimal rents or purchase prices must build in places such as the ones described above. In some cities, such as Bogota, Manila, São Paulo, and the cities of Indonesia,

---

Box 10.4   Abandoned properties as sites for spontaneous settlement

Manila, Philippines. The current pattern of squatting began immediately after the Second World War. The fighting in the rural areas, as well as the general insecurity, pushed a lot of people to the cities, many of which had been bombed. Since many houses had been destroyed by bombing or ground-fighting, new migrants settled anywhere on vacant land. It was at this time that the squatter settlements of Tondo and Intramuros were started. Because the government could not police the city, people continued to settle in this way long after the war was over, and the pattern continues to this day.

Lusaka, Zambia. Land once owned by a farmer named George but abandoned at the time of independence in 1964 rapidly developed into a settlement, known as George's Compound, through spontaneous squatting, completely out of control of the authorities. The core of the settlement was formed by the houses of the farm workers; nobody had ever paid rent, and for this reason the question of landownership initially appeared irrelevant to most of the inhabitants.

However, in order to prevent further spontaneous occupations of this kind, the Zambian Government, through its political organization, the United National Independence Party (UNIP), tried to channel urban arrivals to areas where they were allowed to build. Often, local UNIP officials acted as urban headmen. Later, this arrangement was superseded by the creation of a special unit of the local government administration to oversee the improvement of existing settlements and to provide plots for new ones.

Box 10.5   Marginal land in Indonesia and Morocco

Jakarta, Indonesia. A special type of settlement in the northern part of Jakarta is the marshland squatter *kampung*. The encroachment on marshlands by settlers is carried out systematically along the marsh fringes, progressively adding dry land as new arrivals move into these areas.

River sites in the central city also provide rent-free accommodation, but they are among the poorest choices for living space in the city. Characteristically, river dwellers settle on levees, terraces, and steep embankments. Seasonal flooding is a chronic problem, causing extensive damage to settlements each year. In Bidara Cina and Kampung Melaya, the Ciliwung River has cut deep into bedrock, forming steep banks. In such places, the stilt houses are linked by plank bridges.

Rabat, Morocco. Under the French Protectorate in Morocco, laws were passed declaring certain portions of Rabat off-limits for permanent housing. These zones were on the steep slopes and adjacent salt marshes bordering the river that divides Rabat from Sale. These 'protected' sites became the location for *bidonvilles*. Since the land could not be used for conventional shelter, these regulations in fact had the effect of attracting squatter settlements; and owing to the fact that the construction of permanent housing on such sites was illegal, the normal transformation of these jerry-built shacks to improved and habitable shelter was actually prevented.

the land supply is so commercialized that the non-commercial supply is restricted to marginal land. Another common reason for the increasing use of marginal land for low-income settlements is where such land is centrally located, giving easy access to employment opportunities in the heart of the city. Even when free or cheap land is available for construction on the urban fringe, transport costs are prohibitively high for the many urban poor looking for casual employment or working in the informal sector. If marginal land, for whatever reason, is available near the inner city, it becomes an economically strategic location for shelter.

Two processes, however, tend to erode the use of marginal urban areas as a supply of free land for the construction of shelter. In many of these settlements, the pioneering core of squatter families turn, over time, into petty land-lords, and new arrivals have to purchase shares in the plots. Surveys conducted in well-established squatter areas in marginal locations routinely document an intricate hierarchy of ownership and tenancy patterns both for dwell-

---

Box 10.6   Marginal land: from squatters to landlords in India and Lebanon

Madras, India. A group of 10 or more people living in rented huts will find an unguarded spot of vacant land on the river margins, between industrial sites, infrastructure ease-ments, and the like. First they put up only the bamboo poles for each hut and wait to see if anybody objects. If, for a few days, nobody resists the encroachment, they build the huts overnight. In a period of six months to a year, if not removed, the settlement will start growing as residents encourage their relatives and friends to come and occupy the remaining area. After a year or so, the original settlers gain confidence and begin to sell plots on the remaining land.

Beirut, Lebanon. Originally, the area of Quarantina in central Beirut was the place where persons entering the country were quartered for health reasons. When this institution was abandoned, the land was pre-empted by squatters, even though it was by then adjacent to the city garbage dump and was considered unsuitable for habitation. Quarantina became a classic squatter settlement, densely laid out on a grossly unhealthy site with houses of semi-permanent construction. Over the years, many of the orig-inal settlers experienced social mobility, and, by the 1970s, the houses they owned were being rented to newcomers, many of them Kurds.

Box 10.7   Marginal land: from tolerance to eviction in the Philippines

'Pursuant to Proclamation No. 1081 dated September 21, 1972, and in my capacity as Commander-in-Chief of all the Armed Forces of the Philippines and in the interest of public health, safety and peace and order, you and the subordinate officials and employees under you are hereby ordered:

1. To remove all illegal constructions including buildings on and along estuaries and riverbanks, those along railroad tracks and those built without permits on public or private properties;
2. To relocate, assist in the relocation or return to their home provinces, and determine relocation sites for squatters and other persons to be displaced or evicted from cited estuaries and places and
3. To closely coordinate among yourselves and other agencies and assist in the prompt and effective implementation of these instructions.

The PAHRA [Presidential Assistance on Housing and Resettlement Agency] shall determine the [new] squatter relocation areas. City Engineers, Mayors and other Officials authorized to issue building permits are enjoined to be careful in the issuance of such permits to prevent construc-tions affecting or encroaching upon properties devoted to public use or service and they shall be held to strict account-ability for authorizing or tolerating illegal constructions.

This order shall constitute standing instructions to cover present and future constructions, unless otherwise direc-ted by me or my authorized representative, and shall be executed without regard to any contrary order from any other source or authority.'

Source: Presidential Assistance on Housing and Resettlement Agency, *Terminal Report* (Manila, October 1975), app. 7.

---

ings and land. The second and more serious process is the increasing determination of urban administrations to remove squatters for health and safety reasons. As municipal governments become efficient in the application of building regulations and zoning laws, the tendency has been to evict settlements and block the formation of new ones. The massive eviction programmes in Colombo, Dhaka, Jakarta, Manila, and Delhi are examples of this assertive behaviour on the part of municipal authorities.

Commercial sources

The supply of land for the urban poor through established market mechanisms usually takes three forms: 'miniplots' (minimum-sized plots carved out of the spare land surrounding existing houses), land rental, and 'substandard' sub-divisions, so called because the land is sub-divided without the approval of the proper authorities and is not provided with infra-structure.

Those who sell miniplots do so as a means of capitalizing their urban land assets, usually in the form of a one-time transaction, and using the money to improve their own housing or move to a more secure or up-market settlement. In the land-rental system, landowners are interested in generating a constant cash flow while they await profitable investment opportunities for their property. Substandard subdivisions, on the other hand, constitute an organized commercial activity in which parcels of land are bought, as-sembled into large estates, and subdivided into uniform plots, usually without infrastructure.

Miniplots

When the supply of vacant land is limited or only available at distant fringe locations, the purchase of miniplots may be the only way low-income families can acquire land for the construction of shelter. These small plots, carved out of the spare land surrounding existing houses, usually allow for only enough space to build the most basic shelter for new arrivals.

This fragmentation of land in existing low-income settlements has probably been the main source of financing for the original settlers to improve their shelter situation. In fact, the sale of these miniplots carries with it some advantages. First, it is the poor who benefit financially from the sale of part of their land. Secondly, there is a wide margin of negotiation between sellers and buyers as to the size of the plot, terms of pay-ment, and the price itself. Finally, increasing the population of the settlement through the sale of minimum-size plots to new arrivals strengthens the community's bargaining power to maintain or improve security of tenure and to press the authorities for the provision of basic services.

Another trend in many countries is for the sale of miniplots to give way to the conversion of houses into rental units as increasing densities physically restrict the sale of miniplots. Owner-builders then look for other means to sup-plement their incomes, or use the additional income from rental to seek housing in other parts of the city.

Land rental

While the sale of miniplots is a commercial activity usually restricted to small landowners,

---

Box 10.8 Minimum-sized plots and land rental

Lusaka, Zambia. The first settlers who came to the settlement known as 'George's Compound' built their own houses, sometimes with the help of a bricklayer. They were, at the same time, builders, owners, and occupants of the houses. As far as is known, no houses were built with the conscious purpose of renting them, but mobility was considerable in the compound, and when the builder/owner left the house, he would sell it or rent it. In 1969, about 80 per cent of the houses were occupied by the builders; by 1977, only one-third were builder-occupied. In some cases, two tenant households shared one house, or the main tenant house-hold had a secondary tenant. It also appeared, at that time, as if most absentee owners had lived in the house at one time, and every indication is that petty landlordism has increased up to the present day.

Maputo, Mozambique. Before independence, land tenure and possession of houses could be arranged in different ways. A landowner might own a certain area of land on which he allowed a number of families to build a shelter of their own. In this way, the settlers paid rent to the land-owner for the land but not for the house. Sometimes, the landowner himself arranged for the houses to be built, and in these cases the tenant paid rent for the house but not for the land. Sometimes, individuals rented land from large landholders, which they in turn leased to tenants for profit.

Bangkok, Thailand. Thirty per cent of the total population of Bangkok was found to be living in slums and squatter settlements in 1974. Of these, only 19 per cent were squatters, mostly on government land. The remainder were legal tenants on government and private land, who had constructed temporary houses with the permission of the owners. Of these, the majority were found on private land, and a survey by the National Housing Authority in 1979 revealed that, out of 246 slum communities, 74 per cent were located on private land. Land rental, however, is a transitional form of urban land use and is replaced over time by either 'illegal' land subdivision or corporate hous-ing development.

Butterworth, Malaysia. Most of the private landowners are neither land speculators nor developers. Before the Second World War and immediately thereafter, these landowners encouraged settlers to put up houses on their land, so that they could collect land rents in addition to the revenue from the coconuts already being produced on the land. In the late 1970s, however, these same landowners became reluctant to allow new settlers on their land: there was increasing demand for land by housing developers, and the presence of settlers greatly reduced the price such land could command.

land rentals are most often the domain of large landowners who rent their land for the construction of shelter by the poor while they await either investment opportunities or price increases, so they can sell the land to a large commercial property developer. For this reason, land rental is usually a transitory phenomenon in the urban settlements of developing countries, often replaced by either substandard land subdivision or by large-scale corporate housing development.

Substandard subdivisions

The subdividing of land into regular, unserviced plots for sale to low-income house-builders is an increasing phenomenon in the cities of developing countries, particularly on the urban periphery. The procedure usually runs along the following lines:

1. Land is subdivided without approval by the proper authorities and usually without the urban services required in conventional subdivisions.
2. Plots are purchased from persons who have a legal title.
3. Some 'colour of title' is given to the purchaser, often in the form of an instalment contract with a promise of recordable title at the end of the payment period.
4. Housing is constructed by the purchasers without an official building permit.

The agents responsible for substandard subdivisions are usually property developers who are not, in most cases, the original owners of the land. Rather, they identify parcels of vacant land, assemble them, and then proceed to subdivide the assembled project into plots.

Substandard subdivisions became a source of land supply in Latin American cities approximately two decades ago. In Asia the practice is more recent and given the level of poverty in Asian cities, unauthorized subdivisions are likely to become a land-supply mechanism for middle-income groups rather than the urban poor. This is because the very logic of the land market, with competition for land for industrial and commercial development as well as for middle-income housing, eventually prices out the low-income sector as plots in the subdivisions become too expensive for the poor.

In many countries, developers of such subdivisions are likely to be eclipsed over time by the

Box 10.9   'Pirate' subdivisions in Bogota, Colombia

Nearly half of the new shelter units built in Bogota in recent years have been constructed illegally, most of them in unauthorized 'pirate developments'. These pirate developments differ from squatter settlements, which are not common in Bogota, in that prospective residents purchase lots from developers. The developer usually buys vacant, often rural, land and subdivides it without obtaining an official permit or complying with zoning laws or infrastructure standards. The lots are usually sold with little or no infrastructure or services. Buyers are usually upwardly mobile former renters entering the houseownership market for the first time, with an average age of 35 years. The demand for lots in pirate subdivisions indicates that families are willing to forego some essential services, at least initially, in order to obtain building sites which they can afford.

Pirate subdividers offer instalment credit and accept delayed payments, critical factors for low-income buyers who lack access to conventional sources of credit. In 1978, a survey demonstrated that 63 per cent of households in pirate subdivisions had bought their lot on credit. According to the same survey, approximately two-thirds of the buyers built their house in several stages. Since they lack access to building loans, some households wait up to five years to begin construction. During this time, they often purchase building materials and stockpile them on their plot. Despite the often expressed fear that substandard subdivisions give rise to makeshift housing, research conducted in the early 1980s indicates that shacks and core units are only transitional and give way over time to conventional houses.

Contrary to general belief, pirate development is a competitive business and not a monopoly, and developers earn a normal rate of return on their investment. What pirate land developers do is simply ignore legal regulations and standards. In the past, Bogota has eventually legalized these subdivisions, often by relaxing standards, thus enabling residents to gain access to basic public services and to security of tenure.

The conclusion that can be drawn from Bogota's experience with pirate subdividers is that the existing regulatory framework has become inappropriate and must be modified to conform with actual practice and conditions. Since plots in these subdivisions are acceptable to buyers who could not afford plots developed according to legal standards, pirate subdivisions should be seen as an efficient means of increasing the supply of land for the construction of shelter by low-income groups. However, it is also clear that this process must receive some co-operation and guidance from public authorities, in order to maximize its benefits.

formal, corporate private sector, which usually works in close collaboration with public authorities and employs a strategy of assembling vacant rural land long before urban pressures manifest themselves. These concerns are therefore easily able to pre-empt the 'pirate' operators.

Administrative mechanisms

Public authorities can influence and regulate the supply of land for low-income settlements in two ways: projects and administrative regulations. *Projects* usually take the form of land which is released or sold in a planned fashion to specific groups of owner-builders. *Regulations* represent a form of administrative intervention in the urban land market. Given the limited success of public projects in supplying sufficient public housing or land to build on, rules and regulations may yet prove to be the most effective measures that public authorities can utilize to influence the land supply to the benefit of low-income urban dwellers.

Projects

In most developing countries, even before independence, governments accepted some form of responsibility for the construction of public housing for low-income groups. These programmes were expanded after independence, although the supply of public housing still lagged far behind demand. In the 1970s, governments began to shift towards sites-and-services projects, in the hope that their low costs would allow projects to reach an expanded number of low-income beneficiaries. These projects, consisting of plots with various degrees of basic services and access to other urban infrastructure, were basically a technocratic response to the shelter problems of the urban poor. They were based on the assumption that, given this assistance, recipients would construct their own shelter, ultimately producing a consolidated low-income neighbourhood, with access to basic urban services, roads, transport, etc.

Although sites-and-services projects have been implemented in many developing countries, it would be very difficult to name one in which this form of project represents a significant source of land for the urban low-income majority. In many cases, sites-and-services projects, rather than reaching the core of the urban poor, have given access to building sites for middle-income groups. In other cases, they have eventually become rental housing for low-income groups and a source of income for middle-class builder-owners. This situation is likely to continue as long as employment and income criteria prevent many of the urban poor from participating in such projects. However, even if these eligibility requirements were lowered, it would be impossible for sites-and-services projects to fill the needs gap.

There are many reasons why allocation of land by public authorities through such projects will remain a negligible source of land supply for shelter construction by low-income groups, especially in cities where there exist no substantial parcels of land in the hands of public authorities. First, land for government-sponsored subdivision needs to be acquired at its market price or close to it: this makes it expensive. Secondly, projects must have a level of infrastructure provision high enough not to embarrass the government: this makes them expensive. Thirdly, the acquisition of private land through the exercise of 'eminent domain' is cumbersome and time-consuming: this makes the development of projects slow. Fourthly, projects must be planned, approved, engineered, costed, tendered, supervised, and co-ordinated with other bureaucratic decision-making bodies: this slows down implementation. Fifthly, when implementation is slow, there are budget overruns owing to inflation: these also add to the cost.

However, in countries where governments control land resources around cities and are prepared to release them to low-income housebuilders in a rather rudimentary form of subdivision, projects could provide a significant source of land supply for low-income housing.

Regulations

Over the past decades, governments have used their regulatory powers to intervene in the urban land market in order to release for low-income housing land which would otherwise remain vacant or be designated for other uses. Examples of such regulations are the Land Ceiling Act in India and the decrees nationalizing land in such African states as Mozambique, the United

Republic of Tanzania, and Zambia. However, such sweeping measures do not guarantee that land is actually delivered into the hands of low-income groups, particularly if the administrative machinery is not in place to execute such land-delivery schemes. Moreover, if these mechanisms do not include some provision for formal title which allows for the easy transfer of the property and for its use as a form of security in the granting of credit, potential builders will be hampered in mobilizing resources for the building of houses.

Regulatory actions also include decrees which have legalized unauthorized land occupations. Examples of this are to be found in Peru and Turkey, where unauthorized settlements were legalized by decree. These *ex-post facto* measures are essentially a formal government recognition of what is, in most instances, an irreversible situation, particularly from a practical political standpoint. Such actions are, however, an expedient measure and cannot be looked on as a realistic answer to the land-access problem.

Where squatting has to be dealt with, one systematic possibility which can be pursued by governments is land-sharing. This is primarily a mechanism for resolving conflicts over land tenure, and has been so far successfully applied in Bangkok. It provides for the partitioning of a plot of land owned by one set of people and occupied by another (either illegally by squatting or legally through rental agreement) into two portions, one to be immediately retrieved by the owner for commercial utilization, the other to rehouse the original occupiers. The strategy implies that each of the two parties has to give up a total claim to the land and settle for something less. The trade-off for the owner is the possibility of short-cutting a long and costly bureaucratic and legal battle to force eviction of the occupiers; for the occupiers it is the right to stay on the land and thereby consolidate their housing situation. Although land-sharing schemes up to now have been *ad hoc* arrangements initiated by the private parties concerned, there is room for public authorities to regularize the process by establishing rules and procedures. Moreover, governments could adopt a mediating role during the negotiating process and act as a guarantor, to ensure compliance once the arrangement has been agreed to.

Other administrative means to make land available for shelter construction include regulations requiring that excess land acquired by agencies in the process of executing public projects be made available through sale or lease, and rules which stipulate that governmental agencies must trade or exchange land when that land is needed for the construction of housing.

The establishment of regulations and procedures for the bartering or exchange of parcels of land can also facilitate land transfers between the public and the private sector. For example, authorities often find that the public land available for the construction of facilities, infrastructure, or housing is not suited for these purposes. Land exchange allows these tracts of land to be offered to the owners of more suitable land as compensation. Canada, Chile, India, Mexico, Peru, and Romania are among the countries which have established mechanisms for the barter and exchange of land.

A more elaborate scheme is land readjustment. Under this system, an area of land, usually on the urban periphery, will be declared a land readjustment zone. The landowners are informed, and asked to pool their land for the project. The object then is to divide the pooled parcels into three groups: public land, which will be used for social and physical infrastructure; land that will be sold by the government to cover the costs of servicing the entire project area; and finally, land which will be returned to the original owners after it has been serviced. In this manner, both the public and the private sector benefit, and the outcome is more serviced land available for housing development. In the Republic of Korea, where land readjustment is most widely practised, the Korean Land Development Corporation has proposed that regulatory changes be introduced to increase the percentage of land held back for public use in the land readjustment site plan, as well as that the percentage of serviced land sold to the general public to recover servicing costs be expanded and that the extra income generated from the public sale of additional 'adjusted' land be used for low-income housing construction.

Conclusions

Access to land by all income groups should and must be an integral component of urban development strategies, so that all sectors can make a maximum contribution to economic and social development. In the past, cities have demonstrated a remarkable ability to absorb large numbers of new migrants. For the most part, this was due not to governmental actions to meet demand for land and shelter, but to the existence of informal arrangements which were able to respond to needs, particularly of low-income groups. As the land market becomes formalized and commercialized and informal arrangements gradually lose efficiency as land-supply mechanisms, public authorities must develop the will and capacity to assume an active role and adopt measures of the type illustrated in this chapter. Without such purposive and innovative policies to increase the urban land supply and enact regulatory and administrative reforms, the problems discussed here will become ever more acute, not only threatening social stability but also undermining the success of urban and national economic development policies.

As far as land for low-income housing is concerned, the era of non-commercialized or cheap commercial land is drawing to an end in the developing countries. The development of low-income settlements based on land supplies for which nothing or very little was paid must be regarded as a passing phenomenon. As urbanization proceeds, public authorities assume control over customary lands, government land reserves, and marginal locations, and they effectively cease to become a settlement resource. However, these authorities are not able to offer an alternative source of land. A parallel development has been the commercialization of the private land supply: as corporate developers have begun to make their influence felt, land-rental systems have become obsolete and small developers have been pushed out of the market. Finally, a trend observable almost everywhere in developing countries is that the owner-builders who were the original residents of low-income neighbourhoods are increasingly being replaced by renters. In fact, it is very likely that the developing countries are entering an era in which the bulk of the population will consist of those who rent.

11 Infrastructure

The promotion of improved human settlements development in the developing countries requires the adoption of new technologies conducive to the delivery of services on the massive scale required. From the point of view of human settlements policy, the key service sectors which should be the focus of such an approach are water supply, sanitation, waste disposal, transportation, communications, and energy.

Policy considerations

Human settlements require integrated development and upgrading of all infrastructure components if satisfactory living conditions are to be achieved and social and economic development of the inhabitants promoted. Improving a single component of infrastructure will not support the level of community development which could be achieved if a combination of components were to be integrally upgraded at a cost affordable by the community covered.

The priority a community attaches to the various options for infrastructure upgrading will vary with local conditions, and it is prudent to establish priorities before proceeding with any programme. However, it has been found that most low-income communities in developing countries place a high priority on a safe and adequate water supply and will be interested in improved community health. Waste disposal will not always rate high on the list of priorities because of lack of awareness of health hazards and lack of sensitivity about the quality of the environment. In such cases, public education should be an essential component of any infrastructure project in low-income communities.

The experience in many countries of the failure of infrastructure projects indicates that there is a need to involve the target community at all stages of a project, from conception, through planning and design to implementation and operation. Planning from the community upwards is a practical means of improving a project's chances of success, and therefore of making best use of resources. Public participation can also serve as an input to project financing, usually in the form of labour. The development of community skills to create an informal-sector manufacturing capability for the production of essential components at low cost has in some cases led to the creation of self-reliance. For this approach to be successful, strict quality standards for materials and components have to be relaxed.

The active participation of women in the development and operation of water and sanitation systems has often been neglected. Since women are chiefly responsible for activities related to water collection, use, and disposal, and for the handling of domestic wastes, they are a vital link in the water–sanitation–waste–health chain. Drinking-water supply, sanitation, and waste-disposal programme design could benefit from components introduced to promote the participation of women in achieving the maximum benefits in the provision of these services.

To ensure the coverage of the greatest numbers within available budgets, the standards and regulations for infrastructure services need to be reconsidered. This often entails the development of innovative technologies and project implementation strategies, the adoption of lowered standards for materials and design, and the relaxation of restrictive regulations. The technologies used will have a crucial effect on the pace at which adequate water-supply, sanitation, and waste-disposal services can be provided. Simple, cheap technologies will ensure rapid installation and wide coverage with limited resources.

Initiatives to strengthen infrastructure institutions and establish intersectoral co-ordination are necessary for the efficient delivery of infrastructure services. The creation of special units under each service sector to develop and test innovative, low-cost technological options and project-implementation strategies will increase each institution's capability to address the needs of underprivileged people. Dynamic institutional attitudes towards the expansion of the service to meet the needs of those not yet served, taking into consideration their socio-cultural backgrounds and inviting their participation at the various stages of project planning and implementation in such a way as to develop affordable services is crucial if the provision of cost-effective infrastructure is to be extended to include low-income groups. With regard to waste management, in many developing countries responsibility for refuse disposal has been entrusted to medical officers, public-health inspectors, or sanitary officers, who manage solid waste among other duties such as control of epidemics and endemic diseases, food inspections, and immunization. To provide and maintain a sound service, however, it is necessary to create a department concerned solely with refuse disposal, with staff devoted exclusively to this task and possessing the various skills required.

The identification of manpower training needs at all levels and adoption of measures to develop adequate manpower resources must be considered a priority. Benefits from manpower investment are only likely to be fully realized with appropriate institutional development and reform. The development of sector-related, long-term training strategies is essential in sustaining the supply of trained manpower.

Constraints in the delivery of infrastructure

Many factors affect the delivery of infrastructure to human settlements, especially to low-income settlements. Quite often, institutional arrangements are very complex, and unco-ordinated. In the absence of comprehensive human settle-ments policies and plans, the provision of water supply, sanitation, and waste disposal has been approached on an *ad hoc* basis, in terms of the selection and implementation of projects. Target communities have rarely been involved in the planning and implementation of projects, and after completion they demonstrate little interest in the continuing success of what they perceive as a governmental responsibility. Agencies generally fail to budget for system maintenance, with the result that systems fail rapidly and fall into disuse.

Qualified manpower is in short supply in most developing countries; imaginative approaches are rarely adopted, and costly and inexpedient developed-country technologies are promoted. Design criteria and standards used in the provision of water supply, sanitation, and waste disposal for low-income groups in particular are often inappropriate. As a result, the coverage achieved with the limited budgets usually available is extremely inadequate.

If, by the year 2000, both the urban and rural populations in developing countries are to have safe water and sanitation, water supply must be extended to an additional 2.5 billion people, and sanitation to over 3 billion people. The scale of investment required to cover the capital and recurrent costs involved in a 100 per cent service provision, as shown in Table 11.1, represents a substantial portion of the gross domestic product of developing countries. These calculations suggest that the levels of investment needed for water supply and sanitation are unlikely to be met in most developing countries—particularly considering the demands for other unsatisfied basic needs, such as food, housing, health, and education, which combined can represent approximately four times the cost of water supply

Table 11.1 Average annual costs of hill water supply and sanitation, 1980–2000 (1978 prices)

	Capital cost ($ millions)	Recurrent cost ($millions)	Total cost per capita[a] ($)	GDP per capita[b] ($)	Cost as % GDP
All developing regions	34,000	20,400	24.32	430	6
South Asia	20,800	12,500	23.29	560	4
Africa	7,800	4,700	26.60	330	8
Latin America	5,400	3,200	23.63	1,040	2

Source: UNCHS (Habitat), *A Review of Technologies for the Provision of Basic Infrastructure in Low-income Settlements* (Nairobi, 1984).

[a] Assuming 1980 population.
[b] Assuming 1979 GDP.

and sanitation. If developing countries were to satisfy these basic needs employing conventional standards and technologies, they would have to forego opportunities to invest in the energy, transport, and industrial sectors.

Clearly, few governments are likely to choose this option. Since available resources are not likely to provide full coverage of the whole population, it is essential they be used in the most rational way. This can be achieved, *inter alia*, through the right selection of standards and technologies.

One proven option is to plan infrastructure services in a way which ensures future upgradability but within the constraints of available resources and projected demand, while effective and timely maintenance will ensure best utilization of limited capital resources and reduce the demand for replacements investments. In addition, efficient cost-recovery procedures are necessary to ensure that revolving funds are made available for extending the service coverage.

The selection of technologies will have a crucial effect on the pace at which adequate water supply, sanitation, and waste disposal can be provided. It should also be emphasized that the process of technology selection should be carried out, as far as possible, in consultation with the community, to ensure the acceptance and proper maintenance of the service introduced. The selection of the appropriate technology for a given community depends on a number of cultural, social, physical, technical, economic, and financial factors.

High-technology systems are often very expensive, and their use in developing countries, where limited investment budgets are available, implies that only a small number of people can be reached. Equally, however, it should be borne in mind that the cheapest technical solution is not always the most cost-effective one, since immediate savings from using low-cost technologies may be offset by long-term costs over the life of a project. The optimal exploitation of *all* available resources, including the provision of labour through community participation for the construction and operation of infrastructure services, is fundamental to a solution to the problem.

Water supply

Providing a water supply to a community involves tapping the most suitable source of water, ensuring that the water is fit for domestic consumption, and supplying it in adequate quantities. Besides ensuring that the water is both chemically and biologically safe for consumption (water-quality standards less directly related to health—such as hardness—are often relaxed for economic reasons), it is often necessary to establish whether it is acceptable to the community returning to its traditional sources for drinking water.

The per capita quantity of water consumed daily varies with physical and socio-cultural conditions, and consequently varies widely from region to region. The level of service provided has also been found to have a marked influence on water usage. For example, where communal taps are provided within a maximum walking distance of 200 metres, per capita daily water consumption levels of between 20 and 40 litres are common. Where house connections are provided by means of a single yard tap, consumption levels rise to the 40–60 litres range. Where multiple fixtures are provided within the houses, such as is common in high-income areas, daily water consumption levels can reach 200 litres per capita.

Ground- and surface-waters comprise the most important sources for purposes of human consumption and personal usage. Where only limited quantities of water are required, such as for use in small rural communities, springs are often adequate. Where larger quantities of water are required to meet the demand, groundwater obtained through hand-dug open wells, or, where drilling equipment is available, through deeper, covered wells, is a common source. Groundwater requires little or no treatment prior to distribution. This is especially true for the deep, covered wells, which are less susceptible to contamination than the open, hand-dug wells. A variety of hand pumps have recently been developed to deliver water from wells and have been successfully introduced in many developing countries, including Bangladesh, India, Malawi, and the United Republic of Tanzania. Many rural water-supply programmes currently executed in various countries rely on the introduction of suitably protected springs and, more commonly, on the introduction of simple and locally manufactured and maintained hand pumps.

Most of the water used to supply domestic and industrial needs in developing countries, however, comes from surface sources, such as rivers and reservoirs. Such water requires extensive treatment before consumption, often involving complex and expensive plants. The slow sand filter is perhaps the only cheaper alternative to the more conventional treatment processes involving storage, sedimentation, and disinfection, but their use requires large land areas which may not be readily available. The sea as a prime source of water has received increasing prominence over the last decade, especially in the Western Asian region, but the plant required for large-scale desalination is sophisticated and expensive. A less important source of water is the interception of rainwater from roofs and other impervious surfaces. Rainwater often forms the only source of supply in many unserved squatter settlements in countries that receive copious annual precipitation.

Water-distribution networks constitute one of the most expensive items in a water-supply system. Service levels vary considerably, from low-pressure supply through standpipes for low-income areas to multi-fixture house connections for high-income areas. House connections, although more expensive than standpipes, have

---

Box 11.1   Philippines: the Barangay Rural Water-supply Programme

Water-supply systems in developing countries sometimes fall into disrepair within a few years of their installation. In the Philippines, however, most of the 1,250 systems installed under the Barangay Rural Water-supply Programme are working efficiently. The main reasons for this success are community involvement and imaginative financing arrangements.

Barangays are the smallest administrative units in the Philippines. To participate in the programme, they must have dependable water resources, a population of less than 10,000, and a high percentage of low-income groups. Users must organize themselves into a Rural Water and Sanitation Association which must agree on the technology, financing, and implementation of the scheme and accept responsibility for the operation, maintenance, and repair of the system as well as for repayment of loans.

When these matters are agreed, the provincial government makes a soft loan available to the barangay. Provincial authorities either build the system or employ contractors to do it for them, and train the users' association in planning, management, operation, and maintenance. The provincial government is reimbursed by the Ministry of Local Government, which has a special fund for this purpose.

In participating barangays, improved water supply has stimulated poultry and pig farming and home gardening, thus contributing to an improvement in income and nutrition levels. The monthly fees paid by users have also earned interest for community associations, generating new funds for loans.

Box 11.2   Supplying water to rural China

A simple technological innovation has been successful in bringing water supplies to 10 million rural dwellers in China. The system—a steel tank that drives water under pressure—is so simple that all the materials required are at hand in rural areas, and it costs only a sixth of the cost of a conventional overhead water tank. The successful introduction of the new system has enabled the supply of good-quality water to rural communities, to replace their contaminated surface sources which often contained harmful concentrations of chemicals such as fluorides.

Basically the system is composed of a hermetically sealed steel tank, 1.8 metres high and 1.1 metres wide, which is installed above ground, beside a deep well. Water is pumped into the tank, compressing the air inside, and the pressure sends the water to users through pipes. Automatically controlled electric gauges cut off the power when the water in the tank reaches a predetermined maximum level and restart the pumps when water levels drop to the minimum limit. In this way, the tank maintains a 24-hour water supply.

The device is capable of pumping water to buildings six storeys high and providing water to 200 to 300 households scattered over half a hectare. This is equivalent to a 30-metre high water tower storing 20–30 cubic metres of water which would cost approximately $4,600, take months to construct, and require materials such as timber, reinforcing bars, and cement, which are often hard to obtain in rural areas. The pressure tank only costs approximately $700 and is readily installed within a week: consequently, it lends itself to rapid replication. Of the 55 million rural residents having access to water supply in China, 10 million have benefited from the pressure tank system: since 1969, 4,000 projects have been completed by a 40-strong team assisting installation in rural areas.

Source: N. Zhang, 'Putting Rural China on tap', *South: The Third World Magazine* (London), 60 (Oct. 1985), 178–9.

Table 11.2   Characteristics and costs of standpipes and charges for house connections

	Standpipes				Connection cost ($)
	Min.–max. cost	Persons served	Maximum distance (m)	Consumption (lpcd)	
Africa					
Benin	74^a–140^c	500	400	25	163
Botswana	350–$530^{a,c}$	120	100	—	73
Burkima Faso	1,170–$4,300^c$	1,000	250	20	210
Central African Republic (Bangui)	$1,200^b$	240	500	10	316–333
Egypt	$2,000^d$–$3,000^e$	100–600	—	40	140
Gabon	$5,000^f$	250–700	—	25	—
Liberia	680–$800^{a,c}$	300	100	—	—
Madagascar	700–$2,297^c$	500–900	100–400	19–20	150–429
Malawi	612–$1,155^d$	140–300	250	30	35–225
Mali	$1,044^{a,c}$	200	300	25	—
Senegal	702–$1,000^c$	200–700	—	—	200–230
Togo	$667^{a,d}$–$1,029^a$	2,260–$6,600^h$	—	—	200–250
Zaire	4,675–$13,298^{a,c}$	400	330	2ι	283
Zambia	$360^{a,g}$	250	—	—	—
South America					
Chile	167–210	150	65	55	123–202
Guatemala	60^c–100^f	30–100	200	40–60	40–60
Haiti	370^c	600	250	20–30	50
Mexico	206^c	36	50	100	44–95
Peru	400	300–500	150	25–45	75
Asia					
Bangladesh	$92^{a,c}$	220	150	44	60
India	$56^{a,c}$	50–300	300	40	34
Iraq	300^a	100	100	20–30	360
Yemen	478^a–$689^{b,d}$	200–300	100	10–15	—

Source: World Bank, *Sites and Services Projects: Survey and Analysis of Urbanization Standards and On-site Infrastructure* (Washington DC, 1982).

[a] 2 taps. [b] 4 taps. [c] 1982. [d] 1981. [e] 1978. [f] 1980. [g] 1976. [h] Ratio of standpipe availability to total population.

been found to pay dividends in terms of reducing wastage of water and improving cost recovery. Table 11.2 outlines some costs of standpipes and charges for house connections in several countries, as reported by the World Bank in 1982.

Detecting and repairing defects in distribution systems has been found to be one of the most vital measures for minimizing service costs and maximizing service, but the need is still largely ignored in developing countries. A further problem is that water pressures in most developing countries tend to be low, and conventional means for maintaining pressure are expensive and technologically difficult. However, simple means by which pressures can be increased, without recourse to expressive overhead tanks, have been recently developed in China.

Sanitation

A study published in 1980 by the World Bank identified over 20 systems for sanitation, varying from simple on-site latrines to waterborne sewerage.[1] Waterborne sewerage represents a high level of user convenience but is extremely costly and demands large quantities of water for trouble-free operation. Sanitation, more than any other infrastructure service, offers prospects for reducing costs through the use of alternatives to conventional sewerage systems. These alternatives can meet all public-health requirements for only a third to a tenth of the cost of the conventional sewerage. Table 11.3 gives an indication of the financial costs per household for several sanitation technologies, and suggests that most of these options are not affordable by low-income groups.

Table 11.3   Financial requirements for investment in sanitation and recurrent cost per household (1978 dollars)

	Total investment cost	Monthly recurrent cost	Monthly water cost	Total monthly cost[a]	% of income of average low-income household[b]
Low-cost					
Pour-flush toilet	70.7	0.2	0.3	2.0	2
Pit latrine	123.0	—	—	2.6	3
Communal toilet[c]	355.2	0.3	0.6	8.3	9
Vacuum truck cartage	107.3	1.6	—	3.8	4
Low-cost septic tank	204.5	0.4	0.5	5.2	6
Composing toilet	397.7	0.4	—	8.7	10
Bucket cartage[c]	192.2	2.3	—	5.0	6
Medium-cost					
Sewer aqua privy	570.4	2.0	0.9	10.0	11
Aqua privy	1,100.4	0.3	0.2	14.2	16
Truck cartage	709.9	5.0	—	13.8	15
High-cost					
Septic tanks	1,645.0	5.0	5.9	46.2	51
Sewerage	1,478.6	5.1	5.7	41.7	46

Source: Kalbermatten *et al.*, *Appropriate Technology for Water Supply and Sanitation, Technical and Economic Options* (Washington DC: World Bank, 1980).

[a] Assumes that investment cost is financed by loans of 8 per cent for 5 years for the low-cost system, 10 years for the medium-cost system, and 20 years for the high-cost system.
[b] Assumes that average annual income is $180 per capita with six persons in a household.
[c] Based on per capita costs scaled up to household costs to account for multiple household use in some of the case studies.

Dry, on-site systems, such as overhung latrines, improved, ventilated pit latrines, and composting latrines, are some of the sanitation options available, and information regarding these and other options have been presented in a comprehensive series of publications prepared by the World Bank.[2] The most widely used dry on-site sanitation system is the improved, ventilated pit latrine: a vent pipe connected to the pit helps reduce odour and fly nuisance, and increases the acceptability of this simple technology. Various forms of pit latrines have found widespread acceptance in rural and urban communities in many African and Latin American countries. Composting latrines have been traditionally adopted in many cultures where the practice of human-waste recycling is common. Operational rather than design factors, often based on a cultural reaction against handling excreta, have led to disappointing results of attempts to introduce this technology in Africa and Latin America.

Pour–flush WC latrines and twin-leachpit systems have proved to be amongst the most successful of the low-cost sanitation systems, because, unlike other wet on-site systems of sanitation, such as aquaprivies and septic tanks,

they are inexpensive. They are widely used and promoted in the South Asia subcontinent, and recent efforts to introduce them in parts of urban Africa have had encouraging results. They are eminently suited for use in cultures where water is used for anal cleansing. Aquaprivies, because of their ability to cope with bulky anal cleansing materials, such as corn-cobs and stones, have been adopted with some success in parts of Africa. Their high costs have, however, precluded their wide usage. Septic tanks, despite their high costs, have been widely adopted in high-income areas in developing countries and the use of a single tank to serve many households has been found to reduce considerably the cost of this form of sanitation. A three-compartment septic tank, which receives only excreta and a minimum of flush water, has been used as a means of producing fertilizer in parts of China, but care is necessary in the application of the effluent to prevent contamination.

Vault and bucket latrines are dry off-site sanitation systems. Wastes collected in receptacles are removed either manually or, in the case of vault latrines, by vacuum tanker. Bucket latrines are widely used in the South Asian subcontinent and other parts of Asia and Africa. Because they are unhygienic and involve demeaning manual handling of human wastes, they are now being upgraded to other systems, such as the pour–flush WC pan and leachpit. Vault toilets, on the other hand, are hygienic and are used extensively in East Asia. Organizational capacity to operate the vacuum tankers necessary for this form of sanitation is, however, rarely available in least-developed countries.

Communal toilets have been tried in many developing countries, but the results have not proved encouraging, owing to the lack of user-care. Public motivation and education programmes are often necessary to ensure the success of communal toilets. In India, communal toilets operated by a non-governmental organization, which levies a charge for their use, have proved financially self-sustaining.

As densities of settlements increase and water supplies become freely available, the ability of individual plots to retain and dispose of all waste waters is reduced considerably. The use of some wet off-site system of sanitation, such as small-bore (diameter) or conventional sewerage, becomes necessary. Small-bore sewers are designed to convey sewage which has been either settled or digested in a septic tank or aqua-privy; they can therefore be laid at flatter gradients and require less maintenance than conventional sewerage. However, studies undertaken in certain developing countries have revealed that small-bore sewers are often only marginally cheaper than conventional sewerage. The two systems are often unaffordable to even middle-income groups of most developing countries.

Perhaps the most promising of recent low-cost sanitation technologies for use in low-income urban areas is the shallow-sewer system. Initially developed by the Rio Grande do Norte State Water Company in Brazil for application in a high-density squatter settlement, the system consists of sewers laid at a shallow depth (with 0.3-metre cover and away from imposed vehicular loading) with small inspection chambers used to replace manholes. Such a system has been operated successfully in many low-income areas during the past five years. This is the only form of sewerage which in some instances has been found to be more cost effective than on-site systems in settlements above densities of about

---

Box 11.3   Shallow sewers in Brazil and Pakistan

Cities in developing countries cannot afford the conservative design standards adopted in industrialized countries. Faced with the high costs of conventional sewerage, governments postpone investment decisions indefinitely; as a result, low-income people are left with no improvements at all. New breakthroughs in low-cost sewer technology have been achieved in Brazil and Pakistan, where shallow sewers have been installed at a fraction of the cost of conventional sewerage.

About 15,000 people, two-thirds of them below Brazil's poverty line, live on 50 acres of land just outside the city of Natal in the communities of Rocas and Santos Reis. Frustrated by appalling sanitary conditions and having few other technically feasible sanitation options, they opted for sewer designs they could afford.

With the full backing of the community, design standards were 'lowered': minimum pipe sizes were reduced to 4 inches (100 mm), and minimum slopes relaxed to 1:167. Common house connections serving over 20 houses at a time were laid under backyards, with the householders accepting responsibility for their maintenance. In this way, 97 per cent of the population was covered. Five years after installation, the shallow sewers continue to function well and the people are paying the entire capital, operating, and maintenance costs. The idea has spread, and dozens of communities in Natal and elsewhere in Brazil have improved their sanitation conditions with shallow sewers.

Relaxation of technical standards was only one of the factors. Others were:

- Community participation at all stages of the project.
- Redesign of tariff schedules for repayment.
- Removal of unnecessarily restrictive legislation and standards.

The shallow-sewer concept has also been introduced to Pakistan, where it was successfully used in Chisty Nagar, a Bihari community on the outskirts of Karachi. The project was executed by the Bank of Credit and Commerce International and UNCHS (Habitat). Water availability is very low in Chisty Nagar, but only 27 litres/capita/day are needed to flush sewage solids down the pipes. Despite the low flows, the system has operated satisfactorily for over nine months without blocking.

Chisty Nagar's sewers cost less than $45 per household to build, including the squat-plate toilet, grease/sand trap, house connection, lateral sewers, collector main, and primary-treatment facility. Shallow sewers are affordable, and the concept is bound to spread as Karachi plans an ambitious upgrading programme for its peripheral settlements.

150 persons per hectare. This system was adopted by a UNCHS (Habitat) technical co-operation project in a large squatter settlement in Karachi, Pakistan, with a capital cost of only $45 per unit (including primary treatment in communal septic tanks). While conventional sewerage systems require large quantities of water for trouble-free operation, shallow-sewer systems have been successfully introduced in communities where the per capita daily water consumption was as low as 25 litres. Cost-recovery has proved extremely good, because of the low costs involved and the high motivation on the part of urban communities to be provided with sewerage.

All forms of waterborne sewerage require some kind of treatment for the sewage. Waste-stabilization ponds are, perhaps, the only non-mechanical cheap means of treatment capable of producing high-quality effluents with few disease-causing organisms in them.

Domestic waste disposal

Rural households tend to handle used materials of all kinds very frugally and hence have little problem with their disposal. This is not the case with urban households, and some effective means of waste storage, collection, processing, and disposal becomes necessary. The quantities of waste generated are generally lower in developing countries than in developed countries because of the complete consumption of food and goods and the high incidence of scavenging and salvage. However, the densities of waste are high, and because of the low content of paper, plastics, glass, etc., there is a high concentration of putrescible matter.

The characteristics of a particular refuse determines the appropriateness of collection vehicles and the system for its treatment and disposal. A variety of containers are used for storing domestic refuse, varying from plastic and paper bags, through bamboo or straw baskets, to metal containers, cardboard boxes, and the like. A fly-proof, washable, low-cost domestic refuse container made from used car tyres was successfully developed on a technical co-operation project executed by UNCHS (Habitat).

The level of refuse-collection service can vary considerably. Door-to-door collection facilities are often provided in high-income areas, while communal storage facilities are the norm in low-income settlements. Masonry storage facilities are usually provided in these areas but are rarely used as intended and necessitate double handling to reload the wastes into a refuse vehicle. Large-capacity (5–10 cubic metre) roll-off containers capable of being loaded directly on to the refuse vehicle have been successfully used as an alternative to masonry storage facilities, and a range of such vehicles and containers has recently been introduced in many developing countries. The containers often need to be so designed as to dissuade scavenging, which tends to scatter refuse around the facility.

Many different refuse-collection systems are adopted in different parts of the world. The 'block' system, where residents within a block of houses bring their refuse to a vehicle parked at a predetermined point at given times of the day, has been used satisfactorily in some Asian countries, such as Burma. The kerbside refuse-loading system is often used in high-income areas, but because good access roads are rarely available, it is not usually possible to adopt this method of waste collection in low-income areas. Vehicles such as animal-drawn carts, handcarts, and three-wheel cycles are used to remove solid waste from such areas.

The side-loading collection vehicles widely used in many developing countries are unsuitable for loading light refuse because of their high load-height and the fact that they rarely carry a reasonable payload. 'Roll-off' refuse-container vehicles usually carry high payloads as a result of the high density that refuse attains through compaction under its own weight. Also, the time saved by obviating double-handling of the refuse has been found to be considerable. Most motorized refuse-collection vehicles are designed and produced in developed countries and are unable to meet the heavy demands made on them in developing countries, especially when they are intended for use in low-income areas. Custom-made vehicles have, however, been successfully developed for use in low-income areas with narrow vehicular access in countries such as Trinidad and Tobago.

Open dumping accompanied by burning is the most prevalent form of waste disposal in developing countries. Of the various processes avail-

Box 11.4   Shanghai, Cairo, Karachi: putting waste to work

Many cities in developing countries have no provision for the collection and disposal of solid wastes, and the accumulation of garbage represents a growing health hazard. Some cities do, however, make efforts to collect and recycle wastes; and in some cities there are groups of people who earn their living collecting, sorting, and selling waste, performing a useful social and economic service in the process. Shanghai, Cairo, and Karachi serve as cases in point.

● *Shanghai* produces around 4,000 tons of domestic garbage daily. Of this, around 2,500 tons is organic, and this is systematically collected and converted into compost in simple treatment plants. Wastes such as paper and cloth are also collected and, wherever possible, recycled. The costs involved in collecting, transporting, and processing the wastes are borne entirely by city and state authorities.

● *In Cairo*, much of the waste produced by the city's 9 million inhabitants is controlled by two groups: the *wayiha*, who have rights to the city's domestic refuse, and the *zabaleen*, who rent the right to undertake the removal and processing of the waste materials. The *zabaleen* extract about 2,000 tons of paper a month, which is reprocessed into some 1,500 tons of paper and cardboard. Cotton and woollen rags are converted into upholstery and blankets, and bones are used to produce such goods as glue, paints, and high-grade carbon for use in sugar refining. Most organic wastes are fed to pigs, and the remainder is converted into compost.

● *In Karachi* the group responsible for sorting and recycling wastes is known as the *cabadiwallas*. Whole families work in garbage dumps—both official and unofficial ones—extracting metal (some *cabadiwallas* use magnets), plastic, rags, bones, and *rotis*. Estimates suggest that 98 per cent of all the material that can be recycled is actually removed. A family working a garbage dump is able to earn up to Rs300 per day, whereas the country's minimum wage is only Rs900 per month.

Sources: D. Hayes, *Repairs, Re-use, Recycling: First Steps Toward a Sustainable Society*, Worldwatch Paper 23 (Washington DC, Worldwatch Institute, 1978); and ESCAP/UNCHS (Habitat), *Physical Profile of Cities in the ESCAP Region* (Yokohama, 1982).

Table 11.4   Unit costs (excluding land) of various solid-waste processing methods in Hong Kong (June 1978 prices, in dollars)

Method	Cost per ton
Sanitary landfill	4.74
Baling (excluding disposal)	4.52
Composting	9.30
Incineration	10.74

Note: The ratios implied here may differ with local conditions.

mechanization, have demonstrated some potential for cost-effective reuse of the organic fraction of solid wastes. Table 11.4 shows the costs of alternative methods of processing solid wastes in Hong Kong.

The potential to reuse waste materials has yet to be explored fully in most developing countries. Where efforts have been made in this direction, the results have been promising. In Cairo, for over 70 years the *zabaleens* have collected refuse from certain parts of the city, using animal-drawn carts for transport. The organic fraction of the waste collected is used to fatten pigs, while other materials, such as bottles, bones, tins, paper, rags, and plastics, are recovered for resale. The income generated by these activities and the nominal fee charged to the residents served have demonstrated the economic viability of private-sector collection of wastes with total cost-recovery. Similarly, families salvaging materials from refuse tips in north Karachi, Pakistan, are reported to be able to earn in three days as much as the minimum wage for one month.

Transportation

In many developing countries, transportation planning is carried out using methodologies which evolved in developed countries. Such applications have serious limitations because conditions in developing countries are different from those in developed countries, particularly with respect to financial and human resources, the level of motorization, and the political context of the decision-making process. Many comprehensive land-use/transport studies have been undertaken for large metropolitan areas, but few, if any, have considered the poorest sections

able for waste treatment and disposal, only sanitary landfill and, in some cases, composting are economically feasible in most developing countries. The high organic content of developing-country refuse (which can reach up to two-thirds of the total weight) makes composting a feasible option, but mechanical processes are often uneconomical. Recently, traditional means of producing compost, with little or no

of the population for specific analysis. Such studies have tended to address the needs of the upper 50 per cent of the population, in income terms, and, in many cases, the top 25 per cent. Moreover, plans have a poor record for effectiveness. They are seldom accepted by all the authorities, and even when accepted they are often implemented only after a long delay (or not at all) because of lack of funds and limited executing capabilities. All these drawbacks should not lead to the conclusion that successful planning is not possible. On the contrary, they highlight the need to adopt a modified approach to planning.

The size, density, and shape of a city determine the pattern and intensity of travel demand. As city size increases, the quantity of movement (in terms of person-kilometres or ton-kilometres) grows geometrically, and demand for extra capacity grows in parallel. In large cities, transport solutions require construction of complex structures in difficult conditions. Since transport difficulties increase exponentially with city size, the first response is almost invariably to propose shifting population and economic growth from the largest agglomerations by accelerating the development of small- and medium-sized towns in which most parts are accessible on foot or by unmotorized modes of transport, such as bicycles.

Unfortunately, while such policies are easy to advocate, they are difficult to implement, and experience in achieving the scale of redistribution necessary has been discouraging. Even if it could be achieved, there is no certainty that the overall impact would be positive: any gains in the transportation sector could easily be more than offset by losses in other sectors. This is why many experts advocate the restructuring of metropolitan regions as a more practical goal than decentralization. Broadly speaking, the idea of restructuring is to break up metropolitan agglomerations into largely self-contained modules, so as to minimize the need for long-distance journeys between modules and reverse the geometric relationship between city-size and travel-demand growth. Since most cities of developing countries will have to be substantially rebuilt and renovated in the next few decades, a great opportunity exists for rationalization of land-use/transportation patterns.

In most cities of the developed world, the main economic activities tend to concentrate in or near the centre and in a few large industrial and commercial zones, with the remainder of the city being devoted to housing and social services. Separation of functions imposes long trips for practically all purposes. Moreover, concentration of movement in central areas and on radial roads leads to traffic congestion and pressure for the provision of very expensive, high-capacity transport infrastructure. In most cities of the industrialized countries, such a pattern is already deeply established, although its desirability is open to serious question. In cities of the developing countries, it is not only superimposed on existing patterns of economic and social behaviour but is also counterproductive from an economic efficiency point of view.

The first way to counteract such an undesirable trend is to avoid single-purpose zoning patterns (e.g. large residential areas separated from zones of concentrated employment and service centres) which create the need for long journeys and for expensive and energy-consuming transport systems. Structuring urban areas in the form of medium-sized, self-sustained modules, with arrangements for neighbourhoods which allow people to live, work, educate, and entertain within easy walking distances, would appear to be a solution to meeting the needs of different socio-economic groups. In many developing countries, where the informal sector of the economy is often inextricably mixed with low-income settlements, mixed land uses seem to be more rational than strict single-purpose zones. In addition, a balanced density is desirable, i.e. high enough to conserve land, reduce distances between activities, make efficient use of settlements services, and facilitate community cohesion, but low enough to avoid damaging effects on the population and the environment, as well as excessive costs of construction and operation of buildings and infrastructure.

An example of the way in which transport planning can be used to induce development is found in Curitiba, Brazil. Experiences such as those of Brazil cannot be easily transferred to the poorest developing countries, but elements of a co-ordinated land-use/transportation development strategy can be found in other places. However, the implementation of plans for co-ordinated human settlement/transport development is a difficult task, and it would be unrealistic to expect that transport problems can be completely solved by settlement restructuring. Careful examination of other possibilities to affect the magnitude and structure of transport demand through modifying travel behaviour is also needed. If, as usually happens, the focus is mainly on the supply side of transport, it is very unlikely that balance will be attained; in spite of expenditures and efforts, transport difficulties will continue.

Box 11.5   Curitiba, Brazil: transport as an instrument of development policy

An example of the way in which transport proposals can be used to promote development is to be found in Curitiba, Brazil. The Curitiba strategy is based on 'structural axes'. Each axis is made up of a 'trinary' road system, comprising three parallel routes, one block apart. The land fronting the central road is zoned for high-density commercial and residential development. The central carriageway (two lanes) is reserved for a high-capacity busway. Its physical separation from the other carriageways allows, should future demand require it, for a sophisticated mass-transport system, such as a tramway or light railway. Situated on either side of the busway are carriageways for local access traffic, including parking facilities to serve commercial development. Two lateral roads (four lanes each) provide for through traffic and for access to adjacent development. The inner frontage of the lateral highways are zoned for medium-density residential and commercial uses, while the outer frontages are reserved for low-density residential development. In this concept, development is oriented towards the high-density corridors that are a prerequisite for mass transport, while the high levels of accessibility provided by the trinary system encourage development to concentrate along the corridors.

Three such structural axes have so far been built in Curitiba—Structural North, Structural South, and the Boqueirao axis. The system has demonstrated its effectiveness in promoting high densities along the structural axes. Whereas the population of Curitiba grew by 22 per cent between 1970 and 1974, the population along the axes increased by 67 per cent over the same period. In the period 1975–8, the figures were 42 per cent and 31 per cent, respectively. Commercial development along the axes has not been as rapid as expected but is now beginning to accelerate, especially near the transfer points between the conventional transport and express bus systems.

Sources: World Bank, *Brazil: Urban Transport Project*, Staff Appraisal Report no. 1917-BR (Washington DC, 1978); and United Nations Economic Commission for Latin America, *Integracion de Sistema de transporte urbano: la experiencia de curitiba* (July 1984).

There is no simple answer to the question of the selection of the most appropriate modes of urban transport. Nevertheless, although generalization is difficult, experience has shown that the following considerations have proved useful in the decision-making process:

• There is no single means of transport which can solve transport problems in any type of city. Therefore, what should be looked for is a rational combination of modes complementing one another.

• In developing countries where both public and private resources are limited, economic efficiency has become even more crucial than in developed countries.

• In conditions of rapid growth of cities, there is a shortage of space in central areas, and, as a result, land prices are extremely high. Therefore, modes of transport should be promoted that make the most efficient use of space. The superiority of mass transport is therefore beyond question.

Given the economic circumstances of most cities of developing countries, railways have to be considered with care. If a network of existing railways can be improved or expanded at relatively modest cost, it can be a viable development proposal. The construction of metro systems is rarely justified in most developing countries, not only because of the high costs of construction and maintenance but also because of the heavy governmental subsidies and drains on national development funds, including foreign-exchange reserves. Only for very large cities which are expected to grow quite substantially, might it be appropriate to consider introducing new metro systems, and then only if the population density along some corridors can justify the high passenger capacity of underground rail-transport systems.

These considerations lead to the conclusion that, for the majority of cities in developing countries, a combination of walking, cycling, bus, and paratransit may constitute a correct mix of transport modes. In addition, because of its unquestionable merits and the strong preference exhibited by some sectors of the population, the private automobile will continue to have a role to play. However, as far as possible, the users of cars must meet the costs involved.

Box 11.6   Should cities invest in underground rail (metro) systems?

For most of this century, the metro was identified with cities in developed countries. Up to the Second World War, 17 metro systems had been built, all but one (Buenos Aires) in industrialized countries. However, metro construction since the 1950s has rapidly accelerated, with more than 40 systems being constructed in the period 1954–81. Beijing, Caracas, Calcutta, Hong Kong, Mexico City, Rio de Janeiro, São Paulo, and Santiago have joined Buenos Aires as metro cities in developing countries, and Abidjan, Bogota, Cairo, Lagos, and Singapore are among cities that have heavy-rail systems in advanced stages of planning or under construction.

At first sight, the metro option appears particularly attractive as an answer to transport problems in the rapidly growing cities of developing countries. Its main advantage is its capacity to transport large numbers of people quickly—the São Paulo system can handle 90,000 passengers per hour per track—in relative comfort. Furthermore, it is regarded as a symbol of progress, and foreign suppliers of metro technology, supported by their governments, are often able to make financing readily available.

Despite such advantages, there are good reasons for developing countries to exercise considerable caution in selecting the metro option. The main disadvantage is the enormous sums of money that are required. The construction of Hong Kong's 12.5-kilometre underground/elevated Island Line cost $86 million per kilometre and Caracas's first 12-kilometre underground line cost $117.1 million per kilometre (1983 dollars). In both developed and developing countries, metro construction has required high capital investments and has very often resulted in large cost overruns.

Given the limits of available financial resources, the only option available for transport investment may often be one of conservation and improvement through incremental changes, so as to make the best use of what already exists. In cities where pedestrians and cyclists often account for over half of all personal trips, it is a hindrance to economic development to neglect facilities for these low-cost transport modes. The resources required to correct the balance will be moderate, if investment priorities are assessed with proper regard to social and economic effects.

Urban traffic management has been found to be a powerful tool which can both avoid unnecessary investment and produce an increase in benefits for all groups. Attempts to incorporate traffic-restraint measures and poli-

cies in comprehensive urban-transport projects have, in general, not been very successful. However, there are other ways in which traffic-management measures can help those who do not own vehicles but who comprise the majority of the users of transport facilities in most cities in developing countries, such as the granting of priority for buses and other high-occupancy vehicles within traffic circulation systems, the segregation of motorized and unmotorized modes of travel, the reservation of space for pedestrians and cyclists, and the review of unjustified legislation and procedures hindering the use of slow-moving vehicles. There are numerous examples of highly successful applications of traffic-management measures. Abidjan, Bombay, Kuala Lumpur, and Tunis are only some of the cities where low-cost traffic measures have deferred proposed investments in expensive highways, reduced traffic congestion, and benefited public-transport passengers, cyclists, and pedestrians, and, in many instances, also private vehicles.

The very important place of public transport in the cities of developing countries is rarely questioned, but the means by which the provision of public transport can be stimulated and safeguarded by governmental action represents a rather controversial issue. With regard to ownership, there is evidence that, in many developing countries, privately owned firms, especially when subject to competition, can operate mass transport at a profit, while public agencies run at a substantial deficit. Although there may be cases where public ownership is the only solution, governments should be aware of the financial implications. A solution to the conflict between fares set up by measures of economic efficiency or affordability by beneficiary groups is found by clearly identifying the social objectives to be met through fare and subsidy policies.

Governmental policy with regard to public-transport ownership and subsidies is often reflected in the treatment of intermediate transport services, often called 'paratransit'. From the experience of many countries, it is clear that paratransit, properly promoted, may play an important role in reducing the need for conventional, subsidized public-transport services, increasing the options available to users and generating employment. To make use of that potential, governments and local authorities will often have to reformulate their policies by removing constraints to small-scale transport enterprises and focusing regulations on matters concerning insurance and safety.

Policy measures available to national and local governments include investment, taxation, pricing, financing, and regulation. Decisions on investment may lead to a shift from providing road facilities for automobiles to equitably developing all components of the transportation system and from investing in new facilities to making good use of what is available. Taxation,

pricing, and financing measures which can help to meet policy objectives are, *inter alia*, import tariffs and quotas for vehicles and spare parts, production quotas, general licence fees, fuel taxes, provision of credit facilities for the purchase of transport equipment, and cost recovery of public investment through imposing betterment charges. Taxation of commercial transport and subsidies for public transport constitute two measures that are used to promote desirable services by public and private operators. Road and parking pricing seems to be the best answer to the urban congestion problem, because it is

---

Box 11.7   Paratransit: a neglected policy option

In many developing countries, intermediate transport services (paratransit) are one of the most important means of transporting people and goods. Paratransit flourishes in different forms and under various names, such as *collectivos* (Argentina and Chile), *jeepneys* (Philippines), *peseros* (Mexico), *sherut* (Israel), *por puestos* (Venezuela), *dolmus* (Turkey), *matatus* (Kenya), and *trotros* (Ghana). All these

services can be divided into two categories: *bus-like services*, in which vehicles are used on relatively fixed routes with a fare predetermined for any given journey; and *taxi-like services* in which users hire the vehicle and have control over its destination. Table 1 indicates the importance of such paratransit services.

Opinions on paratransit tend to be polarized. Supporters

Table 1. Importance of paratransit services, selected locations

	Vehicles per 1,000 population	% of public transport trips
Bus-type paratransit		
Tempos (Jaipur, India)	0.3	72
Jeepneys (Manila, Philippines)	3.2	64
Bemos (Surabaya, Indonesia)	0.9	39
Taxi-type paratransit		
Cycle-rickshaws (Kampur, India)	33.0	88
Auto-rickshaws (Jakarta, Indonesia)	0.9	20

Source: G. D. Jacobs, P. R. Fouracre, D. A. C. Maunder, 'Public Transport Services in Third World Cities', *The Highway Engineer* (Mar. 1982).

of public bus services oppose informal modes of transport on the grounds that they undermine the efficiency of conventional bus services by concentrating upon high-density traffic corridors and ignoring spare flows of passengers elsewhere, who have to be served by municipal bus operators. On the other hand, there are those who point to the relative efficiency of paratransit, reflected in the willingness of individuals to supply services and of the public to make use of them. In many developing countries, public authorities do little or nothing to promote paratransit, but tolerate its often defective operating procedures and poor safety record because of public demand for the service.

There are sound reasons why paratransit should be actively promoted. It not only serves a large section of the population but is also a significant source of employment. It

has a very valuable role to play in cities where public policy discourages the use of private automobiles. Most important of all, paratransit is able to operate without public subsidies, although it is often viable only because it functions without special licences and is not fully taxed.

Past and present experience shows that paratransit, properly promoted and sensibly regulated, can play an important role in meeting mobility needs in developing countries, reducing the need for unprofitable conventional public-transport services and increasing the options available to the travelling public.

Source: UNCHS (Habitat), *Transportation Strategies for Human Settlements in Developing Countries*, HS/36/84/E (Nairobi, 1984).

the only way to reduce the discrepancy between the private and the social cost of operating a vehicle on congested roads. Charging road users the marginal social cost of operating their vehicles would result in a reduction in the use of private vehicles in critical areas and improvement of the traffic conditions in which public transport operates. Unfortunately, selective area-specific and time-specific pricing, as for instance in Singapore, appears to be very difficult to implement.

Communications

One of the forces behind the formation and growth of human settlements is the need to communicate. Communications cover a wide range of activities, including personal contacts, broadcasting, postal service, and telecommunications. The role of communication in social, economic, and cultural development is well known. In particular, it has been shown that high levels of income, education, and social status are strongly associated with high levels of access to mass communications. However, the potentials of modern communication media, which have recently been multiplied by technological breakthroughs, are not fully utilized to eradicate inequalities between various income groups, countries, and regions.

Of the mass communications media, radio is the most widely used, with over 4 billion receivers in the world. In many developing countries, radio is the only means of communication that can properly be termed a mass medium; it is an easy and economical way to reach even the most isolated settlements. Newspapers, which are often considered a particularly important medium contributing to the solution of political, social, and economic problems, are not available to most of the population in developing countries. While in most developed countries, daily newspaper circulation reaches 600 copies per 1,000 inhabitants, in Africa an average is 14 copies per 1,000. Postal services, the traditional way of interpersonal communication, are far from adequate in many countries. While in Norway there is one post office for every 1,000 persons, in some African countries, such as Rwanda, the figure is one for 300,000.

The demand for telecommunications services in developing countries has grown rapidly over the past 10 years, but the quality of telecommunications services in many of them has remained poor. Growth in demand has tended to exceed supply, which has to date been concentrated in urban areas. Available statistics also make clear the gap between the developed and the developing countries. Penetration—the number of telephones per 100 population—ranges from 60 to 85 in the developed countries to 0.07–0.15 in the least developed countries, such as Bangladesh, Burma, Burundi, Mali, Nepal, and Rwanda.

Disparities in levels of access to communication media between regions and countries are unaccompanied by even more acute disparities between rural and urban areas. This is particularly true for newspapers and television. In the area of telecommunications, in Côte d'Ivoire, Ethiopia, and the United Republic of Tanzania, urban penetration in 1980 was more than 100 times higher than rural penetration. The higher profitability of telecommunications in urban areas as compared to rural areas is one of the main reasons for these disparities. Where supply is restricted, there is a great incentive to place investment in financially attractive locations.

Technological developments in the various elements of communications are generating changes in the overall technical and economic characteristics of communications systems and are offering economic and human settlements planners increasing flexibility in the allocation of resources. In particular, the expansion of telecommunications services utilizing a combination of satellite, terrestrial, and advanced subscriber-access and switching technologies, may now be contemplated as part of co-ordinated programmes directed towards the integration and growth of previously underdeveloped and spatially dispersed central-place systems.

However, communications as a way to solve problems in human settlements development is critically dependent on the formulation of communications-supply policies, which should be based on considerations of demand for services, benefits from supplying various forms of communications, tariffs policies, human settlements and regional development criteria, and the identification of target groups, regions, or communities. Consideration must be given to how communications *per se* can be used as an independent catalyst to bring about efficient use of resources, and which supporting parallel investments and strategies in other sectors must be initiated. Furthermore, thought must be given to how the various technical components are to be integrated, and to the allocation of resources for the expansion of communication services.

The question of tariffs is particularly important. For example, telecommunications tariffs are the main mechanism for linking demand and supply, and many countries which have implemented successful supply strategies have employed differential tariff structures to enable remote and disadvantaged settlements and regions to have access to telecommunications. This form of discriminatory pricing is used in over 50 countries. Tariffs are therefore a means whereby telecommunications can be directed to aid human settlements development. Low tariffs for target groups of potential users, such as medium-sized centres, which provide a connection between rural areas and main urban centres, can be applied to encourage the development of economic and welfare links to form the basis for equitable development. Cross-subsidization can also guarantee the availability of financial resources from within the sector, thus eliminating the need to seek outside financing.

Because communications can have a significant impact on human settlements development, it should be considered in a framework of integrated development planning, and be regarded as a catalytic agent which can encourage the development of human settlements in a desirable way.

Energy

Priorities at national and international levels regarding the energy requirements of human settlements should be established on the basis of the short-term (5–10 years), medium-term (10–20 years), and long-term (over 20 years). Long-term objectives should establish the overall framework within which other decisions are taken. Some of the critical factors which will have to be considered are:

- Ecological impacts of energy systems (such as the deforestation of large areas).
- Pressure on land use.
- Energy requirements for food production.
- Economic and social impacts of introducing new technologies and systems in rural settlements.
- Changes in the pattern of energy requirements and consumption of the urban and rural poor.
- Long-term capital-intensive and energy-intensive industrialization policies.

In spite of sharp increases in oil prices, petroleum products will continue to play a central role in the economic development of most countries. This fact is sometimes lost during the current wave of interest in new sources of energy. Apart from oil, the most immediate and practical fuel option is coal, which can be used for the generation of thermal electric power and for transport. However, according to present estimates, coal reserves (including coke, bituminous and subbituminous coal, as well as lignite) in developing countries amount to less than 6.5 per cent of the world total.

Given the profiles of energy consumption patterns in the rural and urban settlements of the developing world, it is necessary to examine options for introducing new technologies or upgrading existing technologies for improved fuel-conversion efficiency. Policies for the introduction of new and innovative energy technologies for the general development of human settlements should include the following objectives:

- *To reduce the human labour involved in meeting domestic energy needs*, thus improving the quality of life of the urban and rural poor—and especially of the women and children engaged in the collection of primary energy resources such as fuelwood, vegetable, and animal wastes.

- *To manage non-commercial fuels efficiently* and substantially increase their conversion efficiencies.

- *To minimize the negative environmental impact* of current practices of using fuelwood and agricultural wastes.

- *To increase the energy base* with a view to increasing productivity in various economic sectors.

The use of non-petroleum energy technologies is particularly relevant to the needs of oil-importing developing countries. In order to shift the energy patterns of an oil-based economy to those of a non-oil-based one and to ensure an adequate and uninterrupted supply of energy to the domestic sector, it is necessary to consider renewable energy resource options, such as solar, wind, biogas, small-scale hydro systems, and decentralized non-oil-based integrated energy systems. At the current level of development, renewable sources of energy probably play a very limited role globally, but their importance at the local level should not be underestimated, and their use should be promoted. The present state-of-the-art of renewable energy sources can be subsumed under two main categories: (a) technologies that are technically viable but are not sufficiently developed for adoption on a wide scale; and (b) technologies that have been fully developed and tested, but are still not being extensively used.

In order to provide methodologies for planning human settlements which pay adequate attention to energy requirements and conservation, it is essential that planning criteria embodying energy requirements be developed for various types of climatic zones, social groups, and economic areas. Given the subsistence levels of domestic energy consumption in rural settlements and in low-income urban settlements, any new energy policies and plans to increase the energy base should emphasize the rational use of non-commercial fuels and the adoption of new technologies to maximize the benefits derived from harnessing renewable energy sources. An integrated approach involving the exploitation of all potential, locally available energy resources would not only optimize the benefits that could be obtained from renewable energy sources but also ensure an uninterrupted supply of energy to meet the needs of the domestic, agricultural, and small-scale industrial sectors.

Research and development projects on non-conventional energy sources have, until now, concentrated on developing individual products which would enable solar, wind, or other decentralized sources of energy to be utilized productively. The emphasis has been on establishing the technical viability of concepts and on testing prototypes to demonstrate that they can work. Briefly, an analysis of the results of the research and development activities undertaken so far shows that, while the technical feasibility of many products has been established, it is far from certain that it will be possible to bring their costs down to levels which will make them economically attractive for large-scale usage. In order to solve the energy problems of low-income groups, new strategies emphasizing the rational use of non-commercial alternative energy resources by integrating the products of solar, wind, and other sources and adopting new technologies are needed.

The development and large-scale introduction of an integrated total energy package can be successfully achieved as part of a national programme with assistance from multilateral organizations. Such an energy programme will have to form a part of the total development plan of a subnational region, since an energy package can only be one component of the efforts for the development of that region. The varying needs of each region must be taken into account, and the technological solutions will have to be adapted and modified to suit local needs in each case.

In most developing countries, there is a poor understanding of energy pricing. In view of the important contribution of non-commercial fuels to the rural domestic-energy sector and the present energy policies (promotion of kerosene, rural electrification, subsidies) of some developing countries, pricing policies for fuels, particularly those used by low-income groups in rural and urban settlements, should be rationalized.

Notes

1. World Bank, *Water Supply and Waste Disposal Poverty and Basic Needs Series* (Washington DC, 1980).
2. World Bank, *Appropriate Technology for Water Supply and Sanitation* (Washington DC, 1980).

12 Building Materials and Construction Technologies

National options

In the brief review of the building materials sector in developing countries in Chapter 5, several constraints were identified, mainly relating to limited supply, high costs, low quality, and, in some cases, inappropriate use of building materials. There are proved and established ways of minimizing such constraints, but the options for solving these problems are so diverse that the approach must vary from one situation to another. There are marked differences in the technological and resource capacities of individual developing countries, and these differences must be taken into consideration in the choice of an option for improvements in building materials and construction technologies.

The range of building materials obtainable in a country can be expanded as a means of overcoming deficits in supply of a particular material. For instance, it may be desirable to find alternatives to concrete blocks as a walling material. There are several options open, including the use of clay bricks, timber components, wooden composites, agricultural and industrial residues, reinforced-glass material, or even sheets from base metals. However, if the type of building material to promote is to be determined by the availability of basic raw materials, a material such as timber may not be a viable option in a country such as Namibia, whereas it may be worth promoting in Papua New Guinea. In Africa, the strategy of promoting rice-husk ash as an alternative cementitious material may be feasible only in the 14 rice-growing countries where the output of rice husk is estimated to be a minimum of 10,000 tons per year. If natural pozzolanas were to be promoted as an alternative to rice husk, there are only six countries with known deposits, whereas, with the alternative of using pulverized coal ash, there are hardly any recognized deposits.[1] Even within a country, there are likely to be variations in the availability of raw materials and peculiarities of climate which may make particular building materials suitable for different areas.

For almost every building material currently being produced, several production technologies are feasible, with varying scales of production ranging from petty-scale units through a series of small- and medium-scale plants to large complex production units. What constitutes a small-scale production unit will vary from country to country and from one building material to the next. For instance, in the industrialized countries, a small-scale cement plant will refer to an output of 500 tons per day or more, whereas in developing countries, an output of about 20 tons per day will be applicable. Thus, the choice of a particular technology or scale of production should normally depend on the need and technological capacity of a country. In several industrialized countries, there has been an evolutionary growth process from cottage-scale technologies, which were consistent with the level of advancement during the pre-industrial revolution era, to the present day, where large sophisticated plants are backed by advanced technological capacities (see Table 12.1).

The problems of inadequate supply, high cost, and low quality of building materials and of inappropriateness of techniques of construction are so complex that solutions have to be sought at different levels, even though different sets of solutions are often required to be applied simultaneously. There are at least four sets of solutions which can be applied in an interrelated manner, but depending on the nature of the problem in a country and the state of development of the construction sector, emphasis will tend to vary from one set of solutions to another. First, an expansion in output can be achieved by promoting the type of production technologies which are consistent with the resource constraints of developing economies. Secondly, improvements can be obtained solely by promoting appropriate codes, regulations, and standards. Thirdly, cost efficiency in construc-

Table 12.1   Characteristics of various scales of cement production

Scale of production	Output (tons/day)	Kiln type	Availability of technology to developing countries	Raw materials	Type of cement produced	Quality and uses of product
Medium–large	500–3,000	Rotary	Primarily imported	Limestone; a siliceous or aluminous material such as clay or blast-furnace slag; additive such as gypsum or pozzolana	Portland cement, Portland pozzolana cement, Portland slag cement	Satisfies international (ISO) standard for strength; may be used for any building projects (Q = 0.9–1.0)
Small	100–500	Rotary or vertical shaft	Primarily imported	As above	As above	As above
Mini	20–100	Vertical shaft	Indigenous	Generally as above with some variation	As above	May be full-strength or less; uses vary accordingly (Q = 0.8–1.0)
Village	<20	Vertical shaft	Indigenous rural	Limestones of inferior quality, volcanic tuffs, ground-brick waste, ash from burnt agricultural waste	Hydraulic limes and lime–pozzolana mixture	Low-grade cements, weaker and slower setting than Portland cement, but well suited to mortars, plasters, soil-stabilizing concrete blocks, and foundation concretes (Q = 0.6)

Source: 'Optimum Scale Production in Developing Countries: A Preliminary Review of Prospects and Potentialities in Industrial Sectors', *Sectoral Studies Series* no. 12 (1984), 45–8.

Note: The Q-index is a measure of the strength of cements in relation to their ability to substitute for Portland cement. It is the amount of Portland cement which can be replaced by the substitute.

tion and durability of building materials can be achieved by promoting appropriate construction techniques. Fourthly, by rationalizing the existing supply capacity, it is possible to achieve expansion of the sector without investing in new production units.

Expanding output through appropriate-scale production technologies

Considerable improvements in the construction sector can be achieved if new production units are established with the objective of making adequate supplies of basic building materials available at affordable costs. Most small-scale production technologies are particularly suited to the resource limitations of developing countries. One way of judging the suitability of small-scale production plants to developing economies is to review the main factor inputs required for production, i.e. raw materials, labour, capital investment, and energy.

The task of expanding the capacity of the building materials industry is facilitated by small-scale production units in terms of the nature of raw materials available in most countries. The production of a multitude of basic building materials is largely determined by the availability of the primary raw material at the local level. For large-scale plants, production is only justified if there is a large local reserve of the raw material and if the raw material is of high quality. In most countries, there is limited occurrence of large deposits of high-quality raw materials but an abundance of small deposits of raw materials, often of an inferior quality. Small deposits of raw materials, despite being inferior in quality, are often suited to small-scale technologies. Only 30 per cent of the world's known deposits of iron ore and 5.2 per cent of the supplies of high-quality coking coal are in developing countries. However, as long as a country does not view large, integrated steel mills with coke-fuelled blast furnaces as its only option, it is possible, with mini-plants, to develop a basic steel industry, utilizing readily available supplies of raw materials such as scrap metal. The suitability of small-scale technologies is enhanced by their ability to use a multitude of industrial and agricultural wastes in the production of building materials. Lime, for example, can be produced in small-scale units using a variety of residues, such as sea shells, press mud waste from the sugar industry, lime sludge from the paper industry, and acetylene sludge.

In most developing countries, capital scarcity coexists with an abundance of unskilled and semi-skilled labour. Large-scale plants are typically capital intensive, but most small-scale production units are labour-intensive, and, where operational skills are required, they are usually basic and easy to acquire (see Table 12.2). Several basic building materials, such as lime, concrete blocks, fired-clay bricks and tiles, and fibre-cement roofing tiles, can be produced by predominantly labour-based technologies. For instance, the production of fired-clay bricks at a small scale requires skills in digging the clay, preparing the mix of clay, moulding, drying, and firing the bricks, but these skills can easily be acquired on the job, so that new production units can quickly be set up to expand output. Some small-scale technologies, such as the clamp kiln for brick or lime production, operate intermittently, so that in farming communities or similar areas, the production cycle can be planned in such a manner that the available labour is shifted between building materials production and farming as appropriate.

In developing countries, because of the high cost of investment for large-scale plants, the

---

Box 12.1   Low-cost cement production

Portland cement can be produced in small-scale plants with little or no imported inputs. Several of these plants are already in existence in countries such as China and India. In China, small-scale cement plants, ranging from 20 to 100 tons per day capacity, have made an impact on the performance of the cement industry. In 1975, 28.5 million tons of cement, amounting to more than half of the total national output, was produced in small-scale plants.

Such plants can be locally manufactured, brought on line in a period of about one year, and their kilns can operate with low-grade limestone deposits. The high energy consumption characteristic of conventional cement-production processes can be reduced with small-scale technologies. Small-scale plants can also function on solid fuels with a high ash content. The low cost of initial investment, the low operational costs, both involving little or no foreign exchange, and the ability to operate at installed capacity all contribute to cost reduction. Furthermore, this technology permits the dispersal of plants, thus reducing distribution costs.

Another cost-reducing concept based on small-scale cement technology already adopted in some developing countries is that of split-location cement plants. Clinker is produced in a large-scale centralized plant and distributed to a series of small-scale grinding plants at various locations in the country, so that the finished product is close to market sources.

---

expansion of the building materials industry using this means is only possible through direct governmental investment or through foreign investors. In small-scale operations, building materials can be produced with low investment in capital items. The main capital investment for small-scale production of building stones is a blasting device to loosen the rocks. This requires explosives and hand drills, but the producer need not invest in these capital items, because he can hire the services of a blaster. The main input for production in this case is semi-skilled and

---

Table 12.2   Labour generation in large- and small-scale brick production

Method type	Output per plant (bricks/day)	Labour input per 10 million bricks (person–years)
Small-scale, traditional manual	2,000	160
Small-scale, intermediate technology	2,000	200
Soft-mud machine, otherwise manual	14,000	76
Moderately mechanized	64,000	20
Highly automated	180,000	8

Source: J. Keddie and W. Cleghorn, 'Least-cost Brickmaking', *Appropriate Technology*, 5/3 (1978).

Table 12.3   Investment cost requirements for small- and large-scale cement plants, India

	25 tons/day, vertical shaft	1,200 tons/day rotary
Annual production (tons)	8,000	340,000
Capital investment (Rs millions)	2.5	240
Capital investment per worker (Rs)	48,000	381,000
Capital per unit of output (Rs)	312	706
Jobs per Rs million invested	21	2.6
Ratio : rotary method	8.08 :1	—
Jobs per thousand tons produced annually	6.5	1.84
Ratio : rotary method	3.51 :1	—
Population supplied by one plant	250,000	11 million
Raw material reserve required by one plant (40 years' output) (tons)	496,000	24 million

Source: Intermediate Technology Development Group, London.

unskilled labour, the returns to which represent about 80 per cent of the total cost of production. Because of this, it is easy to enter the industry and to expand production by opening up new quarries. In the production of lime–pozzolana, a comparison between a 25-tons/day plant and a 1,200-tons/day plant shows that the difference in investment cost is as high as 96 times in favour of small-scale production (see Table 12.3). Moreover, materials such as gypsum, clay bricks, tiles, and lime are being produced in several countries in small-scale units, with no foreign-exchange requirements in production.[2]

For products such as fired-clay bricks, lime, and a variety of pozzolanas, energy is a crucial factor of production. The cost of energy in the production of such energy-intensive building materials could be as high as 63 per cent of the total production cost. However, most small-scale production technologies are capable of operating on inexpensive forms of energy, such as firewood and a multitude of residual products, most of which are renewable and occur as waste products. In general, small-scale plants are flexible and adaptable to changes in the use of energy, so

that a shortage in firewood can be overcome by substituting rice husk, coffee husk, or coconut husk.

The low cost of small-scale units, in terms of the factors of production, leads to a relatively low cost of production (see Table 12.4).

However, because of the low value-to-weight

Table 12.4   Unit cost of output for different scales of brick production (cents per brick)

Method type	Medium-wage countries	Low-wage countries
Capital-intensive, year round	6.5	6.2
'Least-cost', year round	3.1	2.3
'Least-cost', seasonal only	2.9	2.0

Source: J. Keddie and W. Cleghorn, 'Least-cost Brickmaking', *Appropriate Technology*, 5/3 (1978).

Box 12.2   Using waste products to produce low-cost binders for construction

Natural and artificial pozzolanas—materials which, even though not a cement on its own, reacts with other materials under conditions to acquire cementitious properties—are readily available in most developing countries, and can be mixed with small proportions of Portland cement or hydrated lime to produce low-cost binders for multiple uses in construction. An example of a natural pozzolana is the residual ash resulting from a volcanic ash. Artificial pozzolanas are widespread and occur either as agricultural residues or industrial by-products. For example, rice-husk ash is obtained after burning the residual husk from rice mills, while fly-ash is the residual ash when coal is burnt as a source of fuel. Similarly, residuals from the manufacture of clay bricks and tiles can be fired and pulverized to obtain an artificial pozzolana.

The production of low-cost binders based on pozzolanas involves drying and grinding the pozzolana to a fine powder and mixing it with lime. The resulting mixture is ready for use in mortars, plasters, or blocks. The production process is relatively simple, requiring little or no imported inputs, and the basic capital items are usually an incinerator and a ball mill. There are numerous examples of this technology in countries such as China, India, Malaysia, Nepal, Rwanda, and the United Republic of Tanzania. The predominant technologies are small-scale, some operating at less than 10 tons per day installed capacity.

ratio of building materials, the cost of transport and distribution is as significant as the production cost. In some countries, because of the underdeveloped transport infrastructure and the high cost of fuel, the cost of distribution of building materials produced in centrally located large-scale plants exceeds the production cost. The high cost of transporting building materials, which results when large-scale plants have to serve large markets over a wide area, could be the most important factor which makes small-scale units more economical than large-scale units. The price of cement in the up-country areas of the United Republic of Tanzania can be as much as three times that in Dar es Salaam where the factory is situated. In most parts of Indonesia, the price of cement is above $100 per ton, but in some parts of Sumatra it can be as high as $500. Sometimes, governments have to subsidize the cost of transporting and distributing materials from large-scale plants, in order to make the final unit-cost affordable. For instance, the 3.2 million square kilometres of India are served by 53 predominantly large-scale plants, approximately the same number serving the United Kingdom with an area of 230,000 square kilometres. In order to overcome the problem of high cost of transport and distribution, the government has equalized the distribution charges throughout the country, with a freight equalization charge of approximately 15 per cent. Small-scale plants have the advantage of being able to locate close to market points, so that the final product does not have to be transported over long distances. In some instances, it is even possible to organize a production unit on-site for a specific construction project; once the construction is completed, the production apparatus can be dismantled and moved to the next site.

In addition to having benefits of low cost of production and distribution, small-scale plants can be set up and brought on the production line in a relatively short period of time, so that they provide the only means of expanding domestic production in the short term. For instance, a mini-plant for cement can be brought on the production line in 1–1.5 years, whereas a standard large-scale plant will take 4–5 years to be set up for production. Innovations in the building materials industry have been favourable to small-scale production: in particular,

recent technological innovations have ensured that large-scale systems are no longer the only means of producing Portland cement and steel, so that it is now possible to develop an entire building materials industry based on small-scale technologies.

Improvements through building standards, codes, and regulations

The regulatory aspects of construction can be promoted in a manner to bring about improve-

---

Box 12.3 Innovations in low-cost building materials

Several innovations have been introduced to improve the low quality, low levels of production or, at times, relatively high cost of producing materials in the traditional sector. In India and in a few other countries, improvements in traditional lime-burning and clay-firing kilns have led to high-quality products. Some of these innovations have also led to fuel efficiency, thereby minimizing costs of production, and there are yet other innovations using non-conventional or renewable forms of energy for firing kilns. In the clay industry, improved techniques for mixing the clay and drying the 'green' bricks can be applied to the traditional small-scale sector to improve production quality. In the field of earth construction, innovations have taken into consideration improvements in the production of soil products, in the techniques for design and construction, and in the technologies for surface protection of earth walls.

The production of traditional materials such as lime, clay bricks, earth products, wood products, and gypsum blocks can be adapted to mobile plants. There are at least two advantages of such mobile plants. If located at the source of raw materials, they can be moved after the deposit has been exhausted; if located at the market for the finished products, they can be moved from one market point to another in order to minimize distribution costs.

Materials for roof cladding are, in most cases, limited to the high-technology options of asbestos-cement, aluminium, or galvanized iron roofing sheets. However, fibre-cement is an excellent substitute for the production of low-cost roofing materials. Initial investments are low, skill requirements are basic, the entire production cycle can be labour intensive, and the only capital item, at times, is a hand-operated vibrator run by a 6-volt battery. Fibre-cement roofing tiles can be produced on individual construction sites, thus reducing distribution costs to the bare minimum. Fibre-cement roofing technology has already been widely introduced in several African countries (Kenya, Malawi, the United Republic of Tanzania, and Zambia), in Latin America (Colombia and Nicaragua), and in Asia (India, Indonesia, and Malaysia).

ments in the building materials situation, through expansion in supply capacity, improvement in quality of production, and reduction in cost of output. For example, the durability of traditional materials such as sun-dried earth blocks can be improved if quality-control procedures are formulated and disseminated to local producers of the material. Similarly, by formulating standards for local building materials, such as lime, fired-clay bricks and tiles, and stabilized soil blocks, and adopting these standards in tender or contract documents, an opportunity is created for expanded production and use. In most developing countries, efforts have been made at promoting relatively new building materials. Most of these efforts have ended only in research findings, because their commercial-scale adoption is hindered by the fact that they have not been incorporated in building codes.

The import-dependence of the construction sector in developing countries is a serious defect in the economy which can be minimized by modifications to regulations and standards. For example, codes of practice can be formulated with a view to promoting an indigenous construction technology, even to the extent of supplementing codes of practice on installations of air conditioners with designs based on passive solar energy. Standards and regulations, if appropriately formulated, can bring about

---

Box 12.4   Innovative building materials yet to be adopted on a wide scale

In most developing countries, efforts are continuing to improve the indigenous construction sector through innovations in low-cost building materials and construction techniques. With regard to the search for low-cost building materials, attention has continued to focus on the use of locally available raw materials, often those that occur as wastes or by-products. In most cases, efforts at promoting the materials have ended at the research and laboratory stage, even though experiments have proved successful.

Sulphur is an example of a raw material which has potential for useful application as a building material in a variety of forms. In most countries with volcanic conditions, the material occurs in natural deposits of raw or elemental sulphur. In recent times, large supplies of sulphur have been made available from the desulphurization of natural gas, smelter gas, and petroleum, and even in coal-producing countries it is possible to obtain sulphur as a residue. Melted sulphur can be used in place of Portland cement for concrete or masonry products. It may also be used as an impregnating material to improve the properties of masonry units and timber. Similarly, sulphur can be used in the construction of pavements, especially in conjunction with asphalt, to provide superior road beds.

There are promising results in using bamboo as a reinforcing material in concrete, in place of steel rods. Bamboo has a relatively high tensile strength, and although not comparable to steel, it is good enough for low-tension applications such as in reinforcement of concrete walls.

The search for indigenous low-cost building materials has often led to the establishment of national institutions with specific responsibilities in this field, but in other instances the private sector has co-operated fruitfully. Notable examples include the following:

• In Papua-New Guinea, the National Building Research Station has developed a simple hand-operated loom that can be used by unskilled workers for weaving sago-palm wall matting. The matting has a life expectancy of up to 20 years and is competitive in price and usefulness with hardboard, asbestos sheets, and galvanized iron, most of which are at present imported.

• A process to manufacture building panels from rice, wheat, and barley straw has been developed. The straw, mixed with glue and lined with paper, is compressed under heat in a process that releases natural resin. Standard panel sizes are $1.5\,m \times 1.2\,m \times 50\,mm$, suitable for many applications. There are plans to construct plants which use this process in China, India, Pakistan, and Thailand.

• In Mexico, a process based on simple equipment has been developed for converting cellulose material, such as refuse paper and cardboard, into corrugated roofing material. The material is waterproof, and finished sheets are hardened in hot air. Used like traditional roofing sheets, they are placed on the roof by standard side-lapping and overlapping arrangements on a wooden support structure.

• The Central Building Research Institute of India has developed a new method of laying thatch roofing by using manually pressed thatch panels. The roof is made waterproof and fire-retardant by applying non-erodable mud plaster over the thatch.

• Many agricultural residues can be used for the production of building materials and components. For example, high-grade building boards have been manufactured on pilot-plant scale from coconut-shell chips. These boards are then bonded with conventional glue, ready for use. When dry, reeds, stalks, and straw can be used for walls for low-cost housing. suitable dry reeds and stalks can be woven or assembled in a variety of designs and then fixed in a wooden or bamboo frame to form wall panels. Bagasse, a waste from sugar-cane processing, can also be used to manufacture building boards.

reductions in the high cost of construction. Codes and regulations can be used to achieve significant changes in the cost of construction, particularly for the low-income population.

Promoting appropriate construction techniques

Improvements in the skill capabilities of local construction manpower and the adoption of appropriate construction techniques can expand the output capacity of the construction industry, minimize cost of construction, and ensure quality in output. Earth as a building material has been frequently identified with non-durable construction, as exemplified in the shelter condi-

---

Box 12.5   Innovations in construction techniques

The use of load-bearing brickwork is gaining considerable attention in India as a means of saving on cost of construction, and particularly as an alternative to reinforced concrete technology. The Central Building Research Institute, Roorkee, has published designs for load-bearing brick construction for multi-storey buildings and, for this purpose, the Institute is engaged in the development of good-quality bricks using a newly designed, semi-mechanized brick machine. In addition, research work has been undertaken on the design and construction of various types of structures, including low-cost housing using brick masonry construction for seismic regions. To complement all these efforts, the Indian Standards Institution has published codes of practice on brick masonry construction, dealing with such items as strength of bricks and strength of mortars. Three successful case studies on use of brick masonry construction in seismic areas are worth mentioning:

- A 23-cm thick load-bearing wall for five-storey residential construction.
- A 19-cm thick load-bearing wall for one- and two-storey buildings.
- An 11.5-cm thick load-bearing wall for one- and two-storey buildings.

The main features of the five-storey construction are: (*a*) adoption of 23-cm load-bearing walls for all floors; (*b*) planning on the basis of cross-wall construction; (*c*) reduction in ceiling heights (total height of the building being 15 metres; and (*d*) provision of adequate strenthening measures for seismic conditions, such as bricks having a crushing strength of 75 kg/cm^2 and similarly designed mortar mixtures.

---

tions of most low-income settlements, but one reason why houses built of mud have become synonymous with low-quality construction is that, in most instances, those who build with the material do not possess the requisite skills. With good construction practice, earth can be durable in simple shelter construction.

Good construction skills and appropriate construction techniques are important for cost saving in construction. For instance, the use of ordinary fired-clay bricks in structural masonry, in place of reinforced concrete, is a cost-saving technique which is simple but requires some basic skills. There are numerous examples where incompetence in craftsmanship has led to wrong mix of mortars on site, leading to excessive use of cement. Again, in an attempt to improve the durability of earth walls, some craftsmen have been limited to the option of stabilizing soils with Portland cement, to the extent that they have turned a 'peasant' product into an industrial product, unnecessarily strong for the function for which it was intended. However, with good construction techniques, the durability of an unstabilized earth wall can be improved simply by adopting appropriate roof overhangs and applying waterproof outer-surface treatments.

In most instances, the promotion of appropriate skills and techniques for the construction industry can be facilitated if basic tools such as those for weights and measures are widely available. In addition, the adoption of standardized building components or the use of co-ordinated sizes in construction will, among other benefits, minimize waste of materials in construction. Typical examples of materials which are wasted on site, as a result of lack of co-ordinated sizes, are timber elements and concrete blocks. With timber elements, the absence of dimensional co-ordination is worsened by inappropriate jointing techniques, so that a considerable amount of timber is cut off as waste material.

Rationalizing the existing capacity of the construction industry

Without investing in any new production units, the supply of building materials can be extended and the cost of construction minimized by simply rationalizing the existing system. One important task will involve rationalizing the installed capacities of production units operating below capacity. There are numerous cases of cement, lime, and fired-clay-brick-producing plants operating far below installed capacities, and these will require a minimal effort to increase output and reduce costs.

Rationalization is also necessary as a means of controlling the use or misuse of scarce and expensive building materials. Portland cement has become ubiquitous as a building material and probably the most widely used item in construction, but at the same time it is the main cause for several construction projects being abandoned or delayed, owing to escalating costs in construction because of its scarcity and high cost. In low-income housing projects, increases in the cost of Portland cement or problems of scarcity and intermittent supply have often led to cost overruns and frequent revisions of afford-ability and cost-recovery criteria, so that, by the completion of the project, the beneficiaries have shifted to a high-income group. Despite the scarcity and high cost of Portland cement, a large proportion of the material is wasted or wrongly applied. For instance, it has been estimated that, in India, about 45 per cent of the cement used in building construction is applied in mortars and plasters, all of which could be replaced by lime and pozzolana. Global estimates are that only 20 per cent of world-wide consumption of cement requires the full strength of international Port-land cement.[3]

The construction process is complex, requiring interaction of several independent activities for a single end-product. This requires co-ordination and planning to avoid duplication and ineffi-ciency. Programmes can be promoted for ration-alization of construction projects at individual construction sites: this, on its own, will go a long way to minimizing the cost of construction and achieving savings in the use of materials. However, a comprehensive approach is desir-able, involving the planning of the interaction of all production factors for multiple construction projects. This will require co-ordination and planning of several agencies and institutions, because each production factor is normally the responsibility of one or more separate agencies. While it may not be easy to rationalize produc-tion factors for private-sector construction, pro-

jects in the public sector are amenable to co-ordination and planning. In adopting this approach, it should be borne in mind that, in developing countries, unlike most developed countries, the public sector makes a higher demand on construction than the private sector. Planning of the construction sector in this manner may require that an agency be established or an existing institution be designated to co-ordinate the various activities within the construction sector, eliminating duplicating functions, stepping up the activities of certain vital agencies, and filling in gaps where they exist. This may also involve operating a mechanism to fit construction targets in the public sector within realistic limits of the national

---

Box 12.6   Efforts in international co-operation to promote building materials and construction technologies

Some of the problems of the building materials and con-struction sectors in developing countries are such that they require efforts in international co-operation to tackle them. For instance, while, in some countries, problems of low-quality production, insufficient output, and high cost of production prevail, solutions to these problems are known in other countries and in international agencies. For this reason, the transfer of technologies within the international community is always a desirable objective. It was with this in the background that UNCHS (Habitat) and UNIDO jointly organized the first consultation on the building materials industry in March 1985. The consultation brought together representatives of 72 developing and developed countries, as well as several international governmental and non-governmental organizations. The purpose was to agree on the main issues confronting the building materials sector and to discuss the most feasible strategies to resolve these issues, based on international co-operation. In a similar manner, efforts in co-operation have developed among some developing countries. Twelve nations in Asia and the Pacific have, for example, joined froces to create the Regional Network in Asia for Low-cost Building Material Technologies and Construction Systems (RENAS-BMTC). As a result of a workshop held in Beijing, hosted by the Government of China and supported by UNIDO, the Net-work will function as a focal point for the exchange of information in indigenous building materials and low-cost building systems appropriate for low-cost housing. The Network will draw exclusively upon the skills and know-ledge of local experts. The participating countries are Afghanistan, Bangladesh, China, Indonesia, Malaysia, Nepal, Pakistan, the Philippines, Sri Lanka, Thailand, Tonga, and Tuvalu.

construction capacity, thereby encouraging an innovative approach to approval of construction projects in the national budget.

The construction needs of the low-income population are such that additional measures will be required in order to have an impact on the situation. In view of the limited available resources, the existing delivery system will have to be rationalized in order to obtain full benefits. A large proportion of the construction requirements of the low-income population is often fulfilled by non-conventional delivery systems, and it is not likely that this trend will change over a reasonable period of time. In this connection, efforts should concentrate on the informal construction sector, including the use of self-help methods and other modes of community participation in upgrading existing settlements and providing new construction. Because of the close relationship between the informal construction sector and the remainder of the construction industry, efforts to rationalize the formal sector may have to be integrated with comprehensive improvement strategies. However, specific measures can be promoted for improvements in low-income construction through the existing informal or traditional sector. Encouraging the widespread use of non-conventional savings facilities or promoting the development of such savings and credit systems in the sector will be a great benefit.

International co-operation is also a valuable means of rationalizing the capacity of the building materials and construction sector. In some countries, the existing capacity of the sector can be expanded if improvement measures are transferred from other countries and applied or adapted to the local situation. This calls for the recipient country to identify areas of need and initiate international co-operation with other countries and relevant international organizations.

Notes

1. Economic Commission for Africa. *Development of the Production of Lime, Pozzolana, and Lime–Pozzolana Products in the African Region* (Addis Ababa, 1983).
2. R. J. S. Spence, *Small-scale Production of Cementitious Materials* (London: Intermediate Technology Publications, 1980).
3. UNIDO, *Optimum-scale production in developing countries*, Sectoral Studies Series no. 12 (Vienna, 1984).

13 Shelter

The Habitat Conference identified the provision of shelter and its supporting infrastructure and services as one of the key issues to be addressed by human settlements policies. 'The overriding objectives of settlements policies', the Conference's Plan of Action affirmed, 'should be to make shelter, infrastructure, and services available to those who need them, in the sequence in which they are needed and at a monetary or social cost they can afford. Social justice depends on the way in which these facilities are distributed among the population and the extent to which they are made available.'[1]

There can be little doubt that since the Conference the vast majority of developing countries have increased their commitment to providing shelter for low-income groups. Some have defined their human settlements policies largely in terms of support for shelter. There can be little doubt, that, despite the commitment and efforts made, shelter is an area in which most settlements are visibly losing ground, with policies failing to respond to the needs they must meet. The evidence points to a general decline in living and shelter standards in the past decade—trends which are most evident in the developing countries but are in no way limited to them. The evidence also clearly indicates that the commitment made by governments to the provision of affordable housing has been progressively eroded by persistent economic and financial difficulties, with resulting reductions in public expenditure—another trend visible in both developed and developing countries.

This chapter examines the routes through which shelter strategies have evolved, evaluates the current state of thinking and action, and, most important, suggests how shelter strategies must further evolve if negative trends are to be reversed and millions of people allowed to exercise the basic right to a decent place in which to live. The chapter requires four introductory observations, each of which qualifies its scope:

• *The focus is on shelter for low-income groups in the developing countries.* This is not meant to imply that the housing conditions of the poor in the developed countries do not constitute a problem. Such a problem not only exists but also has become measurably worse in recent years, with nearly one in six of the populations of some developed market-economy countries today living below officially defined poverty lines. The city of the poor in the developed world remains, however, the city of the minority: in the developing countries, it is the city of the vast majority.

• *The emphasis is on shelter in towns and cities,* not in rural settlements. This emphasis is explained, if not wholly justified, by the pace of urbanization. For every person that will be added to the rural population of the developing countries in the next three decades, more than four persons may be added to the population of its towns and cities. In urban settlements, shelter conditions can become worse, and almost certainly will do so, if present policies are continued. It is in urban areas that developing countries have made the greatest efforts to come to terms with shelter problems, and it is here that the limitations of policies have become most evident.

• *There is no 'one' shelter strategy.* The many types of low-income accommodation and the great variety in housing-delivery systems for the urban poor preclude the possibility of 'one' shelter strategy. This chapter focuses on two main types of low-income settlement—the squatter settlement and the inner-city slum —both of which display considerable internal variation. Each raises its own complex set of issues and each demands its own policy responses.

• The chapter deals with shelter strategies for low-income groups, not with the causes of poverty. Shelter problems cannot be seen in isolation from broad issues of economic and social development and the choices embedded in a nation's development strategy, an argument that has been stressed throughout this study. Poor shelter, like poor nutrition, poor health, and poor education, has its roots in poverty and the processes that give rise to it and maintain it. It follows that strategies aimed at improving shelter conditions for low-income groups cannot be divorced from and may have limited impacts without efforts to generate income and distribute it equitably.

Changing policy responses

Policy responses to the provision of shelter have undergone a number of significant changes, reflecting different perceptions of squatter settlements and slums and of the process of rural–urban migration that has partly fuelled their growth. Attitudes to all three have tended to be negative, and the earliest response to the problem of shelter was essentially a non-response. Its main characteristics were apathy, toleration, and indifference.

This response coincided with the view that migrants constituted little more than surplus labour and had little to offer the city in terms of background and skills or to contribute to growth and development. According to this view, migrants belonged on the farm, and authorities assumed or hoped that if nothing were done to accommodate them in the city, they would return to where they had come from. However, migrants remained in the city and were joined by others.

The growth of low-income settlements began to accelerate, demanding an active policy response. In many cases the response was eviction, and in many cities, squatters were rounded up, dumped into trucks, and taken to camps that were ill-equipped to receive them and located at great distances from sources of employment. Some governments sought to combine eviction with stringent migration controls, a few going as far as imposing restrictions on travel between villages and the nation's capital. Some others enacted legislation requiring all unemployed youth either to perform some useful service or to return to the countryside. All such measures proved singularly ineffective, and not infrequently spawned corruption.

It eventually became apparent to governments that eviction and demolition hardly constituted an appropriate way to add to a city's housing stock at a time of acute shortage. The realization also gradually spread that demolition amounted to a destruction of assets, and entailed large losses to poor families who had invested in their dwellings. Also the demolition of dwellings often meant the destruction of informal-sector jobs, with people losing not only their house but also their source of livelihood.

The majority of governments became somewhat tolerant of low-income settlements and not quite so restrictive in their approach to rural–urban migration. Most sought an answer to the problem of meeting growing shelter needs through public low-cost housing schemes, but the answer proved to be a very inadequate one. The main problem was one of affordability: the poor were simply unable to afford what the government was able to provide. As a general rule, families required to earn about four or five times subsistence-level wages in order to qualify for a government-built house, but in many cities 50 per cent or more of the people were unable to meet this requirement.[2]

If the poor were to have houses, the houses would have to be subsidized, but this placed governments in a dilemma. They could build houses with high subsidies, which meant that few houses could be built; or build houses with low subsidies, which meant that the houses would be too expensive for the poor. People who were relatively well-off in slums and squatter settlements slipped below subsistence level when they moved into government-provided low-cost houses—or tried to capitalize on their newly acquired asset, thus reverting to their original shelter conditions. In the slum, they could afford to pay for shelter and to eat, but in a government-built house they were sometimes unable just to keep up their rental or mortgage payments.

The experience was one of massive defaults on payments and of middle-income groups taking over the houses built with large subsidies for the poor. These subsidies were usually obtained from indirect taxes and, sometimes, from compulsory savings schemes: social security contributions and payroll taxes were typically earmarked as sources of housing finance. Such taxes and contributions were paid by everyone, including the poor employed in the formal sector, but the better-off qualified for the houses built, and the poor often did not. Those who could never afford a government-built house ended up subsidizing those who could.

In addition, governments often chose to use their public housing programmes as a means of rewarding special groups. Civil servants, military personnel, and war veterans, for example, often headed the lists of housing beneficiaries. The mass of the urban poor came low on the list, sometimes occupying a place where the supply of low-cost houses had already dried up. In short, governmental programmes that promised housing for the many ended up providing houses for the few. They were unable to provide houses at prices the poor could afford, and in all but a handful of countries failed to make any inroads into the problem of providing shelter for the poor.

The growing disenchantment with public low-cost housing schemes as an answer to growing shelter needs coincided with the emergence of positive attitudes towards the poor, the work they engaged in, and the settlements they built. A growing library of empirical research studies demonstrated that the poor were far from marginal to the city but rather an integral part of it.[3] The work of most of the poor, defined in terms of the informal economy, constituted neither a separate nor a parasitic enclave but an integrated part of the urban economy and a positive contributor to economic growth. Much informal-sector economic activity was found to be economically efficient and profitable, and, because of its labour-absorptive capacities, able to sustain large numbers of people, although at very low levels of consumption.

Squatters also demonstrated that they possessed the skills, motivation, and sometimes the resources to provide basic shelter for themselves. In favourable circumstances, they were able to produce solid houses as well as to improve and consolidate their communities, even when exposed to the perpetual risks of eviction. They were able to develop their own market mechanisms, provide themselves with building materials largely appropriate to their needs, and use self-help and mutual aid in building not only houses but also community facilities. It was also shown that squatter communities were able to serve as 'base camps' that enabled some of the poor to climb out of poverty.

Governments increasingly came to accept the principles of self-help and mutual aid, although acceptance at first tended to be grudging. They were naturally reluctant to relinquish their control over the housing process, and had difficulty in dispelling the prejudices that had coloured early perceptions of the squatter and slum dweller. Self-help should be promoted but also regulated, and the policy response became known as 'aided self-help'.

Governments provided building materials and supervised the use made of them. Specialists were employed to advise the poor on how best to build a house, sometimes preparing plans that the poor were expected to follow. The consequence was an approach that demanded much in terms of supervision and management, both of which proved expensive. With the adoption of high standards, aided self-help systems resulted in houses that cost almost as much as those built in conventional housing schemes.

In the mid-1970s, a new response to the shelter problem emerged that was anchored in the principles of self-help and mutual aid. Vigorously propagated by the World Bank, which had entered the urban sector in the early 1970s, and by other important multilateral and bilateral donors, the approach was a two-pronged one: squatter-settlement upgrading, and sites-and-services schemes. Projects in these two areas, the Bank argued in 1975, 'should be the prime instruments for improving the housing conditions of the urban poor'.[4]

In squatter-settlement upgrading projects, basic services are introduced to the squatter community. Typically, water supply, sanitation, electricity reticulation, surface drainage, streets, and footpaths are provided, along with such social facilities as schools, clinics, and community centres. Where some of these already exist, they are improved. Because some squatter settlements evolved without the benefit of a plan, the installation of services often requires the demolition of some houses in the rationalization of plots—a process known in some countries as 'reblocking' or 'replotting'.

Sites-and-services schemes involve the opening up of new land and its subdivision into serviced residential plots. Service standards may vary, as may plot sizes. Some projects may have water piped directly into each house; others have common water standpipes shared by up to five families. In some cases, only the serviced plot is provided; in others there is a 'core house'; in others still, a finished house can be purchased. In cases where only a plot or core house is provided, it is assumed that the owner will either build or extend the house, as his or her financial situation permits.

Both squatter-settlement upgrading projects and sites-and-services schemes seek to restore formal control over land subdivision and house-building processes, while seeking to mobilize the energies and resources of low-income groups for

---

Box 13.1   Gaborone, Botswana: squatter-settlement upgrading in Old Naledi

Botswana's main towns, as with many others in Africa, are growing rapidly, partly as a consequence of rural–urban migration. The government's attitude towards the squatter settlements that have resulted from rapid growth has been particularly enlightened. Its approach has been one of progressive upgrading, and the results achieved testify to the effectiveness of the programmes it has adopted.

Botswana's experience with squatter-settlement upgrading started in Old Naledi, a squatter settlement on the fringe of Gaborone, the nation's capital. The decision to legalize and upgrade the community was taken in 1974, following the failure of an attempt to relocate its 10,000 residents to a nearby new settlement. When upgrading work started, the community was served by only four water taps located on its periphery, and only 100 households had erected latrines.

Assisted by the Canadian International Development Agency (CIDA), the government worked in close co-operation with the residents of Old Naledi in drawing up and implementing improvement plans. Today, there is one standpipe for every 15 households, and over 1,600 latrines. Approximately 25 kilometres of roads have been built, as well as an extensive stormwater drainage system with 60 dish drains and 8 culverts. Two seven-room primary schools, a health clinic, a community hall, a shopping centre, and a market have also been built, and the community has a system of street lighting that extends for 2 kilometres. About two-thirds of the families in Old Naledi have either improved their houses or built new ones. Every household pays 9 pula (about $8) per month to defray the cost of water supply, garbage collection, latrine-emptying, electricity reticulation, and other essential services.

The experience gained in Old Naledi is being applied in other squatter settlements in Gaborone and in Francistown, Selebi, Pikwa, Lobatse, and settlements in the north of the country. The government is currently implementing one of the largest low-cost sanitation projects in Africa.

Source: J. van Nostrand, *Old Naledi: The Village Becomes a Town*. (Toronto, James Lorimer, 1982).

Box 13.2   Douala, Cameroon: upgrading infrastructure and services

Douala is the largest city in Cameroon. Of its several squatter settlements, Nylon, with 90,000 inhabitants, is the city's largest, and its levels of infrastructure and urban services are particularly poor. Located on low-lying land that receives run-off and waste from surrounding areas, parts of it are frequently flooded, making the need for an efficient system of drainage a high priority. Garbage collection also constitutes a problem, since the lack of motorable roads prevents garbage removal by truck.

In 1984, the government announced an improvement programme for Nylon. Under a World Bank-supported project, primary infrastructure, including main drainage, roads, refuse bins, water, and street lighting will be provided throughout the community. In addition, one of the settlement's 13 neighbourhoods will be upgraded as a pilot project to demonstrate the feasibility and effects of full upgrading.

The project also includes the construction of community facilities, including Nylon's first public health facilities and a large retail market, and technical assistance to artisans and small-scale businessmen living and working in the settlement.

Source: L. Bret, 'La Zoue Nylon à Dovala', *Project*, No. 162 (Feb. 1982) pp. 163–174.

---

either the improvement or creation of shelter. In squatter-settlement upgrading programmes, such mobilization is seen to depend upon granting security of tenure to the squatter. In sites-and-services programmes, the process seeks to make use of the resources the low-income settler may otherwise invest in squatting or in buying in an illegal subdivision. In this way, the growth of illegal settlement and occupation can be slowed.

While some developing countries continue to afford priority to public low-cost housing programmes, an increasing number of them have adopted the squatter-settlement upgrading and sites-and-services approach as the principal instruments for providing shelter for low-income groups. So widely is the approach endorsed in principle that it can be legitimately termed the 'new orthodoxy'.

Squatter-settlement upgrading and sites-and-services schemes: issues and experience

Experience with squatter-settlement upgrading and sites-and-services projects must be evaluated on the basis of their own objectives. Typically, the most important set of objectives for such projects, especially in cases where they were supported by multilateral and bilateral agencies, have been the following:

• Projects should be 'affordable' for the urban poor.

• Projects should be self-financing and have high levels of cost recovery.

• Projects should lead to the gradual improvement of housing on the basis of realistic standards as well as low overall costs.

• Projects should provide for income generation and employment creation.

• Projects should be 'integrated', providing for the systematic and co-ordinated delivery of physical and social infrastructure.

• Programme and project impacts should be extensive in terms of coverage and reach.

A sufficient number of evaluation studies have now been conducted, including studies by the World Bank, the Canadian International Development Research Centre, and USAID, to enable reasonably precise assessments to be made. The findings may be summarized as follows:[5]

Affordability

While more sensitive to urban poverty than conventional low-cost housing schemes, squatter-settlement upgrading and sites-and-services projects are unable to reach the poorest. Sites-and-services schemes typically meet demands from the third to the sixth decile, while squatter-settlement upgrading projects are sometimes able to reach below the second decile. Given the 'mix' often found in squatter settlements, upgrading programmes tend to affect the broadest range of incomes.

The affordability of sites-and-services projects is frequently defeated for poor groups by problems of site location. The need for large areas of land at low cost has often resulted in projects being situated on the periphery of a city, a location that disadvantages the poor and makes life costly and inconvenient for them. Securing sites

for projects often proves a formidable obstacle, and delays of up to four years have been encountered as a result of difficulties in obtaining land. Delays have often resulted in the need to revise project cost levels and affordability criteria.

Affordability, usually defined within the range of 15–25 per cent of household income, has been reduced by excessively high building and construction standards, by the application of rigid requirements for mutual aid, by restrictions on the use of houses for commercial and informal-sector activities, and by limitations imposed on the way in which loans could be used. This has led in recent years to a softening of requirements—for example, a change from building-material loans to construction loans, and to a wide acceptance of the need for rental accommodation.

Both squatter-settlement upgrading and sites-and-services projects have displayed a tendency to serve the most able and enterprising among the urban poor. This has led to suggestions that they may have a 'creaming-off' as well as polarizing effect among the poor.[6] The most disturbing feature remains, however, the inability of programmes to help those most in need of assistance. In some cities, those unreached and unreachable by the programmes in their present form amount to hundreds of thousands of people. Their numbers will almost certainly grow.

Cost recovery

This has proved to be the most serious of all problems, as well as one of the most complex. Cost-recovery records range from good in a few cases to bad in the majority and appalling in a not insignificant number. Cost-recovery records are nearly always better in sites-and-services than upgrading projects.

The best record appears to have been attained in projects such as the World Bank-supported scheme in El Salvador where repayment procedures were characterized by the existence of both incentives and penalties, and when participants were carefully selected on the basis of both ability and willingness to pay; payment schedules were convenient; discounts were given for early repayment; computerized systems were used for monitoring debt; and community organizations assisted in the collection of payments. In addition, beneficiaries who had fallen more than three months behind with repayments were visited by project lawyers and advised of their position. Housing loans were withheld from families defaulting on lot instalments, and, in the case of persistent default, families were evicted.

Apart from such exceptions, poor cost-recovery records in squatter-upgrading projects appear to be linked to problems in the granting of land tenure and the speed at which services are provided. Squatters are reluctant to make repayments until tenure has been provided, but legal problems surrounding tenure can be very complex. This is especially the case in countries with land legislation dating from colonial times, which has often proved cumbersome and unsuitable for rapid transfer of land titles and occupancy rights. Similarly, families are inclined to pay for such services as water, electricity, and sanitation only after they have been provided and are working satisfactorily. By the time this has been achieved, families may have become accustomed to 'free' services and refuse to pay when collection is finally started. There is little evidence to suggest that poor cost-recovery records are directly linked to people's inability to pay. Families with high incomes are usually equally represented among defaulters.

Other problems related to cost recovery are weak capacities for administration and debt collection and, notably in the case of some African projects, the lack of 'political will' on the part of local authorities to encourage cost recovery.

Mutual aid and community development

Experience in the areas of mutual aid and community development tends to be positive in squatter-settlement upgrading projects. This is not surprising, since sites-and-services schemes often bring together a 'community of strangers', whereas squatter settlements are usually well organized, may have a tradition of mutual aid, and have their own recognized leaders. Squatters are usually prepared and able to assist one another.

There are, however, constraints on mutual aid processes, some of which are inherent in both upgrading and sites-and-services projects. Projects tend to stress a rapid rate of construction, the choice of modern and permanent materials, material-loan programmes, technical assistance, and 'sound' construction procedures and methods. Such tendencies, rooted in the conventional approach to housing construction, discourage self-help and mutual aid. While some projects, for example, provide the bulk-buying of building materials, they seldom cover used galvanized iron sheets, old oil drums that can be flattened out, discarded wood from crates, and old cardboard. Such materials may be most familiar to the low-income builder and have a special role to play in the early stages of construction.

Some upgrading projects have experienced difficulties in sustaining community efforts. Community action is most effective when focused on short-term issues, especially those that are emotionally charged, such as confronting a 'common enemy' when faced with eviction, or mobilizing to build a settlement literally overnight. When community resources, skills, and initiative are required for routine and commonplace activities they are difficult to sustain, yet many of the activities involved in upgrading projects are of this type.

Communal efforts have been found wanting, for example, in such cases as site preparation, digging of ditches for sewerage and drainage, improvement of roads, and, in sites-and-services projects, building of core houses, especially in cases where such activities have to be completed within specified time periods. Squatter motivation is lowest when there is distrust of project agencies and where promises of security of tenure and services are slow in being kept. Poor squatters may also be too preoccupied with surviving today to be very concerned with building for tomorrow.

In some sites-and-services projects, there has been very little in the way of self-help and mutual aid. Better-off families, as well as those who lack time and construction skills, have hired local contractors or skilled workers to build houses for them. This has created employment and generated income, although not necessarily within the informal sector.

Consolidation and reduced standards

Experience with consolidation in squatter settlements has shown that it may take 10 to 15 years before a rudimentary dwelling is transformed into a permanent one. In formal squatter-settlement upgrading and sites-and-services projects, there is a great temptation to try to reduce this period to just a few years. This finds expression in a general tendency to rely on modern materials put together in standardized designs. Project authorities have a natural preference for 'modern' houses made of permanent materials and a natural inclination to see houses 'finished' in the shortest possible time. Such preoccupations lead them to dictate the use of a limited range of building materials and to 'tie' building-material loans to materials of their choice, as well as to make them impatient with self-help and mutual-aid approaches. While such preoccupations are understandable, they run counter to the principles that underlie the projects.

The issue of realistic standards has often proved a contentious one. The building acts and regulations of many developing countries were handed down from colonial administrations and were prepared for circumstances that are no longer valid. The standards they embrace and the type of building materials and construction techniques they promote are not affordable by the majority of the population, while at the same time these specific requirements of the existing low-income settlements are completely ignored. In most cases the authorities responsible for building acts and regulations are yet to respond to the anomalies in the existing regulatory instruments, but the few attempts which have been made at reformating the acts, regulations, and codes have had only a limited impact on low-income settlements.

Unrealistic codes and standards can severely constrain shelter programmes for the urban poor by limiting the number of dwellings that can be made available, making housing unnecessarily expensive, and either condemning the materials used by the poor as substandard or declaring them illegal. Concerns for codes and standards also result in delays, arising from the need for site inspections and building supervision. In some sites-and-services projects, families have been prevented from moving into the houses they have built themselves until they were finished to minimum acceptable standards.

The delays may also stem from interagency disagreements. Progress in the Dandora sites-and-services project in Nairobi was, for example, set back in 1976/7 by a controversy over standards. The City Health Department ruled that the entire first phase of the project failed to conform with health regulations and was therefore unacceptable to the city. This meant that the second phase of the project could not be started as planned, since it incorporated similar design principles. The dispute, which involved the siting of sewers, could not be solved until several revisions had been made to the city's building codes.

Income generation and employment creation

These have been stressed in both squatter-settlement upgrading and sites-and-services projects because the urban poor require money not only to live but also to make their repayments. They are areas in which both types of projects have been unsuccessful, sites-and-services generally more so than squatter-settlement upgrading projects.

Squatter-settlement upgrading projects have had the better record by virtue of the fact that the location of squatter settlements usually reflects proximity to employment opportunity, and that a great deal of income-generating activity takes place within them. It is not unusual to find that a quarter or even a third of all dwellings are the houses of tradesmen who use them as places of business. Such businesses typically include part-time carpenters, bricklayers, and plumbers who form part of the backbone of self-help systems. Squatter-settlement upgrading projects do not remove people from their place of work and can serve to promote small-scale enterprise.

The reverse may be the case with sites-and-services projects. These are often located on the periphery of the city, remote from areas of employment. Numerous projects have attempted to bring work to the new sites by designating areas either within or near the project as industrial estates, but the results have been far from encouraging, even in cases where incentives have been offered to industry. Projects

Box 13.3   Reformulating building acts, regulations, and codes

Building acts, regulations, and codes are the three main regulatory instruments for ensuring safety, health, and comfort in construction of the built environment. They can also be instruments for promoting the use of indigenous inputs in the construction process.

Building acts are issued by law or authoritative decree to control physical development of the built environment. *Regulations* are usually based on building acts, and provide more detailed rules to control the construction of buildings and they are equally statutory. *Building codes*, on the other hand, are not normally mandatory as they provide a set of practical, technical, and administrative rules or requirements for construction.

The reformulation of regulatory instruments is an intricate and resource-demanding activity, however. If the appropriate methodology is not adopted, reformulation could be expensive and time-consuming but yield little or no results. On the other hand, it is possible successfully to reformulate regulations with minimal resources, but only if the appropriate approach is adopted. There are marked differences between the construction practices of the low-income population and those of the remainder of the construction market, and this justifies the need to reformulate regulations specifically for the low-income groups.

In the few developing countries where efforts have been made at reformulating the existing regulations or codes, no standard approach has been adopted. None the less, certain fundamental issues of relevance to the success or failure of a reformulation exercise can be identified, as follows:

● *Low-cost expertise for low-cost building methods*. In a reformulation programme, money may have to be spent on specialist skills or specialized information which may not be locally available. The drafting of building regulations alone may involve several professional groups—notably lawyers, architects, town planners, sanitation engineers, and structural engineers—and for each of these disciplines specialist skills are required. In Jordan, for example, the cost of reformulating codes was originally estimated at $600,000, but by the time the first few volumes had been published this figure had already been exceeded. The cost of drafting model building regulations for low-income housing in Kenya was estimated at $200,000, 40 per cent of which was paid in foreign currency to consultants. However, in the case of India, it was demonstrated that it is possible to mobilize local resources and thus avoid the cost of hiring foreign expertise.

● *Institutional support*. The reformulation of regulatory instruments involves the interaction of several agencies and institutions. Typically, a Ministry of Works and Housing, Electricity Department, Water and Sewerage Agency, City Engineer's Department, Town Planning Department, Building Research Unit, Standards Institution, and a great many other agencies will be involved. In Jordan, for example, apart from the Ministry of Public Works and the Building Research Centre, other agencies involved in the task of reformulating the codes included consulting firms from different sections of the construction industry, the Engineers' Associations, contractors, university professors, and building companies. It is important not to underestimate the role of any single agency in this interacting network. In addition to ensuring that all the relevant agencies, groups, and institutions are represented, a single agency must be assigned the overall responsibility of co-ordinating the activities and providing the end-product. Regulations and codes require frequent amendments, so that such institutional responsibility should ideally be on a permanent basis.

● *Enforcement*. Regulatory instruments are meaningless unless they are enforceable. For this reason, the drafting of codes and regulations should give equal consideration to their enforcement in terms of restructuring the existing enforcement machinery. Enforcement of regulations also places some responsibilities on the enforcement agencies themselves, which if not fulfilled can be disastrous to objectives of safety and health in construction. In many countries, efforts in reformulation of regulations and codes have paid little attention to enforcement implications. An interesting exception is India, where a special national panel was set up to provide a framework for the implementation of the newly formulated codes.

● *Back-up services*. If the fundamental objective of reformulating building regulations is to promote the adoption of local building materials and in general improve low-income shelter construction, certain back-up services must be provided before the regulations are redrafted, or possibly taken care of at the time of reformulation. For instance, it is important to formulate standards for those local building materials which are to be incorporated in the newly formulated regulatory instruments, and to ensure that they are available on the market. It is equally important to provide for skill upgrading and possibly new skills or techniques in the local labour force. In the Indian example, such basic back-up services existed at the time of the reformulating exercise, and this might have contributed to the success of the programme.

Source: UNCHS (Habitat), *The Reformulation of Building Acts, Regulations, and Codes in African Countries* (Nairobi, 1986).

typically forbid dwellings being used as workplaces, requiring that even small-scale activity be conducted in the industrial estates specifically reserved for this purpose. Few small-scale entrepreneurs, however, can afford the rents, even though they may be subsidized.

Regulations have not been able to prevent the establishment of businesses in the houses built on serviced plots. In the Dandora project, for instance, about one in three of all dwellings are used for income-generating activities, while the project's industrial estates remain virtually empty. Women especially, who account for nearly one-half of all beneficiaries in the Dandora project, are dependent upon their houses as places of work and usually need to combine income-generating activities with domestic obligations.

Problems caused by peripheral project locations have caused some implementing agencies to look for small sites close to sources of employment. Since the land needs to be cheap, the sites found have been characterized by such building restrictions as steep slopes and poor drainage. The constraints on construction have not infrequently resulted in false economies, with significantly increased costs for serviced plots.

Where some sites-and-services scheme allottees have been able to increase their incomes is in the rental of rooms. Those who can afford to do so usually build additional rooms for rental purposes, and, for this reason, beneficiaries in the majority of sites-and-services projects have expressed a preference for large plot sizes, even at the cost of reduced levels of services. Such developments have not been entirely positive, since some projects have given rise to a new class of landlords who treat their sites as objects of speculation. In many sites-and-services projects, the majority of inhabitants are tenants.

The need for integrated approaches

Efforts to promote integrated approaches have been frustrated by many factors. These have included conflicts of interest between public agencies, overlapping mandates, lack of co-ordination, disagreements between project agencies and community groups, and the political nature of decision-making and resource-allo-

cation procedures. Many of these problems have their roots in project design and implementation procedures. Such problems might be regarded as inevitable, since many governments have had little experience with either squatter-settlement upgrading or sites-and-services projects, and the urban poor, used to fending for themselves, have had little direct experience of being 'helped'.

Experience has also shown that the stress on integrated approaches can result in expensive shelter. Integration makes great demands on planning, administration, and supervision, which may easily translate into high costs. Analysis of some sites-and-services projects, especially in Latin America, shows that the direct costs resulting from interagency efforts to co-ordinate their activities can be so high that ultimate project cost levels differ little from those of conventional low-cost housing projects.

Project procedures can be improved and made cost effective through learning-by-doing—by building upon the experience gained. The World Bank has attributed some disappointments to poorly developed design and implementation procedures in project agencies, and its lending programmes now stress the strengthening of institutions responsible for urban shelter and infrastructure. The Bank believes that large projects could also help in this respect.

Project impacts

Squatter-settlement upgrading and sites-and-services projects have been presented as 'the prime instrument for improving the housing conditions of the urban poor'. However, their impacts have been very modest indeed. While there have been some cities, such as Lusaka, in which nearly one-half of the urban poor have been positively affected by upgrading and sites-and-services projects, the reach of the programmes has been almost insignificant when measured against growing shelter needs. Viewed globally, programmes have reached no more than 1 in 10 of the urban poor and represent an investment of around $5 per capita in their future. The investment has, of course, been concentrated in no more than 150 projects around the world. For poor people living outside the boundaries of these projects, the world has hardly changed. They exist and improve their habitat, if and when they can, by virtue of their own efforts.

Unresolved issues

Squatter-settlement upgrading and sites-and-services programmes are a considerable improvement on the shelter policies that precluded them. Experience gained with both approaches has been both positive and negative, although squatter-settlement upgrading experience has on the whole tended to be the more favourable. The biggest limitation with squatter-settlement upgrading has been in the area of cost recovery, a factor that appears to be leading the World Bank and other multilateral and bilateral donors to favour sites-and-services projects, where the recovery record is better.

Their achievements notwithstanding, it is clear that neither squatter-settlement upgrading nor sites-and-services projects in their present form provide a long-term answer to the problems of accommodating growing numbers of urban poor at decent standards. As conceived at present, they will not be able to turn the tide of illegal occupation and guarantee that very large numbers of people will be able to satisfy their basic rights with respect to shelter. Attempts to fashion responsive approaches will need to take account of the unresolved issues that continue to surround shelter policies for the urban poor.

The nature of government commitment

Virtually all the upgrading and sites-and-services projects so far undertaken have been supported by multilateral and bilateral aid agencies. Indeed, it can be argued that the entry of the World Bank and other donors into the shelter sector diverted the attention of governments away from the business of 'getting on with the job' to the business of getting a large project funded. This has helped to create the impression that nothing can be done without considerable outside support, and has led to projects on which attention and resources are lavished to the virtual exclusion of everything else. Such projects tend to be non-replicable, and, for this reason, some of the lessons learnt from them

---

Box 13.4   The issue of replicability

The replicability of a shelter project for low-income groups is determined by the extent to which a government is financially and administratively able to duplicate the project and build on the experience gained. In financial terms, replicability is closely linked to the success of efforts aimed at generating revolving funds within the implementation process, and at reducing delivery costs.

The recovery of project costs from beneficiaries is influenced by so many variables, mainly political and social, as to make forecasting recovery rates either hazardous or next to impossible. While there have been projects with successful recovery records, performance in this area has generally been far from satisfactory. Not only have recovery rates tended to be poor, but internal cross-subsidies at the project level have also frequently amounted to little more than transfers from one poor group to another, and the total amounts involved have often been negligible. While the application of appropriate and inexpensive technology for shelter and services is able to reduce costs, experience has shown that such gains have often been offset by rising costs of land and labour.

Administratively, the experience of internationally funded projects has proved hard to replicate once external project support is withdrawn or phased out. There are several reasons for this: in many projects, the emphasis of the sponsoring agency has been on achieving quantitative targets rather than institution building; and governments have been reluctant to mobilize resources for 'social' projects. Moreover, revolving funds are based on the principle that funds be generated through ventures which are able to secure a level of return that can be re-invested at a later stage for the benefit of the poor. This may have some negative consequences, one of which is to prevent national housing and urban development authorities from straying off the 'profitable course', if they wish to keep afloat.

The above considerations help make the issue of replicability a particularly complex one and point to the need for innovative approaches. One area which still needs to be adequately explored by governments is the application of a comprehensive system of cross-subsidization as a way of covering the inevitable element of subsidy inherent in projects aimed at the poor. Such a system could, for example, involve urban property taxation or differential charges for services according to classes of users, designed and administered to subsidize low-income groups.

---

may be of dubious value when applied elsewhere. Such considerations notwithstanding, the fact remains that very few governments have embraced squatter-settlement upgrading and sites-and-services schemes to the extent of funding projects exclusively from their resources.

Government attitudes to settlement upgrading

In some cases, government attitudes appear ambivalent. The 'inevitability' of squatter-settlement upgrading is certainly widely accepted: squatter settlements virtually everywhere are now tolerated, and there are obvious reasons why they should be. The low cost of the shelter provided and the income derived from informal-sector activities enable masses of people to survive with only minimal demands on an often shrinking public exchequer. At the same time, squatter-settlement upgrading improves a country's housing statistics at very little cost and may help to defuse political agitation and social demands. While the positive values as well as the inevitability of squatter-settlement upgrading are widely recognized, there are forces of various kinds that may be arrayed against the vigorous application of the approach.

The illegal nature of many aspects of squatter life, for example, enables public authorities to retain control over squatters, and governments may be naturally reluctant to relinquish such control. As long as laws are contravened, the squatter and the operator of a clandestine business remain in a precarious position—a position that some public authorities may, for their own reasons, prefer to see maintained. At the same time, however, it can be argued that once squatting has taken place, the squatter, by placing himself outside the law, has greater freedom for action than those who occupy substandard but 'legal' housing, for instance in the inner-city slum.

Even though the inevitability of squatter-settlement upgrading and slum improvement is widely accepted, there is a reluctance on the part of some governments to be seen spending money on either an illegal dwelling or a slum, especially when demands on the public purse are great and growing. Many still prefer to be seen building new low-cost housing, an activity that helps buttress an image of modernity. For some governments, slums and squatter settlements represent a past they would prefer to leave behind, even in cases where evidence suggests that the past may represent the shape of things to come.

The reluctance of governments to weld shelter policies to the improvement of slums and squatter settlements finds expression in the pre-occupation, still very much in evidence, with defining shelter needs in terms of housing deficits, and housing deficits in terms of 'dwelling units'. Most national development plans still contain such estimations, even when the figures stretch the imagination to insupportable lengths. They also find expression in an interest in imported prefabricated building systems and in unnecessarily high standards of construction and layout.

This ambivalence might in part be explained by the nature of the ties that link governments with powerful special-interest groups, such as landowners, contractors, and producers of building materials. Such groups may be hostile to the principles of self-help, mutual aid, gradual construction, and reduced standards, since such principles are in direct conflict with the interests of such groups. This is especially so in the case of squatter-settlement upgrading, which demands little in the way of new land, contractors with mechanized equipment, and industrially produced building materials.

The existence of such links may help explain the slow progress in some developing countries in producing appropriate building materials based on indigenous resources. The main requirements of such materials are that they be low cost and usable by semi-skilled workers with simple tools; although there is no shortage of 'good ideas', these all too often fail to get outside the research laboratory. There generally seems to be little interest in 'commercializing' the ideas—bringing them from the laboratory to the building site.

Land-owning, contracting, and building-material groups can be expected to be less hostile to sites-and-services projects than to upgrading. These projects make large claims on land, and a single contractor is usually hired to build the 'core house' or 'wet cell'—in some cases, the entire house. Similarly, the bulk-buying of building materials, a feature of many schemes, enables the large supplier to penetrate an informal market and to sell his products, through state credit, directly to the poor. While such procedures and practices offer a 'second-best' solution to contractors and material suppliers—building new low-cost housing is obviously preferable—they have few attractions for those dependent upon informal-sector operations, since they can only lead to a reduction in informal-sector employment, and hence to erosion of the survival strategies of the poor.

There are unresolved issues at other levels. One of the most contentious of them is security of tenure for squatters. The dominant view is that squatters cannot be expected to improve their housing conditions without first being certain that they will be allowed to remain where they are, and there is a great deal of empirical evidence to support this view. There are also so many exceptions as to require its qualification.

Some of Rio de Janeiro's *favelas* have been improved almost beyond recognition without security of tenure ever being formally conferred on the *favelados*. Indonesia's Kampung Improvement Programme has positively affected nearly 3 million people without changes in tenurial status. There are also cities, such as Colombo, Mexico City, and Port Moresby, where improved security of tenure in squatter settlements has failed to bring about house improvement and consolidation.

Security of tenure is likely to be most important where the squatter's situation is most insecure. In cases where *de facto* rights have already been obtained, it will be least important. It is also likely to be unimportant where the squatter retains a basic mistrust of the intentions of public authorities and is reluctant to accept security out of fear of taxation, displacement by high-income groups, high rents, the possibility of governmental interference, or the need to surrender certain traditional holdings. Land tenure for squatters makes most sense when it is

---

Box 13.5   Improving Rio's *favelas*: three decades of progress

The formation of Brazil's squatter settlements—*favelas*—started well before the Second World War, and the country's experience with upgrading now extends over three decades. Some of the most impressive results have been achieved in Rio de Janeiro, one of Brazil's most rapidly growing cities. In 1920 there was one *favela* in Rio; by 1947, there were more than 100, home to 138,000 people; by 1964, there were 1,370,000 *favelados*, one-third of the city's population. By the late 1970s, the city had grown to 6 million people, but the number of people living in *favelas* had fallen to around 1 million.

One of the first *favelas* to be improved was Penha. When improvement started in 1954, the 1,400 families living in Penha had no water, sewage disposal, electricity, schools, or garbage collection. In that year, some of the community's residents set up a co-operative association, one of the first of its kind in Brazil. The association levied a subscription of 2 cruzeiros a month. It bought a shack for 12 cruzeiros for use as a meeting hall at night and a school by day, found two teachers to give classes to the children, and, from the first day, started rebuilding houses in permanent materials.

By 1976, Penha's population had grown to 7,000 families. Even so, 80 per cent of the houses were built in brick or concrete and had been laid out in streets to provide proper access. Every house had running water and electric light and was linked to a main sewer—remarkable in view of the fact that Penha is built on ground once designated as a cemetery but abandoned because it was considered too rocky for graves. Upgrading had involved the demolition of one-third of all houses, with those displaced being found land elsewhere in the *favela*.

Almost all the work had been planned, financed, and carried out by the *favelados* working through their co-operative. The co-operative carries out all the maintenance on the services, employing some 50 people to do the work. It has even built and owns the police station: only the policemen are provided by the state.

The improvement of Penha was facilitated by the fact that not all its inhabitants were poor. However, most of the families living in another *favela*, the 'Scorpion's Nest'—one of Rio's worst *favelas* built on a swamp—were poor. But they formed an association which prepared its own plans and was able to fill the swamp, pouring rubble into it until the land was raised by nearly 2 metres. When the swamp had been reclaimed, the land was redivided, and families constructed new houses on a regular pattern. When the work was completed, the *favelados* gave their *favela* a new name: they called it Happiness Park.

Such experience has been repeated many times over in Rio de Janeiro. By the late 1970s, 153 of Rio's 376 *favelas* had their own co-operative association, and a Federation of Favela Associations for the state of Rio had been established. About three-quarters of all *favelas* had safe running water, and about one-third had gone some way to rebuilding and replanning the communities.

Two features of Rio's experience need to be stressed. First, almost all improvement work has been planned, financed, and carried out by the *favelados* themselves, and achievements have become the source of considerable pride. Secondly, the upgrading has been achieved without any change in the legal status of the *favelas* and *favelados*. At the end of the 1970s, not one of Rio's *favelas* owned the legal title to its land.

Source: G. Lenn, *Rich World, Poor World* (London: George Allen and Unwin, 1978), ch. 16.

perceived by the squatter as a means to enhance living conditions and is, when necessary, supplemented by other measures that enable the squatter to turn security of tenure into a real advantage.

Another issue still to be adequately resolved is the crucial one of affordability. Sites-and-services projects can theoretically cater for income groups above the third decile who have the regular employment required to enable them to meet service charges and loan repayments, but even squatter-settlement upgrading projects usually leave the poorest 20 per cent of the population untouched. In short, both approaches have little to offer the very poor, and nothing to offer the destitute. If such people are to be reached, something more than squatter-settlement upgrading and sites-and-services projects in their present form is required.

Some governments realize this and have looked for low-cost alternatives. The Sudan and the United Republic of Tanzania, for example, have provided unserviced sites for the very poor and virtually abandoned the application of standards. Individuals are granted leases of 'rights of occupancy'; in both countries, such approaches are made possible by the fact that virtually all land is publicly owned. The Tanzanian case is particularly interesting, since the application of sites-and-services principles has undergone a marked transformation. The earliest schemes were built to too high a standard and were beyond the reach of the poor, but the latest schemes are based on the concept of progressive standards. This is a flexible interpretation in which standards are not viewed as a once-and-for-all affair but assumed to improve over time as consolidation takes place.

Problems of affordability are compounded, in the vast majority of sites-and-services projects, by problems of land transfer. The land allocated to the poor is sold to wealthy persons who are usually able to meet their housing needs in the formal market place. Serviced plots are frequently objects of speculation, and sites-and-services projects provide opportunities for the better-off to increase the size of their land holdings. The poor have their own reasons for disposing of the land allocated to them, ranging from inability to keep up payments on a serviced site that has become a financial burden to a once-in-a-lifetime opportunity to make money from an exercise in speculation.

Improving inner-city slums: issues and experience

The slums of large cities in the developing countries present a set of shelter issues that differ in important respects from those of squatter settlements. They are issues that have received nothing like the same degree of attention, and experience with slum-improvement policies is limited by the fact that little has so far been tried. This is remarkable in view of the fact that, in many large cities, notably in Asia, inner-city slums are the main province of the urban poor. In such cities as Bombay, Calcutta, Colombo, Lahore, and Madras, up to 70 per cent of the urban poor live in the inner cities; Bangkok also has a very large slum population. In North Africa and Western Asia, the urban poor are often concentrated in the *medina*, old cities that are increasingly being transformed into low-income ghettos. Even in Latin America, the inner city can house very large numbers of urban poor. In Lima, for example, which has the most studied squatter settlements in the world, 40 per cent of the urban poor are to be found in the *tugurios* of the inner city. As a general rule, the older the city, the more likely it is to have a large slum population. Slum populations are largest in the old cities of Asia, Latin America, and Western Asia, and smallest in the young cities of Africa, especially sub-Saharan Africa.

While 'formal' housing in the inner-city slum displays great variation, it falls broadly into two main groups derived from the original intended use of the structures. The first category consists of housing produced by the conversion and subdivision of structures originally intended for non-residential purposes or for high-income groups. This category includes the *conventillos* of Santiago and Lima, the *havelis* and *mohallas* (old mansions) of Old Delhi, and the *funduks*, *waggalas*, and *khans* (warehouses-cum-hotels) in the *medinas* of the Arab region. The second category is made up of building types that were, from the beginning, intended for occupation by low-income groups. This category includes the *chawls* of Bombay (three- to four-storey tenements), the shop-house tenements and row tenements of South-east Asia, the *corralones*, *callejones*, and *quintas* of Lima, and the *vecindades* of Mexico City.

The physical form of the inner city in developing countries has been largely determined by its informal economic mode of production. Small firms operating with little capital and manpower require propinquity between places of production, retail, and sale; the informal nature of the operations often implies that residence and workplace are located in the same unit. An economy of this type is likely to generate a variety of casual employment opportunities which in turn tend to attract low-income families to the inner city. This results in the densely packed, mixed-use central neighbourhoods to be found mainly in the traditional Asian city. Increasing modernization of the economy generates demand for space for formal commercial enterprises which may look to the inner city for its potential redevelopment value. This may translate into pressure on the poor, direct or indirect as the case may be, to leave their traditional locations. Alternatively, the modernization of the economy may lead to development of alternative growth poles, when redevelopment interest in the inner city remains low, often as a result of the high opportunity costs implied in protracted legal struggles to gain access to inner-city properties. This often translates into an economic stagnation of central neighbourhoods, accompanied by disinvestment and generalized blight, where demand for housing has slackened and demand for commercial space has not yet appeared.

Inner-city rehabilitation and slum improvement

The critical issues in planning for inner-city rehabilitation and slum improvement relate to competing sets of interests and the ways in which interests are presented and defended. Planning strategies always reflect the pressure that interest groups are able to exert; because interests are great and the stakes usually high in the inner city, this applies to the central area perhaps more than anywhere else. The position of the poor in the inner city is particularly weak, and it is inevitable that they stand to lose most from the changes that take place, especially from changes that squeeze the space that is accessible to them.

Increasing commercialization of inner cities is, in most cases, the dominant threat to slum dwellers. This often results in their expulsion from the legal city into the illegal one, a phenomenon that has been observed in many Asian cities. Such pressures may be accompanied and exacerbated by processes of 'gentrification', whereby areas and floorspace traditionally occupied by low-income groups are gradually taken over by higher-income groups. The slum dweller is typically unable to resist commercialization and gentrification, although there have been isolated instances of organized industrial workers who have been able to prevent 'take-over' of the relatively small areas in which they lived.

Governments have traditionally done very little to prevent the erosion of the position of the inner-city poor. The opposite is, in fact, usually the case, since some of the policies and measures they have implemented have, sometimes unintentionally, served to weaken the position of the slum dweller. Land use and density zoning aimed at promoting decongestion and 'rationalizing' land use, for example, has often resulted in reductions in floorspace, which has harmed the poor as well as resulting in the destruction of informal-sector jobs. Policies that have sought to promote high-rise commercial and residential development have often had similar effects.

Governments and city authorities have adopted three main policy approaches to the inner-city slum. These may be summarized as *resettlement*, *redevelopment*, and *rent control*:

- *Resettlement schemes* have had a twofold purpose. Governments have resorted to them either in the hope that they would help decongest overcrowded central neighbourhoods or with the intention of freeing valuable real estate that could be turned to profitable use. Such schemes share the logic and procedures of squatter evictions and have similar effects. These include increasing the distance between those resettled and their place of work, so that the poor try to return to their original locations for mainly economic reasons.

- *Redevelopment schemes*, whether public or private, have also done more harm than good to the poor. They almost always result in displacement, and in accommodation that few among the poor can afford. This applies, with only few exceptions, not only in the case of private sector development but also in the case of governmental redevelopment schemes that have been shaped in part by a genuine concern for the improvement of the city's housing stock and the living conditions of the poor.

Even efforts to develop co-operative forms of housing in redevelopment schemes have had disappointing results. Experience from such cities as Lima and Mexico City has shown that such initiatives can get caught up in the complex mechanisms of market interests which the projects themselves help to activate. More often than not such schemes backfire, accelerating the very process of expulsion of low-income residents that they are specifically intended to prevent.

• *Rent control* is, in most developing countries, the most important if not the only instance of the public sector intervening on behalf of the poor, whether at the national or city level. The experience of such cities as Bombay, Colombo, Delhi, Karachi, Lima, and Mexico City leaves little doubt that by maintaining rents at affordable levels, rent control has helped stabilize residential neighbourhoods that would otherwise have been lost by low-income groups. Rent control has, however, become one of the most contentious issues in the inner city. Its critics point to the following negative consequences:

- Relatively affluent tenants find themselves in the privileged position of paying rent far below what they can reasonably afford.
- Rent control serves to subsidize the business and commercial establishments that manage to penetrate residential buildings.
- Controls generate extra-rental mechanisms, such as key money (sometimes as high as the purchase price of the house), which, when tenure is transferred, accrues to the outgoing tenant rather than being invested in the property.
- Stabilization of low-income groups in the inner city may be offset by a management stalemate—the situation in which government, houseowners, and residents all refuse to accept responsibility for the maintenance and improvement of the housing stock.

The greatest objection to rent control, however, is that it greatly discourages property owners from investing in the improvement of their property, and new investors from investing in rental housing for low-income groups. Those who voice this objection point to the progressive deterioration in the inner-city housing stock and to the sharp decline over the past three decades in the production of rental housing for low-income groups. This leads them to argue that the abolition or relaxation of rent control would result in improved housing for the urban poor.

In this connection, it is instructive to compare the experience in cities where rent control is in force and cities where it is not. In Bombay, for example, rents are frozen at the levels that prevailed in 1947; in Bangkok, there is no rent control legislation. The housing stock of the inner city in Bangkok is in no better condition, however, than Bombay's housing stock, and there is no evidence of more building for low-income groups in Bangkok than there is in Bombay. This would seem to suggest that property owners in both cities have lost interest in rental returns, probably preferring instead to wait until such time as the property can be demolished and its site turned to more profitable use. If this is so, the most appropriate tactic is simply to buy time: any investment made in the building would simply be a waste of money, irrespective of the existence of rent control.

Nevertheless, it would be superficial to maintain that rent control has no effect at all on investment in housing. The relationship no doubt varies from country to country, even from city to city within the same country. One step that governments could take, therefore, is to review rent control schemes, with a view to removing disincentives for rehabilitation. This could be achieved by allowing rents to rise periodically by a percentage related to costs, by carefully reviewing rates and property taxes and, at the same time, introducing other fiscal measures, such as depreciation allowances on poorly developed residential sites, with the aim of actively encouraging rehabilitation. In any event, rent control should be targeted at low-income groups only, and should not subsidize high-income groups, such as affluent civil servants, company tenants, and others who can afford to pay higher levels of rent.

Governmental responses and user initiatives

Clearly, the abolition of rent control is not the sole answer to the problem of the inner-city slum. Refined policy responses are called for, and, in formulating them, governments and city authorities will need to keep in mind that any form of intervention has the potential to disturb the precarious balance built into the lives of low-income residents. If the issue is how to rehabilitate inner-city slums without endangering the locational stability of low-income dwellers, the question of the best way to channel funds becomes a crucial one.

Subsidies may be necessary to ensure the access of low-income groups, especially the poorest, to decent housing. They may involve direct cash transfers, charging of below-market rates for land and credit, or differential charges for services, and they may be directed at different actors in the housing system. A strategy aimed at increasing the supply of low-rental accommodation, for example, would be directed to the producers of housing and might involve the manipulation of land prices or subsidized loans to builders. Alternatively, subsidies could be extended to individuals, as they increasingly are in the developed countries, in the form of payments to help cover housing expenses. Mixed forms may be appropriate in the case of programmes which seek to promote the improvement of housing by the occupants themselves.

Other possibilities may reside in the application of differential pricing within a single project. Land or housing, for example, could be sold at market rates to high-income residents or to commercial developers, and the proceeds used to finance housing for low-income groups. Still another possibility involves the extension of subsidies through the differential pricing of services. In the cases of water and electricity, for example, it is common to have different tariffs for different types of users. The basic principle underlying such cross-subsidies is to secure the transfer of resources from upper- to low-income groups.

All subsidy systems have their own inherent difficulties, both technical and political. Direct grants to users have the obvious advantage of going straight to the poor, reducing the risk that they will be syphoned off by intermediaries.

However, it is usually difficult to ensure that the grant will be used for the purpose intended. Most important, direct grants are almost bound to be self-limiting in their coverage, as well as opening the door to political manipulation of the kind that keeps them out of the hands of those for whom they are intended. Cross-subsidies within a project will also be limited by the range of incomes represented in a project, so that the transfers generated will inevitably be small.

In central-city programmes, technical difficulties and other problems are complicated by a variety of other factors. Density of occupation and the frequent lack of vacant land, for example, greatly reduce the scope for owner-builder programmes. The fact that the buildings most in need of repair and maintenance are usually owned by one group of people—the relatively affluent—and are occupied by another—the poor—only adds to the complications.

A programme aimed at repairing and improving buildings, even if carried out by tenants, immediately raises the question of who will benefit most from it. Should it result in substantial additions to the capital value of the building, the owner may be encouraged to raise rents, if he is able to do so. A preoccupation with improving the quality of the housing stock tends to translate into programmes that disregard the users, so that if programmes are to reach those most in need, the emphasis will need to shift to subsidizing services. Most important, unless forms of co-operative ownership and control are developed, there is a real risk that subsidies, however well-intended, will be misdirected.

As far as the poor themselves are concerned, they may have little experience of self-help and mutual-aid processes. Community organization tends to be well developed in squatter settlements, where communities, especially new ones, are often deficient in everything and are faced with an ever-present risk of eviction. There is evidence, however, of community organization within slum communities with demonstrated capacities to mobilize human and material resources for the improvement of the living and working environment. In the Chinatown area of Bangkok, for example, an estimated 41 per cent of all households have made improvements to their dwellings, and, of these, 61–75 per cent (depending upon the area

---

Box 13.6   Bombay: involving residents in repairs and reconstruction

The city of Bombay has traditionally provided shelter and employment to low-income groups. The typical rental-housing solution for poor groups are *chawls*—four- and five-storey tenements, built by the private and public sector, which dominate the city's central area. Around 60 per cent of Bombay's low-income population live in *chawls*.

A Rent Control Act enacted by the colonial administration in 1939 followed by a rent freeze in 1947 established a system of protected tenancy that has ensured to this day the survival of the poor in Bombay's central area. In 1969, the Maharashtra Government passed an Act that established the Building Repairs and Reconstruction Board. The Board was responsible for ensuring the timely repair and reconstruction of buildings occupied by tenants and not owned by co-operative housing societies or public bodies and used solely for residential purposes. Under the provisions of the Act, the Board can undertake the repair of buildings when improvement costs do not exceed Rs120 (approximately $10) per square metre, or when tenants are prepared to meet costs in excess of this amount. The occupants are encouraged to repair the buildings themselves, at the expense of the Board, by obtaining a 'no-objection certificate'.

The performance of the Board between 1969, the year of its inception, and 1975 was as follows:

	Number of cases
Building entered on the priority list	7,387
Building accepted for repair by the Board	3,993
Repairs by tenants	693
Number of works completed	2,524
Number of works in progress	2,162

A repair cess was levied on all buildings requiring repair, effective from 1969; in the case of buildings repaired, the owners were required to pay a higher repair cess. In 1977, this legislation was repealed and replaced by the Maharashtra Housing and Area Development Act, under which the state assumed responsibility for repair and reconstruction of the buildings. Most of the buildings affected are in the four congested inner-city wards which, while accounting for only 26.8 per cent of the total area of the city, contain 60 per cent of the 'cessed' buildings.

In 1981, the priority list contained 2,936 buildings, of which 1,136 were considered beyond economic repair. Whereas the repairs programme has proved manageable, reconstruction has proved very difficult. To construct 1,136 replacement buildings with 28,500 tenements would require an investment of Rs630 million—a figure equal to four times the total investment made by Maharashtra Housing and Area Development Authority in the four years following its creation.

One of the most interesting aspects of the repair efforts made in Bombay is that tenants have been allowed and encouraged to undertake repairs themselves. As indicated in the table, there have been cases where the tenants were provided with financial subsidy and loan assistance to undertake repairs through contractors chosen by them and with technical assistance in part provided by the Board. The experiments were considered successful, proving that tenants are willing to contribute their own resources in the case of 'self-managed' repairs. In such cases, the tenants have demonstrated a high degree of willingness to pay the monthly repair cess levied by the Board. The positive results obtained have prompted the Authority to pursue the system of self-managed repairs.

The value of the Bombay experience lies in the efforts to preserve and rehabilitate the existing housing stock in central neighbourhoods, while ensuring the right of low-income groups to remain in the neighbourhoods. The experience also points to the value of directly involving the poor in rehabilitation programmes.

---

surveyed) used either self-help or mutual help. Only 25–30 per cent of households hired skilled labour for the purpose.

There have also been notable cases in Bangkok, Bombay, and Karachi, for instance, of residents' associations effectively blocking attempts at eviction, their efforts sometimes resulting in new measures that increased tenants' security. Residents' associations and other community-based groups have typically received little in the way of support or encouragement from city authorities, since governmental bodies have, on the whole, been reluctant to promote grass-roots organizations and slow in recognizing the role they are able to play in inner-city rehabilitation and housing improvement. The legislative and administrative processes that include inner-city residents in decision-making have yet to achieve satisfactory forms. The slow progress in this direction can no doubt in part be explained by the belief, widely held but seldom articulated, that action in this area runs counter to the logic of centralized planning instruments, and thus curtails possibilities for 'effective' planning.

Such beliefs are being challenged, and there is a growing awareness among some city authorities that it makes sense to promote the establishment of user-groups at the community level for the effective delivery of basic services. A notable example of this is the effort currently being made by the Colombo City Council to establish community development councils charged with responsibility for the provision and improvement of basic services as well as health education.

Guidelines for a positive approach

If the problem of the inner-city slum was posed in terms of making available to the poor unlimited access to space and services in the central city, there would obviously be no solution to it. In the inner city, the poor must compete with others for access to space, services, and resources from a position of weakness. This position has been eroded in most cities by governmental efforts to manipulate the inner city, be it through planning and zoning instruments, resettlement programmes, or redevelopment and reconstruction schemes. In such schemes, social and economic costs are levied against those who can least afford them, and city authorities have been unable to find equitable solutions that incorporate appropriate compensation.

Demolition followed by resettlement is clearly no solution. This simply exacerbates the shelter problems of the poor, and only serves to reduce the supply of low-cost housing and raise rents for the remainder of the housing stock. Similarly, clearance followed by rebuilding at high costs, with concomitantly high rents, simply amounts to proposing that people with limited means should live beyond them.

The pressures on governments to clear and redevelop the inner city are very strong. Some governments engage directly in the land market and derive substantial revenues from it. Where this is the case, governments inevitably seek the most profitable uses for land. Even when they have little direct involvement in the land market, however, they are subject to pressures to promote the kind of redevelopment that results in high urban rents. Governments cannot be seen to be against economic growth, and are thus bound to respond to proposals that promise high rates of economic return: where they derive

revenues from taxes on property, they also have every interest in high property values. Governments, finally, are the guardians of a nation's image, and, for most people, the image is one of the city. The promotion of the image, for internal as well as external consumption, leads to a tendency to replace things old with things new, to improve the image of the city with modern buildings and facilities, and to eradicate 'unsightly slums'.

Governments, however, are also responsible for promoting the welfare of their people: in this, they must demonstrate a responsiveness to the needs of the poor. The ways in which they respond to and reconcile competing interests are, in large measure, determined by ideological preferences and the nature of the political system. Nevertheless, not all governments have strong ideological persuasions, and many have preferred to place their trust in the efficacies of a 'mixed economy'—but this does not automatically dispense solutions to the problems of the inner city. This is evident in many countries where governments are caught in the dilemma of adopting either a 'welfare approach' or a 'market approach' to inner-city problems.

While the welfare approach suggests that it is the responsibility of the public sector to provide shelter for the inner-city poor, the inability to do so without recourse to large subsidies has crippled official capacities to deal with shelter problems. The reaction to this has been an insistence that implementing agencies finance their programmes through revolving funds or other conventional methods, implying that preference be given to financially 'viable' and profitable schemes that make it possible to generate surpluses for future investments. In reality, this version of the welfare approach may differ little from the market approach which governments may be reluctant to embrace officially. Requiring programmes to be self-financing inevitably means that public authorities are reluctant to deviate from a profitable course; as a result, the capacity of public authorities to invest in shelter for the poor becomes increasingly undermined.

There are no clear-cut solutions which resolve all difficulties at once. The best hope is for a series of arrangements that strike realistic compromises between sets of competing interests. In seeking to establish such compromises, it is essential that governments and public authorities recognize the legitimacy of the claims and needs of the inner-city poor, since this is a prerequisite to reversing the prevailing negative trends. There appear to be two main channels through which the required changes can be brought about: one is technical, the other political.

The technical direction aims at making 'replacement housing' affordable and at providing incentives to low-income households to move from congested inner-city neighbour-hoods. The political choice is a difficult but important one: it aims at the stabilization of inner-city neighbourhoods, and provides for governmental intervention through administrative arrangements that resolve tenure problems in favour of the poor. An essential element of this approach is the devolution of some decision-making prerogatives to the user. Ultimately, governments and public authorities must decide whether the inner city is to be treated for its use value—as a place to live and work—or for its exchange value on the market.

Box 13.7   Colombo: upgrading inner-city slums

Sri Lanka provides an interesting example of public-sector legislative intervention, followed by subsequent upgrading programmes, aimed at stabilizing the low-income population of the inner city. The Ceiling on Housing and Property Law, enacted in 1973, controlled the ownership of housing property by specifying the permitted number of houses an individual, family, or group of persons could own. The surplus could be purchased by tenants or be transferred to the ownership of the Department of National Housing. The housing transferred became the responsibility of the National Housing Commissioner, and was later to be offered for purchase to tenants. In 1977, policy changes were enforced to the effect that all tenants who paid a monthly rent of Rs25 (approximately $1.50) or below would receive their housing units free of charge from the government, as a further step towards the socialization of housing.

The transfer of a large share of the existing housing stock to the government automatically bound the public sector to catering for the provision and maintenance of basic services in low-income neighbourhoods, and, for this purpose, the Common Amenities Board Law was adopted in 1973. Under its provisions, the government assumed responsibility for providing basic services to the slum tenement areas (buildings originally intended for single-family use or for commercial purposes, later subdivided into very small single-room rental units) and the slum gardens (usually, one-storey units facing a common alley) that had been transferred to the Housing Commissioner as a result of the Ceiling on Housing and Property Law.

Under a UNICEF-assisted programme, the target for 1980 was to improve the water-supply and toilet facilities in 453 slum tenements in the central areas. The performance of the Board by 1980 was as follows:

	Target	Actual
Toilets	453	348
Bathrooms	230	162
Standpipes	300	271
Children's parks	6	6
Slum gardens	150	139

The performance by 1980 for slum garden improvement was as follows:

Slum gardens benefited	73
Houses benefited	1,240
Latrines improved or constructed	260
Bathrooms improved or constructed	110
Water taps fixed	277
Total cost	Rs1,500,000
Dollar equivalent	(approx. $75,000)

Two pilot upgrading projects in central low-income areas, Steuart Street and Kew Lane, helped establish an alternative model to the original practice of redevelopment through direct construction. The first scheme, Steuart Street (population 900), provided for repair of existing structures, improvement of lighting and ventilation, construction of new units to replace those demolished to accommodate common amenities, delivery of sanitation services, and improvement of footpaths and drainage. The total cost of the project was in the order of $100,000. Such issues as cost effectiveness, affordability, and replicability were largely overlooked, and the upgrading and repair works were totally subsidized. Kew Lane marked a notable step forward, with the emphasis shifting to provision of basic services and environmental upgrading. A total population of 1,924 benefited from the project which provided or improved a total of 45 toilets, 29 bathrooms, and 25 water taps, in addition to paved footpaths, drains, and garbage containers. The total cost was approximately $32,500 (approximately $130 for each of the 251 units), with no provision for cost recovery.

These projects have paved the way for a realistic approach to public-sector intervention in inner-city areas. The value of the Sri Lanka experience is the lesson derived from the enacting of appropriate legal mechanisms which effectively stabilized the low-income groups in the inner city through the enforcement of tenurial changes.

The first set of policy issues that must be addressed concerns tenure arrangements. Governmental concern for the repair and improvement of inner-city housing stock is unlikely to be best served by the maintenance of the *status quo*, since leaving ownership in the hands of landlords has not resulted in desired improvements, even in cases where rent control was not in force. Public-sector attempts to upgrade slum accommodation while leaving tenure arrangements untouched are almost certain to backfire, adding to rather than reducing risks of displacement.

Granting tenure to individual users has few attractions in the inner city, with its multistorey tenements, compared to squatter settlements, with their separate structures. Collective forms of tenure would appear to be appropriate, and, while there are no known cases where this has been conferred, examples of *de facto* transfer of tenure to residents where the owners' interest in the property has slackened suggest its clear potential. In such cases, residents have assumed responsibility for repairs to and maintenance of communal spaces and services: they have also been able to use organized action to resist eviction. The formalization of such arrangements through the *de jure* transfer of tenure could only serve to strengthen positive trends and realize latent potentials.

The second set of issues concerns efforts to promote community and neighbourhood organizations, for it is clear that user groups are able to develop the organizational forms required to initiate and perform complex tasks even when there is a scarcity of financial resources. Community organizations have been formed for purposes other than resisting eviction, and have demonstrated their ability to formulate and implement self-help and mutual-aid programmes that lead to the sustained improvement of living conditions. Organized capacities for self-help and mutual aid are today recognized in squatter settlements, but they are as yet largely unrecognized in inner-city slums, reflecting the fact that governments and public authorities almost everywhere have so far given very little support to the development of residents' groups and community-based organizations in central neighbourhoods. While governments may be reluctant to devolve decision-making

---

Box 13.8 Bangkok: land sharing in the inner city

Land-sharing schemes in Bangkok, implemented or in the design stage, represent an interesting and realistic approach in countries where the urban land market is largely unregulated. The schemes tackle one of the main constraints on inner-city rehabilitation efforts—landlords' opposition to the upgrading of slum areas which they are seeking to recover for private redevelopment. The schemes are based on a trade-off between conflicting interests —owners' versus residents'—which allows the landlord to recover part of his property while permitting the residents to retain possession of the remaining part. In inner-city areas, where growing demands on valuable land increase the threat of expulsion for low-income groups, land sharing is able to break a deadlock by legitimizing the right of the poor to remain where they are.

The assumption underlying land-sharing arrangements is that each party stands to gain in the process of resolving legal conflicts which affect both users and owners—the former in terms of constant insecurity, the latter in terms of being unable to put property to profitable use. Experience has shown that arrangements can be flexibly adapted to suit the conditions prevailing in each location. In a land-sharing scheme in Sam Yod, for example, 'bonus' floorspace was generated which the owner could sell on the open market for commercial utilization while accommodating the occupants in the area within the premises. In a scheme in Lad Buakao, part of the area is being offered to the community to undertake reconstruction through self-help efforts, while the remaining land can be put to commercial use by the owner.

Land-sharing schemes have inherent limitations and their own uncertainties. The physical structure of most inner-city neighbourhoods, for example, may make densification problematic, giving rise to the need for selection among residents. Proximity to an area where commercial development will take place may produce an indirect threat of expulsion of the residents at a later stage, as a result of a general increase in land values.

Tenurial arrangements based on individual freehold rights may also expose families to the risk of progressive displacement. Co-operative and communal forms of tenure, an alternative so far very largely neglected, would enable the community to face external pressures and should be pursued vigorously. Communal tenure combined with community development activities may provide for efficient management and lay the foundation for a sustained process of upgrading and improvement.

The Bangkok experiments with land sharing appear to have considerable potential, not only for stabilizing the position of low-income groups in the inner city. It could be applied to government-owned land, with land sharing used by the public sector as an effective tool for securing cross-subsidization in upgrading programmes.

prerogatives to groups in the inner city, they can no longer afford not to recognize the advantages of self-help and mutual aid and the value of community and neighbourhood organizations that give expression to these principles.

Efforts to promote self-help and mutual aid in the inner city will have to display the same sensitivities to the problems and needs of the poor as those in squatter settlements. This sensitivity demands that attention be given to, among other things, informal processes and arrangements, and to the form and modalities of 'assistance packages'. In squatter settlements, community organizations usually exist: in inner-city slums, they may need to be created or positively encouraged.

This provides a new logic for the use of governmental subsidies, the third issue in the inner city. The difficulties in channelling public funds to the poor were discussed above. Part of the difficulty resides in the absence of appropriate channels, but the existence of strong community-based groups willing and able to work for the improvement of inner-city slums would establish the 'terminal points' for the channels that still require delineation. In this way, governments and public authorities could use public funds to create the local bodies required for the efficient and cost-effective use of public money, turning the vexing question of subsidies into a positive instrument for community development and self-directed change.

The idea of transferring public funds directly to community-based groups in the inner city will no doubt be a difficult one for some governments to accept. The degree of acceptance will in part be conditioned by the importance attached to the principles of self-help and mutual aid, and by the determination to see negative trends reversed. The acceptance will also be conditioned by the formal arrangements that govern transfers. These must require that community groups be fully accountable for the funds they receive, as well as provide for sanctions against 'improper use'. Community-based groups would, in other words, need to be conceived, sooner or later, as planning and implementation bodies that share in decisions on how public funds can best be used.

Such a development would have the potential of changing the relationship between the city and the slum. It is also one that provides for the transformation of the position of the slum dweller from one of 'recipient' to one of 'participant'. The progressive transformation of community-based groups into local-level planning and implementation bodies would open the way to forms of participation responsive to the requirements of the poor and establish a forum in which self-help could, over time, become self-determination. Alliances and coalitions of such bodies could lead to a significant strengthening of the power position of the inner-city poor, enabling them to be more on an equal footing with an interest and pressure groups.

Notes

1. *Report of Habitat: United Nations Conference on Human Settlements* (United Nations publication).
2. See World Bank, *Housing Sector Policy Paper* (Washington DC, 1975), annex 7.
3. For a review of the literature on these themes, see Lisa Peattie and Jose A. Aldrete-Hass, 'Marginal Settlements in Developing Countries: Research, Advocacy of Policy, and Evolution of Programs', *Annual Review of Sociology*, 7 (1981), 157–75.
4. World Bank, *op. cit.*
5. The review of experience with squatter upgrading and sites-and-services projects draws upon: Aprodicio A. Laquian, *Basic Housing: Policies for Urban Sites, Services, and Shelter in Developing Countries* (Ottawa: International Development Research Centre, 1983); Douglas Keare and Scott Parris, *Evaluation of Shelter Programs for the Urban Poor: Principal Findings*, World Bank Staff Working Paper 548 (Washington DC, 1982); and Michael Cohen, *Learning by Doing: World Bank Lending for Urban Development, 1972–1982* (Washington DC: World Bank, 1983).
6. See Lisa R. Peattie and William A. Doebele, 'Second Thoughts on Sites and Services', Massachusetts Institute of Technology, 1976 (mimeo).

Part IV

Conclusion

14 Towards Enabling Settlement Strategies

Human settlements policies in the 1970s were almost exclusively focused on the problem of housing the poor. The strategy most widely advocated was to rely on squatter-settlement upgrading as a crisis-containment action, and sites-and-services production to meet current and future needs. This strategy has been so generally accepted, at least in theory, that it could be called the 'new orthodoxy'.

Unfortunately, in practice, the new orthodoxy has revealed two fatal flaws. First, the administrative and financial problems associated with squatter-settlement upgrading have proved insuperable in the legal and bureaucratic context of most developing countries; and, secondly, hardly any developing country has been able to produce affordable sites-and-services plots on a scale remotely approaching housing needs. The new orthodoxy, while a significant improvement on the old, still constitutes an inadequate basis for human settlements strategies. It has made only an expensive and much-publicized dent in human settlements problems, and settlements needs are growing many times more quickly than they are being met by present programmes. While more sensitive to the poor than the responses that preceded it, the new orthodoxy is typically unable to respond to the needs of the poorest 20 per cent of the population and it has little or nothing to offer the urban poor of inner-city slums.

However, the most significant defect of the programme was that it assumed the problems of low-income housing to be synonymous with the problems of human settlements. In fact, shelter is only one of many settlement elements, and low-income shelter is only one aspect of the total housing picture. Therefore, an almost exclusive focus on this one issue has distorted the use of resources and diverted attention from fundamental human settlements needs which require co-ordinated attention. Furthermore, it implied a role for government which was beyond the capacity of most administrations. Even though direct intervention in the construction process was to be abandoned by government, an enormous range of responsibilities was retained by the public sector, and this has proved to be still an insurmountable obstacle to workable human settlements programmes.

Several conclusions are inescapable: First, despite the efforts made, the poor have done immeasurably more for themselves than governments have been able to do for them, particularly in terms of the best use of available resources. Secondly, something more than squatter-settlement upgrading and sites-and-services programmes in their present form is required if settlement needs are to be met. Thirdly, governments may wish to do a great deal through formal programmes in future, but persistent resource constraints are likely to make this increasingly difficult. The main objective of a new strategy must be one of making conditions for self-help and mutual aid as favourable as possible, through sets of enabling action in support of locally determined, self-organized, and self-managed settlement programmes.

As part of this effort, it is imperative that governments chart new directions in shelter strategies, and one of these directions is the promotion of rental housing as a vehicle for mass shelter provision, particularly in urban areas. Up to now, on the levels of both research and policy, rental housing options have been largely ignored, but the evaluation of rental options requires detailed research on local housing markets and needs, on suitable rental housing programmes for various income groups, and on methods of promoting the construction of rental housing, particularly for low-income groups. Such an effort is required by the very fact that the tendency in developing countries is in the direction of rental housing as the predominant form of shelter provision for most, if not all, income groups.

In considering this new policy path, what has to be borne in mind is that the preoccupation with owner-occupied housing, particularly for low-income groups, was not solely based on a concern with shelter provision. There are two other considerations in choosing the option of owner-occupancy, although these were often implicit rather than explicit. The first of these was political: owner-occupancy was seen as an instrument to create political and social stability, especially of low-income groups. The second was economic: house ownership, in whatever form, was seen as a way to 'enrich' low-income urban residents. In other words, house ownership was simply the means to provide them with physical capital to be translated into income. The house could be used (wholly or partly) to generate rental income or as the location for informal economic activities. Finally, it could be used as an asset to be employed as a surety for the extension of credit for engaging in small-scale businesses or enterprises. In other words, the goals behind shelter programmes for low-income groups were never simply the provision of shelter, and for this reason rental housing as an option was put aside from the beginning. If, however, the goal is to provide shelter, rental housing must now be explored fully, especially in light of the fact that the political and economic goals of owner-occupied housing programmes have apparently materialized.

The shift to enabling settlement strategies implies a reorientation as great as, if not greater than, the shift that has taken place from conventional low-cost housing programmes to squatter-settlement upgrading and sites-and-services programmes. It is not a question of 'improving' and expanding squatter-settlement upgrading and sites-and-services programmes, but one of going beyond them. This is not meant to imply that the experience gained with the programmes has proved inconsequential; on the contrary, many valuable lessons have been learnt. The path to enabling settlement strategies passes through squatter-settlement upgrading and sites-and-services approaches, but does not stop there.

The main elements of enabling settlement strategies

Enabling settlement strategies cannot begin with estimates of 'settlement needs' and 'settlement deficits', nor deal exclusively with the requirements of middle- and upper-income groups that are able to satisfy their requirements through formal mechanisms. Their prime purpose will be to state the sets of measures that are to be used to enable communities to help themselves.[1]

Enabling settlement strategies must contain a response to two main challenges: how to deal with problems posed by very large numbers of poor people, and how to provide for effective autonomy of community-based groups. It will be impossible to find answers to the first challenge without the adoption of a settlement-wide approach, while the second challenge can only be met at the local level. Enabling settlement strategies must therefore fuse settlement-wide action with local initiative. Decisions taken at the local level will establish the framework required for mobilizing and guiding local initiative and action.

Settlement-wide action

The main issue to be addressed at the settlement level is restructuring. If enabling strategies are to work, settlements must be progressively restructured, both spatially and organizationally. When projects are planned and implemented in isolation from settlement-wide processes, they tend to have little impact. Part of the problem is that the relationships between houses, jobs, services, and transport are crucial to the success of enabling settlement strategies, and efforts to consolidate and improve these relationships demand decisions that can only be taken at the settlement level. The decisions required are basic ones concerning the location of public-utility and transport networks, with the aim of establishing a spatial framework that creates opportunities for shaping settlement growth and development. The required spatial framework will not resemble traditional master plans: it will not seek to designate a desired 'end-state' for the simple reason that there is none, and it will not be based on zoning regulations and density standards, since the aim is to create conditions and not to impose restrictions.

Spatial restructuring must be accompanied by organizational restructuring. Organizational restructuring has the aim of establishing and promoting community-based and neighbour-hood groups, with decision-making autonomy. Such groups would effectively serve as community-based planning and implementing agencies that initiate their own programmes and projects and have a large measure of independence in managing their own affairs. It is in such communities that responsibilities for the provision and improvement of shelter should be largely vested.

Enabling actions at the local level

The purpose of action at the local level is to increase access to basic resources for locally determined and self-managed programmes. Enabling actions are, essentially, institutional changes in administrative rules and regulations. They will typically cover changes in the ways in which funds are allocated and used, the ways in which credit is generated and disbursed, and, most important, the ways in which decisions are made and responsibility exercised. These are changes that only governments can authorize. Enabling actions with respect to tenure, services, credit, and building materials will be particularly important. There is considerable positive experience in all these areas, and there is considerable scope for experimentation.

The aim of governmental intervention in the area of services is to make available at reasonable cost what self-help communities are unable to provide for themselves. Such services fall into two main categories. The first is physical infrastructure, especially water, electricity, and low-cost sanitation. The second category includes social services, notably primary education and basic health-care facilities, and garbage collection and disposal.

With respect to credit, governments must intervene to provide initial capital and to assist in creating institutions that mobilize the often meagre resources of those involved in self-help and mutual-aid processes. The overwhelming need is for small loans that can be extended to those without collateral and without regular employment. Credit should be flexible and non-discriminatory, and can include material loans, construction loans, and loans at below market rates adjusted to incorporate the contribution of

self-help. Such loans can be extended to both individuals and self-help communities.

Credit aimed at income generation and employment creation in the informal sector can be extended to individuals, although there appears to be scope for loans to 'solidarity groups' modelled on the delivery systems pioneered in a few developing countries. The greatest potential of all, however, resides in the extension of credit to autonomous communities responsible for its disbursement and use within the framework of self-guided and self-managed programmes. However difficult this may prove in practice, it is likely to be one of the most important of all supportive actions.

Governmental action with respect to building materials must have a twofold purpose. The first is to ensure adequate supplies of low-cost materials that can be used by self-help communities with relatively simple tools. This will require that priority be given to getting 'good ideas' out of the laboratory and on to the building site through low-cost processes of commercialization: in this, there will be considerable scope for private initiative. The second requirement is that governments relax building codes and regulations when they constitute an impediment to self-help and mutual-aid programmes. The urban poor have good reasons for choosing to use salvaged and recycled materials at the early stage of construction and they should not be prevented from doing so. It must be recognized, also, that the lowering of building standards in part of a settlement may translate into an improvement of shelter standards in the settlement as a whole.

Enabling settlement strategies must be based on a new division of responsibilities between governmental agencies and community-based self-help groups. The main responsibilities of government at the settlement level reside in managing the growth of the settlement. These are responsibilities that settlement authorities have always sought to exercise, and they can only be vested in governments. The main responsibilities of community-based self-help groups reside in the carrying out of improvements at the local level. These are responsibilities that the poor have traditionally *de facto* exercised, even though they are not formally recognized. Enabling settlement strategies are based on the recognition that such a division exists, and seek to turn it to advantage by allowing each party to do what it is best equipped to do. In this new division, public authorities do not abrogate their responsibilities but rather assume new ones: these new ones reside in the area of supportive and enabling actions for the self-determined, self-organized, and self-managed programmes of community and neighbourhood groups.

Models of participation

Community participation is frequently seen as merely the provision of residents' labour. In this case, community participation may be conceived of in terms of individuals building their own houses or groups of individuals digging a trench for water pipes. An interpretation that goes further is one in which the community, rather than the individual, is seen as an actor. This would apply, for example, to collective discussions of development plans between the initiating project agency and a settlement's residents, so as to modify the plans to incorporate the expressed wishes of the intended beneficiaries. The principle underlying this approach is that if people agree to a plan, they will be prepared to assist in the process of implementation as well as subsequent maintenance of the buildings and infrastructure provided. Such a pragmatic incentive is often the main motivation behind participation policies. A third conception of community participation goes one step further. This places final decision-making power in the hands of the residents themselves, usually in the form of neighbourhood organizations. In this case, agencies and technicians assume the role of advisers in processes that are designed to give concrete expression to residents' needs and desires. While this mode represents community participation in its most complete form, it implies a transfer of authority from 'planners' to 'planned', and poses a challenge to professional control by technical experts.

Experiments with this last model have mainly been tried in developing countries. Fruitful environments for the application of the model have been countries with strong co-operative movements, such as Portugal and Uruguay in the 1960s, and those involved in social change,

such as Nicaragua, where community organizations have led the planning and implementation process in the upgrading of 26 low-income neighbourhoods in Managua. The developed countries have not proved a fertile ground for the model, although there have been cases where it has been applied. In Denmark and Finland, for example, future residents, usually of rural areas, have practised 'self-planning', with experts acting solely as advisers. In the United States, too, there were cases in the 1960s and early 1970s of citizen groups acting as partners with city authorities under the Model Cities Programme.

Degrees of participation

Even though carried out in slums, squatter settlements, and sites-and-services areas, some housing and infrastructure schemes involve little more than contractor-built operations. All works are undertaken by construction companies or public enterprises, and it is assumed that, upon completion, the residents of the 'new' neighbourhoods will participate in the scheme to the extent of adding to and improving their dwellings and maintaining some of the new services delivered, by cleaning streets and clearing blocked drains. Since all self-help housing projects include dwelling improvements, the special feature of this type of scheme is that it assumes maintenance will be undertaken by the population 'served'. The frequent failure of such schemes lies in the inability to realize that residents are unlikely to maintain facilities which they see as 'officially' provided, and therefore as to be maintained by public authorities. The exclusion of participation in almost all other respects virtually guarantees the absence of commitment to project maintenance. Large-scale schemes of this nature can, however, be seen repeated time and time again, with the same disappointing results.

Other projects allow for participation in implementation. While it is likely that people will be willing to maintain something they have helped to construct (apart from their own houses), this approach may backfire. Implementation means effort and time, and any sense of pride in achievement may be absent if the ideas originate from the project agency. In this case,

Box 14.1   Participation that worked: Villa El Salvador, Lima

In May 1971, a squatter-resettlement project for some 9,000 families was established on the fringes of Lima. The residents were faced with the task of developing their houses and community on a stretch of desert land with no services of any kind. It was expected that the settlement would eventually accommodate approximately 250,000 people.

Resettling squatters on uninviting terrain in poor locations is nothing new; nor is there any novelty in the growth of substandard settlements to massive proportions, while authorities look on helplessly or are forced to turn a blind eye. In the case of Villa El Salvador, however, the government promoted settlement growth, and within five years the desert village was transformed into a strongly organized settlement, with water and electricity connections, street lighting, a community-run bank, a building materials supply depot, kerosene pumps, a nascent popular health centre, and a commonly owned productive enterprise. By this time, it had renamed itself CUAVES—an acronym for the Autonomous Urban Community of Villa El Salvador.

'Autonomy', as represented in the decision-making power of an elected community organization, was a central principle in this remarkable experience of community participation. The principle of autonomous decision-making had been encouraged by government authorities after 1968, and it was felt that, through the development of organizations of industrial and rural workers and residents of low-income settlements, a basis would be established for the transfer of political power to the masses, the government would support these organizations but not control them —self-management was essential.

In CUAVES, self-management took the form of a community-organization structure, with leaders at block, 'residential-group' (grouping of blocks), and settlement levels, each level having different responsibilities. With governmental approbation and assistance, participation took on a structured hierarchical form: house construction was essentially the role of the plot-holder, blocks of households would collect common refuse (for example), residential groups were charged with the development of communal open spaces (community centres, etc.), and the community leadership formulated policies affecting the settlement as a whole (including employment generation, materials supply, clinic operation, and financing of projects to benefit all residents).

The role of governmental authorities was defined as that of partner and 'facilitator'—they would provide what the community could not—but an equally important role was to create an environment in which participation could work. The people could provide the ideas, efforts, and even substantial financing, while the governmental authorities ensured that obstacles to the realization of this commitment were kept to a minimum. Thus, governmental authorities initially offered social workers and community-development support, provided direct access (bypassing middlemen) to essentials, such as cement and kerosene, and made legal provision for a community-controlled bank and health centre.

By April 1976, Villa El Salvador's population numbered approximately 130,000, and its community-participation achievements at block, residential-group, and settlement levels could be summarized as:

- Construction and financing over 200 classrooms, mainly of temporary materials.

- Payment of many of the teachers in schools.

- Conducting of an adult-literacy campaign.

- Conducting of health campaigns, such as vaccination programmes and rabies control.

- Establishment of a health centre, with clinic and pharmacy.

- Establishment of a community bank.

- Establishment of a building materials depot.

- Establishment of a hardware store.

- Provision of a small bus fleet.

- Operation of a cultural centre, with library, films, theatre, etc.

- Improvement of small parks in open spaces.

---

participation may be perceived by the residents purely in terms of cheap labour which they are donating to a project that is not their own. The result is likely to be resentment and a refusal to participate.

The greatest degree of community participation is seen in projects in which planning (decision-making) is added to the implementation and maintenance spheres of collective activity. Settlement development now acquires a character denied it in the other two approaches: people who decide what they want and who play a part in the design of the project, together with the trained, professional agency team, are likely to be willing to assist in implementation and, thereafter, have some psychological commitment to project maintenance. The Villa El Salvador settlement in Lima is a prime example of how participation from the planning stage encouraged participation in the implementation and maintenance stages.

- Provision of community centres in 'residential groups'.
- Setting-up of a self-managed clothing workshop.
- Arrangement of direct fruit and vegetable supplies from the countryside to local markets.
- Installation of kerosene pumps.

However, as community efforts grew, so did the demands made upon the government. Government had provided modern street lighting, half of all families enjoyed access to domestic electricity, water from standpipes was being replaced by domestic connections, and a start was to be made on a sewerage system, but the community demanded increased commitments, on the grounds that it had already provided more than its share. Demands ranged from schools, doctors, and road improvements to employment creation on a massive scale, as well as participation in national economic policy-making. This level of participation, however, extended beyond the limits acceptable to the government.

The main lessons from the Villa El Salvador experience include:

- However willing residents are and however independently minded, participation is given greatest scope with the active support of government.
- Participation in local development as part of a process of national change benefiting the poor is a stimulus to full commitment to community participation.
- Even 'populations of strangers' are capable of collective efforts, if there are perceived common interests, an adequate community organizational structure, and tangible results at the end of participatory efforts.
- Successful participation creates fertile ground for ambitious participatory ventures, from building classrooms to organizing a bank, and when sufficient momentum is created, the process can accelerate.
- This acceleration may lead participation to its ultimate destination: demands for national-level participation.

Source: R. Skinner, 'Self-Help, Community Organization and Politics: Villa El Salvador, Lima', in P. Ward (ed), *Self-Help Housing. A Critique* (London, Mansell, 1982).

Towards effective community-participation strategies

Given the severe limitations of institutional blueprints, proposals for community-participation strategies must be presented in the form of guidelines. The most important are presented below:

- *Government commitment should be publicized.* The intended participants in community-participation programmes are often sceptical about or unclear as to the purpose of participation. This attitude can be reduced by a publicized commitment of government to community participation in settlement development as part of a broad concept of democracy at the national level. This can be expressed by relating settlement-oriented community participation to city and national level decision-making in a wide range of social, economic, cultural, and political spheres. Community participation then ceases to be merely a discrete 'tool' and becomes a part of the development process as a whole.

- *Maximum is not synonymous with optimum.* There should be no assumption that community participation is most effective when it has reached maximum proportions. In some countries, the population may appreciate a limited direct involvement in settlement development, with elected representatives or officials exercising responsibilities for the remainder. In other countries, there will be populations anxious to become involved in an almost unlimited range of community-participation activities. Community-participation strategies which work against these strongly held feelings weaken rather than strengthen the scope for success of community participation. The most 'appropriate' level for any country can only be determined through dialogue with the people at the local level—this is one principle of community-participation strategies which is universally valid.

- *Supporting legislation is required.* Whatever the type or extent of community participation, its effectiveness will be severely hampered without supporting legislation. The issue of tenure regularization for squatters is often raised in this connection. Similarly, the lowering of building and construction standards to levels appropriate to the requirements and payment capacities of the poor is important. The essential point is that, if provisions are made to facilitate the improvement of settlements, residents may be disposed to participation, but collective action cannot be assumed to precede the solution of individual problems. While some countries have clear requirements for recognizing community organizations, others have not. Effective participation requires the existence of laws to which residents' groups can refer when pursuing recognition. In addition to providing for recog-

Box 14.2   Participation that worked: Labadi, Accra

Although community participation is often stressed as an essential ingredient in government-sponsored low-income housing projects, in practice some of the most notable examples of participation are to be found where governmental initiative has been absent. The Labadi settlement in Accra is one such example. Originating as a village and augmented by unplanned accretion, Labadi had, by 1945, formally fallen under the capital city's administration. Its history had been characterized by improvement and demolition plans, none of which was implemented. It was into this policy vacuum that a small group of Labadi residents stepped in order to stimulate action in 1973.

At that time, the population of the settlement numbered over 45,000, of whom six began the venture under the name 'The Alpha Expedition'. The aim was at first limited to providing recreational facilities to local youth, but residents hit upon this scheme as a rallying point for wide-ranging activities over the following years. The provision of recreation space necessitated the clean-up of designated sports areas, but this action quickly expanded with the recognition that other areas of Labadi would benefit from the same action, as well as from refuse collection. Residents successfully negotiated the supply of refuse lorries from the City Council at weekends, and within a year the association was committed to the goal of general improvement. This included the building of a community library and postnatal clinic, the mounting of a health-education campaign (cholera had been detected in Labadi), the provision of manpower for trench-digging to accelerate the City Council's provision of drainage, the maintenance of street and other public lighting, as well as the organization of dances, games, and sports events. While the hope of securing municipal assistance was never abandoned, most of the activities drew on residents' own resources, either through membership dues or donations. The latter were provided in part by some of the better-off residents, such as businessmen and teachers, who also offered advice and persuaded the city authorities to support the Alpha Expedition.

The strength of the association was its ability to get results, despite the limited involvement of the authorities, and the high degree of homogeneity of residents—most members came from the same region of the country and were born in the settlement, although a wide range of occupations was represented. Its weakness was the scarcity of financial resources—the most feasible projects were the most labour intensive—and lack of formalized links with official agencies. This meant that negotiations on joint projects had to be undertaken on an *ad hoc* basis, without any long-term development plan.

The main lesson is clear. Although spontaneous improvement efforts may be extremely effective, there comes a time when a threshold of resource needs is reached. It can only be crossed by the active collaboration of governmental agencies with the people's own organizations.

Source: L. Kooperman, 'Community Action in West Africa', *African Urban Studies*, No. 1, pp. 1–17.

---

nition, laws must specify the powers, rights, and responsibilities of community-based organizations and individual residents.

• *Laws cannot work without effective institutions.* Established institutions are often ill-equipped to deal with new programmes, such as those involving community participation. The attitudes of administrators, technicians, and the people themselves must be adapted to the opportunities of community participation, and new skills have to be acquired within official agencies and by residents and their organizations.

• *Systematic training.* Provision for the acquisition of new skills by professionals and residents (preferably at individual as well as leadership levels) should be made when formulating community-participation programmes and projects. Training should not be undertaken on an *ad hoc* basis; if it remains an afterthought, it will prove impossible to co-ordinate training efforts and project execution. Training should preferably be organized on-site or at local or national training centres, already existing or specially established for this purpose. Other options include training in centres in neighbouring countries or, when absolutely necessary, in centres outside the region.

• *Project support communication.* In order to clarify statutory or other rights and obligations of residents and staff, and to make clear the demarcation of responsibilities of different actors in community-participation programmes, attention must be paid to establishing a system of project support communication (PSC). PSC would involve communications within agencies and among residents, and should be planned as an integral part of programmes and projects. This will help ensure that risks of misinformation, inadequate communication, and distortion of facts crucial to the success of community participation are minimized.

• *Local information offices.* Another form of communication is the establishment of local information offices near or on project sites and easily accessible to residents. Their tasks would include disseminating information or documents as well as answering questions from individuals on such complex issues as legal rights and obligations and loan-repayment schedules. A local office would not only serve to smooth out problems in the community-participation process but also help to narrow the gap that often exists between staff and residents. Numerous countries have experimented with such types of offices. Developed countries

---

Box 14.3   Participation that worked: Hackney, London

In 1979, the United Kingdom's Department of the Environment launched a five-year Priority Estates Project aimed at improving run-down public housing in about 40 urban areas throughout the country. It identified direct tenant involvement as crucial to success. The Wenlock Improvement Scheme (WIS) was one of the high-priority estates chosen for the project. Built in London's inner city some 30 years earlier, it housed 2,000 people. At the start of the project, the existing Tenants' Association served purely as a social club, but, with the encouragement of local and central government staff, a Tenant Board was elected in 1981 and became involved in management and decision-making as well as to a limited degree in implementing the improvement of the estate.

By 1984, the year the project ended, the Tenant Board had organized resident participation in the following activities:

• Re-equipping of playgrounds and a small park.

• Construction of individual and communal gardens and a tree nursery.

• Painting of murals on buildings.

• Establishing and running of a youth club and play scheme.

• Cleaning of shared spaces within the blocks of flats.

In addition, the Tenant Board had been responsible for:

• Joint decision-making regarding improvement priorities with the local authority.

• Organization of general clean-ups in the estate, from the repainting of public interiors and the establishment of new refuse-disposal systems to rat extermination and removal of graffiti.

• Securing and management of public funds for landscaping works and materials purchase; hiring an animal warden; employment of a small group of jobless school-leavers in estate improvements; handling of a small budget of its own for *ad hoc* works; and payment of two part-time staff members.

At the same time, the local authority undertook tasks which the Board could not, such as the installation of security floodlighting and entryphones at the foot of every stairwell and the carrying out of plumbing, heating, and structural repairs. However, the Board was involved in at least a consultative capacity in all management matters leading to these activities and made claims for the allocation of a maintenance grant which it believed it could use more cost effectively than local government to hire contractors.

There are several lessons to be drawn from this experiment:

• Participation does not necessarily imply any physical labour contribution. In the WIS case, involvement was mainly participation in planning and management. The availability of funds made it possible to contract out most physical works.

• The project staff stimulated the residents to establish an active Tenant Board, where a dormant association-cum-social-club had hitherto been the only organized centre in the community. This process started on the right foot with attention to a visible and felt need, in the form of external structural repairs which both symbolized the advent of improvements and showed the good faith of the local-authority staff.

• The area had been becoming increasingly heterogeneous with respect to age, length of stay in the estate, ethnic origin, and family structure. Vandalism was rife, and the area was regarded by many residents as a place in which they found themselves against their will—a last resort. With the activation of the Tenant Board and neighbourhood improvements, this attitude began to change. The Board met all newcomers and introduced them to the estate, making them aware of their responsibilities but also of their new rights. Youths found the improvements offered alternatives to antisocial behaviour, and in general the area appeared at last to have a future.

• From the start of the project, it was recognized by the government that it shared an interest with both the local authority and residents in community participation; indeed it was regarded as a *sine qua non*. This facilitated the decentralization of both fund management and decision-making. In this, the on-site location of project offices proved essential as a means of rapidly dealing with local problems and promoting interaction and understanding amongst officials and residents.

Source: R. Skinner, research notes (1983).

include the Netherlands, the United Kingdom, and the United States; among the developing countries, Latin America is notable for its informal links between NGOs or individual private professionals and community groups. There are also numerous cases in Asia.

• *Budget*. No progress in community participation will take place if governments do not pay close attention to its budgetary implications. The ideal situation would be across-the-board increases in settlement budgets, but, realistically, budgets can be progressively adjusted to favour community-participation types of programmes. While some countries have added significantly to their housing-production statistics by such adjustments—community-participation projects tend to have the lowest costs per unit—the vast majority have yet to take up this option.

• *Strengthening of community organizations*. There is a need for governments to promote the establishment or strengthening of community organizations representing residents as a whole, but in a facilitating rather than a dominating manner. Tools must be found which reduce community organizations' dependency on or domination by state agencies and which stimulate residents to take up the community-participation challenge as a worth while, organized effort. Such tools can include laws establishing spheres of autonomy for recognized organizations, the involvement of NGOs as third parties in collaborative projects, and the allocation to community organizations of a 'freely disposable budget' as part of total project budgets, the use of these funds reflecting the residents' own improvement priorities and not being subject to veto from any state agency.

• *Utilization of local resources*. To date, community-participation projects have neglected many of the resources which exist within settlements. There have been inadequate efforts to identify and capitalize upon the potential of women and youth or of managerial skills of residents. In a number of schemes, children have been active in such areas as inventorying local socio-economic conditions and maintenance requirements. Women have been unnoticed communicators of health and sanitation messages. Groups established for educational reasons

---

Box 14.4   Zimbabwe: aided self-help in low-income housing schemes

Community participation, mainly in the form of aided self-help, is a feature of the low-income housing pilot projects being implemented in the secondary towns of Kwekwe and Gutu in Zimbabwe. UNCHS (Habitat) provides technical assistance to this programme of the Ministry of Construction and National Housing (MCNH), with USAID providing the capital costs for infrastructure works. Under this project, over 1,000 serviced plots for low-income housing have been developed in Kwekwe, an intermediate urban centre, and over 200 plots in Gutu, a rapidly expanding rural growth centre. The pilot character of these projects is underlined by the fact that they are expected to contribute the required technical options for the development of a national housing policy.

Three modes of house construction are being used in the pilot projects—aided self-help, housing co-operatives, and building brigades. Individual families participated in the house-design process by selecting from a range of house-design options, with the use of models and standardized plans. The design concept gives the family a range of choices in terms of room size and functional requirements for indoor and outdoor spaces.

Aided self-help is the most widely selected mode of construction. Each allottee receives a building loan for the purchase of building materials, tools, and equipment, and the hiring of transport. Most families have been able to mobilize their own labour force, assisted by small-scale builders, friends, and relatives. Those who had additional savings have usually opted for hiring the services of the local-authority brigade. The building-materials loans are being recovered over a period of 25 years, with an average monthly rate of $Z20–25, representing approximately 20 per cent of the monthly income of most families.

---

have mobilized and led otherwise inactive communities. Such examples reflect a few of the opportunities for community participation: there are many others, and they merit investigation. It is already accepted that co-operatives, after a period of membership and training, should manage their own activities, and the same could apply to other forms of neighbourhood organizations. Well-trained and self-regulating community organizations could assume responsibility for certain aspects of building materials supply and management, financial administration, project supervision, and technical assistance, thereby relieving pressures on project agencies.

• *Non-governmental organization involvement*. Many community-participation success stories

---

Box 14.5 Burundi: upgrading of the Musaga community

Community participation was an essential part of the upgrading project for Musaga, a semi-urban neighbourhood on the outskirts of Bujumbura. At the request of the government, UNCHS (Habitat) developed a project for improving the housing, environmental, and living conditions of a low-income urban area, designed to develop full involvement of the residents in project planning and implementation. During the five years of project implementation (1978–83), the participation of the community focused mainly on two components: the process of land regularization, and the establishment of co-operatives for plot allocation and house construction.

The process of land regularization, aimed at developing a rational plan with appropriate plot sizes and a network of roads, footpaths, and public spaces for community services, was based on the participation of residents and community leaders. The constant presence of project workers, building technicians, and social workers permitted a gradual evolution of plans which allowed integrated development of the area to take place. A revolving fund for house construction became operational in a pilot block of 104 plots, the allottees of which were organized in a housing co-operative. This first block consisted of regularized parcels of land as well as newly established and allocated plots.

Although co-operative development was not new in Burundi, it was the first time that this type of organized participation was applied to urban development and house construction, with the co-operative becoming fully responsible for plot development. The members of the co-operative were organized in groups of 20 families that built up their plots through mutual aid, with the financial assistance of building-materials loans granted by the revolving fund.

Box 14.6 Lusaka, Zambia: making project support communication work

Project support communication (PSC), a term originally coined by UNICEF for rural-based health and education programmes, was applied in an urban context for the first time in the World Bank's First Urban Project in Lusaka, Zambia, between 1974 and 1978. In an urban environment, PSC requires a special approach, mainly because urban-housing projects are confronted with an array of complex legal, financial, and administrative issues for which elaborate information campaigns need to be organized. In the case of Zambia, four squatter settlements in different parts of Lusaka, with a total of 100,000 inhabitants, were upgraded. The upgrading programme provided for such services as roads, standpipes, clinics, schools, and loans to encourage house improvement.

The Housing Project Unit in charge of the project created, with the assistance of UNICEF, a Communication Section which organized PSC in two stages. First, a public relations campaign was mounted, to secure the support of policy-makers for the project, to inform the public at large and to generate general interest in the project. Secondly, a continuous dialogue was set up with project participants through all stages of planning and implementation, a process in which the local party organization (UNIP) played an important role. Meetings, briefings, and seminars were the most widely and frequently used channels of communication, on-site as well as off-site.

The Housing Project Unit's Evaluation Section carried out surveys to assess the impact of the communication effort. Regular meetings were found to be the most important communication channel, with audiovisuals playing a valuable supporting role. Portable, battery-powered,

---

have involved non-governmental organizations, and their support of projects should be encouraged. NGOs tend to develop strong local ties to the projects in which they become involved and are usually able to respond to changing conditions and new problems. The commitment and effort displayed by many NGO members are indisputable, and the very fact that an NGO is involved in a project indicates that it is providing a service or filling a role not covered by governmental agencies. The relationships between NGOs and governmental agencies may be co-operative, but they can also be strained. Where tensions are the result of deep political divisions, there is little that can be done to improve the situation, but when relationships are not antag-

onistic, ways should be explored to enlarge the contribution of NGOs to participatory processes. Parts of projects can, for example, be subcontracted to a specialized NGO, and projects proposed by community groups through an NGO can be supported financially, administratively, and with equipment. Such types of NGO involvement would not diminish the responsibilities of governmental agencies but would capitalize on the close ties that exist between the NGO and the community.

• *Flexibility in planning and implementation*. Participatory programmes and projects should provide for flexibility in planning as well as implementation. Flexibility is a particularly important consideration in timing and budgeting. Flexibility in timing is necessary because of

Box 14.6 continued

small-format video systems proved particularly useful and have emerged as a powerful interactive communication tool. A growing need was, however, identified for simple-to-operate, durable audiovisual equipment that can withstand rigorous field conditions.

A play, entitled *It Will be Better Tomorrow*, was written by the Communication Section and performed on open-air stages in the upgrading areas. The play showed how an individual, who initially felt suspicious about the motives of the Housing Project Unit, gradually changed his perception and became co-operative. The performance not only solicited a large number of spontaneous audience responses that proved useful to the Communication Section but also contributed significantly to shaping public opinion in favour of the project. A band was also formed that wrote songs in the popular local style, with lyrics on such topics as the advantages of soil-cement blocks over standard blocks, thereby making dull subjects interesting.

Experience in Lusaka and other places indicates that, if PSC is to be successful, at least some of the following conditions should be fulfilled:

● PSC should be planned and budgeted with other project components before the start of a project.

● PSC should continue in the post-implementation stage of the project to optimize maintenance of services and cost recovery.

● PSC should be institutionalized by creating special PSC units and by training officers in PSC methods and techniques.

uncertainties about the speed at which projects can be implemented: some projects may start quickly and with much enthusiasm, only to lose momentum; while others may start slowly and gain speed as they progress. With respect to budgeting, similar unpredictability necessitates the option of modifying budget lines in accordance with the changing priorities of the residents and the needs of the project. This is not to suggest that there should be no planning in terms of time and budget, only that the planning that takes place should not become a straitjacket against community participation.

While the future is full of uncertainties, it is not a hopeless one. Through their own processes of trial and error, governments will be able to arrive at their own kinds of participation strategies.

Preconditions for and limitations of enabling settlement strategies

All strategies have their own preconditions. In the case of enabling settlement strategies, they are undeniably very large ones. Four, in particular, need to be stressed.

First, they imply that governments and public authorities are prepared to take unambiguous decisions that provide for autonomy at the local level. They imply acceptance of the principles of self-help and mutual aid and of the value and potential of participatory approaches to the development of settlements. This acceptance must find concrete expression in the deliberate transfer of certain decision-making prerogatives to local organizations that are vested with the authority to initiate, implement, and manage settlement programmes.

Secondly, they require that measures designed to foster initiative at the local level are complemented by other actions that address the problems and obstacles that stand in the way of local initiatives. This must find expression in the readiness on the part of governments and public authorities to take decisions that may conflict with conventional views on such matters as land and financing.

Thirdly, enabling settlement strategies imply that governments and public authorities are ready to accept social demands of communities as legitimate expressions of hopes and aspirations and as a valid guide for community development and the provision and improvement of shelter. The strategy is unequivocally one of listening and responding to the people.

Fourthly, the strategy implies that those professionally engaged in settlements development are willing and able to redefine their roles. At the local level, the role becomes one of 'enabling' rather than one of 'providing', of working with and for groups in support of self-determined and self-managed programmes. The professional's task is not to impose but to facilitate, to innovate rather than to dictate. It is a concept of professional practice that creates new opportunities and needs for professionals skilled not in the art of building but in the techniques of mobilization.

These preconditions may be too demanding for some developing countries at present. This

Box 14.7   Asia's many signs of hope

All over South and East Asia, there are men and women who have chosen to devote their lives and professional skills to helping others to help themselves. Almost every large city has stories to tell of individuals and non-governmental organizations (NGOs) working with poor and underprivileged groups either in co-operation with or in opposition to local authorities. The stories range from a single individual who works with a handful of poor families in an effort to improve the quality of their daily lives to city-wide attempts to develop the community organizations required to challenge the processes that keep poor people poor.

India is rich in such experiences. In Kerala, the Quilon Social Service Society (QSSS) initiated a scheme in 1984 designed to enable families with joint incomes of under $250 a year to build their own houses. Under this scheme, every Rs1,000 raised by QSSS is matched by another Rs1,000 from the state government, while HUDCO contributes Rs3,000. The funds are lent at 5 per cent interest to poor families who build 21 m² houses on the basis of preselected designs. The families receive the loan in three instalments, following the completion of foundations, walls, and roof. QSSS serves as the intermediary, organizing the loan and assisting the families to obtain permission to build.

In 1984, the Indian government passed an anti-encroachment act designed to prevent rich persons grabbing land, but the act has also been used against squatters. In New Delhi, some 25 NGOs and people's organizations have come together to protest the use of the act against the urban poor. Meetings of the group, which represents some 1 million people, are convened by the Indian Social Institute. The work of the group is reportedly attracting the attention of other groups in Bombay and Calcutta.

In Dharavi, Bombay, groups representing 400,000 people of different races and castes have joined together to form PROUD (People's Responsible Organization for United Dharavi). It is a highly democratic body, with each member organization electing its own representative to PROUD which is itself organized to address specific issues. PROUD has its own team of professionals that prepare schemes for the upgrading of squatter communities and for the regularization of land. While efforts are made to ensure that schemes will be acceptable to city authorities, PROUD makes use of civil disobedience to press its claims. PROUD's technical team has so far worked without pay.

Not far from Dharavi is Nagar, where a small group of individuals is assisting 270 families to install water mains and latrines in the area in which they live. Well organized and innovative, the group has received positive responses from the city government and is in the process of organiz-ing an association of Slum Dwellers of India. It has already organized the first National Meeting of Slum Dwellers.

Active advocacy has also spread to the legal profession. In New Delhi, for example, lawyers at the Indian Social Institute have so far prepared 14 pamphlets explaining the rights of the poor in such areas as bonded labour, and abuses against 'untouchables', as well as leaflets designed to help the poor prepare legal cases. The preparation of the pamphlets has been supported by the Indian government which has assisted in their wide distribution. In Bombay, the People's Union of Civil Liberties has launched a campaign to educate the city's élites on the realities of slum and squatter-settlement life, and the Lawyer's Collective is fighting, through the courts, a city decision to evict many of the city's estimated 200,000 pavement dwellers. In 1981, two Bombay journalists were able to prevent the demolition of several squatter settlements by filing a petition in the Bombay High Court. As a result of their action, the Supreme Court in Delhi decided that no settlement built before 1976 could be demolished, and that the demolition of temporary shelter built after that date must be approved by a special court-appointed officer.

Pakistan is also the scene of much NGO activity. In March 1983, the Bank of Credit and Commerce (BCCI) Foundation, in collaboration with UNCHS (Habitat), initiated a three-year community-development project aimed at improving living conditions in Orangi, Karachi's largest squatter settlement. Within Orangi, which has a population of 800,000 people, the project identified an area containing 375,000 people and aimed at servicing 144,000 people with neighbourhood facilities. With regard to sanitation, the project identified and installed, with community participation and finance, an innovative low-cost sanitation technology, known as 'shallow sewerage'. Investigations conducted by the project revealed a self-financing potential for refuse collection and resource recovery within the community, to be exploited by suitably trained informal operators already working in this sector. Programmes to promote literacy amongst women and train and upgrade their skills were initiated under the project, and health clinics and first-aid centres were established to introduce primary health care through a programme of immunization and health education. Action-oriented research into suitable low-cost building materials and prototype houses was also introduced to assist community members with cost-effective means of improving their dwellings.

Another project is taking place in Belldia, Karachi. Selecting sanitation as its entry point, it has extended its programme of activities to cover health programmes for children and women, education and training, and employment creation. Supported by UNICEF within the framework of

Box 14.7 continued

its Urban Services Programme, the project has resulted in the installation of 3,200 pit latrines—600 by UNICEF, 2,600 by the people themselves—over a four-year period ending in 1983.

In Bangladesh, a religious order assisted a group of squatters in Demra to resist eviction. As a result of their efforts, the squatters were relocated very close to their original houses and received compensation—the first time in Bangladesh that urban squatters were acknowledged to have rights in relocation schemes.

Non-government organization projects in the Philippines include Freedom to Build, at Los Marinos some 40 kilometres south of Manila, the location of a sites-and-services scheme for 8,000 families evicted from squatter settlements in the nation's capital. Freedom to Build provides cheap building materials bought from suppliers at wholesale prices, the materials being sold at cost, with an overhead charge of 4–5 per cent. Sales average $20,000 per month, and a simple savings scheme has been developed for those who wish to make use of it.

At Sorsogon in the Philippines, a one-night's bus journey from Manila, the Centre for Housing and Human Ecology, an NGO based in Legaspi, is working with a group of squatters threatened with eviction. The Centre was able to determine that those who claimed the land were in possession of false titles, and it has not only been able to prevent eviction but also assisted the poor in obtaining water, sanitation, and other services. At the end of 1984, the community was in the process of getting itself fully legalized.

At Cebul in the Philippines, a group buys cheap land from the city and resells it at cost to poor people. A revolving fund has been established for this purpose, and some 600 plots have so far been made available. The plots are sold without services in order to minimize costs.

At Booum Jahri in the Republic of Korea, community organizers are living with very poor people evicted from slums in Seoul. Plots for 200 people have been developed, with the emphasis on creating the community organizations required to make the new community a self-reliant one.

The above are just a few of Asia's many signs of hope. There are as many in Latin America, West Asia, and Africa. Together, they serve to show that there are groups able to work with and for the urban poor, challenging governments as well as co-operating with them. They show also that there are professionals who have been prepared to redefine their disciplines, creating a new practice in the process.

does not mean that situations cannot change and that the ground for enabling strategies cannot become fertile. As the limitations of present settlements strategies become apparent and the problems of unmet shelter needs become acute, governments may increasingly come to accept that there is no realistic alternative to the one of enabling people to help themselves. As the realization grows, preconditions will be moulded by the sheer force of circumstances, and enabling strategies will emerge. As they do so, and countries discover the most appropriate 'mix' of government and people, governments may perceive a future that offers at least the hope that the great majority of the people can have decent settlement conditions.

Conclusions

The potential of enabling settlement strategies is great. They represent the final realization that all else has failed and that, in the majority of developing countries, anything else is bound to fail. Governments, especially those reluctant to relinquish the promises they have made to their people concerning houses, work, and social conditions, will understandably look for other options. They may regard enabling strategies as a denial of the responsibilities they feel bound to exercise, but most will find that the paths that today appear open will resemble cul-de-sacs when viewed 10 years hence. Enabling settlement strategies should not be seen as a denial of traditional responsibilities but rather as a vehicle for creating new ones.

Some will point out that enabling settlement strategies also have limitations of reach. In most developing countries, a distinction must increasingly be made between the poor, the very poor, and the destitute. The number of desperately poor people in some countries is already large and will almost certainly grow, and enabling settlement strategies have little to offer those who live in destitution. They will need to be assisted directly through programmes shaped by principles other than those of affordability and cost recovery. However, part of the logic of enabling strategies is to be found in the very growth of poverty: when conditions are created whereby those who are able to help themselves can do so, resources can be freed for those who are unable to help themselves.

Such limitations notwithstanding, there appears to be no alternative to the one of governmental support for self-determined, self-organized, and self-managed programmes within the framework of settlement-wide action. There can be no guarantees that enabling settlement strategies will work. The problems are too great and the uncertainties too high for such assurances. It does seem certain, however, that they carry the greatest hope and promise.

Governments that make a commitment to enabling settlement strategies will make a commitment to travel untried paths through policy territory that is still largely uncharted.

Note

1. On enabling shelter strategies, see Aprodicio A. Laquian, *Basic Housing: Policies for Urban Sites, Services, and Shelter in Developing Countries* (Ottawa: International Development Research Centre, 1983).

15 The Role of Human Settlements

This study has documented some of the main trends and developments in human settlements in both the developed and developing countries. While it has been able to record encouraging progress in a number of areas, there is disturbingly little evidence in the vast majority of countries to suggest that negative trends are being reversed and that the human settlements situation in either urban or rural areas is being improved. The picture that emerges is overwhelmingly one of a challenge not being met, and of governments losing ground in their efforts to meet it. When demographic and urbanization trends are superimposed upon the present human settlements situation and the conditions that prevail in cities, towns, and villages, the problems threaten to take on forms that render them unmanageable. When likely trends in the growth of poverty are further added to the picture, the problems constitute a challenge not only to decision-making but also to the imagination.

The consensus that appeared to exist, at the time of the United Nations Conference on Human Settlements in Vancouver, 1976, on the need for concerted action in the field of human settlements has been eroded by international economic trends and the crisis in development strategies. The narrowing of planning horizons, weakening of belief in comprehensive planning, disenchantment with the limited efficacy of past policies, and discovery of serious weaknesses in the theories that shaped conventional thinking on the development process have figured prominently among the factors that have eroded support for human settlement policies and plans. The conditions, trends, and prospects outlined in this study leave little doubt that the time has come to rebuild the consensus. The challenge posed by human settlements in the coming decades is one of unprecedented dimensions, but one that can be met. However, success will depend upon the capacity to fashion new strategies, and, more important still, to fuse them with a fresh commitment and determination. If governments fail to meet the challenge that confronts them, a great opportunity to improve the quality of life of countless numbers of people may be irretrievably lost.

The economic role of human settlements[1]

Investments in human settlements are not only investments in the quality of life and the well-being of people: they also put labour that might otherwise be idle to work at a low opportunity cost. Investments in human settlements are investments in construction, and the labour content in construction is high, providing substantial opportunities for labour absorption and the creation of employment. Investments in human settlements also have broad employment effects through direct and indirect multiplier effects.[2] The size of the multiplier effect varies from country to country and by type of project but tends to be highest in the case of housing for low-income groups.

Investments in human settlements are supportive of informal-sector economic activity. Squatter-settlement upgrading programmes, in particular, can give an important stimulus to informal-sector construction activity, while the provision of basic services, especially water and electricity, can increase the competitiveness and productivity of informal-sector enterprises. Around 50 per cent of the urban population of the developing countries—some 500 million people—are dependent upon the informal sector, while employment in the informal sector accounts for a growing share of total urban employment.[3]

Investments in human settlements, especially in housing, have a low import component, thus conserving foreign exchange. They are also non-inflationary, the wage-level effects of increased activity being negligible when unemployed or underemployed labour is used. The main inflationary factor is the use of imported building materials, especially those such as cement, steel, and plastics, which have a high energy content. As illustrated elsewhere in this study, the wide application of indigenous building materials both contains this inflationary force and creates local employment, especially in the informal sector.

The widely canvassed view that investments in human settlements should be regarded as welfare expenditures that absorb rather than generate resources has no basis in fact. There is ample evidence to show that such investments not only serve to stimulate economic growth but also can be used to affect both the pace and direction of growth. Countries with large settlement development and shelter programmes tend to have faster economic growth, and often faster industrial growth, than countries without them. Singapore is the classic case of a country that chose construction as a lead sector for its economic development, building houses for 40 per cent of its population between 1960 and 1974.

Experience has shown that developing countries which invest little in human settlements development typically find that around 3.5 per cent of recorded economic activity goes to all forms of construction. With a few exceptions, most poor countries with this level of construction have slow or even zero rates of economic growth. Deliberate encouragement is able to raise the share of construction to between 6 and 9 per cent—Singapore maintained it for many years at around 15 per cent. With few exceptions, countries that stimulate construction activities and make high allocations to settlement development and housing programmes achieve fast rates of economic growth, low rates of unemployment, and an equitable income distribution.[4]

Human settlements, as focal points for economic activity and for interaction between people, are a nation's principal economic asset and centres of wealth creation. Almost everyone gains from investments in human settlements, although not in the same proportion. The urban poor and urban migrants are usually able to benefit from increased income-earning opportunities that accompany human settlements development, but even the rural poor can profit from remittances sent home by migrants. Governments can also profit when they demonstrate readiness to recover the value

added by their own investments, to collect property taxes, and to charge for the use of the services they provide.

Human settlements development programmes are also compatible with population management, often a key element in economic development. The relationships between urbanization, economic development, and declines in fertility rates are well established, and could, in many countries, be beneficially pursued as a matter of public policy. Furthermore, it will prove impossible to secure appropriate population distributions except on the basis of human settlements development. A well-planned programme of investments in human settlements infrastructure and employment-generating activities would help not only to create conditions for planning population distribution but also to secure the fertility declines compatible with economic growth and development.

The social development role of human settlements

However important the economic reasons for human settlements policies and plans may be, they are balanced by the role that human settlements play in promoting social development, in improving the quality of life, and in meeting basic human needs. Such considerations recognize that the promotion of the well-being of the people is the central concern and purpose of all development efforts. There can be no discussion of increasing the welfare of human beings without consideration of the role and contribution of human settlements, no concept of social fulfilment without a concept of the way in which human beings meet and interact. Human settlements are history's most tangible evidence of efforts to meet individual and collective needs and to improve the quality of life.

Human settlements policies and plans also promote social development in highly pragmatic ways. Investments in human settlements are investments in the development of human resources, the benefits of which accrue not only to groups and individuals but also to the nation as a whole. The planned development of human settlements contributes to minimizing the risks of contagious disease, of fire, and of natural disasters, all of which carry heavy public costs. For example, without concerted efforts to improve living conditions in human settlements, there is an ever-present and growing risk of an epidemic which could claim the lives of people not only in the area of initial infection but also in other countries far removed from it.

Human settlements policies and plans are supportive of efforts to secure social and political stability—considerations that assume some importance, given trends of growth in poverty and inequality in many countries. The possibility of a violent reaction to persistent poverty and inequality, most visible in towns and cities, cannot be discounted by governments on the grounds that it has generally so far failed to take place. If cities continue to be unable to meet the modest expectations of those who live in them, it may well be in cities that poor and disprivileged groups will confront the structures they see as the cause of their predicament. One of the greatest challenges confronting governments is to find ways of harnessing creative energies, which might otherwise fuel social protest and political unrest, to broad-based processes of social and economic development. This search must take place within human settlements— again pointing to the importance of policies for their development. No less important, this search must be for approaches to settlement development that are genuinely participatory and which enable people to make the contribution to the improvement of settlements which experience has repeatedly shown they are able to make.

Human settlements and the development process

One of the themes of this study has been that the prevailing crisis in development has diverted attention and resources from human settlements development goals. Increased investments in human settlements in periods of economic difficulty and other uncertainty, however, may offer a way out of the present predicament.[5] Development strategies are in crisis because they have sought to build development around a narrow concept of economic growth, with progress clumsily expressed in terms of GNP per capita.

The new concept of development that is urgently called for has human settlements as one of its central elements. Development strategies shaped by a concern for human settlements build development around people and the places in which they live and work. Development cannot be defined in terms other than these.

Human settlements are an integrating concept that makes it possible to reconcile economic growth with the need for sustainable development. Being an integrative concept, human settlements provide a framework for reconciling sectoral concerns and for furnishing them with a spatial dimension. Rather than being regarded as a residual consideration, human settlements development should be conceived of as the main framework for social and economic development, for public-sector investment, and for resource allocations.

The reaffirmation of the determination to build development around people must result in a commitment to human settlements development. This will make it possible to chart courses out of the present predicament, and it will be a new concern for human settlements that will lead the way.

Notes

1. For a detailed presentation of these arguments, see L. Grebler, 'The Role of Housing in Economic Development', Third World Congress of Engineers and Architects, Tel Aviv, 1973 (mimeo); L. Burns, 'The World Housing Problem: Towards Second-best Solutions', University of Southern California, Los Angeles, 1974 (mimeo); and the United Nations Centre for Human Settlements (Habitat), *The Construction Industry in Developing Countries*. Vol. 1, *Contributions to Socio-Economic Growth* (Nairobi, 1984).
2. On the multiplier effects of building and construction, see, for example, E. D. Makanas, 'Interindustry Analysis of the Housing Construction Industry', *NEDA Journal of Development* (1974–5), 150–73; and J. Gorynski, 'Modern and Traditional Design Techniques in Construction and Housing', *Ekistics*, 11/186 (1971), 353–9.
3. On the growth of the informal sector, see Institute of Social Studies Advisory Service, *The Informal Sector: Concepts, Issues, and Policies* (The Hague, 1985).
4. See H. Stretton, *Urban Planning in Rich and Poor Countries* (Oxford University Press, 1978), 112–13.
5. Welcoming address by the Executive Director of UNCHS (Habitat) to the participants in the sixth session of the Commission on Human Settlements, Helsinki, Finland, 1983.

Statistical Annex

General Disclaimer

The designations employed and the presentation of the material in this publication do not imply the expression of any opinion whatsoever on the part of the Secretariat of the United Nations concerning the legal status of any country, territory, city or area or of its authorities, or concerning the delimitation of its frontier or boundaries.

Contents

List of Tables

Population

Households

Demographic and social characteristics

Land use

Housing

Infrastructure

Technical Notes

Introduction

This Statistical Annex to the *Global Report on Human Settlements* has been prepared to provide updated versions of the tables contained in the previous issue, *Global Review of Human Settlements, Statistical Annex* (A/CONF.70/A/1/1 Add. 1), published by the United Nations Statistical Office in 1976. Data have been obtained from many different secondary sources and are the product of several data-collection methods. These Technical Notes are designed to give relevant information on the arrangement of tables, sources, coverage, methodology, and the quality and comparability of the data.

It should be noted, however, that owing to lack of relevant current data, it has not been possible to update certain tables of the previous issue of the *Statistical Annex*: Tables 12 (land use); 18 (growth of slums and squatter settlements); 20 (average daily water consumption by house connections and public standposts); 22 (investment for construction of water-supply and sewage-disposal facilities), and 23 (environmental pollution). The main reasons for not updating these tables were as follows:

- *Table 12*. The source of the data for this table, the International Statistical Institute, was not in a position to update it.
- *Table 18*. The data needed for updating this table are available from informal sources only and differ greatly in terms of the variety of sources, underlying concepts, definitions, and survey techniques. The comparability, consistency, and reliability of these data are therefore questionable.
- *Tables 20 and 22*. The World Health Organization is in the process of compiling data on the subjects covered by both tables but they could not yet be released for publication.
- *Table 23*. Data on these subjects are being collected by UNEP but they are not yet in a usable format. In addition, the relevance of the table's indicators for the purpose of the Global Report is questionable.

As the earlier tables are no longer up to date they have not been included in the present publication. Users interested in the historical data are referred to the previous *Annex*.

Sources of data

The Statistical Annex to the *Global Report on Human Settlements* covers 8 geographical regions, 24 subregions, and 210 countries and areas in both the developed and developing regions of the world. Tables have been compiled by the United Nations Centre for Human Settlements (Habitat) from several United Nations statistical publications. Notable among these are *Urban and Rural Population Projections: the 1984 Assessment* (New York, 1986); *Selected Characteristics of the Population of Urban, Rural, Capital City, and Urban Agglomerations in Countries With More Than 2 Million in 1985: The 1984 Assessment* (New York, 1986); *Demographic Yearbook 1982*, ST/ESA/STAT/SER. R/12 (New York, 1984); *UNESCO Statistical Yearbook 1984* (Paris, 1984); *World Population Prospects as Assessed in 1984*, ST/ESA/SER. A/98 (New York, 1986); *Patterns of Urban and Rural Population Growth*, ST/ESA/SER. A/68 (New York, 1980); *Estimates and Projections of Urban, Rural, and City Populations 1950–2025: The 1982 Assessment*, ST/ESA/SER. R/58 (New York, 1985); *Demographic Yearbook 1984*, ST/ESA/STAT/SER. R/14 (New York, 1986); *FAO Production Yearbook 1985*, vol. 39 (Rome, 1986). *Compendium of Housing Statistics 1975–1977*, ST/ESA/STAT/SER. N/3 (New York, 1980); *Compendium of Human Settlements Statistics 1983*, ST/ESA/STAT/SER. N/4 (New York, 1985). The World Health Organization's *International Drinking Water Supply and Sanitation Decade, Review of National Baseline Data (as at 31 December 1980)* (Geneva, 1983) was also utilized.

Publications of the United Nations Statistical Office are prepared from data received in response to annual questionnaires circulated by the Office or obtained from official publications. Such data sources have their limitations but they provide the most reliable estimates in the circumstances. For census and survey data, the latest available year is presented. The respective source is shown at the end of each table.

The United Nations Population Division makes three population projection variants—high, medium, and low. The three variants are established by combining assumed levels of fertility, mortality, and international migration. Throughout this Annex, the population estimates and projections refer to the *medium* projection variant.

Geographical coverage, definitions, and classification

Data have been presented for as many individual countries or areas and cities as the secondary sources could provide. The presentation of tables follows an internationally accepted format. However, owing to marked differences among countries in concepts, definitions, and classifications, this format could not be followed throughout. Table 1, which presents data on population estimates and projections for the period 1950–2025, is the most comprehensive in geographical coverage, since it covers almost every country or area in the world. A few tables include estimates for regions and macro regions only, and several others give data pertaining to developing countries or areas only.

Data definitions as recommended by the United Nations, together with national definitions where appropriate, are given in the following section.

Nomenclature and order of presentation

Owing to space limitations, the countries or areas listed in the tables are generally listed by the commonly employed short titles in use in the United Nations as of 30 June 1985; for example, the United Kingdom of Great Britain and Northern Ireland is referred to as 'United Kingdom', the United States of America as 'United States', the Mongolian People's Republic as 'Mongolia',

and the Union of Soviet Socialist Republics as 'USSR'. Countries or areas are listed in English alphabetical order within the following macro regions: Africa, the Americas, Asia, Europe, Oceania, and the Union of Soviet Socialist Republics. In most cases, cities are listed in English alphabetical order.

The arrangement of data by country or area, region, and city, is done irrespective of political status, and the geographical designations employed were adopted solely for statistical convenience. 'Cities' are defined according to the legal/political boundaries established by the country concerned.

Quality of data

Primary data are incomplete for several countries or areas, and only in Tables 8 and 9 are measures of coverage or quality given. For population data, it is widely recognized that statistics produced by many developing countries are still inadequate. Many of the most recent censuses or surveys are seriously affected by under-enumeration of the total population and misreporting of fundamental population characteristics, such as age. The Population Division of the United Nations has therefore evaluated and adjusted the demographic data presented in this Annex for all the countries or areas given.

For vital statistics, quality codes have been given to indicate the completeness of the births, deaths, etc., recorded in civil registration. Code C refers to data estimated to be virtually complete (at least 90 per cent of the events occurring each year). Code U refers to data estimated to be incomplete (that is, representing less than 90 per cent of the events occurring each year). In addition, deaths tabulated by date of registration and not by date of occurrence, have been indicated by a (+) sign. Whenever the lag between the date of occurrence and the date of registration is prolonged, and therefore a large proportion of the registration is delayed, death statistics for any given year may be seriously affected. Most of the data from the developed countries are more reliable than those from the developing countries. The various derived rates are, of course, also affected by the quality and limitations of the population estimates used.

Comparability of data

The comparability of population data is affected by several factors: the definition of the total population, the definitions used to classify the population into urban/rural components, the extent of over-enumeration or under-enumeration in the most recent census or other source of bench-mark population statistics, and the quality of population estimates. For example, countries or areas may collect information on a *de facto* or *de jure* basis, or both. A *de facto* population includes all persons physically present in the country or area at the reference date; the *de jure* population, by contrast, includes all usual residents of the given country or area, whether or not they were physically present at the reference date. However, some so-called *de facto* counts do not include foreign military, naval, and diplomatic personnel present in the country or area on official duty and their accompanying family members, nor foreign visitors in transmit through the country or area. Further, *de facto* counts may include such persons as merchant seamen and fishermen who are out of the country or area working at their trade. The population of data presented in the tables are *de facto*; those reported as *de jure* are identified as such.

Explanation of symbols

The meaning of symbols used in each table of the Annex is given under the footnotes of that table. The following symbols carry general meaning throughout the Annex:

Data not available	. . .
Magnitude zero	—
Magnitude not zero, but less than unit employed	0, 0.0
Provisional	*

Relevant Definitions

To facilitate international comparisons, as far as possible the terminology used in this report follows the United Nations recommended definitions as set forth here, and departures from these definitions are noted where they occur. In particular, international comparability of urban/rural distributions is seriously impaired by the wide variation among national definitions of the concept of 'urban', so definitions used by individual countries or areas are given here too.

AGRICULTURAL POPULATION is defined as all persons depending for their livelihood on agriculture. This comprises all persons actively engaged in agriculture and their non-working dependants.

A BUILDING is an independent structure comprising one or more rooms or other spaces, covered by a roof, enclosed with external walls or dividing walls which extend from the foundation to the roof. A building may be intended for residential, commercial, or industrial purposes or for the provision of services. It may therefore be a factory, shop, detached dwelling, apartment building, warehouse, garage, barn, and so forth.

CONSTRUCTION RATES are the number of conventional dwellings constructed each year per thousand mid-year population for the year.

A CONVENTIONAL DWELLING is a room or suite of rooms and its accessories in a permanent building or structurally separated part thereof, which, by the way it has been built, rebuilt, or converted, is basically intended for habitation by one household and is not, at the time of the census, used wholly for other purposes. It should have separate access to a street (direct or via a garden or grounds), or to a common space within the building (staircase, passage, gallery, and so on). Examples of dwellings are houses, flats, suites of rooms, apartments, etc.

CROPLAND is defined as arable land and land under permanent crops.

(a) *Arable land* refers to all land under temporary crops, temporary meadows for mowing or pasture, land under market and kitchen gardens (including cultivation under glass), and land temporarily fallow or lying idle. Wide variations occur, particularly between the precise definitions of temporary and permanent meadows and the fallow period.

(b) *Land under permanent crops* refers to land cultivated with crops that occupy the land for long periods and need not be replanted after each harvest, such as cocoa, coffee, and rubber. It includes land under shrubs, fruit trees, nut trees, and vines, but excludes land under trees grown for wood or timber.

(c) *Permanent meadows and pastures* refers to land used permanently (five years or more) for herbaceous forage crops, either cultivated or growing wild (wild prairie or grazing land). Savannahs should be included here but some countries include them under forests.

(d) *Forest land* refers to land under natural or planted stands of trees, whether or not productive. It includes land from which forests have been cleared but which will be reforested in the foreseeable future.

(e) *Other area* refers to unused but potentially productive land, built-on areas, wasteland, parks, ornamental gardens, roads, lanes, barren land, water bodies, and any other land not specifically listed above.

(f) *Total area* refers to the total area of the country, including area under inland water bodies.

(g) *Land area* refers to total area of a country less the area under inland water bodies. Inland water bodies include major rivers and lakes.

GROSS DOMESTIC PRODUCT (GDP), defined from the production side, refers to the sum of the value added of resident producers, in producers' values, plus import duties. The value added of resident producers is equivalent to the difference between the value of their gross output in producers' values and the value of their intermediate consumption in purchasers' values; or to the sum of their compensation of employees, operating surplus, consumption of capital assets, and excess of indirect taxes over subsidies.

GROSS FIXED CAPITAL FORMATION is defined to include outlays (i.e. purchases and own-account production) of industries, government, and private non-profit institutions on additions of new durable goods to their stocks of fixed assets, reduced by the proceeds of their net sales (sales less purchases) of similar second-hand or scrapped goods. Government outlays on durable goods that are primarily used for military purposes are excluded.

A HOUSING UNIT is a separate and independent place of abode basically intended for habitation by one household, or one not intended for habitation (e.g. an occupied mobile or improvised housing unit) but occupied as living quarters by a household at the time of the census.

A HOUSEHOLD is a unit reflecting the arrangements made by persons, individually or in groups, for providing themselves with food or other essentials for living. A household may consist of one or more persons. A one-person household is a person who makes provision for his or her own food or other essentials for living without combining with any other person to form part of a multiperson household.

LIGHTING refers to the principal type of lighting used in the living quarters being enumerated. In most countries electric lighting is of special interest.

LITERACY is defined as the ability both to read and to write; hence unless otherwise specified, semi-literates (persons able to read but not to write) are included with the illiterate population.

NATIONAL DEFINITIONS OF URBAN/RURAL. The criteria, in so far as they are known, used nationally to distinguish urban areas from rural areas appear below:

Africa

Algeria: All communes having as *chef-lieu* either a city, a rural town, or an urban agglomeration.

Angola: Localities with 2,000 or more population.

Benin: Towns of Cotonou, Porto-Novo, Quidah, Parakou, and Djougou.

Botswana: Cities of Gaberone and Lobatse and urban agglomeration of Francistown.

Burkina faso: Five cities.

Burundi: Commune of Bujumbura.

Cameroon: All administrative capitals (of provinces, departments, districts, and subdistricts), including a few agglomerations having a population of 5,000 or more inhabitants which have urban characteristics such as certain public and municipal services.

Central African Republic: 20 principal centres with a population of over 3,000 inhabitants.

Chad: Towns of 5,000 or more inhabitants.

Comoros: Cities of Dzaoudzi and Moroni.

Congo: Three largest communes, consisting of Brazzaville, Pointe-Noire, and Dolisiez.

Côte d'Ivoire: Not available.

Djibouti: The capital city.

Egypt: Governorates of Cairo, Alexandria, Port Said, Ismailia, Suez, frontier governorates, and district capitals (*markaz*).

Ethiopia: Localities of 2,000 or more inhabitants.

Gambia: Banjul only.

Gabon: Towns with over 2,000 inhabitants.

Ghana: Localities of 5,000 or more inhabitants.

Guinea: Urban centres.

Guinea-Bissau: The two main ports, Bissau and Cacheu.

Kenya: Towns with 2,000 or more inhabitants.

Lesotho: Capital city agglomeration.

Liberia: Localities having more than 2,000 inhabitants.

Libyan Arab Jamahiriya: Total population of Tripoli and Benghazi, plus the urban parts of Beida and Dema.

Madagascar: Centres with more than 5,000 inhabitants.

Malawi: All townships and town-planning areas and all district centres.

Mali: Localities of 5,000 or more inhabitants, and district centres.

Mauritania: Urban centres.

Mauritius: Towns with proclaimed legal limits with 20,000 or more population.

Morocco: 184 urban centres.

Mozambique: Concelho of Maputo and Beira.

Namibia: Localities (towns, villages, and townships) large enough to be treated as separate units, whether or not they have local government.

Niger: Urban centres.

Nigeria: Towns with 20,000 or more inhabitants whose occupations are not mainly agrarian.

Reunion: Administrative centres of communes with more than 2,000 inhabitants.

Rwanda: Kigali, the capital; administrative centres of prefectures; important agglomerations of 10,000 or more inhabitants and their surroundings.

Saō Tomé and Principe: Capital city.

Senegal: Agglomerations of 10,000 or more inhabitants.

Seychelles: Victoria, the capital.

Sierra Leone: Towns with 2,000 or more inhabitants.

Somalia: Towns with 5,000 or more inhabitants.

South Africa: All population agglomerations of an urban nature, without regard to local boundaries and status.

Sudan: Localities of administrative and/or commercial importance or with population of 5,000 or more inhabitants.

Swaziland: Localities proclaimed as urban.

Togo: Seven urban communes.

Tunisia: Population living in communes.

Uganda: Population of all settlements as small as trading centres with as few as 100 inhabitants.

United Republic of Tanzania: Sixteen gazetted townships.

Western Sahara: Not available.

Zaire: Agglomerations of 2,000 or more inhabitants where the predominant economic activity is of the non-agricultural type, and also mixed agglomerations which are considered urban because of their type of economic activity but are actually rural in size.

Zambia: Localities of 5,000 or more inhabitants, the majority of whom depend on non-agricultural activities.

Zimbabwe: Before 1982: 14 main towns. From 1982: 19 main towns.

Americas

Antigua: St John's.

Argentina: Population centres with 2,000 or more inhabitants.

Bahamas: Island of New Providence.

Barbados: Parish of Bridgetown.

Belize: Not available.

Bermuda: Totally urban.

Bolivia: Localities of 2,000 or more inhabitants.

Brazil: Urban and suburban zones of administrative centres of municipios and districts.

Canada: Incorporated cities, towns, and villages of 1,000 or more inhabitants, and their urbanized fringes; unincorporated places of 1,000 or more inhabitants having a population density of at least 1,000 per square mile or 390 per square kilometre, and their urbanized fringes.

Cayman Islands: Totally urban.

Chile: Populated centres which have definite urban characteristics such as certain public and municipal services.

Colombia: Population living in a nucleus of 1,500 or more inhabitants.

Costa Rica: Administrative centres of cantons, except cantons of Coto Brus, Guatuso, Los Chiles, Sarapiquin, and Upala.

Cuba: Population living in a nucleus of 2,000 or more inhabitants.

Dominican Republic: Administrative centres of municipios and municipal districts, some of which include suburban zones of rural character.

Ecuador: Capitals of provinces and cantons.

El Salvador: Administrative centres of municipios.

French Guiana: Communes of Cayenne and Saint Laurent du Maroni.

Greenland: Localities proclaimed as urban.

Guadeloupe: All communes with an administrative centre or 2,000 or more inhabitants.

Guatemala: Municipios of Guatemala Department and officially recognized centres of other departments and municipalities.

Guyana: Agglomeration of Georgetown.

Haiti: Administrative centres of communes.

Honduras: Localities of 2,000 or more inhabitants having essentially urban characteristics.

Jamaica: Kingston metropolitan area and selected main towns.

Martinique: Total population of the commune of Fort-de-France plus the agglomeration of other communes with more than 2,000 inhabitants.

Mexico: Localities of 2,500 or more inhabitants.

Montserrat: Town of Plymouth.

Netherlands Antilles: Not available.

Nicaragua: Administrative centres of departments and municipios.

Panama: Localities of 1,500 or more inhabitants having essentially urban characteristics. As of 1970, localities of 1,500 or more inhabitants with such urban characteristics as streets, water-supply systems, sewerage systems, and electric light.

Paraguay: Cities, towns, and administrative centres of departments and districts.

Peru: Populated centres with 100 or more occupied dwellings.

Saint Christopher and Nevis and the Territory of Anguilla: Town of Basse-terre.

Saint Vincent and the Grenadines: Towns with 1,000 or more inhabitants.

Suriname: Greater Paramaribo.

Trinidad and Tobago: Capital city.

United States of America: Places of 2,500 or more inhabitants and urbanized areas.

United States Virgin Islands: Localities with 2,500 or more inhabitants.

Uruguay: Areas defined as urban.

Venezuela: Centres with a population of 2,500 or more inhabitants.

Asia

Afghanistan: 63 localities.

Bahrain: Towns of Al Manamah, Al Muharraq, Al Hadd, Jidd Hafs, Sitrah, Ar Rifa, and Awali.

Bangladesh: Places having a municipality (*pourashava*), a town committee (*shahar* committee), or a cantonment board.

Bhutan: Not available.

Brunei Daryssalam: Not available.

Burma: 301 towns.

China: Cities (including suburbs) and towns based on estimates prepared in the Population Division of the Department of International Economic and Social Affair of the United Nations Secretariat.

Cyprus: Six district towns and Nicosia suburbs.

Democratic Kampuchea: Municipalities of Phnom-Penh, Bokor, Kep, and 13 urban centres.

Democratic People's Republic of Korea: Not available.

Democratic Yemen: Entire former colony of Aden, excluding the oil refinery and villages of Al Burayqah and Bir Fuqum.

East Timor: Dili, the capital.

Hong Kong: Hong Kong Island, Kowloon, New Kowloon, and the Tsuen Wan area of the New Territories.

India: Towns (places with municipal corporation, municipal area committee, town committee, notified area committee, or cantonment board); also all places having 5,000 or more inhabitants, a density of not less than 1,000 persons per square mile or 390 per square kilometre, pronounced urban characteristics, and at least three-fourths of the adult male population employed in pursuits other than agriculture.

Indonesia: Municipalities, regency capitals, and other places with urban characteristics.

Iran (Islamic Republic of): All population centres with 5,000 or more inhabitants.

Iraq: Area within the boundaries of municipality councils.

Israel: All settlements of more than 2,000 inhabitants, except those where at least one-third of the heads of households participating in the civilian labour force earn their living from agriculture.

Japan: A city (*shi*) having 50,000 or more inhabitants with 60 per cent or more of the houses and 60 per cent or more of the population (including their dependants) located in the main built-up areas. Alternatively, a *shi* having urban facilities and conditions as defined by prefectural order is considered as urban.

Jordan: Localities of 10,000 or more inhabitants, and subdistrict centres irrespective of size of population.

Kuwait: Cities with 10,000 or more inhabitants.

Lao People's Democratic Republic: Five largest towns: Vientiane, Louang Phrabang, Savannakhet, Khammouan, and Pakse.

Lebanon: Localities with 5,000 or more inhabitants.

Macau: Concelho of Macau (Macau City), including maritime area.

Malaysia: Gazetted areas with 10,000 or more population.

Maldives: Malé, the capital.

Mongolia: Capital and district centres.

Nepal: Areas with a population of 5,000 or more having some district urban characteristics, such as secondary schools, colleges, government and private offices, mills and factories, and facilities of transport and communication.

Oman: Two main towns (Muscat and Matrah).

Pakistan: Municipalities, civil lines, cantonments not included within municipal limits, any other continuous collection of houses inhabited by not less than 5,000 persons and having urban characteristics, and also a few areas having urban characteristics but with fewer than 5,000 inhabitants.

Philippines: Baguio, Cebu, and Quezon City; all cities and municipalities with a density of at least 1,000 persons per square kilometre; administrative centres, barrios of at least 2,000 inhabitants, and those barrios of at least 1,000 inhabitants which are contiguous to the administrative centre, in all cities and municipalities with a density of at least 500 persons per square kilometre; administrative centres and those barrios of at least 2,500 inhabitants which are conti-

guous to the administrative centre, in all cities and municipalities with at least 20,000 inhabitants; all other administrative centres with at least 2,500 inhabitants.

Qatar: Doha, the capital.

Republic of Korea: Seoul and municipalities with 50,000 or more inhabitants whose usual residence is in cities (*si*) designated by municipality, regardless of the size of the population in a specific administrative district.

Saudi Arabia: Cities with 5,000 or more inhabitants.

Singapore: City of Singapore.

Sri Lanka: Municipalities, urban councils, and towns.

Syrian Arab Republic: Cities, *mohafaza* centres, and *mantika* centres.

Thailand: Municipalities.

Turkey: Population of localities within the municipal limits of administrative centre of provinces and districts.

United Arab Emirates: Dubai, the main city.

Vietnam: Unavailable. For what was formerly the Republic of South Vietnam, estimates for large cities provided in a 1974 letter from the Statistical Office were used to adjust the 1960 urban estimate to correspond with the figures on urban and large city populations provided for 1970. For what was formerly the Democratic Republic of Vietnam, figures are available for 1960 and 1970, but no urban definition is provided.

Yemen: Six main towns.

Europe

Albania: Towns and other industrial centres of more than 400 inhabitants.

Austria: Communes (*Gemeinden*) having more than 5,000 inhabitants.

Belgium: Cities, urban agglomerations, and urban communes.

Bulgaria: Towns, i.e. localities legally established as urban.

Channel Islands: Guernsey: civil parish of St Peter Port; Jersey: civil parish of St Helier.

Czechoslovakia: Large towns, usually with 5,000

or more inhabitants, having a density of more than 100 persons per hectare of built-up area; piped water and a sewage system for the major part of the town; at least five physicians and a pharmacy; a nine-year secondary school; a hotel with at least 20 beds; a network of trade and distributive services which serve more than one town; job opportunities for the population of the surrounding area; the terminal for a system of omnibus lines; and not more than 10 per cent of the total population active in agriculture. Small towns, usually with 2,000 or more inhabitants, having a density of more than 75 persons per hectare of built-up area; three or more living quarters in at least 10 per cent of the houses; piped water and a sewerage system for at least part of the town; at least two physicians and a pharmacy; other urban characteristics to a lesser degree; and not more than 15 per cent of the total population active in agriculture. Agglomerated communities which have the characteristics of small towns in regard to size, population density, housing water supply, and sewerage, and percentage of the total population active in agriculture, but which lack such town characteristics as educational facilities, cultural institutions, health services, and trade and distributive services because these facilities and services are supplied by a town in the vicinity.

Denmark: 1965: Localities of over 2,000 inhabitants. As of 1970: agglomerations of 2,000 or more inhabitants.

Faeroe Islands: Thorshavn, the capital.

Finland: Urban communes.

France: Communes containing an agglomeration of more than 2,000 inhabitants living in contiguous houses or with not more than 200 metres between houses; also, communes of which the major portion of the population is part of a multicommunal agglomeration of this nature.

German Democratic Republic: Communities with 2,000 or more inhabitants.

Germany, Federal Republic of: Communes with 2,000 or more inhabitants.

Gibraltar: City of Gibraltar.

Greece: Population of municipalities and communes in which the largest population centre has 10,000 or more inhabitants; including also the population of the 12 urban agglomerations as defined at the census of 1961: Greater Athens, Salonica, Patras, Volos, Iraklion, Canea, Kalamata, Katerini, Agrinion, Chios, Airyion, and Ermoupolis in their entirety, irrespective of the population size of the largest locality in them.

Hungary: Budapest and all legally designated towns.

Iceland: Localities of 200 or more inhabitants.

Ireland: Cities and towns, including suburbs of 1,500 or more inhabitants.

Isle of Man: Borough of Douglas, town, and village districts.

Italy: Communes with 10,000 or more inhabitants.

Liechtenstein: Vaduz, the capital city.

Luxembourg: Communes with more than 2,000 inhabitants in the administrative centre.

Malta: 1948: Built-up areas devoid of agricultural land, including adjacent suburban areas. As of 1967: urban agglomeration of Valletta.

Monaco: City of Monaco.

Netherlands: Municipalities with a population of 2,000 or more; also, municipalities with a population of less than 2,000 but with not more than 20 per cent of their economically active male population engaged in agriculture, and specific residential municipalities of commuters.

Norway: Town municipalities.

Poland: Towns and settlements of urban type, e.g. workers' settlements, fisherfolk settlements, and health resorts.

Portugal: Agglomerations of 10,000 or more inhabitants.

Romania: Cities, towns, and 183 other localities (comprising 13 per cent of total urban population) having urban socio-economic characteristics.

Spain: Municipios with 10,000 or more inhabitants.

Sweden: Built-up areas with at least 200 inhabitants and usually not more than 200 metres between houses.

Switzerland: Communes with 10,000 or more inhabitants, including suburbs.

United Kingdom
England and Wales: Areas classified as urban for

local government purposes, that is, county boroughs, municipal boroughs, and urban districts.

Northern Ireland: Administrative county boroughs, municipal boroughs, and urban districts.

Scotland: Administrative county boroughs, municipal boroughs and urban districts.

Yugoslavia: Localities with 15,000 or more inhabitants; localities with 5,000 to 14,999 inhabitants of whom at least 30 per cent are not engaged in agriculture; localities with 3,000 to 4,999 inhabitants of whom at least 70 per cent are not engaged in agriculture; and localities with 2,000 to 2,999 inhabitants of whom at least 80 per cent are not engaged in agriculture.

Oceania

American Samoa: Places of 2,500 or more inhabitants and urbanized areas.

Australia: Population clusters of 1,000 or more inhabitants and some areas of lower population (e.g. holiday areas) if they contain 250 or more dwellings of which at least 100 are occupied.

Cook Islands: Avarua.

Fiji: Suva, Lautoka, Nandi, Lambasa, Nausori, and Mba, plus urban localities.

French Polynesia: Urban agglomeration of Papeete.

Guam: Localities with 2,500 or more inhabitants.

Kiribati: Tarawa and Ocean Island.

New Caledonia: Centres with population of 500 or more with commerce, administrative centres, or other public places.

New Zealand: All cities, plus boroughs, town districts, townships, and country towns with a population of 1,000 or more. Estimates: central cities or boroughs, including neighbouring boroughs and town districts, and parts of countries which are regarded as suburban to the centre of population.

Samoa: Urban areas of Apia, comprising the Faipule districts of Vaimauga West and Foleata East.

Tonga: Places with more than 1,400 inhabitants.

Vanuatu: Cities of Vila and Santo.

Union of Soviet Socialist Republics

USSR: Urban-type localities officially designated as such by each of the constituent republics, usually according to the criteria of number of inhabitants and predominance of agriculture or number of non-agricultural workers and their families.

Byelorussian SSR: See USSR.

Ukrainian SSR: See USSR.

OCCUPANCY STATUS is determined on the basis of whether living quarters are occupied or vacant at the time of the census.

OCCUPANTS are persons usually resident in a housing unit or other living quarters. However, since housing censuses are usually carried out simultaneously with population censuses, the possibility of applying this definition depends upon whether the information collected and recorded in the population census indicates where individuals spent the census night or whether it refers to their place of usual residence.

PERSONS NOT LIVING IN HOUSEHOLDS are persons who are not members of households. This includes persons in military installations, penal institutions, the dormitories of schools, universities, hospitals, and religious institutions.

PIPED WATER refers to water provided to within housing units by pipe from community-wide systems or from individual installations such as pressure tanks and pumps. Housing units with piped water outside and beyond 100 metres are considered as being without piped water.

SEWAGE DISPOSAL may include collection and disposal, with or without treatment, of human excreta and waste water by waterborne systems, or the use of pit privies and similar installations.

SQUATTER SETTLEMENT generally refers to areas where groups of housing units have been constructed on land to which the occupants have no legal claim. In many cases housing units located in squatter settlements are shelters or structures built of waste materials and without a predetermined plan. Squatter settlements are usually found in urban and suburban areas, particularly at the peripheries of principal cities.

TENURE STATUS indicates whether the household occupies the housing unit as owner, renter, or under other types of arrangement.

TOILET FACILITIES refers to an installation connected with piped water for humans to discharge their wastes and from which the wastes are flushed by water.

URBAN AGGLOMERATION refers to the populated area falling within the contours of a cluster of dense, contiguous settlement. The boundaries of an agglomeration frequently extend beyond the administrative boundaries of the corresponding city but they may also be more restricted. In some highly urbanized areas an urban agglomeration may include more than one city.

VITAL STATISTICS AND RATES
The following definitions are used:

(a) *Crude birth rate* is the average annual number of live births per 1,000 mid-year population.

(b) *Crude death rate* is the average annual number of deaths per 1,000 mid-year population.

(c) *Death* is the permanent disappearance of all evidence of life at any time after live birth has taken place. This excludes foetal deaths.

(d) *Infant mortality rates* are the annual number of deaths of infants under one year of age per 1,000 live births in the same year.

(e) *Live birth* is the complete expulsion or extraction from its mother of a product of conception, irrespective of the duration of pregnancy, which after such separation breathes or shows any other evidence of life such as beating of the heart, pulsation of the umbilical cord, or definite movement of voluntary muscles.

NB The crude birth and death rates presented in this Annex were calculated by using the numbers of live births and of deaths obtained from civil registers. First priority was given to estimated rates provided by the individual countries or areas. If suitable official estimated rates were not available, then estimated rates prepared by the Population Division of the United Nations Secretariat are presented.

Table 1

Population estimates and projections and average annual rate of growth: world total, regions, countries, or areas, urban and rural, 1950–2025 (medium variant)

WORLD TOTAL, REGIONS, COUNTRIES OR AREAS	TOTAL: T URBAN: U RURAL: R	TOTAL POPULATION (IN THOUSANDS) ANNUAL RATE OF GROWTH (PERCENTAGE)														
		1950	RATE	1960	RATE	1970	RATE	1980	RATE	1990	RATE	2000	RATE	2010	RATE	2025
WORLD TOTAL	T	2515652	1.83	3018877	2.02	3693221	1.86	4449567	1.65	5246209	1.55	6121813	1.32	6989129	1.18	8205765
	U	734208	3.40	1031514	2.85	1371058	2.53	1764113	2.37	2234276	2.45	2853655	2.39	3622921	2.23	4931799
	R	1781444	1.09	1987363	1.55	2322163	1.46	2685454	1.15	3011933	0.82	3268158	0.29	3366208	-0.01	3273965
MORE DEVELOPED REGIONS (*) (**)	T	831857	1.28	944909	1.03	1047392	0.82	1136668	0.62	1209777	0.54	1276647	0.42	1331200	0.36	1396476
	U	447324	2.45	571426	2.00	697862	1.34	798180	0.94	877166	0.80	949939	0.62	1011376	0.54	1086597
	R	384533	-0.29	373483	-0.67	349530	-0.32	338488	-0.18	332611	-0.18	326708	-0.21	319824	-0.24	309879
LESS DEVELOPED REGIONS (*) (+)	T	1683795	2.08	2073968	2.44	2645829	2.25	3312899	1.97	4036432	1.83	4845166	1.51	5657929	1.00	6809289
	U	286884	4.73	460088	3.81	673196	3.61	965933	3.40	1357110	3.39	1903716	3.16	2611546	2.84	3845202
	R	1396911	1.45	1613880	2.00	1972633	1.74	2346966	1.32	2679322	0.94	2941450	0.35	3046383	0.01	2964086
A. AFRICA	T	224361	2.22	280051	2.54	360751	2.85	479456	2.97	645282	3.01	871817	2.83	1157528	2.53	1616515
	U	35295	3.99	52598	4.35	81238	4.65	129253	4.88	210498	4.79	340050	4.40	527996	3.92	894171
	R	189066	1.85	227453	2.06	279513	2.25	350204	2.17	434784	2.02	531767	1.69	629532	1.28	722344
1. EASTERN AFRICA	T	63358	2.35	80073	2.78	105686	2.99	142540	3.17	195636	3.30	272244	3.15	373097	2.79	536859
	U	3301	5.70	5832	6.21	10847	6.85	21499	6.70	42009	6.12	77453	5.38	132643	4.67	246280
	R	60057	2.12	74241	2.45	94839	2.44	121041	2.39	153627	2.38	194791	2.10	240454	1.67	290579
BRITISH INDIAN OCEAN TERRITORY	T	2	0.00	2	0.00	2	0.00	2	0.00	2	0.00	2	0.00	2	0.00	2
	U	N/A	N/A	N/A	N/A	N/A	N/A	N/A	N/A	N/A	N/A	N/A	N/A	N/A	N/A	N/
	R	N/A	0.00	N/A	0.00	N/A	0.00	N/A	0.00	N/A	0.00	N/A	0.00	N/A	0.00	N/
BURUNDI	T	2456	1.76	2927	1.66	3456	1.71	4100	2.83	5443	2.83	7226	2.48	9262	1.91	1181
	U	54	1.76	64	1.66	76	7.98	169	8.54	397	7.34	827	5.99	1506	5.17	304
	R	2402	1.76	2863	1.66	3380	1.51	3931	2.36	5046	2.38	6399	1.93	7757	1.21	877
COMOROS	T	173	2.18	215	2.34	271	3.40	381	3.06	518	2.94	695	2.09	857	1.50	104
	U	6	4.40	9	12.43	31	10.60	89	4.81	143	4.95	235	4.15	355	3.34	55
	R	167	2.09	206	1.56	241	1.96	293	2.47	375	2.06	460	0.86	501	0.09	49
DJIBOUTI	T	103	2.03	126	2.37	160	6.60	310	3.27	430	3.39	604	3.21	832	2.82	120
	U	42	3.95	63	4.60	99	8.33	228	4.18	347	3.82	509	3.50	722	3.07	108
	R	61	0.46	64	-0.46	61	2.92	82	0.18	83	1.35	95	1.48	110	1.10	12
ETHIOPIA	T	19573	2.12	24191	2.36	30623	2.29	38521	2.62	50087	2.83	66509	2.77	87795	2.54	12228
	U	893	5.53	1551	5.30	2634	4.27	4038	4.73	6477	5.48	11203	5.77	19953	5.39	4132
	R	18680	1.93	22640	2.12	27989	2.09	34483	2.35	43610	2.38	55305	2.04	67843	1.61	8096
KENYA	T	5822	3.06	7903	3.57	11290	3.95	16766	4.16	25413	4.16	38534	3.71	55801	3.06	8285
	U	325	5.81	582	6.92	1162	8.42	2696	7.98	5990	7.15	12240	5.93	22149	4.98	426
	R	5496	2.87	7322	3.25	10128	3.29	14069	3.23	19424	3.02	26295	2.47	33652	1.69	4020
MADAGASCAR	T	4428	1.92	5362	2.25	6716	2.59	8704	2.85	11575	2.95	15550	2.80	20573	2.43	2812
	U	345	4.97	568	5.12	947	5.50	1641	5.69	2897	5.54	5043	5.00	8308	4.32	1465
	R	4082	1.60	4794	1.85	5769	2.02	7063	2.06	8678	1.91	10507	1.55	12265	1.04	1346
MALAWI	T	2881	2.03	3529	2.47	4518	2.75	5950	3.21	8198	3.29	11387	3.06	15452	2.67	2185
	U	101	4.22	155	5.67	273	7.47	576	7.43	1210	6.83	2394	5.91	4322	5.21	867
	R	2779	1.94	3374	2.29	4245	2.36	5375	2.62	6988	2.52	8993	2.13	11129	1.59	1317
MAURITIUS (1)	T	487	3.04	660	2.50	848	1.19	955	1.77	1140	1.29	1298	1.04	1439	0.87	160
	U	140	4.47	219	4.87	356	1.40	410	1.64	483	2.02	591	2.43	753	2.22	100
	R	347	2.40	441	1.08	492	1.04	545	1.87	658	0.72	707	-0.29	687	-0.72	60
MOZAMBIQUE	T	5710	1.36	6545	2.18	8140	3.98	12123	2.75	15972	2.79	21104	2.66	27521	2.32	3715
	U	135	5.74	240	6.57	463	12.34	1589	9.12	3954	6.42	7510	4.77	12102	3.87	1953
	R	5575	1.23	6305	1.97	7677	3.16	10534	1.32	12017	1.24	13594	1.26	15419	1.01	1761
REUNION	T	257	2.77	339	2.63	441	1.44	510	1.18	573	1.35	656	1.04	728	0.84	8
	U	60	6.12	111	5.50	193	3.71	280	2.69	366	2.27	459	1.70	544	1.40	65
	R	197	1.47	228	0.85	248	-0.65	230	-1.03	207	-0.50	197	-0.71	184	-0.91	15
RWANDA	T	2125	2.59	2753	3.00	3718	3.25	5144	3.33	7179	3.44	10123	3.27	14042	2.90	2021
	U	38	5.46	66	5.86	119	7.74	257	7.61	551	7.36	1150	6.79	2266	6.17	51
	R	2087	2.53	2687	2.93	3599	3.06	4886	3.04	6628	3.03	8973	2.72	11776	2.21	1503
SEYCHELLES	T	34	2.11	42	2.14	52	2.23	65	3.27	90	3.39	127	3.21	174	2.82	25
	U	9	1.51	11	2.39	14	7.21	28	6.02	51	4.91	83	4.02	124	3.23	18
	R	25	2.33	31	2.05	38	-0.34	37	0.57	39	1.00	43	1.43	50	1.75	6
SOMALIA	T	1803	1.74	2143	2.06	2634	4.23	4019	2.52	5169	2.55	6671	2.75	8778	2.49	1219
	U	229	4.81	371	4.95	609	6.89	1212	4.87	1971	4.47	3081	4.28	4724	3.78	779
	R	1573	1.20	1772	1.33	2025	3.27	2807	1.30	3198	1.16	3590	1.22	4054	0.88	439
UGANDA	T	4762	3.21	6562	4.02	9806	2.90	13106	3.41	18425	3.54	26262	3.41	36907	3.06	5519
	U	163	7.51	344	7.96	763	4.07	1146	5.34	1955	6.39	3706	6.72	7255	6.10	166
	R	4600	3.02	6218	3.73	9044	2.79	11960	3.20	16470	3.15	22556	2.73	29652	2.24	385
UNITED REPUBLIC OF TANZANIA	T	7886	2.40	10026	2.99	13513	3.33	18867	3.58	26998	3.71	39129	3.53	55670	3.11	8338
	U	285	5.27	483	6.62	937	12.00	3110	9.35	7919	6.94	15853	5.38	27171	4.28	4712
	R	7601	2.28	9543	2.76	12576	2.25	15758	1.92	19078	1.99	23277	2.02	28500	1.93	366
ZAMBIA	T	2440	2.52	3141	2.88	4189	2.99	5648	3.37	7912	3.51	11237	3.42	15807	3.10	237
	U	216	9.15	541	8.55	1272	6.42	2416	5.99	4398	5.12	7336	4.30	11277	3.76	185
	R	2224	1.57	2600	1.15	2917	1.03	3232	0.84	3514	1.04	3901	1.50	4530	1.36	52
ZIMBABWE	T	2415	4.00	3605	3.87	5308	3.28	7368	3.56	10511	3.64	15130	3.50	21456	3.19	326
	U	257	5.70	454	6.82	898	5.85	1613	5.86	2898	5.91	5233	5.55	9113	4.98	176
	R	2158	3.78	3150	3.36	4410	2.66	5755	2.80	7613	2.62	9897	2.21	12343	1.76	150
2. MIDDLE AFRICA	T	27185	1.95	33031	1.88	39857	2.66	51997	2.77	68607	2.93	91996	2.82	122013	2.51	1695
	U	3879	4.25	5935	5.11	9886	5.08	16426	5.04	27205	4.78	43856	4.26	67157	3.72	1099
	R	23307	1.51	27097	1.01	29971	1.71	35570	1.52	41402	1.51	48140	1.31	54856	0.91	596

Table 1 (continued)

WORLD TOTAL, REGIONS, COUNTRIES OR AREAS	TOTAL: T / URBAN: U / RURAL: R	1950	RATE	1960	RATE	1970	RATE	1980	RATE	1990	RATE	2000	RATE	2010	RATE	2025
ANGOLA	T	4131	1.53	4816	1.49	5588	3.24	7723	2.59	10002	2.80	13234	2.76	17439	2.58	24482
	U	313	4.74	503	5.08	836	6.62	1621	5.57	2831	5.25	4787	4.76	7703	4.29	13611
	R	3818	1.22	4314	0.97	4752	2.50	6101	1.61	7171	1.64	8447	1.42	9735	1.12	10872
CAMEROON	T	4528	1.92	5483	2.07	6745	2.46	8623	2.75	11359	2.89	15168	2.79	20065	2.51	27763
	U	443	5.41	760	5.89	1369	7.80	2988	6.31	5616	4.82	9089	3.79	13273	3.34	20515
	R	4085	1.45	4723	1.29	5375	0.47	5635	0.19	5744	0.57	6080	1.11	6792	0.79	7248
CENTRAL AFRICAN REPUBLIC	T	1417	1.25	1605	1.55	1875	2.04	2298	2.35	2907	2.54	3750	2.47	4799	2.17	6339
	U	226	4.75	364	4.48	570	4.33	879	4.33	1355	4.12	2044	3.66	2946	3.16	4445
	R	1190	0.42	1241	0.51	1305	0.83	1419	0.90	1553	0.94	1706	0.83	1853	0.48	1894
CHAD	T	2658	1.42	3064	1.76	3652	2.04	4477	2.36	5668	2.54	7308	2.45	9337	2.14	12356
	U	112	6.50	214	6.65	415	8.07	931	7.08	1889	5.39	3238	4.06	4861	3.50	7717
	R	2546	1.12	2850	1.28	3237	0.91	3546	0.64	3779	0.74	4070	0.95	4476	0.56	4639
CONGO	T	812	1.79	972	2.12	1201	2.42	1529	2.66	1994	2.82	2643	2.71	3467	2.36	4732
	U	254	2.34	321	2.65	418	3.10	570	3.91	842	4.41	1309	4.10	1972	3.53	3145
	R	558	1.53	651	1.84	783	2.02	958	1.84	1152	1.48	1335	1.14	1495	0.72	1587
EQUATORIAL GUINEA	T	226	1.12	252	1.45	291	1.89	352	2.23	440	2.40	559	2.35	708	2.16	937
	U	35	6.11	64	5.69	114	5.08	189	4.08	284	3.34	396	3.00	535	2.69	761
	R	191	-0.14	188	-0.56	178	-0.86	163	-0.45	156	0.43	163	0.61	173	0.41	176
GABON	T	812	0.66	867	0.92	950	1.14	1064	1.79	1273	2.31	1603	2.10	1978	1.97	2607
	U	93	4.89	151	4.79	244	4.46	380	4.24	581	3.94	862	3.31	1201	2.99	1814
	R	719	-0.05	716	-0.13	706	-0.33	683	0.12	691	0.70	741	0.47	777	0.29	793
SAO TOME AND PRINCIPE	T	60	0.65	64	1.45	74	1.39	85	2.73	112	2.88	149	2.85	198	2.67	284
	U	8	2.75	10	5.21	17	4.75	28	5.29	47	4.66	75	4.20	115	3.80	191
	R	52	0.29	54	0.54	57	0.08	57	1.20	64	1.34	74	1.26	84	1.01	93
ZAIRE	T	12542	2.38	15908	2.02	19481	2.83	25847	2.99	34852	3.12	47581	2.97	64024	2.59	90097
	U	2396	3.93	3548	5.09	5903	4.04	8840	4.42	13760	4.72	22055	4.49	34553	3.87	57717
	R	10146	1.98	12360	0.94	13578	2.25	17007	2.16	21092	1.91	25526	1.44	29471	0.98	32380
3. NORTHERN AFRICA	T	51798	2.29	65115	2.45	83158	2.59	107749	2.62	139943	2.27	175563	1.83	210895	1.56	260767
	U	14871	3.40	20880	3.75	30369	3.48	43021	3.72	62376	3.53	88773	3.03	120169	2.62	171575
	R	36927	1.81	44235	1.77	52789	2.04	64728	1.81	77567	1.12	86790	0.45	90726	0.07	89192
ALGERIA	T	8753	2.10	10800	2.42	13746	3.06	18666	3.12	25494	2.72	33444	1.94	40586	1.57	50611
	U	1948	5.23	3288	5.02	5430	3.48	7684	3.95	11402	3.96	16945	3.27	23511	2.69	34074
	R	6805	0.99	7512	1.02	8316	2.78	10982	2.49	14092	1.57	16500	0.35	17075	-0.09	16537
EGYPT	T	20330	2.43	25922	2.43	33053	2.28	41520	2.35	52536	1.97	63941	1.63	75263	1.41	90399
	U	8695	2.52	11188	2.52	14395	2.54	18554	3.23	25623	3.26	35499	2.78	46875	2.37	64033
	R	11635	2.36	14734	2.36	18658	2.08	22966	1.59	26913	0.55	28442	-0.02	28388	-0.29	26366
LIBYAN ARAB JAMAHIRIYA	T	1029	2.71	1349	3.87	1986	4.04	2973	3.77	4331	3.40	6082	2.83	8068	2.33	11090
	U	191	4.72	307	8.43	712	8.61	1683	5.91	3038	4.21	4630	3.31	6451	2.75	9377
	R	838	2.19	1042	2.00	1274	0.12	1290	0.02	1292	1.17	1452	1.08	1617	0.59	1713
MOROCCO	T	8953	2.61	11626	2.75	15310	2.36	19382	2.39	24616	1.81	29512	1.36	33835	1.21	40062
	U	2345	3.74	3409	4.42	5300	4.12	8000	4.00	11927	3.22	16455	2.51	21147	2.16	28447
	R	6608	2.18	8217	1.98	10010	1.28	11382	1.08	12689	0.29	13057	-0.29	12688	-0.49	11615
SUDAN	T	9190	1.95	11165	2.16	13859	2.99	18681	2.88	24895	2.80	32926	2.44	42002	2.04	55379
	U	579	6.86	1150	6.80	2271	4.85	3688	3.97	5482	4.65	8721	4.79	14085	4.28	25197
	R	8611	1.51	10015	1.46	11588	2.58	14993	2.58	19413	2.21	24206	1.43	27917	0.81	30183
TUNISIA	T	3530	1.79	4221	1.95	5127	2.21	6392	2.11	7894	1.77	9429	1.41	10858	1.24	12860
	U	1102	3.22	1521	3.83	2229	4.06	3345	3.62	4803	2.83	6379	2.15	7905	1.86	10169
	R	2427	1.06	2699	0.71	2898	0.51	3048	0.14	3090	-0.14	3049	-0.32	2953	-0.50	2691
WESTERN SAHARA	T	14	8.57	32	8.57	76	5.69	135	2.79	178	2.48	229	2.11	282	1.86	365
	U	9	6.64	18	6.01	33	7.00	67	4.14	101	3.60	144	2.99	195	2.59	278
	R	4	11.71	14	11.09	43	4.57	68	1.27	78	0.82	84	0.40	88	0.13	87
4. SOUTHERN AFRICA	T	17274	1.85	20787	2.21	25914	2.35	32774	2.56	42370	2.53	54553	2.32	68803	2.09	90991
	U	6541	2.95	8783	2.64	11432	3.52	16258	3.66	23445	3.49	33234	3.14	45474	2.82	66670
	R	10733	1.12	12004	1.88	14483	1.32	16515	1.36	18925	1.19	21319	0.90	23329	0.57	24321
BOTSWANA	T	389	2.12	481	2.58	623	3.83	915	3.76	1332	3.65	1917	3.51	2724	3.20	4151
	U	1	18.36	8	18.26	53	9.78	140	8.11	314	6.96	630	5.81	1125	5.04	2199
	R	388	1.98	473	1.88	571	3.06	775	2.73	1018	2.35	1287	2.17	1599	1.79	1952
LESOTHO	T	734	1.71	870	2.01	1064	2.30	1339	2.57	1731	2.65	2255	2.52	2903	2.25	3877
	U															
	R	2402	1.76	2863	1.66	3380	1.51	3931	2.48	5046	2.38	6399	1.93	7757	1.21	8772
	R	727	1.46	841	1.47	973	1.74	1157	1.76	1381	1.64	1626	1.40	1869	0.97	2033
NAMIBIA	T	666	2.09	821	2.39	1042	2.58	1349	2.85	1793	2.98	2415	2.87	3216	2.51	4474
	U	103	6.23	191	6.01	349	5.58	610	5.16	1021	4.45	1594	3.71	2311	3.15	3505
	R	563	1.11	629	0.97	693	0.65	739	0.43	771	0.62	821	0.98	905	0.76	969
SOUTH AFRICA	T	15219	1.83	18281	2.20	22760	2.29	28612	2.50	36754	2.44	46918	2.21	58525	1.98	76381
	U	6426	2.85	8541	2.44	10898	3.33	15217	3.46	21508	3.30	29915	2.97	40254	2.67	57802
	R	8794	1.03	9741	1.97	11862	1.22	13396	1.30	15246	1.09	17003	0.72	18271	0.38	18579
SWAZILAND	T	265	2.28	333	2.43	425	2.75	559	3.08	760	3.22	1048	3.15	1435	2.90	2107
	U	4	12.70	13	11.51	41	9.87	111	8.21	251	6.20	467	4.75	750	4.25	1320
	R	262	2.02	320	1.80	383	1.56	448	1.27	509	1.33	581	1.64	685	1.31	787
5. WESTERN AFRICA	T	64746	2.25	81045	2.70	106137	3.08	144397	3.19	198726	3.33	277461	3.22	382720	2.87	558302
	U	6704	5.11	11168	5.16	18705	5.38	32049	5.49	55463	5.56	96734	5.19	162553	4.59	299731
	R	58041	1.85	69877	2.25	87432	2.51	112348	2.43	143263	2.33	180727	1.98	220167	1.49	258571
BENIN	T	2046	0.95	2251	1.85	2708	2.55	3494	3.04	4733	3.23	6532	3.10	8910	2.72	12701
	U	136	4.57	215	7.03	433	8.22	985	7.02	1987	5.52	3451	4.36	5336	3.77	8753
	R	1910	0.65	2036	1.10	2274	0.98	2508	0.90	2745	1.16	3081	1.49	3574	1.05	3949
BURKINA FASO	T	3652	1.58	4279	1.71	5076	1.94	6159	2.52	7923	2.85	10538	2.91	14096	2.68	20106
	U	140	3.62	201	3.71	292	3.92	431	5.04	714	6.01	1303	6.35	2458	5.87	5490
	R	3512	1.50	4078	1.60	4785	1.80	5727	2.30	7209	2.48	9235	2.31	11638	1.94	14616
CAPE VERDE	T	148	2.98	200	3.04	271	0.87	296	2.15	367	2.48	470	2.01	575	1.59	712
	U	12	1.27	13	1.31	15	-0.01	15	3.29	21	5.87	38	5.77	67	5.16	139
	R	137	3.12	187	3.16	256	0.92	281	2.08	346	2.23	432	1.60	508	1.07	573

Table 1 (continued)

WORLD TOTAL, REGIONS, COUNTRIES OR AREAS	TOTAL: T URBAN: U RURAL: R	1950	RATE	1960	RATE	1970	RATE	1980	RATE	1990	RATE	2000	RATE	2010	RATE	2025
COTE D'IVOIRE	T	3241	1.41	3731	3.98	5553	3.86	8172	3.55	11658	3.17	16006	2.98	21567	2.53	29978
	U	427	5.24	720	7.48	1522	6.89	3031	5.84	5433	4.74	8732	4.17	13247	3.53	21030
	R	2815	0.68	3011	2.92	4031	2.44	5141	1.92	6225	1.56	7274	1.34	8319	0.84	8949
GAMBIA	T	331	1.22	374	2.26	469	2.19	583	2.04	715	2.27	898	2.29	1129	2.16	1494
	U	35	2.85	46	4.17	70	4.06	106	4.19	161	4.71	258	4.69	412	4.24	723
	R	296	1.01	327	1.95	398	1.82	478	1.49	554	1.45	641	1.14	718	0.86	771
GHANA	T	4242	4.68	6772	2.41	8614	2.94	11560	3.29	16072	3.42	22607	3.31	31460	3.03	47020
	U	614	9.42	1575	4.60	2494	3.51	3544	4.04	5305	4.79	8563	5.08	14238	4.69	26595
	R	3628	3.60	5197	1.64	6120	2.70	8017	2.95	10767	2.66	14045	2.04	17222	1.55	20424
GUINEA	T	3245	1.21	3660	1.81	4388	2.09	5407	2.41	6876	2.56	8879	2.53	11430	2.34	15561
	U	178	7.08	362	5.17	608	5.28	1031	5.37	1763	5.14	2947	4.68	4705	4.19	8224
	R	3066	0.72	3298	1.36	3780	1.47	4376	1.56	5113	1.49	5932	1.26	6725	0.94	7337
GUINEA-BISSAU	T	505	0.67	540	-0.25	526	4.29	809	2.00	987	2.19	1229	2.15	1523	2.00	2014
	U	51	3.73	73	2.61	95	7.02	192	4.58	304	4.46	474	4.03	709	3.60	1163
	R	454	0.26	466	-0.79	431	3.58	616	1.04	684	0.98	754	0.76	814	0.50	851
LIBERIA	T	855	2.02	1047	2.66	1365	3.15	1871	3.21	2577	3.39	3615	3.35	5052	3.00	7517
	U	111	5.65	195	6.00	355	6.09	653	5.52	1135	5.06	1882	4.63	2990	4.08	5138
	R	744	1.35	852	1.70	1010	1.86	1217	1.70	1443	1.83	1733	1.74	2062	1.33	2379
MALI	T	3850	1.85	4635	2.04	5685	2.11	7023	2.88	9362	3.02	12658	2.95	16992	2.69	24142
	U	327	4.52	513	4.61	814	4.00	1214	3.90	1793	4.92	2932	5.48	5069	5.13	10064
	R	3523	1.57	4122	1.67	4872	1.76	5809	2.65	7568	2.51	9726	2.04	11922	1.55	14078
MAURITANIA	T	796	2.08	981	2.40	1247	2.68	1631	3.01	2202	3.08	2998	2.96	4030	2.74	5780
	U	24	9.91	65	9.80	174	9.26	439	7.48	926	5.51	1608	4.18	2442	3.76	4016
	R	772	1.70	916	1.59	1073	1.05	1192	0.68	1276	0.86	1391	1.33	1588	1.06	1764
NIGER	T	2868	1.20	3234	2.49	4146	2.48	5311	2.92	7109	3.16	9750	3.08	13266	2.72	18940
	U	139	2.97	187	6.33	353	6.87	701	6.81	1385	6.35	2613	5.58	4567	4.91	8786
	R	2729	1.10	3047	2.19	3793	1.95	4610	2.17	5725	2.21	7138	1.98	8699	1.47	10154
NIGERIA	T	32935	2.50	42305	3.02	57221	3.43	80555	3.42	113343	3.56	161930	3.40	227539	3.01	338105
	U	3449	4.77	5558	5.21	9361	5.63	16436	5.86	29535	6.04	54060	5.54	94111	4.85	179299
	R	29486	2.20	36747	2.65	47860	2.93	64120	2.68	83808	2.52	107871	2.12	133428	1.60	158806
ST. HELENA (2)	T	5	0.00	5	0.00	5	0.00	5	3.18	7	3.31	10	3.15	13	2.77	19
	U	1	0.00	1	-1.44	1	-3.95	1	3.18	1	4.33	2	6.13	3	5.45	5
	R	4	0.00	4	0.55	4	1.06	4	3.18	6	3.08	8	2.29	10	1.76	12
SENEGAL	T	2500	1.96	3041	2.77	4008	3.47	5672	2.63	7377	2.81	9765	2.74	12837	2.52	17872
	U	762	2.43	971	3.22	1340	3.92	1982	3.58	2834	4.27	4345	4.34	6705	3.87	11118
	R	1738	1.75	2070	2.54	2669	3.24	3689	2.08	4543	1.76	5421	1.24	6133	0.93	668
SIERRA LEONE	T	2198	1.19	2475	1.35	2835	1.51	3296	1.85	3968	2.04	4867	2.02	5957	1.75	741
	U	203	4.65	322	4.64	513	4.56	809	4.56	1277	4.27	1957	3.83	2868	3.27	438
	R	1995	0.76	2153	0.76	2322	0.69	2487	0.79	2691	0.79	2910	0.60	3089	0.22	303
TOGO	T	1329	1.30	1514	2.89	2020	2.35	2554	3.01	3449	3.11	4709	2.98	6344	2.62	892
	U	96	4.32	148	5.83	265	5.92	479	6.16	888	5.72	1573	5.12	2625	4.46	473
	R	1233	1.03	1366	2.51	1755	1.67	2075	2.11	2561	2.02	3136	1.71	3719	1.21	418
B. AMERICAS	T	330885	2.27	415416	2.06	509972	1.85	613329	1.69	726397	1.50	843730	1.28	959199	1.16	112407
	U	173747	3.47	245737	2.95	329953	2.48	422534	2.25	529623	1.93	642402	1.61	754858	1.46	92257
	R	157137	0.77	169679	0.59	180019	0.58	190795	0.31	196775	0.23	201328	0.15	204342	0.02	20149
B1. LATIN AMERICA	T	164810	2.74	216753	2.68	283407	2.43	361372	2.22	451072	1.92	546395	1.61	641978	1.42	77866
	U	67643	4.57	106860	4.21	162741	3.73	236343	3.19	325139	2.56	419783	2.04	514774	1.78	65569
	R	97167	1.23	109893	0.94	120666	0.35	125030	0.08	125933	0.06	126612	0.05	127204	-0.09	12296
6. CARIBBEAN	T	16933	1.86	20394	1.98	24858	1.75	29600	1.60	34754	1.65	40985	1.49	47572	1.41	5783
	U	5770	3.09	7861	3.70	11372	3.25	15742	2.75	20709	2.49	26552	2.10	32765	1.95	4298
	R	11164	1.16	12533	0.73	13485	0.27	13858	0.14	14045	0.28	14433	0.26	14808	0.16	1485
ANGUILLA	T	5	0.74	6	0.86	6	0.79	7	1.01	7	1.28	8	1.14	9	1.05	1
	U	N/A	N/A	N/A	N/A	N/A	N/A	N/A	N/A	N/A	N/A	N/A	N/A	N/A	N/A	N/
	R	N/A	0.74	N/A	0.86	N/A	0.79	N/A	1.01	N/A	1.28	N/A	1.14	N/A	1.05	N/
ANTIGUA & BARBUDA	T	46	1.74	55	1.89	66	1.33	75	1.35	86	1.35	99	1.11	110	0.96	12
	U	21	0.26	22	0.25	22	0.46	23	1.73	28	3.21	38	3.00	51	2.56	7
	R	25	2.85	33	2.83	44	1.75	52	1.18	59	0.34	61	-0.28	59	-0.55	5
BAHAMAS	T	79	3.58	113	4.13	171	2.07	210	1.61	247	1.34	282	1.11	315	0.95	35
	U	49	3.23	68	3.76	99	1.88	119	2.01	146	2.23	182	1.95	221	1.64	27
	R	30	4.13	45	4.67	72	2.33	91	1.06	101	-0.12	100	-0.60	94	-0.79	8
BARBADOS	T	211	0.89	231	0.35	239	0.42	249	0.46	261	0.87	284	0.83	309	0.76	34
	U	71	1.34	82	0.80	89	1.22	100	1.54	117	2.21	145	2.15	180	1.87	21
	R	140	0.65	149	0.09	150	-0.08	149	-0.34	144	-0.36	139	-0.77	129	-0.90	11
BRITISH VIRGIN ISLANDS	T	6	1.77	7	2.92	10	1.93	12	1.33	14	1.36	16	1.14	18	0.89	2
	U	N/A	N/A	N/A	N/A	N/A	N/A	N/A	N/A	N/A	N/A	N/A	N/A	N/A	N/A	N/
	R	N/A	1.77	N/A	2.92	N/A	1.93	N/A	1.33	N/A	1.36	N/A	1.14	N/A	0.89	N/
CAYMAN ISLANDS	T	6	3.00	9	1.72	10	5.21	17	2.30	21	1.32	24	1.12	27	0.93	3
	U	6	3.00	9	1.72	10	5.21	17	2.30	21	1.32	24	1.12	27	0.93	3
	R	N/A	N/A	N/A	N/A	N/A	N/A	N/A	N/A	N/A	N/A	N/A	N/A	N/A	N/A	N/
CUBA	T	5858	1.82	7029	1.99	8572	1.27	9732	0.80	10540	1.06	11718	0.71	12584	0.60	1357
	U	2893	2.87	3855	2.92	5161	2.50	6628	1.75	7897	1.71	9364	1.13	10482	0.93	1182
	R	2965	0.68	3173	0.72	3411	-0.94	3104	-1.61	2642	-1.16	2354	-1.14	2101	-1.13	175
DOMINICA	T	51	1.60	60	1.61	71	0.35	73	1.02	81	1.35	93	1.36	107	1.22	12
	U	N/A	N/A	N/A	N/A	N/A	N/A	N/A	N/A	N/A	N/A	N/A	N/A	N/A	N/A	N/
	R	N/A	1.60	N/A	1.61	N/A	0.35	N/A	1.02	N/A	1.35	N/A	1.36	N/A	1.22	N/
DOMINICAN REPUBLIC	T	2409	2.92	3224	2.85	4289	2.60	5558	2.27	6971	1.88	8407	1.68	9945	1.52	1215
	U	572	5.33	975	5.72	1727	4.86	2807	4.05	4209	3.08	5729	2.44	7313	2.11	967
	R	1837	2.02	2249	1.30	2562	0.71	2751	0.04	2762	-0.30	2678	-0.18	2632	-0.23	24
GRENADA	T	76	1.73	90	0.42	94	1.26	107	1.14	120	1.35	137	1.37	157	1.21	1
	U	N/A	N/A	N/A	N/A	N/A	N/A	N/A	N/A	N/A	N/A	N/A	N/A	N/A	N/A	N
	R	N/A	1.73	N/A	0.42	N/A	1.26	N/A	1.14	N/A	1.35	N/A	1.37	N/A	1.21	N

Table 1 (continued)

WORLD TOTAL, REGIONS, COUNTRIES OR AREAS	TOTAL: T URBAN: U RURAL: R	1950	RATE	1960	RATE	1970	RATE	1980	RATE	1990	RATE	2000	RATE	2010	RATE	2025
GUADELOUPE	T	210	2.70	275	1.51	320	0.20	327	0.41	340	0.40	354	0.72	380	0.70	418
	U	88	1.98	108	1.90	130	0.87	142	1.50	165	1.74	196	1.87	237	1.67	296
	R	122	3.19	167	1.26	190	-0.27	185	-0.53	175	-1.05	158	-0.93	144	-0.99	122
HAITI	T	3097	1.84	3723	2.12	4605	2.33	5809	2.56	7509	2.73	9860	2.67	12868	2.52	18312
	U	377	4.32	580	4.50	910	4.50	1427	4.65	2272	4.81	3675	4.58	5807	4.18	10337
	R	2720	1.44	3142	1.62	3695	1.71	4382	1.79	5236	1.67	6185	1.32	7060	1.04	7975
JAMAICA	T	1403	1.50	1629	1.38	1869	1.51	2173	1.49	2521	1.33	2880	1.07	3206	1.01	3704
	U	375	3.83	550	3.46	777	3.31	1082	2.94	1452	2.42	1850	1.92	2240	1.71	2845
	R	1028	0.49	1079	0.12	1092	-0.01	1091	-0.20	1069	-0.37	1030	-0.65	966	-0.73	859
MARTINIQUE	T	222	2.39	282	1.45	326	0.02	326	0.15	331	0.45	346	0.56	366	0.57	397
	U	62	6.07	113	4.39	175	2.12	217	1.32	247	1.05	274	0.97	302	0.91	344
	R	160	0.51	169	-1.17	150	-3.16	110	-2.69	84	-1.55	72	-1.18	64	-1.17	53
MONTSERRAT	T	14	-1.09	12	-0.74	11	0.33	12	0.90	13	1.32	15	1.10	16	0.96	18
	U	3	-4.42	2	-4.19	1	0.32	1	1.99	2	3.75	2	4.31	4	3.88	6
	R	11	-0.34	10	-0.22	10	0.33	10	0.76	11	0.93	12	0.38	13	0.07	12
NETHERLANDS ANTILLES	T	162	1.71	192	1.44	222	1.26	252	1.17	283	1.34	323	1.11	361	0.95	410
	U	80	1.78	96	1.52	111	1.47	129	1.89	156	2.40	198	2.06	243	1.74	307
	R	82	1.63	97	1.36	111	1.03	123	0.35	127	-0.15	125	-0.58	118	-0.78	103
PUERTO RICO	T	2219	0.61	2358	1.42	2718	1.63	3199	1.48	3707	1.21	4185	0.94	4595	0.82	5121
	U	901	1.53	1050	4.12	1585	3.02	2144	2.46	2741	1.85	3298	1.35	3778	1.18	4419
	R	1318	-0.08	1308	-1.44	1133	-0.71	1056	-0.89	966	-0.86	886	-0.81	818	-0.92	703
ST. CHRISTOPHER AND NEVIS	T	44	1.43	51	-1.03	46	-0.31	45	1.08	50	1.33	57	1.11	64	0.95	72
	U	10	3.65	14	1.01	16	1.56	18	2.77	24	2.75	32	2.23	40	1.89	51
	R	34	0.69	37	-1.95	30	-1.44	26	-0.30	25	-0.23	25	-0.55	24	-0.75	21
ST. LUCIA	T	79	1.08	88	1.40	101	1.73	120	1.45	139	1.36	159	1.37	183	1.22	215
	U	N/A	N/A	N/A	N/A	N/A	N/A	N/A	N/A	N/A	N/A	N/A	N/A	N/A	N/A	N/A
	R	N/A	1.08	N/A	1.40	N/A	1.73	N/A	1.45	N/A	1.36	N/A	1.37	N/A	1.22	N/A
ST. VINCENT-THE GRENADINES	T	67	1.78	80	0.90	88	1.22	99	1.14	111	1.35	127	1.38	145	1.20	171
	U	N/A	N/A	N/A	N/A	N/A	N/A	N/A	N/A	N/A	N/A	N/A	N/A	N/A	N/A	N/A
	R	N/A	1.78	N/A	0.90	N/A	1.22	N/A	1.14	N/A	1.35	N/A	1.38	N/A	1.20	N/A
TRINIDAD AND TOBAGO	T	636	2.82	843	1.25	955	1.36	1095	1.59	1283	1.38	1473	1.15	1652	1.04	1897
	U	146	2.65	190	6.70	371	5.20	623	3.52	886	2.21	1105	1.67	1305	1.48	1590
	R	490	2.87	653	-1.11	584	-2.15	471	-1.73	396	-0.74	368	-0.60	347	-0.70	306
TURKS AND CAICOS ISLANDS	T	6	-0.52	6	-0.17	6	2.79	7	1.39	9	1.32	10	1.07	11	1.08	12
	U	2	-0.54	2	-0.20	2	3.83	3	2.63	4	2.58	6	2.12	7	1.96	9
	R	4	-0.49	3	-0.16	3	1.99	4	0.23	4	-0.21	4	-0.60	4	-0.63	3
U.S. VIRGIN ISLANDS	T	27	1.89	33	6.70	63	4.31	98	1.42	113	1.34	129	1.12	144	0.95	163
	U	16	1.35	18	-1.34	16	9.00	39	4.50	61	3.00	82	1.99	100	1.67	125
	R	11	2.61	15	11.90	48	2.12	59	-1.26	52	-1.02	47	-0.59	44	-0.79	39
7. CENTRAL AMERICA	T	36602	3.02	49521	3.19	68079	3.01	91949	2.60	119206	2.24	149059	1.85	179296	1.59	222589
	U	14565	4.62	23118	4.62	36693	4.14	55510	3.48	78598	2.92	105246	2.40	133830	2.09	177893
	R	22036	1.81	26403	1.73	31386	1.50	36439	1.08	40609	0.76	43813	0.37	45467	0.06	44696
BELIZE	T	67	3.02	91	2.76	120	1.91	145	2.25	182	1.94	221	1.62	259	1.43	315
	U	38	2.47	49	2.17	61	1.60	72	2.68	94	3.07	127	2.69	167	2.32	228
	R	29	3.71	42	3.41	59	2.22	74	1.80	88	0.57	93	-0.05	93	-0.28	87
COSTA RICA	T	858	3.65	1236	3.37	1732	2.74	2279	2.54	2937	2.02	3596	1.65	4239	1.41	5099
	U	288	4.51	452	4.20	687	4.21	1047	4.08	1575	3.29	2188	2.62	2842	2.20	3803
	R	570	3.18	784	2.87	1045	1.64	1231	1.01	1362	0.34	1408	-0.08	1398	-0.32	1296
EL SALVADOR	T	1940	2.83	2574	3.31	3582	2.92	4797	3.01	6484	2.95	8708	2.51	11188	2.18	15048
	U	708	3.32	987	3.58	1412	2.88	1883	3.16	2581	3.87	3799	3.99	5663	3.60	9215
	R	1232	2.54	1587	3.14	2171	2.95	2914	2.93	3904	2.30	4909	1.19	5524	0.62	5833
GUATEMALA	T	2969	2.89	3964	2.81	5246	2.77	6917	2.85	9197	2.85	12222	2.59	15827	2.30	21668
	U	904	3.70	1308	3.58	1871	3.54	2664	3.71	3862	4.07	5800	3.98	8634	3.55	13986
	R	2065	2.52	2655	2.40	3375	2.31	4253	2.27	5336	1.85	6422	1.13	7193	0.68	7682
HONDURAS	T	1401	3.27	1943	3.07	2639	3.35	3691	3.25	5105	3.12	6978	2.97	9394	2.56	13293
	U	246	5.84	442	5.46	763	5.57	1331	5.23	2245	4.79	3625	4.28	5559	3.63	9084
	R	1155	2.62	1501	2.23	1876	2.29	2360	1.92	2860	1.59	3353	1.34	3835	0.89	4208
MEXICO	T	27376	3.03	37073	3.23	51176	3.04	69393	2.49	89012	2.04	109180	1.61	128241	1.36	154085
	U	11677	4.77	18816	4.74	30205	4.21	46044	3.39	64604	2.69	84492	2.06	103887	1.75	131528
	R	15698	1.51	18257	1.39	20971	1.07	23349	0.45	24407	0.12	24688	-0.14	24354	-0.38	22557
NICARAGUA	T	1098	3.08	1493	3.19	2053	3.00	2771	3.34	3871	3.07	5261	2.60	6824	2.24	9219
	U	384	4.32	591	4.91	965	4.28	1480	4.47	2313	4.04	3466	3.39	4864	2.90	7181
	R	714	2.33	902	1.87	1088	1.72	1291	1.88	1558	1.42	1796	0.87	1960	0.49	2038
PANAMA	T	893	2.52	1148	2.89	1531	2.46	1956	2.12	2418	1.79	2893	1.39	3324	1.14	3862
	U	319	3.95	473	4.32	729	3.04	989	2.93	1324	2.78	1749	2.36	2214	1.95	2868
	R	573	1.62	674	1.73	802	1.89	968	1.22	1094	0.45	1144	-0.30	1110	-0.58	994
8. TEMPERATE SOUTH AMERICA	T	25482	1.89	30765	1.64	36229	1.55	42275	1.48	48996	1.22	55354	1.05	61439	0.92	69599
	U	16513	3.04	22373	2.32	28205	2.10	34807	1.91	42132	1.52	49065	1.26	55599	1.09	64462
	R	8969	-0.67	8392	-0.45	8024	-0.72	7468	-0.84	6864	-0.88	6289	-0.74	5839	-0.77	5137
ARGENTINA	T	17150	1.84	20616	1.51	23962	1.64	28237	1.52	32880	1.24	37197	1.10	41507	0.98	47421
	U	11206	3.04	15176	2.13	18784	2.17	23346	1.94	28337	1.53	33014	1.30	37599	1.15	43952
	R	5944	-0.89	5440	-0.50	5178	-0.57	4891	-0.73	4543	-0.82	4183	-0.68	3909	-0.71	3469
CHILE	T	6091	2.23	7609	2.17	9456	1.62	11127	1.55	12987	1.30	14792	1.00	16348	0.86	18301
	U	3559	3.72	5162	3.21	7113	2.38	9021	2.09	11120	1.65	13112	1.22	14803	1.03	16957
	R	2532	-0.34	2447	-0.44	2343	-1.06	2106	-1.21	1867	-1.06	1680	-0.84	1545	-0.83	1344
FALKLAND ISLAND (MALVINAS)	T	2	-0.41	2	-0.47	2	-1.05	2	0.00	2	0.00	2	0.00	2	0.00	2
	U	N/A	N/A	N/A	N/A	N/A	N/A	N/A	N/A	N/A	N/A	N/A	N/A	N/A	N/A	N/A
	R	N/A	-0.41	N/A	-0.47	N/A	-1.05	N/A	0.00	N/A	0.00	N/A	0.00	N/A	0.00	N/A
URUGUAY	T	2239	1.26	2538	1.01	2808	0.35	2908	0.73	3128	0.72	3364	0.62	3581	0.56	3875
	U	1746	1.52	2034	1.26	2306	0.56	2438	0.93	2673	0.94	2937	0.84	3196	0.76	3552
	R	492	0.24	504	-0.02	503	-0.67	470	-0.34	455	-0.64	427	-1.01	386	-1.14	324

Table 1 (continued)

WORLD TOTAL, REGIONS, COUNTRIES OR AREAS	TOTAL: T URBAN: U RURAL: R	1950	RATE	1960	RATE	1970	RATE	1980	RATE	1990	RATE	2000	RATE	2010	RATE	2025
9. TROPICAL SOUTH AMERICA	T	85793	3.02	116074	2.84	154242	2.48	197549	2.28	248115	1.94	300997	1.61	353671	1.42	4286
	U	30795	5.53	53508	4.80	86471	4.10	130284	3.44	183700	2.62	238921	2.02	292580	1.74	3703
	R	54997	1.29	62566	0.80	67771	-0.07	67264	-0.43	64415	-0.37	62076	-0.16	61091	-0.21	582
BOLIVIA	T	2766	2.15	3428	2.33	4325	2.54	5570	2.73	7314	2.85	9724	2.77	12820	2.55	182
	U	1045	2.53	1346	2.70	1762	3.37	2468	4.21	3759	4.14	5687	3.81	8321	3.42	133
	R	1721	1.91	2082	2.08	2562	1.92	3103	1.36	3554	1.28	4038	1.08	4499	0.84	49
BRAZIL	T	53444	3.06	72594	2.78	95847	2.35	121286	2.15	150368	1.77	179487	1.45	207454	1.26	2458
	U	18430	5.71	32608	4.95	53500	4.26	81888	3.45	115674	2.49	148391	1.81	177963	1.53	2187
	R	35014	1.33	39986	0.57	42346	-0.72	39398	-1.27	34694	-1.09	31090	-0.53	29490	-0.46	270
COLOMBIA	T	11597	2.93	15538	2.92	20803	2.15	25794	2.10	31820	1.78	37999	1.43	43840	1.23	51
	U	4301	5.54	7489	4.63	11899	3.31	16568	3.00	22371	2.44	28557	1.95	34694	1.66	434
	R	7296	0.99	8049	1.01	8904	0.36	9226	0.24	9448	-0.01	9441	-0.32	9147	-0.52	83
ECUADOR	T	3310	2.88	4413	3.16	6051	2.94	8123	2.83	10782	2.57	13939	2.22	17403	1.99	229
	U	935	4.85	1519	4.54	2392	4.75	3844	4.68	6136	3.88	9042	3.08	12303	2.66	177
	R	2375	1.97	2894	2.35	3659	1.56	4280	0.82	4645	0.53	4898	0.41	5099	0.25	51
FRENCH GUIANA	T	25	2.12	31	4.46	48	3.54	69	2.87	92	1.97	112	1.64	131	1.45	
	U	13	3.78	20	5.08	33	4.02	49	3.40	68	2.48	88	2.07	108	1.81	
	R	12	-0.22	11	3.29	16	2.45	20	1.47	23	0.28	24	-0.11	24	-0.29	
GUYANA	T	423	2.96	568	2.21	709	1.98	865	1.84	1040	1.40	1196	1.22	1351	1.11	15
	U	119	3.31	165	2.35	209	2.35	264	3.10	360	3.30	501	2.94	671	2.57	9
	R	304	2.82	404	2.16	501	1.82	601	1.24	680	0.23	696	-0.24	679	-0.45	
PARAGUAY	T	1371	2.60	1778	2.53	2290	3.25	3168	2.89	4231	2.45	5405	2.08	6653	1.84	85
	U	474	2.89	632	2.94	849	4.42	1321	4.20	2008	3.75	2921	3.26	4047	2.85	59
	R	897	2.45	1146	2.29	1441	2.48	1847	1.85	2223	1.11	2484	0.48	2607	0.15	2
PERU	T	7632	2.63	9931	2.84	13193	2.71	17295	2.56	22332	2.25	27952	1.80	33479	1.52	41
	U	2711	5.28	4597	5.00	7574	3.87	11153	3.41	15681	2.93	21014	2.33	26519	1.95	34
	R	4922	0.81	5334	0.52	5619	0.89	6142	0.80	6651	0.42	6938	0.04	6960	-0.22	6
SURINAME	T	215	3.00	290	2.50	372	-0.48	355	1.28	403	1.50	469	1.31	534	1.16	
	U	101	3.08	137	2.21	171	-0.74	159	1.88	192	2.79	254	2.50	326	2.17	
	R	114	2.93	153	2.74	201	-0.27	196	0.77	212	0.16	215	-0.33	208	-0.53	
VENEZUELA	T	5009	4.04	7502	3.46	10604	3.48	15024	2.73	19735	2.26	24715	1.94	30006	1.73	37
	U	2667	6.28	4996	4.82	8082	4.42	12572	3.28	17451	2.53	22462	2.07	27629	1.81	35
	R	2342	0.68	2507	0.06	2522	-0.28	2452	-0.70	2284	-0.14	2253	0.54	2377	0.79	2
B2. NORTHERN AMERICA	T	166075	1.79	198663	1.31	226565	1.06	251956	0.89	275325	0.77	297335	0.65	317222	0.63	345
	U	106105	2.69	138877	1.86	167212	1.08	186191	0.94	204484	0.85	222619	0.76	240084	0.77	268
	R	59970	-0.03	59786	-0.07	59353	1.03	65765	0.74	70841	0.54	74716	0.32	77137	0.22	78
BERMUDA	T	39	1.31	46	2.17	55	2.46	71	2.10	87	1.70	103	1.35	118	1.20	
	U	39	1.31	45	2.17	55	2.46	71	2.10	87	1.70	103	1.35	118	1.20	
	R	N/A	N/A	N/A	N/A	N/A	N/A	N/A	N/A	N/A	N/A	N/A	N/A	N/A	N/A	
CANADA	T	13737	2.66	17909	1.79	21406	1.18	24090	1.05	26744	0.79	28927	0.61	30739	0.59	33
	U	8356	3.90	12340	2.72	16195	1.19	18227	1.11	20373	0.88	22242	0.72	23914	0.71	28
	R	5381	0.34	5569	-0.66	5211	1.18	5863	0.84	6373	0.48	6685	0.21	6825	0.14	6
GREENLAND	T	23	3.61	33	3.54	47	1.01	52	0.74	56	0.69	60	0.65	64	0.62	
	U	18	3.42	25	3.33	34	1.30	39	1.05	44	0.98	48	0.92	53	0.88	
	R	5	4.20	8	4.12	13	0.15	13	-0.27	12	-0.42	12	-0.55	11	-0.67	
ST. PIERRE AND MIQUELON	T	5	0.00	5	0.77	5	1.05	6	0.00	6	0.00	6	0.00	6	0.00	
	U	4	0.63	4	1.05	5	1.25	5	0.15	5	0.09	5	0.05	6	0.03	
	R	N/A	-3.01	N/A	-1.04	N/A	-0.49	N/A	-1.37	N/A	-0.94	N/A	-0.53	N/A	-0.34	
UNITED STATES OF AMERICA	T	152271	1.71	180671	1.27	205051	1.05	227738	0.87	248429	0.77	268329	0.66	286294	0.64	311
	U	97688	2.58	126463	1.77	150923	1.06	167849	0.92	183974	0.85	200220	0.76	215994	0.77	24
	R	54583	-0.07	54208	-0.01	54128	1.01	59889	0.73	64455	0.54	68019	0.33	70300	0.23	7
C. ASIA	T	1375729	1.93	1668165	2.31	2102044	2.06	2583891	1.69	3057649	1.49	3548994	1.15	3982358	0.97	453
	U	225817	4.64	359093	3.37	502802	3.14	688234	2.85	915117	3.06	1242498	2.96	1670427	2.66	239
	R	1149912	1.29	1309072	2.00	1599241	1.70	1895658	1.23	2142532	0.74	2306496	0.02	2311931	-0.35	213
C1. EAST ASIA	T	671391	1.64	791292	2.20	986255	1.76	1176115	1.19	1324149	1.08	1475034	0.74	1588553	0.57	172
	U	112476	5.66	198095	2.93	265549	2.19	330558	1.68	390765	2.17	485178	2.42	618022	2.27	84
	R	558915	0.60	593196	1.95	720706	1.60	845557	0.99	933384	0.59	989857	-0.20	970531	-0.60	87
11. CHINA	T	554760	1.70	657492	2.34	830675	1.82	996134	1.21	1123815	1.11	1255895	0.76	1354942	0.59	1475
	U	60969	7.17	124892	2.91	166966	1.97	203351	1.70	240971	2.67	314610	3.14	430695	2.93	64
	R	493791	0.76	532600	2.21	663709	1.78	792783	1.07	882845	0.64	941285	-0.18	924247	-0.59	83
12. JAPAN	T	83625	1.18	94096	1.03	104331	1.13	116807	0.59	123865	0.47	129725	0.25	133049	0.00	133
	U	42065	3.35	58812	2.34	74296	1.80	88990	0.68	95233	0.58	100888	0.39	104871	0.14	100
	R	41506	-1.64	35284	-1.61	30035	-0.77	27818	0.29	28633	0.07	28837	-0.23	28179	-0.53	2
13. OTHER EAST ASIA	T	33006	1.84	39704	2.56	51249	2.09	63173	1.91	76468	1.56	89415	1.18	100562	0.95	11
	U	9442	4.21	14392	5.23	24287	4.53	38217	3.56	54562	2.45	69680	1.69	82456	1.32	9
	R	23564	0.71	25312	0.63	26962	-0.78	24956	-1.31	21906	-1.04	19735	-0.86	18106	-0.86	
HONG KONG	T	1974	4.43	3075	2.49	3942	2.46	5039	1.80	6034	1.16	6775	0.61	7205	0.47	
	U	1747	4.50	2739	2.55	3534	2.67	4614	1.97	5616	1.26	6370	0.68	6817	0.51	
	R	227	3.93	336	1.92	408	0.41	424	-0.14	418	-0.33	405	-0.43	388	-0.36	
KOREA	T	30097	1.66	35529	2.54	45815	2.04	56149	1.88	67767	1.55	79146	1.18	89052	0.95	10
	U	7371	4.15	11160	5.81	19953	4.86	32437	3.79	47353	2.55	61113	1.74	72728	1.36	8
	R	22726	0.70	24369	0.59	25862	-0.87	23712	-1.50	20414	-1.24	18033	-0.99	16325	-0.95	
DEMOCRATIC REPUBLIC OF KOREA	T	9740	0.78	10526	2.77	13892	2.60	18025	2.41	22939	2.06	28166	1.62	33110	1.34	
	U	3024	3.36	4231	4.98	6958	4.36	10759	3.62	15459	2.83	20523	2.19	25565	1.82	
	R	6716	-0.65	6295	0.97	6934	0.47	7266	0.29	7480	0.21	7643	-0.13	7545	-0.41	
REPUBLIC OF KOREA	T	20357	2.06	25003	2.45	31923	1.78	38124	1.62	44828	1.28	50981	0.93	55942	0.72	
	U	4347	4.66	6929	6.29	12995	5.12	21678	3.86	31894	2.41	40590	1.50	47162	1.10	
	R	16010	1.21	18075	0.46	18928	-1.41	16446	-2.40	12934	-2.19	10391	-1.69	8780	-1.43	

Table 1 (continued)

WORLD TOTAL, REGIONS, COUNTRIES OR AREAS	TOTAL: T URBAN: U RURAL: R	TOTAL POPULATION (IN THOUSANDS) ANNUAL RATE OF GROWTH (PERCENTAGE)													
		1950	RATE	1960	RATE	1970	RATE	1980	RATE	1990	RATE	2000	RATE	2010	RATE	2025
MACAU	T	188	-1.06	169	3.71	245	2.75	323	3.95	479	3.15	656	1.72	780	0.75	820
	U	182	-1.23	161	3.90	238	2.86	316	4.00	472	3.17	649	1.73	771	0.75	811
	R	6	3.08	8	-0.91	7	-1.62	6	0.92	7	1.28	8	0.85	8	0.34	9
MONGOLIA	T	747	2.19	931	2.94	1248	2.88	1663	2.75	2188	2.60	2837	2.17	3525	1.81	4539
	U	142	8.52	332	5.26	562	4.13	850	2.77	1121	3.23	1548	3.23	2141	2.83	3159
	R	606	-0.12	599	1.35	686	1.71	813	2.71	1067	1.89	1289	0.72	1384	0.13	1380
C2. SOUTH ASIA	T	704338	2.19	876873	2.41	1115789	2.33	1407777	2.08	1733500	1.79	2073960	1.44	2393805	1.23	2813766
	U	113341	3.51	160998	3.88	237254	4.11	357676	3.83	524352	3.68	757321	3.29	1052405	2.88	1547634
	R	590997	1.92	715876	2.04	878535	1.78	1050101	1.41	1209148	0.85	1316639	0.18	1341400	-0.17	1266132
14. SOUTHEASTERN ASIA	T	182191	2.14	225666	2.43	287650	2.27	360718	1.96	439122	1.68	519500	1.32	593106	1.12	688477
	U	26891	3.89	39681	3.79	58009	4.00	86581	3.85	127328	3.71	184438	3.27	255755	2.82	373824
	R	155300	1.80	185986	2.11	229641	1.77	274137	1.29	311794	0.72	335062	0.07	337351	-0.27	314653
BRUNEI	T	46	6.00	84	4.40	130	4.10	196	3.23	271	1.75	323	0.85	351	0.45	369
	U	12	10.84	36	7.92	80	3.80	118	2.86	156	1.96	190	1.72	226	1.34	268
	R	34	3.43	47	0.50	50	4.55	79	3.75	114	1.46	132	-0.55	125	-1.26	102
BURMA	T	17832	1.99	21746	2.20	27102	2.18	33714	1.92	40843	1.72	48499	1.41	55842	1.22	65960
	U	2876	3.76	4189	3.93	6190	2.64	8058	2.20	10042	3.08	13664	3.61	19606	3.37	31046
	R	14955	1.60	17557	1.75	20912	2.04	25656	1.82	30801	1.23	34835	0.40	36236	-0.05	34914
DEMOCRATIC KAMPUCHEA	T	4346	2.23	5433	2.45	6938	-0.80	6400	2.54	8246	1.70	9772	0.89	10676	1.07	12337
	U	443	2.32	559	3.73	812	-2.08	659	3.75	959	3.93	1421	3.94	2106	4.11	3724
	R	3903	2.22	4874	2.29	6126	-0.65	5741	2.39	7287	1.36	8352	0.26	8570	0.25	8613
EAST TIMOR	T	433	1.44	500	1.89	604	-0.39	581	2.37	737	1.73	876	1.11	978	1.19	1144
	U	43	1.64	51	2.08	62	0.16	63	4.27	97	4.79	157	4.17	237	3.95	407
	R	391	1.42	450	1.86	542	-0.46	518	2.11	640	1.16	719	0.30	741	0.22	737
INDONESIA	T	79538	1.90	96194	2.24	120280	2.28	150958	1.84	181539	1.52	211367	1.21	238605	1.01	272744
	U	9871	3.52	14032	3.81	20534	4.90	33514	4.45	52270	3.88	77068	3.20	106135	2.70	152381
	R	69667	1.65	82162	1.94	99746	1.64	117444	0.96	129269	0.38	134299	-0.14	132470	-0.46	120364
LAO PEOPLE'S DEMOCRATIC REPUBLIC	T	1894	2.18	2355	2.49	3019	1.99	3683	2.33	4648	2.20	5789	1.85	6969	1.60	8576
	U	137	3.11	187	4.41	291	5.33	495	5.58	865	5.20	1454	4.46	2271	3.89	3820
	R	1757	2.10	2168	2.30	2728	1.56	3188	1.71	3783	1.36	4335	0.81	4697	0.40	4756
MALAYSIA	T	6256	2.71	8205	2.81	10863	2.37	13763	2.29	17298	1.70	20497	1.31	23349	1.12	26844
	U	1274	4.86	2070	3.49	2932	4.75	4713	4.40	7319	3.44	10321	2.66	13460	2.25	18011
	R	4982	2.08	6136	2.56	7931	1.32	9050	0.97	9979	0.20	10176	-0.28	9889	-0.54	8833
PHILIPPINES	T	20552	3.06	27904	2.97	37540	2.52	48317	2.33	60973	1.95	74057	1.54	86344	1.30	102787
	U	5577	4.16	8454	3.82	12380	3.77	18052	3.58	25824	3.40	36292	2.94	48712	2.48	67929
	R	14975	2.62	19450	2.58	25160	1.85	30265	1.50	35150	0.72	37765	-0.04	37632	-0.34	34858
SINGAPORE	T	1022	4.69	1634	2.39	2075	1.52	2415	1.12	2701	0.87	2947	0.64	3141	0.52	3323
	U	1022	4.69	1634	2.39	2075	1.52	2414	1.12	2701	0.87	2947	0.64	3141	0.52	3323
	R	N/A	6.93	N/A	0.00	N/A	0.00	N/A	4.05	N/A	0.00	N/A	-4.05	N/A	0.00	N/A
THAILAND	T	20320	2.80	26867	3.03	36370	2.46	46516	1.81	55712	1.62	65503	1.32	74795	1.05	85929
	U	2129	4.57	3362	3.64	4834	5.11	8053	4.49	12611	4.24	19277	3.68	27862	3.09	42239
	R	18191	2.56	23505	2.94	31536	1.99	38463	1.14	43101	0.70	46225	0.15	46933	-0.27	43690
VIET NAM	T	29954	1.49	34743	2.07	42729	2.38	54175	2.00	66153	1.89	79870	1.42	92056	1.23	108462
	U	3507	3.76	5107	4.25	7820	2.89	10442	3.27	14482	4.02	21647	3.91	31999	3.40	50675
	R	26447	1.14	29636	1.64	34910	2.26	43733	1.67	51671	1.19	58224	0.31	60057	-0.03	57787
15. SOUTHERN ASIA	T	479715	2.16	595352	2.37	754468	2.29	948830	2.05	1164618	1.75	1386872	1.38	1591827	1.18	1854601
	U	76322	2.99	102927	3.60	147428	4.03	220407	3.77	321546	3.70	465579	3.37	651839	2.97	968428
	R	403393	2.00	492425	2.10	607040	1.82	728430	1.47	843071	0.89	921293	0.20	939988	-0.16	886173
AFGHANISTAN	T	8958	1.84	10775	2.35	13623	1.65	16063	2.70	21033	2.13	26035	1.79	31134	1.55	37917
	U	520	5.05	861	5.57	1503	5.13	2512	5.99	4570	5.05	7570	4.20	11513	3.60	18540
	R	8438	1.61	9914	2.00	12120	1.11	13551	1.94	16462	1.15	18465	0.60	19620	0.23	19378
BANGLADESH	T	42284	1.99	51585	2.57	66671	2.80	88219	2.67	115244	2.35	145800	1.95	177053	1.61	219383
	U	1840	3.67	2656	6.47	5073	5.94	9189	5.37	15711	5.27	26617	4.91	43469	4.36	78757
	R	40444	1.91	48829	2.35	61597	2.49	79030	2.31	99532	1.80	119183	1.15	133584	0.63	140626
BHUTAN	T	734	1.68	867	1.85	1045	2.04	1281	2.03	1569	1.88	1893	1.64	2229	1.40	2662
	U	15	3.42	22	4.01	32	4.38	50	5.14	84	5.66	148	5.41	254	4.98	507
	R	718	1.64	846	1.80	1012	1.96	1230	1.88	1485	1.61	1745	1.24	1975	0.89	2156
INDIA	T	357561	2.13	442344	2.27	554911	2.16	688856	1.83	827152	1.53	964072	1.16	1081821	0.99	1228829
	U	61695	2.53	79413	3.23	109616	3.87	161402	3.61	231604	3.54	330018	3.19	453724	2.80	658218
	R	295866	2.04	362931	2.04	445295	1.70	527454	1.22	595548	0.62	634054	-0.10	628097	-0.43	570611
ISLAMIC REPUBLIC OF IRAN	T	14206	3.57	20301	3.35	28397	3.08	38635	2.83	51259	2.40	65161	1.93	79044	1.61	97011
	U	3937	5.50	6828	5.34	11648	4.87	18956	3.95	28142	3.47	39806	2.87	53019	2.40	72392
	R	10269	2.72	13474	2.18	16749	1.61	19679	1.61	23117	0.92	25355	0.26	26025	-0.12	24620
MALDIVES	T	82	1.18	92	2.16	114	3.04	155	3.26	215	2.75	283	2.15	350	1.70	432
	U	9	1.70	10	4.06	16	7.20	32	3.27	44	4.08	66	4.58	105	4.13	181
	R	73	1.11	82	1.89	99	2.19	123	3.25	171	2.38	216	1.27	246	0.56	252
NEPAL	T	8182	1.39	9404	2.00	11488	2.44	14667	2.31	18470	2.22	23048	1.82	27651	1.55	33946
	U	187	4.46	292	4.32	450	6.91	897	6.81	1772	6.21	3297	5.20	5544	4.57	10380
	R	7995	1.31	9112	1.92	11039	2.21	13770	1.93	16698	1.68	19750	1.12	22107	0.72	23565
PAKISTAN	T	40031	2.24	50093	2.72	65706	2.71	86143	2.65	112226	2.28	140961	1.92	170702	1.63	209976
	U	7014	4.57	11073	3.90	16354	3.90	24173	3.95	35890	3.96	53305	3.75	77506	3.28	119044
	R	33017	1.67	39020	2.35	49352	2.27	61970	2.08	76336	1.39	87656	0.61	93196	0.15	90932
SRI LANKA	T	7678	2.53	9889	2.35	12514	1.69	14819	1.64	17451	1.18	19620	1.08	21843	0.95	24443
	U	1106	4.71	1772	4.35	2736	1.56	3196	1.54	3729	2.43	4751	3.45	6704	3.34	10410
	R	6572	2.12	8117	1.86	9778	1.73	11623	1.66	13723	0.81	14869	0.18	15138	-0.21	14033
16. WESTERN ASIA	T	42432	2.75	55856	2.77	73670	2.88	98221	2.79	129760	2.56	167588	2.21	208872	1.90	270689
	U	10128	5.97	18390	5.48	31817	4.66	50688	3.98	75478	3.52	107304	3.00	144811	2.58	205382
	R	32304	1.48	37465	1.10	41854	1.27	47533	1.33	54282	1.05	60284	0.60	64061	0.28	65307
ARAB COUNTRIES	T	19871	2.56	25659	3.04	34760	3.48	49246	3.49	69793	3.21	96173	2.71	126086	2.26	170997
	U	4726	5.73	8377	6.15	15491	5.74	27493	4.79	44424	4.01	66403	3.29	92313	2.77	134021
	R	15145	1.32	17282	1.09	19269	1.21	21753	1.54	25370	1.60	29770	1.26	33773	0.81	36976

Table 1 (continued)

WORLD TOTAL, REGIONS, COUNTRIES OR AREAS	TOTAL: T URBAN: U RURAL: R	TOTAL POPULATION (IN THOUSANDS) ANNUAL RATE OF GROWTH (PERCENTAGE)														
		1950	RATE	1960	RATE	1970	RATE	1980	RATE	1990	RATE	2000	RATE	2010	RATE	2025
BAHRAIN	T	116	3.01	156	3.42	220	4.58	347	4.05	520	2.87	693	2.08	853	1.68	
	U	74	5.12	123	3.37	172	4.86	279	4.34	431	3.13	590	2.31	743	1.90	
	R	42	-2.29	33	3.57	48	3.48	68	2.77	89	1.50	104	0.70	110	0.17	
DEMOCRATIC YEMEN	T	992	1.97	1208	2.15	1497	2.17	1861	2.88	2484	3.08	3379	2.56	4367	2.12	
	U	187	5.96	338	3.53	481	3.56	687	4.47	1075	4.67	1715	3.90	2534	3.23	
	R	805	0.77	870	1.55	1016	1.45	1174	1.83	1409	1.66	1663	0.97	1833	0.46	
GAZA STRIP (PALESTINE)	T	245	2.12	303	1.44	350	2.24	438	2.22	547	2.00	668	1.79	799	1.56	
	U	124	5.16	207	3.27	287	3.15	394	2.62	512	2.19	637	1.89	769	1.62	
	R	121	-2.37	96	-4.25	63	-3.46	44	-2.27	35	-1.24	31	-0.30	30	-0.01	
IRAQ	T	5158	2.83	6847	3.12	9356	3.51	13291	3.45	18760	3.02	25377	2.59	32866	2.14	43
	U	1812	4.83	2937	5.82	5254	5.18	8819	4.56	13915	3.69	20127	3.00	27154	2.48	37
	R	3347	1.56	3910	0.48	4102	0.86	4472	0.80	4844	0.81	5250	0.84	5712	0.40	5
JORDAN	T	1237	3.15	1695	3.05	2299	2.40	2923	3.84	4291	4.06	6437	3.56	9186	2.88	13
	U	429	5.25	724	4.73	1162	4.12	1756	5.10	2923	4.89	4764	4.11	7180	3.34	11
	R	808	1.83	971	1.58	1137	0.26	1166	1.59	1368	2.02	1673	1.81	2005	1.14	2
KUWAIT	T	152	6.02	278	9.85	744	6.14	1375	4.83	2230	2.99	3007	2.26	3769	1.91	4
	U	90	8.05	201	10.57	579	7.62	1240	5.44	2136	3.21	2942	2.35	3721	1.96	4
	R	62	2.10	77	7.67	165	-2.04	135	-3.62	94	-3.77	65	-2.85	48	-1.74	
LEBANON	T	1443	2.52	1857	2.85	2469	0.78	2669	1.06	2967	1.99	3617	1.60	4246	1.45	5
	U	327	8.09	735	6.91	1466	3.08	1996	2.15	2474	2.52	3183	1.87	3837	1.63	
	R	1115	0.06	1122	-1.12	1003	-3.98	673	-3.14	492	-1.25	435	-0.60	409	-0.26	
OMAN	T	413	2.02	505	2.58	654	4.08	984	3.93	1457	3.04	1973	2.68	2580	2.24	3
	U	10	5.79	18	6.31	33	7.76	72	7.60	154	6.58	298	5.93	539	5.20	3
	R	403	1.90	487	2.42	621	3.84	912	3.56	1302	2.52	1675	1.97	2041	1.37	2
QATAR	T	25	5.88	45	9.06	111	7.01	224	6.11	413	3.19	569	2.38	722	2.00	
	U	16	7.29	33	10.10	89	7.70	193	6.52	370	3.45	523	2.54	674	2.12	
	R	9	2.90	12	5.70	22	3.64	32	3.14	43	0.68	46	0.34	48	0.20	
SAUDI ARABIA	T	3201	2.42	4075	3.44	5745	4.90	9372	4.00	13988	3.48	19824	2.87	26397	2.32	3
	U	508	8.69	1211	8.37	2796	7.93	6174	5.53	10724	4.25	16408	3.25	22715	2.57	3
	R	2693	0.61	2864	0.29	2949	0.81	3198	0.20	3263	0.46	3415	0.75	3682	0.67	4
SYRIAN ARAB REPUBLIC	T	3495	2.66	4561	3.17	6258	3.41	8800	3.62	12634	3.43	17809	2.68	23284	2.33	3
	U	1071	4.49	1677	4.81	2713	4.31	4174	4.50	6548	4.46	10228	3.71	14835	3.24	2
	R	2424	1.74	2884	2.06	3545	2.66	4626	2.75	6086	2.19	7580	1.08	8449	0.62	
UNITED ARAB EMIRATES	T	70	2.60	90	9.04	223	14.81	980	4.76	1578	2.06	1939	1.63	2283	1.39	
	U	17	7.29	36	9.61	94	21.32	796	3.96	1182	1.33	1351	1.13	1512	1.04	
	R	52	0.37	54	8.65	129	3.60	184	7.64	395	3.97	588	2.70	771	2.08	
YEMEN	T	3324	1.95	4039	1.80	4835	2.13	5981	2.81	7925	3.17	10881	3.04	14735	2.54	2
	U	63	7.77	137	9.74	364	9.21	913	7.74	1978	6.09	3636	5.17	6099	4.38	1
	R	3261	1.80	3902	1.36	4471	1.26	5068	1.60	5947	1.98	7245	1.76	8635	1.13	
NON-ARAB COUNTRIES	T	22561	2.92	30196	2.54	38910	2.30	48975	2.02	59967	1.75	71415	1.48	82786	1.34	9
	U	5402	6.17	10013	4.88	16326	3.52	23195	2.92	31054	2.76	40901	2.50	52498	2.24	7
	R	17159	1.62	20183	1.12	22584	1.33	25780	1.15	28913	0.54	30513	-0.07	30288	-0.33	2
CYPRUS	T	494	1.49	573	0.71	615	0.23	629	1.11	703	0.80	762	0.80	825	0.74	
	U	147	3.27	204	2.06	251	1.51	291	2.43	372	2.02	455	1.80	544	1.57	
	R	347	0.61	369	-0.12	364	-0.75	338	-0.18	332	-0.78	307	-0.89	281	-0.98	
ISRAEL	T	1258	5.19	2114	3.42	2974	2.66	3878	1.75	4617	1.39	5302	1.16	5952	1.05	
	U	813	6.94	1627	4.32	2504	3.16	3436	2.06	4224	1.58	4949	1.29	5627	1.15	
	R	445	0.91	487	-0.36	470	-0.60	443	-1.20	393	-1.07	353	-0.81	325	-0.67	
TURKEY	T	20809	2.80	27509	2.50	35321	2.31	44468	2.06	54647	1.78	65351	1.51	76008	1.37	9
	U	4442	6.11	8182	5.06	13571	3.61	19468	3.06	26459	2.94	35498	2.66	46327	2.38	6
	R	16367	1.66	19327	1.18	21750	1.39	25000	1.20	28188	0.58	29853	-0.06	29681	-0.32	2
D. EUROPE	T	391955	0.81	425129	0.78	459425	0.53	484547	0.29	498592	0.28	512474	0.14	519521	0.07	52
	U	220817	1.59	259021	1.68	306329	1.05	340330	0.65	363162	0.58	384839	0.40	400337	0.30	4
	R	171137	-0.30	166107	-0.82	153096	-0.60	144218	-0.63	135430	-0.59	127635	-0.69	119185	-0.73	10
17. EASTERN EUROPE	T	88500	0.89	96713	0.66	103312	0.58	109397	0.50	114952	0.46	120366	0.40	125216	0.32	13
	U	37077	2.23	46347	1.77	55278	1.61	64930	1.17	72958	0.97	80323	0.77	86717	0.62	9
	R	51423	-0.20	50366	-0.48	48034	-0.78	44467	-0.57	41994	-0.48	40043	-0.40	38499	-0.37	3
BULGARIA	T	7251	0.82	7867	0.79	8514	0.40	8862	0.42	9246	0.30	9535	0.24	9760	0.22	
	U	1856	4.91	3034	3.84	4453	2.18	5537	1.60	6498	1.08	7238	0.74	7795	0.56	
	R	5395	-1.10	4833	-1.75	4061	-2.00	3325	-1.90	2748	-1.80	2296	-1.56	1965	-1.20	
CZECHOSLOVAKIA	T	12389	0.98	13654	0.51	14362	0.64	15311	0.34	15829	0.47	16581	0.43	17307	0.34	
	U	4634	3.25	6411	2.12	7923	1.85	9538	1.16	10710	1.02	11857	0.79	12828	0.61	
	R	7755	-0.68	7243	-1.18	6439	-1.09	5773	-1.21	5119	-0.80	4724	-0.54	4479	-0.47	
GERMAN DEMOCRATIC REPUBLIC (3)	T	18387	-0.65	17240	-0.10	17066	-0.19	16737	0.09	16889	0.15	17149	0.16	17431	0.12	
	U	13013	-0.44	12456	0.10	12582	0.13	12747	0.30	13144	0.37	13644	0.39	14177	0.33	
	R	5374	-1.16	4784	-0.65	4484	-1.17	3991	-0.64	3745	-0.67	3504	-0.74	3253	-0.84	
HUNGARY	T	9338	0.67	9984	0.37	10353	0.34	10711	-0.05	10658	0.06	10714	-0.01	10703	-0.08	
	U	3440	1.49	3990	1.69	4725	1.94	5735	0.91	6280	0.70	6735	0.41	7016	0.17	
	R	5898	0.16	5994	-0.63	5628	-1.23	4976	-1.28	4379	-0.96	3979	-0.77	3687	-0.55	
POLAND	T	24824	1.75	29561	0.99	32657	0.85	35574	0.80	38513	0.58	40816	0.51	42943	0.40	
	U	9607	3.88	14160	1.88	17077	1.92	20687	1.62	24325	1.14	27246	0.86	29691	0.67	
	R	15217	0.12	15401	0.12	15580	-0.46	14887	-0.49	14188	-0.45	13570	-0.23	13252	-0.20	
ROMANIA	T	16311	1.21	18407	1.01	20360	0.86	22201	0.70	23816	0.71	25571	0.57	27073	0.51	
	U	4525	3.31	6297	3.02	8517	2.27	10687	1.16	12002	1.25	13601	1.12	15209	1.05	
	R	11786	0.27	12110	-0.22	11843	-0.28	11515	0.26	11814	0.13	11970	-0.09	11863	-0.20	
18. NORTHERN EUROPE	T	72477	0.46	75834	0.57	80310	0.22	82114	0.12	83112	0.07	83735	0.00	83730	0.01	
	U	53852	0.77	58176	1.28	66144	0.54	69829	0.34	72231	0.24	73956	0.12	74838	0.11	
	R	18625	-0.54	17658	-2.20	14166	-1.43	12284	-1.22	10881	-1.06	9779	-0.95	8892	-0.85	

Table 1 (continued)

WORLD TOTAL, REGIONS, COUNTRIES OR AREAS	TOTAL: T URBAN: U RURAL: R	1950	RATE	1960	RATE	1970	RATE	1980	RATE	1990	RATE	2000	RATE	2010	RATE	2025
CHANNEL ISLANDS	T	104	0.56	110	1.04	122	0.86	133	0.72	143	0.61	152	0.58	161	0.49	175
	U	27	-0.20	27	-0.04	26	0.06	27	0.33	28	1.76	33	3.06	45	3.05	69
	R	77	0.82	83	1.35	96	1.07	106	0.82	115	0.32	119	-0.24	116	-0.58	106
DENMARK	T	4271	0.70	4581	0.73	4929	0.39	5123	-0.01	5120	-0.08	5082	-0.23	4969	-0.32	4690
	U	2904	1.51	3375	1.52	3929	0.95	4321	0.35	4476	0.15	4546	-0.08	4510	-0.23	4305
	R	1367	-1.26	1206	-1.88	1000	-2.20	802	-2.20	644	-1.84	536	-1.56	459	-1.23	385
FAEROE ISLANDS	T	31	1.22	35	1.08	39	0.50	41	0.47	43	0.46	45	0.43	47	0.42	50
	U	5	3.21	7	3.73	11	0.59	12	1.31	13	2.12	16	2.44	21	2.13	28
	R	26	0.73	28	0.23	28	0.47	29	0.14	30	-0.38	29	-0.90	26	-1.04	22
FINLAND	T	4009	1.00	4430	0.39	4606	0.37	4780	0.38	4966	0.18	5055	0.03	5072	-0.03	4994
	U	1283	2.74	1687	3.17	2315	2.08	2849	1.69	3372	1.06	3751	0.60	3985	0.42	4170
	R	2726	0.06	2743	-1.80	2291	-1.71	1931	-1.92	1594	-2.01	1304	-1.82	1087	-1.78	824
ICELAND	T	143	2.08	176	1.48	204	1.11	228	1.09	254	0.72	273	0.54	289	0.44	304
	U	106	2.92	141	2.04	173	1.49	201	1.33	230	0.88	251	0.64	267	0.52	283
	R	37	-0.78	35	-1.20	31	-1.32	27	-0.93	25	-0.85	23	-0.59	21	-0.47	20
IRELAND	T	2969	-0.47	2834	0.41	2954	1.41	3401	1.22	3843	1.17	4320	0.97	4759	0.84	5326
	U	1219	0.63	1299	1.62	1528	2.09	1882	1.87	2269	1.96	2760	1.79	3299	1.56	4068
	R	1750	-1.31	1535	-0.74	1426	0.63	1519	0.35	1573	-0.08	1560	-0.67	1460	-0.89	1258
ISLE OF MAN	T	55	-1.36	48	1.54	56	1.79	67	0.58	71	0.28	73	0.40	76	0.26	79
	U	29	-0.95	26	1.67	31	0.38	32	0.58	34	0.86	37	1.72	45	1.36	54
	R	26	-1.84	22	1.39	25	3.34	35	0.58	37	-0.31	36	-1.20	31	-1.40	25
NORWAY	T	3265	0.93	3581	0.80	3877	0.53	4086	0.23	4177	0.09	4215	0.04	4229	0.07	4261
	U	1051	0.90	1150	7.83	2513	1.37	2882	0.76	3109	0.44	3249	0.25	3330	0.22	3404
	R	2214	0.94	2431	-5.78	1364	-1.25	1203	-1.20	1068	-1.00	966	-0.73	898	-0.52	856
SWEDEN	T	7014	0.64	7480	0.73	8043	0.33	8310	0.00	8305	-0.17	8166	-0.21	8000	-0.21	7707
	U	4618	1.61	5429	1.84	6525	0.57	6905	0.08	6964	-0.07	6920	-0.09	6857	-0.09	6727
	R	2396	-1.55	2051	-3.00	1518	-0.77	1406	-0.48	1340	-0.73	1246	-0.86	1142	-0.92	980
UNITED KINGDOM	T	50616	0.38	52559	0.54	55480	0.09	55945	0.04	56190	0.03	56354	-0.04	56129	-0.01	55919
	U	42609	0.55	45034	0.87	49091	0.33	50719	0.20	51736	0.12	52393	0.01	52479	0.03	52452
	R	8007	-0.62	7525	-1.64	6389	-2.01	5226	-1.60	4454	-1.17	3962	-0.82	3650	-0.58	3467
19. SOUTHERN EUROPE	T	108539	0.84	118069	0.78	127665	0.89	139507	0.43	145710	0.45	152354	0.26	156329	0.13	159390
	U	48358	1.89	58413	2.05	71714	1.62	84376	1.06	93790	1.02	103810	0.78	112143	0.60	121893
	R	60180	-0.09	59656	-0.64	55952	-0.15	55131	-0.60	51920	-0.68	48543	-0.94	44186	-1.09	37496
ANDORRA	T	6	2.88	8	8.94	20	4.61	31	1.77	37	0.78	40	0.72	43	0.46	47
	U	N/A	N/A	N/A	N/A	N/A	N/A	N/A	N/A	N/A	N/A	N/A	N/A	N/A	N/A	N/A
	R	N/A	2.88	N/A	8.94	N/A	4.61	N/A	1.77	N/A	0.78	N/A	0.72	N/A	0.46	N/A
ALBANIA	T	1230	2.70	1611	2.84	2138	2.45	2731	2.16	3388	1.92	4102	1.53	4776	1.34	5772
	U	250	6.78	493	3.75	717	2.42	913	2.71	1197	3.14	1638	3.20	2256	2.91	3365
	R	979	1.32	1118	2.40	1421	2.46	1818	1.86	2191	1.17	2463	0.23	2521	-0.17	2407
GIBRALTAR	T	23	0.42	24	0.80	26	1.09	29	1.29	33	0.59	35	0.56	37	0.53	40
	U	23	0.42	24	0.80	26	1.09	29	1.29	33	0.59	35	0.56	37	0.53	40
	R	N/A	N/A	N/A	N/A	N/A	N/A	N/A	N/A	N/A	N/A	N/A	N/A	N/A	N/A	N/A
GREECE	T	7566	0.96	8327	0.55	8793	0.93	9643	0.45	10084	0.35	10437	0.20	10643	0.10	10789
	U	2821	2.37	3572	2.57	4617	1.87	5567	1.26	6317	1.14	7079	0.91	7753	0.71	8535
	R	4745	0.03	4755	-1.29	4176	-0.25	4075	-0.79	3768	-1.15	3358	-1.50	2890	-1.64	2254
HOLY SEE	T	1	0.00	1	0.00	1	0.00	1	0.00	1	0.00	1	0.00	1	0.00	1
	U	1	0.00	1	0.00	1	0.00	1	0.00	1	0.00	1	0.00	1	0.00	1
	R	N/A	N/A	N/A	N/A	N/A	N/A	N/A	N/A	N/A	N/A	N/A	N/A	N/A	N/A	N/A
ITALY	T	46769	1.60	50223	1.44	53565	0.97	57070	0.36	57563	0.48	58642	0.26	58435	0.13	57178
	U	25402	-0.46	29813	-0.65	34428	0.00	37932	-0.49	39334	-0.48	41252	-0.78	42348	-0.96	43319
	R	21367	0.53	20410	-0.10	19137	1.26	19138	0.70	18229	0.55	17390	0.48	16087	0.41	13860
MALTA	T	312	0.71	329	0.64	326	0.64	369	0.09	396	0.18	418	-0.04	439	-0.16	459
	U	191	1.87	230	0.92	252	1.96	307	1.14	344	0.83	373	0.67	399	0.54	424
	R	121	-2.04	99	-2.99	73	-1.62	62	-1.81	52	-1.54	45	-1.16	40	-1.02	35
PORTUGAL	T	8405	0.49	8826	-0.23	8628	1.36	9884	0.65	10542	0.61	11211	0.46	11742	0.38	12334
	U	1619	2.06	1990	1.29	2263	2.52	2912	1.88	3513	2.22	4385	2.23	5479	1.97	7130
	R	6786	0.07	6836	-0.71	6366	0.91	6971	0.09	7030	-0.29	6826	-0.86	6262	-1.12	5208
SAN MARINO	T	13	1.43	15	2.36	19	1.01	21	0.91	23	0.83	25	0.77	27	0.73	30
	U	N/A	N/A	N/A	N/A	N/A	N/A	N/A	N/A	N/A	N/A	N/A	N/A	N/A	N/A	N/A
	R	N/A	1.43	N/A	2.36	N/A	1.01	N/A	0.91	N/A	0.83	N/A	0.77	N/A	0.73	N/A
SPAIN	T	27868	0.83	30303	1.09	33779	1.03	37430	0.60	39748	0.60	42237	0.44	44133	0.29	45983
	U	14453	1.71	17142	2.64	22307	2.00	27245	1.29	31020	1.06	34498	0.73	37127	0.52	39688
	R	13415	-0.19	13161	-1.38	11471	-1.19	10185	-1.55	8728	-1.21	7740	-1.00	7006	-0.96	6295
YUGOSLAVIA	T	16346	1.19	18402	1.02	20371	0.91	22299	0.69	23895	0.54	25206	0.33	26053	0.20	26756
	U	3589	3.58	5137	3.21	7081	2.88	9438	2.40	11993	1.90	14504	1.41	16692	1.10	19333
	R	12757	0.39	13265	0.02	13290	-0.33	12861	-0.78	11901	-1.06	10701	-1.34	9361	-1.51	7423
20. WESTERN EUROPE	T	122439	0.94	134513	0.96	148138	0.36	153530	0.09	154818	0.08	156019	-0.12	154246	-0.17	150148
	U	81530	1.64	96085	1.64	113194	0.68	121194	0.24	124183	0.20	126749	-0.01	126638	-0.07	124986
	R	40909	-0.62	38428	-0.95	34944	-0.78	32335	-0.54	30635	-0.46	29269	-0.58	27607	-0.62	25161
AUSTRIA	T	6935	0.16	7048	0.55	7447	0.08	7505	0.00	7507	0.01	7517	-0.10	7446	-0.10	7279
	U	3407	0.33	3520	0.91	3853	0.62	4101	0.55	4332	0.56	4579	0.43	4781	0.41	5035
	R	3528	0.00	3528	0.19	3594	-0.55	3404	-0.70	3175	-0.78	2938	-0.98	2665	-1.04	2244
BELGIUM	T	8639	0.58	9153	0.52	9638	0.22	9852	0.10	9949	0.06	10011	0.03	10033	0.03	10054
	U	7902	0.69	8463	0.71	9090	0.34	9365	0.25	9632	0.14	9763	0.06	9817	0.05	9850
	R	737	-0.66	690	-2.30	548	-1.83	456	-3.65	317	-2.45	248	-1.42	215	-0.91	204
FRANCE	T	41736	0.90	45684	1.04	50670	0.59	53714	0.32	55475	0.30	57162	0.14	57929	0.08	54831
	U	23442	1.96	28501	2.33	35989	0.89	39334	0.40	40925	0.41	42609	0.27	43742	0.22	45144
	R	18294	-0.63	17183	-1.57	14681	-0.21	14380	0.12	14550	0.00	14553	-0.25	14187	-0.36	13288
GERMANY FEDERAL REPUBLIC OF (3)	T	49989	1.03	55430	0.91	60700	0.14	61566	-0.21	60332	-0.15	59484	-0.39	57200	-0.45	53490
	U	36138	1.72	42885	1.41	49371	0.51	51935	0.03	52104	0.00	52126	-0.31	50532	-0.40	47411
	R	13851	-0.99	12548	-1.03	11329	-1.62	9631	-1.57	8228	-1.11	7358	-0.98	6668	-0.86	6079

Table 1 (continued)

WORLD TOTAL, REGIONS, COUNTRIES OR AREAS	TOTAL: T URBAN: U RURAL: R	1950	RATE	1960	RATE	1970	RATE	1980	RATE	1990	RATE	2000	RATE	2010	RATE	2025
		TOTAL POPULATION (IN THOUSANDS) ANNUAL RATE OF GROWTH (PERCENTAGE)														
LIECHTENSTEIN	T	14	1.33	16	2.72	21	2.14	26	1.43	30	1.25	34	1.13	38	1.05	
	U	3	1.58	3	2.97	4	2.66	6	2.98	8	3.61	11	3.32	15	2.93	
	R	11	1.28	13	2.66	17	1.99	20	0.95	22	0.29	23	-0.12	23	-0.34	
LUXEMBOURG	T	296	0.59	314	0.78	339	0.71	364	-0.07	361	-0.10	358	-0.20	351	-0.22	3.
	U	175	1.09	195	1.65	230	2.06	282	0.61	300	0.25	308	-0.04	307	-0.13	2
	R	121	-0.17	119	-0.86	109	-2.93	82	-2.90	61	-2.01	50	-1.24	44	-0.84	
MONACO	T	22	0.45	23	0.42	24	0.80	26	0.74	28	0.69	30	0.65	32	0.60	
	U	22	0.45	23	0.42	24	0.80	26	0.74	28	0.69	30	0.65	32	0.60	
	R	N/A	N/A	N/A	N/A	N/A	N/A	N/A	N/A	N/A	N/A	N/A	N/A	N/A	N/A	N
NETHERLANDS	T	10114	1.27	11480	1.27	13032	0.82	14150	0.42	14748	0.22	15082	-0.02	15057	-0.11	146
	U	8362	1.55	9759	1.40	11221	1.08	12508	0.42	13048	0.24	13373	0.02	13399	-0.06	131
	R	1752	-0.18	1721	0.51	1811	-0.98	1641	0.35	1701	0.05	1709	-0.30	1658	-0.45	15
SWITZERLAND	T	4694	1.33	5362	1.56	6267	0.10	6327	0.10	6387	-0.07	6341	-0.29	6160	-0.37	57
	U	2081	2.74	2736	2.21	3413	0.55	3606	0.54	3805	0.38	3951	0.15	4013	0.07	40
	R	2613	0.05	2626	0.83	2854	-0.48	2721	-0.52	2582	-0.77	2391	-1.07	2147	-1.21	17
E. OCEANIA	T	12647	2.22	15782	2.03	19329	1.67	22850	1.47	26467	1.28	30062	1.05	33402	0.93	378
	U	7759	3.00	10467	2.69	13690	1.76	16336	1.40	18791	1.34	21470	1.24	24316	1.20	288
	R	4888	0.84	5315	0.59	5639	1.45	6514	1.65	7676	1.12	8591	0.56	9086	0.19	89
21. AUSTRALIA-NEW ZEALAND	T	10127	2.26	12687	1.92	15371	1.50	17864	1.22	20172	1.04	22377	0.82	24287	0.73	267
	U	7565	2.91	10118	2.49	12979	1.61	15244	1.21	17202	1.10	19198	0.95	21096	0.87	238
	R	2562	0.02	2569	-0.71	2393	0.91	2620	1.26	2971	0.68	3179	0.04	3191	-0.28	28
AUSTRALIA (4)	T	8219	2.27	10315	1.97	12552	1.57	14695	1.29	16708	1.09	18628	0.87	20319	0.78	225
	U	6181	2.97	8315	2.52	10692	1.65	12603	1.26	14285	1.14	16005	0.99	17677	0.93	20
	R	2038	-0.19	2000	-0.72	1860	1.18	2093	1.47	2423	0.79	2623	0.07	2643	-0.27	2
NEW ZEALAND	T	1908	2.18	2372	1.73	2820	1.17	3169	0.89	3464	0.79	3749	0.57	3968	0.46	4
	U	1384	2.65	1803	2.38	2287	1.44	2641	0.99	2917	0.91	3192	0.69	3420	0.58	3
	R	524	0.82	569	-0.67	533	-0.10	528	0.36	548	0.17	557	-0.14	549	-0.31	
22. MELANESIA	T	2119	1.98	2583	2.45	3300	2.40	4196	2.45	5361	2.12	6622	1.81	7941	1.56	9
	U	117	6.17	217	8.33	498	4.57	787	3.98	1171	3.90	1729	3.86	2544	3.54	4
	R	2002	1.67	2366	1.69	2802	1.97	3409	2.06	4190	1.55	4892	0.98	5397	0.55	5
FIJI	T	289	3.10	394	2.78	520	1.90	629	1.73	748	1.08	834	0.81	904	0.57	
	U	70	5.08	117	4.36	181	2.98	244	3.01	329	2.51	423	2.15	524	1.70	
	R	219	2.37	277	2.04	339	1.27	386	0.83	419	-0.20	411	-0.79	380	-1.08	
NEW CALEDONIA	T	59	2.90	79	3.29	110	2.30	139	1.71	165	1.36	189	1.02	209	0.65	
	U	24	2.90	32	5.23	54	5.63	95	3.31	133	2.02	162	1.28	184	0.87	
	R	35	2.90	47	1.73	56	-2.50	44	-3.08	32	-1.89	27	-0.70	25	-1.05	
PAPUA NEW GUINEA	T	1613	1.74	1920	2.32	2422	2.42	3086	2.48	3955	2.21	4933	1.93	5981	1.65	7
	U	11	15.26	51	15.29	237	5.29	403	4.41	625	4.67	997	4.71	1596	4.27	2
	R	1602	1.54	1869	1.56	2185	2.06	2683	2.16	3330	1.68	3936	1.08	4385	0.61	
SOLOMON ISLANDS	T	105	1.66	124	2.79	164	3.19	225	3.79	329	3.08	447	2.48	573	2.15	4
	U	9	2.02	11	3.17	15	3.56	21	5.17	35	5.71	62	5.81	110	5.21	
	R	96	1.62	113	2.77	149	3.15	204	3.64	294	2.72	386	1.82	463	1.34	
VANUATU	T	52	2.21	65	2.43	83	3.39	117	3.37	164	2.87	218	2.27	274	2.05	
	U	3	7.16	6	7.15	11	7.79	25	6.98	49	5.51	85	4.12	129	3.62	
	R	50	1.86	60	1.85	72	2.49	92	2.15	115	1.48	133	0.86	145	0.53	
23. MICRONESIA-POLYNESIA	T	401	2.44	512	2.51	658	1.82	790	1.67	933	1.30	1063	0.99	1173	0.76	
	U	77	5.45	132	4.76	213	3.64	306	3.11	418	2.64	543	2.18	676	1.79	
	R	324	1.57	380	1.60	445	0.83	484	0.65	516	0.07	520	-0.44	497	-0.73	
MICRONESIA	T	162	2.20	202	2.50	259	2.28	325	1.81	390	1.41	449	1.03	498	0.74	
	U	29	5.33	49	5.36	83	5.16	140	3.85	205	2.76	270	2.00	330	1.55	
	R	133	1.38	153	1.38	176	0.57	186	-0.05	185	-0.34	179	-0.64	168	-0.97	
GUAM	T	60	1.20	67	2.52	86	2.08	106	1.36	122	1.15	137	0.77	148	0.46	
	U	10	3.24	14	4.53	22	6.43	42	4.28	65	2.79	86	1.66	101	1.20	
	R	49	0.72	53	1.90	64	-0.02	64	-1.20	57	-1.12	51	-0.94	46	-1.27	
KIRIBATI (5)	T	32	2.40	41	1.80	49	1.82	59	1.42	68	1.25	77	0.81	84	0.53	
	U	3	7.58	7	6.50	13	3.90	19	2.74	25	2.92	33	2.50	42	1.96	
	R	29	1.66	35	0.59	37	0.97	40	0.75	44	0.16	44	-0.66	41	-1.03	
NAURU	T	3	3.45	4	4.13	7	1.38	8	0.97	8	1.05	9	0.90	10	0.83	
	U	N/A	N/A	N/A	N/A	N/A	N/A	N/A	N/A	N/A	N/A	N/A	N/A	N/A	N/A	
	R	N/A	3.45	N/A	4.13	N/A	1.38	N/A	0.97	N/A	1.05	N/A	0.90	N/A	0.83	
PACIFIC ISLANDS (6)	T	58	3.06	78	2.80	103	2.73	136	2.39	173	1.70	204	1.31	233	1.00	
	U	13	6.22	24	5.57	42	5.01	69	3.99	103	2.74	136	2.09	167	1.65	
	R	45	1.93	54	1.27	62	0.83	67	0.39	69	-0.10	69	-0.41	66	-0.75	
TUVALU	T	5	1.21	5	0.82	6	2.67	8	1.41	9	1.12	10	0.77	10	0.56	
	U	N/A	N/A	N/A	N/A	N/A	N/A	N/A	N/A	N/A	N/A	N/A	N/A	N/A	N/A	
	R	N/A	1.21	N/A	0.82	N/A	2.67	N/A	1.41	N/A	1.12	N/A	0.77	N/A	0.56	
OTHER MICRONESIA (7)	T	5	1.89	6	3.07	8	1.65	9	1.59	11	1.13	12	0.79	13	0.60	
	U	N/A	N/A	N/A	N/A	N/A	N/A	N/A	N/A	N/A	N/A	N/A	N/A	N/A	N/A	
	R	N/A	1.89	N/A	3.07	N/A	1.65	N/A	1.59	N/A	1.13	N/A	0.79	N/A	0.60	
POLYNESIA	T	239	2.60	310	2.52	399	1.51	464	1.57	543	1.22	614	0.95	675	0.78	
	U	48	5.52	83	4.40	129	2.52	166	2.45	213	2.51	273	2.35	346	2.02	
	R	191	1.71	227	1.74	270	1.00	298	1.05	331	0.29	341	-0.34	329	-0.62	
AMERICAN SAMOA	T	19	1.03	21	2.55	27	1.69	32	1.62	38	1.24	43	0.85	46	0.83	
	U	7	1.87	8	3.35	11	2.55	15	2.77	19	2.50	25	1.92	30	1.71	
	R	12	0.53	13	2.00	16	1.01	17	0.55	18	-0.27	18	-0.82	16	-0.88	
COOK ISLANDS	T	15	1.93	18	1.44	21	-1.49	18	1.20	20	0.55	21	0.32	22	0.24	
	U	5	1.65	6	1.12	6	-1.15	6	2.43	7	2.44	9	2.03	11	1.64	
	R	10	2.04	13	1.57	15	-1.65	12	0.59	13	-0.62	12	-1.14	11	-1.36	

Table 1 (continued)

WORLD TOTAL, REGIONS, COUNTRIES OR AREAS	TOTAL: T URBAN: U RURAL: R	TOTAL POPULATION (IN THOUSANDS) ANNUAL RATE OF GROWTH (PERCENTAGE)														
		1950	RATE	1960	RATE	1970	RATE	1980	RATE	1990	RATE	2000	RATE	2010	RATE	2025
FRENCH POLYNESIA	T	62	2.87	82	2.83	109	3.06	148	2.02	181	1.75	216	1.30	246	0.94	277
	U	17	6.74	34	5.87	61	3.82	89	2.74	117	2.49	150	1.98	183	1.51	222
	R	45	0.84	48	-0.03	48	2.01	59	0.85	64	0.24	66	-0.44	63	-0.81	55
NIUE	T	5	0.65	5	0.57	5	-4.66	3	-0.10	3	0.00	3	-0.03	3	0.00	3
	U	1	0.11	1	0.02	1	-4.86	1	1.12	1	2.41	1	2.31	1	2.03	2
	R	3	0.80	4	0.71	4	-4.61	3	-0.45	2	-0.86	2	-1.22	2	-1.33	2
SAMOA	T	82	3.05	111	2.58	143	0.78	155	0.89	169	0.62	180	0.56	191	0.51	200
	U	11	6.88	21	3.27	29	1.32	33	1.54	39	2.23	48	2.86	64	2.73	91
	R	71	2.33	90	2.40	114	0.64	122	0.70	131	0.10	132	-0.44	126	-0.73	108
TONGA	T	50	2.62	65	2.63	85	1.34	97	2.12	120	1.46	139	1.11	155	0.99	174
	U	6	6.07	12	4.25	18	0.53	19	2.49	25	3.29	34	3.75	50	3.31	77
	R	44	1.99	53	2.23	67	1.56	78	2.02	95	0.93	105	0.08	105	-0.20	98
WALLIS AND FUTUNA ISLANDS	T	7	1.27	8	1.05	9	2.25	11	0.78	12	0.00	12	-0.04	12	0.00	12
	U	N/A	N/A	N/A	N/A	N/A	N/A	N/A	N/A	N/A	N/A	N/A	N/A	N/A	N/A	N/A
	R	N/A	1.27	N/A	1.05	N/A	2.25	N/A	0.78	N/A	0.00	N/A	-0.04	N/A	0.00	N/A
F. 24. U.S.S.R.	T	180075	1.74	214335	1.20	241700	0.94	265493	0.95	291822	0.76	314736	0.69	337120	0.64	368234
	U	70772	3.91	104598	2.71	137047	2.00	167426	1.63	197086	1.21	222395	0.97	244988	0.85	272788
	R	109303	0.04	109737	-0.47	104653	-0.65	98067	-0.34	94736	-0.26	92341	-0.03	92133	0.09	95445

Source: United Nations, *Urban and Rural Population Projections 1950–2025: The 1984 Assessment* (New York, 1986).

Notes: Estimates of population trends are derived by using direct and indirect demographic estimation techniques, and are in a continuous process of revision. Consequently the figures may differ from those published in other United Nations publications. For composition of macro regions and regions and for the methodology relating to calculation of population growth rates, see the source cited above and the introductory chapters of United Nations, *Estimates and Projections of Urban, Rural, and City Populations 1950–2025: The 1982 Assessment* (New York, 1984). Due to rounding, totals may differ slightly from the sum of the parts.

N/A Not available.

* This classification is intended for statistical convenience and does not necessarily express a judgement about the stage reached by a particular country or area in the development process.

** 'More developed regions' includes Northern America, Japan, all regions of Europe, Australia–New Zealand, and the USSR.

† 'Less developed regions' includes all regions of Africa, all regions of Latin America, China, Other East Asia, all regions of South Asia, Melanesia, and Micronesia–Polynesia.

[1] Including Agalesa, Roorigues, and St Brandon.

[2] Including Ascension and Tristan Da Cunha.

[3] The data which relate to the Federal Republic of Germany and the German Democratic Republic include the relevant data relating to Berlin for which separate data have not been supplied. This is without prejudice to any question of status which may be involved.

[4] Including Cocos (Keeling) Islands, Christmas Island, and Norfolk Island.

[5] Also includes Canton and Enderpury Islands.

[6] Comprising the Caroline, Mariana and Marshall Islands.

[7] Including Johnston Island, Midway Islands, Pitcairn, Tokelau, and Wake Islands.

Table 2

Component rates of population growth per thousand: world total, macro regions, and regions, 1980–1985

MACRO REGIONS AND REGIONS	GROWTH RATE	BIRTH RATE	DEATH RATE	NATURAL INCREASE RATE	TRANSFER RATE[1]
(1)	(2)	(3)	(4)	(5)	(6)
WORLD	16.7	27.1	10.5	16.6	0.1
MORE DEVELOPED REGIONS[2,3]	6.4	15.5	9.6	5.9	0.5
LESS DEVELOPED REGIONS[2,4]	20.1	31.0	10.8	20.2	-0.1
AFRICA	29.2	45.9	16.6	29.3	-0.1
WESTERN AFRICA	31.2	49.2	18.3	31.0	0.2
EASTERN AFRICA	31.0	49.4	18.3	31.1	-0.1
NORTHERN AFRICA	26.4	39.3	12.3	27.0	-0.6
MIDDLE AFRICA	27.1	44.7	17.7	27.0	0.1
SOUTHERN AFRICA	25.4	39.6	14.2	25.4	0.0
NORTHERN AMERICA	9.0	15.9	8.9	7.0	2.0
LATIN AMERICA	22.7	31.6	8.2	23.4	-0.7
TROPICAL SOUTH AMERICA	23.5	32.1	8.4	23.6	-0.1
MIDDLE AMERICA (MAINLAND)	26.7	35.4	7.5	27.9	-1.2
TEMPERATE SOUTH AMERICA	15.2	23.7	8.3	15.4	-0.2
CARIBBEAN	15.3	27.0	8.3	18.7	-3.4
EAST ASIA	12.2	18.8	6.6	12.1	0.1
CHINA	12.3	19.0	6.7	12.3	0.0
JAPAN	6.6	13.0	6.5	6.6	0.0
OTHER EAST ASIA	19.1	25.1	6.2	18.9	0.2
SOUTH ASIA	21.6	34.1	12.4	21.7	-0.1
MIDDLE SOUTH ASIA	21.4	34.7	13.3	21.4	0.0
SOUTH EAST ASIA	20.5	31.6	10.8	20.8	-0.3
SOUTH WEST ASIA	27.9	36.8	11.7	26.6	1.3
EUROPE	3.0	13.8	10.9	3.0	0.0
WESTERN EUROPE	0.9	12.2	11.5	0.7	0.2
SOUTHERN EUROPE	4.4	14.0	9.5	4.5	-1.0
EASTERN EUROPE	5.3	16.5	11.2	5.3	0.0
NORTHERN EUROPE	1.5	13.4	11.9	1.6	-0.1
OCEANIA	15.1	20.7	8.3	12.4	2.7
AUSTRALIA & NEW ZEALAND	12.5	15.9	7.8	8.1	4.4
MELANESIA	25.5	37.8	11.1	26.7	-1.2
MICRONESIA AND POLYNESIA	17.5	36.0	5.6	30.4	-12.9
U.S.S.R.	9.7	19.0	9.3	9.6	0.1

Source: United Nations, *World Population Prospects as Assessed in 1984* (New York, 1986).

Notes: These estimated rates are in a continuous process of revision, and the figures may differ from some published in other United Nations publications. For composition of macro regions and regions, see the source cited above.

[1] Transfer rates are assumed net interregional migrations (per 1,000 population).

[2] This classification is intended for statistical convenience and does not necessarily express a judgement about the stage reached by a particular country or area in the development process.

[3] 'More developed regions' includes Northern America, Japan, all regions of Europe, Australia–New Zealand, and the USSR.

[4] 'Less developed regions' includes all regions of Africa, all regions of Latin America, China, Other East Asia, all regions of South Asia, Melanesia, and Micronesia–Polynesia.

Table 3

Estimated and projected percentage of population in urban areas: world total, macro regions, and regions, 1950–2025

MACRO REGIONS AND REGIONS	1950	1960	1970	1980	1990	2000	2010	2025
WORLD TOTAL	29.2	34.2	37.1	39.6	42.6	46.6	51.8	60.1
MORE DEVELOPED REGIONS (*)[1]	53.8	60.5	66.6	70.2	72.5	74.4	76.0	77.8
LESS DEVELOPED REGIONS (+)[1]	17.0	22.2	25.4	29.2	33.6	39.3	46.2	56.5
AFRICA	15.7	18.8	22.5	27.0	32.6	39.0	4.6	55.3
EASTERN AFRICA	5.2	7.3	10.3	15.1	21.5	28.4	35.6	45.9
MIDDLE AFRICA	14.3	18.0	24.8	31.6	39.7	47.7	55.0	64.8
NORTHERN AFRICA	28.7	32.1	36.5	39.9	44.6	50.6	57.0	65.8
SOUTHERN AFRICA	37.9	42.3	44.1	49.6	55.3	60.9	66.1	73.3
WESTERN AFRICA	10.4	13.8	17.6	22.2	27.9	34.9	42.5	53.7
LATIN AMERICA	41.0	49.3	57.4	65.4	72.1	76.8	80.2	84.2
CARIBBEAN	34.1	38.5	45.7	53.2	59.6	64.8	68.9	74.3
CENTRAL AMERICA	39.8	46.7	53.9	60.4	65.9	70.6	74.6	79.9
TEMPERATE SOUTH AMERICA	64.8	72.7	77.9	82.3	86.0	88.6	90.5	92.6
TROPICAL SOUTH AMERICA	35.9	46.1	56.1	66.0	74.0	79.4	82.7	86.4
NORTHERN AMERICA	63.9	69.9	73.8	73.9	74.3	74.9	75.7	77.3
EAST ASIA	16.8	25.0	26.9	28.1	29.5	32.9	38.9	49.3
CHINA	11.0	19.0	20.1	20.4	21.4	25.1	31.8	43.7
JAPAN	50.3	62.5	71.2	76.2	76.9	77.8	78.8	80.6
OTHER EAST ASIA	28.6	36.2	47.4	60.5	71.4	77.9	82.0	85.7
SOUTH ASIA	16.1	18.4	21.3	25.4	30.2	36.5	44.0	55.0
SOUTHEASTERN ASIA	14.8	17.6	20.2	24.0	29.0	35.5	43.1	54.3
SOUTHERN ASIA	15.9	17.3	19.5	23.2	27.6	33.6	40.9	52.2
WESTERN ASIA	23.9	32.9	43.2	51.6	58.2	64.0	69.3	75.9
EUROPE	56.3	60.9	66.7	70.2	72.8	75.1	77.1	79.5
EASTERN EUROPE	41.9	47.9	53.5	59.4	63.5	66.7	69.3	71.9
NORTHERN EUROPE	74.3	76.7	82.4	85.0	86.9	88.3	89.4	90.5
SOUTHERN EUROPE	44.6	49.5	56.2	60.5	64.4	68.1	71.7	76.5
WESTERN EUROPE	66.6	71.4	76.4	78.9	80.2	81.2	82.1	83.2
OCEANIA	61.4	66.3	70.8	71.5	71.0	71.4	72.8	76.3
AUSTRALIA-NEW ZEALAND	74.7	79.8	84.4	85.3	85.3	85.8	86.9	89.2
MELANESIA	5.5	8.4	15.1	18.8	21.8	26.1	32.0	42.4
MICRONESIA-POLYNESIA	19.2	25.8	32.4	38.7	44.8	51.1	57.6	66.4
UNION OF SOVIET SOCIALIST REPUBLICS	39.3	48.8	56.7	63.1	67.5	70.7	72.7	74.1

Source: United Nations, *Urban and Rural Population Projections 1950–2025: The 1984 Assessment* (New York, 1986).

Notes: These estimates are in a continuous process of revision, and the figures may differ from some published in other United Nations publications. For composition of macro regions and regions, see source cited above.

[1] This classification is intended for statistical convenience and does not necessarily express a judgement about the stage reached by a particular country or area in the development process.

* 'More developed regions' includes Northern America, Japan, all regions of Europe, Australia–New Zealand, and the USSR.

† 'Less developed regions' includes all regions of Africa, all regions of Latin America, China, Other East Asia, all regions of South Asia, Melanesia, and Micronesia–Polynesia.

Table 4

Sex–age composition of population: number and percentage, world total, macro regions, and regions, 1980

MACRO REGIONS, REGIONS AND AGE GROUPS	TOTAL POPULATION			MACRO REGIONS, REGIONS AND AGE GROUPS	TOTAL POPULATION		
	MALE	FEMALE	BOTH SEXES		MALE	FEMALE	BOTH SEXES
(1)	(2)	(2)	(4)	(1)	(2)	(2)	(4)
WORLD TOTAL				**AFRICA**			
	POPULATION (IN THOUSANDS)						
					POPULATION (IN THOUSANDS)		
ALL AGES	2,233,705	2,219,453	4,453,158				
0 - 4	278,659	267,659	546,512	ALL AGES	236,010	239,973	475,983
5 - 14	530,376	510,556	1,040,932	0 - 4	44,231	43,653	87,884
15 - 24	433,895	415,641	849,536	5 - 14	63,977	63,435	127,412
25 - 44	563,335	546,927	1,110,262	15 - 24	45,220	45,015	90,235
45 - 64	319,032	330,945	649,977	25 - 44	51,729	53,460	105,189
65+	108,408	147,531	255,939	45 - 64	24,305	26,403	50,708
				65+	6,548	8,006	14,554
	PERCENTAGE DISTRIBUTION						
					PERCENTAGE DISTRIBUTION		
ALL AGES	100.0	100.0	100.0				
0 - 4	12.5	12.1	12.3	ALL AGES	100.0	100.0	100.0
5 - 14	23.8	23.0	23.4	0 - 4	18.7	18.2	18.5
15 - 24	19.4	18.7	19.1	5 - 14	27.1	26.4	26.8
25 - 44	25.2	24.7	24.9	15 - 24	19.2	18.8	18.9
45 - 64	14.3	14.9	14.6	25 - 44	21.9	22.3	22.0
65+	4.9	6.6	5.7	45 - 64	10.3	11.0	10.7
				65+	2.8	3.3	3.1
MORE DEVELOPED REGIONS [1,2]				**NORTHERN AMERICA**			
	POPULATION (IN THOUSANDS)						
					POPULATION (IN THOUSANDS)		
ALL AGES	549,356	586,550	1,135,907				
0 - 4	43,559	41,625	85,184	ALL AGES	122,899	128,988	251,887
5 - 14	90,276	86,048	176,324	0 - 4	9,389	8,973	18,362
15 - 24	97,986	94,075	192,061	5 - 14	19,695	18,841	38,536
25 - 44	158,943	158,286	317,229	15 - 24	24,111	23,434	47,545
45 - 64	109,048	126,270	235,318	25 - 44	34,991	35,517	70,508
65+	49,542	80,249	129,791	45 - 64	23,399	25,664	49,063
				65+	11,312	16,560	27,872
	PERCENTAGE DISTRIBUTION						
					PERCENTAGE DISTRIBUTION		
ALL AGES	100.0	100.0	100.0				
0 - 4	7.9	7.0	7.5	ALL AGES	100.0	100.0	100.0
5 - 14	16.5	14.7	15.5	0 - 4	7.6	7.0	7.3
15 - 24	17.8	16.1	16.9	5 - 14	16.0	14.6	15.3
25 - 44	28.9	27.0	27.9	15 - 24	19.6	18.2	18.9
45 - 64	19.9	21.5	20.8	25 - 44	28.5	27.5	28.0
65+	9.0	13.7	11.4	45 - 64	19.0	19.9	19.5
				65+	9.3	12.8	11.0
LESS DEVELOPED REGIONS [1,3]				**LATIN AMERICA**			
	POPULATION (IN THOUSANDS)				POPULATION (IN THOUSANDS)		
ALL AGES	1,684,348	1,632,903	3,317,251	ALL AGES	181,093	181,037	362,130
0 - 4	235,100	226,228	461,328	0 - 4	26,443	25,730	52,173
5 - 14	440,100	424,508	864,607	5 - 14	45,729	44,760	90,489
15 - 24	335,911	321,565	657,476	15 - 24	37,114	36,559	73,673
25 - 44	404,391	388,642	793,033	25 - 44	43,175	43,263	86,438
45 - 64	209,983	204,676	414,659	45 - 64	21,488	22,362	43,850
65+	58,862	67,286	126,148	65+	7,145	8,363	15,508
	PERCENTAGE DISTRIBUTION				PERCENTAGE DISTRIBUTION		
ALL AGES	100.0	100.0	100.0	ALL AGES	100.0	100.0	100.0
0 - 4	14.0	13.8	13.9	0 - 4	14.6	14.2	14.4
5 - 14	26.1	26.0	26.1	5 - 14	25.3	24.7	25.0
15 - 24	19.9	19.7	19.8	15 - 24	20.5	20.2	20.3
25 - 44	24.0	23.8	23.9	25 - 44	23.8	23.9	23.9
45 - 64	12.5	12.6	12.5	45 - 64	11.9	12.4	12.1
65+	3.5	4.1	3.8	65+	3.9	4.6	4.3

Table 4 (continued)

MACRO REGIONS, REGIONS AND AGE GROUPS	TOTAL POPULATION			MACRO REGIONS, REGIONS AND AGE GROUPS	TOTAL POPULATION		
	MALE	FEMALE	BOTH SEXES		MALE	FEMALE	BOTH SEXES
(1)	(2)	(2)	(4)	(1)	(2)	(2)	(4)

EAST ASIA

POPULATION (IN THOUSANDS)

ALL AGES	601,226	581,283	1,182,510
0 - 4	59,288	57,184	116,472
5 - 14	153,661	149,090	302,751
15 - 24	116,552	109,099	225,651
25 - 44	156,955	145,687	302,642
45 - 64	88,330	86,552	174,882
65+	26,439	33,673	60,112

PERCENTAGE DISTRIBUTION

ALL AGES	100.0	100.0	100.0
0 - 4	9.9	9.8	9.8
5 - 14	25.6	25.6	25.6
15 - 24	19.4	18.8	19.1
25 - 44	26.0	25.1	25.6
45 - 64	14.7	14.9	14.8
65+	4.4	5.8	5.1

SOUTH ASIA

POPULATION (IN THOUSANDS)

ALL AGES	720,735	687,452	1,408,187
0 - 4	109,123	103,477	212,600
5 - 14	185,702	175,779	361,481
15 - 24	144,640	138,276	282,916
25 - 44	170,609	164,283	334,892
45 - 64	87,557	82,370	169,927
65+	23,106	23,265	46,371

PERCENTAGE DISTRIBUTION

ALL AGES	100.0	100.0	100.0
0 - 4	15.1	15.1	15.1
5 - 14	25.8	25.6	25.7
15 - 24	20.1	20.1	20.0
25 - 44	23.7	23.9	23.8
45 - 64	12.1	12.0	12.1
65+	3.2	3.4	3.3

EUROPE

POPULATION (IN THOUSANDS)

ALL AGES	235,981	247,957	483,938
0 - 4	17,218	16,402	33,620
5 - 14	38,080	36,148	74,228
15 - 24	39,042	37,238	76,280
25 - 44	66,879	65,354	132,233
45 - 64	49,637	54,896	104,533
65+	24,124	37,920	63,044

SOUTH ASIA (continued)

PERCENTAGE DISTRIBUTION

ALL AGES	100.0	100.0	100.0
0 - 4	7.3	6.6	6.9
5 - 14	16.2	14.6	15.3
15 - 24	16.5	15.0	15.8
25 - 44	28.4	26.4	27.3
45 - 64	21.0	22.1	21.6
65+	10.6	15.3	13.1

OCEANIA

POPULATION (IN THOUSANDS)

ALL AGES	11,642	11,388	23,030
0 - 4	1,183	1,125	2,308
5 - 14	2,303	2,187	4,490
15 - 24	2,154	2,045	4,199
25 - 44	3,165	3,009	6,174
45 - 64	2,042	1,993	4,035
65+	798	1,027	1,825

PERCENTAGE DISTRIBUTION

ALL AGES	100.0	100.0	100.0
0 - 4	10.2	9.9	10.0
5 - 14	19.8	19.2	19.5
15 - 24	18.5	18.0	18.2
25 - 44	27.2	26.4	26.8
45 - 64	17.5	17.5	17.5
65+	6.8	9.0	8.0

U. S. S. R.

POPULATION (IN THOUSANDS)

ALL AGES	124,118	141,375	265,493
0 - 4	11,785	11,308	23,093
5 - 14	21,230	20,315	41,545
15 - 24	25,062	23,974	49,036
25 - 44	35,834	36,353	72,187
45 - 64	22,272	30,705	52,978
65+	7,935	18,719	26,654

PERCENTAGE DISTRIBUTION

ALL AGES	100.0	100.0	100.0
0 - 4	9.5	8.0	8.7
5 - 14	17.1	14.4	15.6
15 - 24	20.2	17.0	18.5
25 - 44	28.9	25.7	27.2
45 - 64	17.9	21.7	19.9
65+	6.4	13.2	10.1

Source: United Nations, *World Population Prospects as Assessed in 1982* (New York, 1983).

Notes: These estimates are in a continuous process of revision, and the figures may differ from some published in other United Nations publications. For composition of macro regions and regions, see the source cited above.

[1] This classification is intended for statistical convenience and does not necessarily express a judgement about the stage reached by a particular country or area in the development process.

[2] 'More developed regions' includes Northern America, Japan, all regions of Europe, Australia–New Zealand, and the USSR.

[3] 'Less developed regions' includes all regions of Africa, all regions of Latin America, China, Other East Asia, all regions of South Asia, Melanesia, and Micronesia–Polynesia.

Table 5

Estimated and projected population in urban agglomerations of 100,000 inhabitants and over as of 1980: and number of agglomerations by size category: world total, macro regions, and regions, 1950–2025 (medium variant, in thousands)

MACRO REGIONS, REGIONS AND SIZE CATEGORY OF URBAN AGGLOMERATIONS	ESTIMATED AND PROJECTED POPULATION IN URBAN AGGLOMERATIONS OF 100,000 INHABITANTS AND OVER AND NUMBER OF URBAN AGGLOMERATIONS							
	1950	1960	1970	1980	1985	1990	2000	2025
(1)	(2)	(3)	(4)	(5)	(6)	(7)	(8)	(9)
WORLD TOTAL								
URBAN POPULATION	735,232	1,013,115	1,360,974	1,775,752	2,013,324	2,286,090	2,951,633	5,107,434
IN URBAN AGGLOMERATIONS:								
4,000,000+	87,825	136,262	186,922	281,389	341,583	405,557	587,267	1,255,062
NUMBER OF AGGLOMERATIONS	13	19	23	35	42	48	66	135
2,000,000 - 3,999,999	46,955	66,966	109,242	140,890	154,482	197,966	290,335	493,175
NUMBER OF AGGLOMERATIONS	17	26	39	51	56	72	106	182
1,000,000 - 1,999,999	65,470	95,930	136,070	182,337	219,128	242,702	282,645	. .
NUMBER OF AGGLOMERATIONS	48	69	98	136	158	350	402	. .
500,000 - 999,999	69,551	94,764	120,049	176,331	207,274	195,991	. .	. .
NUMBER OF AGGLOMERATIONS	101	136	173	258	300	557	. .	. .
250,000 - 499,999	66,050	90,210	133,148	170,731	188,272	. .	. .	. .
NUMBER OF AGGLOMERATIONS	192	263	384	496	539	. .	. .	. .
100,000 - 249,999	86,716	115,350	145,548	148,142	. .	. .	. .	. .
NUMBER OF AGGLOMERATIONS	575	749	930	910	. .	. .	. .	. .
REST OF URBAN	312,665	413,634	529,996	675,932	. .	. .	. .	. .
MORE DEVELOPED REGIONS[1,2]								
URBAN POPULATION	445,669	569,785	695,428	801,957	849,061	896,812	992,148	1,192,400
IN URBAN AGGLOMERATIONS:								
4,000,000+	55,781	80,688	98,945	113,253	119,458	125,302	132,514	152,921
NUMBER OF AGGLOMERATIONS	8	10	11	13	14	15	16	21
2,000,000 - 3,999,999	30,100	41,635	55,506	63,670	70,838	78,416	93,825	101,104
NUMBER OF AGGLOMERATIONS	11	16	20	23	26	29	34	37
1,000,000 - 1,999,999	39,869	50,946	71,583	91,131	95,892	94,570	111,132	134,678
NUMBER OF AGGLOMERATIONS	28	36	52	67	70	67	79	95
500,000 - 999,999	40,474	53,150	65,079	74,975	83,257	99,164	109,654	. .
NUMBER OF AGGLOMERATIONS	59	77	93	111	123	143	159	. .
250,000 - 499,999	41,356	52,316	64,829	82,285	90,997	100,805	. .	. .
NUMBER OF AGGLOMERATIONS	121	151	189	241	265	294	. .	. .
100,000 - 249,999	49,634	65,352	81,144	81,888	. .	. .	. .	. .
NUMBER OF AGGLOMERATIONS	333	429	520	496	. .	. .	. .	. .
REST OF URBAN	188,456	225,697	258,343	294,755	. .	. .	. .	. .

Table 5 (continued)

MACRO REGIONS, REGIONS AND SIZE CATEGORY OF URBAN AGGLOMERATIONS	ESTIMATED AND PROJECTED POPULATION IN URBAN AGGLOMERATIONS OF 100,000 INHABITANTS AND OVER AND NUMBER OF URBAN AGGLOMERATIONS							
	1950	1960	1970	1980	1985	1990	2000	2025
(1)	(2)	(3)	(4)	(5)	(6)	(7)	(8)	(9)
LESS DEVELOPED REGIONS[1,3]								
URBAN POPULATION	289,563	443,330	665,540	973,795	1,164,264	1,389,278	1,959,485	3,915,034
IN URBAN AGGLOMERATIONS:								
4,000,000+	32,045	55,574	87,977	168,137	222,125	280,255	454,753	1,102,142
NUMBER OF AGGLOMERATIONS	5	9	12	22	28	33	50	114
2,000,000 - 3,999,999	16,855	25,331	53,735	77,220	83,644	119,550	196,509	392,071
NUMBER OF AGGLOMERATIONS	6	10	19	28	30	43	72	145
1,000,000 - 1,999,999	25,601	44,984	64,487	91,206	123,236	152,161	215,228	322,438
NUMBER OF AGGLOMERATIONS	20	33	46	69	88	111	157	227
500,000 - 999,999	29,077	41,614	54,971	101,356	124,017	143,538	172,990	..
NUMBER OF AGGLOMERATIONS	42	59	80	147	177	207	243	..
250,000 - 499,999	24,694	37,894	68,319	88,446	97,275	..	..	..
NUMBER OF AGGLOMERATIONS	71	112	195	255	274	..	..	..
100,000 - 249,999	37,083	49,997	64,404	66,254	..	..	..	..
NUMBER OF AGGLOMERATIONS	242	320	410	414	..	..	..	..
REST OF URBAN	124,210	187,936	271,653	381,177	..	..	..	..
AFRICA								
URBAN POPULATION	32,899	51,062	81,750	136,787	177,402	228,886	370,247	957,898
IN URBAN AGGLOMERATIONS:								
4,000,000+	0	0	5,406	7,290	12,892	20,515	73,431	324,719
NUMBER OF AGGLOMERATIONS	0	0	1	1	2	3	11	36
2,000,000 - 3,999,999	2,451	3,727	2,015	10,732	16,043	31,661	49,649	101,212
NUMBER OF AGGLOMERATIONS	1	1	1	4	6	11	18	37
1,000,000 - 1,999,999	2,135	3,926	8,045	19,477	26,663	30,787	41,603	48,106
NUMBER OF AGGLOMERATIONS	2	3	6	15	18	21	30	35
500,000 - 999,999	2,608	4,926	6,648	15,888	22,112	25,469	30,850	..
NUMBER OF AGGLOMERATIONS	4	7	10	24	32	36	43	..
250,000 - 499,999	1,908	4,042	12,170	15,815	17,030	15,958	..	..
NUMBER OF AGGLOMERATIONS	5	12	36	46	49	42	..	..
100,000 - 249,999	5,943	10,086	11,956	9,763	..	..	..	..
NUMBER OF AGGLOMERATIONS	38	63	72	57	..	..	..	..
REST OF URBAN	17,855	24,354	35,509	57,821	..	..	..	..

Table 5 (continued)

MACRO REGIONS, REGIONS AND SIZE CATEGORY OF URBAN AGGLOMERATIONS	ESTIMATED AND PROJECTED POPULATION IN URBAN AGGLOMERATIONS OF 100,000 INHABITANTS AND OVER AND NUMBER OF URBAN AGGLOMERATIONS							
	1950	1960	1970	1980	1985	1990	2000	2025
(1)	(2)	(3)	(4)	(5)	(6)	(7)	(8)	(9)
EASTERN AFRICA								
URBAN POPULATION	3,158	5,587	10,616	21,436	30,299	42,220	78,269	254,228
IN URBAN AGGLOMERATIONS:								
4,000,000+	0	0	0	0	0	0	17,497	97,769
NUMBER OF AGGLOMERATIONS	0	0	0	0	0	0	3	10
2,000,000 - 3,999,999	0	0	0	0	4,489	9,155	9,050	8,983
NUMBER OF AGGLOMERATIONS	0	0	0	0	2	3	3	3
1,000,000 - 1,999,999	0	0	0	4,206	4,216	5,817	8,560	7,393
NUMBER OF AGGLOMERATIONS	0	0	0	3	3	4	6	5
500,000 - 999,999	0	0	1,355	3,508	4,701	4,422	3,597	..
NUMBER OF AGGLOMERATIONS	0	0	2	5	7	6	5	..
250,000 - 499,999	0	385	2,676	2,532	1,397	1,610	..	..
NUMBER OF AGGLOMERATIONS	0	1	8	7	4	4	..	..
100,000 - 249,999	513	1,667	1,295	1,201	..	..	..	..
NUMBER OF AGGLOMERATIONS	3	10	8	8	..	..	..	..
REST OF URBAN	2,645	3,535	5,290	9,989	..	..	..	..
MIDDLE AFRICA								
URBAN POPULATION	4,198	6,355	10,561	18,769	24,551	31,644	50,187	125,189
IN URBAN AGGLOMERATIONS:								
4,000,000+	0	0	0	0	4,347	5,761	8,905	34,392
NUMBER OF AGGLOMERATIONS	0	0	0	0	1	1	1	3
2,000,000 - 3,999,999	0	0	0	3,151	0	2,191	6,641	17,124
NUMBER OF AGGLOMERATIONS	0	0	0	1	0	1	2	6
1,000,000 - 1,999,999	0	0	1,367	2,161	3,022	2,991	5,783	10,444
NUMBER OF AGGLOMERATIONS	0	0	1	2	2	2	4	7
500,000 - 999,999	0	560	0	578	3,137	4,198	5,820	..
NUMBER OF AGGLOMERATIONS	0	1	0	1	5	6	8	..
250,000 - 499,999	0	0	2,077	3,298	2,741	2,324	..	..
NUMBER OF AGGLOMERATIONS	0	0	6	9	8	6	..	..
100,000 - 249,999	869	1,933	1,694	1,042	..	..	..	..
NUMBER OF AGGLOMERATIONS	5	11	11	6	..	..	..	..
REST OF URBAN	3,329	3,861	5,423	8,538	..	..	..	..

Table 5 (continued)

MACRO REGIONS, REGIONS AND SIZE CATEGORY OF URBAN AGGLOMERATIONS	ESTIMATED AND PROJECTED POPULATION IN URBAN AGGLOMERATIONS OF 100,000 INHABITANTS AND OVER AND NUMBER OF URBAN AGGLOMERATIONS							
	1950	1960	1970	1980	1985	1990	2000	2025
(1)	(2)	(3)	(4)	(5)	(6)	(7)	(8)	(9)
NORTHERN AFRICA								
URBAN POPULATION	12,667	19,514	30,706	47,637	59,592	73,787	107,841	213,304
IN URBAN AGGLOMERATIONS:								
4,000,000+	0	0	5,406	7,290	8,545	9,959	26,752	54,439
NUMBER OF AGGLOMERATIONS	0	0	1	1	1	1	4	6
2,000,000 - 3,999,999	2,451	3,727	2,015	4,787	5,651	9,363	4,800	19,217
NUMBER OF AGGLOMERATIONS	1	1	1	2	2	3	2	8
1,000,000 - 1,999,999	1,031	2,608	2,575	3,759	5,922	5,901	10,590	15,182
NUMBER OF AGGLOMERATIONS	1	2	2	3	4	4	8	12
500,000 - 999,999	721	1,473	1,953	3,018	4,995	6,301	8,972	..
NUMBER OF AGGLOMERATIONS	1	2	3	5	8	9	14	..
250,000 - 499,999	1,211	2,085	3,673	4,838	5,368	6,288	..	..
NUMBER OF AGGLOMERATIONS	3	7	12	14	16	17	..	..
100,000 - 249,999	2,595	3,030	3,494	3,381	..	..	..	..
NUMBER OF AGGLOMERATIONS	17	19	21	18	..	..	..	..
REST OF URBAN	4,659	6,591	11,590	20,563	..	..	..	..
SOUTHERN AFRICA								
URBAN POPULATION	6,540	8,767	11,369	16,107	19,359	23,304	33,257	66,595
IN URBAN AGGLOMERATIONS:								
4,000,000+	0	0	0	0	0	0	5,229	9,042
NUMBER OF AGGLOMERATIONS	0	0	0	0	0	0	2	2
2,000,000 - 3,999,999	0	0	0	0	0	2,097	4,560	8,087
NUMBER OF AGGLOMERATIONS	0	0	0	0	0	1	3	3
1,000,000 - 1,999,999	1,104	1,318	2,660	4,256	4,732	4,359	1,150	3,290
NUMBER OF AGGLOMERATIONS	1	1	2	3	3	3	2	3
500,000 - 999,999	1,354	1,670	1,476	1,479	1,737	924	..	..
NUMBER OF AGGLOMERATIONS	2	2	2	2	2	1	..	..
250,000 - 499,999	338	813	498	324	912	1,651	..	..
NUMBER OF AGGLOMERATIONS	1	2	1	1	3	5	..	..
100,000 - 249,999	724	937	1,317	1,479	..	..	..	..
NUMBER OF AGGLOMERATIONS	5	6	8	8	..	..	..	..
REST OF URBAN	3,020	4,029	5,417	8,569	..	..	..	..

Table 5 (continued)

MACRO REGIONS, REGIONS AND SIZE CATEGORY OF URBAN AGGLOMERATIONS	ESTIMATED AND PROJECTED POPULATION IN URBAN AGGLOMERATIONS OF 100,000 INHABITANTS AND OVER AND NUMBER OF URBAN AGGLOMERATIONS							
	1950	1960	1970	1980	1985	1990	2000	2025
(1)	(2)	(3)	(4)	(5)	(6)	(7)	(8)	(9)
WESTERN AFRICA								
URBAN POPULATION	6,336	10,838	18,499	32,839	43,601	57,930	100,691	298,581
IN URBAN AGGLOMERATIONS:								
4,000,000+	0	0	0	0	0	4,795	20,277	129,076
NUMBER OF AGGLOMERATIONS	0	0	0	0	0	1	3	15
2,000,000 - 3,999,999	0	0	0	2,794	5,903	8,855	23,928	47,801
NUMBER OF AGGLOMERATIONS	0	0	0	1	2	3	9	17
1,000,000 - 1,999,999	0	0	1,444	5,095	8,771	11,720	12,110	11,797
NUMBER OF AGGLOMERATIONS	0	0	1	4	6	8	9	8
500,000 - 999,999	533	1,223	1,864	7,305	7,543	9,624	11,310	..
NUMBER OF AGGLOMERATIONS	1	2	3	11	10	14	14	..
250,000 - 499,999	359	759	3,247	4,823	6,612	4,085	..	..
NUMBER OF AGGLOMERATIONS	1	2	9	15	18	10	..	..
100,000 - 249,999	1,243	2,519	4,155	2,661	..	..	..	..
NUMBER OF AGGLOMERATIONS	8	17	24	17	..	..	..	..
REST OF URBAN	4,201	6,338	7,789	10,161	..	..	..	..
LATIN AMERICA								
URBAN POPULATION	67,707	106,909	162,891	236,507	279,675	325,748	421,335	662,147
IN URBAN AGGLOMERATIONS:								
4,000,000+	5,251	22,052	33,089	51,699	73,984	89,016	118,448	196,666
NUMBER OF AGGLOMERATIONS	1	4	4	5	8	9	11	21
2,000,000 - 3,999,999	9,285	0	10,380	23,214	18,981	27,493	42,821	52,585
NUMBER OF AGGLOMERATIONS	3	0	4	8	7	10	15	19
1,000,000 - 1,999,999	4,688	11,214	14,043	17,611	26,099	30,857	42,696	63,694
NUMBER OF AGGLOMERATIONS	4	8	10	13	19	23	31	45
500,000 - 999,999	3,444	7,873	11,656	19,757	23,663	28,997	32,666	..
NUMBER OF AGGLOMERATIONS	5	12	17	27	34	43	45	..
250,000 - 499,999	6,049	7,008	12,807	19,727	20,006	20,820	..	..
NUMBER OF AGGLOMERATIONS	17	20	37	56	56	61	..	..
100,000 - 249,999	6,293	10,234	15,884	15,918	..	..	..	..
NUMBER OF AGGLOMERATIONS	41	70	104	96	..	..	..	..
REST OF URBAN	32,696	48,528	65,030	88,581	..	..	..	..

Table 5 (continued)

MACRO REGIONS, REGIONS AND SIZE CATEGORY OF URBAN AGGLOMERATIONS	ESTIMATED AND PROJECTED POPULATION IN URBAN AGGLOMERATIONS OF 100,000 INHABITANTS AND OVER AND NUMBER OF URBAN AGGLOMERATIONS							
	1950	1960	1970	1980	1985	1990	2000	2025
(1)	(2)	(3)	(4)	(5)	(6)	(7)	(8)	(9)
CARIBBEAN								
URBAN POPULATION	5,765	7,890	11,302	15,448	17,683	20,282	26,140	42,717
IN URBAN AGGLOMERATIONS:								
4,000,000+	0	0	0	0	0	0	0	10,646
NUMBER OF AGGLOMERATIONS	0	0	0	0	0	0	0	2
2,000,000 - 3,999,999	0	0	0	0	2,052	4,535	7,843	4,781
NUMBER OF AGGLOMERATIONS	0	0	0	0	1	2	3	2
1,000,000 - 1,999,999	1,220	1,450	1,752	4,606	4,306	2,840	4,131	3,493
NUMBER OF AGGLOMERATIONS	1	1	1	3	3	2	3	2
500,000 - 999,999	0	546	2,134	1,527	1,461	1,734	0	..
NUMBER OF AGGLOMERATIONS	0	1	3	2	2	2	0	..
250,000 - 499,999	797	899	1,000	824	630	681	..	..
NUMBER OF AGGLOMERATIONS	2	2	3	2	2	2	..	..
100,000 - 249,999	878	995	985	1,537	..	..	..	..
NUMBER OF AGGLOMERATIONS	6	6	7	10	..	..	..	..
REST OF URBAN	2,870	4,001	5,432	6,954	..	..	..	..
CENTRAL AMERICA								
URBAN POPULATION	14,563	23,119	36,742	55,984	67,223	79,579	106,691	179,688
IN URBAN AGGLOMERATIONS:								
4,000,000+	0	5,220	9,152	15,009	18,123	25,365	31,528	49,621
NUMBER OF AGGLOMERATIONS	0	1	1	1	1	2	2	4
2,000,000 - 3,999,999	3,054	0	0	4,864	5,969	3,035	6,048	10,544
NUMBER OF AGGLOMERATIONS	1	0	0	2	2	1	2	4
1,000,000 - 1,999,999	0	0	2,878	1,030	2,259	6,013	13,120	22,327
NUMBER OF AGGLOMERATIONS	0	0	2	1	2	5	10	15
500,000 - 999,999	0	2,147	1,272	4,797	8,880	9,776	..	..
NUMBER OF AGGLOMERATIONS	0	3	2	7	13	14	..	..
250,000 - 499,999	1,201	1,707	4,320	7,165	5,366	5,040	..	..
NUMBER OF AGGLOMERATIONS	3	6	12	20	15	14	..	..
100,000 - 249,999	1,978	2,365	3,464	1,500	..	..	..	..
NUMBER OF AGGLOMERATIONS	13	15	21	8	..	..	..	..
REST OF URBAN	8,330	11,679	15,657	21,619	..	..	..	..

Table 5 (continued)

MACRO REGIONS, REGIONS AND SIZE CATEGORY OF URBAN AGGLOMERATIONS	ESTIMATED AND PROJECTED POPULATION IN URBAN AGGLOMERATIONS OF 100,000 INHABITANTS AND OVER AND NUMBER OF URBAN AGGLOMERATIONS							
	1950	1960	1970	1980	1985	1990	2000	2025
(1)	(2)	(3)	(4)	(5)	(6)	(7)	(8)	(9)
TEMPERATE SOUTH AMERICA								
URBAN POPULATION	16,513	22,357	28,139	34,802	38,473	42,152	49,074	64,773
IN URBAN AGGLOMERATIONS:								
4,000,000+	5,251	6,027	8,545	10,062	15,317	16,634	18,790	21,148
NUMBER OF AGGLOMERATIONS	1	1	1	1	2	2	2	2
2,000,000 - 3,999,999	0	0	2,889	3,932	0	0	0	0
NUMBER OF AGGLOMERATIONS	0	0	1	1	0	0	0	0
1,000,000 - 1,999,999	2,415	3,102	1,212	1,178	3,323	3,534	3,987	6,970
NUMBER OF AGGLOMERATIONS	2	2	1	1	3	3	3	5
500,000 - 999,999	546	1,267	1,633	3,635	1,858	2,603	3,127	..
NUMBER OF AGGLOMERATIONS	1	2	2	5	3	4	4	..
250,000 - 499,999	721	1,306	2,199	2,063	2,346	2,641	..	..
NUMBER OF AGGLOMERATIONS	2	4	6	7	7	8	..	..
100,000 - 249,999	1,502	1,728	2,188	2,039	..	..	..	..
NUMBER OF AGGLOMERATIONS	9	12	14	12	..	..	..	..
REST OF URBAN	6,077	8,026	9,473	11,894	..	..	..	..
TROPICAL SOUTH AMERICA								
URBAN POPULATION	30,866	53,543	86,707	130,273	156,297	183,734	239,429	374,970
IN URBAN AGGLOMERATIONS:								
4,000,000+	0	9,904	15,392	26,629	40,544	47,017	68,130	115,251
NUMBER OF AGGLOMERATIONS	0	2	2	3	5	5	7	13
2,000,000 - 3,999,999	6,232	0	7,491	14,418	10,960	19,923	28,930	37,259
NUMBER OF AGGLOMERATIONS	2	0	3	5	4	7	10	13
1,000,000 - 1,999,999	1,053	6,662	8,201	10,797	16,211	18,470	21,458	30,904
NUMBER OF AGGLOMERATIONS	1	5	6	8	11	13	15	23
500,000 - 999,999	2,898	3,913	6,618	9,798	11,464	14,883	20,748	..
NUMBER OF AGGLOMERATIONS	4	6	10	13	16	23	29	..
250,000 - 499,999*	3,331	3,096	5,289	9,675	11,664	12,458	..	..
NUMBER OF AGGLOMERATIONS	10	8	16	27	32	37	..	..
100,000 - 249,999	1,934	5,147	9,247	10,843	..	..	..	..
NUMBER OF AGGLOMERATIONS	13	37	62	66	..	..	..	..
REST OF URBAN	15,419	24,821	34,469	48,114	..	..	..	..

Table 5 (continued)

MACRO REGIONS, REGIONS AND SIZE CATEGORY OF URBAN AGGLOMERATIONS	ESTIMATED AND PROJECTED POPULATION IN URBAN AGGLOMERATIONS OF 100,000 INHABITANTS AND OVER AND NUMBER OF URBAN AGGLOMERATIONS							
	1950	1960	1970	1980	1985	1990	2000	2025
(1)	(2)	(3)	(4)	(5)	(6)	(7)	(8)	(9)
NORTHERN AMERICA								
URBAN POPULATION	106,105	138,877	167,211	185,980	195,654	206,816	232,161	297,839
IN URBAN AGGLOMERATIONS:								
4,000,000+	21,458	26,787	35,531	36,060	36,356	36,889	38,397	58,262
NUMBER OF AGGLOMERATIONS	3	3	4	4	4	4	4	8
2,000,000 - 3,999,999	10,037	14,151	19,467	23,163	24,130	35,560	41,268	39,416
NUMBER OF AGGLOMERATIONS	4	5	7	8	8	12	14	14
1,000,000 - 1,999,999	10,270	16,070	23,350	28,206	31,108	24,942	28,823	39,501
NUMBER OF AGGLOMERATIONS	8	11	17	20	21	17	20	29
500,000 - 999,999	9,371	13,084	15,502	19,809	22,958	27,285	28,310	..
NUMBER OF AGGLOMERATIONS	14	19	23	30	34	39	39	..
250,000 - 499,999	9,678	13,638	15,444	17,046	16,417	18,053	..	..
NUMBER OF AGGLOMERATIONS	27	38	43	49	46	52	..	..
100,000 - 249,999	11,977	14,634	16,547	17,497	..	..	..	..
NUMBER OF AGGLOMERATIONS	78	93	104	113	..	..	..	..
REST OF URBAN	33,314	40,513	41,371	44,200	..	..	..	..
EAST ASIA								
URBAN POPULATION	119,134	185,318	258,560	330,646	361,503	398,106	503,148	868,658
IN URBAN AGGLOMERATIONS:								
4,000,000+	29,103	40,426	54,507	66,606	73,434	81,138	96,003	168,149
NUMBER OF AGGLOMERATIONS	4	5	6	7	8	9	10	18
2,000,000 - 3,999,999	6,057	12,011	13,794	19,749	22,095	25,843	45,936	92,974
NUMBER OF AGGLOMERATIONS	2	5	5	7	8	10	18	35
1,000,000 - 1,999,999	9,019	18,439	27,984	35,915	37,857	41,072	48,251	78,707
NUMBER OF AGGLOMERATIONS	7	14	20	26	27	30	36	54
500,000 - 999,999	13,540	17,059	20,465	29,064	33,674	39,029	48,900	..
NUMBER OF AGGLOMERATIONS	20	24	29	42	48	56	70	..
250,000 - 499,999	6,025	11,498	21,057	27,094	29,532	28,385	..	..
NUMBER OF AGGLOMERATIONS	19	36	62	78	81	77	..	..
100,000 - 249,999	13,728	15,450	15,693	15,750	..	..	..	..
NUMBER OF AGGLOMERATIONS	91	94	96	97	..	..	..	..
REST OF URBAN	41,662	70,436	105,061	136,469	..	..	..	..

Table 5 (continued)

MACRO REGIONS, REGIONS AND SIZE CATEGORY OF URBAN AGGLOMERATIONS	ESTIMATED AND PROJECTED POPULATION IN URBAN AGGLOMERATIONS OF 100,000 INHABITANTS AND OVER AND NUMBER OF URBAN AGGLOMERATIONS							
	1950	1960	1970	1980	1985	1990	2000	2025
(1)	(2)	(3)	(4)	(5)	(6)	(7)	(8)	(9)
CHINA								
URBAN POPULATION	67,627	112,115	159,977	203,677	223,680	249,595	333,669	665,015
IN URBAN AGGLOMERATIONS:								
4,000,000+	22,366	23,990	26,569	28,592	28,871	34,162	45,205	116,445
NUMBER OF AGGLOMERATIONS	3	3	3	3	3	4	5	13
2,000,000 - 3,999,999	2,229	6,881	10,260	16,560	18,027	19,423	32,126	71,023
NUMBER OF AGGLOMERATIONS	1	3	4	6	6	7	12	26
1,000,000 - 1,999,999	4,117	13,296	20,316	25,393	30,049	31,287	37,390	66,037
NUMBER OF AGGLOMERATIONS	3	10	15	19	22	23	28	45
500,000 - 999,999	11,109	15,756	17,523	24,948	25,890	29,240	34,162	..
NUMBER OF AGGLOMERATIONS	17	22	25	36	37	42	48	..
250,000 - 499,999	4,563	8,748	14,616	14,261	13,734	11,391	..	..
NUMBER OF AGGLOMERATIONS	14	28	42	40	36	29	..	..
100,000 - 249,999	8,925	7,111	3,538	240	..	..	..	..
NUMBER OF AGGLOMERATIONS	57	39	16	1	..	..	..	..
REST OF URBAN	14,319	36,333	67,155	93,682	..	..	..	..
JAPAN								
URBAN POPULATION	42,065	58,812	74,296	88,909	91,834	94,588	101,242	110,218
IN URBAN AGGLOMERATIONS:								
4,000,000+	6,737	16,436	22,520	24,996	25,218	24,970	24,813	22,616
NUMBER OF AGGLOMERATIONS	1	2	2	2	2	2	2	2
2,000,000 - 3,999,999	3,828	0	0	0	4,068	4,153	6,406	6,444
NUMBER OF AGGLOMERATIONS	1	0	0	0	2	2	3	3
1,000,000 - 1,999,999	1,001	3,974	4,751	6,526	2,859	3,044	2,334	2,404
NUMBER OF AGGLOMERATIONS	1	3	3	4	2	2	2	2
500,000 - 999,999	1,891	0	1,392	1,946	2,676	3,482	7,476	..
NUMBER OF AGGLOMERATIONS	2	0	2	3	4	5	12	..
250,000 - 499,999	789	1,758	3,902	7,785	9,978	12,926	..	..
NUMBER OF AGGLOMERATIONS	3	5	13	24	29	37	..	..
100,000 - 249,999	3,496	6,572	9,181	11,993	..	..	..	..
NUMBER OF AGGLOMERATIONS	25	44	61	73	..	..	..	..
REST OF URBAN	24,322	30,071	32,549	..	..	..	..	..

Table 5 (continued)

MACRO REGIONS, REGIONS AND SIZE CATEGORY OF URBAN AGGLOMERATIONS	ESTIMATED AND PROJECTED POPULATION IN URBAN AGGLOMERATIONS OF 100,000 INHABITANTS AND OVER AND NUMBER OF URBAN AGGLOMERATIONS							
	1950	1960	1970	1980	1985	1990	2000	2025
(1)	(2)	(3)	(4)	(5)	(6)	(7)	(8)	(9)
OTHER EAST ASIA								
URBAN POPULATION	9,442	14,392	24,287	38,061	45,989	53,923	68,237	93,424
IN URBAN AGGLOMERATIONS:								
4,000,000+	0	0	5,417	13,017	19,345	22,006	25,985	29,088
NUMBER OF AGGLOMERATIONS	0	0	1	2	2	3	3	3
2,000,000 - 3,999,999	0	5,130	3,534	3,189	0	2,267	7,404	15,506
NUMBER OF AGGLOMERATIONS	0	2	1	1	0	1	3	6
1,000,000 - 1,999,999	3,901	1,169	2,917	3,996	4,950	6,741	8,527	10,266
NUMBER OF AGGLOMERATIONS	3	1	2	3	3	5	6	7
500,000 - 999,999	540	1,303	1,550	2,169	5,108	6,307	7,263	..
NUMBER OF AGGLOMERATIONS	1	2	2	3	7	9	10	..
250,000 - 499,999	672	991	2,539	5,048	5,820	4,068	..	..
NUMBER OF AGGLOMERATIONS	2	3	7	14	16	11	..	..
100,000 - 249,999	1,308	1,767	2,973	3,517	..	..	..	..
NUMBER OF AGGLOMERATIONS	9	11	19	23	..	..	..	..
REST OF URBAN	3,021	4,032	5,357	7,125	..	..	..	..
SOUTH ASIA								
URBAN POPULATION	111,701	158,507	235,928	357,620	436,127	529,442	763,580	1,531,199
IN URBAN AGGLOMERATIONS:								
4,000,000+	4,428	9,532	17,495	67,537	87,032	114,557	191,684	435,224
NUMBER OF AGGLOMERATIONS	1	2	3	11	12	14	20	41
2,000,000 - 3,999,999	2,890	9,592	27,547	23,525	30,594	38,706	64,509	151,745
NUMBER OF AGGLOMERATIONS	1	4	9	9	11	14	24	57
1,000,000 - 1,999,999	10,760	15,379	19,166	24,729	35,476	52,488	85,012	133,252
NUMBER OF AGGLOMERATIONS	8	11	13	19	26	39	62	94
500,000 - 999,999	11,376	11,756	17,594	38,593	47,244	53,524	68,050	..
NUMBER OF AGGLOMERATIONS	15	16	26	57	67	77	97	..
250,000 - 499,999	11,501	17,104	26,186	33,594	40,684	42,949	..	..
NUMBER OF AGGLOMERATIONS	33	49	73	99	117	120	..	..
100,000 - 249,999	14,614	20,800	30,053	36,550	..	..	..	..
NUMBER OF AGGLOMERATIONS	97	137	199	235	..	..	..	..
REST OF URBAN	56,132	74,344	97,888	133,091	..	..	..	..

Table 5 (continued)

MACRO REGIONS, REGIONS AND SIZE CATEGORY OF URBAN AGGLOMERATIONS	ESTIMATED AND PROJECTED POPULATION IN URBAN AGGLOMERATIONS OF 100,000 INHABITANTS AND OVER AND NUMBER OF URBAN AGGLOMERATIONS							
	1950	1960	1970	1980	1985	1990	2000	2025
(1)	(2)	(3)	(4)	(5)	(6)	(7)	(8)	(9)
SOUTHEASTERN ASIA								
URBAN POPULATION	26,510	39,204	57,456	85,576	104,377	127,066	185,603	374,252
IN URBAN AGGLOMERATIONS:								
4,000,000+	0	0	4,480	17,232	20,378	24,085	43,379	96,079
NUMBER OF AGGLOMERATIONS	0	0	1	3	3	3	5	9
2,000,000 - 3,999,999	0	7,316	9,145	6,699	9,673	13,772	16,536	24,036
NUMBER OF AGGLOMERATIONS	0	3	3	3	4	5	6	9
1,000,000 - 1,999,999	5,831	2,761	5,734	5,729	4,857	6,807	9,225	25,548
NUMBER OF AGGLOMERATIONS	4	2	4	4	3	5	7	18
500,000 - 999,999	4,517	4,262	3,226	5,750	10,036	10,889	14,697	..
NUMBER OF AGGLOMERATIONS	6	5	5	9	15	16	20	..
250,000 - 499,999	4,208	5,052	5,830	7,280	7,486	9,052	..	..
NUMBER OF AGGLOMERATIONS	12	14	16	21	23	27	..	..
100,000 - 249,999	3,010	4,203	7,127	7,816	..	..	..	..
NUMBER OF AGGLOMERATIONS	22	27	48	48	..	..	..	..
REST OF URBAN	8,944	15,609	21,913	35,070	..	..	..	..
SOUTHERN ASIA								
URBAN POPULATION	75,063	100,913	146,590	220,951	*268,538*	325,027	467,687	948,322
IN URBAN AGGLOMERATIONS:								
4,000,000+	4,428	9,532	13,015	39,246	32,619	73,099	119,080	270,584
NUMBER OF AGGLOMERATIONS	1	2	2	6	7	9	12	24
2,000,000 - 3,999,999	2,890	2,276	13,115	14,606	18,190	17,228	27,595	104,986
NUMBER OF AGGLOMERATIONS	1	1	4	5	6	6	10	40
1,000,000 - 1,999,999	4,930	10,140	11,093	10,577	17,745	33,176	62,462	76,518
NUMBER OF AGGLOMERATIONS	4	7	7	8	14	26	44	54
500,000 - 999,999	5,312	4,971	10,546	28,098	31,020	32,642	40,273	..
NUMBER OF AGGLOMERATIONS	7	7	16	41	42	46	57	..
250,000 - 499,999	5,651	10,623	15,972	18,080	24,124	25,673	..	..
NUMBER OF AGGLOMERATIONS	16	31	44	54	69	72	..	..
100,000 - 249,999	10,220	12,551	18,359	25,811	..	..	..	..
NUMBER OF AGGLOMERATIONS	65	84	124	171	..	..	..	..
REST OF URBAN	41,632	50,820	64,491	84,533	..	..	..	..

Table 5 (continued)

MACRO REGIONS, REGIONS AND SIZE CATEGORY OF URBAN AGGLOMERATIONS	ESTIMATED AND PROJECTED POPULATION IN URBAN AGGLOMERATIONS OF 100,000 INHABITANTS AND OVER AND NUMBER OF URBAN AGGLOMERATIONS							
	1950	1960	1970	1980	1985	1990	2000	2025
(1)	(2)	(3)	(4)	(5)	(6)	(7)	(8)	(9)
WESTERN ASIA								
URBAN POPULATION	10,128	18,390	31,882	51,094	63,211	77,349	110,291	208,625
IN URBAN AGGLOMERATIONS:								
4,000,000+	0	0	0	11,059	14,036	17,373	29,231	68,561
NUMBER OF AGGLOMERATIONS	0	0	0	2	2	2	3	8
2,000,000 - 3,999,999	0	0	5,286	2,220	2,730	7,706	20,378	22,722
NUMBER OF AGGLOMERATIONS	0	0	2	1	1	3	8	8
1,000,000 - 1,999,999	0	2,478	2,340	8,423	12,875	12,505	13,325	31,186
NUMBER OF AGGLOMERATIONS	0	2	2	7	9	8	11	22
500,000 - 999,999	1,547	2,523	3,822	4,746	6,188	9,995	13,080	..
NUMBER OF AGGLOMERATIONS	2	4	5	7	10	15	20	..
250,000 - 499,999	1,642	1,429	4,384	8,235	9,074	8,225	..	..
NUMBER OF AGGLOMERATIONS	5	4	13	24	25	21	..	..
100,000 - 249,999	1,384	4,045	4,566	2,923	..	..	..	..
NUMBER OF AGGLOMERATIONS	10	26	27	16	..	..	..	..
REST OF URBAN	5,556	7,915	11,484	13,488	..	..	..	..
EUROPE								
URBAN POPULATION	219,162	257,380	303,895	343,866	360,587	376,327	405,096	452,638
IN URBAN AGGLOMERATIONS:								
4,000,000+	22,744	31,180	33,819	39,342	44,130	48,805	48,966	49,217
NUMBER OF AGGLOMERATIONS	3	4	4	5	6	7	7	8
2,000,000 - 3,999,999	13,611	21,882	27,058	31,991	31,430	28,663	32,328	30,478
NUMBER OF AGGLOMERATIONS	5	9	10	12	12	11	12	11
1,000,000 - 1,999,999	25,462	25,815	33,503	32,281	33,258	35,352	39,298	44,589
NUMBER OF AGGLOMERATIONS	17	18	24	23	24	25	28	32
500,000 - 999,999	22,323	24,549	27,334	32,817	35,904	39,030	41,275	..
NUMBER OF AGGLOMERATIONS	32	36	40	47	52	56	60	..
250,000 - 499,999	20,776	23,826	28,430	35,118	37,462	40,876	..	..
NUMBER OF AGGLOMERATIONS	62	70	84	103	111	121	..	..
100,000 - 249,999	23,724	27,878	32,837	32,195	..	..	..	..
NUMBER OF AGGLOMERATIONS	160	181	208	192	..	..	..	..
REST OF URBAN	90,522	102,251	120,914	140,122	..	..	..	..

Table 5 (continued)

MACRO REGIONS, REGIONS AND SIZE CATEGORY OF URBAN AGGLOMERATIONS	ESTIMATED AND PROJECTED POPULATION IN URBAN AGGLOMERATIONS OF 100,000 INHABITANTS AND OVER AND NUMBER OF URBAN AGGLOMERATIONS							
	1950	1960	1970	1980	1985	1990	2000	2025
(1)	(2)	(3)	(4)	(5)	(6)	(7)	(8)	(9)
EASTERN EUROPE								
URBAN POPULATION	37,077	46,347	55,222	65,468	70,756	75,858	85,828	106,308
IN URBAN AGGLOMERATIONS:								
4,000,000+	0	0	0	0	0	0	0	4,403
NUMBER OF AGGLOMERATIONS	0	0	0	0	0	0	0	1
2,000,000 - 3,999,999	0	2,442	2,767	7,340	9,946	10,588	11,811	9,147
NUMBER OF AGGLOMERATIONS	0	1	1	3	4	4	4	3
1,000,000 - 1,999,999	7,721	6,862	7,535	5,256	4,470	5745	7,265	10,398
NUMBER OF AGGLOMERATIONS	6	5	5	4	4	5	6	8
500,000 - 999,999	1,903	3,235	5,314	5,518	4,855	4,643	6,317	..
NUMBER OF AGGLOMERATIONS	3	5	8	8	7	7	10	..
250,000 - 499,999	3,315	3,705	3,330	5,063	7,182	8,977	..	..
NUMBER OF AGGLOMERATIONS	10	11	11	16	22	27	..	..
100,000 - 249,999	3,736	4,542	6,210	6,652	..	..	..	..
NUMBER OF AGGLOMERATIONS	27	30	39	38	..	..	..	..
REST OF URBAN	20,402	25,562	30,065	35,637	..	..	..	..
NORTHERN EUROPE								
URBAN POPULATION	53,868	58,192	65,275	69,853	71,523	72,968	75,263	78,079
IN URBAN AGGLOMERATIONS:								
4,000,000+	10,366	10,726	10,587	10,030	9,775	9,543	9,114	7,962
NUMBER OF AGGLOMERATIONS	1	1	1	1	1	1	1	1
2,000,000 - 3,999,999	5,064	5,198	5,338	5,281	5,245	5,206	5,109	4,740
NUMBER OF AGGLOMERATIONS	2	2	2	2	2	2	2	2
1,000,000 - 1,999,999	7,796	7,979	9,116	8,896	8,759	7,651	9,662	8,187
NUMBER OF AGGLOMERATIONS	5	5	6	6	6	5	7	6
500,000 - 999,999	5,067	6,961	8,256	9,752	10,051	11,851	9,963	..
NUMBER OF AGGLOMERATIONS	8	11	13	15	15	17	15	..
250,000 - 499,999	6,219	5,343	5,486	5,967	6,144	6,274	..	..
NUMBER OF AGGLOMERATIONS	17	15	16	18	18	19	..	..
100,000 - 249,999	5,723	6,024	6,429	6,352	..	..	..	..
NUMBER OF AGGLOMERATIONS	36	36	40	37	..	..	..	..
REST OF URBAN	13,634	15,961	20,062	23,574	..	..	..	..

Table 5 (continued)

MACRO REGIONS, REGIONS AND SIZE CATEGORY OF URBAN AGGLOMERATIONS	ESTIMATED AND PROJECTED POPULATION IN URBAN AGGLOMERATIONS OF 100,000 INHABITANTS AND OVER AND NUMBER OF URBAN AGGLOMERATIONS							
	1950	1960	1970	1980	1985	1990	2000	2025
(1)	(2)	(3)	(4)	(5)	(6)	(7)	(8)	(9)
SOUTHERN EUROPE								
URBAN POPULATION	48,358	58,413	71,807	86,429	92,991	99,305	110,950	133,111
IN URBAN AGGLOMERATIONS:								
4,000,000+	0	4,510	5,553	11,208	16,220	21,153	22,095	21,374
NUMBER OF AGGLOMERATIONS	0	1	1	2	3	4	4	4
2,000,000 - 3,999,999	6,390	9,963	14,631	15,179	11,961	8,545	11,163	16,591
NUMBER OF AGGLOMERATIONS	2	4	5	5	4	3	4	6
1,000,000 - 1,999,999	6,370	4,099	4,766	7,405	9,206	11,023	11,366	11,911
NUMBER OF AGGLOMERATIONS	4	3	4	6	7	8	8	9
500,000 - 999,999	4,459	4,716	6,219	6,131	8,390	8,715	10,436	..
NUMBER OF AGGLOMERATIONS	6	7	9	9	13	13	15	..
250,000 - 499,999	5,579	6,443	7,501	10,562	10,374	11,138	..	..
NUMBER OF AGGLOMERATIONS	17	19	22	30	31	32	..	..
100,000 - 249,999	5,199	5,903	7,258	6,002	..	..	..	..
NUMBER OF AGGLOMERATIONS	35	39	47	36	..	..	..	..
REST OF URBAN	20,360	22,779	25,879	29,942	..	..	..	..
WESTERN EUROPE								
URBAN POPULATION	79,859	94,428	111,591	122,116	125,316	128,195	133,055	135,140
IN URBAN AGGLOMERATIONS:								
4,000,000+	12,378	15,943	17,679	18,104	18,135	18,110	17,757	15,477
NUMBER OF AGGLOMERATIONS	2	2	2	2	2	2	2	2
2,000,000 - 3,999,999	2,157	4,279	4,321	4,191	4,278	4,324	4,245	0
NUMBER OF AGGLOMERATIONS	1	2	2	2	2	2	2	0
1,000,000 - 1,999,999	3,575	6,875	12,086	10,722	10,822	10,934	11,004	14,093
NUMBER OF AGGLOMERATIONS	2	5	9	7	7	7	7	9
500,000 - 999,999	10,894	9,637	7,545	11,416	12,608	13,820	14,560	..
NUMBER OF AGGLOMERATIONS	15	13	10	15	17	19	20	..
250,000 - 499,999	5,663	8,336	12,114	13,526	13,763	14,487	..	..
NUMBER OF AGGLOMERATIONS	18	25	35	39	40	43	..	..
100,000 - 249,999	9,067	11,409	12,940	13,189	..	..	..	..
NUMBER OF AGGLOMERATIONS	62	76	82	81	..	..	..	..
REST OF URBAN	36,126	37,950	44,906	50,969	..	..	..	..

Table 5 (continued)

MACRO REGIONS, REGIONS AND SIZE CATEGORY OF URBAN AGGLOMERATIONS	ESTIMATED AND PROJECTED POPULATION IN URBAN AGGLOMERATIONS OF 100,000 INHABITANTS AND OVER AND NUMBER OF URBAN AGGLOMERATIONS.							
	1950	1960	1970	1980	1985	1990	2000	2025
(1)	(2)	(3)	(4)	(5)	(6)	(7)	(8)	(9)
OCEANIA								
URBAN POPULATION	7,752	10,464	13,692	16,489	17,793	19,176	22,225	30,990
IN URBAN AGGLOMERATIONS:								
4,000,000+	0	0	0	0	0	0	4,166	4,809
NUMBER OF AGGLOMERATIONS	0	0	0	0	0	0	1	1
2,000,000 - 3,999,999	0	2,141	5,021	6,280	6,580	6,880	3,416	3,981
NUMBER OF AGGLOMERATIONS	0	1	2	2	2	2	1	1
1,000,000 - 1,999,999	3,136	1,880	0	2,139	3,482	3,815	5,536	8,833
NUMBER OF AGGLOMERATIONS	2	1	0	2	3	3	4	6
500,000 - 999,999	0	1,171	2,843	2,268	1,480	2,244	1,701	..
NUMBER OF AGGLOMERATIONS	0	2	4	3	2	3	2	..
250,000 - 499,999	1,402	864	272	593	1,290	1,158	..	..
NUMBER OF AGGLOMERATIONS	4	2	1	2	4	4	..	..
100,000 - 249,999	566	899	1,180	1,346	..	..	..	..
NUMBER OF AGGLOMERATIONS	4	6	8	8	..	..	..	..
REST OF URBAN	2,647	3,509	4,376	3,862	..	..	..	..
AUSTRALIA AND NEW ZEALAND								
URBAN POPULATION	7,565	10,118	12,979	15,345	16,403	17,491	19,808	25,639
IN URBAN AGGLOMERATIONS:								
4,000,000+	0	0	0	0	0	0	4,166	4,809
NUMBER OF AGGLOMERATIONS	0	0	0	0	0	0	1	1
2,000,000 - 3,999,999	0	2,141	5,021	6,280	6,580	6,880	3,416	3,981
NUMBER OF AGGLOMERATIONS	0	1	2	2	2	2	1	1
1,000,000 - 1,999,999	3,136	1,880	0	2,139	3,482	3,815	5,536	7,750
NUMBER OF AGGLOMERATIONS	2	1	0	2	3	3	4	5
500,000 - 999,999	0	1,171	2,843	2,268	1,480	2,244	1,701	..
NUMBER OF AGGLOMERATIONS	0	2	4	3	2	3	2	..
250,000 - 499,999	1,402	864	272	593	1,290	1,158	..	..
NUMBER OF AGGLOMERATIONS	4	2	1	2	4	4	..	..
100,000 - 249,999	566	899	1,180	1,081	..	..	..	..
NUMBER OF AGGLOMERATIONS	4	6	8	6	..	..	..	..
REST OF URBAN	2,461	3,163	3,662	2,984	..	..	..	..

Table 5 (continued)

MACRO REGIONS, REGIONS AND SIZE CATEGORY OF URBAN AGGLOMERATIONS	ESTIMATED AND PROJECTED POPULATION IN URBAN AGGLOMERATIONS OF 100,000 INHABITANTS AND OVER AND NUMBER OF URBAN AGGLOMERATIONS							
	1950	1960	1970	1980	1985	1990	2000	2025
(1)	(2)	(3)	(4)	(5)	(6)	(7)	(8)	(9)
MELANESIA ‡‡								
URBAN POPULATION	110	214	498	809	988	1,210	1,802	4,431
IN URBAN AGGLOMERATIONS:								
4,000,000+	0	0	0	0	0	0	0	0
NUMBER OF AGGLOMERATIONS	0	0	0	0	0	0	0	0
2,000,000 - 3,999,999	0	0	0	0	0	0	0	0
NUMBER OF AGGLOMERATIONS	0	0	0	0	0	0	0	0
1,000,000 - 1,999,999	0	0	0	0	0	0	0	1,083
NUMBER OF AGGLOMERATIONS	0	0	0	0	0	0	0	1
500,000 - 999,999	0	0	0	0	0	0	0	..
NUMBER OF AGGLOMERATIONS	0	0	0	0	0	0	0	..
250,000 - 499,999	0	0	0	0	0	0	..	..
NUMBER OF AGGLOMERATIONS	0	0	0	0	0	0	..	..
100,000 - 249,999	0	0	0	265	..	..	..	..
NUMBER OF AGGLOMERATIONS	0	0	0	2	..	..	..	..
REST OF URBAN	110	214	498	543	..	..	..	..
MICRONESIA AND POLYNESIA ‡‡								
URBAN POPULATION	77	132	215	335	402	474	615	920
IN URBAN AGGLOMERATIONS:								
4,000,000+	0	0	0	0	0	0	0	0
NUMBER OF AGGLOMERATIONS	0	0	0	0	0	0	0	0
2,000,000 - 3,999,999	0	0	0	0	0	0	0	0
NUMBER OF AGGLOMERATIONS	0	0	0	0	0	0	0	0
1,000,000 - 1,999,999	0	0	0	0	0	0	0	0
NUMBER OF AGGLOMERATIONS	0	0	0	0	0	0	0	0
500,000 - 999,999	0	0	0	0	0	0	0	..
NUMBER OF AGGLOMERATIONS	0	0	0	0	0	0	0	..
250,000 - 499,999	0	0	0	0	0	0	..	..
NUMBER OF AGGLOMERATIONS	0	0	0	0	0	0	..	..
100,000 - 249,999	0	0	0	0	..	..	..	..
NUMBER OF AGGLOMERATIONS	0	0	0	0	..	..	..	..
REST OF URBAN	77	132	215	335	..	..	..	..

Table 5 (continued)

MACRO REGIONS, REGIONS AND SIZE CATEGORY OF URBAN AGGLOMERATIONS	ESTIMATED AND PROJECTED POPULATION IN URBAN AGGLOMERATIONS OF 100,000 INHABITANTS AND OVER AND NUMBER OF URBAN AGGLOMERATIONS							
	1950	1960	1970	1980	1985	1990	2000	2025
(1)	(2)	(3)	(4)	(5)	(6)	(7)	(8)	(9)
U. S. S. R.								
URBAN POPULATION	70,772	104,598	137,047	167,857	184,583	201,590	233,841	306,065
IN URBAN AGGLOMERATIONS:								
4,000,000+	4,841	6,285	7,074	12,855	13,754	14,638	16,172	18,017
NUMBER OF AGGLOMERATIONS	1	1	1	2	2	2	2	2
2,000,000 - 3,999,999	2,623	3,462	3,961	2,236	4,631	5,160	10,408	20,786
NUMBER OF AGGLOMERATIONS	1	1	1	1	2	2	4	8
1,000,000 - 1,999,999	0	3,207	9,978	21,980	25,185	27,417	35,141	40,435
NUMBER OF AGGLOMERATIONS	0	3	8	18	20	20	25	27
500,000 - 999,999	6,889	14,347	18,008	18,135	20,239	27,123	30,892	..
NUMBER OF AGGLOMERATIONS	11	20	24	28	31	40	46	..
250,000 - 499,999	8,711	12,230	16,781	21,742	25,850	27,792	..	..
NUMBER OF AGGLOMERATIONS	25	36	48	63	75	80	..	..
100,000 - 249,999	9,870	15,369	21,398	19,122	..	..	..	..
NUMBER OF AGGLOMERATIONS	66	105	139	112	..	..	..	..
REST OF URBAN	37,837	49,699	59,847	71,785	..	..	..	..

Source: United Nations, *Estimates and Projections of Urban, Rural, and City Populations 1950–2025: The 1982 Assessment* (New York, 1984). Projections are not available for cities with population up to 249,999 in 1980, and only to a limited extent for cities with population up to 999,999 in 1980.

Notes: The Population Division of the United Nations estimates (for 1950–1980) and projects (for 1980–2025) the population of cities with at least 100,000 inhabitants, as far as possible, for all countries or areas of the world. Wherever possible, cities are considered in terms of agglomerations, that is, within the contours of dense urban settlement. These estimates and projections are in a continuous process of revision, and the figures here may differ from some published in other United Nations Publications. For composition of macro regions and regions, see the source cited above.

** Melanesia, Micronesia, and Polynesia do not have sufficient cities over 100,000 population for estimates and projections to be meaningful.

[1] This classification is intended for statistical convenience and does not necessarily express a judgement about the stage reached by a particular country or area in the development process.

[2] 'More developed regions' includes Northern America, Japan, all regions of Europe, Australia–New Zealand, and the USSR.

[3] 'Less developed regions' includes all regions of Africa, all regions of Latin America, China, Other East Asia, all regions of South Asia, Melanesia, and Micronesia–Polynesia.

Table 6

Estimated and projected population in urban agglomerations of 500,000 inhabitants and over as of 1980;
countries or areas and urban agglomerations, 1950–2000 (medium variant, in thousands)

URBAN AGGLOMERATIONS	ESTIMATED AND PROJECTED POPULATION IN URBAN AGGLOMERATIONS OF 500,000 INHABITANTS AND OVER AS OF 1980						
	1950	1960	1970	1975	1980	1990	2000
(1)	(2)	(3)	(4)	(5)	(6)	(7)	(8)
AFRICA							
ANGOLA							
LUANDA	140	220	460	710	1,030	1,900	3,170
ALGERIA							
ALGIERS	450	870	1,190	1,580	2,090	3,380	5,090
BENIN							
COTONOU	. .	. .	204	400	685	1,512	2,306
CAMEROON							
DOUALA	137	173	250	365	526	983	1,490
EGYPT							
CAIRO-GIZA-IMBABA	3,500	4,460	5,690	6,250	6,900	8,640	11,130
ALEXANDRIA	1,030	1,510	2,020	2,280	2,580	3,350	4,400
ETHIOPIA							
ADDIS ABABA	230	470	860	1,040	1,270	1,880	2,960
GHANA							
ACCRA	230	396	754	880	1,090	1,630	2,500
KUMASI	. .	221	350	447	563	907	1,411
GUINEA							
CONAKRY	50	130	370	600	820	1,470	2,430
IVORY COAST							
ABIDJAN	. .	180	356	503	685	1,189	1,800
KENYA							
NAIROBI	130	230	530	700	920	1,700	3,220
MADAGASCAR							
TANANARIVE	180	250	360	420	500	770	1,280
MOZAMBIQUE							
LOURENCO MARQUES	90	182	370	530	780	1,470	2,680
MOROCCO							
CASABLANCA	721	1,101	1,525	1,850	2,220	3,240	4,490
FEZ	205	256	369	451	553	844	1,239
MARRAKECH	250	288	383	449	533	782	1,140
MEKNE'S	199	261	355	420	503	746	1,091
RABAT-SALE'	180	280	510	640	770	1,150	1,620
NIGERIA							
LAGOS	360	700	1,440	2,100	2,790	4,790	8,340
ADO-EKITI	. .	. .	346	709	1,002	1,955	3,445
IBADAN	432	578	725	839	970	1,296	1,733
ILA	. .	. .	200	347	531	1,096	1,952
ILORIN	. .	119	396	730	1,168	2,542	4,518
KADUNA	. .	. .	239	388	562	1,084	1,907
KANO	140	214	335	424	503	758	1,278
MUSHIN	. .	. .	259	452	696	1,447	2,571
OGBOMOSHO	147	242	410	539	658	1,028	1,735
LIBYAN ARAB JAMAHIRIYA							
TRIPOLI	120	170	390	640	950	1,720	2,580
SENEGAL							
DAKAR	250	360	580	750	980	1,480	2,270
SOUTH AFRICA							
CAPE TOWN	760	920	1,160	1,370	1,620	2,250	3,040
DURBAN	488	650	847	953	1,082	1,444	2,040
EAST RAND	548	682	899	1,019	1,163	1,563	2,208
JOHANNESBURG	904	1,148	1,438	1,587	1,772	2,310	3,224
PORT ELIZABETH	193	289	472	596	742	1,116	1,620
PRETORIA	276	419	564	645	742	1,010	1,439
WEST RAND	209	307	423	489	568	785	1,127
SUDAN							
KHARTOUM	180	350	680	920	1,170	1,800	2,790
TUNISIA							
TUNIS	481	600	760	870	1,090	1,630	2,200

Table 6 (continued)

URBAN AGGLOMERATIONS	ESTIMATED AND PROJECTED POPULATION IN URBAN AGGLOMERATIONS OF 500,000 INHABITANTS AND OVER AS OF 1980						
	1950	1960	1970	1975	1980	1990	2000
(1)	(2)	(3)	(4)	(5)	(6)	(7)	(8)
UGANDA							
KAMPALA	50	130	340	400	480	730	1,260
ZAIRE							
KANANGA	..	154	449	746	1,109	2,113	3,283
KINSHASA	190	500	1,230	1,640	2,200	3,300	5,040
UNITED REPUBLIC OF TANZANIA							
DAR-ES-SALAAM	80	164	375	620	870	1,820	3,430
ZAMBIA							
LUSAKA	20	80	280	380	530	1,030	1,820
ZIMBABWE							
HARARE	100	170	340	460	610	1,060	1,850
AMERICA, NORTH							
CANADA							
CALGARY	133	264	391	472	523	602	677
EDMONTON	164	320	480	586	656	762	856
HAMILTON	264	384	492	540	555	581	642
MONTRE'AL	1,349	2,043	2,701	2,790	2,820	2,860	2,900
OTTAWA	284	417	585	680	710	760	800
QUEBEC	269	351	470	540	577	632	703
TORONTO	1,073	1,755	2,551	2,770	2,960	3,330	3,580
VANCOUVER	621	215	1,051	1,260	1,388	1,572	1,738
WINNIPEG	346	466	538	564	560	561	615
CUBA							
LA HABANA	1,198	1,448	1,751	1,880	1,940	2,040	2,210
DOMINICAN REPUBLIC							
SANTO DOMINIGO	250	470	890	1,140	1,440	2,170	2,950
SANTIAGO DE LOS CABALLEROS	..	140	270	376	504	850	1,315
HAITI							
PORT-AU-PRINCE	130	260	500	540	540	580	740
COSTA RICA							
SAN JOSE'	200	300	450	530	630	880	1,210
NICARAGUA							
MANAGUA	110	210	420	530	640	950	1,390
PANAMA							
PANAMA	120	260	350	390	420	520	660
GUATEMALA							
CIUDAD DE GUATEMALA	400	544	733	850	1,020	1,460	2,100
JAMAICA							
KINGSTON-ST.ANDREW	328	430	540	620	720	950	1,190
MEXICO							
CIUDAD JUA'REZ	127	273	434	548	672	1,006	1,428
GUADALAJARA	430	930	1,580	1,950	2,360	3,200	4,110
LE'ON	127	225	399	532	682	1,077	1,544
MEXICO CITY	3,050	5,220	9,120	11,610	14,470	20,250	25,820
MONTERREY	380	930	1,280	1,650	2,090	3,010	3,970
PUEBLA DE ZARAGOZA	234	318	522	668	830	1,260	1,787
TIJUANA	..	159	299	411	541	883	1,278
PUERTO RICO							
SAN JUAN	470	550	700	890	1,090	1,490	1,830
UNITED STATES OF AMERICA							
AKRON	369	501	618	673	707	794	881
ALBANY/SCHENECTADY/TROY	416	497	552	571	576	615	679
ALLENTOWN	227	281	416	497	562	692	784
ATLANTA	513	845	1,344	1,661	1,928	2,431	2,714
AURORA/ELGIN	..	125	269	386	506	751	882
BALTIMORE	1,168	1,549	1,796	1,896	1,940	2,089	2,267
BIRMINGHAM	447	577	644	667	674	719	792
BOSTON	2,250	2,480	2,670	2,680	2,690	2,740	2,830
BRIDGEPORT	240	401	471	500	515	566	629
BUFFALO	900	1,149	1,233	1,252	1,243	1,294	1,404
CHICAGO	4,970	6,000	6,760	6,770	6,800	6,900	7,030
CINCINNATTI	817	1,084	1,263	1,337	1,371	1,485	1,622
CLEVELAND	1,393	1,948	2,227	2,335	2,374	2,535	2,737

Table 6 (continued)

URBAN AGGLOMERATIONS	ESTIMATED AND PROJECTED POPULATION IN URBAN AGGLOMERATIONS OF 500,000 INHABITANTS AND OVER AS OF 1980						
	1950	1960	1970	1975	1980	1990	2000
(1)	(2)	(3)	(4)	(5)	(6)	(7)	(8)

UNITED STATES OF AMERICA (continued)

	1950	1960	1970	1975	1980	1990	2000
COLUMBUS (OHIO)	441	676	901	1,021	1,105	1,283	1,424
DALLAS	870	1,160	2,040	2,240	2,470	2,870	3,130
DAYTON	350	551	784	916	1,018	1,222	1,365
DENVER	505	881	1,195	1,365	1,488	1,738	1,921
DETROIT	2,790	3,560	3,990	3,900	3,810	3,860	3,960
FAYETTEVILLE	..	..	188	346	555	1,053	1,290
FORT LAUDERDALE	..	354	707	981	1,249	1,772	2,034
FORT WORTH	319	551	773	898	993	1,185	1,323
HARTFORD	303	417	530	585	622	709	791
HONOLULU	250	384	505	567	611	708	792
HOUSTON	710	1,160	1,700	2,040	2,440	3,190	3,650
INDIANAPOLIS	505	700	935	1,060	1,149	1,335	1,481
JACKSONVILLE	246	409	606	722	816	1,000	1,126
KANSAS CITY	703	1,007	1,255	1,374	1,448	1,621	1,779
LAS VEGAS	..	100	274	445	644	1,076	1,285
LOS ANGELES/LONG BEACH	4,070	6,560	8,430	8,960	9,530	10,480	10,990
LOUISVILLE	476	664	843	930	988	1,120	1,240
MEMPHIS	409	596	756	836	888	1,009	1,118
MIAMI	466	936	1,396	1,671	1,890	2,308	2,562
MILWAUKEE	836	1,254	1,423	1,486	1,508	1,611	1,752
MINNEAPOLIS-ST. PAUL	995	1,507	1,942	2,162	2,307	2,615	2,856
NASHVILLE/DAVIDSON	261	380	511	582	633	742	832
NEW ORLEANS	664	923	1,094	1,168	1,206	1,320	1,447
NEW YORK	12,410	14,230	16,290	15,940	15,610	15,690	15,780
NORFOLK/PORTSMOUTH	388	556	763	876	960	1,132	1,262
OKLAHOMA CITY	278	470	662	770	853	1,020	1,143
OMAHA	312	427	561	631	680	788	881
ORLANDO	..	221	350	433	503	641	732
OXNARD/VENTURA	..	..	289	688	1,350	3,279	4,146
PHILADELPHIA	2,960	3,660	4,050	4,080	4,130	4,240	4,360
PHOENIX	221	607	990	1,239	1,453	1,859	2,090
PITTSBURGH	1,540	1,965	2,095	2,120	2,096	2,164	2,326
PORTLAND	516	714	941	1,059	1,142	1,318	1,459
PROVIDENCE	585	722	906	995	1,052	1,186	1,310
RICHMOND	260	365	474	530	569	656	734
ROCHESTER	411	540	685	756	803	913	1,013
SACRAMENTO	216	496	725	858	964	1,172	1,314
SALT LAKE CITY	230	382	548	643	717	867	975
SAN ANTONIO	454	702	880	966	1,020	1,150	1,270
SAN BERNARDINO	139	416	669	832	971	1,240	1,402
SAN DIEGO	440	919	1,371	1,642	1,857	2,269	2,520
SAN FRANCISCO/OAKLAND	2,040	2,450	3,010	3,100	3,200	3,400	3,550
SAN JOSE	182	665	1,178	1,537	1,862	2,477	2,794
SEATTLE/EVERETT	627	949	1,416	1,696	1,919	2,343	2,601
SPRINGFIELD	359	491	585	626	649	716	794
ST. LOIUS	1,408	1,822	2,142	2,278	2,342	2,536	2,746
ST. PETERSBURG	118	357	567	700	814	1,034	1,171
TACOMA	169	236	381	474	555	713	815
TOLEDO	366	478	555	586	600	654	724
TULSA	208	328	424	473	507	584	655
WASHINGTON D.C.	1,310	1,830	2,500	2,640	2,780	3,030	3,220
WEST PALM BEACH	..	191	330	426	513	683	786
WILMINGTON	189	311	424	485	531	627	706

AMERICA, SOUTH

ARGENTINA

	1950	1960	1970	1975	1980	1990	2000
BUENOS AIRES	5,251	6,930	8,550	9,290	10,060	11,710	13,180
CORDOBA	419	590	800	927	1,051	1,285	1,426
LA PLATA	301	379	485	547	608	726	810
MENDOZA	247	356	486	566	644	794	890
ROSARIO	546	677	818	896	971	1,122	1,234

BOLIVIA

	1950	1960	1970	1975	1980	1990	2000
LA PAZ	270	380	550	660	810	1,210	1,770

Table 6 (continued)

URBAN AGGLOMERATIONS		ESTIMATED AND PROJECTED POPULATION IN URBAN AGGLOMERATIONS OF 500,000 INHABITANTS AND OVER AS OF 1980						
		1950	1960	1970	1975	1980	1990	2000
	(1)	(2)	(3)	(4)	(5)	(6)	(7)	(8)
BRAZIL								
	BELE'M	239	382	616	781	949	1,357	1,825
	BELO HORIZONTE	480	890	1,620	2,050	2,590	3,890	5,110
	BRASILIA	40	140	540	800	1,190	2,400	3,720
	CAMPINAS	103	181	338	463	597	923	1,269
	CURITIBA	141	358	914	1,456	2,119	3,772	5,212
	FORTALEZA	263	487	906	1,235	1,586	2,422	3,270
	GOIANIA	..	131	371	622	946	1,788	2,530
	MANAUS	113	156	290	396	511	791	1,089
	PORTO ALEGRE	670	1,040	1,550	1,880	2,280	3,180	4,020
	RECIFE	830	1,240	1,820	2,090	2,400	3,040	3,650
	RIO DE JANEIRO	3,480	5,070	7,170	8,150	9,210	11,370	13,260
	SALVADOR	450	730	1,160	1,450	1,800	2,650	3,450
	SANTOS	244	367	559	689	818	1,139	1,527
	SAO PAULO	2,760	4,840	8,220	10,290	12,820	18,770	23,970
CHILE								
	SANTIAGO	1,430	2,120	3,010	3,380	3,740	4,550	5,260
COLOMBIA								
	BARRANQUILLA	307	473	767	982	1,221	1,775	2,336
	BOGOTA	700	1,320	2,370	3,020	3,720	5,270	6,530
	BUCARAMANGA	130	223	366	457	558	797	1,059
	CALI	288	529	954	1,260	1,606	2,402	3,165
	MEDELLI'N	469	835	1,474	1,929	2,439	3,601	4,703
ECUADOR								
	GUAYAQUIL	258	461	730	892	1,093	1,638	2,370
	QUITO	220	340	530	660	810	1,220	1,800
PERU								
	AREQUIPA	..	131	271	393	533	881	1,232
	LIMA-CALLAO	1,050	1,750	2,920	3,700	4,590	6,780	9,140
PARAGUAY								
	ASUNCION	210	280	450	610	820	1,350	2,010
URUGUAY								
	MONTEVIDEO	1,070	1,150	1,210	1,190	1,190	1,220	1,270
VENEZUELA								
	CARACAS	680	1,310	2,120	2,610	3,170	4,180	5,030
	MARACAIDO	239	423	636	764	895	1,200	1,515
	VALENCIA	..	164	344	492	662	1,059	1,387
	ASIA							
BANGLADESH								
	CHITTAGONG	286	368	722	971	1,293	2,322	3,946
	DACCA	430	660	1,540	2,350	3,400	6,530	11,160
	KHULNA	..	123	323	494	730	1,497	2,629
BURMA								
	MANDALAY	170	251	380	472	586	899	1,336
	RANGOON	660	960	1,420	1,760	2,200	3,170	4,320
CHINA								
	AMOY	150	280	400	471	554	763	1,037
	ANSHAN	425	849	1,050	1,168	1,312	1,694	2,247
	ANTUNG	240	350	480	542	617	815	1,099
	CHANGCHUN	784	1,016	1,200	1,305	1,438	1,813	2,391
	CHANGSHA	618	726	825	879	955	1,186	1,569
	CHENGCHOW	502	816	1,050	1,191	1,358	1,787	2,377
	CHENGCHOW (KIANGON)	260	320	480	591	720	1,035	1,413
	CHANGTU	722	1,134	1,250	1,312	1,406	1,713	2,246
	CHINCHOW	260	350	600	800	1,039	1,612	2,218
	CHINGTEHCHEN	125	230	350	438	540	791	1,088
	CHINHUANGTAO	130	230	350	438	540	791	1,088
	CHUNGKING	1,573	2,150	2,460	2,590	2,640	2,710	3,060
	FOOCHOW	515	628	680	707	753	914	1,210
	FOUHSIN	140	280	400	471	554	763	1,037
	FUSHUN	530	1,003	1,080	1,121	1,190	1,436	1,884
	HAIKOW	114	350	480	549	630	843	1,137
	HANGCHOW	644	816	960	1,042	1,147	1,446	1,914
	HANTAN	167	330	480	576	688	965	1,312

Table 6 (continued)

URBAN AGGLOMERATIONS	ESTIMATED AND PROJECTED POPULATION IN URBAN AGGLOMERATIONS OF 500,000 INHABITANTS AND OVER AS OF 1980						
	1950	1960	1970	1975	1980	1990	2000
(1)	(2)	(3)	(4)	(5)	(6)	(7)	(8)
CHINA (continued)							
HARBIN	940	1,550	2,000	2,240	2,430	2,790	3,340
HOFEI	131	352	630	843	1,097	1,706	2,347
HSIANGTAN	130	230	350	438	540	791	1,088
HUHEHOT	122	349	530	653	797	1,146	1,562
HWAINAN	242	408	600	727	876	1,237	1,678
KAIFENG	300	340	480	562	658	901	1,220
KALGAN	170	523	750	879	1,030	1,404	1,888
KAOSHIUNG	261	448	803	1,098	1,456	2,308	3,173
KIRIN	365	596	720	792	881	1,129	1,505
KUNMING	600	920	1,100	1,203	1,332	1,692	2,236
KUANG CHOU	1,456	1,956	2,500	2,826	3,208	4,174	5,468
KWEIYANG	179	532	660	735	826	1,072	1,434
LANCHOW	273	809	1,450	1,941	2,526	3,899	5,288
LOYANG	138	283	580	831	1,142	1,900	2,645
LUTA	488	1,535	1,650	1,710	1,814	2,177	2,835
MUTANKIANG	180	270	400	485	584	829	1,132
NANCHANG	339	538	675	757	856	1,119	1,498
NANKING	917	1,480	1,750	1,904	2,098	2,637	3,456
NANNING	159	306	550	738	963	1,504	2,075
PANGFU	180	300	450	547	661	940	1,282
PAOTING	160	270	400	485	584	829	1,132
PAOTOW	118	688	920	1,063	1,232	1,654	2,211
PEKING	6,740	7,310	8,290	8,910	9,060	9,290	10,360
PENKI	427	506	600	653	722	919	1,226
SHANGHAI	10,420	10,670	11,410	11,590	11,750	11,960	13,260
SHENYANG	2,250	2,470	3,140	3,530	3,800	4,340	5,170
SHIHKIACHWANG	273	634	800	899	1,018	1,332	1,777
SIAN	561	1,363	1,600	1,733	1,904	2,387	3,131
SINING	..	332	500	613	745	1,065	1,452
SOOSHOW	391	651	730	772	834	1,029	1,364
SUCHOW	251	681	700	710	742	879	1,158
SWATOU	240	270	400	485	584	829	1,132
TAICHUNG	189	291	439	534	645	917	1,251
TAINAN	223	329	468	548	641	877	1,189
TAIPEI	600	970	1,500	1,840	2,160	2,910	3,800
TAIYUAN	572	1,079	1,350	1,510	1,702	2,205	2,915
TANGSHAN	630	828	950	1,018	1,109	1,382	1,825
TIENTSIN	2,392	3,363	4,000	4,363	4,810	6,015	7,775
TSINAN	581	905	1,100	1,213	1,352	1,730	2,289
TSINGTAO	802	1,155	1,300	1,380	1,492	1,836	2,410
TSITSIHAR	222	685	760	800	860	1,056	1,397
TZEKUNG	250	300	450	563	694	1,014	1,389
TZEPO	154	815	850	869	912	1,086	1,427
URUMCHI	116	310	500	635	793	1,173	1,608
WUHAN	1,270	2,170	2,730	3,010	3,190	3,530	4,140
WUSIH	561	620	650	665	700	837	1,106
HONG KONG							
HONG KONG	1,750	2,740	3,530	3,980	4,610	5,620	6,370
INDIA							
AGRA	368	499	624	698	794	1,087	1,592
AHMEDABAD	870	1,210	1,740	2,130	2,600	3,760	5,280
ALLAHABAD	327	423	506	553	617	828	1,213
AMRITSAR	332	394	453	486	535	706	1,033
BANGALORE	780	1,200	1,660	2,210	2,970	5,140	7,960
BHOPAL	..	212	370	487	630	1,016	1,537
BOMBAY	2,950	4,150	5,980	7,170	8,530	11,790	16,000
CALCUTTA	4,520	5,620	7,120	8,250	9,540	12,540	16,530
COCHIN	187	303	428	507	604	879	1,306
COIMBATORE	265	417	707	925	1,189	1,896	2,834
DELHI	1,410	2,330	3,640	4,630	5,870	9,130	13,240
DHANBAD	..	188	410	602	850	1,525	2,341
GWALIOR	238	296	397	462	542	775	1,150
HUBLI-DHARWAR	193	245	367	453	557	845	1,267
HYDERABAD	1,410	1,270	1,800	2,180	2,620	3,700	5,130
INDORE	306	389	546	651	779	1,137	1,684

Table 6 (continued)

URBAN AGGLOMERATIONS	ESTIMATED AND PROJECTED POPULATION IN URBAN AGGLOMERATIONS OF 500,000 INHABITANTS AND OVER AS OF 1980						
	1950	1960	1970	1975	1980	1990	2000
(1)	(2)	(3)	(4)	(5)	(6)	(7)	(8)
INDIA (continued)							
JABALPUR	251	358	520	629	761	1,127	1,674
JAIPUR	285	395	616	775	966	1,485	2,212
JAMSHEDPUR	212	319	445	525	623	902	1,339
KANPUR	700	970	1,290	1,510	1,760	2,350	3,170
LUCKNOW	488	644	801	894	1,012	1,379	2,008
LUDHIANA	149	237	387	497	631	995	1,499
MADRAS	1,420	1,740	3,120	3,770	4,440	6,030	8,150
MADURAI	358	420	685	888	1,133	1,791	2,675
NAGPUR	474	674	910	1,058	1,238	1,753	2,564
PATNA	279	359	480	558	654	932	1,378
POONA	600	740	1,130	1,410	1,740	2,580	3,690
SALEM	200	246	401	518	661	1,048	1,579
SRINAGAR	248	292	412	493	592	870	1,296
SURAT	219	283	474	621	799	1,281	1,928
TIRUCHIRAPALLI	217	248	444	606	808	1,349	2,047
TRIVANDRUM	192	294	400	466	548	785	1,164
ULHASNAGAR	. .	106	360	695	1,220	2,866	4,594
VADODARA	207	289	452	569	710	1,096	1,641
VARANASI	348	480	597	666	754	1,029	1,506
VISAKHAPATNAM	104	176	345	487	667	1,154	1,766
INDONESIA							
BANDUNG	764	936	1,204	1,370	1,583	2,227	3,265
JAKARTA	1,820	2,810	4,480	5,530	6,650	9,480	13,250
MAKASAR	333	374	440	479	536	729	1,079
MALONG	268	329	423	482	558	794	1,185
MEDAN	370	470	640	910	1,390	3,010	5,360
PALEMBANG	376	458	585	663	765	1,080	1,602
SEMARANG	378	482	645	748	880	1,269	1,886
SURABAJA	613	942	1,517	1,931	2,440	3,823	5,676
SURAKARTA	321	358	420	456	509	691	1,024
IRAN							
ISFAHAN	199	311	501	641	808	1,232	1,725
MASHHAD	188	298	489	637	813	1,260	1,769
RAI	. .	. .	176	374	709	1,796	2,762
TABRIZ	255	332	465	576	708	1,046	1,459
TAJRISH	. .	. .	228	384	604	1,217	1,800
TEHERAN	1,126	1,905	3,264	4,267	5,447	8,331	11,329
IRAQ							
BAGHDAD	579	1,024	2,510	3,830	5,138	8,203	11,125
BASRA	116	205	453	680	903	1,440	2,006
MOSUL	144	204	335	435	514	713	978
ISRAEL							
TEL-AVIV/YAFO	359	740	982	1,091	1,220	1,501	1,727
JAPAN							
CHIBA	. .	166	357	554	784	1,231	1,412
HIROSHIMA	266	403	502	540	570	622	672
KITAKYUSHU	935	1,311	1,593	1,759	1,891	2,096	2,228
KYOTO	1,001	1,164	1,298	1,376	1,432	1,528	1,620
NAGOYA	956	1,499	1,847	2,010	2,135	2,330	2,464
OSAKA/KOBE	3,828	5,749	7,595	8,649	9,496	10,686	11,109
SAPPORO	254	489	815	1,016	1,203	1,512	1,655
SENDAI	269	334	436	516	587	705	774
TOKYO-YOKOHAMA	6,736	10,685	14,865	17,668	20,045	23,372	24,172
KOREA							
DEMOCRATIC PEOPLES' REPUBLIC OF KOREA							
HAMHUNG	203	281	475	613	775	1,156	1,509
PYONGYANG	540	635	911	1,084	1,283	1,755	2,240
REPUBLIC OF KOREA							
INCHEON	283	394	628	794	978	1,372	1,708
KWANGCHU	191	307	488	603	730	1,003	1,250
MASAN	118	156	185	361	629	1,365	1,851
PUSAN	1,040	1,170	1,850	2,470	3,190	4,900	6,200
SEOUL	1,113	2,390	5,420	6,950	8,470	11,660	13,770
TAEGU	389	659	1,050	1,303	1,579	2,163	2,660

Table 6 (continued)

URBAN AGGLOMERATIONS		ESTIMATED AND PROJECTED POPULATION IN URBAN AGGLOMERATIONS OF 500,000 INHABITANTS AND OVER AS OF 1980						
		1950	1960	1970	1975	1980	1990	2000
	(1)	(2)	(3)	(4)	(5)	(6)	(7)	(8)
LEBANON								
	BEIRUT	200	480	1,070	1,480	1,610	2,060	2,600
MALAYSIA								
	KUALA LUMPUR	210	350	470	680	970	1,750	2,630
PAKISTAN								
	GUJRANWALA	128	206	323	410	520	830	1,302
	HYDERABAD	255	454	589	675	787	1,137	1,727
	KARACHI	1,040	1,820	3,140	4,030	5,170	8,160	12,000
	LAHORE	830	1,240	1,970	2,420	2,980	4,350	6,160
	LYALLPUR	185	437	730	947	1,219	1,987	3,064
	MULTAN	200	373	504	589	697	1,030	1,572
	RAWALPINDI	254	360	553	698	878	1,396	2,153
PHILIPPINES								
	CEBU	185	256	356	425	507	745	1,096
	DAVAO	128	232	404	539	703	1,152	1,720
	MANILA	1,570	2,320	3,600	5,040	5,960	8,260	11,070
SAUDI ARABIA								
	JEDDAH	116	236	504	746	1,044	1,772	2,462
	MECCA	216	283	393	472	559	775	1,048
	RIYADH	50	130	400	730	1,180	2,380	3,650
SINGAPORE								
	SINGAPORE	810	1,270	1,580	2,260	2,410	2,700	2,950
SRI LANKA								
	COLOMBO	410	490	560	580	590	630	730
SYRIAN ARAB REPUBLIC								
	ALEPPO	299	424	632	766	935	1,405	2,031
	DAMASCUS	389	583	912	1,060	1,210	1,640	2,320
THAILAND								
	BANGKOK-THONBURI	1,440	2,190	3,270	4,050	4,960	7,380	10,710
TURKEY								
	ANKARA	281	640	1,270	1,670	2,200	3,630	5,200
	BURSA	149	221	374	470	575	851	1,167
	ISTANBUL	969	1,453	2,780	2,870	2,910	2,980	3,290
	IZMIR	314	564	710	904	1,115	1,658	2,254
VIET NAM								
	DA-NHANG	..	105	456	921	1,635	3,864	6,269
	HAIPHONG	112	184	316	405	500	759	1,158
	HANOI	700	740	840	830	830	910	1,190
	HO CHI MINH	1,070	1,530	2,300	2,380	2,480	2,850	3,750
	EUROPE							
AUSTRIA								
	VIENNA	1,780	1,790	1,810	1,770	1,710	1,660	1,680
BELGIUM								
	ANTWERP	607	649	671	667	666	683	722
	BRUSSELS	969	1,020	1,074	1,057	1,010	960	960
BULGARIA								
	SOFIA	550	710	890	1,070	1,270	1,600	1,820
CZECHOSLOVAKIA								
	PRAGUE	1,003	1,067	1,079	1,092	1,121	1,180	1,270
DENMARK								
	COPENHAGEN	1,212	1,346	1,381	1,310	1,220	1,220	1,240
FINLAND								
	HELSINKI	364	465	620	750	900	1,220	1,450
FRANCE								
	BORDEAUX	313	465	574	617	662	744	806
	LILLE	739	807	925	1,024	1,125	1,298	1,401
	LYONS	581	878	1,107	1,178	1,253	1,388	1,484
	MARSEILLE	671	810	999	1,079	1,161	1,304	1,400
	NANTES	294	340	413	458	504	586	641
	PARIS	5,525	7,230	8,340	8,620	8,660	8,680	8,720
	TOULOUSE	256	346	462	515	569	664	725

Table 6 (continued)

URBAN AGGLOMERATIONS	ESTIMATED AND PROJECTED POPULATION IN URBAN AGGLOMERATIONS OF 500,000 INHABITANTS AND OVER AS OF 1980						
	1950	1960	1970	1975	1980	1990	2000
(1)	(2)	(3)	(4)	(5)	(6)	(7)	(8)
GERMAN DEMOCRATIC REPUBLIC - #							
BERLIN	1,189	1,090	1,090	1,100	1,150	1,260	1,330
DRESDEN	494	495	502	517	531	560	588
LEIPZIG	617	595	585	579	576	584	609
FEDERAL REPUBLIC OF GERMANY - #							
BONN	210	410	480	490	500	510	510
BREMEN/DELMENHORST	500	725	801	806	813	839	867
FRANKFURT AM MAIN	946	1,381	1,661	1,753	1,833	1,965	2,019
HAMBURG	1,796	2,092	2,200	2,190	2,190	2,190	2,190
HANNOVER	567	764	832	835	840	864	891
MANNHEIM/LUDWIGSHAFEN	584	750	859	888	915	968	1,003
MUENCHEN	963	1,333	1,710	1,869	2,012	2,180	2,220
NUERNBERG/FUERTH	549	746	838	855	871	909	940
RHEIN/RUHR	6,853	8,712	9,337	9,311	9,275	9,252	9,151
STUTTGART	988	1,355	1,620	1,710	1,787	1,916	1,969
WIESBADEN/MAINZ	393	542	634	661	685	733	764
BERLIN	2,157	2,186	2,121	2,026	2,030	2,030	2,030
GREECE							
ATHENS	1,345	1,813	2,100	2,250	2,570	2,800	3,040
THESSALONIKI	291	372	541	647	739	904	1,002
HUNGARY							
BUDAPEST	1,623	1,812	1,950	2,062	2,060	2,060	2,090
IRELAND							
DUBLIN	632	662	769	860	930	1,100	1,300
ITALY							
BOLOGNA	346	460	543	582	616	686	745
CATANIA	381	452	507	532	553	604	654
FLORENCE	649	772	911	984	1,047	1,169	1,259
GENOA	909	1,034	1,108	1,137	1,161	1,230	1,310
MILAN	3,637	4,510	5,520	6,150	6,730	7,530	8,150
NAPLES	2,753	3,196	3,590	3,830	4,000	4,150	4,300
PALERMO	523	623	689	718	742	801	861
ROME	1,570	2,330	3,070	3,360	3,550	3,750	3,870
TURIN	881	1,251	1,628	1,840	2,060	2,400	2,610
NETHERLANDS							
AMSTERDAM	862	913	1,040	1,000	960	920	920
ROTTERDAM	747	830	1,064	1,027	1,003	995	1,056
'S GRAVENHAGE	619	692	715	677	652	638	680
NORWAY							
OSLO	492	580	630	640	640	650	650
POLAND							
BYDGOSZCZ	264	362	444	489	537	636	726
GDANSK	371	543	702	792	887	1,073	1,220
KATOWICE	1,716	2,442	2,770	2,920	3,090	3,460	3,770
KRAKOW	368	525	628	683	742	866	982
LODZ	736	861	923	949	986	1,086	1,212
POZNAN	361	457	536	577	623	721	818
WARSAW	1,031	1,487	1,690	1,660	1,630	1,620	1,680
WROCLAW	314	436	531	582	636	750	853
PORTUGAL							
LISBON	842	936	1,009	1,290	1,590	2,200	2,830
ROMANIA							
BUCURESTI	1,160	1,400	1,690	1,870	2,050	2,370	2,640
SPAIN							
BARCELONA	1,550	1,940	2,660	2,870	3,070	3,240	3,350
BILBAO	375	537	887	1,135	1,375	1,821	2,082
MADRID	1,540	2,220	3,370	3,820	4,290	4,950	5,360
SEVILLE	477	574	822	981	1,125	1,394	1,579
VALENCIA	654	704	1,020	1,228	1,416	1,766	1,996
ZARAGOZA	260	321	463	554	638	796	912
SWEDEN							
GOTEBORG	351	398	535	631	674	721	754
MALMO	190	224	372	582	779	1,103	1,210
STOCKHOLM	741	805	1,094	1,220	1,380	1,540	1,540
SWITZERLAND							
ZURICH	494	532	715	802	870	1,004	1,123

Table 6 (continued)

URBAN AGGLOMERATIONS	ESTIMATED AND PROJECTED POPULATION IN URBAN AGGLOMERATIONS OF 500,000 INHABITANTS AND OVER AS OF 1980						
	1950	1960	1970	1975	1980	1990	2000
(1)	(2)	(3)	(4)	(5)	(6)	(7)	(8)
UNITED KINGDOM							
BIRMINGHAM	2,530	2,670	2,810	2,830	2,850	2,890	2,930
BRISTOL	603	640	695	717	739	779	813
CARDIFF	597	607	620	620	624	639	665
COVENTRY/RHONDDA	525	604	679	712	742	795	832
EDINBURGH	593	601	614	614	618	633	659
GLASGOW	1,898	1,921	1,903	1,871	1,852	1,846	1,880
LEEDS/BRADFORD	1,930	1,929	1,989	1,990	1,990	2,000	2,020
LEICESTER	430	464	519	544	568	610	641
LIVERPOOL	1,619	1,626	1,606	1,578	1,561	1,557	1,590
LONDON	10,369	10,727	10,588	10,310	10,310	10,400	10,510
MANCHESTER	2,538	2,527	2,529	2,490	2,488	2,510	2,530
MIDDLESBROUGH/ HARTLEPOOL	485	534	580	597	614	648	678
NEWCASTLE-UPON-TYNE	1,139	1,159	1,144	1,123	1,111	1,110	1,141
NOTTINGHAM	607	642	684	699	714	746	777
PORTSMOUTH	371	407	459	483	506	546	576
SHEFFIELD	771	785	794	790	791	804	832
SOUTHAMPTON	358	399	457	484	510	555	586
STOKE-ON-TRENT	494	504	519	521	525	541	565
YUGOSLAVIA							
BELGRADE	393	570	760	870	980	1,212	1,430
SKOPLJE	106	161	298	408	529	789	980
ZAGREB	324	423	555	633	710	881	1,054
<u>OCEANIA</u>							
AUSTRALIA							
ADELAIDE	355	565	796	881	964	1,133	1,286
BRISBANE	436	605	801	906	1,009	1,211	1,380
MELBOURNE	1,490	1,880	2,344	2,610	2,880	3,230	3,410
PERTH	277	407	613	782	958	1,296	1,510
SYDNEY	1,646	2,141	2,680	3,010	3,390	3,930	4,230
NEW ZEALAND							
AUCKLAND	334	457	634	728	825	1,015	1,169
UNION OF SOVIET SOCIALIST REPUBLICS							
ALMA-ATA	286	494	744	895	1,055	1,357	1,543
BAKU	708	1,014	1,274	1,395	1,523	1,777	1,974
BARNAUL	205	324	446	514	585	725	826
CHELYABINSK	517	723	882	954	1,033	1,194	1,333
DNEPROPETROVSK	485	697	872	956	1,046	1,226	1,371
DONETSK	541	742	887	951	1,022	1,171	1,306
DUSHANBE	139	247	382	466	556	729	841
FRUNZE	118	245	443	585	744	1,055	1,228
GORKY	718	986	1,180	1,265	1,359	1,554	1,724
IRKUTSK	223	383	455	486	521	599	674
IZHEVSK	190	306	429	498	572	715	816
KARAGANDA	221	368	531	625	724	914	1,042
KAZAN	491	704	878	961	1,049	1,228	1,373
KHABAROVSK	232	344	442	492	545	653	740
KHARKOV	710	1,004	1,235	1,343	1,459	1,691	1,878
KIEV	743	1,189	1,650	1,920	2,240	2,920	3,440
KISHINEV	133	236	367	449	536	705	814
KRASNODAR	208	336	472	548	629	785	896
KRASNOYARSK	280	445	660	787	922	1,176	1,339
KRIVOY ROG	275	428	581	664	752	922	1,045
KUIBYSHEV	595	850	1,058	1,158	1,265	1,478	1,648
LENINGRAD	2,623	3,462	3,960	4,310	4,690	5,430	5,930
LVOV	297	435	560	623	690	825	932
MINSK	291	560	938	1,190	1,462	1,975	2,256
MOSCOW	4,841	6,285	7,070	7,600	8,200	9,540	10,400
NOVOKUZNETSK	280	404	504	552	604	711	803
NOVOSIBIRSK	645	934	1,174	1,291	1,415	1,659	1,847
ODESSA	477	703	903	1,003	1,110	1,318	1,477

Table 6 (continued)

URBAN AGGLOMERATIONS	ESTIMATED AND PROJECTED POPULATION IN URBAN AGGLOMERATIONS OF 500,000 INHABITANTS AND OVER AS OF 1980						
	1950	1960	1970	1975	1980	1990	2000
(1)	(2)	(3)	(4)	(5)	(6)	(7)	(8)
U.S.S.R. (continued)							
OMSK	402	620	832	944	1,061	1,287	1,448
PERM	454	671	860	955	1,056	1,253	1,405
RIGA	437	609	740	799	864	999	1,118
ROSTOV-NA-DONU	448	634	798	879	966	1,138	1,276
RYAZAN	132	232	358	436	519	680	784
SARATOV	424	611	766	840	920	1,080	1,211
SVERDLOVSK	569	823	1,037	1,141	1,251	1,469	1,640
TASHKENT	613	1,000	1,400	1,610	1,850	2,360	2,740
TBILISI	530	739	897	969	1,047	1,210	1,350
TOLYATTI	. .	. .	264	452	708	2,299	1,586
TULA	257	371	467	514	565	669	757
UFA	378	583	784	891	1,005	1,222	1,377
ULYANOVSK	123	225	359	444	536	713	825
VILNIUS	150	255	379	453	532	683	786
VLADIVOSTOK	190	314	450	528	611	771	882
VOLGOGRAD	415	629	829	933	1,043	1,255	1,411
VORONEZH	298	480	670	776	888	1,101	1,248
YAROSLAVL	306	428	522	565	613	712	803
YEREVAN	315	532	781	926	1,080	1,368	1,552
ZAPOROZHYE	301	481	668	778	894	1,115	1,265
ZHDANOV	191	305	423	489	558	693	791

Source: United Nations, *Patterns of Urban and Rural Population Growth;* United Nations, *Selected Characteristics of the Population of Urban, Rural, Capital City, and Urban Agglomerations in countries with More than 2 million in 1985: The 1984 Assessment* (New York, 1986).

Notes: The Population Division of the United Nations estimates (for 1950–1980) and projects (for 1980–2000) the population of cities with at least 500,000 inhabitants, as far as possible, for all countries or areas of the world. Wherever possible, cities are considered in terms of agglomerations, that is, within the contours of dense urban settlement. These estimates and projections are in a continuous process of revision, and the figures here may differ from some published in other United Nations publications.

Urban agglomerations and the capital cities are arranged in alphabetical order within the country.

‡ The data which relate to the Federal Republic of Germany and the German Democratic Republic include the relevant data relating to Berlin for which separate data have not been supplied. This is without prejudice to any question of status which may be involved.

. . Figures not available.

Table 7

Households (urban and rural): distribution by number of persons per household and average number of persons per household (number and percentage, latest available census)

REGIONS, COUNTRIES AND CENSUS DATES (1)	TOTAL: T URBAN: U RURAL: R	POPULATION LIVING IN HOUSEHOLDS (2)	HOUSEHOLDS BY SIZE CATEGORY TOTAL (3)	1 (4)	2 (5)	3 (6)	4 OR MORE (7)	AVERAGE NUMBER OF PERSONS PER HOUSE-HOLD (8)
AFRICA								
EGYPT - 3	T	36,346,702	6,946,391	418,997	761,265	837,793	4,928,336	5.2
23-XI-1976	%	..	100.0	6.0	11.0	12.1	70.9	
	U	15,780,336	3,213,056	206,923	380,803	417,068	2,208,262	4.9
	%	..	100.0	6.4	11.9	13.0	68.7	
	R	20,566,366	3,733,335	212,074	380,462	420,725	2,720,074	5.5
	%	..	100.0	5.7	10.2	11.3	72.8	
AMERICA								
BRAZIL - %,6,8	T	118,322,184	27,966,748	1,771,618	4,912,400	5,531,934	15,750,796	4.2
1-IX-1980	%	..	100.0	6.3	17.6	19.8	56.3	
	U	79,717,653	19,384,528	1,195,785	3,510,850	3,957,260	10,720,633	‡‡ 4.1
	%	..	100.0	6.2	18.1	20.4	55.3	
	R	38,604,531	8,582,220	575,833	1,401,550	1,574,674	5,030,163	‡‡ 4.5
	%	..	100.0	6.7	16.3	18.4	58.6	
ASIA								
AFGHANISTAN - 7	T	13,051,358	2,110,044	54,737	149,452	206,296	1,699,559	‡‡ 6.2
23-VI-1979	%	..	100.0	2.6	7.1	9.8	80.5	
	U	1,976,738	313,269	12,434	21,648	27,831	251,356	‡‡ 6.3
	%	..	100.0	4.0	6.9	8.9	80.2	
	R	11,074,620	1,796,775	42,303	127,804	178,465	1,448,203	‡‡ 6.2
	%	..	100.0	2.4	7.1	9.9	80.6	
IRAN - 7	T	33,046,623	6,709,068	376,122	766,696	887,520	4,678,730	4.9
23-VI-1979	%	..	100.0	5.6	11.4	13.2	69.8	
	U	15,448,263	3,264,193	209,006	391,212	467,769	2,196,206	4.7
	%	..	100.0	6.4	12.0	14.3	67.3	
	R	17,598,360	3,444,875	167,116	375,484	419,751	2,482,524	5.1
	%	..	100.0	4.9	10.9	12.2	72.0	
ISRAEL - 6	T	2,929,621	744,179	94,521	172,152	137,899	339,607	3.9
20-V-1972	%	..	100.0	12.7	23.1	18.5	45.7	
	U	2,622,598	716,605	91,274	164,112	130,733	330,486	3.7
	%	..	100.0	12.7	22.9	18.2	46.2	
	R	307,023	57,574	3,247	8,040	7,166	39,121	5.3
	%	..	100.0	5.6	14.0	12.4	68.0	
JAPAN - 10	T	115,450,540	35,823,609	7,105,246	6,001,075	6,475,220	16,242,068	3.2
1-X-1980	%	..	100.0	19.8	16.8	18.1	45.3	
	U	87,920,200	28,364,105	6,225,939	4,752,527	5,149,356	12,236,283	3.1
	%	..	100.0	22.0	16.8	18.2	43.0	
	R	27,530,340	7,459,504	879,307	1,248,548	1,325,864	4,005,785	3.7
	%	..	100.0	11.8	16.7	17.8	53.7	
KOREA, REPUBLIC OF - 9,1	T	36,230,762	7,969,201	382,743	839,839	1,152,569	5,594,050	4.5
1-XI-1980	%	..	100.0	4.8	10.5	14.5	70.2	
	U	20,652,868	4,669,976	220,088	499,643	714,045	3,236,200	4.4
	%	..	100.0	4.7	10.7	15.3	69.3	
	R	15,577,894	3,299,225	162,655	340,196	438,524	2,357,850	4.7
	%	..	100.0	4.9	10.3	13.3	71.5	
EUROPE								
BULGARIA - 6	T	8,608,514	2,755,022	461,896	642,384	579,230	1,071,512	3.1
2-XII-1975	%	..	100.0	16.8	23.3	21.0	38.9	
	U	4,989,228	1,654,379	334,706	305,772	385,832	628,069	3.0
	%	..	100.0	20.2	18.5	23.3	38.0	
	R	3,619,286	1,100,643	127,190	336,612	193,398	443,443	3.3
	%	..	100.0	11.6	30.6	17.6	40.2	

Table 7 (continued)

REGIONS, COUNTRIES AND CENSUS DATES	TOTAL: T URBAN: U RURAL: R	POPULATION LIVING IN HOUSEHOLDS	HOUSEHOLDS BY SIZE CATEGORY					AVERAGE NUMBER OF PERSONS PER HOUSE-HOLD
			TOTAL	1	2	3	4 OR MORE	
(1)		(2)	(3)	(4)	(5)	(6)	(7)	(8)
EUROPE (continued)								
FINLAND - 6 ....T	T	4,495,487	1,644,018	427,900	405,083	329,398	481,637	2.7
31-XII-1975	%	. .	100.0	26.0	24.6	20.0	29.3	
	U	2,639,305	1,037,083	301,721	265,278	210,672	259,412	2.5
	%	. .	100.0	29.1	25.6	20.3	25.0	
	R	1,856,182	606,935	126,179	139,805	118,726	222,225	3.1
	%	. .	100.0	20.8	23.0	19.6	36.6	
FRANCE - 2,4,5 ....T	T	51,151,300	17,744,985	3,935,260	4,937,025	3,401,060	5,471,640	2.9
20-II-1975	%	. .	100.0	22.2	27.8	19.2	30.8	
	U	37,199,125	13,187,565	3,012,165	3,661,250	2,619,125	3,895,025	2.8
	%	. .	100.0	22.8	27.8	19.9	29.5	
	R	13,952,175	4,557,420	923,095	1,275,775	781,935	1,576,615	3.1
	%	. .	100.0	20.3	28.0	17.2	34.5	
HUNGARY ....T	T	10,377,223	3,719,349	730,741	1,043,798	830,093	1,114,717	2.8
1-I-1980	%	. .	100.0	19.6	28.1	22.3	30.0	
	U	5,437,464	2,049,854	451,379	582,662	469,261	546,552	2.7
	%	. .	100.0	22.0	28.4	22.9	26.7	
	R	4,939,759	1,669,495	279,362	461,136	360,832	568,165	3.0
	%	. .	100.0	16.7	27.6	21.6	34.1	
POLAND ....T	T	34,095,024	10,947,081	1,903,923	2,371,409	2,502,119	4,169,630	3.1
7-XII-1978	%	. .	100.0	17.4	21.7	22.9	38.0	
	U	19,327,886	6,788,925	1,407,251	1,512,358	1,672,499	2,196,817	2.8
	%	. .	100.0	20.7	22.3	24.6	32.4	
	R	14,767,138	4,158,156	496,672	859,051	829,620	1,972,813	3.6
	%	. .	100.0	11.9	20.7	20.0	47.4	
U.S.S.R. ....T	T	262,436,227	66,307,213	-	19,663,525	19,127,843	27,515,845	*** 4.0
17-I-1979	%	. .	100.0	-	29.7	28.8	41.5	
	U	163,585,944	42,440,151	-	12,364,229	13,649,547	16,426,375	*** 3.9
	%	. .	100.0	-	29.1	32.2	38.7	
	R	98,850,283	23,867,062	-	7,299,296	5,478,296	11,089,470	*** 4.1
	%	. .	100.0	-	30.6	23.0	46.4	

Source: United Nations, Demographic Yearbook 1982, special topic.

Notes: Only countries or areas for which separate urban and rural data are available have been included.

. . Data not available.

* Provisional.

** Ratio of total population to number of households.

[1] Excluding alien armed forces, civilian aliens employed by armed forces, and foreign diplomatic personnel and their dependents.

[2] De jure population, but excluding diplomatic personnel outside country and including members of alien armed forces not living in military camps and foreign diplomatic personnel not living in Embassies.

[3] For classification of urban/rural residence, see end of Table 6 of the Demographic Yearbook 1982.

[4] Based on a 5 per cent sample of census returns.

[5] Data on households include persons living in institutions who have given an address of a household as their personal residence: but excluding persons living in mobile homes.

[6] De jure population.

[7] Excluding nomads.

[8] Excluding Indian jungle population.

[9] For private households only.

[10] Excluding diplomatic personnel outside country, and foreign military and civilian personnel and their dependants stationed in the area.

Table 8

Crude death rates: urban and rural, 1978–1984

COUNTRIES OR AREAS	TOTAL:T URBAN:U CODE - 1 RURAL:R		RATE (PER 1000 MID-YEAR POPULATION)						
			1978	1979	1980	1981	1982	1983	1984
(1)	(2)		(3)	(4)	(5)	(6)	(7)	(8)	(9)
AFRICA									
EGYPT.....................T	C		10.4	10.9	..	10.1	10.3	*9.0	..
U			9.7	9.6	..	..	..	..	..
R			11.0	11.8	..	..	..	..	..
AMERICA, NORTH									
EL SALVADOR [2].................T	C		6.9	7.4	8.2	7.7	6.7	6.2	..
U			8.7	9.2	11.0	10.4	9.3	..	..
R			5.5	5.8	6.4	5.9	5.0	..	..
HONDURAS [2]...................T	+U		--------- ‡‡‡ 11.8---------				-------------- 10.1 -------		
U			6.7	..	..	..	..	..	..
R			4.5	..	..	..	..	..	..
MEXICO [2]....................T	C		6.4	6.4	6.3	6.0	..	..	..
U			6.2	5.7	..	..	..	..	..
R			6.4	6.7	..	..	..	..	..
NICARAGUA....................T	+U		--------- ‡‡‡ 12.1---------				-------------- 19.5 -------		
U			6.8	..	10.2	..	..	..	..
R			3.7	..	10.8	..	..	..	..
PUERTO RICO..................T	C		6.4	6.5	6.4	6.5	6.6	6.6	..
U			..	..	5.2	..	..	..	..
R			..	..	8.8	..	..	..	..
TURKS AND CAICOS ISLANDS...........T	+C		8.5	..	6.2	..	6.2	6.2	6.2
U			..	..	‡‡ 7.0	..	..	..	..
R			..	..	‡‡ 5.6	..	..	..	..
PANAMA.......................T	U		--------- ‡‡‡ 6.0---------			4.1	..	5.4	..
U			4.0	4.2	4.5	..	..	..	..
R			4.4	4.6	4.2	..	..	..	..
AMERICA, SOUTH									
BOLIVIA [2]...................T	U		--------- ‡‡‡ 17.5---------				-------------- 15.9 -------		
U			5.3	..	4.4	..	..	..	..
R			6.5	..	5.1	..	..	..	..
ECUADOR [2,3]...................T	U		--------- ‡‡‡ 10.4---------				-------------- 8.9 -------		
U			9.0	..	..	..	..	..	..
R			5.8	..	..	..	..	..	..
FALKLAND ISLANDS (MALVINAS) ....T	+C		12.9	9.0	5.4	5.4	..	..	..
U			..	..	7.3	..	..	..	..
R			..	..	1.3	..	..	..	..
ASIA									
AFGHANISTAN [2].................T	..		23.2	18.7	..	..	..	27.3	..
U			..	4.5	..	..	..	..	..
R			..	33.8	..	..	..	..	..
IRAN [2]......................T	U		----------‡‡‡13.6---------				-------------- 10.4 ---------		
U			4.2	4.4	4.7	5.1	5.6	5.7	..
R			3.0	3.1	3.8	3.9	4.2	4.2	..
ISRAEL [2,5]....................T	C		6.8	6.8	6.8	6.6	6.9	6.8	..
U			7.2	..	..	..	..	6.9	..
R			4.4	..	..	..	..	6.6	..
JAPAN [2,6]....................T	C		6.1	6.0	6.2	6.1	6.0	6.2	..
U			..	..	5.6	..	..	..	..
R			..	..	8.0	..	..	..	..
JORDAN [2,7]...................T	+U		---------‡‡‡ 10.5---------				-------------- 8.4 -------		
U			..	3.0	..	..	..	..	..
R			..	3.1	..	..	..	..	..

Table 8 (continued)

COUNTRIES OR AREAS	TOTAL:T URBAN:U CODE - 1 RURAL:R	RATE (PER 1000 MID-YEAR POPULATION)						
		1978	1979	1980	1981	1982	1983	1984
(1)	(2)	(3)	(4)	(5)	(6)	(7)	(8)	(9)
ASIA								
(continued)								
MONGOLIA[2] ....T	..	----------‡‡‡8.3---------			---------------- 7.2 --------			
U		..	8.8	..	..	..	..	..
R		..	10.5	..	..	..	..	..
INDIA[2,4] ....T	..	14.2	12.8	12.6	12.5	11.9	..	..
U		9.4	8.4	7.9	7.8	7.4	..	..
R		15.3	13.9	13.7	13.7	13.1	..	..
EUROPE								
BULGARIA[2] ....T	C	10.5	10.7	11.1	10.7	11.2	11.4	‡11.3
U		7.9	8.0	8.2	7.9	8.2	8.2	8.1
R		14.4	15.0	15.7	15.6	16.7	17.1	‡17.2
FINLAND[2,8] ....T	C	9.2	9.2	9.3	9.2	9.0	9.3	..
U		8.5	9.2	8.6	8.6	8.3	8.7	..
R		10.3	9.4	10.3	10.2	10.0	10.3	..
GERMAN DEMOCRATIC REPUBLIC-‡.......T	C	13.9	13.9	14.2	13.9	13.7	13.3	‡13.3
U		13.6	13.6	13.9	13.4	13.2	13.0	..
R		14.8	15.0	15.4	15.3	15.0	14.6	..
EUROPE								
HUNGARY[2] ....T	C	13.1	12.8	13.6	13.5	13.5	13.9	‡13.7
U		12.0	12.0	12.6	12.5	12.2	12.5	..
R		14.3	13.7	14.6	14.6	15.1	15.7	..
ICELAND[2] ....T	C	6.4	6.6	6.7	7.1	6.8	7.0	..
U		6.2	6.4	6.6	..	6.6	6.9	..
R		7.5	7.4	7.6	..	8.2	7.5	..
LUXEMBOURG[2] ....T	C	11.6	11.0	11.3	11.2	11.3	11.9	‡11.2
U		..	10.4	..	..	..	..	..
R		..	13.0	..	..	..	..	..
NETHERLANDS[2,9] ....T	C	8.2	8.0	8.1	8.1	8.2	8.2	‡8.3
U		9.1	9.0	9.1	9.0	9.2	..	..
R		7.3	6.8	7.0	7.1	7.2	..	..
NORWAY[2,10] ....T	C	10.0	10.2	10.1	10.2	10.1	10.2	‡10.2
U		..	..	6.7	..	..	..	..
R		..	..	18.3	..	..	..	..
POLAND[2] ....T	C	9.3	9.2	9.8	9.2	9.2	9.6	‡9.9
U		8.6	8.5	9.2	8.5	8.6	8.9	..
R		10.2	10.0	10.7	10.1	10.2	10.6	..
ROMANIA[2] ....T	C	9.7	9.9	10.4	10.0	10.0	10.4	..
U		7.8	8.0	8.3	8.0	8.2	..	..
R		11.5	11.6	12.6	12.1	11.6	..	..
OCEANIA								
GUAM[2,11] ....T	C	4.2	3.6	3.9	3.7	4.0	4.0	..
U		..	..	7.2	..	..	..	..
R		..	..	1.3	..	..	..	..
SAMOA[2] ....T	U	2.8	..	3.0	..	..	2.1	..
U		3.6	..	2.5	..	..	..	..
R		2.6	..	3.2	..	..	..	..

Source: United Nations, Demographic Yearbook 1984.

Notes: Data exclude foetal deaths. Rates are the number of deaths per 1,000 corresponding population and were computed by the Statistical Office of the United Nations. For method of evaluation and limitations of data, see the source cited above. Only countries or areas for which data on rates for urban rural sectors are available are included here.

Table 8 (continued)

.. Figures not available.

------ Numbers set between dashes are average rates for the period covered by the dashes.

* Provisional.

*** Estimates for 1978–80 prepared by the Population Division of the United Nations.

† The data which relate to the Federal Republic of Germany and the German Democratic Republic include the relevant data relating to Berlin for which separate data have not been supplied. This is without prejudice to any question of status which may be involved.

[1] Code C indicates that the data are estimated to be virtually complete (at least 90 per cent). Code U indicates that the data are estimated to be incomplete (less than 90 per cent). Some deaths are tabulated by date of registration and not by date of occurrence; these have been indicated by a (†), e.g. †C, †U.

[2] For classification by urban/rural residence, see end of Table 6 of the *Demographic Yearbook 1984*. The urban/rural classification of deaths is that provided by each country or area.

[3] Excluding nomadic Indian tribes.

[4] Based on sample Registration scheme.

[5] Including data for East Jerusalem, and Israeli residents in other territories under occupation.

[6] For Japanese nationals in Japan only; however, rates computed on total population.

[7] Excluding foreigners, but including registered Palestinian refugees.

[8] Including nationals temporarily outside the country.

[9] Including residents outside the country if listed in a Netherlands population register.

[10] Including residents temporarily outside the country.

[11] Including United States military personnel and their dependents, and contract employees.

Table 9

Infant mortality rates: urban and rural, 1978–1984

COUNTRIES OR AREAS	TOTAL:T URBAN:U CODE - 1 RURAL:R	RATE (PER 1000 LIVE BIRTHS)						
		1978	1979	1980	1981	1982	1983	1984
(1)	(2)	(3)	(4)	(5)	(6)	(7)	(8)	(9)
AMERICA, NORTH								
EL SALVADOR[4] ....T	C	50.8	53.0	42.0	44.0	42.2	..	..
	U	58.7	61.9	47.0	47.0	43.5	..	..
	R	45.9	47.2	38.4	41.4	41.1	..	..
GUATEMALA[4] ....T	C	67.9	69.7	65.5	63.9	62.5	71.2	..
	U	76.6	79.1	..	..	..	..	..
	R	62.4	64.2	..	..	..	..	..
NICARAGUA[4] ....T	+U	--------- ‡‡ 96.5---------			---------------- 85.0 -------			
	U	..	115.0	96.6	..	..	..	..
	R	..	126.6	106.3	..	..	..	..
PANAMA[2,4] ....T	U	--------- ‡‡ 36.2---------			---------------- 26.0 -------			
	U	22.3	21.5	..	19.7	17.1	..	..
	R	26.2	27.7	..	24.7	22.6	..	..
PUERTO RICO.................T	C	18.5	19.9	19.0	18.6	17.2	17.3	..
	U	..	..	18.1	18.8	17.8	17.0	..
	R	..	..	18.8	18.2	16.4	17.6	..
ASIA								
AFGHANISTAN[4,5] ....T	..	..	181.6	..	---------------- 204.8 -------			
	U	..	129.9	..	..	..	..	..
	R	..	189.0	..	..	..	..	..
ISRAEL[4,7] ....T	C	16.3	15.9	15.1	15.6	13.9	14.4	..
	U	16.1	..	..	..	13.4	13.3	..
	R	22.1	..	..	..	15.6	18.4	..
JAPAN[4,8] ....T	C	8.4	7.9	7.5	7.1	6.6	6.2	..
	U	8.1	7.6	7.3	7.0	6.4	6.0	..
	R	9.4	8.8	8.3	7.6	7.1	6.8	..
JORDAN[4,6] ....T	+U	--------- ‡‡ 75.1 --------			---------------- 63.4 -------			
	U	11.0	11.5	..	..	..	..	..
	R	12.7	15.5	..	..	..	..	..
PENINSULAR MALAYSIA.................T	C	26.7	26.0	24.9	..	..	..	..
	U	19.9	19.1	..	..	..	..	..
	R	29.8	29.2	..	..	..	..	..
SRI LANKA[4] ....T	C	37.1	37.7	34.4	..	..	..	..
	U	40.7	..	41.5	..	..	..	..
	R	33.8	..	28.3	..	..	..	..
THAILAND.................T	U	--------- ‡‡ 58.9---------			---------------- 51.0 ---------			
	U	25.4	22.5	..	..	32.4	32.5	..
	R	13.3	10.9	..	..	8.2	8.2	..
EUROPE								
AUSTRIA[4] ....T	C	15.0	14.7	14.3	12.6	12.8	11.9	‡11.5
	U	15.4	..	..	..	..	..	..
	R	14.6	..	..	..	..	..	..
BULGARIA[4] ....T	C	22.2	19.8	20.2	18.9	18.2	16.8	16.2
	U	19.9	17.6	18.0	17.4	16.4	15.3	14.9
	R	27.0	24.5	24.9	21.9	21.7	19.9	18.9
FINLAND[4,9] ....T	C	7.6	7.7	7.6	6.5	6.0	6.2	..
	U	7.7	7.2	7.5	6.0	6.2	6.2	..
	R	7.3	8.4	7.8	7.3	5.6	6.2	..
GERMAN DEMOCRATIC REPUBLIC-‡.......T	C	13.1	12.9	12.1	12.3	11.4	10.7	‡10.0
	U	13.1	13.0	12.1	12.4	11.3	11.0	..
	R	13.2	12.7	12.0	12.1	11.8	9.7	..

Table 9 (continued)

COUNTRIES OR AREAS	TOTAL:T URBAN:U CODE - 1 RURAL:R		RATE (PER 1000 LIVE BIRTHS)						
			1978	1979	1980	1981	1982	1983	1984
(1)	(2)		(3)	(4)	(5)	(6)	(7)	(8)	(9)
EUROPE									
(continued)									
GREECE[4]	T	C	19.3	18.7	17.9	16.3	15.1	14.9	‡14.1
	U		20.6	20.4	19.3	17.9	17.4	..	..
	R		17.1	15.7	15.4	13.4	11.0	..	..
HUNGARY[4]	T	C	24.4	24.0	23.2	20.8	20.0	19.0	..
	U		23.9	23.6	22.3	19.8	20.2	18.8	..
	R		24.8	24.4	24.1	21.9	19.8	19.3	..
IRELAND[4,10]	T	C	15.0	12.8	11.2	10.3	10.5	9.8	..
	U		14.9	14.2	11.9	10.6	12.5	..	..
	R		14.9	12.1	10.6	10.2	9.6	..	..
NETHERLANDS[4,11]	T	C	9.6	8.7	8.6	8.3	8.3	8.4	‡8.3
	U		10.3	8.8	9.2	8.8	8.7	9.2	..
	R		7.8	7.8	8.4	7.8	6.8	8.1	..
NORWAY[3,4]	T	C	8.6	8.8	8.1	7.5	8.1	7.9	..
	U		8.3	8.8	8.2	..	..	..	..
	R		8.9	8.7	7.9	..	..	..	..
POLAND[4]	T	C	22.5	21.1	21.3	20.6	20.2	19.2	..
	U		22.1	20.3	20.9	20.4	19.7	19.2	..
	R		22.9	22.0	21.7	20.9	20.8	19.2	..
ROMANIA[4]	T	C	30.3	31.6	29.3	28.6	28.0	..	..
	U		26.1	26.7	25.9	24.4	24.4	..	..
	R		33.8	35.9	32.4	32.6	31.6	..	..
OCEANIA									
NEW ZEALAND[4]	T	C	13.8	12.5	12.9	11.7	11.8	12.5	..
	U		..	..	12.2	11.8	11.6	12.6	..
	R		..	..	14.2	11.3	12.1	12.5	..

Source: United Nations, *Demographic Yearbook 1984*.

Notes: Data exclude foetal deaths. Rates are the number of deaths of infants under 1 year of age per 1,000 corresponding live births, and were computed by the Statistical Office of the United Nations. For method of evaluation and limitations of data, see the source cited above. Only countries or areas for which urban/rural data on infant mortality rates are available have been included here.

. . Figures not available.

------ Number set between dashes are average rates for the period covered by the dashes.

* Provisional.

** Estimates for 1978–80 prepared by Population Division of the United Nations.

‡ The data which relate to the Federal Republic of Germany and the German Democratic Republic include the relevant data relating to Berlin for which separate data have not been supplied. This is without prejudice to any question of status which may be involved.

[1] Code C indicates that the data are estimated to be virtually complete (at least 90 per cent). Code U indicates that the data are estimated to be incomplete (less than 90 per cent). Some deaths are tabulated by date of registration and not by date of occurrence; these have been indicated by a (†) e.g. †C or †U.

[2] Prior to 1980, excluding the former Canal Zone.

[3] Including residents temporarily outside the country.

[4] For classification by urban/rural residence, see end of Table 6 of the *Demographic Yearbook 1984*. The urban/rural classification of deaths is that provided by each country or area.

[5] Based on the results of the population census of 1979.

[6] Excluding data for Jordanian territory under occupation.

[7] Including data for East Jerusalem, and Israeli residents in other territories under occupation.

[8] For Japanese nationals in Japan only; however, rates computed on total population.

[9] Including nationals temporarily outside the country.

[10] Infants deaths registered within one year of occurrence.

[11] Including residents outside the country if listed in a Netherlands population register.

Table 10

Percentage of the population illiterate by age group and sex: urban and rural, 1973–1982

COUNTRIES AND CENSUS YEARS	TOTAL:T URBAN:U RURAL:R	AGE GROUP	PERCENTAGE OF ILLITERATE POPULATION		
			BOTH SEXES	MALE	FEMALE
(1)		(2)	(3)	(4)	(5)
AFRICA					
EGYPT 1976	T	15+	61.8	46.4	77.6
	T	10+	56.5	43.2	71.0
	U	10+	39.7	28.5	51.8
	R	10+	70.6	55.5	86.9
TUNISIA 1980	T	15+	53.5	38.9	67.7
	T	10+	47.5	33.8	61.1
	U	10+	35.3	..	..
	R	10+	62.2	..	..
UNITED REPUBLIC OF TANZANIA 1978	T	15+	53.7	37.8	68.6
	U	15+	29.9	16.5	45.5
	R	15+	57.9	42.1	72.2
BURKINA FASO 1975	T	15+	91.2	85.3	96.7
	U	15+	68.5	55.2	81.9
	R	15+	93.3	88.3	98.0
AMERICA, NORTH					
COSTA RICA 1973	T	15+	11.6	11.4	11.8
	U	15+	4.9	4.0	5.7
	R	15+	17.0	16.6	17.5
EL SALVADOR 1975	T	10+	38.0	34.5	41.1
	U	10+	18.0	12.7	22.2
	R	10+	53.0	48.9	57.2
GUATEMALA ‡‡1973	T	15+	54.0	46.4	61.5
	U	15+	28.2	20.0	35.5
	R	15+	68.6	59.9	77.6
HONDURAS ‡‡1974	T	15+	43.1	41.1	44.9
	U	15+	21.1	17.6	24.0
	R	15+	54.4	52.1	56.8
MEXICO 1980	T	15+	17.3	..	..
	U	15+	..	..	..
	R	15+	..	..	..
AMERICA, SOUTH					
BOLIVIA 1976	T	15+	36.8	24.2	48.6
	U	15+	15.2	6.2	23.2
	R	15+	53.2	37.3	68.5
BRAZIL 1978	T	15+	23.9	22.0	25.7
	U	15+	15.6	12.8	18.1
	R	15+	42.4	40.9	43.9
COLOMBIA 1981	T	15+	14.8	13.6	16.1
	U	15+	9.0	..	..
	R	15+	24.8	..	..

COUNTRIES AND CENSUS YEARS	TOTAL:T URBAN:U RURAL:R	AGE GROUP	PERCENTAGE OF ILLITERATE POPULATION		
			BOTH SEXES	MALE	FEMALE
(1)		(2)	(3)	(4)	(5)
AMERICA, SOUTH (continued)					
ECUADOR ‡‡1974	T	15+	25.8	21.8	29.6
	U	15+	9.7	6.9	12.2
	R	15+	38.2	32.3	44.4
URUGUAY 1975	T	15+	6.1	6.6	5.7
	U	15+	5.2	5.1	5.2
	R	15+	11.0	12.6	8.6
ASIA					
AFGHANISTAN 1980	T	15+	80.0	66.8	94.2
	U	15+	60.9	45.5	78.5
	R	15+	83.5	70.9	96.9
BANGLADESH 1974	T	15+	74.2	62.7	86.8
	U	15+	51.9	42.1	66.8
	R	15+	76.5	65.3	88.5
BAHRAIN 1981	T	15+	20.9	17.0	26.3
	U	15+	19.8	16.6	24.0
	R	15+	25.3	19.0	33.7
CHINA ‡‡1982	T	15+	34.5	20.8	48.9
	U	15+	17.6	9.5	26.4
	R	15+	37.8	23.1	53.2
DEMOCRATIC YEMEN 1973	T	10+	72.9	52.3	92.1
	U	10+	59.1	40.0	80.5
	R	10+	77.4	53.8	96.8
INDONESIA 1980	T	15+	32.7	22.5	42.3
	U	15+	16.5	8.8	24.0
	R	15+	37.6	26.8	47.7
IRAN 1976	T	15+	63.5	51.8	75.6
	U	15+	44.0	32.7	56.5
	R	15+	83.0	72.3	93.4
PAKISTAN 1981	T	15+	73.8	64.0	84.8
	U	15+	53.1	43.1	65.3
	R	15+	82.6	73.4	92.7
SRI LANKA ‡‡1981	T	15+	13.9	9.2	18.8
	U	15+	6.7	4.4	9.2
	R	15+	16.0	10.7	21.4
EUROPE					
POLAND 1978	T	15+	1.2	0.7	1.7
	U	15+	0.7	0.3	0.9
	R	15+	2.1	1.3	2.9
UNION OF SOVIET SOCIALIST REPUBLICS					
U.S.S.R. 1979	T	9 - 49	0.2	..	..
	U	9 - 49	0.1	..	..
	R	9 - 49	0.3	..	..
BYELORUSSIAN S.S.R. 1979	T	9 - 49	0.1	0.1	0.1

Source: *UNESCO Statistical Yearbook 1984*.

Notes: Literacy is defined as ability to read and to write; hence, unless otherwise specified, semi-literates (persons able to read but not write) are included with the illiterate population.

It should be noted that mainly countries or areas for which urban/rural data are available have been extracted from the *Statistical Yearbook 1984*.

†† Figures refer to *de jure* population.

. . Figures not available.

Table 11

Land use by area: Part I—Estimates for macro regions and regions, 1974–1984 (millions of hectares)

MACRO REGIONS AND REGIONS	1974-1976 TOTAL AREA	ARABLE LAND AND LAND UNDER PERMANENT CROPS	PERMANENT MEADOWS AND PASTURES	FORESTS	OTHER AREA	1980 TOTAL AREA	ARABLE LAND AND LAND UNDER PERMANENT CROPS	PERMANENT MEADOWS AND PASTURES	FORESTS	OTHER AREA
(1)	(2)	(3)	(4)	(5)	(6)	(7)	(8)	(9)	(10)	(11)
DEVELOPED [1] MARKET ECONOMIES										
NORTHERN AMERICA	1935	232	266	616	722	1,935	236	261	610	731
WESTERN EUROPE	385	96	72	121	91	385	95	71	124	92
OCEANIA	796	43	471	135	140	796	45	466	113	165
OTHER DEVELOPED MARKET ECONOMIES	161	19	83	29	30	161	19	82	29	31
DEVELOPING [1] MARKET ECONOMIES										
AFRICA	2,384	146	636	671	878	2,384	151	635	659	887
LATIN AMERICA	2,055	158	539	1,038	285	2,055	172	547	1,011	290
NEAR EAST	1,208	84	268	99	741	1,208	82	268	97	746
FAR EAST	857	265	36	310	199	857	268	35	306	200
OTHER DEVELOPING MARKET ECONOMIES	90	1	1	43	43	90	1	1	43	43
CENTRALLY PLANNED ECONOMIES										
ASIA	1,179	113	421	166	450	1,179	113	410	172	456
E. EUROPE AND U.S.S.R.	2,342	279	389	926	734	2,342	278	389	945	715

MACRO REGIONS AND REGIONS	1982 TOTAL AREA	ARABLE LAND AND LAND UNDER PERMANENT CROPS	PERMANENT MEADOWS AND PASTURES	FORESTS	OTHER AREA	1984 TOTAL AREA	ARABLE LAND AND LAND UNDER PERMANENT CROPS	PERMANENT MEADOWS AND PASTURES	FORESTS	OTHER AREA
(12)	(13)	(14)	(15)	(16)	(17)	(18)	(19)	(20)	(21)	(22)
DEVELOPED [1] MARKET ECONOMIES										
NORTHERN AMERICA	1935	236	265	591	746	1,935	236	265	591	746
WESTERN EUROPE	385	95	71	126	81	385	95	70	126	82
OCEANIA	796	47	458	116	167	796	49	453	117	171
OTHER DEVELOPED MARKET ECONOMIES	161	19	81	29	31	161	19	81	29	32
DEVELOPING [1] MARKET ECONOMIES										
AFRICA	2,384	152	630	653	896	2,384	154	630	648	900
LATIN AMERICA	2,055	177	549	1,001	293	2,055	177	551	991	300
NEAR EAST	1,208	82	268	96	747	1,208	82	267	96	747
FAR EAST	857	270	35	305	200	857	272	35	303	200
OTHER DEVELOPING MARKET ECONOMIES	90	1	1	43	43	90	1	1	43	43

Table 11 (continued)

MACRO REGIONS AND REGIONS	1982						1984				
	TOTAL AREA	ARABLE LAND AND LAND UNDER PERMANENT CROPS	PERMANENT MEADOWS AND PASTURES	FORESTS	OTHER AREA		TOTAL AREA	ARABLE LAND AND LAND UNDER PERMANENT CROPS	PERMANENT MEADOWS AND PASTURES	FORESTS	OTHER AREA
(12)	(13)	(14)	(15)	(16)	(17)		(18)	(19)	(20)	(21)	(22)
CENTRALLY PLANNED ECONOMIES											
ASIA	1,179	114	410	179	448		1,179	114	410	185	442
E. EUROPE AND U.S.S.R.	2,342	278	388	953	707		2,342	278	388	961	700

Source: Food and Agriculture Organization of the United Nations, *FAO Production Yearbook 1985* vol. 39, 47–58.

Notes: For many developing countries, changes in data from one year to another, particularly for permanent meadows and pastures and forests, might reflect a general improvement in statistical information and better interpretation of land use classification and not an actual change.

[1] The classification is intended for statistical convenience and does not necessarily express a judgement about the stage reached by a particular country or area in the development process.

Land use by area: Part II—Countries for which data are available, 1974–1984 (millions of hectares)

COUNTRIES	1974-1976						1980					
	TOTAL AREA	LAND AREA	ARABLE LAND AND LAND UNDER PERMANENT CROPS	PERMANENT MEADOWS AND PASTURES	FORESTS	OTHER LAND AREA	TOTAL AREA	LAND AREA	ARABLE LAND AND LAND UNDER PERMANENT CROPS	PERMANENT MEADOWS AND PASTURES	FORESTS	OTHER LAND AREA
(1)	(2)	(3)	(4)	(5)	(6)	(7)	(8)	(9)	(10)	(11)	(12)	(13)
AFRICA												
ALGERIA	238	238	7	37	4	190	238	238	8	36	4	190
ANGOLA	125	125	4	29	54	38	125	125	4	29	54	38
BENIN	11	11	2	1	4	5	11	11	2	1	4	5
BOTSWANA	60	59	1	44	1	12	60	59	1	44	1	12
BURKINA FASO	27	27	3	10	8	7	27	27	3	10	8	8
BURUNDI	3	3	1	1	-	1	3	3	1	1	-	1
CAMEROON	47	47	6	8	26	6	47	47	7	8	26	6
CENTRAL AFRICAN REPUBLIC	62	62	2	3	36	21	63	63	2	3	36	21
CHAD	128	126	3	45	14	64	128	126	3	45	14	64
CONGO	34	34	1	10	21	2	34	34	1	10	21	2
COTE D'IVOIRE	32	32	3	3	12	13	32	32	3	3	10	15
EGYPT	100	100	3	-	-	97	100	100	3	-	-	97
EQUATORIAL GUINEA	3	3	-	-	1	1	3	3	-	-	1	1
ETHIOPIA	122	110	14	46	29	22	122	110	14	45	28	23
GABON	27	26	-	5	20	1	27	26	-	5	20	1
GHANA	24	23	3	4	9	8	24	23	3	3	9	9
GUINEA	25	25	2	3	11	9	25	25	2	3	11	9
GUINEA-BISSAU	4	3	-	1	1	1	4	3	-	1	1	1
KENYA	58	57	2	4	4	47	58	57	2	4	4	47
LESOTHO	3	3	-	2	-	1	3	3	-	2	-	1
LIBERIA	11	10	-	-	4	5	11	10	-	-	4	5
LIBYAN ARAB JAMAHIRIYA	176	176	2	12	1	161	176	176	2	13	1	160
MADAGASCAR	58	58	3	34	17	5	58	58	3	34	16	5
MALAWI	12	9	2	2	5	-	12	9	2	2	5	-
MALI	124	122	2	30	9	81	124	122	2	30	9	81
MAURITANIA	103	103	-	39	15	48	103	103	-	39	15	49
MOROCCO	45	45	8	13	5	19	45	45	8	13	5	19
MOZAMBIQUE	80	78	3	44	17	15	80	78	3	44	16	16
NIGER	127	127	2	10	4	111	127	127	4	10	3	111
NIGERIA	92	91	30	21	18	22	92	91	30	21	16	23
RWANDA	3	2	1	1	-	1	3	2	1	1	-	1
SENEGAL	20	19	5	6	6	3	20	19	5	6	6	3
SIERRA LEONE	7	7	2	2	2	1	7	7	2	2	2	1

Table 11 (continued)

COUNTRIES	1974-1976						1980					
	TOTAL AREA	LAND AREA	ARABLE LAND AND LAND UNDER PERMANENT CROPS	PERMANENT MEADOWS AND PASTURES	FORESTS	OTHER LAND AREA	TOTAL AREA	LAND AREA	ARABLE LAND AND LAND UNDER PERMANENT CROPS	PERMANENT MEADOWS AND PASTURES	FORESTS	OTHER LAND AREA
(1)	(2)	(3)	(4)	(5)	(6)	(7)	(8)	(9)	(10)	(11)	(12)	(13)
AFRICA (continued)												
SOMALIA	64	63	1	29	9	24	64	63	1	29	9	24
SUDAN	251	238	12	56	54	119	251	238	12	56	51	120
SWAZILAND	2	2	-	1	-	1	2	2	-	1	-	1
TANZANIA, UNITED REPUBLIC OF	95	89	5	35	43	5	95	89	5	35	43	6
TOGO	6	5	1	-	2	2	6	5	1	-	2	2
TUNISIA	16	16	5	3	1	8	16	16	5	3	1	8
UGANDA	24	20	5	5	6	4	24	20	5	5	6	3
WESTERN SAHARA	27	27	-	5	-	22	27	27	-	5	-	22
ZAIRE	235	227	6	9	179	32	235	227	6	9	178	34
ZAMBIA	75	74	5	35	30	4	75	74	5	35	30	4
ZIMBABWE	39	39	3	5	24	7	39	39	3	5	24	7
SOUTH AFRICA	122	122	13	82	4	23	122	122	13	81	4	24

COUNTRIES	1982						1984					
	TOTAL AREA	LAND AREA	ARABLE LAND AND LAND UNDER PERMANENT CROPS	PERMANENT MEADOWS AND PASTURES	FORESTS	OTHER LAND AREA	TOTAL AREA	LAND AREA	ARABLE LAND AND LAND UNDER PERMANENT CROPS	PERMANENT MEADOWS AND PASTURES	FORESTS	OTHER LAND AREA
(14)	(15)	(16)	(17)	(18)	(19)	(20)	(21)	(22)	(23)	(24)	(25)	(26)
AFRICA												
ALGERIA	238	238	8	32	4	195	238	238	7	32	4	194
ANGOLA	125	125	4	29	54	39	125	125	4	29	54	39
BENIN	11	11	2	1	4	5	11	11	2	1	4	5
BOTSWANA	60	59	1	44	1	12	60	59	1	44	1	12
BURKINA FASO	27	27	3	10	7	7	27	27	3	10	7	8
BURUNDI	3	3	1	1	-	1	3	3	1	1	-	1
CAMEROON	48	47	7	8	25	6	48	47	7	8	25	6
CENTRAL AFRICAN REPUBLIC	62	62	2	3	36	21	62	62	2	3	36	21
CHAD	128	126	3	45	13	64	128	126	3	45	13	64
CONGO	34	34	1	10	21	2	34	34	1	10	21	2
COTE D'IVOIRE	32	32	4	3	9	16	32	32	4	3	8	17
EGYPT	100	100	2	-	-	97	100	100	2	-	-	97
EQUATORIAL GUINEA	3	3	-	-	1	1	3	3	-	-	1	1
ETHIOPIA	122	110	14	45	28	23	122	110	14	45	28	23
GABON	27	26	-	5	20	1	27	26	-	5	20	1
GHANA	24	23	3	3	9	8	24	23	3	3	8	8
GUINEA	25	25	2	3	10	10	25	25	2	3	10	10
GUINEA-BISSAU	4	3	-	1	1	1	4	3	-	1	1	1
KENYA	58	57	2	4	3	47	58	57	2	4	3	47
LESOTHO	3	3	-	2	-	1	3	3	-	2	-	1
LIBERIA	11	10	-	-	4	5	11	10	-	-	4	5
LIBYAN ARAB JAMAHIRIYA	176	176	2	12	1	160	176	176	2	13	1	160
MADAGASCAR	59	58	3	34	15	6	59	58	3	34	15	6
MALAWI	12	9	2	2	5	-	12	9	2	2	5	1
MALI	124	122	2	30	9	81	124	122	2	30	8	82
MAURITANIA	103	103	-	39	15	49	103	103	-	39	15	49
MOROCCO	45	45	8	13	5	19	45	45	8	13	5	19
MOZAMBIQUE	80	78	3	44	16	16	80	78	3	44	15	16
NIGER	127	127	4	9	3	111	127	127	4	9	3	111
NIGERIA	92	91	30	21	16	24	92	91	31	21	15	24
RWANDA	3	2	1	1	-	1	3	2	1	1	-	1
SENEGAL	20	19	5	6	6	2	20	19	5	6	6	2
SIERRA LEONE	7	7	2	2	2	1	7	7	2	2	2	1
SOMALIA	64	63	1	29	9	24	64	63	1	29	9	24
SUDAN	251	238	12	56	48	121	251	238	12	56	48	121
SWAZILAND	2	2	-	1	-	1	2	2	-	1	-	1
TANZANIA, UNITED REPUBLIC OF	95	89	5	35	43	5	95	89	5	35	43	6
TOGO	6	5	1	-	2	2	6	5	1	-	2	2

Table 11 (continued)

	1982						1984					
COUNTRIES	TOTAL AREA	LAND AREA	ARABLE LAND AND LAND UNDER PERMANENT CROPS	PERMANENT MEADOWS AND PASTURES	FORESTS	OTHER LAND AREA	TOTAL AREA	LAND AREA	ARABLE LAND AND LAND UNDER PERMANENT CROPS	PERMANENT MEADOWS AND PASTURES	FORESTS	OTHER LAND AREA
(14)	(15)	(16)	(17)	(18)	(19)	(20)	(21)	(22)	(23)	(24)	(25)	(26)
AFRICA (continued)												
TUNISIA	16	16	5	3	1	7	16	16	5	3	-	7
UGANDA	24	20	6	5	6	3	24	20	6	5	6	3
WESTERN SAHARA	27	27	-	5	-	22	27	27	-	5	-	22
ZAIRE	235	227	6	9	177	34	235	227	6	9	176	35
ZAMBIA	75	74	5	35	30	4	75	74	5	35	29	4
ZIMBABWE	39	39	3	5	24	7	39	39	3	5	24	7
SOUTH AFRICA	122	122	14	80	4	24	122	122	14	80	4	25

	1974-1976						1980					
COUNTRIES	TOTAL AREA	LAND AREA	ARABLE LAND AND LAND UNDER PERMANENT CROPS	PERMANENT MEADOWS AND PASTURES	FORESTS	OTHER LAND AREA	TOTAL AREA	LAND AREA	ARABLE LAND AND LAND UNDER PERMANENT CROPS	PERMANENT MEADOWS AND PASTURES	FORESTS	OTHER LAND AREA
(1)	(2)	(3)	(4)	(5)	(6)	(7)	(8)	(9)	(10)	(11)	(12)	(13)
AMERICA, NORTH												
BAHAMAS	1	1	-	-	-	1	1	1	-	-	-	1
BELIZE	2	2	-	-	1	1	2	2	-	-	1	1
CANADA	998	922	43	23	326	529	998	922	45	23	326	527
COSTA RICA	5	5	1	2	3	1	5	5	1	2	2	1
CUBA	11	11	3	3	2	4	11	11	3	3	2	3
DOMINICAN REPUBLIC	5	5	1	2	1	1	5	5	1	2	1	1
EL SALVADOR	2	2	1	1	1	1	2	2	1	1	-	1
GREENLAND	34	34	-	-	-	34	34	34	-	-	-	34
GUATEMALA	11	11	2	1	5	3	11	11	2	1	5	3
HAITI	3	3	1	1	-	1	3	3	1	1	-	1
HONDURAS	11	11	2	3	4	2	11	11	2	3	4	2
MEXICO	197	192	24	74	51	43	197	192	25	74	48	45
NICARAGUA	13	12	1	5	5	1	13	12	1	5	5	1
PANAMA	8	8	1	1	4	2	8	8	1	1	4	2
PUERTO RICO	1	1	-	-	-	-	1	1	-	-	-	-
UNITED STATES OF AMERICA	936	913	190	244	292	186	936	913	188	242	291	192

	1982						1984					
COUNTRIES	TOTAL AREA	LAND AREA	ARABLE LAND AND LAND UNDER PERMANENT CROPS	PERMANENT MEADOWS AND PASTURES	FORESTS	OTHER LAND AREA	TOTAL AREA	LAND AREA	ARABLE LAND AND LAND UNDER PERMANENT CROPS	PERMANENT MEADOWS AND PASTURES	FORESTS	OTHER LAND AREA
(14)	(15)	(16)	(17)	(18)	(19)	(20)	(21)	(22)	(23)	(24)	(25)	(26)
AMERICA, NORTH												
BAHAMAS	1	1	-	-	-	1	1	1	-	-	-	1
BELIZE	2	2	-	-	1	1	2	2	-	-	1	1
CANADA	998	922	46	24	326	526	998	922	47	24	326	526
COSTA RICA	5	5	-	2	2	1	5	5	-	2	2	1
CUBA	11	11	3	3	2	3	11	11	3	2	2	3
DOMINICAN REPUBLIC	5	5	1	2	1	2	5	5	1	2	1	1
EL SALVADOR	2	2	1	1	-	1	2	2	1	1	-	1
GREENLAND	34	34	-	-	-	34	34	34	-	-	-	34
GUATEMALA	11	11	2	1	4	3	11	11	2	1	4	3
HAITI	3	3	1	1	-	1	3	3	1	1	-	1
HONDURAS	11	11	2	3	4	2	11	11	2	3	4	2

Table 11 (continued)

COUNTRIES	1982						1984					
	TOTAL AREA	LAND AREA	ARABLE LAND AND LAND UNDER PERMANENT CROPS	PERMANENT MEADOWS AND PASTURES	FORESTS	OTHER LAND AREA	TOTAL AREA	LAND AREA	ARABLE LAND AND LAND UNDER PERMANENT CROPS	PERMANENT MEADOWS AND PASTURES	FORESTS	OTHER LAND AREA
(14)	(15)	(16)	(17)	(18)	(19)	(20)	(21)	(22)	(23)	(24)	(25)	(26)
(continued)												
MEXICO	197	192	25	74	47	46	197	192	25	75	46	47
NICARAGUA	13	12	1	5	4	1	13	12	1	5	4	1
PANAMA	8	8	1	1	4	2	8	8	1	1	4	2
PUERTO RICO	1	1	-	1	-	-	1	1	-	1	-	-
UNITED STATES OF AMERICA	936	913	188	242	291	192	936	913	191	238	284	200

COUNTRIES	1974-1976						1980					
	TOTAL AREA	LAND AREA	ARABLE LAND AND LAND UNDER PERMANENT CROPS	PERMANENT MEADOWS AND PASTURES	FORESTS	OTHER LAND AREA	TOTAL AREA	LAND AREA	ARABLE LAND AND LAND UNDER PERMANENT CROPS	PERMANENT MEADOWS AND PASTURES	FORESTS	OTHER LAND AREA
(1)	(2)	(3)	(4)	(5)	(6)	(7)	(8)	(9)	(10)	(11)	(12)	(13)
AMERICA, SOUTH												
ARGENTINA	277	274	35	143	60	35	277	274	35	143	60	35
BOLIVIA	110	108	3	27	56	22	110	108	3	27	56	22
BRAZIL	851	846	61	155	586	40	851	846	71	161	585	38
CHILE	76	75	5	12	15	42	76	75	5	12	15	42
COLOMBIA	114	104	5	30	58	11	114	104	6	30	53	15
ECUADOR	28	28	3	3	15	7	28	28	2	4	15	7
FALKLAND IS. (MALVINAS)	1	1	-	1	-	-	1	1	-	1	-	-
FRENCH GUIANA	9	9	-	-	7	2	9	9	-	-	7	2
GUYANA	21	20	-	1	18	-	21	20	-	1	16	2
PARAGUAY	41	40	1	15	21	3	41	40	2	16	21	2
PERU	129	128	3	27	72	26	129	128	3	27	71	27
SURINAME	16	16	-	-	16	1	16	16	-	-	16	1
URUGUAY	18	17	1	14	1	2	18	17	1	14	1	2
VENEZUELA	91	88	4	17	34	33	91	88	4	17	33	34

COUNTRIES	1982						1984					
	TOTAL AREA	LAND AREA	ARABLE LAND AND LAND UNDER PERMANENT CROPS	PERMANENT MEADOWS AND PASTURES	FORESTS	OTHER LAND AREA	TOTAL AREA	LAND AREA	ARABLE LAND AND LAND UNDER PERMANENT CROPS	PERMANENT MEADOWS AND PASTURES	FORESTS	OTHER LAND AREA
(14)	(15)	(16)	(17)	(18)	(19)	(20)	(21)	(22)	(23)	(24)	(25)	(26)
AMERICA, SOUTH												
ARGENTINA	277	274	36	143	60	35	277	274	36	143	60	35
BOLIVIA	110	108	3	27	56	22	110	108	3	27	56	22
BRAZIL	851	846	75	163	570	38	851	846	75	165	565	40
CHILE	76	75	5	12	15	42	76	75	6	12	15	42
COLOMBIA	114	104	6	30	52	17	114	104	6	30	50	18
ECUADOR	28	28	2	4	14	6	28	28	3	5	14	6
FALKLAND IS. (MALVINAS)	1	1	-	1	-	-	1	1	-	1	-	-
FRENCH GUIANA	9	9	-	-	7	2	9	9	-	-	7	2
GUYANA	21	20	-	1	16	2	21	20	-	1	16	2
PARAGUAY	41	40	2	16	21	2	41	40	2	16	20	2
PERU	129	128	4	27	70	27	129	128	4	27	70	27
SURINAME	16	16	-	-	16	1	16	16	-	-	16	1
URUGUAY	18	17	2	14	1	2	18	17	2	14	1	2
VENEZUELA	91	88	4	17	32	35	91	88	4	17	32	35

Table 11 (continued)

COUNTRIES	1974-1976 TOTAL AREA	LAND AREA	ARABLE LAND AND LAND UNDER PERMANENT CROPS	PERMANENT MEADOWS AND PASTURES	FORESTS	OTHER LAND AREA	1980 TOTAL AREA	LAND AREA	ARABLE LAND AND LAND UNDER PERMANENT CROPS	PERMANENT MEADOWS AND PASTURES	FORESTS	OTHER LAND AREA
(1)	(2)	(3)	(4)	(5)	(6)	(7)	(8)	(9)	(10)	(11)	(12)	(13)
ASIA												
AFGHANISTAN	65	65	8	30	2	25	65	65	8	30	2	25
BANGLADESH	14	13	9	1	2	1	14	13	9	1	2	1
BHUTAN	5	5	-	-	3	1	5	5	-	-	3	1
BURMA	68	66	10	-	32	23	68	66	10	-	32	23
CHINA	960	933	101	286	115	431	960	933	100	286	121	425
EAST TIMOR	1	1	-	-	1	-	1	1	-	-	1	-
INDIA	329	297	168	13	66	51	329	297	168	13	67	49
INDONESIA	190	181	20	12	122	27	190	181	20	12	122	28
IRAN	165	164	16	44	18	85	165	164	14	44	18	88
IRAQ	43	43	5	4	2	32	43	43	5	4	2	32
ISRAEL	2	2	-	1	-	1	2	2	-	1	-	1
JAPAN	37	37	5	-	25	6	37	37	5	-	25	6
JORDAN	10	10	1	-	-	8	10	10	1	-	-	8
KAMPUCHEA, DEMOCRATIC	18	18	3	1	13	1	18	18	3	1	13	1
KOREA, DEMOCRATIC PEOPLE'S REPUBLIC OF	12	12	2	-	9	1	12	12	2	-	9	1
KOREA, REPUBLIC OF	10	10	2	-	7	1	10	10	2	-	7	1
KUWAIT	2	2	-	-	-	2	2	2	-	-	-	2
LAO PEOPLE'S DEMOCRATIC REPUBLIC	24	23	1	1	14	7	24	23	1	1	14	8
LEBANON	1	1	-	-	-	1	1	1	-	-	-	1
MALAYSIA	33	33	4	-	21	8	33	33	4	-	20	8
MONGOLIA	157	157	1	135	15	6	157	157	1	123	17	1
NEPAL	14	14	2	2	4	7	14	14	2	2	4	7
OMAN	21	21	-	1	-	20	21	21	-	1	-	20
PAKISTAN	80	78	20	5	2	51	80	78	20	5	3	50
PHILIPPINES	30	30	10	1	13	6	30	30	10	1	12	5
SAUDI ARABIA	215	215	1	85	2	127	215	215	1	85	2	128
SRI LANKA	7	6	2	-	3	1	7	6	2	-	3	1
SYRIAN ARAB REPUBLIC	19	18	6	8	-	4	19	18	6	8	-	4
THAILAND	51	51	19	-	16	16	51	51	20	-	15	16
TURKEY	78	77	27	9	20	20	78	77	27	9	20	20
UNITED ARAB EMIRATES	8	8	-	-	-	8	8	8	-	-	-	8
VIET NAM	33	33	6	5	13	12	33	33	6	5	13	12
YEMEN	20	20	1	7	2	10	20	20	3	7	2	10
YEMEN, DEMOCRATIC	33	33	-	9	2	22	33	33	-	9	2	22

COUNTRIES	1982 TOTAL AREA	LAND AREA	ARABLE LAND AND LAND UNDER PERMANENT CROPS	PERMANENT MEADOWS AND PASTURES	FORESTS	OTHER LAND AREA	1984 TOTAL AREA	LAND AREA	ARABLE LAND AND LAND UNDER PERMANENT CROPS	PERMANENT MEADOWS AND PASTURES	FORESTS	OTHER LAND AREA
(14)	(15)	(16)	(17)	(18)	(19)	(20)	(21)	(22)	(23)	(24)	(25)	(26)
ASIA												
AFGHANISTAN	65	65	8	30	2	25	65	65	8	30	2	25
BANGLADESH	14	13	9	1	2	2	14	13	9	1	2	2
BHUTAN	5	5	-	-	3	1	5	5	-	-	3	1
BURMA	68	66	10	-	32	23	68	66	10	-	32	23
CHINA	960	933	101	286	128	418	960	933	101	286	135	411
EAST TIMOR	1	1	-	-	1	-	1	1	-	-	1	-
INDIA	329	297	168	12	67	50	329	297	168	12	67	50
INDONESIA	190	181	20	12	122	28	190	181	21	12	122	28
IRAN	165	164	15	44	18	87	165	164	15	44	18	87
IRAQ	43	43	5	4	2	32	43	43	5	4	2	32
ISRAEL	2	2	-	1	-	1	2	2	-	1	-	1
JAPAN	37	37	5	1	25	7	37	37	5	1	25	7
JORDAN	10	10	1	-	-	9	10	10	1	-	-	9

Table 11 (continued)

COUNTRIES	1982						1984					
	TOTAL AREA	LAND AREA	ARABLE LAND AND LAND UNDER PERMANENT CROPS	PERMANENT MEADOWS AND PASTURES	FORESTS	OTHER LAND AREA	TOTAL AREA	LAND AREA	ARABLE LAND AND LAND UNDER PERMANENT CROPS	PERMANENT MEADOWS AND PASTURES	FORESTS	OTHER LAND AREA
(14)	(15)	(16)	(17)	(18)	(19)	(20)	(21)	(22)	(23)	(24)	(25)	(26)
(continued)												
KAMPUCHEA, DEMOCRATIC	18	18	3	1	13	1	18	18	3	1	13	1
KOREA, DEMOCRATIC PEOPLE'S REPUBLIC OF	12	12	2	-	9	1	12	12	2	-	9	1
KOREA, REPUBLIC OF	10	10	2	-	7	1	10	10	2	-	7	1
KUWAIT	2	2	-	-	-	2	2	2	-	-	-	2
LAO PEOPLE'S DEMOCRATIC REPBULIC	24	23	1	1	13	8	24	23	1	1	13	8
LEBANON	1	1	-	-	-	1	1	1	-	-	-	1
MALAYSIA	33	33	4	-	23	5	33	33	4	-	22	6
MONGOLIA	157	157	1	125	15	15	157	157	1	123	15	17
NEPAL	14	14	2	2	4	5	14	14	2	2	4	5
OMAN	21	21	-	1	-	20	21	21	-	1	-	20
PAKISTAN	80	78	20	5	3	50	80	78	20	5	3	50
PHILIPPINES	30	30	10	1	13	6	30	30	10	1	12	7
SAUDI ARABIA	215	215	1	85	2	128	215	215	1	85	2	128
SRI LANKA	7	6	2	-	2	2	7	6	2	-	2	2
SYRIAN ARAB REPUBLIC	19	18	6	9	-	4	19	18	6	8	-	4
THAILAND	51	51	17	-	17	16	51	51	16	-	16	17
TURKEY	78	77	27	9	20	20	78	77	27	9	20	20
UNITED ARAB EMIRATES	8	8	-	-	-	8	8	8	-	-	-	8
VIET NAM	33	33	7	-	13	12	33	33	7	-	13	12
YEMEN	20	20	1	7	2	10	20	20	1	7	2	10
YEMEN, DEMOCRATIC	33	33	-	9	2	22	33	33	-	9	2	23

COUNTRIES	1974-1976						1980					
	TOTAL AREA	LAND AREA	ARABLE LAND AND LAND UNDER PERMANENT CROPS	PERMANENT MEADOWS AND PASTURES	FORESTS	OTHER LAND AREA	TOTAL AREA	LAND AREA	ARABLE LAND AND LAND UNDER PERMANENT CROPS	PERMANENT MEADOWS AND PASTURES	FORESTS	OTHER LAND AREA
(1)	(2)	(3)	(4)	(5)	(6)	(7)	(8)	(9)	(10)	(11)	(12)	(13)
EUROPE												
ALBANIA	3	3	1	1	1	-	3	3	1	1	1	-
AUSTRIA	8	8	2	2	3	1	8	8	2	2	3	1
BELGIUM-LUXEMBOURG	3	3	1	1	1	1	3	3	1	1	1	1
BULGARIA	11	11	5	1	5	1	11	11	4	2	5	1
CZECHOSLOVAKIA	13	13	5	2	4	1	13	13	5	2	4	1
DENMARK	4	4	3	-	-	1	4	4	3	-	-	1
FINLAND	34	31	3	-	22	6	34	31	3	-	23	5
FRANCE	55	55	19	14	14	8	55	55	19	14	15	8
GERMAN DEMOCRATIC REPUBLIC #	11	11	5	1	3	1	11	11	5	1	3	1
GERMANY, FEDERAL REPUBLIC OF #	25	24	8	5	7	4	25	24	8	5	7	4
GREECE	13	13	4	5	3	1	13	13	4	5	3	1
HUNGARY	9	9	5	1	2	1	9	9	5	1	2	1
ICELAND	10	10	-	2	-	8	10	10	-	2	-	8
IRELAND	7	7	1	5	-	1	7	7	1	5	-	1
ITALY	30	29	12	5	6	6	30	29	12	5	6	6
NETHERLANDS	4	3	1	1	-	1	4	3	1	1	-	1
NORWAY	32	31	1	-	8	22	32	31	1	-	8	22
POLAND	31	30	15	4	9	3	31	30	15	4	9	3
PORTUGAL	9	9	4	1	4	1	9	9	4	1	4	1
ROMANIA	24	23	11	4	6	2	24	23	10	4	6	2
SPAIN	50	50	21	11	15	3	50	50	21	11	15	3
SWEDEN	45	41	3	1	26	11	45	41	3	1	26	11
SWITZERLAND	4	4	-	2	1	1	4	4	-	2	1	1
UNITED KINGDOM	24	24	7	11	2	4	24	24	7	11	2	4
YUGOSLAVIA	26	26	8	6	9	3	26	26	8	6	9	3

Table 11 (continued)

COUNTRIES	1982						1984					
	TOTAL AREA	LAND AREA	ARABLE LAND AND LAND UNDER PERMANENT CROPS	PERMANENT MEADOWS AND PASTURES	FORESTS	OTHER LAND AREA	TOTAL AREA	LAND AREA	ARABLE LAND AND LAND UNDER PERMANENT CROPS	PERMANENT MEADOWS AND PASTURES	FORESTS	OTHER LAND AREA
(14)	(15)	(16)	(17)	(18)	(19)	(20)	(21)	(22)	(23)	(24)	(25)	(26)
EUROPE												
ALBANIA	3	3	1	1	1	-	3	3	1	1	1	-
AUSTRIA	8	8	2	2	3	1	8	8	2	2	3	1
BELGIUM-LUXEMBOURG	3	3	1	1	1	-	3	3	1	1	1	-
BULGARIA	11	11	4	2	4	1	11	11	4	2	4	1
CZECHOSLOVAKIA	13	13	5	2	5	1	13	13	5	2	5	1
DENMARK	4	4	3	-	-	1	4	4	3	-	-	1
FINLAND	34	31	2	-	23	5	34	31	2	-	23	5
FRANCE	55	55	19	13	15	5	55	55	19	13	15	5
GERMAN DEMOCRATIC REPUBLIC ‡	11	11	5	1	3	1	11	11	5	1	3	1
GERMANY, FEDERAL REPUBLIC OF ‡	25	24	7	5	7	5	25	24	7	5	7	5
GREECE	13	13	4	5	3	1	13	13	4	5	3	1
HUNGARY	9	9	5	1	2	1	9	9	5	1	2	1
ICELAND	10	10	-	2	-	8	10	10	-	2	-	8
IRELAND	7	7	1	5	-	1	7	7	1	5	-	1
ITALY	30	29	12	5	6	6	30	29	12	5	6	5
NETHERLANDS	4	3	1	1	-	1	4	3	1	1	-	1
NORWAY	32	31	1	-	8	22	32	31	1	-	8	22
POLAND	31	30	15	4	9	2	31	30	15	4	9	2
PORTUGAL	9	9	4	1	4	1	9	9	4	1	4	1
ROMANIA	24	23	11	4	6	2	24	23	10	4	6	2
SPAIN	50	50	21	11	15	3	50	50	21	11	15	3
SWEDEN	45	41	3	1	26	11	45	41	3	1	26	11
SWITZERLAND	4	4	-	2	3	1	4	4	-	2	3	1
UNITED KINGDOM	24	24	7	11	2	4	24	24	7	11	2	4
YUGOSLAVIA	26	26	8	6	9	3	26	26	8	6	9	3

COUNTRIES	1974-1976						1980					
	TOTAL AREA	LAND AREA	ARABLE LAND AND LAND UNDER PERMANENT CROPS	PERMANENT MEADOWS AND PASTURES	FORESTS	OTHER LAND AREA	TOTAL AREA	LAND AREA	ARABLE LAND AND LAND UNDER PERMANENT CROPS	PERMANENT MEADOWS AND PASTURES	FORESTS	OTHER LAND AREA
(1)	(2)	(3)	(4)	(5)	(6)	(7)	(8)	(9)	(10)	(11)	(12)	(13)
OCEANIA												
AUSTRALIA	769	762	42	458	107	163	769	762	44	451	107	158
FIJI	2	2	-	-	1	1	2	2	-	-	1	1
NEW CALEDONIA	2	2	-	-	1	1	2	2	-	-	1	1
NEW ZEALAND	27	27	1	14	7	6	27	27	1	14	7	5
PAPUA NEW GUINEA	46	45	-	-	38	6	46	45	-	-	38	6
SOLOMON ISLANDS	3	3	-	-	3		3	3	-	-	3	
VANUATU	1	1	-	-	-	1	1	1	-	-	-	1
U.S.S.R.												
U.S.S.R.	2,240	2,227	232	374	897	724	2,240	2,227	232	374	916	706

Table 11 (continued)

COUNTRIES	1982 TOTAL AREA	LAND AREA	ARABLE LAND AND LAND UNDER PERMANENT CROPS	PERMANENT MEADOWS AND PASTURES	FORESTS	OTHER LAND AREA	1984 TOTAL AREA	LAND AREA	ARABLE LAND AND LAND UNDER PERMANENT CROPS	PERMANENT MEADOWS AND PASTURES	FORESTS	OTHER LAND AREA
(14)	(15)	(16)	(17)	(18)	(19)	(20)	(21)	(22)	(23)	(24)	(25)	(26)
OCEANIA												
AUSTRALIA	769	762	41	458	127	134	769	762	42	451	106	160
FIJI	2	2	-	-	2	1	2	2	-	-	2	-
NEW CALEDONIA	2	2	-	-	1	1	2	2	-	-	1	1
NEW ZEALAND	27	27	1	13	7	6	27	27	-	14	7	5
PAPUA NEW GUINEA	46	45	-	-	38	6	46	45	-	-	38	6
SOLOMON ISLANDS	3	3	-	-	3	-	3	3	-	-	3	-
VANUATU	1	1	-	-	-	1	1	1	-	-	-	1
U.S.S.R.												
U.S.S.R.	2,240	2,227	232	374	897	724	2,240	2,227	233	374	916	706

Source: Food and Agriculture Organization of the United Nations, *FAO Production Yearbook 1985 Vol. 39*, 47–58.

Notes: Because of rounding, totals do not always correspond to the sum of the component parts. For many developing countries, changes in data from one year to another, particularly for permanent meadows and pastures and forests, might reflect a general improvement in statistical information and better interpretation of land use classification, and not acute change.

Although the areas of the following countries are included in the area estimates of the macro regions depicted in Part I of this table, they are excluded from Part II since their individual areas are less than 1,000,000 hectares:

Africa. British Indian Ocean, Cape Verde, Comoros, Mauritius, Reunion, St Helena, Sao Tomé, Seychelles.

America, North. Antigua-Bare, Barbados, Bermuda, British Virgin Islands, Cayman, Dominica, Grenada, Guadeloupe, Martinique, Montserrat, Netherlands Antille, St Christopher Nevis, St Lucia, St Pierre and Miquelon, St Vincent, Turks and Caicos Islands, and US Virgin Islands.

Asia. Bahrain, Gaza Strip, Hong Kong, Macau, Maldives, Singapore.

Europe. Andorra, Faeroe Islands, Gibraltar, Liechtenstein, Malta, San Marion.

Oceania. American Samoa, Canton Islands, Christmass Island, Cocos Islands, Cook Islands, French Ploynesia, Guam, Kiribati, Nauru, Nieu, Norfolk Islands, Pacific Islands, Samoa and Futuna Islands, Tokelau, Tonga and Tuvalu, Wallis Islands.

- Magnitude zero or negligible.

‡ The data which relate to the Federal Republic of Germany and the German Democratic Republic include the relevant data relating to Berlin for which separate data have not been supplied. This is without prejudice to any question of status which may be involved.

Table 12

Gross urban densities: persons per square kilometre, cities or urban agglomerations, for recent years for which data are available

COUNTRIES, CITIES OR URBAN AGGLOMERATIONS	BOUNDARIES	YEAR	POPULATION (IN THOUSANDS)	AREA (SQ.KM)	GROSS DENSITIES (PERSONS PER SQ.KM)
(1)	(2)	(3)	(4)	(5)	(6)
AFRICA					
EGYPT					
ALEXANDRIA	CITY PROPER	1976	2,318	334	6,940
CAIRO	CITY PROPER	1976	5,074	214	23,710
GUINEA					
CONAKRY	URBAN AGGLOMERATIONS	1967	197	285	6,912
KENYA					
MOMBASA	URBAN AGGLOMERATIONS	1984	426	..	..
NAIROBI	URBAN AGGLOMERATIONS	1984	1,103	695	1,587
MAURITIUS					
PORT-LOUIS	CITY PROPER	1983	148	39	3,795
MOROCCO					
CASABLANCA - 1	CITY PROPER	1981	1,371	113	12,133
AMERICA, NORTH					
HAITI					
PORT-AU-PRINCE	CITY PROPER	1984	461	66	6,985
MEXICO					
MEXICO CITY	CITY PROPER	1979	9,191	272	33,790
MEXICO	AGGLOMERATIONS	1979	14,750	433	34,065
PANAMA					
PANAMA CITY	CITY PROPER	1980	389	100	3,890
UNITED STATES					
CHICAGO	CITY PROPER	1982	2,997	..	..
CHICAGO - 3	AGGLOMERATIONS	1982	8,016	3,307	2,424
DETROIT	CITY PROPER	1982	1,140	..	..
DETROIT - 4	AGGLOMERATIONS	1982	4,605	2,258	2,039
LOS ANGELES	CITY PROPER	1982	3,022	..	..
LOS ANGELES - 5	AGGLOMERATIONS	1982	12,191	4,071	2,995
NEW YORK	CITY PROPER	1983	7,074	..	..
NEW YORK - 6	AGGLOMERATIONS	1983	17,687	..	..
PHILADELPHIA	CITY PROPER	1983	1,663	..	..
PHILADELPHIA	AGGLOMERATIONS	1983	5,738	1,948	2,946
AMERICA, SOUTH					
ARGENTINA					
BUENOS AIRES	CITY PROPER	1980	2,923	200	14,615
BUENOS AIRES	AGGLOMERATIONS	1980	9,968	3,680	2,709
BOLIVIA					
LA PAZ - 7	CITY PROPER	1982	881	..	..
COCHABAMBA	CITY PROPER	1982	282	43	6,558
BRAZIL					
BELO HORIZONTE	CITY PROPER	1980	1,442	335	4,304
CURITIBA	CITY PROPER	1980	844	..	..
FORTALEZA	CITY PROPER	1980	649	336	1,932
RECIFE	CITY PROPER	1980	1,184	209	5,665
RIO DE JANEIRO	CITY PROPER	1980	5,093	1,171	4,349
SALVADOR	CITY PROPER	1980	1,496	..	..
SAO PAULO	CITY PROPER	1980	7,034	1,493	4,711

Table 12 (continued)

COUNTRIES, CITIES OR URBAN AGGLOMERATIONS	BOUNDARIES	YEAR	POPULATION (IN THOUSANDS)	AREA (SQ.KM)	GROSS DENSITIES (PERSONS PER SQ.KM)
(1)	(2)	(3)	(4)	(5)	(6)
CHILE					
CONCEPCION - 8	CITY PROPER	1983	210	150	1,400
SANTIAGO	CITY PROPER	1983	4,132	240	17,217
COLOMBIA					
BOGOTA	CITY PROPER	1973	2,836	1,528	1,856
BOGOTA	AGGLOMERATIONS	1973	2,855	. .	. .
MEDELLIN	CITY PROPER	1973	1,112	358	3,106
ECUADOR					
GUAYAQUIL	CITY PROPER	1982	1,279	. .	. .
QUITO	CITY PROPER	1982	881	. .	. .
PERU					
LIMA - 9	CITY PROPER	1981	4,165	144	28,924
LIMA	AGGLOMERATIONS	1981	4,601	. .	. .
VENEZUELA					
CARACAS - 10	CITY PROPER	1981	1,817	. .	. .
CARACAS	AGGLOMERATIONS	1981	2,944	. .	. .
MARACAIBO	AGGLOMERATIONS	1981	889	. .	. .
ASIA					
CYPRUS					
NICOSIA	CITY PROPER	1982	180	40	4,500
INDIA					
AHMEDABAD	AGGLOMERATIONS	1981	2,515	93	2,704
ALLAHABAD	AGGLOMERATIONS	1981	642	. .	. .
BANGALORE	AGGLOMERATIONS	1981	2,914	134	2,175
BOMBAY	CITY PROPER	1981	8,227	446	18,446
CALCUTTA - 11	AGGLOMERATIONS	1981	9,166	104	88,135
COIMBATORE	AGGLOMERATIONS	1981	917	. .	. .
DELHI	AGGLOMERATIONS	1981	5,714	1,485	3,848
GAYA	CITY PROPER	1981	247	. .	. .
HUBLI	CITY PROPER	1981	526	. .	. .
HYDERABAD	AGGLOMERATIONS	1981	2,528	169	14,959
JAMSHEDPUR	AGGLOMERATIONS	1981	670	. .	. .
KANPUR	AGGLOMERATIONS	1981	1,688	. .	. .
LUCKNOW	AGGLOMERATIONS	1981	1,007	. .	. .
MADRAS	AGGLOMERATIONS	1981	4,277	128	33,414
POONA	AGGLOMERATIONS	1981	1,685	. .	. .
SHOLAPUR	AGGLOMERATIONS	1981	514	. .	. .
TIRUCHIRAPALLI	AGGLOMERATIONS	1981	608	. .	. .
VARANASI	AGGLOMERATIONS	1981	794	. .	. .
INDONESIA					
BANGDUNG	CITY PROPER	1980	1,463	. .	. .
JAKARTA	CITY PROPER	1980	6,503	. .	. .
SURABAJA	CITY PROPER	1980	2,028	. .	. .
IRAN					
ABADAN	CITY PROPER	1976	294	37	7,946
ABADAN	AGGLOMERATIONS	1976	308	. .	. .
AHVAZ	CITY PROPER	1982	471	34	13,853
AHVAZ	AGGLOMERATIONS	1976	340	. .	. .
ESFAHAN	CITY PROPER	1982	927	77	12,039
ESFAHAN	AGGLOMERATIONS	1976	842	. .	. .
KERMANSHAH	CITY PROPER	1982	239	20	11,950
KERMANSHAH	AGGLOMERATIONS	1976	336	. .	. .
MASHHAD	CITY PROPER	1982	1,120	53	21,132

Table 12 (continued)

COUNTRIES, CITIES OR URBAN AGGLOMERATIONS	BOUNDARIES	YEAR	POPULATION (IN THOUSANDS)	AREA (SQ.KM)	GROSS DENSITIES (PERSONS PER SQ.KM)
(1)	(2)	(3)	(4)	(5)	(6)
(continued)					
MASHHAD	AGGLOMERATIONS	1976	743	..	..
RASHT	CITY PROPER	1982	260	24	10,833
RASHT	AGGLOMERATIONS	1976	195	..	..
SHIRAZ	CITY PROPER	1982	800	..	..
SHIRAZ	AGGLOMERATIONS	1976	448	..	..
TABRIZ	CITY PROPER	1982	852	45	18,933
TABRIZ	AGGLOMERATIONS	1976	715	..	..
TEHERAN	CITY PROPER	1982	5,734	283	20,261
TEHERAN	AGGLOMERATIONS	1976	4,589	..	..
JAPAN					
KITAKYUSHU	..	1983	1,064	457	2,328
KOBE	..	1983	1,394	539	2,586
KYOTO	..	1983	1,484	611	2,429
NAGOYA	..	1983	2,100	326	6,642
OSAKA	..	1983	2,625	206	14,668
TOKYO	CITY PROPER	1983	8,361	570	6,839
TOKYO	AGGLOMERATIONS	1983	11,746	..	..
YOKOHAMA	..	1983	2,893	423	6,839
JORDAN					
AMMAN	CITY PROPER	1983	744	67	11,104
KOREA, REPUBLIC OF					
CHUNCHEON	CITY PROPER	1980	155	87	1,782
GWANGJU	CITY PROPER	1980	728	215	3,386
MOGPO	CITY PROPER	1980	222	29	7,655
PUSAN	CITY PROPER	1980	3,160	373	8,472
SEOUL	CITY PROPER	1980	8,364	613	13,644
TAEGU	CITY PROPER	1980	1,605	177	9,068
YAESU	CITY PROPER	1980	161	45	3,578
LEBANON					
BEIRUT [2]	CITY PROPER	1970	475	..	..
BEIRUT	AGGLOMERATIONS	1970	939	..	..
NEPAL					
KATHMANDU	CIYT PROPER	1981	235	..	..
PAKISTAN [13]					
KARACHI	CITY PROPER	1972	3,499	198	17,672
PHILIPPINES [1]					
CALOOCAN	CITY PROPER	1980	468	56	8,357
QUEZON CITY	CITY PROPER	1980	1,166	..	..
MANILA	CITY PROPER	1980	1,630	38	42,895
PASAY	CITY PROPER	1980	288	14	20,571
SINGAPORE					
SINGAPORE [12]	..	‡1984	2,529	586	4,316
SRI LANKA					
COLOMBO	CITY PROPER	1983	623	..	..
SYRIAN ARAB REPUBLIC					
ALEPPO	CITY PROPER	1982	985	..	..
DAMASCUS	CITY PROPER	1982	1,112	..	..
DAMASCUS	AGGLOMERATIONS	1981	923	..	..
THAILAND					
BANGKOK	CITY PROPER	1980	3,077	290	10,610
TURKEY [14]					
ISTANBUL	CITY PROPER	1983	2,903	..	..
ISTANBUL	AGGLOMERATIONS	1983	2,949	..	..

Table 12 (continued)

COUNTRIES, CITIES OR URBAN AGGLOMERATIONS	BOUNDARIES	YEAR	POPULATION (IN THOUSANDS)	AREA (SQ.KM)	GROSS DENSITIES (PERSONS PER SQ.KM)
(1)	(2)	(3)	(4)	(5)	(6)
EUROPE					
AUSTRIA					
GRAZ	CITY PROPER	1981	243	128	1,898
LINZ	CITY PROPER	1981	200	96	2,083
SALZBURG	CITY PROPER	1981	138	66	2,091
WIEN	CITY PROPER	1981	1,531	415	3,689
BELGIUM					
BRUSSELS - 15	AGGLOMERATIONS	1983	990	161	6,149
CHALEROI	CITY PROPER	1983	216	102	2,118
GENT	CITY PROPER	1983	237	156	1,519
LIEGE	CITY PROPER	1983	207	69	3,000
CZECHOSLOVAKIA					
PRAHA	CITY PROPER	1983	1,185	420	2,821
BRATISLAVA	CITY PROPER	1983	398	527	755
BRNO	CITY PROPER	1983	379	265	1,430
OSTRAWA	CITY PROPER	1983	324	140	2,314
DENMARK					
COBENHAGEN	CITY PROPER	1983	487	..	..
COBENHAGEN	AGGLOMERATIONS	1983	1,372	..	..
FINLAND					
HELSINKI	CITY PROPER	1983	484	185	2,616
HELSINKI	AGGLOMERATIONS	1983	927	..	..
ESPOO	CITY PROPER	1983	147	417	353
TAMPERE	CITY PROPER	1983	167	682	245
TURKU	CITY PROPER	1983	163	304	536
FRANCE					
LILLE	CITY PROPER	1982	165	..	..
LILLE	AGGLOMERATIONS	1982	935	304	3,076
MARSEILLE	CITY PROPER	1982	867	..	..
MARSEILLE	AGGLOMERATIONS	1982	1,080	547	1,974
NICE	CITY PROPER	1982	335	..	..
NICE	AGGLOMERATIONS	1982	449	223	2,013
PARIS	CITY PROPER	1982	2,189	105	20,848
PARIS - 16	AGGLOMERATIONS	1982	8,510	761	11,183
TOULOUSE	CITY PROPER	1982	346	..	..
TOULOUSE	AGGLOMERATIONS	1982	523	368	1,421
GERMAN DEMOCRATIC REPUBLIC - #					
BERLIN	CITY PROPER	1983	1,189	403	2,950
DRESDEN	CITY PROPER	1983	520	226	2,301
KARL-MARX-STADT	CITY PROPER	1983	317	129	2,457
LEIPZIG	CITY PROPER	1983	557	141	3,950
GERMANY, FEDERAL REPUBLIC OF					
BONN	CITY PROPER	1983	292	..	..
HAMBURG	CITY PROPER	1983	1,610	747	2,155
HANNOVER	CITY PROPER	1983	523	..	..
MUENCHEN	CITY PROPER	1983	1,283	311	4,125
HUNGARY					
BUDAPEST	CITY PROPER	1983	2,064	525	3,931
DEBRECEN	CITY PROPER	1983	206	446	462
MISKOLC	CITY PROPER	1983	211	224	942
SZEGED	CITY PROPER	1983	175	357	490

Table 12 (continued)

COUNTRIES, CITIES OR URBAN AGGLOMERATIONS	BOUNDARIES	YEAR	POPULATION (IN THOUSANDS)	AREA (SQ.KM)	GROSS DENSITIES (PERSONS PER SQ.KM)
(1)	(2)	(3)	(4)	(5)	(6)
ITALY					
GENOVA	CITY PROPER	1982	758	236	3,212
MILANO	CITY PROPER	1982	1,592	182	8,747
NAPOLI	CITY PROPER	1982	1,210	117	10,342
ROMA	CITY PROPER	1982	2,836	1,507	1,882
TORINO	CITY PROPER	1982	1,104	130	8,492
NETHERLANDS					
EINDHAVEN	CITY PROPER	1983	194	79	2,456
EINDHAVEN	AGGLOMERATIONS	1983	374	..	..
UTRECHT	CITY PROPER	1983	231	57	4,053
UTRECHT	AGGLOMERATIONS	1983	500	..	..
AMSTERDAM	CITY PROPER	1983	682	207	3,295
ROTTERDAM	CITY PROPER	1983	965	270	3,574
GRAVENHAGE	CITY PROPER	1983	447	70	6,386
POLAND					
GDANSK	CITY PROPER	1983	465	261	1,782
KRAKOW	CITY PROPER	1983	734	322	2,280
WARSZAWA	CITY PROPER	1983	1,635	485	3,371
WROCLAW	CITY PROPER	1983	630	293	2,150
ROMANIA					
BUCURESTI	CITY PROPER	1982	1,979	605	3,271
BUCURESTI	AGGLOMERATIONS	1982	1,934	610	3,170
SPAIN					
BARCELONA	AGGLOMERATIONS	1981	1,755	98	17,908
BILBAO	AGGLOMERATIONS	1981	433	114	3,798
MADRID	AGGLOMERATIONS	1981	3,188	608	5,243
SEVILLA	AGGLOMERATIONS	1981	654	49	13,347
VALENCIA	AGGLOMERATIONS	1981	752	136	5,529
SWEDEN					
GOTEBORG	CITY PROPER	1983	424	445	953
GOTEBORG	AGGLOMERATIONS	1983	696	896	777
MALMO	CITY PROPER	1983	229	154	1,519
MALMO	AGGLOMERATIONS	1983	454	..	..
STOCKHOLM	CITY PROPER	1983	651	214	3,042
STOCKHOLM	AGGLOMERATIONS	1983	1,409	..	..
VASTERAYS	CITY PROPER	1983	118	96	1,229
SWITZERLAND					
BALE	CITY PROPER	1982	183	..	..
BALE	AGGLOMERATIONS	1982	365	240	1,521
BERNE	CITY PROPER	1982	146	..	..
BERNE	AGGLOMERATIONS	1982	287	273	1,051
GENEVA	CITY PROPER	1982	161	..	..
GENEVA	AGGLOMERATIONS	1982	335	178	1,882
LAUSANNE	CITY PROPER	1982	128	..	..
LAUSANNE	AGGLOMERATIONS	1982	226	41	5,512
ZURICH	CITY PROPER	1982	368	..	...
ZURICH	AGGLOMERATIONS	1982	706	470	1,502
UNITED KINGDOM					
BIRMINGHAM	CITY PROPER	1981	920	207	4,444
LONDON	CITY PROPER	1981	6,696	1,601	4,182
YUGOSLAVIA					
BEOGRAD	CITY PROPER	1981	1,088	360	3,022
BEOGRAD	AGGLOMERATIONS	1981	775	366	2,117
SKOPJE	CITY PROPER	1981	408	202	2,020

Table 12 (continued)

COUNTRIES, CITIES OR URBAN AGGLOMERATIONS	BOUNDARIES	YEAR	POPULATION (IN THOUSANDS)	AREA (SQ.KM)	GROSS DENSITIES (PERSONS PER SQ.KM)
(1)	(2)	(3)	(4)	(5)	(6)
OCEANIA					
AUSTRALIA					
ADELAIDE	CITY PROPER	1983	970	..	..
ADELAIDE	AGGLOMERATIONS	1983	900	1,852	486
MELBOURNE	CITY PROPER	1983	2,866	..	..
MELBOURNE	AGGLOMERATIONS	1983	2,604	..	..
SYDNEY	CIYT PROPER	1983	3,335	..	..
SYDNEY	AGGLOMERATIONS	1983	3,022	..	..
BRISBONE	CITY PROPER	1983	1,138	..	..
BRISBONE	AGGLOMERATIONS	1983	958	..	..
NEWCASTLE	CITY PROPER	1983	415	..	..
NEWCASTLE	AGGLOMERATIONS	1983	363	2,948	123
CANBERRA	CITY PROPER	1983	256	..	..
CANBERRA	AGGLOMERATIONS	1983	197	..	..
UNION OF SOVIET SOCIALIST REPUBLICS					
GORKY	CITY PROPER	1983	1,382	335	4,125
KHARKOV [18]	CITY PROPER	1983	1,519	272	5,585
KIEV	CITY PROPER	1983	2,355	794	2,966
KUIBYSHEV	CITY PROPER	1983	1,242	360	3,450
LENINGRAD	CITY PROPER	1983	4,779	636	7,514
LENINGRAD	AGGLOMERATIONS	1983	4,588	..	..
MOSKVA	CITY PROPER	1983	8,396	893	9,402
MOSKVA	AGGLOMERATIONS	1983	8,011	..	..
NOVOSIBIRSK	CITY PROPER	1983	1,370	470	2,915
SVERDLOVSK	CITY PROPER	1983	1,269	393	3,229
TASHKENT	CITY PROPER	1983	1,944	251	7,745

Sources: Population data was extracted from United Nations, Demographic Year-book 1984. Current area data was extracted from United Nations.

Compendium of Human Settlements Statistics 1983. In the absence of new data, old area data series were used as estimates.

Notes: Figures not available.

* Where the data for area (col. 5) could not be extracted form the *Compendium of Human Settlements Statistics 1983.* Figures were taken from the *1976 Statistical Annex.*

‡ The data which refer to the Federal Republic of Germany and the German Democratic Republic include the relevant data relating to Berlin for which separate data have not been supplied. This is without prejudice to any question of status which may be involved.

[1] *De jure* population.

[2] Based on sample survey.

[3] Chicago–Gary–Kenosha standard consolidated statistical area, comprising Chicago (1980 population 7,103,624), Gary–Hammond–Bast Chicago, Ind. (642,781), and Kenosha (123,137).

[4] Detroit–Ann Arbor standard consolidated statistical area, comprising Detroit (1980 population 4,353,413) and Ann Arbor (264,748).

[5] Los Angeles–Long Beach–Anaheim standard consolidated statistical area, comprising Los Angeles–Long Beach (1980 population 7,477,503), Anaheim–Santa Ana–Garden Grove (1,932,709), Oxnard–Simi Valley–Ventura (529,174), and Riverside–San Bernardino–Ontario (1,558,182).

[6] New York–Newark–Jersey City standard consolidated statistical area, comprising New York (1980 population 9,120,346), Jersey City, NJ (556,972), Long Branch–Asbury Park, NJ (503,173), Nassa–Suffolk, NY (2,605,813), Newark, NJ (1,965,969), New Brunswick–Perth Amboy–Sayreville, NJ (595,893), Norwalk, Conn. (126,692), Paterson–Clifton–Passaic, NJ (447,585), and Stanford, Conn. (198,854).

[7] La Paz is the actual capital and seat of the government, but Surce is the legal capital and the seat of the judiciary.

[8] Metropolitan area (Gran Santiago).

[9] Metropolitan area (Gran Lima).

[10] Metropolitan area comprising Caracas proper and a part of the district of Surce in the State of Miranda.

[11] Including Bally, Baranagar, Bhatpara, Calcutta Municipal Corporation, Houghlychinsura, Howrah, Kamarhati, Pinihati, Serampore, South Dum Dum, and South Suburban Urban Agglomeration (including Garden Reach).

[12] Excluding transients afloat, non-locally domiciled military, and civilian services personnel and their dependants.

[13] Excluding data for the Pakistan held part of Jammu and Kashmir, (the final status of which has not yet been determined), Junagardh, Manavador, Gilgit, and Baltistan.

[14] Including Adalar, Bakiroy, Besistas, Beykoz, Eminonu, Eyup, Fatih, Gazi, Osman-Pass, Kadikoy, Sariyer, Sisli, Uskudar, and Zeytinburnu.

[15] Including Anderlecht and Schaerbeek.

[16] Data refer to the extended agglomeration, comprising the city of Paris, 73 communes in Department of Essome, 36 communes in Department of Hauts-de-Seine, 13 communes in the Department of Seine-et-Marne, 40 communes in Department of Seine-Saint-Denis, 47 communes in Department of Val-De-Marne, 58 communes in Department of Val-d'Oise, and 42 communes in the Department of Yvelines.

[17] Greater London conurbation as reconstituted in 1965 and comprising 32 new Greater London Boroughs.

[18] Capital of the Ukrainian Soviet Socialist Republic.

Table 13

Cropland and area of cropland in relation to total population and agricultural population, 1984

COUNTRIES	CROPLAND (THOUSAND HECTARES)	% POPULATION		HECTARES OF CROPLAND PER PERSON	
		TOTAL (THOUSANDS)	AGRICULTURAL (THOUSANDS)	TOTAL POPULATION	AGRICULTURAL POPULATION
(1)	(2)	(3)	(4)	(5)	(6)
AFRICA					
ALGERIA	7,440	21,718	5,216	0.34	1.43
ANGOLA	3,500	8,754	6,268	0.40	0.56
BENIN	1,818	4,050	2,581	0.45	0.70
BOTSWANA	1,360	1,107	665	1.23	2.05
BURKINA FASO	2,633	6,942	5,956	0.38	0.44
BURUNDI	1,308	4,721	4,359	0.28	0.30
CAMEROON	6,965	9,873	6,036	0.71	1.15
CAPE VERDE	40	326	148	0.12	0.27
CENTRAL AFRICAN REPUBLIC	1,982	2,576	1,696	0.77	1.17
CHAD	3,150	5,018	3,944	0.63	0.80
COMOROS	94	444	359	0.21	0.26
CONGO	675	1,740	1,064	0.39	0.63
COTE D'IVOIRE	4,025	9,810	5,766	0.41	0.70
EGYPT	2,474	46,909	19,958	0.05	0.12
EQUATORIAL GUINEA	230	392	238	0.59	0.97
ETHIOPIA	13,930	43,557	33,440	0.32	0.42
GABON	452	1,151	842	0.39	0.54
GAMBIA	165	643	531	0.26	0.31
GHANA	2,820	13,588	7,487	0.21	0.38
GUINEA	1,576	6,075	4,744	0.26	0.33
GUINEA-BISSAU	290	889	723	0.33	0.40
KENYA	2,335	20,600	16,242	0.11	0.14
LESOTHO	298	1,520	1,276	0.20	0.23
LIBERIA	371	2,191	1,588	0.17	0.23
LIBYAN ARAB JAMAHIRIYA	2,115	3,605	508	0.59	4.16
MADAGASCAR	3,020	10,012	7,943	0.30	0.38
MALAWI	2,345	6,944	5,440	0.34	0.43
MALI	2,053	8,082	6,734	0.25	0.30
MAURITANIA	195	1,888	1,115	0.10	0.17
MAURITIUS	107	1,050	264	0.10	0.41
MOROCCO	8,331	21,941	8,712	0.38	0.96
MOZAMBIQUE	3,080	13,961	11,647	0.22	0.26
NAMIBIA	662	1,550	616	0.43	1.07
NIGER	3,760	6,115	5,440	0.61	0.69
NIGERIA	31,035	95,198	63,484	0.33	0.49
REUNION	55	531	61	0.10	0.90
RWANDA	1,010	6,070	5,603	0.17	0.18
SENEGAL	5,225	6,444	5,121	0.81	1.02
SEYCHELLES	7	76	..	0.09	..
SIERRA LEONE	1,771	3,602	2,390	0.49	0.74
SOMALIA	1,066	4,653	3,419	0.23	0.31
SOUTH AFRICA	13,630	32,392	3,603	0.42	3.78
SUDAN	12,448	21,550	14,637	0.58	0.85
SWAZILAND	144	650	457	0.22	0.32
TANZANIA, UNITED REPUBLIC OF	5,190	22,499	18,574	0.23	0.28
TOGO	1,427	2,960	2,101	0.48	0.68
TUNISIA	4,687	7,081	2,239	0.66	2.09
UGANDA	6,500	15,477	12,976	0.42	0.50
ZAIRE	6,510	29,938	20,099	0.22	0.32
ZAMBIA	5,158	6,666	4,747	0.77	1.09
ZIMBABWE	2,682	8,777	6,177	0.31	0.43
AMERICA, NORTH					
BAHAMAS	9	230	17	0.04	0.53
BARBADOS	43	253	18	0.17	2.39
CANADA	46,580	25,379	1,099	1.84	42.38
COSTA RICA	637	2,600	666	0.25	0.96
CUBA	3,236	10,038	2,102	0.32	1.54
DOMINICAN REPUBLIC	1,470	6,243	2,574	0.24	0.57

Table 13 (continued)

COUNTRIES	CROPLAND (THOUSAND HECTARES)	POPULATION TOTAL (THOUSANDS)	POPULATION AGRICULTURAL (THOUSANDS)	HECTARES OF CROPLAND PER PERSON TOTAL POPULATION	HECTARES OF CROPLAND PER PERSON AGRICULTURAL POPULATION
(1)	(2)	(3)	(4)	(5)	(6)
AMERICA, NORTH (continued)					
EL SALVADOR	725	5,552	2,095	0.13	0.35
GUADELOUPE	41	334	35	0.12	1.17
GUATEMALA	1,815	7,963	4,346	0.23	0.42
HAITI	904	6,585	4,455	0.14	0.20
HONDURAS	1,777	4,372	2,545	0.41	0.70
MEXICO	24,700	78,996	26,036	0.31	0.95
NICARAGUA	1,267	3,272	1,407	0.39	0.90
PANAMA	564	2,180	598	0.26	0.94
PUERTO RICO	131	3,451	68	0.04	1.93
TRINIDAD AND TOBAGO	160	1,185	87	0.14	1.84
UNITED STATES OF AMERICA	189,915	238,840	7,418	0.80	25.60
AMERICA, SOUTH					
ARGENTINA	35,600	30,564	3,588	1.16	9.92
BOLIVIA	3,385	6,371	2,780	0.53	1.22
BRAZIL	75,250	135,564	34,186	0.56	2.20
CHILE	5,528	12,038	1,691	0.46	3.27
COLOMBIA	5,695	28,714	9,140	0.20	0.62
ECUADOR	2,510	9,378	3,089	0.27	0.81
GUYANA	495	953	233	0.52	2.12
PARAGUAY	1,940	3,681	1,713	0.53	1.13
PERU	3,517	19,698	7,680	0.18	0.46
SURINAME	58	375	67	0.15	0.87
URUGUAY	1,446	3,012	436	0.48	3.32
VENEZUELA	3,758	17,317	2,140	0.22	1.76
ASIA					
AFGHANISTAN	8,054	16,519	9,644	0.49	0.84
BANGLADESH	9,111	101,147	71,774	0.09	0.13
BHUTAN	100	1,417	1,295	0.07	0.08
BURMA	10,061	37,153	18,540	0.27	0.54
CHINA	100,892	1,059,521	762,964	0.10	0.13
CYPRUS	432	669	140	0.65	3.09
EAST TIMOR	80	659	480	0.12	0.17
HONG KONG	8	5,548	80	0.00	0.10
INDIA	168,350	758,927	521,426	0.22	0.32
INDONESIA	20,850	166,440	87,258	0.13	0.24
IRAN	14,830	44,632	14,285	0.33	1.04
IRAQ	5,450	15,898	3,732	0.34	1.46
ISRAEL	437	4,289	212	0.10	2.06
JAPAN	4,780	120,754	9,786	0.04	0.49
JORDAN	415	3,515	205	0.12	2.02
KAMPUCHEA, DEMOCRATIC	3,046	7,284	5,263	0.42	0.58
KOREA, DEMOCRATIC PEOPLE'S REPUBLIC OF	2,312	20,385	7,741	0.11	0.30
KOREA, REPUBLIC OF	2,166	41,258	12,610	0.05	0.17
KUWAIT	2	1,811	36	0.00	0.06
LAO PEOPLE'S DEMOCRATIC REPUBLIC	890	4,117	3,048	0.22	0.29
LEBANON	298	2,668	322	0.11	0.93
MALAYSIA	4,350	15,557	5,446	0.28	0.80
MONGOLIA	1,335	1,908	686	0.70	1.95
NEPAL	2,319	16,482	15,264	0.14	0.15
PAKISTAN	20,280	100,380	52,634	0.20	0.39
PHILIPPINES	11,300	54,498	27,233	0.21	0.41
SAUDI ARABIA	1,156	11,542	4,672	0.10	0.25
SINGAPORE	6	2,559	27	0.00	0.22
SRI LANKA	2,202	16,205	8,491	0.14	0.26
SYRIAN ARAB REPUBLIC	5,654	10,505	2,599	0.54	2.18
THAILAND	19,670	51,411	33,775	0.38	0.58
TURKEY	27,411	49,289	25,477	0.56	1.08
VIET NAM	6,740	59,713	37,192	0.11	0.18
YEMEN	1,351	6,848	4,420	0.20	0.31
YEMEN, DEMOCRATIC	167	2,137	778	0.08	0.21

Table 13 (continued)

COUNTRIES	CROPLAND (THOUSAND HECTARES)	POPULATION *		HECTARES OF CROPLAND PER PERSON	
		TOTAL (THOUSANDS)	AGRICULTURAL (THOUSANDS)	TOTAL POPULATION	AGRICULTURAL POPULATION
(1)	(2)	(3)	(4)	(5)	(6)
EUROPE					
ALBANIA	713	3,050	1,542	0.23	0.46
AUSTRIA	1,523	7,555	526	0.20	2.90
BELGIUM-LUXEMBOURG	824	10,230	228	0.08	3.61
BULGARIA	4,135	8,980	1,117	0.46	3.70
CZECHOSLOVAKIA	5,165	15,498	1,818	0.33	2.84
DENMARK	2,627	5,113	300	0.51	8.76
FINLAND	2,335	4,910	484	0.48	4.82
FRANCE	18,812	55,162	3,722	0.34	5.05
GERMAN DEMOCRATIC REPUBLIC	4,991	16,660	1,619	0.30	3.08
GERMANY, FEDERAL REPUBLIC OF	7,437	61,015	3,087	0.12	2.41
GREECE	3,974	9,970	2,587	0.40	1.54
HUNGARY	5,293	10,642	1,830	0.50	2.89
ICELAND	8	243	19	0.03	0.42
IRELAND	972	3,608	556	0.27	1.75
ITALY	12,233	57,128	5,427	0.21	2.25
MALTA	13	383	17	0.03	0.76
NETHERLANDS	875	14,484	720	0.06	1.22
NORWAY	855	4,150	290	0.21	2.95
POLAND	14,800	37,203	8,928	0.40	1.66
PORTUGAL	3,545	10,212	2,350	0.35	1.51
ROMANIA	10,574	22,710	5,231	0.47	2.02
SPAIN	20,540	38,356	5,065	0.54	4.06
SWEDEN	2,995	8,351	439	0.36	6.82
SWITZERLAND	412	6,520	357	0.06	1.15
UNITED KINGDOM	6,991	56,807	1,426	0.12	4.90
YUGOSLAVIA	7,758	23,120	5,734	0.34	1.35
OCEANIA					
AUSTRALIA	48,108	15,691	1,000	3.07	48.11
FIJI	238	691	301	0.34	0.79
NEW ZEALAND	470	3,271	358	0.14	1.31
PAPUA NEW GUINEA	376	3,511	2,504	0.11	0.15
U.S.S.R.					
U.S.S.R.	232,215	277,570	48,654	0.84	4.77

Source: Cropland and population data extracted from *FAO Production Yearbook 1985, vol. 39.*

Note: Col. 5 is calculated by dividing col. 3 by col. 2; col. 6 by dividing col. 4 by col. 2.

It should be noted that only countries for which agricultural population data are available appear in the table.

* 1985 data.

Table 14

Total population, rate of growth, and population living in households; number, average size, and tenure of households; number of conventional dwellings and occupancy status; size, density of occupation, and facilities of occupied dwellings; rate of dwelling construction; capital formation in residential building construction: urban and rural, as of latest available census[51]

COUNTRIES AND AREAS AND CENSUS YEARS	TOTAL:T URBAN:U RURAL:R	POPULATION[1] TOTAL (IN THOUS- ANDS)[9]	ANNUAL RATE OF GROWTH[19]	LIVING IN HOUSEHOLDS (IN THOUS- ANDS)	HOUSEHOLDS TOTAL NUMBER (IN THOUS- ANDS)	AVERAGE SIZE (PERSONS PER HOUSEHOLD)	TENURE OF HOUSEHOLDS IN CONVENTIONAL DWELLINGS[11] PERCENTAGE OF: OWNER OCCUPANTS	RENTERS	DWELLINGS TOTAL NUMBER (IN THOUS- ANDS)	NUMBER OCCUPIED (IN THOUS- ANDS)	VACANCY PERCENTAGE[13]
		(2)	(3)	(4)	(5)	(6)	(7)	(8)	(9)	(10)	(11)
AFRICA											
ALGERIA [68]1966	T	12,096	1.8[2]	12,040	2,034	5.9	..	..	1,795	1,792	0.2
	U	4,688	6.1[2]	3,736	633	5.6	..	..	634	631	0.3
	R	7,408	0.1[2]	8,304	1,371	6.1	..	..	1,161	1,160	0.1
EGYPT 1976	T	36,656	2.6	36,346	6,946	5.2	..	..	..[6]	..[6]	..
	U	16,036	3.1	15,780	3,213	4.9	..	..	1,111	1,055	5.0
	R	20,590	2.1	20,566	3,733	5.5	..	..	..	..	..
MOROCCO 1971	T	15,379	2.6	..	2,819	5.5	..	..	..	..	..
	U	..	5.2	..	1,113	4.9[3]	28.9	62.8	..	880	..
	R	..	2.7	..	1,706	5.8	..	..	..	..	..
ST. HELENA 1966	T	5	0.2	5	1	4.3	46.6	41.5	..	1	..
	[29]U	2	..	..	..	..	..	..	..	0	..
	[29]R	3	..	..	..	..	..	..	..[6]	1[15]	..[45]
SEYCHELLES [5]1972	T	53	2.2	51	11	4.7	37.2	45.1	10[6]	10[6]	7.3[6]
	U	14	2.2	13	3	4.7	26.9	62.7	2[6]	2[6]	3.0[6]
	R	39	2.4	38	8	4.7	40.8[26]	38.9[26]	8[6]	7[6]	8.6[6]
TUNISIA[15] 1966	T	4,533	1.8[2]	4,437	874	5.1	70.7[26]	15.5[26]	..	836	..
	U	1,820	2.9[2]	1,735	342	5.1	54.5[26]	32.7[26]	..	335	..
	R	2,713	2.9[2]	2,701	532	5.1	81.6[26]	4.0[26]	..	501	..
WESTERN SAHARA [68]1974	T	76	12.4	75	..	..	..	..	4	4	-
	U	..	..	43	..	..	..	..	4	4	-
	R	..	..	32	..	..	..	..	0	0	-
ZAMBIA [69]1969	T	3,881	..	4,016	915	4.4	..	..	879	842	4.2
	U	784	6.5	..	..	..	..	..	188	..	..
	R	3,097	2.0	..	..	..	..	..	691	..	..

Table 14 (continued)

SIZE, DENSITY OF OCCUPATION AND FACILITIES OF OCCUPIED DWELLINGS

COUNTRIES AND AREAS AND CENSUS YEARS	TOTAL:T URBAN:U RURAL:R	SIZE		DENSITY OF OCCUPATION		PERCENTAGE OF DWELLINGS WITH [30]					CAPITAL FORMATION IN RESIDENTIAL BUILDING CONSTRUCTION AS PERCENTAGE OF GROSS DOMESTIC PRODUCT [17]
		AVERAGE SIZE (ROOMS PER DWELLINGS) [23]	PERCENTAGE OF DWELLINGS WITH 1 ROOM [27]	AVERAGE NUMBER OF PERSONS PER ROOM [23]	PERCENTAGE OF DWELLINGS WITH 3 OR MORE PERSONS PER ROOM [27]	WATER PIPED INSIDE DWELLING	TOILET ANY TYPE	FLUSH	ELECTRIC LIGHTING	DWELLINGS CONSTRUCTED PER 1000 POPULATION [37]	
		(13)	(14)	(15)	(16)	(17)	(18)	(19)	(20)	(21)	(22)
(12)											
AFRICA											
ALGERIA [68]1966	T	· 2.2	34.6	2.8	..	22.7	49.1	..	33.7	..	..
	U	2.4	28.3	..	..	53.5	93.1	..	74.0	..	..
	R	2.1	38.1	..	..	5.9	25.1	..	11.8	..	..
EGYPT 1976	T	..	..	..	..	[6]30.2	..	..	[6]45.7	..	..
	U	..	..	..	..	[6]60.7	..	..	[6]76.9	..	..
	R	..	..	..	..	3.7	..	..	18.6	..	..
MOROCCO 1971	T	[24]2.1	[24]35.5	[24]2.4	[24]42.3	..	..	..	..	..	..
	U	[24]2.1	[24]33.2	[24]2.1	[24]34.4	[36]64.8	[36]92.6	..	[36]81.5	..	..
	R	[24]2.0	[24]36.9	[24]2.6	[24]47.4	..	..	..	..	..	..
ST. HELENA 1966	T	[20]3.7	[20]1.2	[20]1.2	[20]4.7	[21]43.9	[21]99.8	[21]38.4	[21]45.1	..	..
	U	..	..	..	..	81.1	100.0	89.6	..	..	..
	R	..	..	..	..	27.8	99.7	16.2	..	..	..
SEYCHELLES [5]1971	T	3.2	14.0	1.6	21.5	23.2	97.7	19.9	..	..	..
	U[29]	3.8	6.3	1.6	16.1	41.6	99.3	36.9	..	..	..
	R[29]	3.1	16.3	1.7	23.1	17.7	97.2	14.8	..	..	..
TUNISIA [15] 1966	T	[20]1.6	[20]60.2	[20]3.2	..	[8]14.8	..	..	23.9	[12]1.2	..
	U	[20]1.9	[20]46.5	[20]2.7	..	[8]35.1	..	..	..	..	..
	R	[20]1.4	[20]69.3	[20]3.6	..	1.8	..	..	..	..	..
WESTERN SAHARA [68]1974	T	4.5	-	1.2	-	78.5	100.0	87.4	95.3	..	..
	U	4.5	-	1.2	-	90.1	100.0	95.9	95.3	..	..
	R	4.5	-	1.6	-	22.8	100.0	46.7	95.3	..	..
ZAMBIA [69]1969	T	1.9	51.3	2.6	47.5	12.4	49.6	15.1	..	..	..
	U	2.4	23.7	..	..	48.6	92.5	57.3	..	..	..
	R	1.7	58.8	..	..	2.5	37.9	3.6	..	..	..

Table 14 (continued)

COUNTRIES AND AREAS AND CENSUS YEARS	TOTAL:T URBAN:U RURAL:R	POPULATION [1]			HOUSEHOLDS		TENURE OF HOUSEHOLDS IN CONVENTIONAL DWELLINGS [11] PERCENTAGE OF:		DWELLINGS		
		TOTAL (IN THOUSANDS) [9]	ANNUAL RATE OF GROWTH [19]	LIVING IN HOUSEHOLDS (IN THOUSANDS)	TOTAL NUMBER (IN THOUSANDS)	AVERAGE SIZE (PERSONS PER HOUSEHOLD)	OWNER OCCUPANTS	RENTERS	TOTAL NUMBER (IN THOUSANDS)	NUMBER OCCUPIED (IN THOUSANDS)	VACANCY PERCENTAGE [13]
(1)		(2)	(3)	(4)	(5)	(6)	(7)	(8)	(9)	(10)	(11)
AMERICA, NORTH											
ANTIGUA AND BARBUDA [22] 1970	T	66	1.9	..	15	4.3	[24]55.9	[21]30.5	[6]17	[6]15	[6]6.7
	U	22	..	..	..	..	[24]49.2	[21]40.4	[6]6	[6]6	[6]3.5
	R	44	..	..	..	..	[24]59.8	[21]24.7	[6]11	[6]10	[6]8.5
BAHAMAS [25] 1963	T	130	4.9	130	32	4.1	[6]55.1	35.3	..	[6]32	..
	U	81	3.6	81	20	4.0	[6]46.2	..	..	[6]20	..
	R	49	6.6	49	12	4.2	[6]70.6	..	..	[6]12	..
BARBADOS 1970	T	238	0.2	231	59	4.0	[24]73.5	[24]20.3	59	..	..
	U	..	..	64	..	..	[24]45.5	[24]43.7	..	..	..
	R	..	..	54	..	..	[24]73.5	[24]6.8	..	..	..
BELIZE 1970	T	121	2.9	118	23	5.2	[24]57.9	[24]27.4	..	..	..
	U	..	..	64	..	..	[24]45.5	[24]3.7	..	..	..
	R	..	..	54	..	..	[24]73.5	[24]6.8	..	..	..
BERMUDA 1970	T	52	2.1	52	16	3.4	[24]39.1	[24]55.4	..	16	..
	U	..	..	4	1	3.1	[24]16.0	[24]76.7	..	1	..
	R	..	..	49	14	3.4	[24]41.0	[24]53.4	..	14	..
BRITISH VIRGIN ISLANDS 1970	T	10	3.0	9	2	3.9	54.5	43.7	..	..	..
	U	..	..	..	1	..	33.1	64.8	..	..	..
	R	..	..	..	2	..	61.6	36.6	..	..	..
CANADA 1971	T	21,568	1.5	..	6,041	3.5	[26]60.0	[26]40.0	6,259	5,970	4.6
	U	16,411	2.2	..	..	..	[26]54.1	[26]45.9	4,923	4,711	4.3
	R	5,158	-0.5	..	..	..	81.9	18.1	1,336	1,259	5.7
1976	T	22,993	1.3	..	7,166	3.1	61.8	38.2	7,364	7,009	4.8
	U	17,367	1.0	..	5,613	3.0	55.6	44.4	5,815	5,570	4.2
	R	5,626	1.7	..	1,553	3.5	84.2	15.8	1,549	1,440	7.1
COSTA RICA [22,29] 1963	T	1,379	[2]3.7	..	[28]231	[28]5.8	[21]56.3	[21]24.0	..	231	..
	U	461	[2]4.9	..	[28]86	[28]5.4	[21]43.1	[21]48.9	..	86	..
	R	918	[2]3.4	..	[28]145	[28]6.0	[21]64.1	[21]9.3	..	145	..
CUBA 1970	T	8,569	2.3	8,502	1,908	4.5	[26]74.7	[26]24.3	1,924	1,901	1.2
	U	5,169	..	5,110	1,241	4.1	[26]67.0	[26]31.9	1,252	1,237	1.2
	R	3,400	..	3,392	667	5.1	[26]89.0	[26]10.2	671	664	1.1
DOMINICAN REPUBLIC 1960	T	3,047	3.6	2,999	594	5.0	[6]70.5	[6]15.6	..	[6]594	..
	U	922	6.0	890	185	4.8	[6]44.9	[6]44.0	..	[6]185	..
	R	2,125	2.0	2,109	409	5.1	[6]22.0	[6]2.8	..	[6]409	..
EL SALVADOR [29] 1971	T	3,549	3.5	..	686	5.2	[21]47.9	[21]26.0	..	655	..
	U	1,403	3.8	..	..	..	[21]35.3	[21]53.3	..	271	..
	R	2,146	3.3	..	..	..	[21]56.7	[21]6.7	..	385	..
GREENLAND 1970	T	..	..	43	10	4.5	[10]46.2	[10]30.0	..	10	..
	U	..	..	32	..	..	[10]38.7	[10]33.8	..	7	..
	R	..	..	12	..	..	[10]72.0	16.9	..	2	..
GUATEMALA 1973	T	5,160	2.1	5,014	998	5.0	56.7	12.8	..	935	..
	U	1,878	..	1,805	368	4.9	52.0	31.3	..	331	..
	R	3,282	..	3,209	629	5.1	59.4	2.0	..	604	..
HAITI 1976	T	..	..	4,673	1,065	4.4	[24]82.9	[24]4.8	..	..	..
	U	..	..	937	226	4.2	[24]53.1	[24]18.1	..	..	..
	R	..	..	3,736	839	4.5	[24]90.9	[24]1.2	..	..	..

Table 14 (continued)

COUNTRIES AND AREAS AND CENSUS YEARS	TOTAL:T URBAN:U RURAL:R	POPULATION[1]		LIVING IN HOUSEHOLDS (IN THOUS-ANDS)	HOUSEHOLDS		TENURE OF HOUSEHOLDS IN CONVENTIONAL DWELLINGS[11] PERCENTAGE OF:		DWELLINGS		
		[9]TOTAL (IN THOUS-ANDS)	ANNUAL[19] RATE OF GROWTH		TOTAL NUMBER (IN THOUS-ANDS)	AVERAGE SIZE (PERSONS PER HOUSEHOLD)	OWNER OCCUPANTS	RENTERS	TOTAL NUMBER (IN THOUS-ANDS)	NUMBER OCCUPIED (IN THOUS-ANDS)	VACANCY[13] PERCENTAGE
(1)		(2)	(3)	(4)	(5)	(6)	(7)	(8)	(9)	(10)	(11)
AMERICA, NORTH (continued)											
HONDURAS	1974 T	2,657	2.7	..	..	..	[35]71.8	[35]16.5	527	463	12.1
	U	833	5.1	..	..	..	[35]49.2	[35]43.4	160	146	8.6
	R	1,824	0.9	..	..	..	[35]82.3	[35]4.0	366	317	13.6
JAMAICA	1970 T	1,814	1.2	..	420	4.3	[21]52.1	[21]38.8	..	420	..
	U	..	..	..	..	..	[21]29.5	[21]63.2	..	189	..
	R	..	..	..	..	..	[21]70.6	[21]18.9	..	231	..
MEXICO	1970 T	48,225	3.4	..	[6]8,286	[6]5.7	66.0	..	..	[6]8,286	..
	U	28,308	5.0	..	[6]4,864	[6]5.7	54.2	..	..	[6]4,864	..
	R	19,917	1.5	..	3,422	5.8	82.8	..	..	3,422	..
MONTSERRAT	1970 T	12	-0.4	11	3	3.5	[24]72.7	[24]16.6	..	..	..
	U	..	..	1	0	3.0	[24]49.9	[24]38.1	..	..	..
	R	..	..	10	3	3.6	[24]76.1	[24]13.4	..	..	..
NICARAGUA	1971 T	1,912	2.8	..	..	..	..	..	..	305	..
	U	917	4.9	..	..	..	..	..	..	148	..
	R	995	1.1	..	..	..	..	..	..	156	..
PANAMA[4,25]	[36]1970 T	1,428	3.1	1,422	288	4.9	62.9	27.8	287	277	3.5
	U	679	4.6	..	..	..	38.8	52.6	138	136	1.8
	R	749	1.9	..	..	..	86.8	3.4	149	141	5.1
CANAL ZONE	1974 T	..	..	16	5	3.2	2.8	97.2	5	5	6.6
	U	..	..	15	5	3.3	1.1	99.0	5	4	6.4
	R	..	..	1	0	2.8	26.5	73.5	0	0	8.5
	1975 T	44	0.5	15	5	3.4	2.9	97.1	5	5	7.1
	U	..	..	14	4	3.4	1	99.0	5	4	6.5
	R	..	..	1	0	3.2	28.6	71.4	0	0	14.5
PUERTO RICO[22]	1970 T	2,712	1.4	2,676	632	4.2	[6]71.5	[6]28.5	[6]714	[6]632	[6]11.4
	U	1,532	4.0	1,548	388	4.0	[6]63.5	[6]36.5	[6]430	[6]388	[6]9.8
	R	1,180	[7]-1.1	1,129	245	4.6	[6]84.1	[6]15.9	[6]284	[6]245	[6]13.8
ST. VINCENT AND THE GRENADINES	1966 T	89	[7]1.1	88	22	4.0	..	..	..	[6]18	..
	U	..	..	23	5	4.4	..	..	..	[6]5	..
	R	..	..	65	17	3.9	..	..	..	[6]13	..
TURKS AND CAICOS ISLANDS	1970 T	6	-0.2	..	1	4.3	70.3	28.9	..	..	..
	U	..	..	..	..	..	62.3	36.7	..	..	..
	R	..	..	..	..	..	76.3	23.1	..	..	..
UNITED STATES	1970 T	203,235	1.3	197,400	63,450	3.1	[6]62.9	[6]37.1	[6]68,679	[6]63,450	[6]7.6
	U	149,332	1.8	144,610	47,563	3.1	[6]58.4	[6]41.6	[6]50,143	[6]47,563	[6]5.1
	R	53,878	-0.0	52,790	15,887	3.4	[6]76.2	[6]23.8	[6]18,536	[6]15,887	[6]14.3
UNITED STATES VIRGIN ISLANDS	[36]1970 T	62	6.9	61	..	..	..	..	21	18	13.8
	U	15	-1.7	15	..	..	..	..	5	5	8.6
	R	47	12.9	46	..	..	..	..	16	13	15.4

Table 14 (continued)

SIZE, DENSITY OF OCCUPATION AND FACILITIES OF OCCUPIED DWELLINGS

COUNTRIES AND AREAS AND CENSUS YEARS	TOTAL:T URBAN:U RURAL:E	SIZE AVERAGE SIZE (ROOMS PER DWELLINGS) [23]	PERCENTAGE OF DWELLINGS WITH 1 ROOM [27]	DENSITY OF OCCUPATION AVERAGE NUMBER OF PERSONS PER ROOM [23]	PERCENTAGE OF DWELLINGS WITH 3 OR MORE PERSONS PER ROOM [27]	PERCENTAGE OF DWELLINGS WITH [30] WATER PIPED INSIDE DWELLING	TOILET ANY TYPE	FLUSH	ELECTRIC LIGHTING	DWELLINGS CONSTRUCTED PER 1000 POPULATION [37]	CAPITAL FORMATION IN RESIDENTIAL BUILDING CONSTRUCTION AS PERCENTAGE OF GROSS DOMESTIC PRODUCT [17]
(12)		(13)	(14)	(15)	(16)	(17)	(18)	(19)	(20)	(21)	(22)
AMERICA, NORTH											
ANTIGUA AND BARBUDA [22] 1970	T	3.6[24]	11.3[24]	..	..	21.0[24]	78.2[24]	17.0	..	..	..
	U	3.8[24]	11.6[24]	..	..	33.2[24]	80.8[24]	21.9	..	..	..
	R	3.5[24]	11.1[24]	..	..	14.0[24]	76.7[24]	14.2	..	..	..
BAHAMAS 1963	T	3.5	12.4	1.2	7.1	30.8	90.7	28.4	57.7	..	..
	U	3.4	13.6	1.2	7.3	..	99.3	35.1	73.1	..	..
	R	3.6	10.3	1.2	6.7	..	75.6	16.8	31.1	..	..
BARBADOS 1970	T	3.8	2.5	1.0	..	40.0	98.7	26.6	59.1	..	..
	U	..	..	..	..	..	..	..	..	..	..
	R	..	..	..	..	..	..	..	..	..	..
BELIZE 1970	T	..	..	..	..	80.0[24]	95.6[24]	1.2[24]	..	..	..
	U	..	..	..	..	..	..	..	..	..	..
	R	..	..	..	..	..	..	..	..	..	..
BERMUDA 1970	T	3.9[24]	5.9[24]	..	..	94.6	99.5	95.8	..	..	..
	U	..	..	..	..	90.5	99.6	96.3	..	..	..
	R	..	..	..	..	95.0	99.5	95.7	..	..	..
BRITISH VIRGIN ISLANDS 1970	T	..	..	..	..	..	..	..	..	..	..
	U	..	..	..	..	..	..	..	..	..	..
	R	..	..	..	..	..	..	..	..	..	..
CANADA 1971	T	5.4	1.5	0.6	0.2	96.0[20]	100.0[20]	94.3[20]	..	9.4	..
	U	5.3	1.6	0.6	0.1	99.3[20]	100.0[20]	98.9[20]	..	..	5.1
	R	5.7	1.3	0.7	0.7	84.2[20]	100.0[20]	77.3[20]	..	..	..
1976	T	5.4	1.4	0.6	..	98.5[70]	97.9[70]	97.4[70]	..	10.3	5.5
	U	..	..	..	..	99.8[70]	..	99.5[70]	..	..	..
	R	..	..	..	..	93.2[70]	..	88.4[70]	..	..	..
COSTA RICA [22,29] 1963	T	3.8	6.6	1.5	13.0	59.0	74.5	29.7	54.6	..	..
	U	4.2	7.0	1.3	7.9	85.1	98.0	63.5	93.5	..	..
	R	3.6	6.5	1.7	16.0	43.6	60.6	9.8	31.6	..	..
CUBA 1970	T	3.7	9.8	1.2	8.4	45.6[26]	82.1[26]	43.9[26]	70.7[26]	0.5[46]	..
	U	3.6	12.8	1.1	9.1	64.2[26]	93.2[26]	64.2[26]	98.1[26]	..	..
	R	3.9	4.3	1.3	7.1	10.9[26]	61.3[26]	6.1[26]	19.6[26]	..	..
DOMINICAN REPUBLIC 1960	T	2.7	9.5	2.0	..	8.1	86.2	11.9	20.0	..	..
	U	3.2	13.3	1.6	..	22.9	94.9	35.7	57.7	..	..
	R	2.4	7.7	2.2	..	1.4	82.3	1.2	3.0	..	..
EL SALVADOR [29] 1971	T	1.7	60.8	3.1	63.1	26.0	41.3	22.5	34.1	0.7[46]	..
	U	2.1	52.5	2.4	50.2	59.5	82.5	52.1	73.0	..	..
	R	1.5	66.6	3.8	72.2	2.5	12.3	1.6	6.7	..	..
GREENLAND 1970	T	2.6	19.7	1.7	..	32.8	84.4	24.5	..	10.4[46]	..
	U	2.8	15.7	1.5	..	41.9	92.9	31.1	..	..	..
	R	2.0	33.4	2.7	..	0.9	54.7	1.3	..	..	..
GUATEMALA 1973	T	2.4	27.5	2.2	43.0	25.4	40.7	14.9	28.5	..	..
	U	3.3	17.7	1.6	26.5	58.1	82.4	39.5	67.8	..	..
	R	2.0	32.9	2.7	52.0	6.3	16.4	0.6	5.4	..	..
HAITI 1976	T	2.2	18.2	..	..	..	..	..	..	..	..
	U	2.3	37.6	..	..	..	..	..	..	..	..
	R	2.2	13.3	..	..	..	..	..	..	..	..

Table 14 (continued)

SIZE, DENSITY OF OCCUPATION AND FACILITIES OF OCCUPIED DWELLINGS

COUNTRIES AND AREAS AND CENSUS YEARS	TOTAL:T URBAN:U RURAL:R	SIZE		DENSITY OF OCCUPATION		PERCENTAGE OF DWELLINGS WITH[30]				DWELLINGS[37] CONSTRUCTED PER 1000 POPULATION	CAPITAL FORMATION IN RESIDENTIAL BUILDING CONSTRUCTION AS PERCENTAGE OF GROSS DOMESTIC PRODUCT[17]
		AVERAGE SIZE[23] (ROOMS PER DWELLINGS)	PERCENTAGE[27] OF DWELLINGS WITH 1 ROOM	AVERAGE[23] NUMBER OF PERSONS PER ROOM	PERCENTAGE[27] OF DWELLINGS WITH 3 OR MORE PERSONS PER ROOM	WATER PIPED INSIDE DWELLING	TOILET ANY TYPE	TOILET FLUSH	ELECTRIC LIGHTING		
(12)		(13)	(14)	(15)	(16)	(17)	(18)	(19)	(20)	(21)	(22)
AMERICA, NORTH (continued)											
HONDURAS	1974 T	2.4	19.8	..	..	15.4	32.2	..	25.0	..	..
	U	3.0	14.5	..	..	39.3	78.8	..	67.1	..	..
	R	2.2	22.3	..	..	4.4	10.6	..	5.5	..	..
JAMAICA	1970 T	2.4	34.7	..	..	21.6	96.7	31.3	..	[38]1.5	..
	U	2.3	45.2	..	..	40.2	99.2	63.0	..	..	..
	R	2.5	26.3	..	..	6.4	94.7	5.5	..	..	..
MEXICO	1970 T	2.3	40.1	2.5	..	38.7	41.5	..	58.9	..	..
	U	2.6	31.1	2.2	..	54.0	61.0	..	80.7	..	..
	R	1.8	53.0	3.2	..	17.1	13.8	..	27.8	..	..
MONTSERRAT	1970 T	3.2	7.9	1.1	6.6	29.2	75.9	..	..	..	..
	U	..	..	..	..	54.8	82.1	..	..	..	..
	R	..	..	..	..	25.4	75.0	..	..	..	..
NICARAGUA	1971 T	2.2	38.3	..	..	27.9	53.9	19.3	40.9	..	1.3
	U	2.3	36.0	..	..	54.1	90.8	38.2	76.7	..	..
	R	2.0	40.5	..	..	3.1	18.8	1.3	6.9	..	..
PANAMA[4,25]	[36]1970 T	2.2	37.4	2.2	38.6	26.1	72.0	41.3	52.4	..	..
	U	2.5	34.4	1.8	30.6	47.6	98.4	77.4	90.4	..	..
	R	2.0	40.2	2.5	46.4	5.5	46.8	6.8	16.0	..	..
CANAL ZONE	1974 T	..	..	..	..	98.2	100.0	98.2	98.2	..	..
	U	..	..	..	..	100.0	100.0	100.0	100.0	..	..
	R	..	..	..	..	73.5	100.0	73.5	73.5	..	..
	1975 T	..	..	..	..	98.1	100.0	98.1	98.1	..	..
	U	..	..	..	..	100.0	100.0	100.0	100.0	..	..
	R	..	..	..	..	71.4	100.0	71.4	71.4	..	..
PUERTO RICO[22]	1970 T	4.7	3.4	0.9	..	62.7	..	64.5	..	[39]8.3	..
	U	4.9	3.2	1.1	..	82.8	..	84.2	..	..	..
	R	4.2	3.7	1.0	..	32.1	..	34.5	..	..	..
ST. VINCENT AND THE GRENADINES	1966 T	2.5	..	..	..	25.0	77.3	22.6	..	..	..
	U	..	..	..	..	..	..	..	..	..	..
	R	..	..	..	..	..	..	..	..	..	..
TURKS AND CAICOS ISLANDS	1970 T	4.0	3.8	..	..	12.0	82.4	12.9	..	..	..
	U	4.3	3.5	..	..	22.3	98.6	22.9	..	..	..
	R	3.8	3.9	..	..	4.3	70.4	6.5	..	..	..
UNITED STATES	1970 T	5.1	1.8	0.6	..	97.5	..	96.0	..	[53]7.1	..
	U	5.0	2.1	0.6	..	99.7	..	99.4	..	..	..
	R	5.3	0.8	0.6	..	91.3	..	86.4	..	..	..
UNITED STATES VIRGIN ISLANDS	[36]1970 T	3.7	13.8	0.9	..	85.5	94.5	83.8	97.6	..	..
	U	3.4	19.1	0.9	..	84.4	88.9	85.0	97.5	..	..
	R	3.8	11.9	0.9	..	85.9	96.4	83.4	97.6	..	..

Table 14 (continued)

COUNTRIES AND AREAS AND CENSUS YEARS	TOTAL:T URBAN:U RURAL:R	POPULATION [1]			HOUSEHOLDS		TENURE OF HOUSEHOLDS IN CONVENTIONAL DWELLINGS [11]		DWELLINGS		
		[9] TOTAL (IN THOUS-ANDS)	ANNUAL [19] RATE OF GROWTH	LIVING IN HOUSEHOLDS (IN THOUS-ANDS)	TOTAL NUMBER (IN THOUS-ANDS)	AVERAGE SIZE (PERSONS PER HOUSEHOLD)	PERCENTAGE OF: OWNER OCCUPANTS	RENTERS	TOTAL NUMBER (IN THOUS-ANDS)	NUMBER OCCUPIED (IN THOUS-ANDS)	VACANCY [13] PERCENTAGE
(1)		(2)	(3)	(4)	(5)	(6)	(7)	(8)	(9)	(10)	(11)
AMERICA, SOUTH											
BRAZIL	1970 T	93,139	2.9	89,963	18,554	4.8	60.4	19.0	..	17,628	..
	U	52,085	4.8	50,363	10,904	4.6	60.0	30.8	..	10,276	..
	R	41,054	[7]0.9	39,600	7,650	5.2	60.9	2.9	..	7,352	..
	1973 T	[7]92,342	[7]2.7	..	..	..	..	..	..	..	..
	U	[7]51,774	..	..	..	..	..	..	..	..	..
	R	40,568	..	..	..	..	..	..	..	..	..
CHILE	[41]1970 T	8,853	1.4	8,601	1,690	5.1	[26]53.3	[26]26.3	1,775	..	..
	U	6,726	3.1	6,519	1,313	5.0	[26]55.5	[26]31.9	..	..	..
	R	2,127	-0.1	2,083	377	5.5	[26]45.5	[26]7.0	..	..	..
COLOMBIA	1964 T	17,485	[3]3.2	16,836	2,798	5.8	61.3	24.4	..	1,928	[6]0.5
	U	9,240	[2]5.9	8,601	..	..	54.1	38.8	..	1,005	[6]0.2
	R	8,245	[2]0.5	8,235	..	..	67.9	11.0	..	924	[6]0.9
	1973 T	22,552	2.8	19,640	3,472	5.7	[24]53.5	[24]30.7	2,956	2,800	5.3
	U	11,004	2.0	12,406	2,249	5.5	[24]49.1	[24]41.4	1,861	1,784	4.1
	R	11,548	3.8	7,234	1,222	5.9	[24]61.6	[24]11.1	1,096	1,016	7.3
ECUADOR	1974 T	6,522	3.0	..	..	..	..	..	1,313	1,189	9.4
	U	2,699	..	..	..	..	..	..	504	484	4.0
	R	3,823	..	..	..	..	..	..	810	706	12.8
FALKLAND ISLANDS (MALVINAS)	1972 T	2	-1.0	2	1	3.1	..	..	1	1	7.7
	U	1	..	1	0	3.0	..	..	0	0	4.8
	R	1	..	1	0	3.3	..	..	0	0	11.3
PARAGUAY	1962 T	1,819	2.6	1,776	[28]328	[28]5.5	[6]69.2	[6]9.9	327	328	..
	U	652	4.2	627	[28]123	[28]5.3	[6]66.0	[6]19.9	122	123	..
	R	1,167	2.7	1,150	[28]206	5.7	[28]71.1	[6]3.9	204	206	..
	1972 T	2,358	2.6	2,325	428	5.4	81.8	8.7	..	427	..
	U	882	3.1	862	172	5.0	73.8	18.2	..	171	..
	R	1,476	1.2	1,464	256	5.7	87.2	2.4	..	255	..
PERU	1961 T	9,907	[2]2.2	9,566	1,962	4.9	[6]56.0	[6]24.7	[6]1,975	[6]1,962	[6]0.7
	U	4,698	[2]4.3	4,428	921	4.8	[6]39.4	[6]44.7	[6]933	[6]921	[6]1.3
	R	5,209	[2]2.0	5,138	1,041	4.9	[6]70.7	[6]7.0	[6]1,042	[6]1,041	[6]0.1
	1972 T	13,538	2.9	..	2,772	4.8	[35]69.5	[35]16.6	2,904	2,771	4.6
	U	8,058	5.0	..	..	..	[35]59.1	[35]27.9	1,620	1,561	3.6
	R	5,480	0.4	..	..	..	[35]83.4	[35]1.5	1,285	1,210	5.8
URUGUAY	1963 T	2,596	1.8	2,545	678	3.8	39.4	47.2	751	666	11.4
	U	2,097	2.3	..	..	..	38.9	51.2	555	560	..
	R	499	-1.2	..	..	..	42.0	26.3	107	106	..
	1975 T	2,782	0.6	[32]2,705	797	3.4	52.1	32.1	[6]848	[6]751	[6]11.0
	U	2,308	0.8	[32]2,316	..	..	..	..	[6]730	[6]647	10.9
	R	474	-0.4	[32]389	..	..	..	..	[6]118	[6]104	11.6

Table 14 (continued)

SIZE, DENSITY OF OCCUPATION AND FACILITIES OF OCCUPIED DWELLINGS

COUNTRIES AND AREAS AND CENSUS YEARS	TOTAL:T URBAN:U RURAL:R	SIZE		DENSITY OF OCCUPATION		PERCENTAGE OF DWELLINGS WITH [30]				DWELLINGS [37] CONSTRUCTED PER 1000 POPULATION	CAPITAL FORMATION IN RESIDENTIAL BUILDING CONSTRUCTION AS PERCENTAGE OF GROSS DOMESTIC PRODUCT [37]
		AVERAGE SIZE [23] (ROOMS PER DWELLINGS)	PERCENTAGE [27] OF DWELL-INGS WITH 1 ROOM	AVERAGE [23] NUMBER OF PERSONS PER ROOM	PERCENTAGE OF DWELL-INGS WITH 3 [27] OR MORE PERSONS PER ROOM	WATER PIPED INSIDE DWELLING	TOILET ANY TYPE	TOILET FLUSH	ELECTRIC LIGHTING		
(12)		(13)	(14)	(15)	(16)	(17)	(18)	(19)	(20)	(21)	(22)

AMERICA, SOUTH

BRAZIL	1970 T	4.7	2.8	1.1	4.8	27.4	60.6	13.2	47.6	..	..
	U	4.8	3.6	1.0	4.9	45.8	85.6	22.3	75.6	..	..
	R	4.5	1.8	1.2	4.7	1.6	25.6	0.4	8.4	..	..
	1973 T	3.9	2.8	..	..	33.8	77.5	24.0	55.6	..	..
	U	4.3	3.3	..	..	51.2	87.4	36.6	79.1	..	..
	R	4.6	1.8	..	..	1.7	31.0	0.8	12.5	..	..
CHILE	[41] 1970 T	[24]2.9	[24]10.9	[24]1.4	[24]17.4	[24]59.6	[24]61.5	[24]43.6	..	..	..
	U	[24]3.0	[24]9.9	[24]1.3	[24]14.7	[24]63.1	[24]68.9	[24]54.4	..	..	..
	R	[24]2.4	[24]14.5	1.7	[24]26.8	12.7	[24]35.8	[24]6.1	..	..	..
COLOMBIA	1964 T	2.9	18.9	..	..	30.0	40.7	30.5	47.4	..	..
	U	3.4	11.5	..	..	54.9	69.1	58.0	83.4	..	..
	R	2.4	25.8	..	..	6.8	14.2	4.9	8.3	..	..
	1973 T	3.4	15.3	1.8	30.3	64.2	..	46.5	58.1	..	..
	U	4.0	9.7	1.6	21.2	87.6	..	72.8	87.5	..	..
	R	2.5	23.9	2.4	44.1	28.5	..	6.5	13.2	..	..
ECUADOR	1974 T	2.4	34.0	2.3	43.2	[44]20.0	[44]42.0	..	[44]41.2	[38]1.8	..
	U	2.8	27.8	1.9	34.6	[44]44.8	[44]84.0	..	[44]84.3	..	..
	R	2.1	38.3	2.6	49.1	[44]3.0	[44]13.2	..	[44]11.6	..	..
FALKLAND ISLANDS (MALVINAS)	1972 T	7.4	-	..	..	98.6	99.7	98.0	..	..	..
	U	5.0	-	..	..	99.1	100.0	99.1	..	..	..
	R	10.6	-	..	..	98.0	99.2	96.4	..	..	..
PARAGUAY	1962 T	2.0	47.5	2.6	53.3	5.9	88.3	5.0	13.2	..	..
	U	..	..	..	..	15.3	95.0	13.1	33.2	..	..
	R	..	..	..	..	0.3	84.3	0.2	1.2	..	..
	1972 T	2.2	41.8	2.4	49.2	..	93.7	14.3	17.5	..	..
	U	2.9	26.3	1.7	30.3	..	97.5	33.6	41.7	..	..
	R	1.8	52.3	3.1	61.8	..	91.2	1.3	1.2	..	..
PERU	1961 T	2.3	37.2	2.3	43.0	14.6	44.3	25.4	26.0	..	..
	U	2.7	30.4	2.0	33.7	30.2	63.3	50.1	50.7	..	..
	R	2.0	43.0	2.7	49.8	0.8	27.5	3.5	4.2	..	..
	1972 T	2.5	33.4	1.9	36.8	25.3	24.7	23.2	32.0	..	..
	U	2.9	25.2	1.7	29.3	43.5	42.5	40.2	54.3	..	..
	R	2.0	44.4	2.4	46.7	1.2	1.2	0.8	2.7	..	..
URUGUAY	1963 T	2.5	27.7	1.5	..	59.4	94.3	58.7	78.4	..	..
	U	2.4	29.3	..	..	67.6	97.7	67.4	87.8	..	..
	R	3.2	19.5	..	..	15.9	76.4	13.1	29.1	..	..
	1975 T	1.7	55.5	2.1	40.4	63.1	92.2	62.7	80.7	..	..
	U	1.7	55.7	2.1	40.3	69.2	94.7	69.0	89.2	..	..
	R	1.8	53.7	2.1	41.0	23.1	75.4	21.3	27.8	..	..

Table 14 (continued)

		POPULATION [1]			HOUSEHOLDS				DWELLINGS		
COUNTRIES AND AREAS AND CENSUS YEARS	TOTAL:T URBAN:U RURAL:R					AVERAGE SIZE	TENURE OF HOUSEHOLDS IN CONVENTIONAL DWELLINGS [11]				
		[9] TOTAL (IN THOUSANDS)	ANNUAL [19] RATE OF GROWTH	LIVING IN HOUSEHOLDS (IN THOUSANDS)	TOTAL NUMBER (IN THOUSANDS)	(PERSONS PER HOUSEHOLD)	PERCENTAGE OF: OWNER OCCUPANTS	RENTERS	TOTAL NUMBER (IN THOUSANDS)	NUMBER OCCUPIED (IN THOUSANDS)	VACANCY [13] PERCENTAGE
(1)		(2)	(3)	(4)	(5)	(6)	(7)	(8)	(9)	(10)	(11)
ASIA											
BAHRAIN [29] 1971	T	216	2.8	216	34	6.4	[24]60.6	[24]33.6	31	..	..
	U	169	1.9	169	..	..	[24]53.7	[24]40.1	25	..	..
	R	47	6.5	47	..	..	[24]93.1	[24]2.6	6	..	..
CYPRUS 1960	T	578	..	..	146	4.0	..	..	157	139	11.7
	U	206	3.2	..	51	4.0	48.5	44.8	49	46	4.9
	R	371	-0.7	..	94	3.9	..	..	109	93	14.8
[36] 1973	T	..	[16]..	628	160	-3.9	[26]86.3	[26]13.7	..	164	..
	U	..	[16]3.2	268	..	..	[26]70.7	[26]29.3	..	71	..
	R	..	[16]-0.7	360	..	..	[26]97.6	[26]2.4	..	93	..
HONG KONG 1971	T	3,948	2.3	3,805	847	4.5	[24]18.1	[24]75.7	651	605	7.0
	U	..	2.8	..	766	..	..	..	564	535	5.3
	R	..	-1.7	..	81	..	..	..	87	71	18.6
1973	T	..	..	4,102	946	4.3	..	..	696	636	8.5
	U	..	..	..	853	..	..	..	634	587	7.4
	R	..	..	..	93	..	..	..	62	49	20.0
INDIA 1971	T	547,950	2.0	[42]543,481	[42]97,057	[42]5.6	[42]84.6	[42]15.4	100,251	92,494	7.7
	U	109,094	3.0	[42]106,888	[42]19,125	[42]5.6	[42]47.1	[42]52.9	20,242	18,416	9.0
	R	438,856	1.8	[42]436,593	[42]77,968	[42]5.6	[42]93.8	[42]6.2	80,009	74,077	7.4
INDONESIA [54] 1971	T	118,460	2.1	118,368	24,507	[3]4.8	[24]87.0	[24]5.0	22,471	..	..
	U	20,765	3.8	20,465	3,873	[3]5.3	[24]59.2	[24]24.7	3,009	..	..
	R	97,695	1.8	97,902	20,634	[3]4.7	[24]92.3	[24]1.3	19,462	..	..
IRAN 1966	T	25,079	3.0	24,920	5,029	5.0	[24]71.6	[24]16.2	[21]3,899	..	..
	U	9,794	5.2	9,645	1,961	4.9	[24]54.9	[24]33.4	[21]1,301	..	..
	R	15,285	1.4	15,275	3,069	5.0	[24]82.4	[24]5.1	[21]2,598	..	..
ISRAEL [25,57] 1971	T	[56]2,919	..	..	[32]788	[32]3.8	[26]64.6	[26]30.5	743	..	..
	U	[56]2,401	2.9	..	[32]678	[32]3.7	[26]63.5	[26]33.4	670	..	..
	R	[56]518	1.1	..	[32]110	[32]4.4	[26]75.2	[26]4.0	73	..	..
JAPAN [40] 1970	T	103,720	1.1	99,055	26,856	3.7	58.2	33.6	31,033	28,714	7.5
	U	74,853	2.3	70,882	20,019	3.5	50.7	40.1	..	..	..
	R	28,867	-1.7	28,173	6,837	4.1	80.0	14.5	..	..	..
[36,58] 1973	T	111,940	1.5	104,327	29,105	3.6	[26]58.8	[26]40.5	31,059	28,731	7.5
	U	84,967	2.6	77,991	22,569	3.5	[26]52.1	[26]47.2	24,186	22,257	8.0
	R	26,973	-1.4	26,336	6,535	4.0	[26]82.0	[26]17.6	6,873	6,474	5.8
RYUKYU ISLANDS [40] 1970	T	945	0.2	928	215	4.3	[24]69.7	[24]29.6	..	..	..
	U	..	3.5	561	135	4.2	[24]59.5	[24]39.8	..	..	..
	R	..	-0.3	367	80	4.6	[24]86.8	[24]12.4	..	..	..
JORDAN 1961	T	1,706	2.7	1,650	314	5.3	[24]48.5	[24]23.3	..	..	..
	U	748	4.3	708	129	5.5	[24]36.6	[24]42.6	111	..	..
	R	958	2.2	942	184	5.1	[24]56.9	[24]9.8	..	..	..
KOREA, REPUBLIC OF 1960	T	24,989	[2]2.9	24,235	4,361	5.6	[21]79.5	[21]15.3	4,175	4,098	1.9
	U	6,997	[2]6.0	6,734	1,252	5.4	[21]61.3	[21]35.3	1,117	1,083	3.1
	R	17,992	[2]1.5	17,501	3,109	5.6	[21]86.8	[21]7.2	3,058	3,015	1.4
1970	T	31,466	1.9	29,236	5,576	5.2	91.7	5.5	4,408	4,334	1.7
	U	12,953	7.2	11,603	..	..	85.7	12.0	1,404	1,379	1.8
	R	18,512	-1.2	17,632	..	..	94.5	2.5	3,004	2,956	1.6

Table 14 (continued)

COUNTRIES AND AREAS AND CENSUS YEARS		POPULATION [1]			HOUSEHOLDS		TENURE OF HOUSEHOLDS IN CONVENTIONAL DWELLINGS		DWELLINGS [11]		
	TOTAL:T URBAN:U RURAL:R	[9] TOTAL (IN THOUS-ANDS)	ANNUAL [19] RATE OF GROWTH	LIVING IN HOUSEHOLDS (IN THOUS-ANDS)	TOTAL NUMBER (IN THOUS-ANDS)	AVERAGE SIZE (PERSONS PER HOUSEHOLD)	PERCENTAGE OF: OWNER OCCUPANTS	RENTERS	TOTAL NUMBER (IN THOUS-ANDS)	NUMBER OCCUPIED (IN THOUS-ANDS)	VACANCY [13] PERCENTAGE
(1)		(2)	(3)	(4)	(5)	(6)	(7)	(8)	(9)	(10)	(11)
ASIA (continued)											
PENINSULAR MALAYSIA [60] 1970	T	8,801	2.6	8,832	1,587	5.6	..	..	[62]1,455	[62]1,323	[62]9.1
	U	2,528	-0.4	2,532	432	5.9	..	..	[62]349	[62]323	[62]7.7
	R	6,264	4.3	6,300	1,155	5.5	..	..	[62]1,106	[62]1,001	[62]9.5
MONGOLIA 1969	T	[13]1,019	..	1,160	252	4.6	[21]100.0	..	242	230	5.0
	U	[13]415	5.1	496	102	4.8	[21]100.0	..	83	..	..
	R	[13]604	2.0	664	150	4.4	[21]100.0	..	159	..	..
PAKISTAN [63,64] [71]1973	T	[18]64,980	..	60,510	10,881	5.6	80.3	6.9	..	..	..
	U	[18]16,558	..	16,743	2,847	5.9	64.7	23.3	..	..	..
	R	[18]48,422	[7]..	43,767	8,034	5.4	85.8	1.1	..	..	..
PHILIPPINES 1967	T	[7]36,684	[7,34]3.1	[34]31,980	[34]5,234	[34]6.1	[34]89.4	[34]6.1	..	..	..
	U	[7]11,678	[7,34]3.7	[34]10,145	[34]1,570	[34]6.5	[34]74.1	[34]19.4	..	..	..
	R	[7]25,007	[7]2.8	[34]21,835	[34]3,664	[34]6.0	[34]96.0	[34]0.4	..	..	..
1970	T	36,685	3.1	36,603	6,163	5.9	[26]83.3	[26]8.1	5,822	5,738	1.5
	U	11,678	..	11,615	1,884	6.2	[26]63.6	[26]23.7	1,763	1,724	2.2
	R	25,007	..	24,987	4,279	5.8	[26]92.1	[26]1.1	4,059	4,013	1.1
SRI LANKA 1971	T	12,711	2.2	..	..	..	[6]63.3	[6]27.4	[6]2,382	[6]2,217	[6]6.9
	U	2,842	..	..	..	..	[6]47.7	[6]47.3	[6]440	421	[6]4.4
	R	9,869	..	..	..	..	[6]67.0	[6]22.8	[6]1,942	[6]1,746	[6]7.5
SYRIAN ARAB REPUBLIC 1970	T	6,305	3.3	6,271	[32]1,061	[32]5.9	81.6	15.5	990	[6]908	[6]8.3
	U	2,741	5.0	2,714	[32]460	[32]6.0	67.7	30.4	405	[6]385	[6]5.0
	R	3,564	2.2	3,557	[32]600	[32]5.9	92.8	3.6	585	[6]523	[6]10.5
THAILAND 1970	T	34,397	2.7	..	5,908	[3]5.8	..	..	..	[6]5,923	..
	U	4,553	-0.5	4,418	762	[3]5.8	..	..	..	[6]754	..
	R	29,844	3.3	..	5,146	[3]5.8	..	..	..	[6]5,168	..

SIZE, DENSITY OF OCCUPATION AND FACILITIES OF OCCUPIED DWELLINGS

COUNTRIES AND AREAS AND CENSUS YEARS		SIZE		DENSITY OF OCCUPATION		PERCENTAGE OF DWELLINGS WITH [30]					CAPITAL FORMATION IN RESIDENTIAL BUILDING CONSTRUCTION AS PERCENTAGE OF GROSS DOMESTIC PRODUCT [17]
	TOTAL:T URBAN:U RURAL:R	AVERAGE SIZE [23] (ROOMS PER DWELLINGS)	PERCENTAGE [27] OF DWELL-INGS WITH 1 ROOM	AVERAGE [23] NUMBER OF PERSONS PER ROOM	PERCENTAGE [27] OF DWELL-INGS WITH 3 OR MORE PERSONS PER ROOM	WATER PIPED INSIDE DWELLING	TOILET ANY TYPE	FLUSH	ELECTRIC LIGHTING	DWELLINGS [37] CONSTRUCTED PER 1000 POPULATION	
(12)		(13)	(14)	(15)	(16)	(17)	(18)	(19)	(20)	(21)	(22)
ASIA											
BAHRAIN [29]1971	T	3.0	15.7	2.3	30.5	92.8	..	..	94.0	..	..
	U	2.9	15.1	2.0	27.9	..	..	..	..	..	..
	R	2.9	18.3	2.5	41.3	..	..	..	..	..	..

Table 14 (continued)

COUNTRIES AND AREAS AND CENSUS YEARS	TOTAL:T URBAN:U RURAL:R	SIZE — AVERAGE SIZE (ROOMS PER DWELLINGS) [23]	SIZE — PERCENTAGE OF DWELLINGS WITH 1 ROOM [27]	DENSITY OF OCCUPATION — AVERAGE NUMBER OF PERSONS PER ROOM [23]	DENSITY OF OCCUPATION — PERCENTAGE OF DWELLINGS WITH 3 OR MORE PERSONS PER ROOM [27]	PERCENTAGE OF DWELLINGS WITH [30] — WATER PIPED INSIDE DWELLING	TOILET — ANY TYPE	TOILET — FLUSH	ELECTRIC LIGHTING	DWELLINGS CONSTRUCTED PER 1000 POPULATION [37]	CAPITAL FORMATION IN RESIDENTIAL BUILDING CONSTRUCTION AS PERCENTAGE OF GROSS DOMESTIC PRODUCT [17]
(12)		(13)	(14)	(15)	(16)	(17)	(18)	(19)	(20)	(21)	(22)
ASIA (continued)											
CYPRUS 1960	T	[28]2.7	[28]24.0	[28]1.5	[28]17.1	[21]26.0	[21]84.0	[21]20.0	[21]43.1	[13]6.2	..
	U	[28]3.1	[28]17.9	[28]1.3	[28]12.3	[21]67.5	[21]96.9	[21]52.6	[21]90.4	..	..
	R	[28]2.5	[28]27.3	[28]1.6	[28]19.7	[21]7.1	[21]78.1	[21]5.2	[21]21.5	..	..
[36]1973	T	4.4	2.3	0.9	2.4	77.3	..	52.7	..	7.0	6.5
	U	4.7	0.5	0.8	1.0	94.8	..	85.6	99.0	..	..
	R	4.1	3.6	1.0	3.5	63.9	..	27.6	..	..	..
HONG KONG 1971	T	3.1	21.8	1.9	32.4	88.9	..	65.2	..	..	3.9
	U	3.1	23.4	..	..	92.5	..	68.0	..	..	..
	R	3.1	9.9	..	..	48.8	..	34.0	..	..	..
1973	T	3.1	22.3	..	..	89.1	..	65.4	..	..	..
	U	3.1	23.4	..	..	92.5	..	68.0	..	..	..
	R	3.3	8.0	..	..	48.8	..	..	..	..	..
INDIA 1971	T	[42]2.0	[42]47.9	[42]2.8	..	..	..	..	..	..	..
	U	[42]2.0	[42]50.2	[42]2.8	..	..	..	..	..	..	..
	R	[42]2.0	[42]47.3	[42]2.8	..	..	..	..	..	..	..
INDONESIA [54]1971	T	3.1	10.9	1.5	16.9	3.3	47.0	12.8	..	..	..
	U	3.2	15.0	1.6	20.3	14.8	64.7	47.8	..	..	..
	R	3.1	10.1	1.5	16.2	1.1	41.8	16.2	..	..	..
IRAN 1966	T	[21]3.0	[21]23.3	2.3	[55]46.5	[21]13.1	..	..	[21]25.4	..	..
	U	[21]3.5	[21]9.8	2.2	[55]42.8	[21]37.8	..	..	[21]68.6	..	..
	R	[21]2.7	[21]30.1	2.4	[55]48.8	[21]0.7	..	..	[21]3.7	..	..
ISRAEL [25,57] 1971	T	[24]2.5	[57]10.6	[24]1.5	[24]8.3	96.5	95.0	..	96.5	..	9.8
	U	[24]2.6	[57]8.4	[24]1.4	[24]6.7	..	..	..	..	..	..
	R	[24]2.3	[57]24.3	[24]2.0	[24]18.2	..	..	..	..	..	..
JAPAN [40]1970	T	3.8	8.7	1.0	2.2	..	..	..	..	15.1	..
	U	3.6	10.8	1.0	2.5	..	..	..	..	..	..
	R	4.5	2.6	0.9	1.2	..	..	..	..	..	..
[36,58]1973	T	4.0	6.5	1.1	1.1	98.3	100.0	31.4	..	18.7	..
	U	3.7	8.0	1.1	1.2	99.3	100.0	38.5	..	..	..
	R	4.8	1.3	1.2	0.5	95.2	100.0	6.8	..	..	..
RYUKYU ISLANDS [40]1970	T	3.6	7.7	1.2	5.7	..	..	..	..	..	..
	U	3.4	8.8	1.2	6.4	..	..	..	..	..	..
	R	3.9	5.8	1.1	4.6	..	..	..	..	..	..
JORDAN 1961	T	..	..	..	..	[24]21.3	[24]55.4	..	[24]17.0	..	..
	U	..	..	..	..	[24]48.6	[24]90.4	..	[24]39.2	..	..
	R	..	..	..	..	[24]2.1	[24]30.8	..	[24]1.4	..	..
KOREA, REPUBLIC OF 1960	T	[24]2.2	[24]27.5	[24]2.5	[24]46.6	[21]12.1	[21]84.4	[21]0.2	[21]28.4	..	..
	U	[24]1.9	[24]45.9	[24]2.8	[24]58.9	[21]18.6	[21]66.2	[21]0.5	[21]67.3	..	..
	R	[24]2.3	[24]20.0	[24]2.4	41.7	[21]9.5	[21]91.9	[21]0.1	[21]12.4	..	..
1970	T	[59]3.0	[59]7.5	[59]2.3	..	35.2	94.8	1.8	49.9	[31]2.5	3.4
	U	[59]3.3	[59]9.3	[59]2.7	..	65.0	92.1	5.0	92.4	..	..
	R	[59]2.8	[59]6.6	[59]2.2	..	19.5	96.0	0.3	29.9	..	..
PENINSULAR MALAYSIA [60,61]1970	T	[59,62]2.3	[59,62]36.5	[59,62]2.6	..	33.8	79.9	18.6	[62]43.4	..	..
	U	[59,62]3.1	[59,62]16.5	[59,62]2.3	..	70.6	94.3	42.1	[62]84.7	..	..
	R	[59,62]2.0	[59,62]42.9	[59,62]2.8	..	22.3	75.4	11.2	[62]30.1	..	..

Table 14 (continued)

SIZE, DENSITY OF OCCUPATION AND FACILITIES OF OCCUPIED DWELLINGS

COUNTRIES AND AREAS AND CENSUS YEARS	TOTAL:T URBAN:U RURAL:R	SIZE AVERAGE SIZE (ROOMS PER DWELLINGS) [23]	PERCENTAGE OF DWELLINGS WITH 1 ROOM [27]	AVERAGE NUMBER OF PERSONS PER ROOM [23]	DENSITY OF OCCUPATION PERCENTAGE OF DWELLINGS WITH 3 OR MORE PERSONS PER ROOM [27]	PERCENTAGE OF DWELLINGS WITH [30] WATER PIPED INSIDE DWELLING	TOILET ANY TYPE	FLUSH	ELECTRIC LIGHTING	DWELLINGS [37] CONSTRUCTED PER 1000 POPULATION	CAPITAL FORMATION IN RESIDENTIAL BUILDING CONSTRUCTION AS PERCENTAGE OF GROSS DOMESTIC PRODUCT [7]
		(13)	(14)	(15)	(16)	(17)	(18)	(19)	(20)	(21)	(22)
ASIA (continued)											
MONGOLIA	1969 T	..	..	..	..	0.3	..	..	47.5	1.6	..
	U	..	..	..	..	0.8	..	..	87.8	..	..
	R	..	..	..	..	-	..	..	26.5	..	..
PAKISTAN[64,65]	[71]1973 T	2.0	41.2	2.8	54.0	8.4	34.1	3.9	17.9	..	..
	U	2.2	39.0	2.7	53.6	28.4	82.6	13.4	54.4	..	..
	R	2.0	[65]42.2	2.8	54.2	1.3	17.0	0.6	4.9	..	..
PHILIPPINES	1967 T	..	[65]20.3	..	[65]38.1	[48]34.4	[65]66.4	[65]19.9	[65]22.9	..	..
	U	..	[65]14.0	..	[65]30.1	[48]62.9	[65]83.9	[65]48.2	[65]62.8	..	..
	R	..	[65]23.1	..	[65]41.7	[48]22.1	[65]59.1	[65]7.8	[65]5.8	..	..
	1970 T	2.4	30.2	2.3	43.6	[6]24.0	[6]63.3	[6]22.6	[6]23.2	..	..
	U	2.8	23.5	2.1	37.6	[6]54.3	[6]82.8	[6]48.4	[6]60.4	..	..
	R	[59]2.3	[59]33.0	[59]2.4	[59]46.2	10.7	54.6	11.2	6.8	..	..
SRI LANKA	1971 T	[59]2.2	[59]35.3	[59]2.5	[59]47.7	4.4	64.5	6.7	9.0	..	9.0
	U	[59]2.4	[59]34.6	[59]2.7	[59]49.9	16.3	79.7	22.8	34.5	..	..
	R	[59]2.2	[59]35.5	[59]2.5	[59]47.3	1.6	[20]61.0	[20]3.0	3.0	..	..
SYRIAN ARAB REPUBLIC	1970 T	6.4	3.8	0.4	0.6	[20]40.2	[20]49.2	[20]36.0	[20]41.7	..	..
	U	6.6	3.5	0.5	1.0	[20]82.6	[20]93.7	[20]77.9	[20]84.7	..	..
	R	6.2	4.0	0.3	0.4	[20]10.5	[20]18.0	[20]6.6	[20]10.2	..	..
THAILAND	1970 T	..	..	..	..	8.6	97.9	1.1	18.9	..	2.7
	U	..	..	..	..	[34]54.7	[34]98.8	[34]5.6	[34]86.1	..	..
	R	..	..	..	..	1.8	97.8	0.5	9.0	..	..

COUNTRIES AND AREAS AND CENSUS YEARS	TOTAL:T URBAN:U RURAL:R	POPULATION [1] TOTAL (IN THOUSANDS) [9]	ANNUAL RATE OF GROWTH [19]	LIVING IN HOUSEHOLDS (IN THOUSANDS)	HOUSEHOLDS TOTAL NUMBER (IN THOUSANDS)	AVERAGE SIZE (PERSONS PER HOUSEHOLD)	TENURE OF HOUSEHOLDS IN CONVENTIONAL DWELLINGS [11] PERCENTAGE OF: OWNER OCCUPANTS	RENTERS	DWELLINGS TOTAL NUMBER (IN THOUSANDS)	NUMBER OCCUPIED (IN THOUSANDS)	VACANCY [13] PERCENTAGE
		(2)	(3)	(4)	(5)	(6)	(7)	(8)	(9)	(10)	(11)
EUROPE											
AUSTRIA	1971 T	7,456	0.6	7,216	2,536	2.9	[10]41.2	[10]46.6	2,666	2,432	8.8
	U	3,867	..	..	..	..	..	..	..	..	..
	R	3,589	..	..	..	..	..	..	..	..	..
	[43]1972 T	..	..	7,294	2,485	2.9	[10]49.4	[10]45.1	2,650	2,460	7.2
	U	..	1.1	2,655	..	..	..	..	..	1,127	..
	R	..	-0.4	4,639	..	..	..	..	..	1,333	..

Table 14 (continued)

COUNTRIES AND AREAS AND CENSUS YEARS	TOTAL:T URBAN:U RURAL:E	POPULATION [1]			HOUSEHOLDS		TENURE OF HOUSEHOLDS IN CONVENTIONAL DWELLINGS		DWELLINGS [11]		
		TOTAL [9] (IN THOUS-ANDS)	ANNUAL RATE OF GROWTH [19]	LIVING IN HOUSEHOLDS (IN THOUS-ANDS)	TOTAL NUMBER (IN THOUS-ANDS)	AVERAGE SIZE (PERSONS PER HOUSEHOLD)	PERCENTAGE OF: OWNER OCCUPANTS	RENTERS	TOTAL NUMBER (IN THOUS-ANDS)	NUMBER OCCUPIED (IN THOUS-ANDS)	VACANCY [13] PERCENTAGE
(1)		(2)	(3)	(4)	(5)	(6)	(7)	(8)	(9)	(10)	(11)
EUROPE (continued)											
BULGARIA 1965	T	[66]8,228	[66]0.9	8,120	2,527	3.2	[24]71.0	[24]17.1	2,055	2,019	1.7
	U	[66]3,823	4.9	3,762	1,278	2.9	[24]51.9	[24]27.9	874	874	0.0
	R	[66]4,405	-2.0	4,358	1,248	3.5	[24]90.1	[24]6.3	1,181	1,145	3.0
CZECHOSLOVAKIA 1970	T	14,345	0.5	14,249	4,632	3.1	50.2	42.8	4,406	4,239	3.8
	U	7,964	2.2	..	..	..	..	65.4	2,560	2,504	2.2
	R	6,381	-1.1	..	..	..	..	10.3	1,846	1,735	6.0
DENMARK 1970	T	4,938	0.7	4,929	1,850	2.7	[26]45.7	[26]49.9	..	1,801	..
	U	..	..	3,294	1,319	2.5	[26]31.6	[26]64.8	..	1,279	..
	R	..	..	1,635	531	3.1	[26]81.0	[26]13.0	..	522	..
FAEROE ISLANDS 1966	T	37	1.3	37	10	3.8	84.3	9.9	..	9	..
	U	32	..	10	3	3.6	67.5	24.0	..	2	..
	R	5	..	27	7	3.9	90.4	4.8	..	6	..
1970	T	39	1.0	38	10	3.7	77.8	18.9	..	10	..
	U	11	..	11	3	3.4	59.6	36.4	..	3	..
	R	28	..	28	7	3.8	85.6	11.4	..	7	..
FINLAND 1970	T	4,598	0.3	[32]4,541	[32]1,494	[32]3.0	[10]58.5	[10]27.7	1,463	1,419	3.0
	U	2,949	1.7	[32]2,311	[32]839	[32]2.8	[10]48.7	[10]38.8	807	785	2.7
	R	1,649	-1.7	[32]2,230	[32]655	[32]3.4	[10]70.7	[10]13.9	656	634	3.4
FRANCE 1968	T	49,779	1.1	48,311	15,778	3.1	43.3	44.4	18,120	15,190	16.2
	U	34,827	2.9	33,628	11,258	3.0	36.0	52.3	12,360	10,732	13.2
	R	14,952	-2.3	14,683	4,519	3.3	61.6	24.5	5,760	4,458	22.6
[43]1973	T	52,656	0.8	..	..	..	45.5	40.1	..	..	..
	U	..	..	..	..	..	38.4	49.1	..	..	..
	R	..	..	..	..	..	64.6	16.1	..	..	..
GREECE 1961	T	8,389	1.0	8,104	2,143	3.8	..	..	[62]2,261	[62]1,919	[62]15.1
	U	3,628	1.8	4,475	1,249	3.6	..	..	[62]1,226	[62]1,081	[62]11.8
	R	4,761	-0.5	3,630	894	4.1	..	..	[62]1,035	[62]838	[62]19.0
1971	T	8,769	0.4	8,455	2,556	3.3	[26]70.6	[26]25.1	3,086	2,483	19.5
	U	4,666	2.5	4,430	1,391	3.2	[26]56.2	[26]39.5	1,551	1,352	12.8
	R	3,083	-4.4	4,024	1,165	3.5	[26]87.9	[26]7.9	1,535	1,131	26.4
HUNGARY 1970	T	10,316	0.3	9,981	3,378	3.0	62.9	29.6	3,150	3,034	3.7
	U	4,648	1.4	4,540	1,663	2.7	40.0	49.8	1,454	1,423	2.1
	R	5,668	-0.5	5,440	1,715	3.2	85.1	10.0	1,696	1,611	5.0
1973	T	10,432	0.4	10,028	3,352	3.0	..	..	3,346	3,209	4.1
	U	5,136	3.4	4,710	1,675	2.8	..	..	1,590	1,549	2.5
	R	5,275	-2.4	5,318	1,677	3.2	..	..	1,756	1,660	5.5
IRELAND 1966	T	2,884	0.5	..	[32]687	[32]4.0	..	..	..	687	..
	U	1,419	1.1	..	[32]325	[32]4.1	..	..	..	325	..
	R	1,465	-0.4	..	[32]362	[32]4.0	..	..	..	362	..
1971	T	2,978	0.6	2,873	731	3.9	68.8	28.9	..	705	..
	U	1,556	1.9	1,471	370	4.0	52.5	45.9	..	348	..
	R	1,423	-0.6	1,402	360	3.9	85.5	11.3	..	357	..
LUXEMBOURG 1970	T	340	0.4	334	108	3.1	55.9	38.8	112	106	5.5
	U	233	1.7	228	78	2.9	47.5	46.8	79	76	3.9
	R	107	3.8	106	30	2.5	77.8	18.1	33	30	9.4

Table 14 (continued)

COUNTRIES AND AREAS AND CENSUS YEARS	TOTAL:T URBAN:U RURAL:R	POPULATION[1]			HOUSEHOLDS		TENURE OF HOUSEHOLDS IN CONVENTIONAL DWELLINGS[11] PERCENTAGE OF:		DWELLINGS		
		TOTAL[9] (IN THOUSANDS)	ANNUAL[19] RATE OF GROWTH	LIVING IN HOUSEHOLDS (IN THOUSANDS)	TOTAL NUMBER (IN THOUSANDS)	AVERAGE SIZE (PERSONS PER HOUSEHOLD)	OWNER OCCUPANTS	RENTERS	TOTAL NUMBER (IN THOUSANDS)	NUMBER OCCUPIED (IN THOUSANDS)	VACANCY[13] PERCENTAGE
(1)		(2)	(3)	(4)	(5)	(6)	(7)	(8)	(9)	(10)	(11)
EUROPE (continued)											
NORWAY	1970 T	3,874	0.8	3,819	1,297	2.9	52.6	42.4	..	[6]1,297	..
	U	2,555	8.3	2,514	890	2.8	41.9	52.9	..	[6]890	..
	R	1,319	-6.3	1,305	407	3.2	76.1	19.5	..	[6]407	..
POLAND	1970 T	32,642	0.9	31,885	[6]9,376	[6]3.4	..	..	8,295	8,081	2.6
	U	17,064	1.9	16,428	[6]5,390	[6]3.0	..	..	4,596	4,507	1.9
	R	15,578	0.2	15,457	[6]3,986	[6]3.9	..	..	3,699	3,574	3.4
ROMANIA[36]	1966 T	19,103	0.9	[28]19,113	[28]5,955	[28]3.2	..	..	5,380	5,250	2.4
	U	7,306	[2]2.9	[28]6,940	[28]2,430	[28]2.8	..	..	1,987	1,956	1.5
	R	11,797	[2]-0.6	[28]12,173	3,524	3.4	..	..	3,394	3,293	3.0
SAN MARINO	1975 T	..	..	20	5	3.6	..	..	6	5	5.2
	U	..	..	18	5	3.7	..	..	5	5	0.8
	R	..	..	1	0	3.0	..	..	1	0	35.1
	1976 T	..	..	20	6	3.6	78.2	17.2	6	6	5.1
	U	..	..	19	5	3.7	81.2	18.8	5	5	0.8
	R	..	..	1	0	3.0	46.3	-	1	0	35.0
SPAIN	1960 T	30,529	0.9	29,815	7,548	4.0	..	..	7,726	..	..
	U	13,090	1.7	..	..	..	..	..	3,151	..	..
	R	17,439	-0.3	..	..	..	..	..	4,575	..	..
	[15]1970 T	34,041	1.2	33,524	8,854	3.8	[24]57.2	[24]24.4	10,659	9,301	10.7
	U	25,322	6.8	..	..	..	[24]50.8	[24]30.9	..	..	..
	R	8,719	-7.2	..	..	..	[24]68.6	[24]13.0	..	..	..
SWEDEN[15]	1970 T	8,077	0.8	8,076	[32]3,050	[32]2.6	[26]35.2	[26]44.3	3,181	3,050	4.1
	U	6,575	1.8	6,574	[32]2,522	[32]2.6	[26]26.8	[26]50.5	2,635	2,522	4.3
	R	1,502	-3.1	1,502	[32]528	[32]2.8	[26]75.6	[26]14.4	546	528	3.2
	1975 T	8,209	0.3	8,016	3,325	2.4	38.9	56.0	[6]3,530	[6]3,320	[6]5.9
	U	6,789	0.6	6,623	2,797	2.4	31.5	64.5	[6]2,990	[6]2,794	[6]6.5
	R	1,419	-1.1	1,393	528	2.6	[26]78.2	[26]10.9	540	526	2.6
SWITZERLAND	1970 T	6,270	1.5	6,014	2,050	2.9	[26]28.5	[26]68.4	2,169	2,012	7.2
	U	3,614	2.6	3,463	1,278	2.7	[26]16.8	[26]81.2	1,283	1,246	2.9
	R	2,656	0.0	2,551	773	3.3	[26]47.6	[26]47.5	886	767	13.5
NORTHERN IRELAND[50]	1971 T	1,528	0.7	1,492	427	3.5	[26]45.6	[26]53.9	454	424	6.6
	U	842	0.9	815	244	3.3	[26]40.5	[26]59.0	259	242	6.5
	R	686	0.5	677	183	3.7	[26]52.4	[26]47.0	195	182	6.7
YUGOSLAVIA	1971 T	20,523	1.0	20,490	5,375	3.8	[26]70.7	[26]29.3	5,110	4,935	3.4
	U	7,915	4.2	7,895	2,459	3.2	[26]46.6	[26]53.4	2,139	2,098	1.9
	R	12,608	-0.5	12,595	2,916	4.3	[26]90.5	[26]9.5	2,971	2,837	4.5

Table 14 (continued)

SIZE, DENSITY OF OCCUPATION AND FACILITIES OF OCCUPIED DWELLINGS

COUNTRIES AND AREAS AND CENSUS YEARS	TOTAL:T URBAN:U RURAL:R	SIZE		DENSITY OF OCCUPATION		PERCENTAGE OF DWELLINGS WITH [30]					CAPITAL FORMATION IN RESIDENTIAL BUILDING CONSTRUCTION AS PERCENTAGE OF GROSS DOMESTIC PRODUCT [17]
		AVERAGE SIZE (ROOMS PER DWELLINGS) [23]	PERCENTAGE OF DWELLINGS WITH 1 ROOM [27]	AVERAGE NUMBER OF PERSONS PER ROOM [23]	PERCENTAGE OF DWELLINGS WITH 3 OR MORE PERSONS PER ROOM [27]	WATER PIPED INSIDE DWELLING	TOILET ANY TYPE	FLUSH	ELECTRIC LIGHTING	DWELLINGS CONSTRUCTED PER 1000 POPULATION [37]	
(12)		(13)	(14)	(15)	(16)	(17)	(18)	(19)	(20)	(21)	(22)
EUROPE											
AUSTRIA	1971 T	..	..	..	..	86.0[42]	70.6[42]	..	..	5.9	..
	U	..	..	..	..	87.7[42]	73.9[42]	..	..	..	..
	R	..	..	..	..	84.5[42]	67.8[42]	..	..	..	..
	1972[43] T	4.1	0.6	0.9	..	87.8[20]	72.8[20]	..	..	6.7	..
	U	3.7	1.1	..	..	89.2[20]	75.5[20]	..	..	..	
	R	4.5	0.2	..	..	86.6[20]	70.4[20]	..	..	..	..
BULGARIA	1965 T	3.2[20]	4.9[20]	1.2[20]	7.1[20]	28.2	100.0	11.8	94.8	5.5	..
	U	3.0[20]	4.0[20]	1.4[20]	8.9[20]	55.0	100.0	25.9	98.1	..	..
	R	3.4[20]	5.7[20]	1.1[20]	5.7[20]	7.8	100.0	1.0	92.2	..	..
CZECHOSLOVAKIA	1970 T	3.1	4.9	1.1	1.9	75.4	99.9	57.6	99.7	8.6	6.1[67]
	U	3.1	5.9	1.0	1.2	89.0	..	..	99.9	..	..
	R	3.2	3.5	1.1	3.0	55.7	..	..	99.4	..	..
DENMARK	1970 T	3.5	3.7	0.8	0.2	98.7	100.0	96.2	..	10.3	4.8
	U	3.2	3.7	0.8	0.1	99.9	100.0	99.2	..	..	..
	R	4.3	0.4	0.7	0.2	95.9	100.0	89.0	..	..	..
FAEROE ISLANDS	1966 T	5.4	1.6	0.8	0.2	95.0	79.5	76.7	..	..	..
	U	4.6	6.0	0.9	0.7	94.9	86.7	77.5	..	..	..
	R	5.7	0.1	0.8	0.1	95.0	77.1	76.5	..	..	..
	1970 T	6.2	2.5	0.7	0.1	99.6	..	94.6	98.2	..	..
	U	5.3	8.2	0.7	0.3	100.0	..	97.5	99.3	..	..
	R	6.6	0.2	0.6	0.1	99.4	..	93.4	97.7	..	..
FINLAND	1970 T	3.1	12.4	1.0	3.0	72.1	..	61.4	95.6	10.8	6.3[16]
	U	2.9	16.8	1.0	2.7	86.6	..	80.9	99.5	..	..
	R	3.3	7.0	1.0	3.2	54.2	..	37.4	90.9	..	..
FRANCE	1968 T	3.3	11.6	0.9	2.8	90.8	54.8	51.8	98.8	8.4[33]	6.4
	U	3.2	13.1	0.9	2.7	95.5	64.2	61.1	99.4	..	..
	R	3.6	7.9	0.9	3.1	79.1	31.3	28.6	97.7	..	..
	1973[43] T	3.6	7.6	1.3	1.0	96.6	69.7	..	..	9.9[33]	..
	U	3.4	8.8	..	..	98.1	76.5	..	..	..	..
	R	4.0	4.5	..	..	92.6	51.7	..	..	..	..
GREECE	1961 T	2.6	20.0	1.5	16.3	28.7	78.9	14.6	53.2	..	..
	U	2.7	22.1	1.4	14.4	46.5	92.8	24.3	81.5	..	..
	R	2.6[26]	17.0[26]	1.6[26]	18.9[26]	3.8	59.4	1.1	13.5	..	..
	1971 T	3.5[26]	7.3[26]	0.9[26]	3.0[26]	65.0	92.5	45.0	88.3	14.1	7.4
	U	3.4[26]	8.1[26]	0.9[26]	2.5[26]	88.1	99.0	70.4	97.6	..	..
	R	3.6[26]	6.2[26]	1.0[26]	3.5[26]	37.2	84.7	14.5	77.2	..	..
HUNGARY	1970 T	2.6[42]	4.1[42]	1.2[42]	3.8[42]	35.6	100.0	32.5	91.7	7.8	4.2[67]
	U	2.6[42]	6.3[42]	1.2[42]	3.5[42]	64.6	100.0	61.0	96.6	..	..
	R	2.6[42]	2.2[42]	1.3[42]	4.1[42]	10.8	100.0	8.1	87.4	..	..
	1973 T	2.8	3.1	1.1	2.6	44.0	100.0	34.1	94.3	8.2	4.9
	U	..	..	..	..	71.8	100.0	57.6	97.6	..	..
	R	..	..	..	..	18.8	100.0	12.9	91.3	..	..

Table 14 (continued)

SIZE, DENSITY OF OCCUPATION AND FACILITIES OF OCCUPIED DWELLINGS

| COUNTRIES AND AREAS AND CENSUS YEARS | TOTAL:T URBAN:U RURAL:R | SIZE | | DENSITY OF OCCUPATION | | PERCENTAGE OF DWELLINGS WITH [30] | | | | DWELLINGS[37] CONSTRUCTED PER 1000 POPULATION | CAPITAL FORMATION IN RESIDENTIAL BUILDING CONSTRUCTION AS PERCENTAGE OF GROSS DOMESTIC PRODUCT[17] |
		AVERAGE[23] SIZE (ROOMS PER DWELLINGS)	PERCENTAGE[27] OF DWELLINGS WITH 1 ROOM	AVERAGE[23] NUMBER OF PERSONS PER ROOM	PERCENTAGE[27] OF DWELLINGS WITH 3 OR MORE PERSONS PER ROOM	WATER PIPED INSIDE DWELLING	TOILET ANY TYPE	TOILET FLUSH	ELECTRIC LIGHTING		
(12)		(13)	(14)	(15)	(16)	(17)	(18)	(19)	(20)	(21)	(22)
EUROPE (continued)											
IRELAND	1966 T	4.5	2.2	0.9	1.2	..	..	..	..	3.5	..
	U	4.6	4.0	0.9	1.5	..	..	..	..	..	..
	R	4.4	0.6	0.9	0.9	..	..	..	..	..	..
	1971 T	4.7	0.8	0.9	0.7	73.2	80.2	70.0	94.7	5.2	[18]5.1
	U	4.9	1.1	0.9	0.7	96.4	99.5	98.4	99.6	..	..
	R	4.5	0.6	0.9	0.8	50.7	61.2	42.3	90.0	..	..
LUXEMBOURG	1970 T	5.3	0.7	0.6	0.0	98.4	98.9	93.0	..	5.2	[52]4.5
	U	..	..	..	..	..	98.8	99.0	95.8	..	..
	R	..	..	..	..	..	97.3	98.5	85.8	..	..
NORWAY	1970 T	4.4	6.0	0.7	0.5	97.5	89.2	71.8	..	10.2	5.3
	U	4.1	7.6	0.7	0.4	99.2	82.9	82.2	..	..	..
	R	5.1	2.3	0.6	0.3	93.5	92.0	49.0	..	..	..
POLAND	1970 T	2.9	10.6	1.4	..	47.3	33.4	32.9	96.2	5.9	[16]4.2
	U	2.8	12.3	1.3	..	75.2	55.6	55.0	99.6	..	..
	R	3.0	8.5	1.4	..	12.1	5.5	5.1	92.0	..	..
ROMANIA[36]	1966 T	2.6	12.0	1.4	9.4	12.3	100.0	12.2	48.6	[14,47]6.1	..
	U	2.7	12.8	1.3	6.7	32.8	100.0	32.4	86.1	7.4	..
	R	2.6	11.5	1.4	11.0	0.4	100.0	0.3	26.6	..	..
SAN MARINO	1975 T	4.7	-	0.8	-	100.0	98.3	96.6	100.0	..	..
	U	4.7	-	0.8	-	100.0	100.0	100.0	100.0	..	..
	R	4.1	-	0.8	-	100.0	82.4	64.6	100.0	..	..
	1976 T	4.7	-	0.8	-	100.0	98.4	96.8	100.0	..	..
	U	4.7	-	0.8	-	100.0	100.0	100.0	100.0	..	..
	R	4.1	-	0.7	-	100.0	82.6	64.9	100.0	..	..
SPAIN	1960 T	4.2	..	..	..	45.0	66.1	..	89.3	[47]10.0	..
	U	4.4	..	0.9	5.1	75.5	92.6	..	97.5	..	..
	R	4.0	..	..	..	24.0	47.8	..	83.6	..	..
	[15]1970 T	4.4	1.4	..	..	77.6	76.9	70.6	..	9.1	5.6
	U	4.4	1.6	..	..	87.7	88.6	83.6	..	..	..
	R	[59]4.5	[59]0.9	..	..	60.0	56.3	47.9	..	..	..
SWEDEN[15]	1970 T	[59]3.8	[59]5.3	0.7	0.1	97.3	..	90.1	..	13.6	[16]5.9
	U	[59]3.7	[59]6.3	0.7	0.1	99.2	..	94.5	..	..	..
	R	4.3	0.6	0.7	0.1	88.3	..	68.7	..	..	..
	1975 T	..	..	..	..	98.7	..	96.3	..	9.1	..
	U	..	..	..	..	99.7	..	98.8	..	..	..
	R	..	..	..	..	93.3	..	82.1	..	..	..
SWITZERLAND	1970 T	4.7	2.2	0.6	0.1	..	..	93.3	..	10.6	6.6
	U	4.3	3.1	0.6	0.1	..	..	98.4	..	..	..
	R	5.2	0.8	0.6	0.1	..	..	84.9	..	..	..
NORTHERN IRELAND[50]	1971 T	5.0	0.3	0.7	0.4	92.6	..	72.8	..	..	..
	U	5.0	0.3	0.7	0.2	98.8	..	74.5	..	..	..
	R	5.0	0.4	0.7	0.6	84.3	..	70.6	..	..	..
YUGOSLAVIA	1971 T	2.8	6.7	1.4	9.2	33.6	91.7	[49]26.1	87.9	6.1	..
	U	2.8	8.3	1.3	6.1	62.0	98.5	[49]52.9	98.4	..	..
	R	2.8	5.5	1.5	11.4	12.4	86.5	[49]6.0	80.1	..	..

Table 14 (continued)

POPULATION [1] — HOUSEHOLDS — DWELLINGS

COUNTRIES AND AREAS AND CENSUS YEARS	TOTAL:T URBAN:U RURAL:R	TOTAL (IN THOUSANDS) [9]	ANNUAL RATE OF GROWTH [19]	LIVING IN HOUSEHOLDS (IN THOUSANDS)	TOTAL NUMBER (IN THOUSANDS)	AVERAGE SIZE (PERSONS PER HOUSEHOLD)	OWNER OCCUPANTS	RENTERS	TOTAL NUMBER (IN THOUSANDS)	NUMBER OCCUPIED (IN THOUSANDS)	VACANCY PERCENTAGE [13]
(1)		(2)	(3)	(4)	(5)	(6)	(7)	(8)	(9)	(10)	(11)
OCEANIA											
AUSTRALIA	1966 T	11,531	1.9	..	[6]3,152	[6]3.5	70.8	26.5	3,085	[6]3,152	[21]7.6
	U	9,611	2.3	..	[6]2,665	[6]3.4	70.8	27.5	2,600	[6]2,665	[21]5.9
	R	1,920	0.6	..	487	[6]3.7	[26]71.0	[26]21.2	486	487	[21]16.1
	1971 T	12,756	2.0	12,155	3,671	3.3	[26]67.3	[26]27.3	[6]4,010	[6]3,671	8.5
	U	10,913	2.6	10,421	3,184	3.3	[26]67.1	[26]28.8	[6]3,421	[6]3,184	6.9
	R	1,825	-1.0	1,735	486	[6]3.6	[26]68.7	[26]17.2	[6]589	486	[6]17.4
GUAM	1970 T	85	2.4	75	[6]16	[6]4.8	46.0	54.0	[6]17	[6]16	6.7
	U	22	..	18	[6]4	[6]4.8	48.2	51.8	[6]4	[6]4	7.2
	R	63	..	57	[6]12	[6]4.9	45.3	54.7	12	12	6.5
NEW ZEALAND	1971 T	2,863	1.4	..	803	3.6	[26]26.5	[26]25.8	878	802	8.7
	U	2,329	4.9	..	..	..	[26]25.7	[26]27.8	..	667	..
	R	534	-9.6	..	..	..	[26]30.3	[26]15.5	..	[6]135	..
SAMOA	1971 T	147	2.3	143	25	5.8	[26]93.4	[26]2.1	[6]29	[6]24	[6]16.1
	U	..	..	29	5	6.5	[26]84.3	[26]9.2	[6]5	[6]4	[6]17.7
	R	..	..	114	20	5.6	[26]95.4	[26]0.6	[6]24	[6]20	[6]15.8

SIZE, DENSITY OF OCCUPATION AND FACILITIES OF OCCUPIED DWELLINGS

COUNTRIES AND AREAS AND CENSUS YEARS	TOTAL:T URBAN:U RURAL:R	AVERAGE SIZE (ROOMS PER DWELLINGS) [23]	PERCENTAGE OF DWELLINGS WITH 1 ROOM [27]	AVERAGE NUMBER OF PERSONS PER ROOM [23]	PERCENTAGE OF DWELLINGS WITH 3 OR MORE PERSONS PER ROOM [27]	WATER PIPED INSIDE DWELLING	TOILET ANY TYPE	TOILET FLUSH	ELECTRIC LIGHTING	DWELLINGS CONSTRUCTED PER 1000 POPULATION [37]	CAPITAL FORMATION IN RESIDENTIAL BUILDING CONSTRUCTION AS PERCENTAGE OF GROSS DOMESTIC PRODUCT [17]
(12)		(13)	(14)	(15)	(16)	(17)	(18)	(19)	(20)	(21)	(22)
OCEANIA											
AUSTRALIA	1966 T	5.2	1.6	0.7	0.3	..	..	..	98.3	9.7	4.7
	U	5.2	1.5	0.7	0.2	..	..	..	99.3	..	..
	R	5.5	2.2	0.7	0.7	..	..	..	92.7	..	..
	1971 T	5.0	1.9	0.7	0.3	..	98.9	89.5	98.4	11.1	5.5
	U	..	..	..	..	..	98.9	93.0	98.9	..	..
	R	..	..	..	..	..	98.8	66.3	95.1	..	..
GUAM	1970 T	4.5	2.1	1.1	..	98.4	96.6	84.2	97.7	..	..
	U	4.5	2.3	1.1	..	99.4	97.7	90.0	99.2	..	..
	R	4.5	2.1	1.1	..	98.0	96.3	82.3	97.2	..	..
NEW ZEALAND	1971 T	4.8	0.8	0.7	0.1	92.7	..	97.1	..	8.0	..
	U	..	..	..	..	..	..	..	..	..	..
	R	..	..	..	..	..	..	..	..	..	..

Table 14 (continued)

SIZE, DENSITY OF OCCUPATION AND FACILITIES OF OCCUPIED DWELLINGS

COUNTRIES AND AREAS AND CENSUS YEARS	TOTAL:T URBAN:U RURAL:R	SIZE		DENSITY OF OCCUPATION		PERCENTAGE OF DWELLINGS WITH [30]					CAPITAL FORMATION IN RESIDENTIAL BUILDING CONSTRUCTION AS PERCENTAGE OF GROSS DOMESTIC PRODUCT [17]
		AVERAGE SIZE [23] (ROOMS PER DWELLINGS)	PERCENTAGE OF DWELL- INGS WITH 1 ROOM [27]	AVERAGE NUMBER OF PERSONS PER ROOM [23]	PERCENTAGE OF DWELL- INGS WITH 3 OR MORE PERSONS PER ROOM [27]	WATER PIPED INSIDE DWELLING	TOILET ANY TYPE	TOILET FLUSH	ELECTRIC LIGHTING	DWELLINGS [37] CONSTRUCTED PER 1000 POPULATION	
(12)		(13)	(14)	(15)	(16)	(17)	(18)	(19)	(20)	(21)	(22)
OCEANIA (continued)											
SAMOA	1971 T	3.9	9.9	1.5	22.2	9.2	100.0	10.1	18.8	..	..
	U	4.4	10.3	1.4	19.7	25.5	100.0	28.9	65.8	..	..
	R	3.5	9.5	1.6	24.0	5.6	100.0	6.0	8.7	..	..

Source: United Nations, *Compendium of Housing Statistics 1975–1977*, and United Nations, *Compendium of Human Settlements Statistics 1983*.

Note: a This table provides an overall view of housing conditions in each country or area and furnishes a general indication of improvement or deterioration in the housing situation over time. An important feature is the possibility it provides for considering over time the level of housing conditions within each country or area in relation to levels of construction attained.

b It should be noted that only countries for which urban and rural data are available appear in the table.

‡ The data which relate to the Federal Republic of Germany and the German Democratic Republic include the relevant data relating to Berlin for which separate data have not been supplied. This is without prejudice to any question of status which may be involved.

[1] Including living quarters other than housing units.

[2] Data are for 1965.

[3] Computed from total population and number of households.

[4] Kitchens are not counted as rooms.

[5] Data in cols. 4–19 exclude outer rings.

[6] Data refer to housing units.

[7] Data are for 1970.

[8] Inside or outside.

[9] Population data have been taken from United Nations, *Demographic Yearbook 1982*. They refer to years for which housing data are available.

[10] Data refer to occupied conventional dwellings.

[11] The data on tenure of households in conventional dwellings shown include the percentage of owner-occupant households and the percentage of households which rent their accommodation either as tenants or subtenants. Percentages ar based on the total number of households occupying dwellings.

[12] Data exclude dwellings made available by partition or conversion of existing structures.

[13] Vacancy ratios are the percentages which vacant units represent of all units.

[14] Data refer to whole country.

[15] A household is defined as the total number of persons occupying a set of living quarters.

[16] Data are for 1971.

[17] Gross domestic product and gross fixed capital formation are in millions of national currency units at constant prices.

[18] Data are for 1972.

[19] Annual rates of growth for total population have been taken from United Nations, *Demographic Yearbook 1982*. Rates of growth for urban and rural populations have been taken from United Nations, *Monthly Bulletin of Statistics*. However, some rates are based on census results and refer to the intercensal period. For detailed information concerning the basis for these rates, reference should be made to the publications from which they have been derived.

[20] Data refer to conventional dwellings.

[21] Data refer to living quarters.

[22] A set of living quarters is defined in terms of the space occupied by a household.

[23] The average number of rooms per dwelling and the average number of persons per room are, in some cases, estimated by the United Nations Statistical Office. Where the aggregate number of rooms was not available, an approximation of the value was obtained by multiplying each room category by its corresponding dwelling frequency, multiplying the residual category by the lowest number of rooms invloved, disregarding the dwellings with an unknown number of rooms, and summing the products. A similar procedure has been used to derive the aggregate number of persons from data on dwellings classified by number of occupants. The resultant estimates are probably low.

[24] Data refer to all households.

[25] Kitchens are not counted as rooms.

[26] Data refer to households in conventional dwellings.

[27] The percentages in cols. 14 and 16 are computed on the basis of dwellings with known number of rooms and occupied dwellings with known number of persons per room, respectively.

[28] Including persons not living in households.

[29] Data in cols. 9–19 refer to living quarters.

[30] The percentages in cols. 17–20 are computed on the basis of total number of occupied dwellings, if available; otherwise, on total dwellings, occupied and unoccupied.

[31] Data refer to residential buildings.

[32] Data refer to occupants of dwellings.

[33] In residential buildings only.

[34] Data based on sample survey of housing.

[35] Data refer to occupied housing units.

[36] Data in cols. 12–19 refer to conventional dwellings.

[37] Data in col. 21 refer to the number of conventional (permanent) dwellings newly constructed or made available during the calendar year as a result of partition or conversion of existing structures. Unless otherwise noted, data refer to dwellings completed.

Table 14 (continued)

[38] Construction of dwellings authorized.

[39] Data refer to dwellings in newly constructed residential buildings only.

[40] Data in cols. 9–19 refer to households.

[41] Data in cols. 4–19 based on sample tabulation.

[42] Data based on sample tabulation of census returns.

[43] Data in cols. 4–19 based on results of sample survey.

[44] Including 2,026 living quarters other than housing units.

[45] Excluding data for Inini and also penal, military, and Indian population.

[46] Data exclude dwellings made available by partition or conversion of existing structures.

[47] Data are for 1973.

[48] Data refer to source of water supply.

[49] Only dwellings with inside flush toilets are included.

[50] Data based on a demographic survey.

[51] Additional current data relevant to this table can be found in Tables 1, 4, 6, 12, 15, 16, 17, 18, and 20 of the *Compendium of Human Settlements Statistics 1983*.

[52] Percentages based on data at current prices.

[53] Data are for 1968.

[54] Excluding data for West Irian.

[55] Data refer to households and exclude nomadic tribes and persons with no fixed place.

[56] Including data relating to certain territories under occupation.

[57] Including households occupying less than one room.

[58] Number of rooms refers to rooms used as principal households.

[59] Number of rooms includes rooms used only for professional or business purposes.

[60] Data are for six major towns. Data in cols. 9–19 refer to conventional dwellings including improvised units.

[61] Data are for towns of Jesselton, Sandakan, Tawaua, and Victoria in 1960 only, and refer to housing units only.

[62] Data refer to conventional dwellings, excluding semi-permanent dwellingsl

[63] Including Bangladesh, Junagardh, Manavador, Gilgit, and Baltistan.

[64] Data in cols. 4–19 include Bangladesh, except for nomads and river boatmen.

[65] Data based on results of households survey and refer to households.

[66] Excluding data for Southern Dobruja.

[67] Not material product; housing, including owner-occupied dwellings.

[68] Data in cols. 9–19 refer to conventional dwellings, excluding semi-permanent dwellings.

[69] Data are for households of African population.

[70] Data based on a household survey conducted in 1975. Excluding households in the Yukon and Northwest Territories.

[71] Data based on sample survey of housing.

Table 15

Occupied housing units by average size and distribution according to number of rooms: urban and rural, as of latest available census

			DISTRIBUTION ACCORDING TO NUMBER OF ROOMS PER HOUSING UNIT									
COUNTRIES OR AREAS AND CENSUS YEARS	TOTAL:T URBAN:U RURAL:R	TOTAL HOUSING UNITS	1	2	3	4	5	6	7+	HOUSING UNITS WITH UNKNOWN NUMBER OF ROOMS	AVERAGE SIZE PER HOUSING UNIT
(1)		(2)	(3)	(4)	(5)	(6)	(7)	(8)	(9)	(10)	(11)

AFRICA

CAMEROON	1976 T	1,390,896	192,434	247,631	228,538	219,009	160,509	114,382	228,393	-	4.1
	%	100.0	13.8	17.8	16.4	15.7	11.5	8.2	16.4	-	..
	U	395,881	61,689	62,259	55,342	65,445	53,933	37,420	59,793	-	4.1
	%	100.0	15.6	15.7	14.0	16.5	13.6	9.5	15.1	-	..
	R	995,015	130,745	185,372	173,196	153,564	106,576	76,962	168,600	-	4.1
	%	100.0	13.1	18.6	17.4	15.4	10.7	7.7	16.9	-	..
LIBYAN ARAB JAMAHIRIYA	1973 T	283,615	23,847	49,225	85,050	74,216	27,914	8,215	4,711	-	3.3
	%	100.0	8.4	17.4	30.0	26.2	9.8	2.9	1.7	-	..
	U	195,190	14,061	31,023	60,735	55,924	19,033	5,046	2,740	-	3.3
	%	100.0	7.2	15.9	31.1	28.7	9.8	2.6	1.4	-	..
	R	88,425	9,786	18,202	24,315	18,292	8,881	3,169	1,971	-	3.2
	%	100.0	11.1	20.6	27.5	20.7	10.0	3.6	2.2	-	..
MOROCCO	1971 T	2,819,213	999,586	1,081,164	461,849	175,146	52,217	28,721	20,530	-	2.1
	%	100.0	35.5	38.4	16.4	6.2	1.9	1.0	0.7	-	..
	U	1,113,386	369,753	419,047	203,086	74,760	24,492	13,313	8,935	-	2.1
	%	100.0	33.2	37.6	18.2	6.7	2.2	1.2	0.8	-	..
	R	1,705,827	629,833	662,117	258,763	100,386	27,725	15,408	11,595	-	2.0
	%	100.0	36.9	38.8	15.2	5.9	1.6	0.9	0.7	-	..
	%	100.0	50.9	25.9	13.3	5.8	2.6	0.9	0.6	-	..
TUNISIA	1975 T	1,009,670	462,480	268,300	133,230	51,690	16,080	5,850	4,400	49,640	1.9
	%	100.0	45.8	28.4	13.2	5.1	1.6	0.6	0.4	4.9	..
	U	507,960	170,600	156,830	98,240	40,720	12,670	4,610	3,550	20,740	2.2
	%	100.0	33.6	30.9	19.3	8.0	2.5	0.9	0.7	4.1	..
	R	501,710	291,880	129,470	34,990	10,970	3,410	1,240	850	28,900	1.5
	%	100.0	58.2	25.8	7.0	2.2	0.7	0.2	0.2	5.8	..

AMERICA, NORTH

ANTIGUA	1970 T	15,405	1,735	4,066	1,760	3,144	2,259	1,505	936	-	3.6
	%	100.0	11.3	26.4	11.4	20.4	14.6	9.8	6.1	-	..
	U	5,649	656	1,145	620	1,227	919	730	352	-	3.8
	%	100.0	11.6	20.3	11.0	21.7	16.3	12.9	6.2	-	..
	R	9,756	1,079	2,921	1,140	1,917	1,340	775	584	-	3.5
	%	100.0	11.1	30.0	11.7	19.6	13.7	7.9	6.0	-	..
CANADA	1971 T	6,034,505	91,575	192,955	611,940	1,083,390	1,363,250	1,153,030	1,538,360	-	5.4
	%	100.0	1.5	3.2	10.1	18.0	22.6	19.1	25.5	-	..
	U	4,737,415	74,360	158,665	535,805	877,200	1,062,475	890,485	1,138,420	-	5.3
	%	100.0	1.6	3.4	11.3	18.5	22.4	18.8	24.0	-	..
	R	1,297,090	17,205	34,295	76,140	206,185	300,775	262,550	399,935	-	5.7
	%	100.0	1.3	2.6	5.9	15.9	23.2	20.2	30.8	-	..
	1981 T	8,063,000	92,000	184,000	706,000	1,272,000	1,725,000	1,624,000	2,460,000	-	5.6
	%	100.0	1.1	2.3	8.8	15.8	21.4	20.1	30.5	-	..
	U	6,743,000	91,000	171,000	656,000	1,129,000	1,417,000	1,335,000	1,943,000	-	5.5
	%	100.0	1.3	2.5	9.7	16.7	21.0	19.8	28.8	-	..
	R	1,321,000	..	13,000	50,000	143,000	308,000	289,000	517,000	-	6.1
	%	100.0	..	1.0	3.8	10.8	23.3	21.9	39.1	-	..
CUBA	1981 T	2,290,176	111,727	262,293	422,117	608,583	505,809	252,043	127,604	-	4.0
	%	100.0	4.9	11.5	18.4	26.6	22.1	11.0	5.6	-	..
	U	1,609,699	96,176	200,958	302,581	428,658	311,420	168,952	100,954	-	4.0
	%	100.0	6.0	12.5	18.8	26.6	19.3	10.5	6.3	-	..
	R	680,477	15,551	61,335	119,536	179,925	194,389	83,091	26,650	-	4.2
	%	100.0	2.3	9.0	17.6	26.4	28.6	12.2	3.9	-	..

Table 15 (continued)

DISTRIBUTION ACCORDING TO NUMBER OF ROOMS PER HOUSING UNIT

COUNTRIES OR AREAS AND CENSUS YEARS	TOTAL:T URBAN:U RURAL:R	TOTAL HOUSING UNITS	1	2	3	4	5	6	7+	HOUSING UNITS WITH UNKNOWN NUMBER OF ROOMS	AVERAGE SIZE PER HOUSING UNIT
(1)		(2)	(3)	(4)	(5)	(6)	(7)	(8)	(9)	(10)	(11)
AMERICA, NORTH (continued)											
DOMINICAN REPUBLIC	1970 T	718,732	38,491	242,422	143,131	113,494	60,975	49,034	64,063	7,122	3.6
	%	100.0	5.4	33.7	19.9	15.8	8.5	6.8	8.9	1.0	..
	U	285,908	15,329	58,056	48,515	49,755	33,499	31,675	47,234	1,845	4.3
	%	100.0	5.4	20.3	17.0	17.4	11.7	11.1	16.5	0.6	..
	R	432,824	23,162	184,366	94,616	63,739	27,476	17,359	16,829	5,277	1.4
	%	100.0	5.4	42.6	21.9	14.7	6.3	4.0	3.9	1.2	..
EL-SALVADOR	1978 T	850,007	614,497	123,093	57,688	33,048	11,991	4,965	4,725	-	1.5
	%	100.0	72.3	14.5	6.8	3.9	1.4	0.6	0.6	-	..
	U	389,744	220,505	68,047	49,418	30,601	11,569	4,965	4,639	-	1.9
	%	100.0	56.6	17.5	12.7	7.9	3.0	1.3	1.2	-	..
	R	460,263	393,992	55,046	8,270	2,447	422	-	86	-	1.2
	%	100.0	85.6	12.0	1.8	0.5	0.1	-	0.0	-	..
GREENLAND	1976 T	11,833	2,185	3,027	2,776	2,336	829	..	..	680	2.7
	%	100.0	18.5	25.6	23.5	19.7	7.0	..	..	5.7	..
	U	9,747	1,754	2,110	2,427	2,086	774	..	..	596	2.8
	%	100.0	18.0	21.6	24.9	21.4	7.9	..	..	6.1	..
	R	2,086	431	917	349	250	55	..	..	84	2.3
	%	100.0	20.7	44.0	16.7	12.0	2.6	..	..	4.0	..
GUATEMALA	1973 T	934,954	257,344	378,717	140,607	65,071	36,398	23,397	33,199	221	2.4
	%	100.0	27.5	40.5	15.0	7.0	3.9	2.5	3.6	0.0	..
	U	331,273	58,547	95,446	57,386	40,463	28,982	20,140	30,173	136	3.3
	%	100.0	17.7	28.8	17.3	12.2	8.8	6.1	9.1	0.0	..
	R	603,681	198,797	283,271	83,221	24,608	7,416	3,257	3,026	85	2.0
	%	100.0	33.0	46.9	13.8	4.1	1.2	0.5	0.5	0.0	..
HAITI	1976 T	1,064,818	187,750	583,648	166,551	61,687	18,350	10,028	3,768	33,035	2.1
	%	100.0	17.6	54.8	15.7	5.8	1.7	0.9	0.4	3.1	..
	U	225,736	78,106	60,604	30,765	19,165	9,122	6,806	3,078	18,090	2.1
	%	100.0	34.6	26.9	13.6	8.5	4.0	3.0	1.4	8.0	..
	R	839,082	109,644	523,044	135,786	42,522	9,228	3,222	690	14,946	2.1
	%	100.0	13.0	62.3	16.2	5.1	1.1	0.4	0.1	1.8	..
HONDURAS	1974 T	463,004	91,840	202,160	90,854	35,438	----------------42,712-------------			-	..
	%	100.0	19.8	43.7	19.6	7.7	9.2			-	..
	U	146,409	21,205	42,635	30,922	19,096	32,551				3.0
	%	100.0	14.5	29.1	21.1	13.1	22.2			-	..
	R	316,595	70,635	159,525	59,932	16,342	10,161			-	2.2
	%	100.0	22.3	50.4	18.9	5.2	3.2			-	..
JAMAICA	1970 T	420,159	137,512	110,365	67,614	35,627	22,385	11,740	10,764	24,152	2.4
	%	100.0	32.7	26.3	16.1	8.5	5.3	2.8	2.6	5.8	..
	U	188,671	79,856	36,916	22,134	14,184	11,099	6,274	6,394	11,814	2.3
	%	100.0	42.3	19.6	11.7	7.5	5.9	3.3	3.4	6.3	..
	R	231,488	57,656	73,449	45,480	21,443	11,286	5,466	4,370	12,338	2.5
	%	100.0	24.9	31.7	19.7	9.3	4.9	2.4	1.9	5.3	..
MEXICO	1970 T	8,286,369	3,326,520	2,395,916	1,144,121	657,459	312,065	174,896	275,932	-	2.3
	%	100.0	40.1	28.9	13.8	7.9	3.8	2.1	3.3	-	..
	U	4,864,160	1,513,762	1,385,247	810,373	515,945	265,739	151,201	221,853	-	2.6
	%	100.0	31.1	28.5	16.7	10.6	5.5	3.1	4.6	-	..
	R	3,422,209	1,812,758	1,010,669	333,748	141,514	46,326	23,695	53,499	-	1.8
	%	100.0	53.0	29.5	9.8	4.1	1.4	0.7	1.6	-	..
NICARAGUA	1971 T	304,580	116,670	92,390	50,620	21,650	-------------23,250-------------			-	2.2
	%	100.0	38.3	30.0	16.6	7.1	7.6				..
	U	148,390	53,430	41,360	23,030	13,900	16,670				2.3
	%	100.0	36.0	27.9	15.5	9.4	11.2				..
	R	156,190	63,240	51,030	27,590	7,750	6,580				2.0
	%	100.0	40.5	32.7	17.7	5.0	4.2				..
MONTSERRAT	1980 T	3,736	155	980	746	1,000	453	236	161	5	3.5
	%	100.0	4.1	26.2	20.0	26.8	12.1	6.3	4.3	0.1	..
	U	532	44	120	99	140	70	35	22	2	3.5
	%	100.0	8.3	22.6	18.6	26.3	13.2	6.6	4.1	0.4	..
	R	3,204	111	860	647	860	383	201	139	3	3.5
	%	100.0	3.5	26.8	20.2	26.8	12.0	6.3	4.3	0.1	..

Table 15 (continued)

DISTRIBUTION ACCORDING TO NUMBER OF ROOMS PER HOUSING UNIT

COUNTRIES OR AREAS AND CENSUS YEARS	TOTAL:T URBAN:U RURAL:R	TOTAL HOUSING UNITS	1	2	3	4	5	6	7+	HOUSING UNITS WITH UNKNOWN NUMBER OF ROOMS	AVERAGE SIZE PER HOUSING UNIT
(1)		(2)	(3)	(4)	(5)	(6)	(7)	(8)	(9)	(10)	(11)
AMERICA, NORTH (continued)											
PANAMA	1970 T	276,708	103,418	81,583	44,707	27,514	11,132	4,698	3,656	-	2.2
	%	100.0	37.4	29.5	16.2	9.9	4.0	1.7	1.3	-	..
	U	135,543	46,622	35,110	22,047	17,330	7,809	3,640	2,985	-	2.5
	%	100.0	34.4	25.9	16.3	12.8	5.8	2.7	2.2	-	..
	R	141,165	56,796	46,473	22,660	10,184	3,323	1,058	671	-	2.0
	%	100.0	40.2	32.9	16.1	7.2	2.4	0.8	0.5	-	..
	1981 T	364,325	98,020	93,625	81,980	52,405	20,955	8,020	4,985	4,335	2.6
	%	100.0	26.9	25.7	22.5	14.4	5.8	2.2	1.4	1.2	..
	U	199,750	48,255	43,570	45,835	34,895	14,880	6,125	4,045	2,145	2.8
	%	100.0	24.2	21.8	22.9	17.5	7.4	3.1	2.0	1.1	..
	R	164,575	49,705	50,055	36,145	17,510	6,075	1,895	940	2,190	2.3
	%	100.0	30.2	30.4	22.0	10.6	3.7	1.2	0.6	1.3	..
PUERTO RICO	1970 T	709,799	24,093	36,167	89,161	170,367	229,213	103,971	56,827	-	4.7
	%	100.0	3.4	5.1	12.6	24.0	32.3	14.7	8.0	-	..
	U	428,638	13,605	16,213	41,034	86,541	151,137	75,380	44,728	-	4.9
	%	100.0	3.2	3.8	9.6	20.2	35.3	17.6	10.4	-	..
	R	281,161	10,488	19,954	48,127	83,826	78,076	28,591	12,099	-	4.2
	%	100.0	3.7	7.1	17.1	29.8	27.8	10.2	4.3	-	..
TURKS AND CAICOS ISLANDS	1970 T	1,270	47	190	233	347	196	123	116	18	4.0
	%	100.0	3.7	15.0	18.4	27.3	15.4	9.7	9.1	1.4	..
	U	542	19	60	101	130	103	63	64	2	4.3
	%	100.0	3.5	11.1	18.6	24.0	19.0	11.6	11.8	0.4	..
	R	728	28	130	132	217	93	60	52	16	3.8
	%	100.0	3.8	17.9	18.2	29.8	12.8	8.2	7.1	2.2	..
UNITED STATES OF AMERICA	1970 T	62,449,747	1,108,398	2,131,502	6,757,879	12,976,505	16,007,056	13,007,834	11,460,573	-	5.1
	%	100.0	1.8	3.4	10.7	20.5	25.2	20.5	18.1	-	..
	U	47,562,681	983,697	1,821,191	5,735,575	9,576,809	11,746,960	9,591,537	8,106,912	-	5.0
	%	100.0	2.1	3.8	12.1	20.1	24.7	20.2	17.0	-	..
	R	15,887,066	124,701	310,311	1,022,304	3,399,696	4,260,096	3,416,297	3,353,661	-	5.3
	%	100.0	0.8	2.0	6.4	21.4	26.8	21.5	21.1	-	..
U.S. VIRGIN ISLANDS	1970 T	17,761	2,400	2,870	2,681	3,161	3,425	1,841	1,383	-	3.7
	%	100.0	13.5	16.2	15.1	17.8	19.3	10.4	7.8	-	..
	U	4,546	857	800	786	791	680	350	282	-	3.4
	%	100.0	18.9	17.6	17.3	17.4	15.0	7.7	6.2	-	..
	R	13,215	1,543	2,070	1,895	2,370	2,745	1,491	1,101	-	3.8
	%	100.0	11.7	15.7	14.3	17.9	20.8	11.3	8.3	-	..
AMERICA, SOUTH											
BRAZIL	1973 T	19,401,867	537,313	1,974,131	3,528,816	4,773,067	3,883,328	2,452,298	2,246,916	5,998	4.3
	%	100.0	2.8	10.2	18.2	24.6	20.0	12.6	11.6	0.0	..
	U	12,574,955	415,945	1,402,693	2,334,196	3,102,981	2,444,397	1,482,281	1,388,702	3,760	4.3
	%	100.0	3.3	11.2	18.6	24.7	19.4	11.8	11.0	0.0	..
	R	6,826,912	121,368	571,438	1,194,620	1,670,086	1,438,931	970,017	858,214	2,238	4.5
	%	100.0	1.8	8.4	17.5	24.4	21.1	14.2	12.6	0.0	..
CHILE	1970 T	1,689,840	184,280	347,560	363,380	352,600	175,780	101,380	164,860	-	2.9
	%	100.0	10.9	20.6	21.5	20.9	10.4	6.0	9.8	-	..
	U	1,312,860	129,680	246,220	278,900	298,500	146,560	85,800	135,200	-	3.0
	%	100.0	9.9	18.8	21.2	22.1	11.2	6.5	10.3	-	..
	R	376,980	54,600	101,340	84,480	62,100	29,220	15,580	29,660	-	2.4
	%	100.0	14.5	26.9	22.4	16.5	7.8	4.1	7.9	-	..
COLOMBIA	1973 T	3,028,051	463,777	805,910	597,281	720,947	----------440,136---------			-	2.9
	%	100.0	18.9	33.2	18.8	19.2	9.9			-	..
	U	1,828,111	177,090	351,634	354,186	555,375	389,826			-	4.0
	%	100.0	9.7	19.2	19.4	30.4	21.3			-	..
	R	1,199,940	286,687	454,276	243,095	165,572	50,310			-	2.5
	%	100.0	23.9	37.8	20.3	13.8	4.2			-	..
ECUADOR	1974 T	1,193,940	406,291	378,679	184,392	104,897	49,644	27,871	42,166	-	2.4
	%	100.0	34.0	31.7	15.5	8.8	4.2	2.3	3.5	-	..
	U	486,534	135,255	132,340	79,983	54,807	32,065	19,233	32,851	-	2.8
	%	100.0	27.8	27.2	16.4	11.2	6.6	4.0	6.8	-	..
	R	707,406	271,036	246,339	104,409	50,090	17,579	8,638	9,315	-	2.1
	%	100.0	38.3	34.8	14.8	7.1	2.5	1.2	1.3	-	..

Table 15 (continued)

DISTRIBUTION ACCORDING TO NUMBER OF ROOMS PER HOUSING UNIT

COUNTRIES OR AREAS AND CENSUS YEARS	TOTAL:T URBAN:U RURAL:R	TOTAL HOUSING UNITS	1	2	3	4	5	6	7+	HOUSING UNITS WITH UNKNOWN NUMBER OF ROOMS	AVERAGE SIZE PER HOUSING UNIT
(1)		(2)	(3)	(4)	(5)	(6)	(7)	(8)	(9)	(10)	(11)
AMERICA, SOUTH (continued)											
FALKLAND ISLANDS (MALVINAS) 1972	T	587	-	13	9	47	95	125	298	-	7.4
	%	100.0	-	2.2	1.5	8.0	16.2	21.3	50.8	-	..
	U	337	-	12	7	41	71	91	115	-	5.0
	%	100.0	-	3.6	2.1	12.2	21.0	27.0	34.1	-	..
	R	250	-	1	2	6	24	34	183	-	10.6
	%	100.0	-	0.4	0.8	2.4	9.6	13.6	73.2	-	..
PARAGUAY 1972	T	428,111	179,116	121,197	57,611	32,163	17,126	9,492	11,406	-	2.2
	%	100.0	41.8	28.3	13.5	7.5	4.0	2.2	2.7	-	..
	U	172,127	45,215	44,942	30,575	21,272	12,866	7,560	9,697	-	2.9
	%	100.0	26.3	26.1	17.8	12.3	7.5	4.4	5.6	-	..
	R	255,984	133,901	76,255	27,036	10,891	4,260	1,932	1,709	-	1.8
	%	100.0	52.3	29.8	10.5	4.2	1.7	0.8	0.7	-	..
PERU 1972	T	2,686,471	883,399	791,528	409,898	271,979	------------286,488------------			43,179	2.5
	%	100.0	32.9	29.5	15.2	10.1	10.7			1.6	..
	U	1,530,335	380,206	411,671	268,606	205,944	242,678			21,230	2.9
	%	100.0	24.8	26.9	17.5	13.5	15.9			1.4	..
	R	1,156,136	503,193	379,857	141,292	66,035	43,810			21,949	2.0
	%	100.0	43.5	32.9	12.2	5.7	3.8			1.9	..
URUGUAY 1975	T	794,501	74,517	146,541	248,595	147,496	100,387	32,407	44,319	239	3.5
	%	100.0	9.4	18.4	31.3	18.6	12.6	4.1	5.6	0.0	..
	U	673,687	63,958	126,456	213,098	125,474	83,014	26,357	35,120	210	3.4
	%	100.0	9.5	18.8	31.6	18.6	12.3	3.9	5.2	0.0	..
	R	120,814	10,559	20,085	35,497	22,022	17,373	6,050	9,199	29	3.7
	%	100.0	8.7	16.6	29.4	18.2	14.4	5.0	7.6	0.0	..
ASIA											
BAHRAIN 1971	T	31,045	4,881	9,371	7,684	4,623	2,088	------2,398------------		-	3.0
	%	100.0	15.7	30.2	24.8	14.9	6.7	7.7			..
	U	25,072	3,787	7,673	6,337	3,721	1,654	1,900		-	2.9
	%	100.0	15.1	30.6	25.3	14.8	6.6	7.6			..
	R	5,973	1,094	1,698	1,347	902	434	498		-	2.9
	%	100.0	18.3	28.4	22.6	15.1	7.3	8.3			..
BANGLADESH 1973	T	12,675,448	5,700,247	3,823,822	1,798,512	820,406	308,432	120,288	103,741	-	2.0
	%	100.0	45.0	30.2	14.2	6.5	2.4	0.9	0.8	-	..
	U	1,064,977	584,835	242,581	125,198	62,039	25,718	11,190	13,416	-	1.9
	%	100.0	54.9	22.8	11.8	5.8	2.4	1.1	1.3	-	..
	R	11,610,471	5,115,412	3,581,241	1,673,314	758,367	282,714	109,098	90,325	-	2.0
	%	100.0	44.1	30.8	14.4	6.5	2.4	0.9	0.8	-	..
CYPRUS 1973	T	163,730	3,723	19,238	28,394	36,746	37,796	22,200	15,633	-	4.4
	%	100.0	2.3	11.8	17.3	22.4	23.1	13.6	9.6	-	..
	U	70,850	344	4,668	9,645	16,752	18,605	12,667	8,169	-	4.7
	%	100.0	.5	6.6	13.6	23.6	26.3	17.9	11.5	-	..
	R	92,880	3,379	14,570	18,749	19,994	19,191	9,533	7,464	-	4.1
	%	100.0	3.6	15.7	20.2	21.5	20.7	10.3	8.0	-	..
HONG-KONG 1973	T	636,428	141,592	133,546	109,721	107,943	75,945	38,206	29,475	-	3.1
	%	100.0	22.3	21.0	17.2	17.0	11.9	6.0	4.6	-	..
	U	587,182	137,642	121,389	95,198	98,103	71,238	36,134	27,478	-	3.1
	%	100.0	23.4	20.7	16.2	16.7	12.1	6.2	4.7	-	..
	R	49,246	3,950	12,157	14,523	9,840	4,707	2,072	1,997	-	3.3
	%	100.0	8.0	24.7	29.5	20.0	9.6	4.2	4.1	-	..
INDIA 1971	T	97,056,737	46,411,738	27,339,615	11,647,240	5,803,074	5,769,022	-	-	86,048	2.0
	%	100.0	47.8	28.2	12.0	6.0	5.9	-	-	0.1	..
	U	19,121,491	9,579,845	5,149,808	2,184,517	1,092,090	1,077,992	-	-	37,239	2.0
	%	100.0	50.1	26.9	11.4	5.7	5.6	-	-	0.2	..
	R	77,935,246	36,831,893	22,189,807	9,462,723	4,710,984	4,691,030	-	-	48,809	2.0
	%	100.0	47.3	28.5	12.1	6.0	6.0	-	-	0.1	..
INDONESIA 1971	T	24,506,742	2,673,864	6,643,801	7,155,049	4,367,903	2,177,043	872,840	616,242	-	3.1
	%	100.0	10.9	27.1	29.2	17.8	8.9	3.6	2.5	-	..
	U	3,872,663	580,647	931,445	1,013,718	645,432	360,880	166,340	174,201	-	3.2
	%	100.0	15.0	24.0	26.2	16.7	9.3	4.3	4.5	-	..
	R	20,634,079	2,093,217	5,712,356	6,141,331	3,722,471	1,816,163	706,500	442,041	-	3.1
	%	100.0	10.1	27.7	29.8	18.1	8.8	3.4	2.1	-	..

Table 15 (continued)

DISTRIBUTION ACCORDING TO NUMBER OF ROOMS PER HOUSING UNIT

COUNTRIES OR AREAS AND CENSUS YEARS	TOTAL:T URBAN:U RURAL:R	TOTAL HOUSING UNITS	1	2	3	4	5	6	7+	HOUSING UNITS WITH UNKNOWN NUMBER OF ROOMS	AVERAGE SIZE PER HOUSING UNIT
(1)		(2)	(3)	(4)	(5)	(6)	(7)	(8)	(9)	(10)	(11)
ASIA (continued)											
IRAN	1978 T	6,709,068	1,908,897	2,287,699	1,242,290	665,374	304,146	155,539	135,371	-	2.4
	%	100.0	28.5	34.1	18.5	9.9	4.5	2.3	2.0	-	..
	U	3,264,193	928,869	973,942	585,597	380,325	197,296	103,541	86,904	-	2.6
	%	100.0	28.5	29.8	17.9	11.7	6.0	3.2	2.7	-	..
	R	3,444,875	980,028	1,313,757	656,693	285,049	106,850	51,998	48,467	-	2.3
	%	100.0	28.4	38.1	19.1	8.3	3.1	1.5	1.4	-	..
ISRAEL	1978 T	930,400	39,100	206,100	459,800	227,000	..	..	..	..	2.9
	%	100.0	4.2	22.2	49.4	24.4	..	..	..	..	..
	U	870,000	35,200	194,400	440,200	199,800	..	..	..	..	2.9
	%	100.0	4.0	22.3	50.6	23.0	..	..	..	..	..
	R	62,400	3,900	11,700	19,600	27,200	..	..	..	..	3.3
	%	100.0	6.3	18.8	31.4	43.6	..	..	..	..	..
JAPAN	1978 T	32,188,700	1,652,600	4,382,900	5,884,300	5,905,400	4,904,500	3,895,700	5,492,100	71,400	4.3
	%	100.0	5.1	13.6	18.3	18.3	15.2	12.1	17.1	0.2	..
	U	25,281,300	1,590,000	3,942,000	5,036,400	4,779,800	3,669,600	2,753,100	3,440,500	69,900	4.1
	%	100.0	6.3	15.6	19.9	18.9	14.5	10.9	13.6	0.3	..
	R	6,907,400	62,600	441,000	848,000	1,125,500	1,234,800	1,142,600	2,051,600	1,300	5.1
	%	100.0	0.9	6.4	12.3	16.3	17.9	16.5	29.7	0.0	..
RYUKYU ISLANDS	1970 T	214,590	16,461	47,709	42,991	45,710	33,963	18,070	9,686	-	3.6
	%	100.0	7.7	22.2	20.0	21.3	15.8	8.4	4.5	-	..
	U	134,635	11,800	35,277	28,467	26,062	17,905	9,465	5,659	-	3.4
	%	100.0	8.8	26.2	21.1	19.4	13.3	7.0	4.2	-	..
	R	79,955	4,661	12,432	14,524	19,648	16,058	8,605	4,027	-	3.9
	%	100.0	5.8	15.6	18.2	24.6	20.1	10.8	5.0	-	..
KOREA, REPUBLIC OF	1970 T	4,359,962	327,201	1,523,531	1,356,722	681,809	260,000	110,449	100,250	-	3.0
	%	100.0	7.5	35.0	31.1	15.6	6.0	2.5	2.3	-	..
	U	1,397,859	130,576	355,983	382,758	274,707	129,144	60,145	64,546	-	3.3
	%	100.0	9.3	25.5	27.4	19.7	9.2	4.3	4.6	-	..
	R	2,962,103	196,625	1,167,548	973,964	407,102	130,856	50,304	35,704	-	2.8
	%	100.0	6.6	39.4	32.9	13.8	4.4	1.7	1.2	-	..
	1980 T	5,340,276	214,729	1,412,791	1,824,085	1,015,927	443,241	205,617	223,886	-	4.1
	%	100.0	4.0	26.5	34.2	19.0	8.3	3.9	4.2	-	..
	U	2,484,476	86,838	444,042	714,569	581,029	314,691	159,394	183,913	-	4.4
	%	100.0	3.5	17.9	28.8	23.4	12.7	6.4	7.4	-	..
	R	2,855,800	127,891	968,749	1,109,516	434,898	128,550	46,223	39,973	-	3.8
	%	100.0	4.5	33.9	38.9	15.2	4.5	1.6	1.4	-	..
MALAYSIA, PENINSULAR	1970 T	1,323,208	482,686	376,409	226,667	129,551	60,498	26,654	20,743	-	2.3
	%	100.0	36.5	28.5	17.1	9.8	4.6	2.0	1.6	-	..
	U	322,501	53,157	76,753	74,930	59,621	30,836	14,711	12,493	-	3.1
	%	100.0	16.5	23.8	23.2	18.5	9.6	4.6	3.9	-	..
	R	1,007,707	429,529	299,656	151,737	69,930	29,662	11,943	8,250	-	2.0
	%	100.0	42.9	29.9	15.2	7.0	3.0	1.2	0.8	-	..
PAKISTAN	1980 T	12,587,648	6,487,461	3,721,239	1,356,690	565,251	213,605	106,797	136,605	-	1.9
	%	100.0	51.5	29.6	10.8	4.5	1.7	.8	1.1	-	..
	U	3,554,173	1,513,465	1,120,401	486,326	231,236	90,811	51,014	60,920	-	2.2
	%	100.0	42.6	31.5	13.7	6.5	2.6	1.4	1.7	-	..
	R	9,033,475	4,973,996	2,600,838	870,364	334,015	122,794	55,783	75,685	-	1.8
	%	100.0	55.1	28.8	9.6	3.7	1.4	0.6	0.8	-	..
PHILIPPINES	1970 T	6,010,837	1,814,349	1,805,473	1,289,968	634,645	261,112	115,010	99,260	-	2.4
	%	100.0	30.2	30.0	21.3	10.6	4.3	1.9	1.7	-	..
	U	1,803,746	424,412	504,271	383,817	240,845	121,136	64,082	65,183	-	2.8
	%	100.0	23.5	28.0	21.3	13.4	6.7	3.6	3.6	-	..
	R	4,207,091	1,389,957	1,301,202	897,151	393,800	139,976	50,928	34,077	-	2.3
	%	100.0	33.0	30.9	21.3	9.4	3.3	1.2	0.8	-	..
SRI LANKA	1981 T	2,811,411	865,227	908,128	501,161	279,432	133,767	64,890	58,806	-	2.5
	%	100.0	30.8	32.3	17.8	9.9	4.8	2.3	2.1	-	..
	U	509,459	157,098	148,662	93,556	53,847	27,897	13,891	14,508	-	2.6
	%	100.0	30.8	29.2	18.4	10.6	5.5	2.7	2.8	-	..
	R	2,301,952	708,129	759,466	407,605	225,585	105,870	50,999	44,298	-	2.4
	%	100.0	30.8	33.0	17.7	9.8	4.6	2.2	1.9	-	..

Table 15 (continued)

COUNTRIES OR AREAS AND CENSUS YEARS	TOTAL:T URBAN:U RURAL:R	TOTAL HOUSING UNITS	1	2	3	4	5	6	7+	HOUSING UNITS WITH UNKNOWN NUMBER OF ROOMS	AVERAGE SIZE PER HOUSING UNIT
(1)		(2)	(3)	(4)	(5)	(6)	(7)	(8)	(9)	(10)	(11)
ASIA (continued)											
SYRIAN ARAB REPUBLIC	1970 T	908,254	34,078	62,511	66,655	84,004	101,336	106,519	453,151	-	6.4
	%	100.0	3.8	6.9	7.3	9.2	11.2	11.7	49.9	-	..
	U	384,905	13,386	24,784	25,770	33,398	40,209	42,631	204,727	-	6.6
	%	100.0	3.5	6.4	6.7	8.7	10.4	11.1	53.2	-	..
	R	523,349	20,692	37,727	40,885	50,606	61,127	63,888	248,424	-	6.2
	%	100.0	4.0	7.2	7.8	9.7	11.7	12.2	47.4	-	..
THAILAND	1976 T	6,863,260	2,651,980	2,587,380	1,242,710	235,630	76,710	..	..	68,850	1.9
	%	100.0	38.6	37.7	18.1	3.4	1.1	..	..	1.0	..
	U	1,011,420	330,070	382,730	194,930	64,010	29,350	..	..	10,330	2.1
	%	100.0	32.6	37.8	19.3	6.3	2.9	..	..	1.0	..
	R	5,851,840	2,321,910	2,204,650	1,047,780	171,620	47,360	..	..	58,520	1.9
	%	100.0	39.7	37.7	17.9	2.9	0.8	..	..	1.0	..
TURKEY	1975 T	6,982,505	1,016,383	2,569,835	1,920,017	941,304	196,454	85,386	42,958	210,668	2.5
	%	100.0	14.6	36.8	27.5	13.5	2.8	1.2	0.6	3.0	..
	U	1,148,112	145,698	145,698	344,012	150,574	25,400	9,031	3,340	51,179	2.5
	%	100	12.7	12.7	30.0	13.1	2.2	0.8	0.3	4.5	..
	R	5,834,393	870,685	2,150,457	1,576,005	790,730	171,054	76,355	39,618	159,489	2.5
	%	100.0	14.9	36.9	27.0	13.6	2.9	1.3	0.7	2.7	..
EUROPE											
AUSTRIA	1972 T	2,460,000	15,000	163,000	634,000	755,000	464,000	----------------420,000		9,000	4.1
	%	100.0	.6	6.6	25.8	30.7	18.9	-------------------17.1		0.4	..
	U	1,127,000	12,000	129,000	404,000	351,000	147,000	----------------80,000		4,000	3.7
	%	100.0	1.1	11.5	35.9	31.1	13.0	--------------------7.1		0.4	..
	R	1,333,000	3,000	34,000	230,000	404,000	317,000	----------------340,000		5,000	4.5
	%	100.0	.2	2.6	17.3	30.3	23.8	-------------------25.5		0.4	..
BULGARIA	1975 T	2,339,380	108,274	317,664	690,438	686,734	345,044	191,226	-	-	3.0
	%	100.0	4.6	13.6	29.5	29.4	14.7	8.2	-	-	..
	U	1,288,613	83,976	201,697	419,119	356,627	151,625	75,569	-	-	3.0
	%	100.0	6.5	15.7	32.5	27.7	11.8	5.8	-	-	..
	R	1,050,767	24,298	115,967	271,319	330,107	193,419	115,657	-	-	3.0
	%		2.3	11.0	25.8	31.4	18.4	11.1	-	-	..
CZECHOSLOVAKIA	1980 T	4,908,778	127,398	835,036	1,610,036	1,515,766	510,503	207,025	103,014	-	3.5
	%	..	2.6	17.0	32.8	30.9	10.4	4.2	2.1	-	..
	U	3,345,973	..	..	..	..	..	..	..	-	3.4
	%	..	..	..	..	..	..	..	..	-	..
	R	1,562,805	..	..	..	..	..	..	..	-	3.7
	%	..	..	..	..	..	..	..	..	-	..
DENMARK	1970 T	1,800,654	64,633	364,886	488,896	431,218	195,854	--------183,657--------		71,510	3.5
	%	100.0	3.6	20.3	27.1	23.9	10.9	10.2		4.0	..
	U	1,278,508	62,428	320,890	359,899	285,112	111,477	78,385		60,317	3.2
	%	100.0	4.9	25.1	28.2	22.3	8.7	6.1		4.7	..
	R	522,146	2,205	43,996	128,997	146,106	84,377	105,272		11,193	4.3
	%	100.0	0.4	8.4	24.7	28.0	16.2	20.2		2.1	..
FAEROE ISLANDS	1970 T	9,619	232	253	449	994	1,522	1,767	4,044	358	6.2
	%	100.0	2.4	2.6	4.7	10.3	15.8	18.4	42.1	3.7	..
	U	2,830	222	180	222	380	439	435	825	127	5.3
	%	100.0	7.8	6.4	7.8	13.4	15.5	15.4	29.2	4.5	..
	R	6,789	10	73	227	614	1,083	1,332	3,219	231	6.6
	%	100.0	0.1	1.1	3.3	9.1	16.0	19.6	47.4	3.4	..
FINLAND	1970 T	1,463,221	180,835	362,890	410,153	260,496	162,184	20,532	28,754	7,377	3.1
	%	100.0	12.4	24.8	28.0	17.8	11.1	3.5	2.0	0.5	..
	U	806,936	135,583	208,276	212,609	134,809	77,988	23,854	11,803	2,014	2.9
	%	100.0	16.8	25.8	26.4	16.7	9.7	3.0	1.5	0.3	..
	R	656,285	45,252	154,614	197,544	125,687	84,196	26,678	16,951	5,363	3.3
	%	100.0	6.9	23.6	30.1	19.2	12.8	4.1	2.6	0.8	..
	1980 T	1,728,100	202,172	292,065	446,358	370,287	264,891	98,959	29,697	23,671	3.4
	%	100.0	11.8	16.9	25.8	21.4	15.3	5.7	1.7	1.4	..
	U	1,098,684	155,657	196,626	289,822	235,031	145,981	50,337	14,764	10,466	3.2
	%	100.0	14.2	17.9	26.4	21.4	13.3	4.6	1.3	0.9	..
	R	629,416	46,515	95,439	156,536	135,256	118,910	48,622	14,933	13,205	3.7
	%	100.0	7.4	15.2	24.8	21.5	18.9	7.7	2.4	2.1	..

Table 15 (continued)

DISTRIBUTION ACCORDING TO NUMBER OF ROOMS PER HOUSING UNIT

COUNTRIES OR AREAS AND CENSUS YEARS	TOTAL:T URBAN:U RURAL:R	TOTAL HOUSING UNITS	1	2	3	4	5	6	7+	HOUSING UNITS WITH UNKNOWN NUMBER OF ROOMS	AVERAGE SIZE PER HOUSING UNIT
(1)		(2)	(3)	(4)	(5)	(6)	(7)	(8)	(9)	(10)	(11)
EUROPE (continued)											
FRANCE	1973 T	17,123,709	1,302,955	2,826,904	4,592,219	4,331,660	2,374,130	-----1,695,841--------		-	3.6
	%	100.0	7.6	16.5	26.8	25.3	13.9	9.9		-	. .
	U	12,441,621	1,092,736	2,205,833	3,501,570	3,111,399	1,554,837	975,246		-	3.4
	%	100.0	8.8	17.7	28.2	25.0	12.5	7.8		-	. .
	R	4,682,088	210,219	621,071	1,090,649	1,220,261	819,293	720,595		-	4.0
	%	100.0	4.5	13.3	23.3	26.0	17.5	15.4		-	. .
	1975 T	17,744,985	1,637,260	3,075,550	4,778,860	4,464,075	2,312,195	1,477,045	. .	-	3.4
	%	100.0	9.2	17.3	26.9	25.2	13.0	8.3	. .	-	. .
	U	13,187,565	1,374,020	2,404,395	3,677,545	3,299,900	1,564,220	867,485	. .	-	3.3
	%	100.0	10.4	18.2	27.9	25.0	11.9	6.6	. .	-	. .
	R	4,557,420	263,240	671,155	1,101,315	1,164,175	747,975	609,560	. .	-	3.7
	%	100.0	5.8	14.7	24.2	25.5	16.4	13.4	. .	-	. .
GREECE	1971 T	2,544,020	184,380	425,820	681,140	719,860	340,080	121,800	68,600	2,340	3.5
	%	100.0	7.3	16.7	26.8	28.3	13.4	4.8	2.7	0.1	. .
	U	1,387,280	112,480	230,400	385,360	396,980	179,200	57,200	24,300	1,340	3.4
	%	100.0	8.1	16.6	27.8	28.6	12.9	4.1	1.8	0.1	. .
	R	1,156,740	71,900	195,420	295,780	322,880	160,880	64,580	44,300	1,000	3.6
	%	100.0	6.2	16.9	25.9	27.9	13.9	5.6	3.8	0.1	. .
IRELAND	1971 T	705,180	5,839	32,738	106,555	217,785	153,093	110,480	77,122	1,568	4.7
	%	100.0	.8	4.6	15.1	30.9	21.5	15.7	10.9	0.2	. .
	U	348,070	3,871	14,867	39,675	93,648	75,825	72,290	47,496	398	4.9
	%	100.0	1.1	4.3	11.4	26.9	21.8	20.8	13.7	0.1	. .
	R	357,110	1,968	17,871	66,880	124,137	77,268	38,190	29,626	1,170	4.5
	%	100.0	.6	5.0	18.7	34.8	21.6	10.7	8.3	0.3	. .
NORWAY	1970 T	1,296,760	77,221	100,020	206,107	306,380	322,781	153,730	130,475	46	4.4
	%	100.0	6.0	7.7	15.9	23.6	24.9	11.8	10.1	0.0	. .
	U	890,101	67,891	80,197	158,079	232,181	215,911	80,921	54,882	39	4.1
	%	100.0	7.6	.9	17.8	26.1	24.2	9.1	6.2	0.0	. .
	R	406,659	9,330	19,823	48,028	74,199	106,870	72,809	75,593	7	5.1
	%	100.0	2.3	4.9	11.8	18.2	26.3	17.9	18.6	0.0	. .
SPAIN	1970 T	9,542,458	130,548	623,163	1,646,570	3,021,337	2,357,926	1,038,409	724,505	-	4.4
	%	100.0	1.4	6.5	17.2	31.7	24.7	10.9	7.6	-	. .
	U	6,067,896	98,568	386,550	1,006,587	2,019,574	1,565,078	601,724	389,815	-	4.4
	%	100.0	1.6	6.4	16.6	33.3	25.8	9.9	6.4	-	. .
	R	3,474,562	31,980	236,613	639,983	1,001,763	792,848	436,685	334,690	-	4.5
	%	100.0	0.9	6.8	18.4	28.9	22.8	12.6	9.6	-	. .
POLAND	1970 T	8,081,054	855,768	2,496,339	2,642,512	1,401,015	428,748	164,875	91,797	-	2.9
	%	100.0	10.6	30.9	32.7	17.3	5.3	2.0	1.1	-	. .
	U	4,507,247	553,090	1,379,173	1,575,852	710,600	184,764	73,653	30,115	-	2.8
	%	100.0	12.3	30.6	35.0	15.8	4.1	1.6	0.7	-	. .
	R	3,573,807	302,678	1,117,166	1,066,660	690,415	243,984	91,222	61,682	-	3.0
	%	100.0	8.5	31.3	30.0	19.3	6.8	2.6	1.7	-	. .
	1977 T	9,326,045	631,899	2,261,563	3,248,794	2,131,561	614,796	281,180	156,252	-	3.1
	%	100.0	6.8	24.2	34.8	22.9	6.6	3.0	1.7	-	. .
	U	5,741,122	456,812	1,375,343	2,099,300	1,270,773	324,000	146,788	68,106	-	3.1
	%	100.0	8.0	24.0	36.6	22.1	5.6	2.6	1.2	-	. .
	R	3,584,923	175,087	886,220	1,149,494	860,788	290,796	134,392	88,146	-	3.3
	%	100.0	4.9	24.7	32.1	24.0	8.1	3.7	2.5	-	. .
SAN MARINO	1976 T	5,575	-	76	1,211	1,137	1,684	914	553	-	4.7
	%	100.0	-	1.4	2179	20.4	3021	1646	9.9	-	. .
	U	5,093	-	76	1,177	775	1,606	909	550	-	4.7
	%	100.0	-	1.5	23.1	15.2	31.6	17.8	10.8	-	. .
	R	482	-	-	34	362	78	5	3	-	4.1
	%	100.0	-	-	7.1	75.1	16.2	1.0	0.6	-	. .
	1979 T	5,769	25	216	960	1,987	1,587	600	394	-	4.5
	%	100.0	0.4	3.7	16.6	34.4	27.5	10.4	6.8	-	. .
	U	5,253	21	185	883	1,806	1,457	543	358	-	4.5
	%	100.0	0.4	3.5	16.8	34.4	27.7	10.3	6.8	-	. .
	R	516	4	31	77	181	130	57	36	-	4.4
	%	100.0	0.8	6.0	14.9	35.1	25.2	11.0	7.0	-	. .

Table 15 (continued)

COUNTRIES OR AREAS AND CENSUS YEARS	TOTAL:T URBAN:U RURAL:R	TOTAL HOUSING UNITS	1	2	3	4	5	6	7+	HOUSING UNITS WITH UNKNOWN NUMBER OF ROOMS	AVERAGE SIZE PER HOUSING UNIT
(1)		(2)	(3)	(4)	(5)	(6)	(7)	(8)	(9)	(10)	(11)
EUROPE (continued)											
SWITZERLAND	1970 T	1,924,629	..	85,317	273,791	589,558	466,168	242,003	244,107	23,685	4.8
	%	100.0	..	4.4	14.2	30.6	24.2	12.6	12.7	1.2	..
	U	1,176,644	..	71,512	206,754	404,882	268,437	113,676	101,568	9,815	4.5
	%	100.0	..	6.1	17.6	34.4	22.8	9.7	8.6	0.8	..
	R	747,985	..	13,805	67,037	184,676	197,731	128,327	142,539	13,870	5.4
	%	100.0	..	1.8	9.0	24.7	26.4	17.2	19.1	1.9	..
SWEDEN	1980 T	3,497,801	162,123	292,174	779,357	856,829	659,795	406,574	276,945	64,004	4.0
	%	100.0	4.6	8.4	22.3	24.5	18.9	11.6	7.9	1.8	..
	U	2,966,022	153,489	271,851	703,963	732,983	533,402	328,394	215,171	26,769	4.0
	%	100.0	5.2	9.2	23.7	24.7	18.0	11.1	7.3	0.9	..
	R	531,779	8,634	20,323	75,394	123,846	126,393	78,180	61,774	37,235	4.0
	%	100.0	1.6	3.8	14.2	23.3	23.8	14.7	11.6	7.0	..
OCEANIA											
GUAM	1970 T	15,569	332	1,047	2,003	3,761	4,827	2,541	1,058	–	4.5
	%	100.0	2.1	6.7	12.9	24.2	31.0	16.3	6.8	–	..
	U	3,882	91	273	627	922	999	608	362	–	4.5
	%	100.0	2.3	7.0	16.2	23.8	25.7	15.7	9.3	–	..
	R	11,687	241	774	1,376	2,839	3,828	1,933	696	–	4.5
	%	100.0	2.1	6.6	11.8	24.3	32.8	16.5	6.0	–	..
SAMOA	1971 T	3,582	353	841	597	587	459	289	456	–	3.9
	%	100.0	9.9	23.5	16.6	16.4	12.8	8.1	12.7	–	..
	U	1,489	154	225	214	243	213	164	276	–	4.4
	%	100.0	10.3	15.1	14.4	16.3	14.3	11.0	18.6	–	..
	R	2,093	199	616	383	344	246	125	180	–	3.5
	%	100.0	9.5	29.4	18.3	16.4	11.8	6.0	8.6	–	..

Sources: United Nations, *Compendium of Housing Statistics 1975–1977* and United Nations, *Compendium of Human Settlements Statistics 1983.*

Notes: Only countries for which urban/rural data for 1969 and after are available are included here.

a Data refer to conventional dwellings. Data by city or urban agglomeration are not available.

b Kitchens with a floor sapce of at least 12 square metres are counted as rooms.

c As indicated, the average number of rooms per housing unit is, in some cases, estimated by the United Nations Statistical Office. Where the aggregate number of rooms was not available, an approximation of this value was obtained by multiplying each room category by its corresponding housing unit frequency, multiplying the residual category by the lowest number of rooms involved, disregarding the housing units with an unknown number of rooms, and summing the products.

Table 16

Conventional dwellings constructed annually: number and rate per thousand mid-year population, countries, areas, cities, or urban agglomerations, 1972–1981

CONVENTIONAL DWELLINGS CONSTRUCTED ANNUALLY: NUMBER AND RATE PER THOUSAND MID-YEAR POPULATION

COUNTRIES, AREAS, CITIES OR URBAN AGGLOMERATIONS	TOTAL:T URBAN:U RURAL:R	1972	1973	1974	1975	1976	1977	1978	1979	1980	1981
(1)		(2)	(3)	(4)	(5)	(6)	(7)	(8)	(9)	(10)	(11)
AFRICA											
CENTRAL AFRICAN REPUBLIC											
BANGUI[1]		232	236	143	83	100	97	118	..	..	..
EGYPT[31,32] ....T		23,529	27,575	19,797	..	..	..	..	..	..	..
		0.7	0.8	0.5	..	..	..	..	..	..	..
MAURITIUS[32,33,34] ....T		2,006	2,623	2,918	3,775	4,141	..	..	..	..	..
		2.4	3.1	3.4	4.3	4.7	..	..	..	..	..
MOZAMBIQUE[31,32,35] ....T		2,788	4,051	1,470	..	..	..	..	..	..	..
		0.3	0.5	0.2	..	..	..	..	..	..	..
REUNION[31,32] ....T		1,921	2,817	3,121	2,640	3,496	..	..	..	..	..
		4.1	6.0	6.7	5.3	6.9	..	..	..	..	..
SWAZILAND											
MBABANE[2]		..	..	..	78	110	94	73	88	62	80
TUNISIA[31,32,33] ....T		8,154	15,474	14,245	13,384	..	..	..	..	..	..
		1.5	2.8	2.5	2.4	..	..	..	..	..	..
AMERICA, NORTH											
BAHAMAS[32,34] ....T		158	316	410	334	412	..	..	..	..	..
		0.9	1.7	2.1	1.7	2.0	..	..	..	..	..
BARBADOS[33,34] ....T		..	998	727	700	753	..	..	..	..	..
		..	4.2	3.0	2.8	3.0	..	..	..	..	..
CANADA[3] ....T		..	268,529	222,123	231,456	273,203	245,724	227,667	197,049	158,601	177,973
		..	12.2	9.9	10.2	11.9	10.6	9.7	8.3	6.6	7.3
MONTREAL[3,4]		..	30,700	24,758	26,702	37,531	27,193	18,300	16,188	12,433	14,643
		..	11.1	8.8	9.6	13.4	9.6	6.5	5.8	4.4	5.2
OTTAWA[3,4]		..	15,511	9,709	7,156	7,059	7,429	7,592	4,777	2,590	4,035
		..	25.1	15.5	10.5	10.2	10.6	10.7	6.7	3.6	5.6
TORONTO[3,4]		..	37,697	29,580	26,457	26,555	27,918	26,051	21,379	20,204	26,133
		..	14.0	10.8	9.6	9.5	9.8	9.0	7.3	6.8	8.7
WINNIPEG[3,4]		..	7,698	5,628	5,294	6,718	6,353	9,706	4,091	1,668	2,088
		..	13.7	9.9	9.2	11.6	10.9	16.6	7.0	2.9	3.6
COSTA RICA[32,33,36] ....T		7,601	9,921	12,784	11,918	..	..	..	..	..	..
		4.1	5.3	6.7	6.0	..	..	..	..	..	..
CUBA[5] ....T		16,807	20,710	18,552	18,602	15,342	20,024	17,072	14,523	20,378	25,361
		1.9	2.3	2.0	2.0	1.6	2.1	1.8	1.5	2.1	2.6
	U	..	..	..	..	..	..	..	..	19,995	23,449
	R	..	..	..	..	..	..	..	..	383	1,912
DOMINICAN REPUBLIC[6] ....T		..	3,059	3,863	5,331	3,625	4,656	7,065	2,795	5,455	3,532
		..	0.7	0.8	1.1	0.7	0.9	1.4	0.5	1.0	0.6
SANTO DOMINGO[6]		..	1,766	2,298	3,029	2,179	3,154	3,777	2,081	3,916	2,216
EL SALVADOR[33,37] ....T		2,426	2,776	2,155	2,730	2,272	..	..	..	..	..
		0.6	0.7	0.5	0.7	0.6	..	..	..	..	..
GREENLAND........................T		656	360	389	428	468	337	335	356	543	469
		13.6	7.3	7.9	8.6	9.4	6.8	6.8	7.2	10.8	9.2
GODTHAB		126	100	85	86	111	36	111	62	165	..
		14.5	11.4	9.7	9.7	12.4	4.0	12.1	6.6	10.9	..

Table 16 (continued)

CONVENTIONAL DWELLINGS CONSTRUCTED ANNUALLY: NUMBER AND RATE PER THOUSAND MID-YEAR POPULATION

COUNTRIES, AREAS, CITIES OR URBAN AGGLOMERATIONS	TOTAL:T URBAN:U RURAL:R	1972	1973	1974	1975	1976	1977	1978	1979	1980	1981
(1)		(2)	(3)	(4)	(5)	(6)	(7)	(8)	(9)	(10)	(11)

AMERICA, NORTH   (continued)

		1972	1973	1974	1975	1976	1977	1978	1979	1980	1981
GUADELOUPE [31,32] ....T		1,222	1,555	1,214	1,712	1,995	..	..	..	..	..
		3.6	4.6	3.6	5.0	5.7	..	..	..	..	..
JAMAICA [33,37] ....T		3,575	3,797	5,878	1,974	..	..	..	..	..	..
		1.9	1.9	2.9	1.0	..	..	..	..	..	..
MARTINIQUE [31] ....T		1,283	951	1,350	900	662	..	..	..	..	..
		3.8	2.8	3.8	2.5	1.8	..	..	..	..	..
PANAMA [7] ....T		3,385	3,767	2,884	2,314	2,244	2,499	2,723	3,175	2,628	2,537
PUERTO RICO [31,32,33,38] ....T		25,817	25,894	24,951	28,993	18,632	..	..	..	..	..
		9.0	8.8	8.2	9.3	5.8	..	..	..	..	..
TRINIDAD AND TOBAGO [32,33] ....T		2,797	3,112	2,995	2,322	2,813	..	..	..	..	..
		2.7	2.9	2.8	2.2	..	..	..	..	..	..
UNITED STATES [8] ....T		2,003,900	2,100,500	1,728,500	1,317,200	1,377,200	1,657,100	1,867,500	1,870,800	1,501,600	1,265,700
		9.6	9.9	8.1	6.1	6.3	7.5	8.4	8.3	6.6	5.5
	U	1,430,900	1,541,000	1,266,100	922,600	950,100	1,161,900	1,313,600	1,332,000	1,078,900	888,400
	R	573,000	559,500	462,400	394,500	427,200	495,200	553,900	538,800	422,700	377,400

AMERICA, SOUTH

BRAZIL

		1972	1973	1974	1975	1976	1977	1978	1979	1980	1981
BELO HORIZONTE		3,392	3,413	..	3,124	2,726	5,777	7,159	7,619	9,585	..
		2.6	2.5	..	2.1	1.8	3.6	4.3	4.5	5.4	..
BRASILIA		4,237	2,213	..	6,793	7,658	3,701	10,117	6,983	10,125	..
		6.6	3.1	..	8.2	8.6	3.9	9.9	6.4	8.7	..
RIO DE JANEIRO		12,025	11,092	..	10,175	8,213	9,958	7,592	8,050	8,766	..
		2.7	2.5	..	2.2	1.7	2.1	1.6	1.6	1.7	..
SAO PAULO		38,894	35,790	..	20,571	24,207	21,787	19,837	21,114	21,112	..
		6.1	5.4	..	2.9	3.3	2.9	2.5	2.6	2.5	..
CHILE [9] ....T		..	35,361	20,381	19,369	37,394	25,043	23,226	37,615	46,284	54,550
		..	3.6	2.0	1.9	3.6	2.4	2.2	3.4	4.2	4.8
SANTIAGO [9]		..	14,575	8,655	6,032	17,189	8,213	10,741	18,376	22,691	33,328
		..	4.5	2.6	1.8	4.9	2.3	2.9	4.9	5.9	8.4
TALCAHUANO [9]		..	1,183	39	85	1,746	329	344	352	253	527
		..	6.6	0.2	0.5	9.3	1.7	1.8	1.8	1.3	2.6
VALPARAISO		..	380	175	104	334	639	410	411	1,169	580
		..	1.4	0.7	0.4	1.3	2.4	1.5	1.5	4.4	2.2
VINA DEL MAR		..	412	2,327	965	1,426	1,063	689	1,497	2,277	2,429
		..	1.9	10.5	4.2	6.0	4.3	2.7	5.7	8.3	8.6
ECUADOR [10] ....U		..	..	..	..	11,492	11,946	15,998	12,972	13,967	..
		..	..	..	..	3.7	3.7	4.8	3.7	3.7	..
FRENCH GUIANA [31,32] ....T		458	164	240	409	175	..	..	..	..	..
		9.2	3.3	4.0	0.3	2.9	..	..	..	..	..
GUYANA [32,34] ....T		1,813	1,622	1,301	1,259	..	..	..	..	..	..
		2.5	2.1	1.7	1.6	..	..	..	..	..	..

Table 16 (continued)

CONVENTIONAL DWELLINGS CONSTRUCTED ANNUALLY: NUMBER AND RATE PER THOUSAND MID-YEAR POPULATION

COUNTRIES, AREAS, CITIES OR URBAN AGGLOMERATIONS	TOTAL:T URBAN:U RURAL:R	1972	1973	1974	1975	1976	1977	1978	1979	1980	1981
(1)		(2)	(3)	(4)	(5)	(6)	(7)	(8)	(9)	(10)	(11)
AMERICA, SOUTH (continued)											
VENEZUELA [11]	T	44,249	93,680	56,440	60,622	65,437	63,916	73,558	82,716	85,728	91,452
		4.0	8.3	4.9	5.1	5.3	5.0	5.6	6.1	6.2	6.4
	U[12]	12,363	61,145	22,065	23,065	20,408	14,320	15,972	27,285	21,952	30,708
	R[12]	9,141	9,340	10,002	11,554	8,824	8,528	17,611	5,004	12,764	14,197
BARQUISIMETO [13]		696	4,460	3,261	2,340	1,773	3,137	4,677	3,975	2,824	3,595
		1.9	11.5	8.1	5.6	4.1	7.1	10.2	8.4	5.8	7.1
CARACAS [4,13]		15,304	21,602	15,176	14,851	17,106	9,687	7,168	6,977	8,337	6,532
		6.8	9.3	6.3	6.0	6.6	3.6	2.6	2.4	2.8	2.1
MARACAIBO [13]		3,118	8,799	3,885	3,704	4,033	5,651	5,877	8,870	4,756	5,790
		4.5	12.3	5.2	4.8	5.1	6.9	7.0	10.1	5.3	6.2
VALENCIA [13]		1,794	5,919	3,836	2,103	3,313	4,948	8,858	9,661	10,923	6,268
		4.7	15.1	9.4	5.0	7.5	10.9	18.8	19.9	21.6	12.0
ASIA											
CYPRUS [41]	T	4,250	4,530	2,785	2,266	2,747	..	..	..	..	..
		6.5	7.0	4.4	3.5	4.3	..	..	..	..	..
HONG KONG [15]	T	22,045[16]	25,565[16]	27,081	24,524	30,255	35,117	42,320	50,196	58,001	64,199
		5.4[16]	6.1[16]	6.3	5.6	6.8	7.8	9.2	10.4	11.6	12.5
HONG KONG ISLAND		9,455[16]	7,620[16]	7,550	7,839	10,376	10,127	16,693	16,419	10,451	13,627
KOWLOON		4,140[16]	6,230[16]	8,966	5,340	3,285	3,340	5,375	6,776	4,212	3,591
NEW KOWLOON		5,475[16]	5,680[16]	6,230	3,380	4,347	4,821	14,271	12,715	10,916	16,987
INDIA [28,17]	U	60,000	61,000	40,000	58,000	67,000	89,000	86,000	63,000	..	..
		0.6	0.5	0.3	0.5	0.5	0.7	0.6	0.4	..	..
IRAN [6]	T	..	..	..	69,587	98,015	68,522	71,637	114,031	152,120	155,543
		..	..	..	2.1	2.9	2.0	2.0	3.1	4.0	4.0
ESFAHAN [6]		..	..	1,961	..	..	..	..	..	5,617	4,610
MASHHAD [6]		..	..	4,324	..	..	..	..	..	4,363	4,179
TABRIZ [6]		..	..	1,004	..	..	..	..	..	6,585	5,636
TEHERAN [6]		..	..	14,763	10,803	12,428	10,078	10,831	15,073	10,198	13,073
IRAQ [32,34]	T	17,141	22,735	22,229	24,674	31,823	..	..	..	..	..
		1.7	2.2	2.1	2.2	2.8	..	..	..	..	..
ISRAEL [29]	T	47,240	50,870	51,710	55,610	55,640	42,830	35,450	30,500	30,740	33,780
		15.0	15.5	15.3	16.1	15.8	11.9	9.6	8.0	7.9	8.6
	U	42,690	45,530	44,050	47,920	48,030	37,380	28,090	23,560	24,860	28,820
		15.9	16.9	16.0	16.2	16.0	11.9	8.7	7.1	..	..
	R	4,550	5,340	7,660	7,690	7,610	5,450	7,360	6,940	5,880	4,960
		9.7	9.1	12.2	15.1	14.6	11.8	15.7	15.1	..	..
BAT-YAM [29]		2,524	1,832	1,846	1,495	1,456	1,144	910	588	430	924
HAIFA [29]		2,770	3,220	2,420	2,600	2,140	1,700	1,450	670	1,070	1,350
JERUSALEM [29,30]		4,764	5,100	3,940	4,250	4,160	3,300	2,250	2,370	2,580	2,930
TEL AVIV-YAFO [29]		3,300	3,090	3,100	3,420	2,730	2,590	1,690	1,680	1,650	1,550
JAPAN	T	1,807,581	1,905,112	1,316,100	1,356,286	1,503,844	1,508,260	1,549,362	1,493,023	1,268,626	1,151,699
		16.9	17.5	11.9	12.2	13.5	13.2	13.5	12.9	10.9	9.8
	U	1,537,721	1,605,368	1,056,901	1,091,654	1,249,950	1,242,831	1,267,367	1,213,946	1,027,310	1,091,078
	R	269,860	299,744	259,199	264,632	273,894	265,429	281,995	279,077	241,316	60,621
NAGOYA		40,476	34,321	22,170	24,760	31,038	34,222	31,477	26,244	23,063	21,751
OSAKA		46,830	46,329	17,380	23,900	33,183	41,017	35,680	37,692	30,452	32,494
TOKYO		228,091	207,126	116,528	135,239	165,587	184,057	194,804	163,621	141,724	135,151
YOKOHAMA		65,225	54,274	34,814	32,856	38,301	38,465	38,060	38,614	35,956	35,002
JORDAN [32,34]	T	4,021	4,063	2,951	4,747	2,202	..	..	..	..	..
		1.6	1.6	1.1	1.8	0.8	..	..	..	..	..

Table 16 (continued)

CONVENTIONAL DWELLINGS CONSTRUCTED ANNUALLY: NUMBER AND RATE PER THOUSAND MID-YEAR POPULATION

COUNTRIES, AREAS, CITIES OR URBAN AGGLOMERATIONS	TOTAL:T URBAN:U RURAL:R	1972	1973	1974	1975	1976	1977	1978	1979	1980	1981
(1)		(2)	(3)	(4)	(5)	(6)	(7)	(8)	(9)	(10)	(11)
ASIA (continued)											
KOREA, REPUBLIC OF[33,34] .... T		60,832	96,551	109,347	101,887	88,323	..	..	..	..	..
		1.8	2.8	3.2	2.9	2.5	..	..	..	..	..
KUWAIT[33] .... T		4,975	5,247	4,208	7,231	8,154	..	..	..	..	..
		5.9	5.9	4.5	7.2	7.9	..	..	..	..	..
MONGOLIA[32] .... T		1,600	1,900	1,600	4,100	1,300	..	..	..	..	..
		1.2	1.4	1.1	2.8	0.9	..	..	..	..	..
SINGAPORE .... T		25,530	25,167	31,806	32,321	35,169	33,318	36,379	29,968	23,369	16,697
		11.9	11.5	14.3	14.3	15.3	14.3	15.5	12.6	9.7	6.8
SRI LANKA .... T		..	..	..	294,422[14]	106,589	94,505	116,942	145,450	148,187	39,510
	U	..	..	..	42,499[14]	12,683	11,224	13,678	19,581	17,956	5,400
	R	..	..	..	251,923[14]	93,906	83,281	103,264	125,869	130,231	34,110
SYRIAN ARAB REPUBLIC[32,39] .... T		27,055	15,579	22,655	24,496	34,653	..	..	..	..	..
		4.1	2.3	3.2	3.3	4.6	..	..	..	..	..
TURKEY .... T		88,231	96,163	84,199	97,431[18]	102,110	119,409	120,615	124,297	139,207[19]	118,778
		2.4	2.5	2.2	2.4[18]	2.5	2.9	2.8	2.9	3.1[19]	2.6
YEMEN SANA'A[6,16]		..	..	..	..	..	2,423	2,862	2,172	1,674	2,362
EUROPE											
AUSTRIA .... T		50,373	44,193	50,131	48,570	44,586	45,447	51,525	52,972	78,457	51,038
		6.7	5.9	6.7	6.5	5.9	6.0	6.9	7.1	10.4	6.8
	U	30,217	24,924	29,865	28,076	25,037	24,977	29,710	31,476	36,416	24,662
	R	20,156	19,269	20,266	20,494	19,549	20,470	21,815	21,496	42,041	26,376
GRAZ		1,718	2,146	3,422	2,647	2,016	3,109	1,586	1,285	2,829	1,790
LINZ		1,174	1,455	2,009	1,659	971	992	1,135	966	671	2,606
SALZBURG		2,842	2,055	2,887	1,943	1,503	983	923	929	1,102	438
WIEN		10,072	6,927	5,813	7,144	6,412	7,568	14,670	15,503	11,259	5,552
BELGIUM[3] .... T		53,494	64,129	67,428	80,258	78,415	74,491	68,100	70,451	48,688	34,113[19]
		5.5	6.6	6.9	8.2	8.0	7.6	6.9	7.2	4.9	3.5[19]
BRUXELLES[3,4]		2,911	7,147	5,298	5,604	6,207	5,540	4,247	4,113	2,480	1,146[19]
		2.7	6.7	5.0	5.3	5.9	5.3	4.1	4.0	2.5	1.1[19]
BULGARIA .... T		46,542	54,209	44,065	57,151	67,626	75,885	67,796	66,223	74,308	71,419
		5.4	6.3	5.1	6.6	7.7	8.6	7.7	7.5	8.4	8.0
	U	38,682	46,424	37,017	51,210	62,074	68,071	60,617	60,169	66,658	64,313
		8.2	9.6	7.3	10.0	12.1	13.0	11.4	11.1	12.1	11.5
	R	7,860	7,785	7,048	5,941	5,552	7,814	7,179	6,054	7,650	7,106
		2.0	2.1	1.9	1.6	1.5	2.2	2.1	1.8	2.3	2.2
PLOVDIV		2,557	2,925	1,596	3,532	3,897	5,035	5,160	5,185	5,059	5,044
		9.9	10.6	5.4	11.7	12.7	15.8	15.7	15.4	14.6	14.2
ROUSSE		1,377	2,600	1,368	1,650	2,226	2,151	2,123	1,818	2,334	2,098
		8.6	15.8	8.1	10.0	13.8	13.0	12.7	10.7	13.6	12.0
SOFIA		6,781	9,608	4,519	13,417	13,795	15,527	12,703	12,176	14,648	16,142
		7.4	10.3	4.7	13.9	14.1	15.7	12.5	11.7	13.9	15.2
VARNA		1,959	2,401	2,860	3,368	4,176	4,146	3,621	3,990	4,169	3,858
		8.0	9.4	10.8	12.9	16.2	15.5	13.1	14.1	14.4	13.2
CHANNEL ISLANDS JERSEY .... T		454	633	458	541	703	661	733	356	194	204
		6.2	8.6	6.2	7.3	9.4	8.8	9.7	4.7	2.5	2.6

Table 16 (continued)

CONVENTIONAL DWELLINGS CONSTRUCTED ANNUALLY: NUMBER AND RATE PER THOUSAND MID-YEAR POPULATION

COUNTRIES, AREAS, CITIES OR URBAN AGGLOMERATIONS	TOTAL:T URBAN:U RURAL:R	1972	1973	1974	1975	1976	1977	1978	1979	1980	1981
(1)		(2)	(3)	(4)	(5)	(6)	(7)	(8)	(9)	(10)	(11)
EUROPE (continued)											
CZECHOSLOVAKIA.....................T		115,559	118,594	128,988	144,678	132,451	134,820	129,330	122,741	128,876	95,387
		8.0	8.1	8.8	9.8	8.9	9.0	8.5	8.1	8.4	6.2
BRATISLAVA		3,692	4,682	4,818	7,480	4,700	6,013	5,768	5,073	6,800	4,316
		11.7	14.6	14.7	22.2	13.6	17.0	15.9	13.6	17.9	11.2
PRAHA		7,065	6,874	10,268	12,512	9,860	11,097	11,451	10,127	8,740	6,077
		6.5	6.3	8.9	10.7	8.4	9.4	9.7	8.5	7.3	5.1
DENMARK..........................T		50,006	55,566	48,595	35,510	39,218	36,276	34,218	31,064	30,345	..
		10.0	11.1	9.6	7.0	7.7	7.1	6.7	6.1	5.9	..
ALBORG		1,873	1,700	1,833	1,193	1,673	1,038	1,027	1,055	970	..
		12.1	11.0	11.9	7.7	10.8	6.7	6.7	6.9	6.3	..
ARHUS		3,362	3,048	2,199	2,164	2,231	1,420	1,249	1,048	1,114	..
		13.8	12.4	8.9	8.8	9.1	5.8	5.1	4.3	4.5	..
COPENHAGEN[4]		8,412	9,217	9,830	5,761	4,125	4,350	4,292	3,647	6,879	..
		6.2	6.9	7.4	4.4	3.2	3.4	3.4	2.6	5.0	..
ODENSE		2,103	2,484	1,515	921	1,411	1,650	1,226	955	974	..
		12.6	14.8	9.0	5.5	8.4	9.8	7.3	5.7	5.8	..
FINLAND...........................T		59,937	62,358	73,033	69,408	57,498	56,966	55,287	50,301	49,648	..
		12.9	13.4	15.6	14.7	12.2	12.0	11.6	10.6	10.3	..
	U	41,020	41,797	49,723	45,684	36,137	36,288	34,142	31,767	31,336	..
		16.6	16.0	18.4	16.6	13.0	12.9	12.0	11.2	11.0	..
	R	18,917	20,561	23,310	23,724	21,361	20,678	21,145	18,534	18,312	..
		8.7	10.0	11.8	12.1	11.0	10.7	11.0	9.7	9.5	..
ESPOO		2,641	2,417	2,429	2,938	1,620	2,057	1,964	2,090	2,414	..
		25.3	22.0	21.2	24.8	13.3	16.4	15.3	15.9	17.8	..
HELSINKI		5,031	4,266	5,508	4,029	3,608	4,272	4,192	3,927	3,771	..
		9.8	8.3	10.9	8.0	7.3	8.7	8.6	8.1	7.8	..
TAMPERE		2,762	2,189	2,860	2,661	2,182	2,366	2,464	1,783	1,852	..
		17.2	13.3	17.3	16.0	13.1	14.3	14.8	10.7	11.2	..
TURKU		2,313	2,563	2,870	2,580	2,235	2,009	1,919	1,358	1,453	..
		14.7	16.0	17.7	15.7	13.6	12.2	11.6	8.3	8.9	..
FRANCE[10] ....T		622,473	667,906	641,038	539,202	566,885	504,248	469,155	461,994	500,679	488,527
	U	462,141	482,163	458,091	396,804	396,889	334,840	301,915	283,179	313,886	318,510
	R	160,332	185,743	182,947	142,398	169,996	169,408	167,240	178,815	186,793	170,017
LYON[4,10]		15,584	11,322	15,725	10,951	9,731	7,140	6,115	5,765	6,425	5,738
MARSEILLE[4,10]		10,033	7,471	6,276	5,927	7,171	6,811	14,027	9,226	6,777	8,809
PARIS[4,10]		87,724	108,135	86,612	64,487	61,828	48,667	41,667	34,887	37,488	45,301
TOULOUSE[4,10]		7,119	5,863	6,086	6,877	5,601	4,362	2,518	3,013	3,446	3,153
GERMANY, FEDERAL REPUBLIC OF-#.....T		660,636	714,226	604,387	436,829	392,380	409,012	368,145	357,751	388,904	365,462
		10.7	11.5	9.7	7.1	6.4	6.7	6.0	5.8	6.3	5.9
	U	216,301	219,095	184,101	136,874	108,428	127,403	90,080	85,179	92,611	92,892
	R	444,335	495,131	420,286	299,955	283,952	281,609	278,065	272,572	296,293	272,570
BERLIN		18,237	17,418	19,822	14,784	13,049	17,381	7,931	6,011	6,783	6,823
HAMBURG		14,856	14,959	12,950	9,104	9,109	10,707	5,407	4,091	5,636	5,676
MUNCHEN		22,083	16,803	14,313	7,719	5,187	5,410	4,379	3,970	6,757	6,726
BONN		2,897	3,594	2,181	1,485	1,510	1,123	1,189	879	1,350	1,284
GERMAN DEMOCRATIC REPUBLIC[31,#].....T		117,026	125,769	138,301	140,793	150,617	..	..	..	..	..
		6.9	7.4	8.2	8.4	9.0	..	..	..	..	..

Table 16 (continued)

CONVENTIONAL DWELLINGS CONSTRUCTED ANNUALLY: NUMBER AND RATE PER THOUSAND MID-YEAR POPULATION

COUNTRIES, AREAS, CITIES OR URBAN AGGLOMERATIONS	TOTAL:T URBAN:U RURAL:R	1972	1973	1974	1975	1976	1977	1978	1979	1980	1981
(1)		(2)	(3)	(4)	(5)	(6)	(7)	(8)	(9)	(10)	(11)
EUROPE (continued)											
GREECE.....................T		178,558	188,105	81,616	120,869	128,601	158,269	186,981	189,195	136,044	108,174
		20.1	21.1	9.1	13.4	14.0	17.0	19.8	19.8	14.1	11.0
	U	128,603	132,205	49,137	82,301	89,759	110,469	134,644	128,096	74,102	50,983
	R	32,416	30,726	20,287	25,844	25,341	30,442	32,665	37,701	38,463	38,102
ATHENS[4]		83,824	75,041	27,947	7,053	48,868	56,878	74,652	62,583	34,116	21,244
		..	..	..	..	..	..	..	..	..	7.0
IRAKLIO[4]		16,647	16,058	4,845	1,486	10,354	17,455	6,950	6,696	8,623	5,259
		..	..	..	..	..	..	..	..	..	7.4
PATRAI[4]		4,051	4,979	1,753	2,699	3,627	3,103	5,421	4,341	1,910	2,585
		..	..	..	..	..	..	..	..	..	18.2
SOLONIQUE[4]		993	1,490	1,510	1,950	2,019	2,071	3,224	2,690	1,316	1,670
		..	..	..	..	..	..	..	..	..	15.0
HUNGARY....................T		90,194	85,211	87,843	99,588	93,905	91,396	88,153	88,196	89,065	76,975[20]
		8.7	8.2	8.4	9.5	8.9	8.8	8.3	8.2	8.3[21]	7.2[20]
	U	51,931	50,733	54,804	61,826	56,879	58,823	55,542	58,308	57,526[21]	49,228[20]
		9.9	9.6	10.3	11.4	10.4	10.6	9.9	10.3	10.1[21]	..[20]
	R	38,263	34,478	33,039	37,762	37,026	34,573	32,611	29,888	31,539[21]	27,747[20]
		7.4	6.7	6.4	7.4	7.3	6.8	6.5	6.0	6.3[21]	..[20]
BUDAPEST		15,503	14,713	15,498	19,916	16,474	17,804	16,386	18,016	16,908	16,938[20]
DEBRECEN		2,787	2,614	2,321	2,781	2,176	2,401	2,298	2,293	2,163	1,576[20]
MISKOLC		1,837	2,334	3,445	2,852	2,726	2,204	2,387	2,270	1,813	1,595[20]
SZEGED		1,833	1,826	1,794	2,918	3,721	2,551	2,617	1,863	2,297	1,963[20]
ICELAND[31,32].................T		1,930	2,220	2,193	2,068	2,172	..	..	..	..	..
		9.2	10.6	10.0	9.4	9.9	..	..	..	..	..
IRELAND[22]...................T		..	..	..	26,892	24,000	24,548	25,444	26,544	27,785	28,917
		..	..	..	8.5	7.4	7.5	7.7	7.9	8.2	8.4
ITALY[41]....................T		259,004	196,640	180,698	219,647	184,276	..	..	..	..	..
		4.8	3.6	3.3	3.9	3.3	..	..	..	..	..
LUXEMBOURG[34,37].............T		2,235	2,468	3,408	3,308	3,300	..	..	..	..	..
		6.4	7.1	9.5	9.2	9.2	..	..	..	..	..
MALTA[41]....................T		2,853	865	1,119	907	1,075	..	..	..	..	..
		8.9	2.7	3.5	3.0	3.6	..	..	..	..	..
NETHERLANDS.................T		152,272	155,412	146,174	120,774	106,813	111,047	105,825	87,522	113,756	117,759
AMSTERDAM		3,096	2,024	4,237	3,312	3,056	4,433	1,203	1,205	1,853	2,983
ROTTERDAM		2,214	1,743	1,996	1,131	753	987	2,078	2,289	4,278	6,306
GRAVENHAGE		695	846	1,180	1,462	2,280	1,177	1,549	1,371	1,685	2,243
UTRECHT		171	45	206	131	341	310	762	936	1,226	931
NORWAY[23]...................T		43,578	44,714	41,557	43,548	42,681	38,597	39,605	37,160	38,092	34,697
		11.1	11.3	10.4	10.9	10.6	9.5	9.8	9.1	9.3	8.5
BERGEN[23]		2,815	2,560	2,010	1,843	1,747	1,308	1,880	1,363	1,526	1,206
		13.2	12.0	9.4	8.6	8.2	6.2	8.9	6.5	7.3	5.8
OSLO[23]		4,419	5,555	3,526	4,409	5,374	3,070	2,269	3,053	3,529	2,851
		9.3	11.8	7.6	9.5	11.6	6.7	4.9	6.7	7.8	6.3
TRONDHEIM[23]		2,058	2,172	1,625	1,570	1,704	949	1,118	1,087	1,115	708
		15.8	16.4	12.2	11.7	12.6	7.0	8.3	8.1	8.3	5.3

Table 16 (continued)

CONVENTIONAL DWELLINGS CONSTRUCTED ANNUALLY: NUMBER AND RATE PER THOUSAND MID-YEAR POPULATION

COUNTRIES, AREAS, CITIES OR URBAN AGGLOMERATIONS	TOTAL:T URBAN:U RURAL:R	1972	1973	1974	1975	1976	1977	1978	1979	1980	1981
(1)		(2)	(3)	(4)	(5)	(6)	(7)	(8)	(9)	(10)	(11)
EUROPE (continued)											
POLAND...........................T		205,500	227,100	249,800	248,100	263,500	266,100	283,600	278,000	217,100	187,000
		6.2	6.8	7.4	7.2	7.6	7.6	8.1	7.8	6.1	5.2
	U	154,900	173,100	194,800	192,100	206,700	206,600	226,200	221,600	171,900	150,500
		8.8	9.6	10.5	10.2	10.7	10.4	11.2	10.8	8.2	7.1
	R	50,600	54,000	55,000	56,000	56,800	59,500	57,400	56,400	45,200	36,500
		3.2	3.5	3.6	3.6	3.7	3.9	3.8	3.7	3.0	2.4
KRAKOW		5,700	6,100	7,200	6,200	5,600	6,000	8,300	6,500	5,200	3,900
		9.4	9.3	10.8	9.1	8.0	8.4	11.5	9.2	7.3	5.4
LODZ		8,300	8,700	9,200	10,000	10,400	8,600	9,000	8,800	4,900	4,100
		10.7	11.1	11.7	12.6	12.9	10.5	10.9	10.6	5.8	4.8
WARSAWA		14,700	18,700	20,100	20,100	14,500	16,200	13,200	13,500	7,900	10,400
		10.9	13.5	14.3	14.1	10.0	10.6	8.5	8.6	4.9	6.4
WROCLAW		3,700	4,800	5,600	5,400	4,100	5,300	6,500	7,100	4,100	3,600
		6.8	8.6	9.9	9.4	7.0	9.0	10.8	11.7	6.6	5.8
PORTUGAL [40]....................T		43,679	44,581	46,784	35,411	33,196	..	..	..	..	..
		5.1	5.2	5.3	3.7	..	..	..	..	..	..
ROMANIA..........................T		135,969	149,128	154,345	165,431	139,443	145,039	166,750	191,566	197,846	..
		6.6	7.2	7.3	7.8	6.5	6.7	7.6	8.7	8.9	..
SAN MARINO.......................T		..	..	..	..	129	144	165	143	136	120
		..	..	..	..	6.7	7.3	..	7.1	6.7	5.8
	U	..	..	..	..	128	144	165	143	134	120
	R	..	..	..	..	1	-	-	-	2	-
SAN MARINO		..	..	..	..	13	13	25	14	47	35
SPAIN............................T		456,058	391,512	421,151	541,867	416,566	410,850	472,803	405,808	435,789[24]	..
		13.2	11.2	12.0	15.3	11.6	11.3	12.9	10.9	11.6	..
BARCELONA		19,337	18,509	18,015	22,570	14,495	14,096	12,567	10,035	14,383[24]	..
		11.1	10.7	10.4	13.0	8.3	..	..	..	8.2	..
MADRID		32,676	28,229	25,903	29,141	20,727	16,326	16,349	14,616	17,079[24]	..
		10.4	8.9	8.2	9.1	6.5	..	..	..	5.4	..
SEVILLA		9,125	5,904	9,471	8,733	7,388	4,574	7,788	5,128	11,209[24]	..
		16.4	10.5	16.6	15.0	12.5	..	..	..	17.4	..
VALENCIA		9,715	8,735	8,884	13,737	11,301	9,201	8,408	6,448	8,735[24]	..
		14.6	13.0	13.0	19.7	16.0	..	..	..	11.7	..
SWEDEN...........................T		104,046	97,484	85,311	74,499	55,812	54,878	53,742	55,491	51,438	51,597
		12.8	12.0	10.5	9.1	6.8	6.7	6.5	6.7	6.2	6.2
STOCKHOLM		2,889	4,226	4,977	5,464	3,187	2,527	1,726	2,676	2,117	2,378
		4.0	6.1	7.4	8.2	4.8	3.8	2.7	4.1	3.3	3.7
GOTEBORG		5,676	3,976	5,118	3,729	2,154	2,089	1,886	1,762	2,203	1,400
		12.3	8.8	11.4	8.4	4.9	4.7	4.3	4.0	5.1	3.3
MALMO		4,673	4,198	2,872	2,031	1,390	1,046	649	1,190	734	826
		4.0	6.1	7.4	8.2	4.8	3.8	2.7	4.1	3.3	3.7
UPPSALA		3,055	2,442	1,359	1,403	1,260	1,143	1,236	908	1,145	1,461
		23.0	18.1	9.9	10.2	9.1	8.1	8.7	6.3	7.8	9.9
SWITZERLAND......................T		74,643	83,273	76,628	57,689	36,920	..	..	..	..	..
		11.7	13.0	11.9	9.0	5.8	..	..	..	..	..

Table 16 (continued)

CONVENTIONAL DWELLINGS CONSTRUCTED ANNUALLY: NUMBER AND RATE PER THOUSAND MID-YEAR POPULATION

COUNTRIES, AREAS, CITIES OR URBAN AGGLOMERATIONS	TOTAL:T URBAN:U RURAL:R	1972	1973	1974	1975	1976	1977	1978	1979	1980	1981
(1)		(2)	(3)	(4)	(5)	(6)	(7)	(8)	(9)	(10)	(11)
EUROPE (continued)											
UNITED KINGDOM-ENGLAND AND WALES...T		287,300	264,000	241,200	278,700	278,700	276,000	254,000	220,700	213,000	179,500
		5.9	5.4	4.9	5.7	5.7	5.6	5.2	4.5	4.3	3.6
BIRMINGHAM[25]		3,000	2,800	3,700	4,400	5,700	5,200	4,000	3,700	2,300	3,200
		2.7	2.6	3.4	4.1	5.4	5.0	3.8	3.6	2.2	3.1
LEEDS[25]		1,800	2,600	3,000	3,400	3,400	2,400	2,500	2,200	2,800	1,800
		3.1	4.5	5.3	6.2	6.2	4.5	3.4	3.1	3.9	2.5
LIVERPOOL[25]		2,900	2,900	1,900	2,400	1,400	1,700	1,400	1,700	1,800	1,200
		4.9	5.0	3.4	4.3	2.6	3.2	2.7	3.3	3.5	2.3
LONDON[25]		28,400	24,700	28,600	30,200	31,600	30,800	26,400	21,200	22,400	18,100
		3.9	3.4	4.0	4.2	4.5	4.4	3.8	3.1	3.3	2.6
SCOTLAND..........................T		31,992	30,033	28,336	34,323	36,527	27,320	25,759	23,665	20,516	19,909
		6.1	5.8	5.4	6.6	7.0	5.3	5.0	4.6	4.0	3.9
ABERDEEN		201	795	241	1,358	1,837	1,678	1,822	1,204	1,210	1,250
DUNDEE		1,183	941	874	468	772	316	388	603	468	511
EDINBURGH		1,876	1,965	1,649	1,575	2,080	1,518	2,159	2,554	1,373	1,723
GLASGOW		2,938	4,094	1,889	2,266	2,733	2,284	2,066	1,528	1,381	3,079
YUGOSLAVIA[32]......................T		133,875	134,819	145,000	145,500	149,900	..	..	..	..	..
		6.4	6.4	6.9	6.8	7.0	..	..	..	..	..
OCEANIA											
AUSTRALIA[26].....................T		143,806	150,610	150,028	141,100	132,026	144,788	128,936	117,134	129,268	145,120
		10.9	11.3	11.0	10.2	9.5	12.3	9.0	8.1	8.7	9.8
	U	97,202	101,867	96,599	86,630	84,968	91,190	78,023	69,897	71,047	81,202
	R	46,604	48,743	53,429	54,470	45,198	53,598	50,913	47,237	58,221	61,990
BRISBANE		11,244	13,681	13,203	9,880	9,533	10,379	10,546	10,116	10,576	11,040
CANBERRA		3,898	4,088	3,669	4,920	4,963	3,484	3,253	2,204	2,013	2,357
MELBOURNE		28,910	30,406	27,913	26,830	23,012	25,647	21,713	17,620	16,364	15,825
SYDNEY		30,120	29,094	26,904	22,850	19,866	19,038	18,582	20,846	24,305	29,519
FIJI[34,37].......................T		477	361	594	468	602	..	..	..	..	..
		0.9	0.7	1.1	0.8	1.0	..	..	..	..	..
NEW CALEDONIA.....................T		2,043	2,774	2,025	1,842	717	575	500	376	390	454
		16.6	22.0	15.7	13.9	5.3	4.2	3.6	2.7	2.8	..
NEW ZEALAND.......................T		..	..	32,088	34,326	33,905	28,638	24,240	19,181	16,003	14,260[27]
		..	..	10.6	11.1	10.5	9.1	7.7	6.1	5.1	4.5[27]
	U	..	..	24,231	29,250	27,436	24,409	20,128	15,685	12,899	11,250[27]
		..	..	9.6	11.3	10.5	9.3	7.6	5.9	4.9	4.2[27]
	R	..	..	7,857	5,076	5,469	4,229	4,112	3,496	3,104	3,010[27]
		..	..	15.5	10.0	10.7	8.2	8.0	6.8	6.0	5.8[27]
AUCKLAND		..	..	851	1,166	532	524	327	472	339	387[27]
		..	..	5.6	7.7	3.5	3.5	2.2	3.2	2.3	2.7[27]
CHRISTCHURCH		..	..	1,772	1,775	2,041	1,703	1,257	771	522	378[27]
		..	..	10.4	10.4	11.9	9.9	7.4	4.6	3.1	2.3[27]
MANUKAU		..	..	2,193	2,619	2,563	2,304	1,459	1,737	1,199	1,243[27]
		..	..	17.2	19.2	18.3	15.9	9.8	11.5	7.7	7.8[27]
WELLINGTON		..	..	983	1,003	1,037	797	495	336	408	248[27]
		..	..	7.1	7.2	7.4	5.7	3.5	2.4	3.0	1.8[27]
PAPUA NEW GUINEA[32,38].............T		1,621	1,313	1,486	1,897	1,913	..	..	..	..	..
		0.6	0.5	0.6	0.7	0.7	..	..	..	..	..

Table 16 (continued)

CONVENTIONAL DWELLINGS CONSTRUCTED ANNUALLY: NUMBER AND RATE PER THOUSAND MID-YEAR POPULATION

COUNTRIES, AREAS, CITIES OR URBAN AGGLOMERATIONS	TOTAL:T URBAN:U RURAL:R	1972	1973	1974	1975	1976	1977	1978	1979	1980	1981
(1)		(2)	(3)	(4)	(5)	(6)	(7)	(8)	(9)	(10)	(11)
U.S.S.R.											
U.S.S.R.	T	..	..	..	..	..	..	..	..	..	1,998,000
		..	..	..	..	..	..	..	..	..	7.5
	U	..	..	..	..	..	..	..	..	..	1,463,000
		..	..	..	..	..	..	..	..	..	8.6
	R	..	..	..	..	..	..	..	..	..	535,000
		..	..	..	..	..	..	..	..	..	5.5
KIEV		..	..	..	..	..	..	..	..	..	27,000
LENINGRAD		..	..	..	..	..	..	..	..	..	26,000
MOSKVA		..	..	..	..	..	..	..	..	..	71,000
TASHKENT		..	..	..	..	..	..	..	..	..	15,000

Sources: United Nations, *Compendium of Housing Statistics 1975–1977* and United Nations, *Compendium of Human Settlements statistics 1983*.

Notes: From 31 on, unless otherwise stated, the number of conventional dwellings constructed refers to all dwellings including extensions and those made available by restoration and conversion.

. . Data not available.

‡ The date which relate to the Federal Republic of Germany and the German Democratic Republic include the relevant data relating to Berlin for which separate data have not been supplied. This is without prejudice to any question of status which may be involved.

[1] Construction of residential buildings only and refer to permits issued.

[2] Construction of modern buildings reported to town councils in Mbabane and Manzini.

[3] Construction work started.

[4] Urban agglomeration.

[5] Data for 1972–9 exclude private construction.

[6] Data refer to building permits issued.

[7] Data refer to residential construction only.

[8] Excluding dwellings in publicly owned structures.

[9] For 1973 and 1974, data on new construction exclude the private sector in certain communes.

[10] Construction authorized.

[11] Data for 1981 are provisional. Private construction is based on permits issued.

[12] Public construction only.

[13] Private construction is based on permits issued.

[14] Dwellings constructed during the period 1971–5.

[15] Data for 1972–5 exclude a small number of units built in new towns and rural areas.

[16] Private construction only.

[17] Official estimates.

[18] Data refer to occupancy permits.

[19] Calculated on census population.

[20] Excluding new construction of secondary dwellings.

[21] Calculated on census population enumerated 1 July 1980.

[22] Including estimated number of flats converted from houses.

[23] Data are provisional.

[24] Calculated on census population enumerated 1 Mar. 1981.

[25] Construction of dwellings authorized by city authorities. Including dwellings beyond urban agglomerations.

[26] Data for 1972–6 and 1981 exclude dwellings constructed in the Northern Territory. Data for 1972 and 1973 include alterations and additions to dwellings. Data for 1981 refer to construction started.

[27] Calculated on census population enumerated 24 Mar. 1981.

[28] Including data for the Indian-held part of Jannu and Kashmir, the final status of which has not yet been determined.

[29] Including data for East Jerusalem and Israeli residents in certain other territories under occupation by Israeli military forces since June 1967.

[30] Designation and data provided by Israel. The position of the United Nations on the question of Jerusalem is contained in General Assembly resolution 181(ii) and subsequent resolutions of the General Assembly and the Security Council concerning this question.

[31] Dwellings in residential buildings (Australia, prior to 1970; Ireland, prior to 1971; Puerto Rico, prior to 1974).

[32] New construction only (Puerto Rico, prior to 1974; Sweden, new construction, excluding extensions).

[33] Construction authorized.

[34] Number of residential buildings.

[35] Excluding construction by the Directorate of Ports, Railways, and Transport.

[36] Number of works.

[37] Construction by the private sector.

[38] Fiscal year ending 30 June of the year started (Puerto Rico: beginning 1974).

[39] Beginning 1972, including unauthorized construction.

[40] Including the adjacent islands.

[41] See general *Notes*.

Table 17

Community water supply: population supplied by house connections and public standposts—number and percentage, developing countries, urban and rural, 1970 and 1980 (thousands)

COUNTRIES COUNTRY OR AREA	URBAN POPULATION SUPPLIED												RURAL POPULATION WITH REASONABLE ACCESS[1]		TOTAL	
	BY HOUSE CONNEXIONS				BY PUBLIC STANDPOSTS				TOTAL URBAN							
	1970		1980		1970		1980		1970		1980		1980		1980	
	NUMBER	PERCENT	NUMBER	PERCENT	NUMBER	PERCENT	NUMBER	PERCENT	NUMBER	PERCENT	NUMBER	PERCENT	NUMBER	PERCENT	NUMBER	PERCENT
(1)	(2)	(3)	(4)	(5)	(6)	(7)	(8)	(9)	(10)	(11)	(12)	(13)	(14)	(15)	(16)	(17)
AFRICA																
BENIN..........................	33	9	165	10	313	86	248	16	346	94	413	26	300	15	713	20
BURKINA FASO...................	40	20	155	16	100	49	100	11	140	68	255	27	1,612	31	1,867	30
BURUNDI........................	15	15	49	..	60	62	148	68	75	77	197	90	799	20	996	24
EGYPT..........................	11,170	75	13,770	69	2,830	19	3,680	19	14,000	94	17,450	88	14,540	64	31,990	75
GHANA..........................	652	22	1,100	26	1,483	51	1,915	46	2,135	73	3,015	72	2,439	33	5,454	47
GUINEA.........................	337	75	180	16	100	22	589	53	437	97	769	69	90	2	859	17
KENYA..........................	1,000	90	1,436	59	72	77	615	26	1,072	97	2,051	85	2,055	15	4,106	26
LESOTHO........................	5	19	36	24	22	81	19	13	27	100	55	37	126	11	181	14
LIBYAN ARAB JAMAHIRIYA.........	650	54	2,466	95	200	17	130	5	850	71	2,596	100	584	90	3,180	98
MADAGASCAR.....................	236	25	330	19	594	63	1,050	61	830	87	1,380	80	500	7	1,880	22
MALI...........................	160	26	248	20	20	3	203	17	180	29	451	37	8	0	459	6
MAURITANIA.....................	80	91	71	20	6	7	212	60	86	98	283	80	925	85	1,208	84
MOROCCO........................	2,200	39	3,704	44	3,000	53	4,715	56	5,200	91	8,419	100	..	..	..	..
NIGER..........................	40	12	203	29	180	55	83	12	220	68	286	41	1,547	32	1,833	33
SENEGAL........................	300	29	600	33	722	69	800	44	1,022	98	1,400	77	980	25	2,380	42
SIERRA LEONE...................	102	27	185	20	180	53	277	30	282	75	462	50	45	2	507	16
TUNISIA........................	1,200	53	2,480	71	850	38	1,020	29	2,050	91	3,500	100	470	17	3,970	63
TOGO...........................	34	13	100	14	214	84	390	56	248	97	490	70	565	31	1,055	42
AMERICA, NORTH																
COSTA RICA.....................	611	91	1,041	95	46	7	55	5	657	98	1,096	100	761	68	1,857	84
DOMINICAN REPUBLIC.............	934	55	1,642	60	291	17	688	25	1,225	72	2,330	85	897	33	3,227	59
EL SALVADOR....................	540	37	1,171	62	446	31	110	6	986	68	1,281	67	1,049	40	2,370	52
GUATEMALA......................	725	45	1,377	51	858	35	1,026	38	1,583	98	2,403	89	828	18	3,231	45
HONDURAS.......................	475	65	719	46	233	32	63	4	708	97	782	50	1,012	40	1,794	44
MEXICO.........................	18,840	64	26,800	62	3,290	11	800	2	22,130	75	27,600	64	10,300	43	37,900	56
NICARAGUA......................	296	34	985	68	227	26	345	24	523	60	1,330	91	125	10	1,455	53
PANAMA.........................	611	87	838	93	66	9	62	7	677	96	900	100	602	65	1,502	82
TRINIDAD AND TOBAGO............	297	54	550	79	59	11	150	21	356	65	700	100	370	93	1,070	98
AMERICA, SOUTH																
ARGENTINA......................	11,800	60	14,146	61	900	5	831	4	12,700	64	14,977	65	787	17	15,764	57
BOLIVIA........................	542	33	599	24	1,009	62	1,129	45	1,551	95	1,728	69	316	10	2,044	37
BRAZIL.........................	28,700	53	64,600	80	12,600	23	..	..	41,300	77	64,600	80	19,600	51	84,200	71
CHILE..........................	4,200	58	8,420	93	800	11	651	7	5,000	69	9,071	100	355	17	9,426	84
COLOMBIA.......................	9,493	73	11,840	74	2,000	15	4,160	26	11,493	88	16,000	100	7,110	79	23,110	92
ECUADOR........................	1,498	61	1,739	47	312	13	1,289	35	1,810	74	3,028	82	745	16	3,773	45
GUYANA.........................	200	75	222	90	60	23	25	10	260	98	247	100	347	60	594	72
PARAGUAY.......................	162	17	448	39	25	3	..	..	187	20	448	39	192	10	640	21
PERU...........................	3,580	51	6,227	57	620	9	1,180	11	4,200	60	7,407	68	1,210	21	8,617	51
URUGUAY........................	1,947	85	2,190	90	216	9	163	7	2,163	95	2,353	96	12	2	2,365	80
VENEZUELA......................	5,400	72	9,804	82	1,520	20	1,200	10	6,920	92	11,004	91	2,010	50	13,014	81

Table 17 (continued)

COUNTRY OR AREA	URBAN POPULATION SUPPLIED												RURAL POPULATION WITH REASONABLE ACCESS[1]		TOTAL	
	BY HOUSE CONNEXIONS				BY PUBLIC STANDPOSTS				TOTAL URBAN							
	1970		1980		1970		1980		1970		1980		1980		1980	
	NUMBER	PERCENT	NUMBER	PERCENT	NUMBER	PERCENT	NUMBER	PERCENT	NUMBER	PERCENT	NUMBER	PERCENT	NUMBER	PERCENT	NUMBER	PERCENT
(1)	(2)	(3)	(4)	(5)	(6)	(7)	(8)	(9)	(10)	(11)	(12)	(13)	(14)	(15)	(16)	(17)
ASIA																
AFGHANISTAN	125	10	136	7	200	15	385	21	325	25	521	28	1,100	8	1,621	10
BANGLADESH	750	16	..	..	1,100	24	..	..	1,850	41	2,600	26	32,000	40	34,600	38
BURMA	369	7	..	..	1,581	30	..	..	1,950	37	3,200	38	3,700	15	6,900	21
INDONESIA	5,000	23	..	..	2,500	12	..	..	7,500	35	17,700	35	18,000	19	35,700	24
INDIA	46,400	39	..	..	19,900	17	..	..	66,300	56	115,000	77	162,000	31	277,000	41
JORDAN	972	88	1,208	78	108	10	342	22	1,080	98	1,550	100	444	65	1,994	89
MALAYSIA	3,257	72	4,130	90	881	19	..	..	4,138	91	4,130	90	4,370	49	8,500	63
NEPAL	13	2	..	..	300	56	..	..	313	59	800	83	900	7	1,700	12
PAKISTAN	5,194	34	7,100	30	6,270	41	9,900	42	11,464	76	17,000	72	12,000	20	29,000	35
PHILIPPINES	7,350	55	9,303	53	1,312	10	2,012	12	8,662	65	11,315	65	13,034	43	24,349	51
REPUBLIC OF KOREA	10,430	84	21,800	86	549	4	0	0	10,979	88	21,800	86	7,800	61	29,600	78
SAUDI ARABIA	1,500	79	2,225	35	330	17	3,607	57	1,830	97	5,832	92	1,000	87	6,832	91
SINGAPORE	1,586	74	2,402	100	..	..	12	0	1,586	74	2,141	100	0	0	2,141	100
SRI LANKA	920	36	..	..	800	31	..	..	1,720	67	2,500	65	2,000	18	4,500	31
SYRIAN ARAB REPUBLIC	2,455	89	3,367	98	244	9	0	0	2,699	98	3,367	98	2,982	54	6,349	71
THAILAND	2,841	52	..	..	435	8	..	..	3,275	60	7,000	65	3,000	10	10,000	21
TURKEY	5,706	45	13,600	69	1,426	11	5	26	7,132	65	18,600	95	15,500	66	34,100	76
YEMEN, DEMOCRATIC	80	23	509	80	75	22	30	5	155	45	539	85	316	25	855	44
OCEANIA																
FIJI	144	100	171	70	..	..	58	24	144	100	229	94	260	66	489	77
WESTERN SAMOA	18	49	34	97	7	19	0	0	25	68	34	97	113	94	147	95

Sources: GWS, WHO, *The International Drinking Water Supply and Sanitation Decade: Review of National Baseline Data (as at 31 December 1980)* (1983), and WHO data in the *Global Review of Human Settlements*, Statistical Annex.

Notes: Only countries for which both 1970 and 1980 data are available are included. The total figures for 1980 are derived.

[1] In rural areas, 'reasonable access' implies that members of the household do not have to spend a disproportionate part of the day in fetching water.

[2] The classification is intended for statistical convenience and does not necessarily express a judgement about the stage reached by a particular country or area in the development process.

Table 18

Sanitation facilities. Population served by sewer connections and other systems: numberand percentage, developing countries or areas, urban and rural, 1980

COUNTRIES OR AREAS	URBAN POPULATION SERVED BY SEWER CONNECTION NUMBER	%	POPULATION SERVED BY OTHER SYSTEMS NUMBER	%	TOTAL URBAN POPULATION SERVED NUMBER	%	RURAL POPULATION WITH ADEQUATE SANITATION NUMBER	%	TOTAL POPULATION SERVED BY SEWAGE SYSTEMS NUMBER	%
(1)	(2)	(3)	(4)	(5)	(6)	(7)	(8)	(9)	(10)	(11)
AFRICA										
ANGOLA............................	240	20	240	20	480	40	1,000	15	1,480	19
BENIN............................	0	0	760	48	760	48	80	4	840	24
BURUNDI..........................	18	8	70	32	88	40	1,393	35	1,481	35
BURKINA FASO.....................	0	0	349	38	349	38	260	5	609	10
CAPE VERDE.......................	12	11	25	23	37	34	19	10	56	19
DJIBOUTI.........................	..	..	..	..	118	43	11	20	129	39
EGYPT............................	8,930	45	..	..	8,930	45	2,280	10	11,210	26
GHANA............................	160	4	1,780	43	1,940	47	1,226	17	3,166	27
GUINEA...........................	145	13	455	41	600	54	40	1	640	13
GUINEA-BISSAU....................	2	1	32	20	34	21	81	13	115	14
KENYA............................	1,180	49	960	40	2,140	89	2,590	19	4,730	30
LESOTHO..........................	15	10	5	3	20	13	162	14	182	14
LIBYAN ARAB JAMAHIRIYA...........	1,146	44	1,450	56	2,596	100	467	72	3,063	94
MADAGASCAR.......................	60	4	90	5	150	9	..	..	..	..
MAURITANIA.......................	18	5	..	..	18	5	..	..	..	..
MAURITIUS........................	225	55	185	45	410	100	492	90	902	94
MALAWI...........................	90	16	486	84	576	100	4,400	81	4,976	83
MALI.............................	10	1	945	78	955	79	6	0	961	13
NIGER............................	..	..	252	36	252	36	145	3	397	7
RWANDA...........................	0	0	140	60	140	60	2,500	50	2,640	51
SENEGAL..........................	91	5	1,720	95	1,811	100	79	2	1,890	33
SIERRA LEONE.....................	7	1	277	30	284	31	134	6	418	13
TOGO.............................	0	0	170	24	170	24	180	10	350	14
TUNISIA..........................	1,600	46	1,900	54	3,500	100	..	..	3,500	56
AMERICA, NORTH										
COSTA RICA.......................	471	43	548	50	1,019	93	916	92	1,935	87
DOMINICAN REPUBLIC...............	691	25	..	..	691	25	110	4	801	15
EL SALVADOR......................	914	48	610	32	1,524	80	688	26	2,212	49
GUATEMALA........................	945	35	270	10	1,215	45	920	20	2,135	29
HONDURAS.........................	672	43	94	6	766	49	658	26	1,424	35
MEXICO...........................	21,500	49	700	2	22,200	51	2,800	12	25,000	37
NICARAGUA........................	505	35	..	..	505	35	..	..	..	..
PANAMA...........................	556	62	..	..	556	62	261	28	817	45
TRINIDAD AND TOBAGO..............	165	24	500	71	665	95	350	88	1,015	93
AMERICA, SOUTH										
ARGENTINA........................	7,390	32	13,154	57	20,544	89	1,532	32	22,076	79
BOLIVIA..........................	579	23	337	14	916	37	116	4	1,032	18
BRAZIL...........................	25,900	32	..	..	25,900	32	..	..	..	..
CAYMAN ISLANDS...................	0	0	16	94	16	94	0	0	16	94
CHILE............................	6,251	69	2,764	30	9,015	99	..	..	..	..
COLOMBIA.........................	9,760	61	6,240	39	16,000	100	370	4	16,370	65
ECUADOR..........................	1,332	36	111	3	1,443	39	651	14	2,094	25
GUYANA...........................	67	27	180	73	247	100	462	80	709	86
PARAGUAY.........................	341	30	750	65	1,091	95	1,703	89	2,794	91
PERU.............................	6,000	55	242	2	6,242	57	24	0	6,265	37
URUGUAY..........................	357	15	1,086	44	1,443	59	300	60	1,743	59
VENEZUELA........................	7,217	60	3,607	30	10,824	90	2,814	70	13,638	85

Table 18 (continued)

COUNTRIES OR AREAS	URBAN						RURAL POPULAT- ION WITH ADEQUATE SANITATION		TOTAL POPULAT- ION SERVED BY SEWAGE SYSTEMS	
	POPULATION SERVED BY SEWER CONNECTION		POPULATION SERVED BY OTHER SYSTEMS		TOTAL URBAN POPULATION SERVED					
	NUMBER	%	NUMBER	%	NUMBER	%	NUMBER	%	NUMBER	%
(1)	(2)	(3)	(4)	(5)	(6)	(7)	(8)	(9)	(10)	(11)
ASIA										
AFGHANISTAN..........................	..	..	..	..	..	..	..	..	..	..
BANGLADESH...........................	..	..	..	..	2,100	21	900	1	3,000	3
BURMA................................	..	..	..	..	3,158	38	3,700	15	6,858	21
HONG KONG............................	3,775	80	944	20	4,719	100	..	..	4,719	93
INDIA................................	..	..	..	..	40,000	27	2,800	0.5	42,800	6
INDONESIA............................	..	..	..	..	14,600	29	20,000	21	34,600	23
JORDAN...............................	280	18	1,178	76	1,458	94	231	34	1,689	76
KOREA, REPUBLIC OF...................	2,200	9	23,200	91	25,400	100	12,700	100	38,100	100
MACAU................................	250	80	63	20	313	100	6	60	319	99
MALAYSIA.............................	700	15	3,895	85	4,595	100	4,850	55	9,445	70
MALDIVES.............................	..	..	..	..	25	60	1	1	26	16
NEPAL................................	..	..	..	..	160	16	130	1	290	2
PAKISTAN.............................	..	..	..	..	10,000	42	1,000	2	11,000	13
PHILIPPINES..........................	206	1	13,955	80	14,161	81	20,486	67	34,647	72
SAUDI ARABIA.........................	1,231	20	3,900	61	5,131	81	575	50	5,706	76
SINGAPORE............................	1,936	80	..	..	1,936	80	0	0	1,936	80
SRI LANKA............................	..	..	..	..	3,040	80	6,900	63	9,940	68
SYRIAN ARAB REPUBLIC.................	2,548	74	0	0	2,548	74	1,533	28	4,081	45
THAILAND.............................	..	..	..	..	7,000	64	15,000	41	22,000	46
UNITED ARAB EMIRATES.................	654	68	245	25	899	93	25	22	924	86
VIET NAM.............................	..	..	..	..	..	..	23,500	55	23,500	44
YEMEN ARAB REPUBLIC..................	71	10	355	50	426	60	..	..	..	..
YEMEN, DEMOCRATIC....................	319	50	127	20	446	70	193	15	639	33
EUROPE										
TURKEY...............................	2,000	10	9,000	46	11,000	56	..	..	..	..
MALTA................................	..	..	..	..	239	100	67	84	306	96
OCEANIA										
FIJI.................................	67	27	141	58	208	85	236	60	444	70
NEW CALEDONIA........................	44	76	14	24	58	100	52	65	110	80
PAPUA NEW GUINEA.....................	156	42	200	54	356	96	75	3	431	14
SOLOMON ISLANDS......................	..	..	..	..	18	82	20	10	38	17
VANAUTU..............................	0	0	19	95	19	95	67	68	86	73
KIRIBATI.............................	10	67	3	20	13	87	32	80	45	82
PACIFIC ISLANDS......................	6	17	21	58	27	75	4	5	31	26
AMERICAN SAMOA.......................	9	45	11	55	20	100	11	92	31	97
COOK ISLANDS.........................	0	0	2	100	2	100	13	76	15	79
TONGA................................	0	0	28	97	28	97	65	94	93	95
TUVALU...............................	0	0	2	100	2	100	4	80	6	86
WESTERN SAMOA........................	0	0	30	86	30	86	100	83	130	84

Source: GWS, WHO, The International Drinking Water Supply and Sanitation Decade: Review of National Baseline Data (as at December 1980) (1983).

[1] The classification is intended for statistical convenience and does not necessarily express a judgement about the stage reached by a particular country or area in the development process.